LAW & PHILOSOPHY

Edited by

Ishani Maitra
Elizabeth Anderson
UNIVERSITY OF MICHIGAN

Kendall Hunt
publishing company

Kendall Hunt
publishing company

www.kendallhunt.com
Send all inquiries to:
4050 Westmark Drive
Dubuque, IA 52004-1840

Copyright © 2010 by Elizabeth Anderson

Revised printing 2013

ISBN 978-1-4652-2933-5

Printed in the United States of America
10 9 8 7 6 5 4 3 2 1

CONTENTS

CHAPTER 1

Individual Liberty vs. State Authority

SUPREME COURT OF THE UNITED STATES

381 U.S. 479

GRISWOLD V. CONNECTICUT

APPEAL FROM THE SUPREME COURT
OF ERRORS OF CONNECTICUT

NO. 496 ARGUED: MARCH 29–30, 1965–DECIDED: JUNE 7, 1965

OPINION: [480] MR. JUSTICE DOUGLAS delivered the opinion of the Court.

Appellant Griswold is Executive Director of the Planned Parenthood League of Connecticut. Appellant Buxton is a licensed physician and a professor at the Yale Medical School who served as Medical Director for the League at its Center in New Haven—a center open and operating from November 1 to November 10, 1961, when appellants were arrested.

They gave information, instruction, and medical advice to married persons as to the means of preventing conception. They examined the wife and prescribed the best contraceptive device or material for her use. Fees were usually charged, although some couples were serviced free.

The statutes whose constitutionality is involved in this appeal are §§ 53-32 and 54-196 of the General Statutes of Connecticut (1958 rev.). The former provides:

"Any person who uses any drug, medicinal article or instrument for the purpose of preventing conception shall be fined not less than fifty dollars or imprisoned not less than sixty days nor more than one year or be both fined and imprisoned."

Section 54-196 provides:

"Any person who assists, abets, counsels, causes, hires or commands another to commit any offense may be prosecuted and punished as if he were the principal offender."

The appellants were found guilty as accessories and fined $100 each, against the claim that the accessory statute, as so applied, violated the Fourteenth Amendment. The Appellate Division of the Circuit Court affirmed. The Supreme Court of Errors affirmed that judgment. 151 Conn. 544, 200 A.2d 479. We noted probable jurisdiction. 379 U.S. 926.

[481] We think that appellants have standing to raise the constitutional rights of the married people with whom they had a professional relationship. . . .

Coming to the merits, we are met with a wide range of questions that implicate the Due Process Clause of the Fourteenth Amendment. . . . We do not sit as a super-legislature to determine the wisdom, need, and propriety of laws that touch economic problems, business affairs, or social conditions. This law, however, operates directly on an intimate relation of husband and wife and their physician's role in one aspect of that relation.

The association of people is not mentioned in the Constitution nor in the Bill of Rights. The right to educate a child in a school of the parents' choice—whether public or private or parochial—is also not mentioned. Nor is the right to study any particular subject or any foreign language. Yet the First Amendment has been construed to include certain of those rights.

By *Pierce v. Society of Sisters*, 268 U.S. 510, the right to educate one's children as one chooses is made applicable to the States by the force of the First and Fourteenth Amendments. By *Meyer v. Nebraska*, 262 U.S. 390, the same dignity is given the right to study the German language in a private school. In other words, the State may not, consistently with the spirit of the First Amendment, contract the spectrum of available knowledge. The right of freedom of speech and press includes not only the right to utter or to print, but the right to distribute, the right to receive, the right to read (*Martin v. Struthers*, 319 U.S. 141, 143) and freedom of inquiry, freedom of thought, and freedom to teach (*see Wiemann v. Updegraff*, 344 U.S. 183, 195)—indeed, the freedom of the entire university community. *Sweezy v. New Hampshire*, 354 U.S. 234, 249–250, 261–263; *Barenblatt v. United States*, 360 U.S. 109, 112; *Baggett v. Bullitt*, 377 U.S. 360, 369. Without [483] those peripheral rights, the specific rights would be less secure. And so we reaffirm the principle of the *Pierce* and the *Meyer* cases.

In *NAACP v. Alabama*, 357 U.S. 449, 462 we protected the "freedom to associate and privacy in one's associations," noting that freedom of association was a peripheral First Amendment right. Disclosure of membership lists of a constitutionally valid association, we held, was invalid "as entailing the likelihood of a substantial restraint upon the exercise by petitioner's members of their right to freedom of association." *Ibid*. In other words, the First Amendment has a penumbra where privacy is protected from governmental intrusion. In like context, we have protected forms of "association" that are not political in the customary sense, but pertain to the social, legal, and economic benefit of the members. *NAACP v. Button*, 371 U.S. 415, 430–431. In *Schware v. Board of Bar Examiners*, 353 U.S. 232, we held it not permissible to bar a lawyer from practice because he had once been a member of the Communist Party. The man's "association with that Party" was not shown to be "anything more than a political faith in a political party" (*id*. at 244), and was not action of a kind proving bad moral character. *Id*. at 245–246.

Those cases involved more than the "right of assembly"—a right that extends to all, irrespective of their race or ideology. *De Jonge v. Oregon*, 299 U.S. 353. The right of "association," like the right of belief (*Board of Education v. Barnette*, 319 U.S. 624), is more than the right to attend a meeting; it includes the right to express one's attitudes or philosophies by membership in a group or by affiliation with it or by other lawful means. Association in that context is a form of expression of opinion, and, while it is not expressly included in the First Amendment, its existence is necessary in making the express guarantees fully meaningful.

[484] The foregoing cases suggest that specific guarantees in the Bill of Rights have penumbras, formed by emanations from those guarantees that help give them life and substance. *See Poe v. Ullman*, 367 U.S. 497, 516–522 (dissenting opinion). Various guarantees create zones of privacy. The right of association contained in the penumbra of the First Amendment is one, as we have seen. The Third Amendment, in its prohibition against the quartering of soldiers "in any house" in time of peace without the consent of the owner, is another facet of that privacy. The Fourth Amendment explicitly affirms the "right of the people to be secure in their persons, houses, papers, and effects, against unreasonable searches and seizures." The Fifth Amendment, in its Self-Incrimination Clause, enables the citizen to create a zone of privacy which government may not force him to surrender to his detriment. The Ninth Amendment provides: "The enumeration in the Constitution, of certain rights, shall not be construed to deny or disparage others retained by the people."

The Fourth and Fifth Amendments were described in *Boyd v. United States*, 116 U.S. 616, 630, as protection against all governmental invasions "of the sanctity of a man's home and the privacies of life."[1] We recently referred [485] in *Mapp v. Ohio*, 367 U.S. 643, 656, to the Fourth Amendment as creating a "right to privacy, no less important than any other right carefully and particularly reserved to the people." *See* Beaney, *The Constitutional Right to Privacy*, 1962 Sup. Ct. Rev. 212; Griswold, *The Right to be Let Alone*, 55 Nw. U.L. Rev. 216 (1960).

We have had many controversies over these penumbral rights of "privacy and repose." *See, e.g., Breard v. Alexandria*, 341 U.S. 622, 626, 644; *Public Utilities Comm'n v. Pollak*, 343 U.S. 451; *Monroe v. Pape*, 365 U.S. 167; *Lanza v. New York*, 370 U.S. 139; *Frank v. Maryland*, 359 U.S. 360; *Skinner v. Oklahoma*, 316 U.S. 535, 541. These cases bear witness that the right of privacy which presses for recognition here is a legitimate one.

The present case, then, concerns a relationship lying within the zone of privacy created by several fundamental constitutional guarantees. And it concerns a law which, in forbidding the use of contraceptives, rather than regulating their manufacture or sale, seeks to achieve its goals by means having a maximum destructive impact upon that relationship. Such a law cannot stand in light of the familiar principle, so often applied by this Court, that a "governmental purpose to control or prevent activities constitutionally subject to state regulation may not be achieved by means which sweep unnecessarily broadly and thereby invade the area of protected freedoms." *NAACP v. Alabama*, 377 U.S. 288, 307. Would we allow the police to search the sacred precincts of marital bedrooms for telltale signs of the use of contraceptives? The [486] very idea is repulsive to the notions of privacy surrounding the marriage relationship.

We deal with a right of privacy older than the Bill of Rights—older than our political parties, older than our school system. Marriage is a coming together for better or for worse, hopefully enduring, and intimate to the degree of being sacred. It is an association that promotes a way of life, not causes; a harmony in living, not political faiths; a bilateral loyalty, not commercial or social projects. Yet it is an association for as noble a purpose as any involved in our prior decisions.

Reversed.

NOTE

[1]The Court said in full about this right of privacy:

> "The principles laid down in this opinion [by Lord Camden in *Entick v. Carrington*, 19 How. St. Tr. 1029] affect the very essence of constitutional liberty and security. They reach farther than the concrete form of the case then before the court, with its adventitious circumstances; they apply to all invasions on the part of the government and its employes [sic] of the sanctity of a man's home and the privacies of life. It is not the breaking of his doors, and the rummaging of his drawers, that constitutes the essence of the offence; but it is the invasion of his indefeasible right of personal security, personal liberty and private property.... Breaking into a house and opening boxes and drawers are circumstances of aggravation; but any forcible and compulsory extortion of a man's own testimony or of his private papers to be used as evidence to convict him of crime or to forfeit his goods is within the condemnation of that judgment. In this regard, the Fourth and Fifth Amendments run almost into each other." 116 U.S. at 630.

SUPREME COURT OF THE UNITED STATES

478 U.S. 186

BOWERS V. HARDWICK

CERTIORARI TO THE UNITED STATES COURT
OF APPEALS FOR THE ELEVENTH CIRCUIT

NO. 85-140 ARGUED MARCH 31, 1986–DECIDED:
JUNE 30, 1986

[187] **JUSTICE WHITE delivered the opinion of the Court.**

In August, 1982, respondent Hardwick (hereafter respondent) was charged with violating the Georgia statute criminalizing [188] sodomy by committing that act with another adult male in the bedroom of respondent's home. After a preliminary hearing, the District Attorney decided not to present the matter to the grand jury unless further evidence developed.

Respondent then brought suit in the Federal District Court, challenging the constitutionality of the statute insofar as it criminalized consensual sodomy. He asserted that he was a practicing homosexual, that the Georgia sodomy statute, as administered by the defendants, placed him in imminent danger of arrest, and that the statute for several reasons violates the Federal Constitution. . . .

[189] . . . .

[190] This case does not require a judgment on whether laws against sodomy between consenting adults in general, or between homosexuals in particular, are wise or desirable. . . . The issue presented is whether the Federal Constitution confers a fundamental right upon homosexuals to engage in sodomy, and hence invalidates the laws of the many States that still make such conduct illegal, and have done so for a very long time. The case also calls for some judgment about the limits of the Court's role in carrying out its constitutional mandate.

We first register our disagreement with the Court of Appeals and with respondent that the Court's prior cases have construed the Constitution to confer a right of privacy that extends to homosexual sodomy and, for all intents and purposes, have decided this case. The reach of this line of cases was sketched in *Carey v. Population Services International*, 431 U.S. 678, 685 (1977). *Pierce v. Society of Sisters*, 268 U.S. 510 (1925), and *Meyer v. Nebraska*, 262 U.S. 390 (1923), were described as dealing with childrearing and education; *Prince v. Massachusetts*, 321 U.S. 158 (1944), with family relationships; *Skinner v. Oklahoma ex rel. Williamson*, 316 U.S.

535 (1942), with procreation; *Loving v. Virginia*, 388 U.S. 1 (1967), with marriage; *Griswold v. Connecticut*, 381 U.S. 479 (1965), and *Eisenstadt v. Baird*, 405 U.S. 438 (1972), with contraception; and *Roe v. Wade*, 410 U.S. 113 (1973), with abortion. The latter three cases were interpreted as construing the Due Process Clause of the Fourteenth Amendment to confer a fundamental individual right to decide whether or not to beget or bear a child. *Carey v. Population Servs. Int'l, supra*, at 688–89.

Accepting the decisions in these cases and the above description of them, we think it evident that none of the rights announced in those cases bears any resemblance to the [191] claimed constitutional right of homosexuals to engage in acts of sodomy that is asserted in this case. No connection between family, marriage, or procreation, on the one hand, and homosexual activity, on the other, has been demonstrated, either by the Court of Appeals or by respondent. Moreover, any claim that these cases nevertheless stand for the proposition that any kind of private sexual conduct between consenting adults is constitutionally insulated from state proscription is unsupportable. Indeed, the Court's opinion in *Carey* twice asserted that the privacy right, which the *Griswold* line of cases found to be one of the protections provided by the Due Process Clause, did not reach so far. 431 U.S. at 688 n.5, 694 n.17.

Precedent aside, however, respondent would have us announce, as the Court of Appeals did, a fundamental right to engage in homosexual sodomy. This we are quite unwilling to do. It is true that, despite the language of the Due Process Clauses of the Fifth and Fourteenth Amendments, which appears to focus only on the processes by which life, liberty, or property is taken, the cases are legion in which those Clauses have been interpreted to have substantive content, subsuming rights that to a great extent are immune from federal or state regulation or proscription. Among such cases are those recognizing rights that have little or no textual support in the constitutional language. *Meyer, Prince*, and *Pierce* fall in this category, as do the privacy cases from *Griswold* to *Carey*.

Striving to assure itself and the public that announcing rights not readily identifiable in the Constitution's text involves much more than the imposition of the Justices' own choice of values on the States and the Federal Government, the Court has sought to identify the nature of the rights qualifying for heightened judicial protection. In *Palko v. Connecticut*, 302 U.S. 319, 325, 326 (1937), it was said that this category includes those fundamental liberties that are "implicit in the concept of ordered liberty," such that "neither [192] liberty nor justice would exist if [they] were sacrificed." A different description of fundamental liberties appeared in *Moore v. East Cleveland*, 431 U.S. 494, 503 (1977) (opinion of Powell, J.), where they are characterized as those liberties that are "deeply rooted in this Nation's history and tradition." *Id.* at 503 (Powell, J.). *See also Griswold v. Connecticut*, 381 U.S. at 506.

It is obvious to us that neither of these formulations would extend a fundamental right to homosexuals to engage in acts of consensual sodomy. Proscriptions against that conduct have ancient roots. *See generally Survey on the Constitutional Right to Privacy in the Context of Homosexual Activity*, 40 U. Miami L. Rev. 521, 525 (1986). Sodomy was a criminal offense at common law, and was forbidden by the laws of the original 13 States when they ratified the Bill of Rights. In 1868, when the Fourteenth Amendment was [193] ratified, all but 5 of the 37 States in the Union had criminal sodomy laws. In fact, until 1961, all 50 States outlawed sodomy, and today, 24 States and the District of Columbia [194] continue to provide criminal penalties for sodomy performed in private and between consenting adults. *See Survey*, U. Miami L. Rev. *supra*, at 524 n.9. Against this background, to claim that a right to engage in such conduct is "deeply rooted in this Nation's history and tradition" or "implicit in the concept of ordered liberty" is, at best, facetious.

Nor are we inclined to take a more expansive view of our authority to discover new fundamental rights imbedded in the Due Process Clause. The Court is most vulnerable and comes nearest to illegitimacy when it deals with judge-made constitutional law having little or no cognizable roots in the language or design of the Constitution. That this is so was painfully demonstrated by the face-off between the Executive and the Court in the 1930's, which resulted in the repudiation [195] of much of the substantive gloss that the Court had placed on the Due Process Clauses of the Fifth and Fourteenth Amendments. There should be, therefore, great resistance to expand the substantive reach of those Clauses, particularly if it requires redefining the category of rights deemed to be fundamental. Otherwise, the Judiciary necessarily takes to itself further authority to govern the country without express constitutional authority. The claimed right pressed on us today falls far short of overcoming this resistance.

Respondent, however, asserts that the result should be different where the homosexual conduct occurs in the privacy of the home. He relies on *Stanley v. Georgia*, 394 U.S. 557 (1969), where the Court held that the First Amendment prevents conviction for possessing and reading obscene material in the privacy of one's home: "If the First Amendment means anything, it means that a State has no business telling a man, sitting alone in his house, what books he may read or what films he may watch." *Id.* at 565.

Stanley did protect conduct that would not have been protected outside the home, and it partially prevented the enforcement of state obscenity laws; but the decision was firmly grounded in the First Amendment. The right pressed upon us here has no similar support in the text of the Constitution, and it does not qualify for recognition under the prevailing principles for construing the Fourteenth Amendment. Its limits are also difficult to discern. Plainly enough, otherwise illegal conduct is not always immunized whenever it occurs in the home. Victimless crimes, such as the possession and use of illegal drugs, do not escape the law where they are committed at home. *Stanley* itself recognized that its holding offered no protection for the possession in the home of drugs, firearms, or stolen goods. *Id.* at 568 n.11. And if respondent's submission is limited to the voluntary sexual conduct between consenting adults, it would be difficult, except by fiat, to limit the claimed right to homosexual conduct [196] while leaving exposed to prosecution adultery, incest, and other sexual crimes even though they are committed in the home. We are unwilling to start down that road.

Even if the conduct at issue here is not a fundamental right, respondent asserts that there must be a rational basis for the law, and that there is none in this case other than the presumed belief of a majority of the electorate in Georgia that homosexual sodomy is immoral and unacceptable. This is said to be an inadequate rationale to support the law. The law, however, is constantly based on notions of morality, and if all laws representing essentially moral choices are to be invalidated under the Due Process Clause, the courts will be very busy indeed. Even respondent makes no such claim, but insists that majority sentiments about the morality of homosexuality should be declared inadequate. We do not agree, and are unpersuaded that the sodomy laws of some 25 States should be invalidated on this basis.

Accordingly, the judgment of the Court of Appeals is

Reversed.

SUPREME COURT OF THE UNITED STATES

539 U.S. 558

Lawrence v. Texas

Certiorari to the Court of Appeals of Texas, Fourteenth District
No. 02-102 Argued: March 26, 2003–Decided: June 26, 2003

[562] JUSTICE KENNEDY delivered the opinion of the Court.

Liberty protects the person from unwarranted government intrusions into a dwelling or other private places. In our tradition the State is not omnipresent in the home. And there are other spheres of our lives and existence, outside the home, where the State should not be a dominant presence. Freedom extends beyond spatial bounds. Liberty presumes an autonomy of self that includes freedom of thought, belief, expression, and certain intimate conduct. The instant case involves liberty of the person both in its spatial and more transcendent dimensions.

I

The question before the Court is the validity of a Texas statute making it a crime for two persons of the same sex to engage in certain intimate sexual conduct.

In Houston, Texas, officers of the Harris County Police Department were dispatched to a private residence in response to a reported weapons disturbance. They entered an apartment where one of the petitioners, John Geddes Lawrence, [563] resided. The right of the police to enter does not seem to have been questioned. The officers observed Lawrence and another man, Tyron Garner, engaging in a sexual act. The two petitioners were arrested, held in custody over night, and charged and convicted before a Justice of the Peace.

The complaints described their crime as "deviate sexual intercourse, namely anal sex, with a member of the same sex (man)." App. to Pet. for Cert. 127a, 139a. The applicable state law is Tex. Penal Code Ann. § 21.06(a) (2003). It provides: "A person commits an offense if he engages in deviate sexual intercourse with another individual of the same sex." The statute defines "[d]eviate sexual intercourse" as follows:

"(A) any contact between any part of the genitals of one person and the mouth or anus of another person; or

"(B) the penetration of the genitals or the anus of another person with an object." § 21.01 (1).

The petitioners exercised their right to a trial de novo in Harris County Criminal Court. They challenged the statute as a violation of the Equal Protection Clause of the Fourteenth Amendment and of a like provision of the Texas Constitution. Tex. Const., Art. 1, § 3a. . . .

[564] We granted certiorari, 537 U.S. 1044 (2002), to consider three questions:

1. Whether Petitioners' criminal convictions under the Texas 'Homosexual Conduct' law—which criminalizes sexual intimacy by same-sex couples, but not identical behavior by different-sex couples—violate the Fourteenth Amendment guarantee of equal protection of laws?

2. Whether Petitioners' criminal convictions for adult consensual sexual intimacy in the home violate their vital interests in liberty and privacy protected by the Due Process Clause of the Fourteenth Amendment?

3. Whether *Bowers v. Hardwick*, 478 U.S. 186 (1986), should be overruled?

Pet. for Cert. i. . . .

II

We conclude the case should be resolved by determining whether the petitioners were free as adults to engage in the private conduct in the exercise of their liberty under the Due Process Clause of the Fourteenth Amendment to the Constitution. For this inquiry we deem it necessary to reconsider the Court's holding in *Bowers*.

There are broad statements of the substantive reach of liberty under the Due Process Clause in earlier cases, including *Pierce v. Society of Sisters*, 268 U.S. 510 (1925), and *Meyer v. Nebraska*, 262 U.S. 390 (1923); but the most pertinent beginning point is our decision in *Griswold v. Connecticut*, 381 U.S. 479 (1965).

In *Griswold* the Court invalidated a state law prohibiting the use of drugs or devices of contraception and counseling or aiding and abetting the use of contraceptives. The Court described the protected interest as a right to privacy and [565] placed emphasis on the marriage relation and the protected space of the marital bedroom. *Id.* at 485.

After *Griswold* it was established that the right to make certain decisions regarding sexual conduct extends beyond the marital relationship. In *Eisenstadt v. Baird*, 405 U.S. 438 (1972), the Court invalidated a law prohibiting the distribution of contraceptives to unmarried persons. The case was decided under the Equal Protection Clause, *id.* at 454; but with respect to unmarried persons, the Court went on to state the fundamental proposition that the law impaired the exercise of their personal rights, *ibid.* It quoted from the statement of the Court of Appeals finding the law to be in conflict with fundamental human rights, and it followed with this statement of its own:

> It is true that in Griswold *the right of privacy in question inhered in the marital relationship. . . . If the right of privacy means anything, it is the right of the individual, married or single, to be free from unwarranted governmental intrusion into matters so fundamentally affecting a person as the decision whether to bear or beget a child.*

Id. at 453.

The opinions in *Griswold* and *Eisenstadt* were part of the background for the decision in *Roe v. Wade*, 410 U.S. 113 (1973). . . . Although the Court held the woman's rights were not absolute, her right to elect an abortion did have real and substantial protection as an exercise of her liberty under the Due Process Clause. The Court cited cases that protect spatial freedom and cases that go well beyond it. *Roe* recognized the right of a woman to make certain fundamental decisions affecting her destiny and confirmed once more that the protection of liberty under the Due Process Clause has a substantive dimension of fundamental significance in defining the rights of the person.

[566] In *Carey v. Population Services International*, 431 U.S. 678 (1977), the Court confronted a New York law forbidding sale or distribution of contraceptive devices to persons under 16 years of age. Although there was no single opinion for the Court, the law was invalidated. Both *Eisenstadt* and *Carey*, as well as the holding and rationale in *Roe*, confirmed that the reasoning of *Griswold* could not be confined to the protection of rights of married adults. This was the state of the law with respect to some of the most relevant cases when the Court considered *Bowers v. Hardwick*.

The facts in *Bowers* had some similarities to the instant case. A police officer, whose right to enter seems not to have been in question, observed Hardwick, in his own bedroom, engaging in intimate sexual conduct with another adult male. The conduct was in violation of a Georgia statute making it a criminal offense to engage in sodomy. One difference between the two cases is that the Georgia statute prohibited the conduct whether or not the participants were of the same sex, while the Texas statute, as we have seen, applies only to participants of the same sex. Hardwick was not prosecuted, but he brought an action in federal court to declare the state statute invalid. He alleged he was a practicing homosexual and that the criminal prohibition violated rights guaranteed to him by the Constitution. The Court, in an opinion by Justice White, sustained the Georgia law. . . .

The Court began its substantive discussion in *Bowers* as follows: "The issue presented is whether the Federal Constitution confers a fundamental right upon homosexuals to engage in sodomy and hence invalidates the laws of the many States that still make such conduct illegal and have done so [567] for a very long time." *Id.* at 190. That statement, we now conclude, discloses the Court's own failure to appreciate the extent of the liberty at stake. To say that the issue in *Bowers* was simply the right to engage in certain sexual conduct demeans the claim the individual put forward, just as it would demean a married couple were it to be said marriage is simply about the right to have sexual intercourse. The laws involved in *Bowers* and here are, to be sure, statutes that purport to do no more than prohibit a particular sexual act. Their penalties and purposes, though, have more far-reaching consequences, touching upon the most private human conduct, sexual behavior, and in the most private of places, the home. The statutes do seek to control a personal relationship that, whether or not entitled to formal recognition in the law, is within the liberty of persons to choose without being punished as criminals.

This, as a general rule, should counsel against attempts by the State, or a court, to define the meaning of the relationship or to set its boundaries absent injury to a person or abuse of an institution the law protects. It suffices for us to acknowledge that adults may choose to enter upon this relationship in the confines of their homes and their own private lives and still retain their dignity as free persons. When sexuality finds overt expression in intimate conduct with another person, the conduct can be but one element in a personal bond that is more enduring. The liberty protected by the Constitution allows homosexual persons the right to make this choice.

Having misapprehended the claim of liberty there presented to it, and thus stating the claim to be whether there is a fundamental right to engage in consensual sodomy, the *Bowers* Court said: "Proscriptions against that conduct have ancient roots." *Id.* at 192. . . . [568] . . . [T]he following considerations counsel against adopting the definitive conclusions upon which *Bowers* placed such reliance.

At the outset it should be noted that there is no longstanding history in this country of laws directed at homosexual conduct as a distinct matter. Beginning in colonial times there were prohibitions of sodomy derived from the English criminal laws passed in the first instance by the Reformation Parliament of 1533. The English prohibition was understood to include relations between men and women as well as relations between men and men. *See, e.g.*, *King v. Wiseman*, 92 Eng. Rep. 774, 775 (K.B. 1718) (interpreting "mankind" in Act of 1533 as including women and girls). Nineteenth-century commentators similarly read American sodomy, buggery, and crime-against-nature statutes as criminalizing certain relations between men and women and between men and men. . . . Thus early American sodomy laws were not directed at homosexuals as such but instead sought to prohibit nonprocreative sexual activity more generally. This does not suggest approval of [569] homosexual conduct. It does tend to show that this particular form of conduct was not thought of as a separate category from like conduct between heterosexual persons.

Laws prohibiting sodomy do not seem to have been enforced against consenting adults acting in private. A substantial number of sodomy prosecutions and convictions for which there are surviving records were for predatory acts against those who could not or did not consent, as in the case of a minor or the victim of an assault. As to these, one purpose for the prohibitions was to ensure there would be no lack of coverage if a predator committed a sexual assault that did not constitute rape as defined by the criminal law. Thus the model sodomy indictments presented in a 19th-century treatise, *see* 2 Chitty, *supra*, at 49, addressed the predatory acts of an adult man against a minor girl or minor boy. Instead of targeting relations between consenting adults in private, 19th-century sodomy prosecutions typically involved relations between men and minor girls or minor boys, relations between adults involving force, relations between adults implicating disparity in status, or relations between men and animals.

. . . [570] . . . .

[F]ar from possessing "ancient roots," *Bowers*, 478 U.S. at 192, American laws targeting same-sex couples did not develop until the last third of the 20th century. . . .

It was not until the 1970's that any State singled out same-sex relations for criminal prosecution, and only nine States have done so. . . . Over the course of the last decades, States with same-sex prohibitions have moved toward abolishing them. *See, e.g., Jegley v. Picado*, 349 Ark. 600, 80 S.W.3d 332 (2002); *Gryczan v. State*, 283 Mont. 433, 942 P.2d 112 (1997); *Campbell v. Sundquist*, 926 S.W.2d 250 (Tenn. App. 1996); *Commonwealth v. Wasson*, [571] 842 S.W.2d 487 (Ky. 1992); *see also* 1993 Nev. Stats. p. 518 (repealing Nev. Rev. Stat. § 201.193).

In summary, the historical grounds relied upon in *Bowers* are more complex than the majority opinion and the concurring opinion by Chief Justice Burger indicate. Their historical premises are not without doubt and, at the very least, are overstated.

It must be acknowledged, of course, that the Court in *Bowers* was making the broader point that for centuries there have been powerful voices to condemn homosexual conduct as immoral. The condemnation has been shaped by religious beliefs, conceptions of right and acceptable behavior, and respect for the traditional family. For many persons these are not trivial concerns but profound and deep convictions accepted as ethical and moral principles to which they aspire and which thus determine the course of their lives. These considerations do not answer the question before us, however. The issue is whether the majority may use the power of the State to enforce these views on the whole society through operation of the criminal law. "Our obligation is to define the liberty of all, not to mandate our own moral code." *Planned Parenthood of Southeastern Pa. v. Casey*, 505 U.S. 833, 850 (1992).

Chief Justice Burger joined the opinion for the Court in *Bowers* and further explained his views as follows: "Decisions of individuals relating to homosexual conduct have been subject to state intervention throughout the history of Western civilization. Condemnation of those practices is firmly rooted in Judeao-Christian moral and ethical standards." 478 U.S. at 196. As with Justice White's assumptions about history, scholarship casts some doubt on the sweeping nature of the statement by Chief Justice Burger as it pertains to private homosexual conduct between consenting adults. *See, e.g.,* Eskridge, *Hardwick and Historiography*, 1999 U. Ill. L. Rev. 631, 656. In all events we think that our laws and traditions in the past half century are of [572] most relevance here. These references show an emerging awareness that liberty gives substantial protection to adult persons in deciding how to conduct their private lives in matters pertaining to sex. "[H]istory and tradition are the starting point but not in all cases the ending point of the substantive due process inquiry." *County of Sacramento v. Lewis*, 523 U.S. 833, 857 (1998) (Kennedy, J., concurring). . . .

In *Bowers* the Court referred to the fact that before 1961 all 50 States had outlawed sodomy, and that at the time of the Court's decision 24 States and the District of Columbia had sodomy laws. 478 U.S. at 192–193. Justice Powell pointed out that these prohibitions often were being ignored, however. Georgia, for instance, had not sought to enforce its law for decades. *Id.* at 197–198 n.2 ("The history of nonenforcement suggests the moribund character today of laws criminalizing this type of private, consensual conduct").

The sweeping references by Chief Justice Burger to the history of Western civilization and to Judeo-Christian moral and ethical standards did not take account of other authorities pointing in an opposite direction. A committee advising the British Parliament recommended in 1957 repeal of laws [573] punishing homosexual conduct. *The Wolfenden Report: Report of the Committee on Homosexual Offenses and Prostitution* (1963). Parliament enacted the substance of those recommendations 10 years later. Sexual Offences Act, 1967, § 1.

Of even more importance, almost five years before *Bowers* was decided the European Court of Human Rights considered a case with parallels to *Bowers* and to today's case. An adult male resident in Northern Ireland alleged he was a practicing homosexual who desired to engage in consensual homosexual conduct. The laws of Northern Ireland forbade him that right. He alleged that he had been questioned, his home had been searched, and he feared criminal prosecution. The court held that the laws proscribing the conduct were invalid under the European Convention on Human Rights. *Dudgeon v. United Kingdom*, 45 Eur. Ct. H.R. (1981) ¶52. Authoritative in all countries that are members of the Council of Europe (21 nations then, 45 nations now), the decision is at odds with the premise in *Bowers* that the claim put forward was insubstantial in our Western civilization.

In our own constitutional system the deficiencies in *Bowers* became even more apparent in the years following its announcement. The 25 States with laws prohibiting the relevant conduct referenced in the *Bowers* decision are reduced now to 13, of which 4 enforce their laws only against homosexual conduct. In those States where sodomy is still proscribed, whether for same-sex or heterosexual conduct, there is a pattern of nonenforcement with respect to consenting adults acting in private. The State of Texas admitted in 1994 that as of that date it had not prosecuted anyone under those circumstances. *State v. Morales*, 869 S.W.2d 941, 943.

Two principal cases decided after *Bowers* cast its holding into even more doubt. In *Planned Parenthood of Southeastern Pa. v. Casey*, 505 U.S. 833 (1992), the Court reaffirmed the substantive force of the liberty protected by the Due Process Clause. The *Casey* decision again confirmed [574] that our laws and tradition afford constitutional protection to personal decisions relating to marriage, procreation, contraception, family relationships, child rearing, and education. *Id.* at 851. In explaining the respect the Constitution demands for the autonomy of the person in making these choices, we stated as follows:

> These matters, involving the most intimate and personal choices a person may make in a lifetime, choices central to personal dignity and autonomy, are central to the liberty protected by the Fourteenth Amendment. At the heart of liberty is the right to define one's own concept of existence, of meaning, of the universe, and of the mystery of human life. Beliefs about these matters could not define the attributes of personhood were they formed under compulsion of the State.

Ibid. Persons in a homosexual relationship may seek autonomy for these purposes, just as heterosexual persons do. The decision in *Bowers* would deny them this right.

The second post-*Bowers* case of principal relevance is *Romer v. Evans*, 517 U.S. 620 (1996). There the Court struck down class-based legislation directed at homosexuals as a violation of the Equal Protection Clause. *Romer* invalidated an amendment to Colorado's constitution which named as a solitary class persons who were homosexuals, lesbians, or bisexual either by "orientation, conduct, practices or relationships," *id.* at 624 (internal quotation marks omitted), and deprived them of protection under state antidiscrimination laws. We concluded that the provision was "born of animosity toward the class of persons affected" and further that it had no rational relation to a legitimate governmental purpose. *Id.* at 634.

As an alternative argument in this case, counsel for the petitioners and some amici contend that *Romer* provides the basis for declaring the Texas statute invalid under the Equal Protection Clause. That is a tenable argument, but we conclude [575] the instant case requires us to address whether *Bowers* itself has continuing validity. Were we to hold the statute invalid under the Equal Protection Clause some might question whether a prohibition would be valid if drawn differently, say, to prohibit the conduct both between same-sex and different-sex participants.

Equality of treatment and the due process right to demand respect for conduct protected by the substantive guarantee of liberty are linked in important respects, and a decision on the latter point advances both interests. If protected conduct is made criminal and the law which does so remains unexamined for its substantive validity, its stigma might remain even if it were not enforceable as drawn for equal protection reasons. When homosexual conduct is made criminal by the law of the State, that declaration in and of itself is an invitation to subject homosexual persons to discrimination both in the public and in the private spheres. The central holding of *Bowers* has been brought in question by this case, and it should be addressed. Its continuance as precedent demeans the lives of homosexual persons.

The stigma this criminal statute imposes, moreover, is not trivial. The offense, to be sure, is but a class C misdemeanor, a minor offense in the Texas legal system. Still, it remains a criminal offense with all that imports for the dignity of the persons charged. The petitioners will bear on their record the history of their criminal convictions. Just this Term we rejected various challenges to state laws requiring the registration of sex offenders. *Smith v. Doe*, 538 U.S. 84 (2003); *Connecticut Dept. of Public Safety v. Doe*, 538 U.S. 1 (2003). We are advised that if Texas convicted an adult for private, consensual homosexual conduct under the statute here in question the convicted person would come within the registration laws of at least four States were he or she to be subject to their jurisdiction. . . . This underscores the consequential nature of the punishment and the state-sponsored condemnation attendant to the criminal prohibition. Furthermore, the Texas criminal conviction carries with it the other collateral consequences always following a conviction, such as notations on job application forms, to mention but one example.

The foundations of *Bowers* have sustained serious erosion from our recent decisions in *Casey* and *Romer*. When our precedent has been thus weakened, criticism from other sources is of greater significance. In the United States criticism of *Bowers* has been substantial and continuing, disapproving of its reasoning in all respects, not just as to its historical assumptions. *See, e.g.*, C. Fried, *Order and Law: Arguing the Reagan Revolution—A Firsthand Account* 81–84 (1991); R. Posner, *Sex and Reason* 341–350 (1992). The courts of five different States have declined to follow it in interpreting provisions in their own state constitutions parallel to the Due Process Clause of the Fourteenth Amendment, *see Jegley v. Picado*, 349 Ark. 600, 80 S.W.3d 332 (2002); *Powell v. State*, 270 Ga. 327, 510 S.E.2d 18, 24 (1998); *Gryczan v. State*, 283 Mont. 433, 942 P.2d 112 (1997); *Campbell v. Sundquist*, 926 S.W.2d 250 (Tenn. App. 1996); *Commonwealth v. Wasson*, 842 S.W.2d 487 (Ky. 1992).

To the extent *Bowers* relied on values we share with a wider civilization, it should be noted that the reasoning and holding in *Bowers* have been rejected elsewhere. The European Court of Human Rights has followed not *Bowers* but its own decision in *Dudgeon v. United Kingdom*. *See P.G. & J.H. v. United Kingdom*, App. No. 00044787/98, ¶ 56 (Eur. Ct. H.R., Sept. 25, 2001); *Modinos v. Cyprus*, 259 Eur. Ct. H.R. (1993); *Norris v. Ireland*, 142 Eur. Ct. H.R. (1988). Other nations, too, have taken action consistent with an affirmation of the protected right of homosexual adults to engage in intimate, consensual conduct. *See* Brief for Mary [577] Robinson et al. as Amici Curiae 11–12. The right the petitioners seek in this case has been accepted as an integral part of human freedom in many other countries. There has been no showing that in this country the governmental interest in circumscribing personal choice is somehow more legitimate or urgent.

The doctrine of *stare decisis* is essential to the respect accorded to the judgments of the Court and to the stability of the law. It is not, however, an inexorable command. *Payne v. Tennessee*, 501 U.S. 808, 828 (1991). . . . In *Casey* we noted that when a Court is asked to overrule a precedent recognizing a constitutional liberty interest, individual or societal reliance on the existence of that liberty cautions with particular strength against reversing course. 505 U.S. at 855–856; *see also id.* at 844 ("Liberty finds no refuge in a jurisprudence of doubt"). The holding in *Bowers*, however, has not induced detrimental reliance comparable to some instances where recognized individual rights are involved. Indeed, there has been no individual or societal reliance on *Bowers* of the sort that could counsel against overturning its holding once there are compelling reasons to do so. *Bowers* itself causes uncertainty, for the precedents before and after its issuance contradict its central holding.

The rationale of *Bowers* does not withstand careful analysis. In his dissenting opinion in *Bowers* Justice Stevens came to these conclusions:

> *Our prior cases make two propositions abundantly clear. First, the fact that the governing majority in a State has traditionally viewed a particular practice as immoral is not a sufficient reason for upholding a law prohibiting the practice; neither history nor tradition could save a law prohibiting miscegenation from constitutional* [578] *attack. Second, individual decisions by married persons, concerning the intimacies of their physical relationship, even when not intended to produce offspring, are a form of "liberty" protected by the Due Process Clause of the Fourteenth Amendment. Moreover, this protection extends to intimate choices by unmarried as well as married persons.*

478 U.S. at 216 (footnotes and citations omitted). Justice Stevens' analysis, in our view, should have been controlling in *Bowers* and should control here.

Bowers was not correct when it was decided, and it is not correct today. It ought not to remain binding precedent. *Bowers v. Hardwick* should be and now is overruled.

The present case does not involve minors. It does not involve persons who might be injured or coerced or who are situated in relationships where consent might not easily be refused. It does not involve public conduct or prostitution. It does not involve whether the government must give formal recognition to any relationship that homosexual persons seek to enter. The case does involve two adults who, with full and mutual consent from each other, engaged in sexual practices common to a homosexual lifestyle. The petitioners are entitled to respect for their private lives. The State cannot demean their existence or control their destiny by making their private sexual conduct a crime. Their right to liberty under the Due Process Clause gives them the full right to engage in their conduct without intervention of the government. "It is a promise of the Constitution that there is a realm of personal liberty which the government may not enter." *Casey, supra,* at 847. The Texas statute furthers no legitimate state interest which can justify its intrusion into the personal and private life of the individual.

Had those who drew and ratified the Due Process Clauses of the Fifth Amendment or the Fourteenth Amendment known the components of liberty in its manifold possibilities, they might have been more specific. They did not presume [579] to have this insight. They knew times can blind us to certain truths and later generations can see that laws once thought necessary and proper in fact serve only to oppress. As the Constitution endures, persons in every generation can invoke its principles in their own search for greater freedom.

The judgment of the Court of Appeals for the Texas Fourteenth District is reversed, and the case is remanded for further proceedings not inconsistent with this opinion.

It is so ordered.

SUPREME COURT OF VERMONT

170 VT. 194

STAN BAKER, ET AL.,
v. STATE OF VERMONT, ET AL.

NO. 98-032 FILED: DECEMBER 20, 1999

OPINION: JEFFREY L. AMESTOY, C.J.

[197] May the State of Vermont exclude same-sex couples from the benefits and protections that its laws provide to opposite-sex married couples? That is the fundamental question we address in this appeal. . . .

We conclude that under the Common Benefits Clause of the Vermont Constitution, which, in pertinent part, reads,

> *That government is, or ought to be, instituted for the common benefit, protection, and security of the people, nation, or community, and not for the particular emolument or advantage of any single person, family, or set of persons, who are a part only of that community. . . .*

Vt. Const., ch. I, art 7., plaintiffs may not be deprived of the statutory benefits and protections afforded persons of the opposite sex who choose to marry. We hold that the State is constitutionally required to extend to same-sex couples the common benefits and protections that flow from marriage under Vermont law. Whether this ultimately takes the form of inclusion within the marriage laws themselves or a parallel "domestic partnership" system or some equivalent statutory [198] alternative, rests with the Legislature. Whatever system is chosen, however, must conform with the constitutional imperative to afford all Vermonters the common benefit, protection, and security of the law.

Plaintiffs are three same-sex couples who have lived together in committed relationships for periods ranging from four to twenty-five years. Two of the couples have raised children together. Each couple applied for a marriage license from their respective town clerk, and each was refused a license as ineligible under the applicable state marriage laws. Plaintiffs thereupon filed this lawsuit against defendants—the State of Vermont, the Towns of Milton and Shelburne, and the City of South Burlington—seeking a declaratory judgment that the refusal to issue them a license violated the marriage statutes and the Vermont Constitution.

. . . [199–201]. . . .

II. THE CONSTITUTIONAL CLAIM

Assuming that the marriage statutes preclude their eligibility for a marriage license, plaintiffs contend that the exclusion violates their right to the common benefit and protection of the law guaranteed by Chapter I, Article 7 of the Vermont Constitution. They note that in denying them access to a civil marriage license, the law effectively excludes them from a broad array of legal benefits and protections incident to the marital relation, including access to a spouse's medical, life, and disability insurance, hospital visitation and other medical decision making privileges, spousal support, intestate succession, homestead protections, and many other statutory protections. They claim the trial court erred in upholding the law on the basis that it reasonably served the State's interest in promoting the "link between procreation and child rearing." They argue that the large number of married couples without children, and the increasing incidence of same-sex couples with children, undermines the State's rationale. They note that Vermont law affirmatively guarantees the right to adopt and raise children regardless of the sex of the parents and challenge the logic of a legislative scheme that recognizes the rights of same-sex partners as parents, yet denies them—and their children—the same security as spouses.

In considering this issue, it is important to emphasize at the outset that it is the Common Benefits Clause of the Vermont Constitution we are construing, rather than its counterpart, the Equal Protection Clause of the Fourteenth Amendment to the United States Constitution. . . .

[202–206]. . . .

. . . Vermont case law has consistently demanded in practice that statutory exclusions from publicly-conferred benefits and protections must be "premised on an appropriate and overriding public interest." *State v. Ludlow Supermarkets*, 141 Vt. 261, 268, 448 A.2d 791, 795 (1982). . . .

[207–208] . . . .

The words of the Common Benefits Clause are revealing. While they do not, to be sure, set forth a fully-formed standard of analysis for determining the constitutionality of a given statute, they do express broad principles which usefully inform that analysis. Chief among these is the principle of inclusion. . . . The affirmative right to the "common benefits and protections" of government and the corollary proscription of favoritism in the distribution of public "emoluments and advantages" reflect the framers' overarching objective "not only that everyone enjoy equality before the law or have an equal voice in government but also that everyone have an equal share in the fruits of the common enterprise." Willi Paul Adams, *The First American Constitutions* 188 (1980) (emphasis added). . . . [209] . . .

. . . [210–211] . . . .

[212] D. ANALYSIS UNDER ARTICLE 7

The language and history of the Common Benefits Clause thus reinforce the conclusion that a relatively uniform standard, reflective of the inclusionary principle at its core, must govern our analysis of laws challenged under the Clause. Accordingly, we conclude that this approach, rather than the rigid, multi-tiered analysis evolved by the federal courts under the Fourteenth Amendment, shall direct our inquiry under Article 7. As noted, Article 7 is intended to ensure that the benefits and protections conferred by the State are for the common benefit of the community and are not for the advantage of persons "who are a part only of that community." When a statute is [213] challenged under Article 7, we first define that "part of the community" disadvantaged by the law. We examine the statutory basis that distinguishes those protected by the law from those excluded from the State's protection. . . .

We look next to the government's purpose in drawing a classification that includes some members of the community within the scope of the challenged law but excludes others. Consistent with Article 7's guiding principle of affording the protection and benefit of the law to [214] all members of the Vermont community, we examine the nature of the classification to determine whether it is reasonably necessary to accomplish the State's claimed objectives.

We must ultimately ascertain whether the omission of a part of the community from the benefit, protection and security of the challenged law bears a reasonable and just relation to the governmental purpose. Consistent with the core presumption of inclusion, factors to be considered in this determination may include: (1) the significance of the benefits and protections of the challenged law; (2) whether the omission of members of the community from the benefits and protections of the challenged law promotes the government's stated goals; and (3) whether the classification is significantly underinclusive or overinclusive. . . .

[215]. . . .

E. THE STANDARD APPLIED

With these general precepts in mind, we turn to the question of whether the exclusion of same-sex couples from the benefits and protections incident to marriage under Vermont law contravenes Article 7. The first step in our analysis is to identify the nature of the statutory classification. As noted, the marriage statutes apply expressly to opposite-sex couples. Thus, the statutes exclude anyone who wishes to marry someone of the same sex.

[216] Next, we must identify the governmental purpose or purposes to be served by the statutory classification. The principal purpose the State advances in support of the excluding same-sex couples from the legal benefits of marriage is the government's interest in "furthering the [217] link between procreation and child rearing." The State has a strong interest, it argues, in promoting a permanent commitment between couples who have children to ensure that their offspring are considered legitimate and receive ongoing parental support. The State contends, further, that the Legislature could reasonably believe that sanctioning same-sex unions "would diminish society's perception of the link between procreation and child rearing . . . [and] advance the notion that fathers or mothers . . . are mere surplusage to the functions of procreation and child rearing." The State argues that since same-sex couples cannot conceive a child on their own, state-sanctioned same-sex unions "could be seen by the Legislature to separate further the connection between procreation and parental responsibilities for raising children." Hence, the Legislature is justified, the State concludes, "in using the marriage statutes to send a public message that procreation and child rearing are intertwined."

. . . .

It is . . . undisputed that many opposite-sex couples marry for reasons unrelated to procreation, that some of these couples never intend to have children, and that others are incapable of having children. Therefore, if the purpose of the statutory exclusion of same-sex couples is to "further[] the link between procreation and child rearing," it is significantly under-inclusive. The law extends the benefits and protections of marriage to many persons with no logical connection to the stated governmental goal.

Furthermore, while accurate statistics are difficult to obtain, there is no dispute that a significant number of children today are actually being raised by same-sex parents, and that increasing numbers of [218] children are being conceived by such parents through a variety of assisted-reproductive techniques. . . .

The Vermont Legislature has not only recognized this reality, but has acted affirmatively to remove legal barriers so that same-sex couples may legally adopt and rear the children conceived through such efforts. *See* Vt. Stat. Ann. tit. 15A, § 1-102(b) (allowing partner of biological parent to adopt if in child's best interest without reference to sex). The State has also acted to expand the domestic relations laws to safeguard the interests of same-sex parents and their children when such couples terminate their domestic relationship. *See* Vt. Stat. Ann. tit. 15A, § 1-112 (vesting family court with jurisdiction over parental rights and responsibilities, parent-child contact, and child support when unmarried persons who have adopted minor child "terminate their domestic relationship").

Therefore, to the extent that the State's purpose in licensing civil marriage was, and is, to legitimize children and provide for their security, the statutes plainly exclude many same-sex couples who are [219] no different from opposite-sex couples with respect to these objectives. If anything, the exclusion of same-sex couples from the legal protections incident to marriage exposes their children to the precise risks that the State argues the marriage laws are designed to secure against. In short, the marital exclusion treats persons who are similarly situated for purposes of the law, differently.

The State also argues that because same-sex couples cannot conceive a child on their own, their exclusion promotes a "perception of the link between procreation and child rearing," and that to discard it would "advance the notion that mothers and fathers . . . are mere surplusage to the functions of procreation and child rearing" Apart from the bare assertion, the State offers no persuasive reasoning to support these claims. Indeed, it is undisputed that most of those who utilize non-traditional means of conception are infertile married couples and that many assisted-reproductive techniques involve only one of the married partner's genetic material, the other being supplied by a third party through sperm, egg, or embryo donation. . . . The State does not suggest that the use of these technologies undermines a married couple's sense of parental responsibility, or fosters the perception that they are "mere surplusage" to the conception and parenting of the child so conceived. . . . Accordingly, there is no reasonable basis to conclude that a same-sex couple's use of the same technologies would undermine the bonds of parenthood, or society's perception of parenthood.

. . . . [220–22] . . . .

The State asserts that a number of additional rationales could support a legislative decision to exclude same-sex partners from the statutory benefits and protections of marriage. Among these are the State's purported interests in "promoting child rearing in a setting that provides both male and female role models" . . . It is conceivable that the Legislature could conclude that opposite-sex partners offer advantages in this area, although we note that child-development experts disagree and the answer is decidedly uncertain. The argument, however, contains a more fundamental flaw, and that is the Legislature's endorsement of a policy diametrically at odds with the State's claim. In 1996, the Vermont General Assembly enacted, and the Governor signed, a law removing all prior legal barriers to the adoption of children by same-sex couples. *See* Vt. Stat. Ann. tit. 15A, § 1-102. At the same time, the Legislature provided additional legal protections in the form of court-ordered child support and parent-child contact in the event that same-sex parents dissolved their "domestic relationship." *Id.* § 1-112. In light of these express policy choices, the State's arguments that Vermont public policy favors opposite-sex over same-sex parents or disfavors the use of artificial reproductive technologies are patently without substance.

. . .

Finally, it is suggested that the long history of official intolerance of intimate same-sex relationships cannot be reconciled with an interpretation of Article 7 that would give state-sanctioned benefits and protection to individuals of the same sex who commit to a permanent domestic relationship. We find the argument to be unpersuasive for several reasons. First, to the extent that state action historically has been motivated by an animus against a class, that history cannot provide a legitimate basis for continued unequal application of the law. *See MacCallum v. Seymour's Adm'r*, 165 Vt. 452, 459–60, 686 A.2d 935, 939 (1996) (holding that although adopted persons had "historically been a target of discrimination," social prejudices failed to support their continued exclusion from intestacy law). As we observed recently in *Brigham v. State*, 166 Vt. 246, 267, 692 A.2d 384, 396 (1997), "equal protection of the laws cannot be limited by eighteenth-century standards." Second, whatever claim may be made [224] in light of the undeniable fact that federal and state statutes—including those in Vermont—have historically disfavored same-sex relationships, more recent legislation plainly undermines the contention. *See, e.g.*, Laws of Vermont, 1977, No. 51, §§ 2, 3 (repealing former § 2603 of Title 13, which criminalized fellatio). In 1992, Vermont was one of the first states to enact statewide legislation prohibiting discrimination in employment, housing, and other services based on sexual orientation. *See* Vt. Stat. Ann. tit. 21, § 495 (employment); Vt. Stat. Ann. tit. 9, § 4503 (housing); Vt. Stat. Ann. tit. 8, § 4724 (insurance); Vt. Stat. Ann. tit. 9, § 4502 (public accommodations). Sexual orientation is among the categories specifically protected against hate-motivated crimes in Vermont. *See* Vt. Stat. Ann. tit. 13, § 1455. Furthermore, as noted earlier, recent enactments of the General Assembly have removed barriers to adoption by same-sex couples, and have extended legal rights and protections to such couples who dissolve their "domestic relationship." *See* Vt. Stat. Ann. tit. 15A, §§ 1-102, 1-112.

Thus, viewed in the light of history, logic, and experience, we conclude that none of the interests asserted by the State provides a reasonable and just basis for the continued exclusion of same-sex couples from the benefits incident to a civil marriage license under Vermont law. Accordingly, in the faith that a case beyond the imagining of the framers of our Constitution may, nevertheless, be safely anchored in the values that infused it, we find a constitutional obligation to extend to plaintiffs the common benefit, protection, and security that Vermont law provides opposite-sex married couples. . . .

F. REMEDY

. . . .

We hold only that plaintiffs are entitled under Chapter I, Article 7, of the Vermont Constitution to obtain the same benefits and protections afforded by Vermont law to married opposite-sex couples. We do [225] not purport to infringe upon the prerogatives of the Legislature to craft an appropriate means of addressing this constitutional mandate, other than to note that the record here refers to a number of potentially constitutional statutory schemes from other jurisdictions. These include what are typically referred to as "domestic partnership" or "registered partnership" acts, which generally establish an alternative legal status to marriage for same-sex couples, impose similar formal requirements and limitations, create a parallel licensing or registration scheme, and extend all or most of the same rights and obligations provided by the law to married partners. . . .

COURT OF APPEALS OF ARIZONA DIVISION ONE, DEPARTMENT E

206 ARIZ. 276

STANDHARDT V. SUPERIOR COURT OF THE STATE OF ARIZONA

MARICOPA COUNTY SUPERIOR COURT; PETITION FOR SPECIAL ACTION 1 CA-SA 03-0150 FILED: OCTOBER 8, 2003

JUDGES: Ann A. Scott Timmer, Presiding Judge; John C. Gemmill; Maurice Portley

OPINION: [278] TIMMER, Presiding Judge

Recently, in *Lawrence v. Texas*, 539 U.S. 558, 123 S. Ct. 2472, 2484 (2003), the United States Supreme Court struck a Texas statute that prohibited certain sexual activity between persons of the [279] same sex. The Court reasoned that the statute impermissibly infringed on homosexuals' liberty interest under the Due Process Clause of the Fourteenth Amendment to the United States Constitution to engage in private, consensual sexual activity without state intervention. *Id.*

In the wake of *Lawrence*, we are asked to declare that Arizona's prohibition of same-sex marriages, Arizona Revised Statutes ("A.R.S.") sections 25-101 (C) and -125(A) (2003), similarly violates the federal and state constitutions. For the reasons that follow, we hold that Arizona's prohibition of such state-licensed unions does not violate Petitioners' rights under either constitution. Therefore, although we accept jurisdiction of this special action, we deny relief to Petitioners.

BACKGROUND

Days after the Supreme Court issued *Lawrence*, Harold Donald Standhardt and Tod Alan Keltner, homosexual men in a committed relationship, applied to the Clerk of the Superior Court of Arizona, Maricopa County, for a marriage license. The Clerk denied the application in light of A.R.S. §§ 25-101(C) and -125(A), which, respectively, prohibit marriages between persons of the same sex and define a valid marriage as one between a man and a woman.

After being turned away by the Clerk, Standhardt and Keltner petitioned this court to both compel the Clerk to issue them a marriage license and declare §§ 25-101(C) and -125(A) unconstitutional under the federal and state constitutions. In light of *Lawrence* and other authorities, Petitioners argue that these provisions violate their fundamental right to marry and their right to equal protection under the laws, both of which are guaranteed by the federal and state constitutions. . . .

DISCUSSION

I. Fundamental Right

Petitioners first argue that Arizona's prohibition of same-sex marriages impermissibly infringes on their right to marry each other, which, they contend, is guaranteed as a fundamental liberty interest by the due process provisions of both the Fourteenth Amendment to the United States Constitution and article 2, section 4 of the Arizona Constitution, and assured as a fundamental privacy right explicitly granted by article 2, section 8 of the Arizona Constitution. The State responds that while Petitioners possess a fundamental right to enter opposite-sex marriages, they do not have an equivalent right to enter same-sex marriages.

Whether entry in state-licensed, same-sex marriages is a constitutionally anointed "fundamental right" is a critical inquiry in deciding the viability of A.R.S. §§ 25-101(C) and -125(A). If participation in such unions is a fundamental right, we must apply a "strict scrutiny" analysis, which permits us to uphold these provisions only if they serve a compelling state interest and are narrowly tailored to achieve that interest. *Washington v. Glucksberg*, 521 U.S. 702, 721 (1997). . . .

If participation in such unions is not a fundamental right, we will assess the constitutionality of §§ 25-101(C) and -125(A) by using a "rational basis" analysis, which requires us to uphold these provisions if they are simply rationally related to a legitimate government interest. *Glucksberg*, 521 U.S. at 728. . . .

Thus, to select the appropriate methodology for resolving Petitioners' arguments, we initially determine whether Petitioners assert a constitutionally protected fundamental right under the Due Process Clauses of the federal and state constitutions or the explicit privacy provision of the Arizona Constitution.

A. DUE PROCESS

We begin with the well-accepted premise that the substantive due process guarantee "provides heightened protection against government interference with certain fundamental rights and liberty interests." *Glucksberg*, 521 U.S. at 720. In addition to the freedoms protected in the Bill of Rights, such rights and interests are those "'deeply rooted in this Nation's history and tradition,' . . . and 'implicit in the concept of ordered liberty,' such that 'neither liberty nor justice would exist if they were sacrificed.'" *Id.* at 720–21 (citations omitted); *see Watson*, 198 Ariz. at 51, ¶ 8, 6 P.3d at 755. Thus, using our Nation's history, legal traditions, and practices as a guidepost, the Supreme Court has conferred fundamental-right status on the right to marry, *Loving v. Virginia*, 388 U.S. 1, 12 (1967), and the right to marital privacy, *Griswold v. Connecticut*, 381 U.S. 479, 485 (1965). [note omitted]

Arizona courts have similarly construed Arizona's Due Process Clause. . . . [281] . . .

Neither the United States Supreme Court nor any Arizona court has explicitly recognized that the fundamental right to marry includes the freedom to choose a same-sex spouse. Petitioners argue, however, that the Court in *Lawrence* implicitly recognized such a right. We therefore turn to that case before considering whether such a right otherwise exists.

In *Lawrence*, the Court held that a Texas statute that prohibited certain same-gender sexual activity violated homosexuals' liberty interests protected by the Due Process Clause. 123 S. Ct. at 2484. . . .

Significantly, during a discussion of cases casting doubt on the ongoing viability of *Bowers*, the Court reflected on the attributes of liberty as follows:

> *In* Planned Parenthood of Southeastern Pennsylvania v. Casey, *505 U.S. 833 (1992), the Court reaffirmed the substantive force of the liberty protected by the Due Process Clause. The Casey decision again confirmed that* **our laws and tradition afford constitutional protection to personal decisions relating to marriage, procreation, contraception, family relationships, child rearing, and education.** *Id. at 851. In explaining the respect the Constitution demands for the autonomy of the person in making these choices, we stated as follows: "These matters, involving the most intimate and personal choices a person may make in a lifetime, choices central to personal dignity and autonomy, are central to the liberty protected by the Fourteenth Amendment. At the heart of liberty is the right to define one's own concept of existence, of meaning, of the universe, and of the mystery of human life. Beliefs about these matters could not define the attributes of personhood were they formed under compulsion of the State." Ibid.* **Persons in a homosexual relationship may seek autonomy for these purposes, just as heterosexual persons do.** *The decision in* Bowers *would deny them this right.*

Id. at 2481–82 (emphasis added). Petitioners seize on the italicized language as expressing the Court's view that persons have a fundamental liberty interest to enter same-sex marriages. We disagree with Petitioners' interpretation for three reasons.

First, as the State points out, elsewhere in its decision the Court explicitly stated that the case before it "[did] not involve whether the government must give formal recognition to any relationship that homosexual persons seek to enter." *Id.* at 2484. . . . It therefore follows that the Court did not intend by its comments to address same-sex marriages.[1]

Second, Petitioners mistakenly equate the "purposes" for which persons in a homosexual relationship may seek autonomy with the personal choices described in *Casey*, including the choice to marry. They do this by stitching together the italicized language from the Court's decision, *supra* ¶ 16, thereby ignoring the language quoted from *Casey* that appears amidst these words and that explains why the Constitution zealously guards an individual's right to make these choices. . . . In light of the context of the quoted discussion, the issue whether *Bowers* remained viable, and the Court's eventual holding, striking the Texas law, we view the language in question as acknowledging a homosexual person's right to define his or her own existence, and achieve the type of individual fulfillment that is a hallmark of a free society, by entering a homosexual relationship. We do not view the language as stating that such a right includes the choice to enter a state-sanctioned, same-sex marriage.

Third, and finally, because other language in *Lawrence* indicates that the Court did not consider sexual conduct between same-sex partners a fundamental right, it would be illogical to interpret the quoted language as recognizing a fundamental right to enter a same-sex marriage. Specifically, the Court applied without explanation the rational basis test, rather than the strict scrutiny review utilized when fundamental rights are impinged, to hold the Texas statute unconstitutional. *Id.* at 2484 ("The Texas statute furthers no legitimate state interest which can justify its intrusion into the personal and private life of the individual."). Although the Court spoke of a person's liberty interest to engage in same-gender sexual relations, and described such conduct as "one element in a personal bond that is more enduring," *id.* at 2478, 2484, the Court did not declare that participation in such conduct is a fundamental right. *See id.* at 2488 (Scalia, J., dissenting). . . .

For the foregoing reasons, we reject Petitioners' contention that *Lawrence* establishes entry in same-sex marriages as a fundamental right. We therefore examine the fundamental right to marry to determine whether it encompasses the right to marry someone of the same gender.

[283] Petitioners argue that because the freedom to enter marriage has long been recognized as a fundamental right, *see Maynard v. Hill*, 125 U.S. 190, 205 (1888), that freedom necessarily includes the right to choose a same-sex spouse. Although marriage traditionally has involved opposite-sex partners, Petitioners contend that this tradition, like others before it, must crumble under our evolving understanding of liberty. *See Lawrence*, 123 S. Ct. at 2484. . . .

To support their contention, Petitioners first rely on *Loving v. Virginia*, wherein the Court held that a Virginia law forbidding interracial marriages deprived the couple in that case of their fundamental right to marry. 388 U.S. at 12. The Court explained that "the freedom of choice to marry [cannot] be restricted by invidious racial discrimination," but must be left to individual preference. *Id.* Thus, although historical custom supported such anti-miscegenation laws . . . Virginia's law was not spared from constitutional attack. *Bowers*, 478 U.S. at 216 (Stevens, J., dissenting) (adopted in *Lawrence*, 123 S. Ct. at 2483–84).

Petitioners assert that because the "freedom of choice to marry" recognized in *Loving* is unrestricted, it encompasses the right to marry anyone, including a same-sex partner, even in the face of traditional, societal disapproval of such unions. We disagree. Implicit in *Loving* and predecessor opinions is the notion that marriage, often linked to procreation, is a union forged between one man and one woman. 388 U.S. at 12 ("Marriage is one of the 'basic civil rights of man,' fundamental to our very existence and survival.") (citation omitted). . . . Thus, while *Loving* expanded the traditional scope of the fundamental right to marry by granting interracial couples unrestricted access to the state-sanctioned marriage institution, that decision was anchored to the concept of marriage as a union involving persons of the opposite sex. In contrast, recognizing a right to marry someone of the same sex would not expand the established right to marry, but would redefine the legal meaning of "marriage." . . .

[284] Petitioners finally argue that the choice to enter a same-sex marriage must be granted fundamental-right status in view of society's evolving acceptance of same-sex unions. . . .

We are mindful of the Supreme Court's admonition to "exercise the utmost care" in conferring fundamental-right status on a newly asserted interest lest we transform the liberty protected by due process into judicial policy preferences rather than principles born of public debate and legislative action. *Glucksberg*, 521 U.S. at 720. In exercising that care, we reject Petitioners' argument.

Although same-sex relationships are more open and have garnered greater societal acceptance in recent years, same-sex marriages are neither deeply rooted in the legal and social history of our Nation or state nor are they implicit in the concept of ordered liberty. *Id.* at 720–21. Despite changing attitudes about both homosexuality and the attributes of "family," no state in this Nation has enacted legislation allowing same-sex marriages. To the contrary, Congress and the majority of states, including Arizona, have enacted legislation in recent years explicitly limiting marriage to opposite-sex unions.

This court does not dispute that a homosexual person's choice of life partner is an intimate and important decision. However, not all important decisions [285] sounding in personal autonomy are protected fundamental rights. *Id.* at 727–28 . . .

C. Rational Basis Review

Because Petitioners do not have a fundamental right to enter a same-sex marriage, we review the constitutionality of A.R.S. §§ 25-101(C) and -125(A) using the [286] rational basis analysis. *See supra* ¶ 9. We presume the prohibition is constitutional and will uphold it if there is "a reasonable, even though debatable, basis for [its] enactment." *State v. Murphy*, 117 Ariz. 57, 61, 505 P.2d 1070, 1074 (1977). . . . Petitioners bear the burden of proving that Arizona's prohibition of same-sex marriages is not rationally related to any conceivable legitimate state interest. *Glucksberg*, 521 U.S. at 728. . . .

The State contends it has a legitimate interest in encouraging procreation and childrearing within the stable environment traditionally associated with marriage, and that limiting marriage to opposite-sex couples is rationally related to that interest. Essentially, the State asserts that by legally sanctioning a heterosexual relationship through marriage, thereby imposing both obligations and benefits on the couple and inserting the State in the relationship, the State communicates to parents and prospective parents that their long-term, committed relationships are uniquely important as a public concern. . . . [citations omitted] . . . Because the State's interest in committed sexual relationships is limited to those capable of producing children, it contends it reasonably restricts marriage to opposite-sex couples. . . .

Petitioners . . . argue that the State's attempt to link marriage to procreation and childrearing is not reasonable because (1) opposite-sex couples are not required to procreate in order to marry, and (2) same-sex couples also raise children, who would benefit from the stability provided by marriage within the family. However, as the State notes, "[a] perfect fit is not required" under the rational basis test, and we will not overturn a statute "merely because it is not made with 'mathematical nicety, or because in practice it results in some inequality.'" *Big D Constr. Corp.*, 163 Ariz. at 566, 789 P.2d at 1067 (citations omitted).

Allowing all opposite-sex couples to enter marriage under Arizona law, regardless of their willingness or ability to procreate, does not defeat the reasonableness of the link between opposite-sex marriage, procreation, and child-rearing. First, if the State excluded opposite-sex couples from marriage based on their intention or ability to procreate, the State would have to inquire about that subject before issuing a license, thereby implicating constitutionally rooted privacy concerns. *See Griswold*, 381 U.S. at 485–86; *Eisenstadt*, 405 U.S. at 453–54; *Adams v. Howerton*, 486 F. Supp. 1119, 1124–25 (C.D. Cal. 1980) (recognizing government inquiry about couples' procreation plans or requiring sterility tests before issuing marriage licenses would "raise serious constitutional questions"). Second, in light of medical advances affecting sterility, the ability to adopt, and the fact that intentionally childless couples may eventually choose to have a child or have an unplanned pregnancy, the State would have a difficult, if not impossible, task in identifying couples who will never bear and/or raise children. Third, because opposite-sex couples have a fundamental right to marry, *Loving*, 388 U.S. at 12, excluding such couples from marriage could only be justified by a compelling state interest, narrowly tailored to achieve that interest, *Glucksberg*, 521 U.S. at 721, which is not readily apparent. . . .

Likewise, although some same-sex couples also raise children, exclusion of these couples from the marriage relationship does not defeat the reasonableness of the link between opposite-sex marriage, procreation, and child-rearing. Indisputably, the only sexual relationship capable of producing children is one between a man and a woman. The State could reasonably decide that by encouraging opposite-sex couples to marry, [288] thereby assuming legal and financial obligations, the children born from such relationships will have better opportunities to be nurtured and raised by two parents within long-term, committed relationships, which society has traditionally viewed as advantageous for children. Because same-sex couples cannot by themselves procreate, the State could also reasonably decide that sanctioning same-sex marriages would do little to advance the State's interest in ensuring responsible procreation within committed, long-term relationships.

Children raised in families headed by a same-sex couple deserve and benefit from bilateral parenting within long-term, committed relationships just as much as children with married parents. Thus, children in same-sex families could benefit from the stability offered by same-sex marriage, particularly if such children do not have ties with both biological parents. But although the line drawn between couples who may marry (opposite-sex) and those who may not (same-sex) may result in some inequity for children raised by same-sex couples, such inequity is insufficient to negate the State's link between opposite-sex marriage, procreation, and child-rearing. *See Big D Constr. Corp.*, 163 Ariz. at 566, 789 P.2d at 1067; *see also Baker v. State*, 170 Vt. 194, 219, 744 A.2d 864, 882 (1999) ("It is, of course, well settled that statutes are not necessarily unconstitutional because they fail to extend legal protection to all who are similarly situated."). The fact that the line could be drawn differently is a matter for legislative, rather than judicial, consideration. . . .

II. Equal Protection

Petitioners finally argue that A.R.S. §§ 25-101(C) and -125(A) deprive them of the equal protection of laws as guaranteed by both the federal and state[2] constitutions. . . .

It is well-established that legislation may discriminate among classes as long as the burden imposed on the affected class is justifiable. *Simat*, 203 Ariz. at 458, ¶ 15, 56 P.3d at 32. One of three levels of scrutiny is applied by the courts to determine whether sufficient justification exists: rational basis analysis, intermediate scrutiny, or strict scrutiny. *Id.*

The rational basis analysis is substantially similar to the analysis employed to determine whether a law violates an individual's liberty interest guaranteed by substantive due process. *Watson*, 198 Ariz. at 51 n.1, ¶ 7, 6 P.3d at 755 n.1. Thus, a law that disparately treats an affected class is presumptively constitutional and will be upheld if the classification rationally furthers a legitimate state interest. *Romer v. Evans*, 517 U.S. 620, 632–33 (1996). . . .

An intermediate level of scrutiny is used for laws that discriminate against quasi-suspect classifications such as those based on gender and illegitimacy of birth. *Id*. . . . Finally, when the challenged law affects a fundamental right or discriminates against a "suspect class," such as one based on race or national origin, we apply a strict scrutiny analysis . . . *Id*.

Petitioners do not argue that homosexuals are a quasisuspect or suspect class. Rather, they contend that because Arizona's prohibition of same-sex marriages impinges the fundamental right to marry, we must apply strict scrutiny analysis and strike A.R.S. §§ 25-101(C) and -125(A) because they do not serve a compelling state interest. As previously explained, *supra* ¶¶ 14–31, Petitioners do not have a fundamental right to marry each other. Thus, we evaluate Petitioners' equal protection arguments using the rational basis analysis. . . .

Petitioners contend that the State's purpose in prohibiting same-sex marriages is to "single out gay persons to impose a particular disability on them," which cannot serve a legitimate state objective for the reasons explained in *Romer v. Evans*. In *Romer*, the Court addressed an equal protection challenge [290] to Colorado's "Amendment 2" to its constitution, which prohibited all legislative, executive, or judicial action designed to protect homosexual persons from discrimination. 517 U.S. at 624. The Court held that Amendment 2 did not bear a rational relation to a legitimate end due to its "peculiar property of imposing a broad and undifferentiated disability on a single named group," with a breadth "so discontinuous with the reasons offered for it that the amendment seems inexplicable by anything but animus toward the class it affects." *Id*. at 632.

In contrast to Amendment 2, A.R.S. §§ 25-101(C) and -125(A) are not so exceptional and unduly broad as to render the State's reasons for their enactment "inexplicable by anything but animus" towards Arizona's homosexual residents. Arizona's prohibition of same-sex marriages furthers a proper legislative end and was not enacted simply to make same-sex couples unequal to everyone else. . . . Consequently, we reject Petitioners' equal protection challenge to A.R.S. §§ 25-101(C) and -125(A).

CONCLUSION

For the foregoing reasons, we hold that the fundamental right to marry protected by our federal and state constitutions does not encompass the right to marry a same-sex partner. Moreover, although many traditional views of homosexuality have been recast over time in our state and Nation, the choice to marry a same-sex partner has not taken sufficient root to receive constitutional protection as a fundamental right. Because Arizona's prohibition against same-sex marriage rationally furthers a legitimate state interest, we further decide that the prohibition does not deprive Petitioners of their constitutional rights to substantive due process, privacy, or equal protection of the laws. Consequently, it is for the people of Arizona, through their elected representatives or by using the initiative process, rather than this court, to decide whether to permit same-sex marriages. Having accepted jurisdiction of this special action, we deny relief.

NOTES

[1]As Petitioners point out, Justice Scalia, in his dissenting opinion in *Lawrence*, admonished the public to disbelieve the Court's assertion that the case did not involve whether governments must formally recognize homosexual relationships. 123 S. Ct. at 2497–98. He considered the Court's comments concerning homosexual autonomy to be "illuminating" regarding the issue of same-sex marriage. *Id*. at 2498; *but see id*. at 2487–88 (O'Connor, J., concurring) (asserting state interest in promoting marriage severable from state disapproval of same-sex relations). As explained hereafter, *infra* ¶ 18, and with due respect to Justice Scalia, we do not read the Court's comments so broadly.

[2]The Equal Privileges and Immunities Clause in the Arizona Constitution provides that "[n]o law shall be enacted granting to any citizen, class of citizens, or corporation other than municipal, privileges or immunities which, upon the same terms, shall not equally belong to all citizens or corporations." Ariz. Const. art. 2, § 13. We have held that this clause provides the same benefits as its federal counterpart, *Empress Adult Video & Bookstore*, 204 Ariz. at 64, ¶ 36, 59 P.3d at 828, and Petitioners do not argue otherwise.

THE DOCTRINE OF LIBERTY IN ITS APPLICATION TO MORALS

—James Fitzjames Stephen—

. . . These explanations enable me to restate without fear of misapprehension the object of morally intolerant legislation. It is to establish, to maintain, and to give power to that which the legislator regards as a good moral system or standard. For the reasons already assigned I think that this object is good if and in so far as the system so established and maintained is good. How far any particular system is good or not is a question which probably does not admit of any peremptory final decision; but I may observe that there are a considerable number of things which appear good and bad, though no doubt in different degrees, to all mankind. For the practical purpose of legislation refinements are of little importance. In any given age and nation virtue and vice have meanings which for that purpose are quite definite enough. In England at the present day many theories about morality are current, and speculative men differ about them widely, but they relate not so much to the question whether particular acts are right or wrong, as to the question of the precise meaning of the distinction, the manner in which the moral character of particular actions is to be decided, and the reasons for preferring right to wrong conduct. The result is that the object of promoting virtue and preventing vice must be admitted to be both a good one and one sufficiently intelligible for legislative purposes.

If this is so, the only remaining questions will be as to the efficiency of the means at the disposal of society for this purpose, and the cost of their application. Society has at its disposal two great instruments by which vice may be prevented and virtue promoted—namely, law and public opinion; and law is either criminal or civil. The use of each of these instruments is subject to certain limits and conditions, and the wisdom of attempting to make men good either by Act of Parliament or by the action of public opinion depends entirely upon the degree in which those limits and conditions are recognized and acted upon.

First, I will take the case of criminal law. What are the conditions under which and the limitations within which it can be applied with success to the object of making men better? In considering this question it must be borne in mind that criminal law is at once by far the most powerful and by far the roughest engine which society can use for any purpose. Its power is shown by the fact that it can and does render crime exceedingly difficult and dangerous. Indeed, in civilized society it absolutely prevents avowed open crime committed with the strong hand, except in cases where crime rises to the magnitude of civil war. Its roughness hardly needs illustration. It strikes so hard that it can be enforced only on the gravest occasions, and with every sort of precaution against abuse or mistake. Before an act can be treated as a crime, it ought to be capable of distinct definition and of specific proof, and it ought also to be of such a nature that it is worth while to prevent it at the risk of inflicting great damage, direct and indirect, upon those who commit it. These conditions are seldom, if ever, fulfilled by mere vices. It would obviously be impossible to indict a man for ingratitude or perfidy. Such charges are too vague for specific discussion and distinct proof on the one side, and disproof on the other.

Moreover, the expense of the investigations necessary for the legal punishment of such conduct would be enormous. It would be necessary to go into an infinite number of delicate and subtle inquiries which would tear off all privacy from the lives of a large number of persons. These considerations are, I think, conclusive reasons against treating vice in general as a crime.

The excessive harshness of criminal law is also a circumstance which very greatly narrows the range of its application. It is the *ratio ultima* of the majority against persons whom its application assumes to have renounced the common bonds which connect men together. When a man is subjected to legal punishment, society appeals directly and exclusively to his fears. It renounces the attempt to work upon his affections or feelings. In other words, it puts itself into distinct, harsh, and undisguised opposition to his wishes; and the effect of this will be to make him rebel against the law. The violence of the rebellion will be measured partly by the violence of the passion the indulgence of which is forbidden, and partly by the degree to which the law can count upon an ally in the man's own conscience. A law which enters into a direct contest with a fierce imperious passion, which the person who feels it does not admit to be bad, and which is not directly injurious to others, will generally do more harm than good; and this is perhaps the principal reason why it is impossible to legislate directly against unchastity, unless it takes forms which every one regards as monstrous and horrible. The subject is not one for detailed discussion, but any one who will follow out the reflections which this hint suggests will find that they supply a striking illustration of the limits which the harshness of criminal law imposes upon its range.

If we now look at the different acts which satisfy the conditions specified, it will, I think, be found that criminal law in this country actually is applied to the suppression of vice and so to the promotion of virtue to a very considerable extent; and this I say is right.

The punishment of common crimes, the gross forms of force and fraud, is no doubt ambiguous. It may be justified on the principle of self-protection, and apart from any question as to their moral character. It is not, however, difficult to show that these acts have in fact been forbidden and subjected to punishment not only because they are dangerous to society, and so ought to be prevented, but also for the sake of gratifying the feeling of hatred—call it revenge, resentment, or what you will—which the contemplation of such conduct excites in healthily constituted minds. If this can be shown, it will follow that criminal law is in the nature of a persecution of the grosser forms of vice, and an emphatic assertion of the principle that the feeling of hatred and the desire of vengeance above-mentioned are important elements of human nature which ought in such cases to be satisfied in a regular public and legal manner.

The strongest of all proofs of this is to be found in the principles universally admitted and acted upon as regulating the amount of punishment. If vengeance affects, and ought to affect, the amount of punishment, every circumstance which aggravates or extenuates the wickedness of an act will operate in aggravation or diminution of punishment. If the object of legal punishment is simply the prevention of specific acts, this will not be the case. Circumstances which extenuate the wickedness of the crime will often operate in aggravation of punishment. If, as I maintain, both objects must be kept in view, such circumstances will operate in different ways according to the nature of the case.

A judge has before him two criminals, one of whom appears, from the circumstances of the case, to be ignorant and depraved, and to have given way to very strong temptation, under the influence of the other, who is a man of rank and education, and who committed the offence of which both are convicted under comparatively slight temptation. I will venture to say that if he made any difference between them at all every judge on the English bench would give the first man a lighter sentence than the second.

What should we think of such an address to the prisoners as this? You, A, are a most dangerous man. You are ignorant, you are depraved, and you are accordingly peculiarly liable to be led into crime by the solicitations or influence of people like your accomplice B. Such influences constitute to men like you a temptation practically all but irresistible. The class to which you belong is a large one, and is accessible only to the coarsest possible motives. For these reasons I must put into the opposite scale as heavy a weight as I can, and the sentence of the court upon you is that you be taken to the place from whence you came and from thence to a place of execution, and that there you be hanged by the neck till you are dead. As to you, B, you are undoubtedly an infamous wretch. Between you and your tool A there can, morally speaking, be no comparison at all. But I have nothing to do with that. You belong to a small and not a dangerous class. The temptation to which you gave way was slight, and the impression made upon me by your conduct is that you really did not care very much whether you committed this crime or not. From a moral point of view, this may perhaps increase your guilt; but it shows that the motive to be overcome is less powerful in your case than in A's. You belong, moreover, to a class, and occupy a position in society, in which exposure and loss of character are much dreaded. This you will have to undergo. Your case is a very odd one, and it is not likely that you will wish to commit such a crime again, or that others will follow your example. Upon the whole, I think that what has passed will deter others from such conduct as much as actual punishment. It is, however, necessary to keep a hold over you. You will therefore be discharged on your own recognizance to come up and receive judgment when called upon, and unless you conduct yourself better for the future, you will assuredly be so called upon, and if you do not appear, your recognizance will be inexorably forfeited.

Caricature apart, the logic of such a view is surely unimpeachable. If all that you want of criminal law is the prevention of crime by the direct fear of punishment, the fact that a temptation is strong is a reason why punishment should be severe. In some instances this actually is the case. It shows the reason why political crimes and offences against military discipline are punished so severely. But in most cases the strength of the temptation operates in mitigation of punishment, and the reason of this is that criminal law operates not merely by producing fear, but also indirectly, but very powerfully, by giving distinct shape to the feeling of anger, and a distinct satisfaction to the desire of vengeance which crime excites in a healthy mind.

Other illustrations of the fact that English criminal law does recognize morality are to be found in the fact that a considerable number of acts which need not be specified are treated as crimes merely because they are regarded as grossly immoral.

I have already shown in what manner Mr Mill deals with these topics. It is, I venture to think, utterly unsatisfactory. The impression it makes upon me is that he feels that such acts ought to be punished, and that he is able to reconcile this with his fundamental principles only by subtleties quite unworthy of him. Admit the relation for which I am contending between law and morals, and all becomes perfectly clear. All the acts referred to are unquestionably wicked. Those who do them are ashamed of them. They are all capable of being clearly defined and specifically proved or disproved, and there can be no question at all that legal punishment reduces them to small dimensions, and forces the criminals to carry on their practices with secrecy and precaution. In other words, the object of their suppression is good, and the means adequate. In practice this is subject to highly important qualifications, of which I will only say here that those who have due regard to the incurable weaknesses of human nature will be very careful how they inflict penalties upon mere vice, or even upon those who make a trade of promoting it, unless special circumstances call for their infliction. It is one thing however to tolerate vice so long as it is inoffensive, and quite another to give it a legal right not only to exist, but to assert itself in the face of the world as an 'experiment in living' as good as another, and entitled to the same protection from law.

I now pass to the manner in which civil law may and does, and as I say properly, promote virtue and prevent vice. This is a subject so wide that I prefer indicating its nature by a few illustrations to attempting to deal with it systematically. It would, however, be easy to show that nearly every branch of civil law assumes the existence of a standard of moral good and evil which the public at large have an interest in maintaining, and in many cases enforcing—a proceeding which is diametrically opposed to Mr Mill's fundamental principles.[1]

The main subject with which law is conversant is that of rights and duties, and all the commoner and more important rights and duties presuppose some theory of morals. Contracts are one great source of rights and duties. Is there any country in the world the courts of which would enforce a contract which the Legislature regarded as immoral? and is there any country in which there would be much difficulty in specific cases in saying whether the object or the consideration of a contract was or was not immoral? Other rights are of a more general nature, and are liable to be violated by wrongs. Take the case of a man's right to his reputation, which is violated by defamation. How, without the aid of some sort of theory of morals, can it be determined whether the publication of defamatory matter is justifiable or not?

Perhaps the most pointed of all illustrations of the moral character of civil law is to be found in the laws relating to marriage and inheritance. They all proceed upon an essentially moral theory as to the relation of the sexes. Take the case of illegitimate children. A bastard is *filius nulius*—he inherits nothing, he has no claim on his putative father. What is all this except the expression of the strongest possible determination on the part of the Legislature to recognize, maintain, and favour marriage in every possible manner as the foundation of civilized society? It has been plausibly maintained that these laws bear hardly upon bastards, punishing them for the sins of their parents. It is not necessary to my purpose to go into this, though it appears to me that the law is right. I make the remark merely for the sake of showing to what lengths the law does habitually go for the purpose of maintaining the most important of all moral principles, the principle upon which one great department of it is entirely founded. It is a case in which a good object is promoted by efficient and adequate means.

These illustrations are so strong that I will add nothing more to them from this branch of the law, but I may refer to a few miscellaneous topics which bear on the same subject. Let us take first the case of sumptuary laws. Mr Mill's principles would no doubt condemn them, and, as they have gone out of fashion, it may be said, that unless my principle does so too, it is the worse for my principle. I certainly should not condemn sumptuary laws on the principle that the object in view is either bad or improper for legislation. I can hardly imagine a greater blessing to the whole community than a reduction in the lavish extravagance which makes life so difficult and laborious. It is difficult for me to look at a lace machine with patience. The ingenuity which went to devise it might have made human life materially happier in a thousand ways, and its actual effect has been to enable a great number of people to wear an imitation of an ornament which derives what little merit it has principally from its being made by hand. If any one could practically solve the problem of securing the devotion of the higher forms of human ingenuity to objects worthy of them, he would be an immense benefactor to his species. Life, however, has become so complicated, vested interests are so powerful and so worthy of respect, it is so clear that the enforcement of any conceivable law upon such a subject would be impossible, that I do not think anyone in these days would be found to propose one. In a simpler age of the world and in a smaller community such laws may have been very useful. The same remarks apply to laws as to the distribution of property and to the regulation of trade.

Laws relating to education and to military service and the discipline of the army have a moral side of the utmost importance. Mr Mill would be the first to admit this; indeed, in several passages of his book he insists on the fact that society has complete control over the rising generation as a reason why it should not coerce adults into morality. This surely is the very opposite of the true conclusion. How is it possible for society to accept the position of an educator unless it has moral principles on which to educate? How, having accepted that position and having educated people up to a certain point, can it draw a line at which education ends and perfect moral indifference begins? When a private man educates his family, his superiority over them is founded principally on his superior age and experience; and as this personal superiority ceases, the power which is founded upon it gradually ceases also. Between society at large and individuals the difference is of another kind. The fixed principles and institutions of society express not merely the present opinions of the ruling part of the community, but the accumulated results of centuries of experience, and these constitute a standard by which the conduct of individuals may be tried, and to which they are in a variety of ways, direct and indirect, compelled to conform. This, I think, is one of the meanings which may be attached to the assertion that education never ceases. As a child grows into a man, and as a young man grows into an old man, he is brought under the influence of successive sets of educators, each of whom sets its mark upon him. It is no uncommon thing to see aged parents taught by their grown-up children lessons learned by the children in their intercourse with their own generation. All of us are continually educating each other, and in every instance this is and must be a process at once moral and more or less coercive.[2]

As to Mr Mill's doctrine that the coercive influence of public opinion ought to be exercised only for self-protective purposes, it seems to me a paradox so startling that it is almost impossible to argue against it. A single consideration on the subject is sufficient to prove this. The principle is one which it is impossible to carry out. It is like telling a rose that it ought to smell sweet only for the purpose of affording pleasure to the owner of the ground in which it grows. People form and express their opinions on each other, which, collectively, form public opinion, for a thousand reasons; to amuse themselves; for the sake of something to talk about; to gratify this or that momentary feeling; but the effect of such opinions, when formed, is quite independent of the grounds of their formation. A man is tried for murder, and just escapes conviction.

People read the trial from curiosity; they discuss it for the sake of the discussion; but if, by whatever means, they are brought to think that the man was in all probability guilty, they shun his society as they would shun any other hateful thing. The opinion produces its effect in precisely the same way whatever was its origin.

The result of these observations is that both law and public opinion do in many cases exercise a powerful coercive influence on morals, for objects which are good in the sense explained above, and by means well calculated to attain those objects, to a greater or less extent at a not inadequate expense. If this is so, I say law and public opinion do well, and I do not see how either the premises or the conclusion are to be disproved.

Of course there are limits to the possibility of useful interference with morals, either by law or by public opinion; and it is of the highest practical importance that these limits should be carefully observed. The great leading principles on the subject are few and simple, though they cannot be stated with any great precision. It will be enough to mention the following:

1. Neither legislation nor public opinion ought to be meddlesome. A very large proportion of the matters upon which people wish to interfere with their neighbours are trumpery little things which are of no real importance at all. The busybody and world-betterer who will never let things alone, or trust people to take care of themselves, is a common and a contemptible character. The commonplaces directed against these small creatures are perfectly just, but to try to put them down by denying the connection between law and morals is like shutting all light and air out of a house in order to keep out gnats and blue-bottle flies.

2. Both legislation and public opinion, but especially the latter, are apt to be most mischievous and cruelly unjust if they proceed upon imperfect evidence. To form and express strong opinions about the wickedness of a man whom you do not know, the immorality or impiety of a book you have not read, the merits of a question on which you are uninformed, is to run a great risk of inflicting a great wrong. It is hanging first and trying afterwards, or more frequently not trying at all. This, however, is no argument against hanging after a fair trial.

3. Legislation ought in all cases to be graduated to the existing level of morals in the time and country in which it is employed. You cannot punish anything which public opinion, as expressed in the common practice of society, does not strenuously and unequivocally condemn. To try to do so is a sure way to produce gross hypocrisy and furious reaction. To be able to punish, a moral majority must be overwhelming. Law cannot be better than the nation in which it exists, though it may and can protect an acknowledged moral standard, and may gradually be increased in strictness as the standard rises. We punish, with the utmost severity, practices which in Greece and Rome went almost uncensured. It is possible that a time may come when it may appear natural and right to punish adultery, seduction, or possibly even fornication, but the prospect is, at present, indefinitely remote, and it may be doubted whether we are moving in that direction.

4. Legislation and public opinion ought in all cases whatever scrupulously to respect privacy. To define the province of privacy distinctly is impossible, but it can be described in general terms. All the more intimate and delicate relations of life are of such a nature that to submit them to unsympathetic observation, or to observation which is sympathetic in the wrong way, inflicts great pain, and may inflict lasting moral injury. Privacy may be violated not only by the intrusion of a stranger, but by compelling or persuading a person to direct too much attention to his own feelings and to attach too much importance to their analysis. The common usage of language affords a practical test which is almost perfect upon this subject. Conduct which can be described as indecent is always in one way or another a violation of privacy.

There is one perfect illustration of this, of which I may say a few words. It is the case of the confessional and casuistry generally. So far as I have been able to look into the writings of casuists, their works appear to contain a spiritual penal code, in which all the sins of act and thought, of intention and imagination, which it is possible for men to commit, are described with legal minuteness and with specific illustrations, and are ranged under the two heads of mortal and venial, according as they subject the sinner to eternal damnation or only to purgatory. Nothing can exceed the interest and curiosity of some of the discussions conducted in these strange works, though some of them (by no means so large a proportion as popular rumour would suggest) are revolting. So far as my observation has gone, I should say that nothing can be more unjust than the popular notion that the casuists explained away moral obligations. Escobar in particular (Pascal's *bete noire*) gives me rather the impression of a sort of half-humorous simplicity.[3]

The true objection to the whole system, and the true justification of the aversion with which it has been regarded, is that it is perhaps the greatest intrusion upon privacy, the most audacious and successful invasion by law of matters which lie altogether out of the reach of law, recorded in history. Of course if the postulate on which it is founded is true—if, in fact, there is a celestial penal code which classifies as felonies or misdemeanours punishable respectively with hell or purgatory all human sins—and if priests have the power of getting the felonies commuted into misdemeanours by confession and absolution—there is no more to be said; but this supposition need not be seriously considered. It is, I think, impossible to read the books in question without feeling convinced that a trial in a court which administers such laws upon evidence supplied exclusively by the criminal must be either a mere form, a delusion of a very mischievous kind, or a process which would destroy all the self respect of the person submitted to it and utterly confuse all his notions of right and wrong, good and evil. That justice should be done without the fullest possible knowledge of every fact connected with every transgression is impossible. That every such fact should be recalled, analyzed, dwelt upon, weighed and measured, without in a great measure renewing the evil of the act itself, and blunting the conscience as to similar acts in future, seems equally impossible. That any one human creature should ever really strip his soul star naked for the inspection of any other, and be able to hold up his head afterwards, is not, I suppose, impossible, because so many people profess to do it; but to lookers-on from the outside it is inconceivable.

The inference which I draw from this illustration is that there is a sphere, none the less real because it is impossible to define its limits, within which law and public opinion are intruders likely to do more harm than good. To try to regulate the internal affairs of a family, the relations of love or friendship, or many other things of the same sort, by law or by the coercion of public opinion, is like trying to pull an eyelash out of a man's eye with a pair of tongs. They may put out the eye, but they will never get hold of the eyelash.

These, I think, are the principal forms in which society can and actually does promote virtue and restrain vice. It is impossible to form any estimate of the degree in which it succeeds in doing so, but it may perhaps be said that the principal importance of what is done in this direction by criminal law is that in extreme cases it brands gross acts of vice with the deepest mark of infamy which can be impressed upon them, and that in this manner it protects the public and accepted standard of morals from being grossly and openly violated. In short, it affirms in a singularly emphatic manner a principle which is absolutely inconsistent with and contradictory to Mr Mill's—the principle, namely, that there are acts of wickedness so gross and outrageous that, self-protection apart, they must be prevented as far as possible at any cost to the offender, and punished, if they occur, with exemplary severity.

As for the influence of public opinion upon virtue and vice, it is incalculably great, but it is difficult to say much as to its extent, because its influence is indefinite, and is shown in an infinite variety of ways. It must also be observed that, though far more powerful and minute than the influence of law, it is infinitely less well instructed. It is also exceedingly liable to abuse, for public opinion is multiform, and may mean the gossip of a village or the spite of a coterie, as well as the deliberate judgment of a section of the rational part of mankind. On the other hand, its power depends on its nature and on the nature of the person on whom it acts. A calm, strong, and rational man will know when to despise and when to respect it, though no rules can be laid down on the subject. It is, however, clear that this much may be said of it in general. If people neither formed nor expressed any opinions on their neighbours' conduct except in so far as that conduct affected them personally, one of the principal motives to do well and one of the principal restraints from doing ill would be withdrawn from the world. . . .

NOTES

[1]Mr Morley says on this: 'A good deal of rather bustling ponderosity is devoted to proving that the actual laws do in many points assume the existence of a standard of moral good and evil, and that this proceeding is diametrically opposed to Mr Mill's fundamental principles. To this one would say first that the actual existence of laws of any given kind is wholly irrelevant to Mr Mill's contention,

which is that it would be better if laws of such a kind did not exist. Secondly, Mr Mill never says, nor is it at all essential to his doctrine to hold, that a government ought not to have "a standard of moral good and evil which the public at large have an interest in maintaining, and in many instances enforcing." He only set apart a certain class of cases to which the right or duty of enforcement of the criminal standard does not extend—self-regarding cases.'

As to the first point, surely it is not irrelevant to show that Mr Mill is at issue with the practical conclusions to which most nations have been led by experience. Those to whom I address myself may be disposed to doubt whether a principle which condemns so many of the institutions under which they live can be right.

As to the second point, Mr Mill says in express words: 'Society, as society, has no right to decide anything to be wrong which concerns only the individual.' This I think is equivalent to denying that society ought to have a moral standard, for by a moral standard I understand a judgment that certain acts are wrong, whoever they concern. Whether they concern the agent only or others as well, is and must be an accident. Mr Morley, however, thinks that Mr Mill's opinion was that society may and ought to have a moral standard, but ought not to enforce it in the case of self-regarding acts. I say, and attempt throughout the whole of this chapter to prove, that as regards the 'moral coercion of public opinion,' this is neither possible nor desirable, and that as regards legal coercion, the question whether it is possible and desirable depends upon considerations drawn from the nature of law, civil and criminal. Whether I am right or wrong I cannot see that I have not understood Mr Mill, or that I have not contradicted him.

[2]Mr Morley says in reference to this passage and the preceding passages from pp. 153–4: 'Mr. Stephen . . . proves the contradictory of assertions which his adversary never made, as when he cites judicial instances which imply the recognition of morality by the law.' I think Mr Morley misunderstands my argument, which nevertheless appears to me very plain. It is simply this: I say laws can and do promote virtue and diminish vice by coercion in the cases and in the ways specified, and their interference does more good than harm. The contradictory of this proposition would be that in the cases specified legal interference does more harm than good. Surely, if Mr Mill's general principle is true, this must follow from it. Therefore in denying it I deny a necessary inference from the principle which I attack.

[3]His habit of putting all his illustrations in the first person has a very strange effect. Here for instance is a catalogue of the mortal sins which an advocate may commit. 'Defendi litem injustam, seu minus probabilem, quando minimè poteram, et debebam de minori probabilitate consulentem admonere. Ob studit defectum falso de probabilitate causae judicavi, quam improbabilem omnino post studium rejicerem. Induxi partem ad pactum, cum nulla justitia inniti cognoscerem, et nihil ab altero posset exigi nisi parum aliquid quod fortasse daretur in vexationis redemptionem.' (I got my client too good terms in a compromise.) 'Plures causaes quam discutere poteram suscepi' (I held briefs in too many committee-rooms at once.) 'Leges, statuta et ordinationes ignoravi' (I did not know all the local government acts), &c., &c.—Escobar, Theol. Mor. 286. The last appears to me to be a very hard law. It is difficult to imagine the state of mind of a man who really thought that he was authorized to declare as a part of the law of God, that a lawyer who did not know all 'laws, statutes, and ordinances' would be eternally damned unless he repented.

DEMOCRACY AND DISTRUST

A Theory of Judicial Review

—John Hart Ely—

The remainder of this chapter will comprise three arguments in favor of a participation-oriented, representation-reinforcing approach to judicial review. The first will take longer than the others, since it will necessitate a tour, albeit brisk, of the Constitution itself. What this tour will reveal, contrary to the standard characterization of the Constitution as "an enduring but evolving statement of general values, is that in fact the selection and accommodation of substantive values is left almost entirely to the political process and instead the document is overwhelmingly concerned, on the one hand, with procedural fairness in the resolution of individual disputes (process writ small), and on the other, with what might capaciously be designated process writ large with ensuring broad participation in the processes and distributions of government. An argument by way of *ejusdem generis* seems particularly justified in this case, since the constitutional provisions for which we are attempting to identify modes of supplying content, such as the Ninth Amendment and the Privileges or Immunities Clause, seem to have been included in a "we must have missed something here, so let's trust our successors to add what we missed" spirit. On my more expansive days, therefore, I am tempted to claim that the mode of review developed here represents the ultimate interpretivism. Our review will tell us something else that may be even more relevant to the issue before us—that the few attempts the various framers *have* made to freeze substantive values by designating them for special protection in the document have been ill-fated, normally resulting in repeal, either officially or by interpretative pretense. This suggests a conclusion with important implications for the task of giving content to the document's more open-ended provisions, that preserving fundamental values is not an appropriate constitutional task.

The other two arguments are susceptible to briefer statement but are not less important. The first is that a representation-reinforcing approach to judicial review, unlike its rival value-protecting approach, is not inconsistent with, but on the contrary (and quite by design) entirely supportive of, the underlying premises of the American system of representative democracy. The second is that such an approach, again in contradistinction to its rival, involves tasks that courts, as experts on process and (more important) as political outsiders, can sensibly claim to be better qualified and situated to perform than political officials.

THE NATURE OF THE UNITED STATES CONSTITUTION

In the United States the basic charter of the law-making process is found in a written constitution . . . [W]e should resist the temptation to clutter up that document with amendments relating to substantive matters . . . [Such attempts] involve the obvious unwisdom of trying to solve tomorrow's problems today. But their more insidious danger lies in the weakening effect they would have on the moral force of the Constitution itself.

—Lon Fuller

Many of our colonial forebears' complaints against British rule were phrased in "constitutional" terms. Seldom, however, was the claim one of deprivation of some treasured good or substantive right: the American colonists, at least the white males, were among the freest and best-off people in the history of the world, and by and large they knew it. "Constitutional" claims thus were often jurisdictional—that Parliament lacked authority, say, to regulate the colonies' "internal commerce"—the foundation for the claim being generally that we were not represented in Parliament. (Obviously the colonists weren't any crazier about being taxed than anyone else is, but what they damned as tyrannical was taxation *without* representation.) Or they were arguments of inequality: claims of entitlement to "the rights of Englishmen" had an occasional natural law flavor, but the more common meaning was that suggested by the words, a claim for equality of treatment with those living in England. Thus the colonists "constitutional" arguments drew on the two participational themes we have been considering: that (1) their input into the process by which they were governed was insufficient, and that (partly as a consequence) (2) they were being denied what others were receiving. The American version of revolution, wrote Hannah Arendt, "actually proclaims no more than the necessity of civilized government for all mankind; the French version . . . proclaims the existence of rights independent of and outside the body public . . .

The theme that justice and happiness are best assured not by trying to define them for all time, but rather by attending to the governmental processes by which their dimensions would be specified over time, carried over into our critical constitutional documents. Even our foremost "natural law" statement, the Declaration of Independence, after adverting to some admirable but assuredly open-ended goals—made more so by using "the pursuit of happiness" in place of the already broad Lockean reference to "property—signals its appreciation of the critical role of (democratic) process:

> We hold these truths to be self-evident, that all men are created equal, that they are endowed by their creator with certain unalienable rights: that among these are life, liberty, and the pursuit of happiness; that to secure these rights governments are instituted among men, deriving their just powers from the consent of the governed . . .

The Constitution, less surprisingly, begins on the same note, not one of trying to set forth some governing ideology—the values mentioned in the Preamble could hardly be more pliable—but rather one of ensuring a durable structure for the ongoing resolution of policy disputes:

> We the People of the United States, in Order to form a more perfect Union, establish Justice, insure domestic Tranquility, provide for the common defence, promote the general Welfare, and secure the Blessings of Liberty to ourselves and our Posterity, do ordain and establish this Constitution for the United States of America.

I don't suppose it will surprise anyone to learn that the body of the original Constitution is devoted almost entirely to structure, explaining who among the various actors—federal government, state government; Congress, executive, judiciary—has authority to do what, and going on to fill in a good bit of detail about how these persons are to be selected and to conduct their business. Even provisions that at first glance might seem primarily designed to assure or preclude certain substantive results seem on reflection to be principally concerned with process. Thus, for example, the provision that treason "shall consist only in levying War against [the United States], or in adhering to their Enemies, giving them Aid and Comfort," appears at least in substantial measure to have been a precursor of the First Amendment, reacting to the recognition that persons in power can disable their detractors by charging disagreement as treason. The prohibitions against granting titles of nobility seem rather plainly to have been designed to buttress the democratic ideal that all are equals in government. The Ex Post Facto and Bill of Attainder Clauses prove on analysis to be separation of powers provisions, enjoining the legislature to act prospectively and by general rule (just as the judiciary is implicitly enjoined by Article III to act retrospectively and by specific decree). And we have seen that the Privileges and Immunities Clause of Article IV, and at least in one aspect—the other being a grant of congressional power—the Commerce Clause as well, function as equality provisions, guaranteeing virtual representation to the politically powerless.

During most of this century the Obligation of Contracts Clause has not played a significant role. Powerful arguments have been made that the clause was intended importantly to limit the extent to which state governments could control the subjects and terms of private contracts. Early in the nineteenth century the Supreme Court rejected this broad interpretation, however, holding that the clause affected only the extent to which the legislature could alter or overrule the terms of contracts in existence at the time the statute was passed, and thus did not affect what legislation could say about future contracts. What's more, though there have been signs of stiffening in the past two years, the Court in general has not been very energetic about protecting existing contracts either, holding in essence that legislatures can alter them so long as they do so reasonably (which virtually denudes the clause of any independent function). It is tempting to conclude that the Court's long-standing interpretation of the clause as protecting only existing contracts reduces it to just another hedge against retroactive legislation and thus, like the Ex Post Facto Clause, essentially a separation of powers provision. That conclusion, however, is a little quick. Legislation effectively overruling the terms of an existing contract is not really "retroactive" in the ex post facto sense of attaching untoward consequences to an act performed before it was enacted; rather it refuses to recognize a prior act (the making of the contract) as a defense to or exemption from a legal regime the legislature now wishes to impose. Thus both interpretations of the clause recognize the existence of a contract as a special shield against legislative regulation of future behavior, though on the long-accepted narrow interpretation only contracts already in existence can serve thus.

At this point another temptation arises, to characterize the Contracts Clause as serving an institutional or "separation of powers" function of cordoning off an extragovernmental enclave, in this case an enclave of decision via contract, to serve as a counterpoise to governmental authority. The problem with this account is not that it does not fit, but rather that it will *always* fit: it is difficult to imagine any purported constitutional right that cannot be described as creating a private space where actions antithetical to the wishes of our elected representatives can be taken. For this reason the account seems incapable of serving as a meaningful explanation (or as a basis from which broader constitutional themes can responsibly be extrapolated). Thus whichever interpretation of the clause was in fact intended, it is difficult to avoid the conclusion that in the Contracts Clause the framers and ratifiers meant to single out for special protection from the political processes—though note that in this case it is only the *state* political processes—a substantive value that is not wholly susceptible to convincing rationalization in terms of either the processes of government or procedure more narrowly conceived. On the broad and rejected interpretation, that value is contract, the ability to arrive at binding agreements. On the narrower and received interpretation, applying the clause only to contracts in existence at the time of the legislation—which I should reiterate is an interpretation the Court has not, at least until very recently, pursued very enthusiastically either—what is protected is a somewhat narrower reliance interest, an assurance that by entering into a contract one can render oneself immune from future shifts in the identity or thinking of one's elected representatives.

This needn't throw us into a tailspin: my claim is only that the original Constitution was principally, indeed I would say over-whelmingly, dedicated to concerns of process and structure and not to the identification and preservation of specific substantive values. Any claim that it was exclusively so conceived would be ridiculous (as would any comparable claim about any comparably complicated human undertaking). And indeed there are other provisions in the original document that seem almost entirely value-oriented, though my point, of course, is that they are few and far between.[1] Thus "corruption of blood" is forbidden as a punishment for treason. Punishing people for their parents' transgressions is outlawed as a substantively unfair outcome: it just can't be done, irrespective of procedures and also irrespective of whether it is done to the children of all offenders. The federal government, along with the states, is precluded from taxing articles exported from any state. Here too an outcome is simply precluded; what might be styled a value, the economic value of free trade among the states, is protected. This short list, however, covers just about all the values protected in the original Constitution—save one. And a big one it was. Although an understandable squeamishness kept the word out of the document, *slavery* must be counted a substantive value to which the original Constitution meant to extend unusual protection from the ordinary legislative process, at least temporarily. Prior to 1808, Congress was forbidden to prohibit the slave trade into any state that wanted it, and the states were obliged to return escaping slaves to their "homes."

The idea of a bill of rights was not even brought up until close to the end of the Constitutional Convention, at which time it was rejected. The reason is not that the framers were unconcerned with liberty, but rather that by their lights a bill of rights did not belong in a constitution, at least not in the one they had drafted. As Hamilton explained in *Federalist* 84, "a minute detail of particular rights is certainly far less applicable to a Constitution like that under consideration, which is merely intended to regulate the general political interests of the nation . . . Moreover, the very point of all that had been wrought had been, in large measure, to preserve the liberties of individuals. "The truth is, after all the declamations we have heard, that the Constitution is itself, in every rational sense, and to every useful purpose, *a Bill of Rights.*" "The additional securities to republican government, to liberty, and to property, to be derived from the adoption of the plan under consideration, consist chiefly in the restraints which the preservation of the Union will impose on local factions . . . in the prevention of extensive military establishments . . . in the express guarantee of a republican form of government to each [state]: in the absolute and universal exclusion of titles of nobility . . ."

Of course a number of the state ratifying conventions remained apprehensive, and a bill of rights did emerge. Here too, however, the data are unruly. The expression-related provisions of the First Amendment—"Congress shall make no law . . . abridging the freedom of speech, or of the press; or the right of the people peaceably to assemble, and to petition the Government for a redress of grievances"—were centrally intended to help make our governmental processes work, to ensure the open and informed discussion of political issues, and to check our government when it gets out of bounds. We can attribute other functions to freedom of expression, and some of them must have played a role, but the exercise has the smell of the lamp about it: the view that free expression per se, without regard to what it means to the process of government, is our preeminent right has a highly elitist cast. Positive law has its claims, and I am not suggesting that such other purposes as are plausibly attributable to the language should not be attributed: the amendment's language is not limited to political speech and it should not be so limited by construction (even assuming someone could come up with a determinate definition of "political"). But we are at present engaged in an exploration of what sort of document our forebears thought they were putting together, and in that regard the linking of the politically oriented protections of speech, press, assembly, and petition is highly informative.

The First Amendment's religious clauses—"Congress shall make no law respecting an establishment of religion, or prohibiting the free exercise thereof"—are a different matter. Obviously part of the point of combining these cross-cutting commands was to make sure the church and the government gave each other breathing space: the provision thus performs a structural or separation of powers function. But we must not infer that because one account fits the data it must be the only appropriate account, and here the obvious cannot be blinked: part of the explanation of the Free Exercise Clause has to be that for the framers religion was an important substantive value they wanted to put significantly beyond the reach of at least the federal legislature.

The Second Amendment, protecting "the right of the people to keep and bear Arms," seems (at least if that's all you read) calculated simply to set beyond congressional control another "important" value, the right to carry a gun. It hasn't been construed that way, however, and instead has been interpreted as protecting only the right of state governments to keep militias (National Guards) and to arm them. The rationalization for this narrow construction has ordinarily been historical, that the purpose the framers talked most about was maintaining state militias. However, a provision cannot responsibly be restricted to less than its language indicates simply because a particular purpose received more attention than others (and in fact that favored purpose of today's firearms enthusiasts, the right of *individual* self-protection, was mentioned more than a couple of times). Arguments can be right for the wrong reasons, however, and though the point is debatable, the conclusion here is probably correct. The Second Amendment has its own little preamble: "A well regulated Militia, being necessary to the security of a free State, the right of the people to keep and bear Arms, shall not be infringed." Thus here, as almost nowhere else, the framers and ratifiers apparently opted against leaving to the future the attribution of purposes, choosing instead explicitly to legislate the goal in terms of which the provision was to be interpreted.

The Third Amendment, undoubtedly another of your favorites, forbids the nonconsensual peacetime quartering of troops. Like the Establishment of Religion Clause, it grew largely out of fear of an undue influence, this time by the military: in that aspect it can be counted a "separation of powers" provision. Again, however, one cannot responsibly stop there. Other provisions provide for civilian control of the military, and although that is surely one of the purposes here, there is obviously something else at stake, a desire to protect the privacy of the home from prying government eyes, to say nothing of the annoyance of uninvited guests. Both process and value seem to be involved here.

Amendments five through eight tend to become relevant only during lawsuits, and we tend therefore to think of them as procedural—instrumental provisions calculated to enhance the fairness and efficiency of the litigation process. That's exactly what most of them are: the importance of the guarantees of grand juries, criminal and civil petit juries, information of the charge, the right of confrontation, compulsory process, and even the assistance of counsel inheres mainly in their tendency to ensure a reliable determination. Unconcerned with the substance of government regulation, they refer instead to the ways in which regulations can be enforced against those they cover. Once again, however, that is not the whole story. The Fifth Amendment's privilege against self-incrimination surely has a lot to do with wanting to find the truth: coerced confessions are less likely to be reliable. But at least as interpreted, the privilege needs further rationalization than that: the argument runs that there is simply something immoral—though it has proved tricky pinning down exactly what it is—about the state's asking somebody whether he committed a crime and expecting him to answer. The same amendment's guarantee against double jeopardy gets complicated. Insofar as it forbids retrial after acquittal, it seems a largely procedural protection, designed to guard against the conviction of innocent persons. But insofar as it forbids additional prosecution after conviction or added punishment after sentence, it performs the quite different (and substantive) function, which obviously is present in the acquittal situation too, of guaranteeing a sense of repose, an assurance that at some definable point the defendant can assume the ordeal is over, its consequences known.

The Fourth Amendment provides: "The right of the people to be secure in their persons, houses, papers, and effects, against unreasonable searches and seizures, shall not be violated, and no Warrants shall issue, but upon probable cause, supported by Oath or affirmation, and particularly describing the place to be searched, and the persons or things to be seized." This provision most often becomes relevant when a criminal defendant tries to suppress evidence seized as the fruit of an illegal search or arrest, but it would be a mistake to infer from that that it is a purely procedural provision. In fact (as thus enforced by the exclusionary rule) it *thwarts* the procedural goal of accurately determining the facts, in order to serve one or more other goals felt to be more important. The standard line is that that other, more important goal is privacy, and surely privacy is sometimes implicated. But the language of the amendment reaches further—so for that matter did the customs abuses we know had a lot to do with its inclusion—and when it is read in its entirety the notion of "privacy" proves inadequate as an explanation. The amendment covers seizures of goods and arrests ("seizures of the person") along with searches, and it does not distinguish public episodes from private: a completely open arrest or seizure of goods is as illegal as a search of a private area if it is effected without probable cause. It thus "protects individual privacy against certain kinds of governmental intrusion, but its protections go further, and often have nothing to do with privacy at all."

A major point of the amendment, obviously, was to keep the government from disrupting our lives without at least moderately convincing justification. That rationale intertwines with another—and the historic customs abuses are relevant here too—namely, a fear of official discretion. In deciding whose lives to disrupt in the ways the amendment indicates—that is, whom to search or arrest or whose goods to seize—law enforcement officials will necessarily have a good deal of low visibility discretion. In addition they are likely in such situations to be sensitive to social station and other factors that should not bear on the decision. The amendment thus requires not simply a certain quantum of probability but also when possible, via the warrant requirement, the judgment of a "neutral and detached magistrate." From this perspective, which obviously is only one of several, the Fourth Amendment can be seen as another harbinger of the Equal Protection Clause, concerned with avoiding indefensible inequities in treatment. The Eighth Amendment's ban on "cruel and unusual punishments" is even more obviously amenable to this account. Apparently part of the point was to outlaw certain understood and abhorred forms of torture, but the decision to use open-ended language can hardly have been inadvertent. It is possible that part of the point also was to ban punishments that were unusually severe in relation to the crimes for which they were being imposed. But much of it surely had to do with a realization that in the context of imposing penalties too there is tremendous potential for the arbitrary or invidious infliction of "unusually" severe punishments on persons of various classes other than "our own."

On first reading, the Fifth Amendment's requirement that private property not be taken for public use without just compensation may appear simply to mark the substantive value of private property for special protection from the political process (though, on the face of the document, from only the state political process). Again, though, we must ask why. Because property was regarded as unusually important? That may be part of the explanation, but note that property is not shielded from condemnation by this provision. On the contrary, the amendment assumes that property will sometimes be taken and provides instead for compensation. Read through it thus emerges—and this account fits the historical situation like a glove—as yet another protection of the few against the many, "a limit on government's power to isolate particular individuals for sacrifice to the general good." Its point is to "spread the cost of operating the governmental apparatus throughout the society rather than imposing it upon some small segment of it." If we want a highway or a park we can have it, but we're all going to have to share the cost rather than imposing it on some isolated individual or group.[2]

With one important exception, the Reconstruction Amendments do not designate substantive values for protection from the political process. The Fourteenth Amendment's Due Process Clause, we have seen, is concerned with process writ small, the processes by which regulations are enforced against individuals. Its Privileges or Immunities Clause is quite inscrutable, indicating only that there should exist some set of constitutional entitlements not explicitly enumerated in the document: it is one of the provisions for which we are seeking guides to construction. The Equal Protection Clause is also unforthcoming with details, though it at least gives us a clue: by its explicit concern with equality among the persons within a state's jurisdiction it constitutes the document's clearest, though not sole, recognition that technical access to the process may not always be sufficient to guarantee good-faith representation of all those putatively represented. The Fifteenth Amendment, forbidding abridgment of the right to vote on account of race, opens the process to persons who had previously been excluded and thus by another strategy seeks to enforce the representative's duty of equal concern and respect. The exception, of course, involves a value I have mentioned before, slavery. The Thirteenth Amendment can be forced into a "process" mold—slaves don't participate effectively in the political process—and it surely significantly reflects a concern with equality as well. Just as surely, however, it embodies a substantive judgment that human slavery is simply not morally tolerable. Thus at no point has the Constitution been neutral on this subject. Slavery was one of the few values the original document singled out for protection from the political branches; *non*slavery is one of the few values it singles out for protection now.

What has happened to the Constitution in the second century of our nationhood, though ground less frequently plowed, is most instructive on the subject of what jobs we have learned our basic document is suited to. There were no amendments between 1870 and 1913, but there have been eleven since. Five of them have extended the franchise: the Seventeenth extends to all of us the right to vote for our Senators directly, the Twenty-Fourth abolishes the poll tax as a condition of voting in federal elections, the Nineteenth extends the vote to women, the Twenty-Third to residents of the District of Columbia, and the Twenty-Sixth to eighteen-year-olds. Extension of the franchise to groups previously excluded has therefore been the dominant theme of our constitutional development since the Fourteenth Amendment, and it pursues both of the broad constitutional themes we have observed from the beginning: the achievement of a political process open to all on an equal basis and a consequent enforcement of the representative's duty of equal concern and respect to minorities and majorities alike. Three other amendments—the Twentieth, Twenty-Second, and Twenty-Fifth—involve Presidential eligibility and succession. The Sixteenth, permitting a federal income tax, adds another power to the list of those that had previously been assigned to the central government.[3] That's it, save two, and indeed one of those two did place a substantive value beyond the reach of the political process. The amendment was the Eighteenth, and the value shielded was temperance. It was, of course, repealed fourteen years later by the Twenty-First Amendment, precisely, I suggest, because such attempts to freeze substantive values do not belong in a constitution. In 1919 temperance obviously seemed like a fundamental value; in 1933 it obviously did not.

What has happened to the Constitution's other value-enshrining provisions is similar, and similarly instructive. Some surely have survived, but typically because they are so obscure that they don't become issues (corruption of blood, quartering of troops) or so interlaced with procedural concerns they seem appropriate in a constitution (self-incrimination, double jeopardy). Those sufficiently conspicuous and precise to be controvertible have not survived. The most dramatic examples, of course, were slavery and prohibition. Both were removed by repeal, in one case a repeal requiring unprecedented carnage. Two other substantive values that at least arguably were placed beyond the reach of the political process by the Constitution have been "repealed" by judicial construction—the right of individuals to bear arms, and freedom to set contract terms without significant state regulation. Maybe in fact our forebears did not intend very seriously to protect those values, but the fact that the Court, in the face of what must be counted at least plausible contrary arguments, so readily read these values out of the Constitution is itself instructive of American expectations of a constitution. Finally, there is the value of religion, still protected by the Free Exercise Clause. Something different has happened here. In recent years that clause has functioned primarily to protect what must be counted as discrete and insular minorities, such as the Amish, Seventh Day Adventists, and Jehovah's Witnesses. Whatever the original conception of the Free Exercise Clause, its function during essentially all of its effective life has been one akin to the Equal Protection Clause and thus entirely appropriate to a constitution.

Don't get me wrong: our Constitution has always been substantially concerned with preserving liberty. If it weren't, it would hardly be worth fighting for. The question that is relevant to our inquiry here, however, is how that concern has been pursued. The principal answers to that, we have seen, are by a quite extensive set of procedural protections, and by a still more elaborate scheme designed to ensure that in the making of substantive choices the decision process will be open to all on something approaching an equal basis, with the decision-makers held to a duty to take into account the interests of all those their decisions affect. (Most often the document has proceeded on the assumption that assuring access is the best way of assuring that someone's interests will be considered, and so in fact it usually is. Other provisions, however—centrally but not exclusively the Equal Protection Clause—reflect a realization that access will not always be sufficient.) The general strategy has therefore not been to root in the document a set of substantive rights entitled to permanent protection. The Constitution has instead proceeded from the quite sensible assumption that an effective majority will not inordinately threaten its own rights, and has sought to assure that such a majority not systematically treat others less well than it treats itself—by structuring decision processes at all levels to try to ensure, first, that everyone's interests will be actually or virtually represented (usually both) at the point of substantive decision, and second, that the processes of individual application will not be manipulated so as to reintroduce in practice the sort of discrimination that is impermissible in theory. We have noted a few provisions that do not comfortably conform to this pattern. But they're an odd assortment, the understandable products of particular historical circumstances—guns, religion, contract, and so on—and in any event they are few and far between. To represent them as a dominant theme of our constitutional document one would have to concentrate quite single-mindedly on hopping from stone to stone and averting one's eyes from the mainstream.

The American Constitution has thus by and large remained a constitution properly so called, concerned with constitutive questions. What has distinguished it, and indeed the United States itself, has been a process of government, not a governing ideology. Justice Linde has written: "As a charter of government a constitution must prescribe legitimate processes, not legitimate outcomes, if like ours (and unlike more ideological documents elsewhere) it is to serve many generations through changing times.

As I have tried to be scrupulous about indicating, the argument from the general contours of the Constitution is necessarily a qualified one. In fact the documentary dictation of particular substantive outcomes has been rare (and generally unsuccessful), but our Constitution is too complex a document to lie still for *any* pat characterization. Beyond that, the premise of the argument, that aids to construing the more open-ended provisions are appropriately found in the nature of the surrounding document, though it is a premise that seems to find acceptance on all sides, is not one with which it is impossible to disagree. Thus the two arguments that follow, each overtly normative, are if anything more important than the one I have just reviewed. The first is entirely obvious by now, that unlike an approach geared to the judicial imposition of "fundamental values," the representation-reinforcing orientation whose contours I have sketched and will develop further is not inconsistent with, but on the contrary is entirely supportive of, the American system of representative democracy. It recognizes the unacceptability of the claim that appointed and life-tenured judges are better reflectors of conventional values than elected representatives, devoting itself instead to policing the mechanisms by which the system seeks to ensure that our elected representatives will actually represent. There may be an illusion of circularity here: my approach is more consistent with representative democracy because that's the way it was planned. But of course it isn't any more circular than setting out to build an airplane and ending up with something that flies.

The final point worth serious mention is that (again unlike a fundamental-values approach) a representation-reinforcing approach assigns judges a role they are conspicuously well situated to fill.[4] My reference here is not principally to expertise. Lawyers *are* experts on process writ small, the processes by which facts are found and contending parties are allowed to present their claims. And to a degree they are experts on process writ larger, the processes by which issues of public policy are fairly determined: lawyers do seem genuinely to have a feel, indeed it is hard to see what other special value they have, for ways of insuring that everyone gets his or her fair say. But too much shouldn't be made of this. Others, particularly the full-time participants, can also claim expertise on how the political process allocates voice and power. And of course many legislators are lawyers themselves. So the point isn't so much one of expertise as it is one of perspective.

The approach to constitutional adjudication recommended here is akin to what might be called an "antitrust" as opposed to a "regulatory" orientation to economic affairs—rather than dictate substantive results it intervenes only when the "market," in our case the political market, is systemically malfunctioning. (A referee analogy is also not far off: the referee is to intervene only when one team is gaining unfair advantage, not because the "wrong" team has scored.) Our government cannot fairly be said to be "malfunctioning" simply because it sometimes generates outcomes with which we disagree, however strongly (and claims that it is reaching results with which "the people" really disagree—or would "if they understood"—are likely to be little more than self-deluding projections). In a representative democracy value determinations are to be made by our elected representatives, and if in fact most of us disapprove we can vote them out of office. Malfunction occurs when the *process* is undeserving of trust, when (1) the ins are choking off the channels of political change to ensure that they will stay in and the outs will stay out, or (2) though no one is actually denied a voice or a vote, representatives beholden to an effective majority are systematically disadvantaging some minority out of simple hostility or a prejudiced refusal to recognize commonalities of interest, and thereby denying that minority the protection afforded other groups by a representative system.

Obviously our elected representatives are the last persons we should trust with identification of either of these situations. Appointed judges, however, are comparative outsiders in our governmental system, and need worry about continuance in office only very obliquely. This does not give them some special pipeline to the genuine values of the American people: in fact it goes far to ensure that they won't have one. It does, however, put them in a position objectively to assess claims—though no one could suppose the evaluation won't be full of judgment calls—that either by clogging the channels of change or by acting as accessories to majority tyranny, our elected representatives in fact are not representing the interests of those whom the system presupposes they are.

Before embarking on his career-long quest for a satisfactory approach to constitutional adjudication, Alexander Bickel described the challenge thus:

> *The search must be for a function . . . which is peculiarly suited to the capabilities of the courts; which will not likely be performed elsewhere if the courts do not assume it; which can be so exercised as to be acceptable in a society that generally shares Judge Hand's satisfaction in a "sense of common venture"; which will be effective when needed; and whose discharge by the courts will not lower the quality of the other departments' performance by denuding them of the dignity and burden of their own responsibility.*

As quoted, it's a remarkably appropriate set of specifications, one that fits the orientation suggested here precisely. Unfortunately, by adding one more specification (where I have put the elipsis) and thereby committing himself to a value orientation—"which might (indeed must) involve the making of policy, yet which differs from the legislative and executive functions"—he built in an inescapable contradiction and thereby ensured the failure of his enterprise.

NOTE

[1] I realize that by stressing the few occasions on which values *were* singled out for protection, I run the risk of conveying the impression that that is the character of much of the Constitution. My point of course is quite the opposite, but I'm not sufficiently sadistic to list all the provisions that are obviously concerned only with process. If you find yourself thinking I'm not making my case here, please read a few pages of the Constitution to assure yourself that I could.

[2]This view of the clause is also of some assistance in deciding whether a given government action should be counted a taking in the first place as opposed to, say, a regulation or a tax. In recent discussions of this issue the Court has begun to ask whether the measure under review singles out a minority for unusually harsh treatment or rather affects a class sufficiently generalized to have a fair shot at protecting itself politically. E.g., *Penn Central Transp. Co. v. New York City*, 438 U.S. 104, 132 (1978).

[3]Moreover, the amendment most likely (though perhaps not likely enough) to become the Twenty-Seventh, the Equal Rights Amendment, is a guarantor of fair distribution akin to the Equal Protection Clause: it does not designate any substantive values as worthy of constitutional protection.

[4]For reasons that are currently obscure, I went through a period of worrying that the orientation here recommended might mean less protection for civil liberties. (Of course it would deny the opportunity to create rights out of whole cloth; that is much of its point and strength. What I had in mind was the possibility that the *same* freedoms might systematically come out thinner if derived from a participational orientation than they would if protected on the ground that they are "good.") Reflection has convinced me that just the opposite is true, that freedoms are more secure to the extent that they find foundation in the theory that supports our entire government, rather than gaining protection because the judge deciding the case thinks they're important. Cf. C. Black, *Structure and Relationship in Constitutional Law* 29–30 (1969). Indeed, the only remotely systematic "Carolene Products" Court we have had was also clearly the most protective of civil liberties.

CHAPTER 2

Multiculturalism and Religion

BELIEVERS AS EQUAL CITIZENS

—Michael W. McConnell—

Until the modern period, citizenship was inextricably tied to religion. The legitimacy of government was based in large part on claims of divine sanction, and those who disputed that sanction could not be trusted. Dissenters could be dealt with tolerantly or harshly, but they could not be full and equal citizens. Throughout most of Europe, Jews, the quintessential dissenters, constituted virtually a state within a state. Subjects of the king but not citizens of the realm, Jews were vulnerable to special exactions and—at the mercy of the sovereign—to violence, insult, and expulsion. At the same time, they typically enjoyed a kind of home rule, running their own schools, courts, hospitals, and social services. Ostracism and indignity were coupled with a kind of communal autonomy.[1] In England, where the Glorious Revolution was predicated on the Protestant succession and the victory over Catholic tyranny, adherence to Catholicism was associated with Jacobitism and hence with treason, and radical Protestants might bring about a return to the Commonwealth and civil war. Under such circumstances, it seemed prudent to confine public offices to adherents of the Church of England.

With the rise of liberal constitutionalism, especially at the American founding and the French Revolution, an attempt was made to sever the connection between citizenship and religion by divorcing the state from its sacred foundations and identification with an established religion and opening the doors of citizenship to all inhabitants, without regard to their religion. No special privileges for adherents of a favored denomination, no special disabilities for anyone else. That individuals of all religious faiths can be full and equal citizens became a fundamental and uncontroversial premise of liberal constitutional order. As stated in the Virginia Bill for Establishing Religious Freedom, "our civil rights have no dependence on our religious opinions; any more than our opinions in physics or geometry."

The problem with this formulation is that it makes it sound too easy. Religion is not like physics and geometry. Religion is connected to conscience and character and loyalty, in a way physics and geometry are not. If we do not grasp why religious convictions pose a problem for citizenship, we may become careless in our interpretation of what it means to treat religious believers, of all faiths, as full and equal citizens. The purpose of this chapter is to recall the nature and seriousness of the problem. The first section will describe the problem, as it has been seen by several noted philosophers and statesmen. The second section will describe two broad approaches to the problem adopted by liberal democracies, and their implications for constitutional questions of church and state.

THE PROBLEM

The essential problem is that religious believers have an allegiance to an authority outside the commonwealth. To be sure, the demands of faith do not necessarily (or even frequently) conflict with the laws of the civil society; often they are mutually reinforcing. Much depends on the nature of the religion and of the state. Religions that place few nonspiritual demands on their adherents, or whose cultural and moral commitments are more or less congruent with the wider community, will create relatively few conflicts. Governments that confine themselves to the few essential functions necessary to peace and good order will generate fewer conflicts than governments active in the educational, cultural, and moral lives of their citizens. But in principle, so long as church and state are separate, there is always the possibility of conflict between spiritual and temporal authorities. Believers inevitably face two sets of loyalties and two sets of obligations. In this respect, they resemble resident aliens, or, at best, persons with dual citizenship. This conflict of loyalties and obligations I will call the problem of "citizenship ambiguity."

The problem of citizenship ambiguity was articulated with characteristic bluntness by Rousseau. He wrote in *The Social Contract* that adherents of certain religions (including Catholic Christianity) cannot be "at the same time both churchmen and citizens." Under Christianity, "men have never known whether they ought to obey the civil ruler or the priest." Christianity gave men "two legislative orders, two rulers, two homelands," and it put them under "two contradictory obligations." This situation is "so manifestly bad," he said, that the "pleasure of demonstrating its badness would be a waste of time."[2] If this sounds overly hostile to Christianity, it is well to remember that Christians have said it of themselves. Paul's *Letter to the Philippians* affirms that "our citizenship is in heaven."[3] Those who live the life of faith, according to the writer of *Hebrews*, are "aliens and strangers on earth." They are "longing for a better country—a heavenly one." "God . . . has prepared a city for them."[4] If believers have one foot in the city that God has prepared for them, the potential for conflict with the city in which they temporarily find themselves is inevitable. How can believers insist upon enjoying the status of equal citizens if they admit that their true citizenship—their ultimate loyalty and allegiance—lies elsewhere?

Citizenship ambiguity is not an oddity of Christian doctrine; it will be present in any religion that recognizes a divine or transcendent normative authority higher than that of earthly institutions. Only if the religion contains no teaching relevant to civil life, or if it is either subordinate to or dominant over the civil regime, will there be no possibility of conflict.

Nor is the diagnosis of the problem an oddity of Rousseau, or of the Old World. In the single most influential document expounding the American theory of relations between religion and government, Madison's *Memorial and Remonstrance Against Religious Assessments*, Madison presupposes a relation between religion and government remarkably similar to Rousseau's. Like Rousseau, he recognizes the potential for conflict between the "claims of Civil Society" and the duty of "every man" to render homage to the Creator. Unlike Rousseau, however, Madison avers that the latter duty "is precedent both in order of time and degree of obligation" to the former.

> Before any man can be considered as a member of Civil Society, he must be considered as a subject of the Governor of the Universe: And if a member of Civil Society, who enters into any subordinate Association, must always do it with a reservation of his duty to the general authority; much more must every man who becomes a member of any particular Civil Society, do it with a saving of his allegiance to the Universal Sovereign.[5]

Madison's terminology draws attention to the question of citizenship: believers are "subjects" of the "Universal Sovereign," to whom they owe "allegiance." In effect, Madison is saying, much like Rousseau, that the problem of church and state is the problem of citizenship ambiguity: How can we deal with the fact that religious believers are both subjects of God and citizens of earthly commonwealths?

The difference between Rousseau and Madison is that Rousseau deplored this "conflict of jurisdiction," while Madison deduced from it the "unalienable right" to worship God in accordance with the dictates of conscience. Rousseau maintained that a properly ordered civil society required suppression of religion as it then existed and substitution of a mandatory civil religion that preaches "the sanctity of the social contract and the law." Rousseau thus created his own new "civil religion," no less intolerant and no less tied to government than the religions and governments of yore. Madison argued, by contrast, that government may not tamper with the dictates of conscience, and he created a new form of government that would protect the believer's dual allegiance. Rousseau thought it essential that loyalty to the state supersede religious faith; Madison maintained

Madison

that religious obligation takes precedence, "both in order of time and degree of obligation," since allegiance to God is primary and civil society is a "subordinate" form of association. Different solutions, different constitutions—but essentially the same understanding of the underlying problem.

Admittedly, not everyone has agreed with Rousseau and Madison that religious conviction and civil obligation are in conflict. There have been important attempts to understand religion and citizenship in such a way as to minimize or eliminate the problem of citizenship ambiguity.

One such attempt may be found in the device of separation between church and state. The philosophical foundation of church-state separationism was laid by John Locke in his *Essay on Toleration*. So long as civil and religious sources of authority are clearly distinguished and given separate jurisdictions, according to Locke, the problem of citizenship ambiguity can be eliminated. The problem is not inherent in the situation of religious people in secular communities, but is a result of either government, or religion, or both, overstepping their proper bounds. If religion and government would stick to their own proper spheres, a believer could be a citizen of both sacred and secular realms—he could enjoy dual citizenship—with no conflict of obligations. That is why Locke "esteem[ed] it above all things necessary to distinguish exactly the business of civil government from that of religion and to settle the just bounds that lie between the one and the other."[6] The religious citizen would obey God within God's proper jurisdiction, and would obey the magistrate within the magistrate's proper jurisdiction. Eliminate the jurisdictional overlap—get the magistrate out of God's business and God out of the magistrate's business—and there would be no further difficulty.

Locke's vision found adherents on this side of the Atlantic. In his noted *Letter to the Danbury Baptists*, Jefferson wrote that he

> contemplate[d] with solemn reverence that act of the whole American people which declared that their legislature should "*make no law respecting an establishment of religion, or prohibiting the free exercise thereof*," thus building a wall of separation between Church and State. Adhering to this expression of the supreme will of the nation in behalf of the rights of conscience, I shall see with sincere satisfaction the progress of those sentiments which tend to restore to man all his natural rights, convinced he has no natural right in opposition to his social duties.[7]

The Lockean character of this profession can be seen not only in the famous metaphor of the "wall of separation," but in Jefferson's faith that man "has no natural right"—presumably including obligations of conscience—"in opposition to his social duties." This obviously presupposes that the realms of conscience and social duty are sufficiently distinct that conflict between them will not legitimately arise.

The flaw in Locke's prescription is not with its desirability but with its congruence to reality. To the extent that church and state *can* be separated, without violence to the just and proper jurisdiction of either, they should be separated. The less overlap there is between sacred and secular authority, the less serious the problem of citizenship ambiguity will be. If it were possible to "distinguish exactly the business of civil government from that of religion," the field of church-state law would be easy, and religious freedom would be secure.

Alas, it is not so. Even conceding, with Locke, that "the care of souls is not committed to the civil magistrate," there remain numerous and inevitable potential conflicts between the demands of civil society and the demands of faith. Indeed, the very boundary between sacred and secular is a point of contention on which persons of various religious and secular persuasions will inevitably disagree. How should children be raised? Parents may wish to pass on the truths and joys of their religious tradition through inculcation of the faith, but the state may think that children are better off with exposure to a multiplicity of views, coupled with science, modernist philosophy, and sex education. Which is overstepping its bounds? What should be the relations between the races? In 1908, a religious college in Kentucky was criminally prosecuted for its insistence on educating black and white students together,[8] and in 1983 the tax-exempt status of a religious college was revoked for forbidding its students to engage in interracial dating.[9] Which should prevail, church or state? What mind-altering substances may be used as a sacrament in worship?[10] What headcovering may be worn by a Jewish officer in the military?[11] Should there be chaplains in public hospitals? Prisons?[12] Legislatures?[13] Military installations?[14] Who should pay for them? Can religious radio stations get free access to the broadcast spectrum? Can they get discretionary construction grants?[15] Should commercial rock climbing be halted on Devil's Tower, sacred to the Sioux, during the month of their holy celebrations there?[16] Can the government prevent the church in Boerne, Texas, from remodeling its sanctuary?[17] Can it force the Bishop of Newark to allow parochial school teachers to unionize?[18] Can it apply discrimination laws to a congregation's choice of clergy?[19] Can believers opposed to alcohol keep their counties dry?[20] Whose side of the "wall of separation" are these questions on?

What happens when civil law does conflict with religious conscience? According to Locke, this "will seldom happen." But if it does, the believer should suffer the punishment. "For the private judgement of any person concerning a law enacted in political matters, for the public good, does not take away the obligation of that law, nor deserve a dispensation."[21] Only if the magistrate has overstepped the bounds of his proper authority is the believer properly entitled to disobey. And since "there is no judge upon earth between the supreme magistrate and the people,"[22] in cases of conflict between religious conscience and the exercise of civil authority, civil authority always prevails, no matter which party to the dispute—believer or magistrate—has overstepped the proper bounds.[23] Moreover, the teachings of some religions—atheism and Roman Catholicism—seemed to Locke to be so inimical to public order that they should be denied toleration altogether. It is not obvious that this is much of an improvement over Rousseau.

The disagreement—if there is a disagreement—is not over what is desirable, but over social reality. Locke and Jefferson profess to believe that religion is essentially irrelevant to the affairs of this world, while Rousseau insists that the opposite is true. In the end, however, their response to conflict is the same. Whether common or rare, conflicts must be resolved in favor of the state.

The greater gulf is between Rousseau and Madison, who, while agreeing about the reality of citizenship ambiguity, respond in different ways to it. Madison does not dwell upon the practical consequences of treating religious obligations as superior to civil obligations, except to say (in another place) that religion should prevail "in every case where it does not trespass on private rights or the public peace."[24] Evidently, Madison is willing to sacrifice some degree of social control (on matters not related to private rights or the public peace) in exchange for liberty of conscience. Indeed, it is possible that Madison viewed citizenship ambiguity as a strength rather than a weakness. Perhaps religion, as an authority independent of the state, would serve much the same function as federalism and separation of powers: to minimize the dangers of tyranny by dividing power. The difference between Madison and Rousseau may have been that the latter had more ambitious plans for government.

With all respect to Locke and Jefferson, it would be naive to assume that civil society is unaffected by the moral and even the theological teachings of its major religions. Locke was well aware that his unorthodox understanding of the afterlife—Locke believed in a future state of rewards but not of punishments—could be expected to have earthly consequences: the divine sanction against evildoers would be weakened, to the detriment of civil order. Today, feminists have no doubt that the patriarchal character of many major religions (in their eyes) has earthly consequences, and they often do not hesitate in asking the civil magistrate to intervene in the internal affairs of churches to solve this problem. Environmentalists are not oblivious to the earthly consequences of the "stewardship" and "dominion" models of man's relation to Creation. Welfare reformers have noticed that ministries preaching spiritual regeneration are markedly more successful in changing the lives of their clients than secular programs that dole out money. Jefferson's comment that "it does me no injury for my neighbor to say that there are twenty gods, or no god. It neither picks my pocket nor breaks my leg" seems oblivious to the fact that religion affects character and character affects conduct.[25] Edmund Burke appears much more realistic when he says that "it is the right of government to attend much to opinions; because, as opinions soon combine with passions, even when they do not produce them, they have much influence on action."[26]

Jefferson may ultimately have been right (I think he was) in saying that "it is time enough for the rightful purposes of civil government for its officers to interfere when principles break out into overt acts against peace and good order."[27] But he was not right because religious opinions are irrelevant to the common good. If he was right, it is because liberty of conscience is precious enough to sacrifice other public goods for its attainment, and because government is not to be trusted in judging which opinions are likely to be injurious to the public good. The danger in Jefferson's "pick my pocket or break my leg" reasoning is that, whenever my neighbor's religion *does* have secular consequences, it will seem appropriate to intervene. Locke's exclusion of atheists and Catholics from toleration cannot be dismissed as a quaint exception to his beneficent liberalism; it follows logically from the ground on which his argument for toleration rested. If religious freedom means nothing more than that religion should be free so long as it is irrelevant to the state, it does not mean very much.

A second response to the problem of citizenship ambiguity is to agree that religion is relevant to citizenship, but to maintain that the teachings of religion, taken as a whole, tend to foster the virtues on which a democratic republic depends. In his Farewell Address, Washington stated that "[o]f all the dispositions and habits which lead to political prosperity, religion and morality are indispensable supports." Religion, in this view, does not undermine good citizenship; rather, religion and morality are the "firmest props of the duties of men and citizens." In "religion," Washington was not using a code word for the dominant religion. His formal letters to the Jewish congregations of Newport, Philadelphia, New York, Richmond, Charleston, and Savannah make clear that his regard extended to them,[28] and he gave instructions to American troops in Canada to respect the rights of conscience of the Catholic French Canadians. Nor was Washington unaware that religious convictions could produce conflicts with civil duties. In writing to "the religious society called Quakers," Washington noted that except in "their declining to share with others the burden of common defense," there was "no denomination among us, who are more exemplary and useful citizens." He insisted that "in my opinion the conscientious scruples of all men should be treated with great delicacy and tenderness; and it is my wish and desire, that the laws may always be as extensively accommodated to them, as a due regard for the protection and essential interests of the nation may justify and permit."[29] In contrast to Locke (as well as Rousseau), Washington thus maintained that conflicts should be minimized by accommodating the laws to religious convictions (where it is possible to do so without excessive injury to the essential interests of the nation), rather than by insisting that in all matters religious citizens conform to the law of the state.

The difference between Washington and Madison was more one of tone than of substance, but the difference in tone is significant. Washington tended to address the situation of minority religions from a posture of toleration by the society toward the dissenter, while Madison tended to see believers of all religions as occupying a similar position in relation to the secular state. Perhaps more strikingly, Madison spoke in more emphatic terms of "unalienable rights," whereas Washington spoke in terms of treating religious conscience with "great delicacy and tenderness"—language of forebearance rather than right. Finally, while Washington and Madison both expressed concern about conscience, Madison placed the rights of conscience at the fore while Washington placed greater emphasis on the contributions of religion to virtue and hence to republican citizenship.

It does not, and did not, follow from the Washingtonian view that government has the authority to use its power directly for the inculcation of religion. The founders of the American regime believed not only that government should not, but also that it cannot, advance the cause of genuine religion by use of state power. A genuine religion is a matter between each believer and his God. "[A]ll attempts to influence it by temporal punishments or burdens, or by civil incapacitations, tend only to beget habits of hypocrisy and meanness."[30] Experience showed that government support for religion produced only "pride and indolence in the Clergy" and "ignorance and servility in the laity."[31] The only effectual support government could give to religion was to guarantee its freedom.

Washington thus combined a favorable posture toward religion as a political matter with a commitment to religious freedom and respect for the "conscientious scruples" of religious minorities.[32] His position is neither separationist nor majoritarian. The central theme is his belief that religion—all religion—is a salutary prop for democratic citizenship, and therefore that the religious commitments of all citizens should be treated with "great delicacy and tenderness." It is important to see the deep congruence between this view and Rousseau's: neither believes that religion is irrelevant to citizenship; neither believes that the spheres of government and religion can be so separated that the state can be indifferent to the influence of religion. But what accounts for the equally profound difference: that Washington sees religion as salutary while Rousseau sees religion as disruptive? One answer may be that Rousseau envisioned a society of much deeper and thicker solidarity, making difference of religion—or even deep commitment to religion as a locus of truth and loyalty—a threat.

Washington, by contrast, desired only enough virtue to allow republican institutions to work. This idea was later developed by Tocqueville, who wrote that "all Americans" think that religion is "necessary to the maintenance of republican institutions."[33] "Despotism may be able to do without faith," Tocqueville wrote, "but freedom cannot. Religion is much more needed in the republic they [French revolutionaries] advocate than in the monarchy they attack, and in democratic republics most of all. How could society escape destruction if, when political ties are relaxed, moral ties are not tightened?"[34] The characteristic vice of the liberal republic is its tendency toward selfish individualism; all republicans of the founding era agreed that republics required a virtuous citizenry, where "virtue" was understood to mean public spiritedness. Religion was thus especially needful to a republic, because, as Tocqueville pointed out, "[e]very religion also imposes on each man some obligations toward mankind, to be performed in common with the rest of mankind, and so draws him away, from time to time, from thinking about himself."[35]

A second reason for the difference is that in France, the dominant religious faith was associated with the *ancien régime*, and hostile to the republican future Rousseau envisioned, while the churches of America were in the forefront of this nation's struggle for independence. When Rousseau thought of religion, he thought principally of Catholicism, whose organization was hierarchical, autocratic, and nonegalitarian. As Tocqueville points out, the situation in America was the reverse: the American colonists had "brought to the New World a Christianity which I can only describe as democratic and republican; this fact singularly favored the establishment of a temporal republic and democracy."[36] American republicans thus never shared the anticlericalism of their republican counterparts in France. In America, unlike France, the dominant Protestant religion reinforced the essential philosophical presuppositions of the republic, and the religious minorities—whatever the details of their doctrine—as a practical matter favored the liberalism of the new regime.[37]

Washington's happy accommodationism must therefore be seen, in significant part, as contingent: contingent both on the principles of the regime and on the principles of religion. Washington saw no conflict between religion and citizenship because the dominant religion of America—Protestant Christianity—preached ideals consistent with the principles of the republic. It was therefore safe to allow religion to be free, and therefore strong. What would happen if, as in France, the ideals espoused by religion were inimical to the principles of the regime? To make matters concrete, but at the risk of exaggerating our current situation, what if the regime were based on such principles as radical feminism, acceptance of homosexuality, and the superiority of modernist philosophy, and if the most prominent and visible religions were opposed to these trends? Far from being the most democratic and egalitarian of citizens, as in Washington and Tocqueville's day, religious individuals might come to be seen as the most retrograde. The happy coincidence of freedom and good citizenship would be broken. It would then be necessary to choose. And which would we choose? Religious freedom, or other ideals closer to the heart of the modern polity? That is the issue raised by modern feminist scholarship critical of religious freedom.[38]

This brings us back to Rousseau, and to the potential for conflict between being a good citizen and being a person of faith. Rousseau proposed one solution: to crush religion that does not reinforce the dogmas of the state. Madison proposed another: to recognize the duty to God as an unalienable right, precedent to the demands of civil society. The easy answer of separationism will only go so far, and the easy answer that religion is good for citizenship is to some degree contingent on historical circumstance. None of the answers will satisfy all legitimate demands; all come at a price.

TWO MODELS OF EQUAL CITIZENSHIP

For the most part, we no longer argue about whether believers should be equal citizens. But we are still far from agreement about how to achieve this objective. According to Rousseau, it is impossible for adherents of traditional religions (such as Catholicism) to be proper citizens. Your citizenship can be in heaven or in France, but not in both. For obvious reasons, that cannot be the answer in a liberal republic. It is not possible for a liberal republic to grant or withhold the privileges or immunities of citizenship on the basis of adherence to one or another religion. Instead, liberal regimes have developed a range of answers to the problem of citizenship ambiguity. Here, I will describe two models of religious citizenship that cast light on the problem: one characterized by insistence on the secular character of the state, the other by the idea of religious pluralism. Both of these have a pedigree in the practice and theory of liberal constitutionalism, but I would contend that the pluralist model best achieves the ideal of full equality of all citizens.

The first model is that of the secular state, sometimes called "strict separation" between church and state. In this model, the public sphere is strictly secular in nature: laws are based on secular premises, government programs and activities are strictly secular in nature, and religion is deemed to be irrelevant to determination of the citizens' civil obligations. Public schools are the favored form of education and should be used to inculcate ideals of democratic citizenship, untainted by sectarian teaching or dogma. Religious exercise is protected, so long as it is confined to the private sphere of home and church. The approach is captured by the saying: "Be a man in the streets and a Jew at home"—with the understanding that the same is true of adherents of every faith.

The assumption underlying this model is that the secular public philosophy of the society is "neutral" toward religion. The approach is generally associated with the idea that politics should be conducted on the basis of public reason, which is accessible to all citizens, and not on the basis of sectarian dogma. One modern exponent of this view has explained: "The establishment clause should be viewed as a reflection of the secular, relativist political values of the Enlightenment, which are incompatible with the fundamental nature of religious faith. As an embodiment of these Enlightenment values, the establishment clause requires that the political influence of religion be substantially diminished."[39] The effect is to force all citizens to put aside their sectarian loyalties and convictions in their capacities as citizen, but to allow everyone complete freedom to practice religion in private. Don't ask, don't tell.

This approach tends to be animated by fear of religious divisiveness, religious warfare, sectarianism, and intolerance. The hope is to domesticate religion by privatizing it. For some, disestablishmentarianism and privatization are the first steps toward reducing attachments to sectarian religion and fostering assimilation and secularization. If religion is understood as largely superstitious, propped up by the force of the state, then disestablishment of religion and the spread of enlightened reason should cause religion to wither away, without the need for coercion. Even the most liberal of gentile supporters of Jewish emancipation in France expected the Jewish religion to disappear as a distinctive group once Jews were given their civil rights.[40] In a similar vein, Jefferson predicted that, with the advent of religious freedom, sectarian religion would decline and within a generation all would become Unitarians.[41]

This model of religious liberty repudiated the enforced difference of the *ancien régime* and substituted an enforced denial of difference. Under the *ancien régime*, religious minorities were treated by the state as radically different and apart from the citizenry, whether they liked it or not. Under emancipation, they were admitted to membership in the citizenry—but at the price of forgoing their distinctiveness: "Jews, according to the terms of emancipation, were expected to divest themselves entirely of their national character—they were to give up the civil aspects of Talmudic law; disavow the political implications of Jewish messianism; abandon the use of Yiddish; and, most importantly, relinquish their semi-autonomous communal institutions. They were to become like other Frenchmen in every respect, save religion."[42] One prominent French legislator explained that no one could be his fellow citizen "who does not wish to drink or eat with me, who cannot give me his daughter in marriage, whose son cannot become my son-in-law, and who, by the religion he professes is separated from all other men. Only when Jews do what other men do," he said, "what the constitution and law requires of us all, will we welcome them as citizens."[43]

This view has not disappeared. An excellent example is the recent controversy in France over whether Muslim girls may wear the traditional head scarf in public school. This touched a nerve, or more precisely, two nerves, in French public opinion. First was the offense against secularity, or what the French call *laïcité*. In a public school, all must put aside forms of dress or conduct that set them apart from others. That was the deal: religious minorities would be full and equal citizens so long as they acted "French" in the public sphere. Second was the offense against modern feminist sensibilities, which reject the notion that Muslim girls must cover their heads. That certain religious traditions are at odds with the feminist ideal in this regard was all the more reason to insist on conformity in school; by this means, children would be encouraged to challenge, and perhaps depart from, the oppressive traditions of their families.

Nor is this attitude toward religious difference confined to France. Although it is unlikely that Muslim head scarves would be prohibited in the freewheeling sartorial atmosphere of American public schools, there have been incidents in which evangelical students were reprimanded for wearing T-shirts with religious slogans, or for engaging in other expression that is deemed inconsistent with the secular character of public schools.

The American version of *laicité* is to insist that religious believers bend their religious conscience to the law, rather than asking government to accommodate the law to religious conscience. It is not uncommon to hear the argument, in various forms, that any exception to generally applicable laws would be a form of "preference" for religious believers.[44] As Justice Felix Frankfurter wrote in his dissenting opinion in *West Virginia Board of Education v. Barnette*, "[t]he constitutional protection of religious freedom terminated disabilities, it did not create new privileges. It gave religious equality, not civil immunity. Its essence is freedom from conformity to religious dogma, not freedom from conformity to law because of religious dogma."[45] According to Isaac Kramnick and R. Laurence Moore in their book *The Godless Constitution*, religion should have "the same rights in the public sphere as General Motors, no more and no less."[46] Since General Motors is subject to extensive regulation in almost every aspect of its operations, short of expropriating its property, this suggests that the authority of the state to regulate or restrain the exercise of religion is substantial, and that free exercise rights are minimal.

While never fully embraced by the Supreme Court, this position has obvious connections to the constitutional doctrine of the past few decades, though less so in recent years. If the state must be strictly secular, then laws based on religious justifications are unconstitutional. This idea is reflected in the first part of the Supreme Court's test for an establishment of religion: that government action must have a "secular purpose."[47] In theory, legislation predicated on religious views (such as religious condemnation of abortion or gambling) could be held to be unconstitutional, even though legislation predicated on competing worldviews (feminism or libertarianism, for example) would pose no constitutional problem. Moreover, if all publicly funded activities must be strictly secular, there can be no public subsidies of religious schools, universities, or social welfare programs—at least, if those programs are identifiably religious in nature. Thus, for many years, the Supreme Court held that public funds could not be provided to any activity that is "specifically religious," or even to secular activities conducted by "pervasively religious" organizations.[48] Finally, the Free Exercise Clause must not be interpreted to require accommodation of religious dissenters.[49] As Suzanna Sherry argues, "the constitutional protection of religion—found primarily in the Free Exercise Clause—is a limited aberration in a secular state, and thus best interpreted narrowly.[50] Indeed—although the Supreme Court has never gone so far—it would seem to follow that the Establishment Clause should forbid religious accommodations as a form of preference for religion.

The alternative to this idea of the secular state is the religiously pluralistic state. The animating purpose of this constitutional position is to enable people of all religious persuasions to be citizens of the commonwealth with the least possible violence to their religious convictions. The Jew can be a Jew not just in his house but in the public square as well. So can the Muslim and the Christian. If this requires accommodation—a relaxation of the general rules of society—it is worth the price. Perhaps the most eloquent statement of the pluralist view came from the Irish lawyer William Sampson in a case in New York in 1813.[51] The question before the court was whether a Roman Catholic priest could be forced to testify to information learned in the confessional.[52] This, it turned out, would be the first recorded decision by any court in the United States that Free Exercise protects believers from laws that would require them to violate their religious conscience. In his argument before the court, Sampson expressed a broad vision of religious liberty in America: "Every citizen here is in his own country," Sampson argued. "To the protestant it is a protestant country; to the catholic, a catholic country; and the jew, if he pleases, may establish in it his New Jerusalem."[53] No talk here of a "secular state," as if only secular individuals can fully be citizens, or as if one had to leave religion behind when entering the public sphere of citizenship. To the Protestant it is a Protestant country, to the Catholic a Catholic country, to the Jew a Jewish country. By accommodating the laws to every citizen, this approach aspires to eliminate citizenship ambiguity: to make everyone at home.

The difference between the secular and pluralist approaches came to the fore in the first recorded case in the United States involving a claim of freedom of religion. In this case, in Pennsylvania in 1793, a Jewish witness, Jonas Phillips, resisted a subpoena to testify in court in a civil case on Saturday, his day of sabbath. Phillips was a leader of the Philadelphia Jewish community and active in the struggle against religious tests for office. It is likely that it was a test case, closely watched by members of the small Jewish community of America, curious to find out what freedom of religion would mean in this new liberal regime. The news was not good: Phillips was fined £10 for refusing to appear in court on Saturday. But the case never was finally resolved, because the party on whose behalf the subpoena was issued excused the fine before an appellate court could review the matter.[54] This may appear to be a minor case, but the implications of Jonas Phillips's position were profound. In effect, he was asking that the civil court system adjust its schedule to the Jewish law. He was asking that civic obligations be accommodated to religious faith. He was, in effect, embracing the pluralist vision of religious citizenship, for he wished to be *both* an American citizen *and* a faithful Jew—even in his public role as a witness in court.

The pluralist model rejects the assumptions that the polity is based on "secular, relativist" Enlightenment values, or that secularism is a "neutral" position. Indeed, what passes for "neutrality," according to pluralist thinkers, is actually a deeply embedded ideological preference for some modes of reasoning and ways of life over others—rationalism and choice over tradition and conscience.[55] No specific law or policy can be "neutral"; all are based on ideological or philosophical positions. "Neutrality," therefore, cannot be achieved by scrutinizing each individual law. Rather, the overall constitutional framework must leave the choice among competing worldviews and perspectives to the people, privileging neither religious nor secular values. This means that religious citizens, like everyone else, are entitled to advocate laws that reflect their best judgment of what will promote the public good, even if their premises derive from religious teachings. The resulting system is "neutral" toward religion not because the laws are based on nonsectarian "reason," but because all citizens are equally free to adopt or reject arguments without any limitation arising from their metaphysical, philosophical, epistemological, or theological foundations. To tell religious citizens that their conceptions of justice or the common good must be "bracketed" is to treat them as second-class citizens.

The claim that religious or theological arguments have no place in democratic politics is especially odd when we consider the unbroken record of religious participation in social and political controversy throughout American history. From the struggle for Independence, abolition, and the Civil War, through women's suffrage and prohibition, to the modern controversies over civil rights, the Vietnam War, and abortion, religious voices and religious arguments have been among the most prominent. It is hard to sympathize with a position that implies that Sam Adams, William Lloyd Garrison, Dorothea Dix, and Martin Luther King were bad citizens, or that someone should have delivered them a lecture on the separation of church and state. Even the Religion Clauses themselves were justified, in large part, on the basis of theological principle. The Virginia Bill for Establishing Religious Freedom begins with the theological assertion that "Almighty God hath made the mind free"; Madison argued against the establishment on the ground that man's duties to the Creator are superior to positive law, and the political muscle for religious freedom came from Baptists and other evangelical Protestants who derived their love of liberty and equality from the sectarian Protestant dogmas of the priesthood of all believers and unmediated access of the soul to the love and grace of God. Advocates of the secular state claim that laws based on religious reasoning demean the status of nonbelievers as equal citizens. The pluralist would respond that no citizen is demeaned by laws that he disagrees with, so long as he has an equal right both to advocate for laws he deems just and to disagree with arguments he does not find persuasive. The pluralist state thus affirms the equality of all citizens by allowing all to participate in public affairs without privileging any particular ideology or mode of persuasion.

By the same token, the pluralist approach encourages communities of conscience to preserve the institutions necessary to perpetuate their distinctive ways of life and to pass these on to future generations. Our long-standing tradition of broad-based tax exemptions and tax-deductible contributions for nonprofit religious and charitable groups is a practical means by which government can support these institutions without government involvement in the selection of worthy recipients or control over their operations. Where government-funded programs duplicate or compete with religious institutions that perform public functions (such as hospitals, universities, schools, or soup kitchens), the pluralist view suggests that, where possible, it should allow a range of choice so that those who wish to educate their children, receive their medical care, or participate in public programs in a manner consistent with their faith can do so. In the past, any financial support of religious institutions was constitutionally suspect, unless it could be shown convincingly that the funded activity had no religious component.[56] The recent trend, however, is to uphold government assistance so long as it is provided to a broad array of beneficiaries, secular as well as religious, on the basis of objective secular criteria.[57] The most difficult problem is how to ensure that the assistance is given in such a way that it does not destroy the autonomy of the institutions. Some thoughtful pluralists think that religious institutions are better off if they continue to be excluded from government assistance, because the threat of regulation and control is more dangerous than the deprivation of resources.

None of this is to deny that pluralism comes at a cost: it dilutes the concept of "citizen," making it difficult to identify what being an "American" is all about. If there is to be a common core of tradition and affection, it must emerge *indirectly*, from what Rawls might call the "overlapping consensus" of different traditions, rather than through conscious inculcation of a public ideology or civil religion. It is for this reason that many thoughtful Americans fear that the pluralist approach will exacerbate an already dangerous balkanization of American public life.

The key battleground between these two approaches to religious freedom has been over the question of education. Advocates of the secular state, following in the tradition of Horace Mann and John Dewey, hold that the government's control over education should be used to inculcate a common set of democratic ideals in keeping with the principles of the regime. In the United States, this usually means commitment to toleration, equality, critical rationality, and liberal democracy. Pluralists, by contrast, think it is better to permit families and subgroups to educate their children in the principles of their own tradition, so long as they satisfy basic educational standards. Strangely, although the United States tends to be the most pluralist of the western liberal democracies, it is alone among these countries in its insistence that government schools enjoy a monopoly over public funding. England, France, Germany, Holland, Belgium, and Canada all permit families to choose among nonreligious and religious schools, of different denominations, without forfeiting their right to a share of public educational funding.[58]

The pluralist idea, especially in education, came under sharp attack during the last half of the nineteenth century and first quarter of the twentieth century, when Protestant, anti-immigrant, and educational reform advocates combined for different reasons to produce the common school and "Americanization" movements.[59] This movement sought to inculcate democratic, supposedly nonsectarian values among the (often Catholic or Jewish) immigrant classes through a combination of control over the public school curriculum and an attack on private education. One prominent educational reformer stated: "The children of this country, of whatever parentage, should . . . be *educated together*,—not as Baptists, or Methodists, or Episcopalians, or Presbyterians; not as Roman Catholics or Protestants, still less as foreigners in language or spirit, but as Americans, as made of one blood and citizens of the same free country,—educated to be one harmonious people."[60]

The most extreme manifestation of this movement—the attempt to mandate public schooling and outlaw private alternatives—was rebuffed by the Supreme Court in *Pierce v. Society of Sisters*, in 1925.[61] "The fundamental theory of liberty upon which all governments in this Union repose," according to the Court, "excludes any general power of the State to standardize its children by forcing them to accept instruction from public teachers only."[62] But while overt coercion was prevented, the power of the purse was used to make it difficult and costly for children from disadvantaged families to take advantage of this constitutional freedom. Whether we will continue this attempt to use control over public resources to induce the families of America to accept instruction from government employees only is one of the most hotly contested constitutional questions of our day.

. . . . .

The great public feast given in 1789 in Philadelphia, then the nation's capital, to celebrate ratification of the Constitution included a fitting symbol of this new pluralistic philosophy: the feast included a special table where the food conformed to Jewish dietary laws.[63] This was a fitting symbol because it included Jewish Americans in the celebration without requiring that they sacrifice their distinctiveness as Jews. In France, by contrast, Napoleon summoned the leaders of the Jewish community to a "Great Sanhedrin," where he insisted that the Jewish law be modified to enable the Jewish people to be integrated into the French nation.[64] In a gesture no less revealing than the kosher table in Philadephia, Napoleon's minister of the interior scheduled the first session to be held on Saturday. Here we see the three alternatives. Under the *ancien régime*, Jews would be excluded from the celebration, for they could not be citizens. Under the secular state, Jews would be welcome to attend, but they would be expected to eat the same food that other citizens eat. If they want to keep kosher, they should do it at home, in private, at their own expense. Under the pluralist vision, multiple tables are provided to ensure that for Protestants, it is a Protestant country, for Catholics a Catholic country, and the Jew, if he pleases, may establish in it his New Jerusalem.

NOTES

[1] See Paul Johnson, *A History of the Jews* (New York: Harper and Row, 1987), 280.

[2] Jean-Jacques Rousseau, *The Social Contract*, trans. Maurice Cranston (Penguin, 1968), 179, 181. In this analysis, Rousseau was anticipated by Hobbes.

[3] Philippians 3:20 (NIV).

[4] Hebrews 11:13–16 (NIV).

[5] James Madison, *Memorial and Remonstrance Against Religious Assessments*, ¶ 1, vol. 2 of *The Writings of James Madison*, ed. G. Hunt (New York: G. P. Putman's Sons, 1901), 183.

[6] John Locke, *Essay on Toleration*, in vol. 6 of *The Works of John Locke* (Locke 1823; photo reprint, 1963), 1, 9.

[7] Thomas Jefferson to the Danbury Baptist Association, I January 1802, *The Founders' Constitution*, ed. P. Kurland and R. Lerner (Chicago: University of Chicago Press, 1987) 5:96.

[8] *Berca College v Kentucky*, 211 U.S. 45 (1908).

[9] *Rob Jones University v United States*, 461 U.S. 574 (1983).

[10] *Employment Division v Smith*, 494 U.S. 872 (1990); *People v Woody*, 61 Cal. 2d 716, 394 P.2d 813 (1964).

[11] *Goldman v Weinberger*, 475 U.S. 503 (1986).

[12] *Cruz v Beto*, 405 U.S. 319 (1972).

[13] *Marsh v Chambers*, 463 U.S. 783 (1983).

[14] *Katcoff v Marsh*, 755 F.2d 223 (1985).

[15] *Fordham Univ. v Brown*, 856 F. Supp. 684 (D. D.C. 1994).

[16] *U.S. v Means*, 858 F.2d 404 (8th Cir. 1988), cert, denied, 492 U.S. 910 (1989).

[17] *City of Boerne v Flores*, 117 S. Ct. 2157 (1997).

[18] *South Jersey Catholic School Teachers Org. v St. Teresa of the Infant Jesus Church Elementary School*, 150 N.J. 575, 696 A.2d 709 (1997).

[19] *Rayburn v General Conference of Seventh-Day Adventists*, 772 F.2d 1164 (4th Cir. 1985), cert, denied, 478 U.S. 1020 (1986).

[20] See Christopher Smith, "Booze Fight Looks Like It Will Go to Trial; Still No Rum at the lnn: Lodge Owner's Fight to Sell Liquor in 'Mormon Country' Appears Headed for a Trial," *Salt Lake Tribune*, 7 February 1997, sec. B.

[21] *Works of John Locke*, 6:43.

[22] Ibid.

[23] For additional discussion of this point in Locke, see Michael W. McConnell, *Freedom from Persecution or Protection of the Rights of Conscience?: A Critique of Justice Scalia's Historical Arguments in City of Boerne v. Flores*, 39 Wm. and Mary L. Rev. 819 (1998).

[24] *Writings of James Madison*, 98–100.

[25] Thomas Jefferson, *Notes on the State of Virginia* (Chapel Hill: University of North Carolina Press, 1955), 159.

[26] Edmund Burke, Speech on the Petition of the Unitarians (11 May 1792), in vol. 7 of *Works of the Right Honorable Edmund Burke* (Little, Brown, 1889), 44. For further discussion of Burke's views on this subject, see Michael W. McConnell, *Establishment and Toleration in Edmund Burke's "Constitution of Freedom,"* 1995 Sup. Ct. Rev. 393.

[27] Thomas Jefferson, A Bill for Establishing Religious Freedom (12 June 1779), reprinted in *The Founders' Constitution*, 5:77.

28Joseph Blau and Salo Baron, eds., *The Jews of the United States 1790–1840: A Documentary History* (New York: Columbia University Press, 1963), 1:9–11.

29George Washington to the Religious Society Called Quakers (October 1789), in *George Washington on Religious Liberty and Mutual Understanding*, ed. E. Humphrey (Washington D.C., 1932), 11.

30*Founders' Constitution*, 5:77.

31*Writings of James Madison*, 2:185.

32Washington's views about the theological truth of religion are harder to determine and are irrelevant to his constitutional position.

33Alexis de Tocqueville, *Democracy in America*, ed. J. P. Mayer, vol. 1, pt. 2, ch. 9 (Garden City, N.Y.: Doubleday, 1969), 293.

34Ibid., 294.

35de Tocqueville, *Democracy in America*, vol. 2, pt. 1, ch. 5, 444–45.

36Ibid., 287.

37Tocqueville explains why, under the social conditions of America, Catholics make good democratic citizens. Ibid., 289. ("Most of the Catholics are poor, and unless all citizens govern, they will never attain to the government themselves. The Catholics are in a minority, and it is important for them that all rights should be respected so that they can be sure to enjoy their own in freedom.")

38See, for example, Jane Rutherford, *Equality as the Primary Constitutional Value: The Case for Applying Employment Discrimination Laws to Religion*, 81 Cornell L. Rev. 1049 (1996); Mary Becker, *The Politics of Women's Wrongs and the Bill of "Rights"; A Bicentennial Perspective, in The Bill of Rights in the Modern State*, ed. Geoffrey R. Stone, Richard A. Epstein, and Cass R. Sunstein (Chicago: University of Chicago Press, 1992), 453.

39Stephen G. Gey, *Why Is Religion Special? Reconsidering the Accommodation of Religion under the Religion Clauses of the First Amendment*, 52 U. Pitt. L. Rev. 75, 79 (1990). To similar effect, see Suzanna Sherry, *Enlightening the Religion Clauses*, 7 J. of Contemp. Legal Issues 473, 483 (1996): "It is historically uncontroversial [!] that the Enlightenment, with its emphasis on rationalism and empiricism and its rejection of religious faith and mysticism, was the primary epistemology of the founding generation. Most scholars consider the Constitution itself to be a product of the Enlightenment." From this premise, Sherry concludes that "our Constitution does—as a matter of history—and ought to—as a matter of policy—privilege reason over faith." Ibid., 477.

40See generally Arthur Hertzberg, *The French Enlightenment and the Jews* (New York: Columbia University Press, 1968).

41Thomas Jefferson to Dr. Benjamin Waterhouse (22 June 1822), in *The Works of Thomas Jefferson*, ed. P. Ford (New York: G. P. Putnam's Sons, 1905), 241–3; Thomas Jefferson to James Smith (3 December 1822), in *The Life and Selected Writings of Thomas Jefferson*, ed. A. Koch and W. Peden (New York: Random House, 1944), 703–4.

42Vicki Caron, "French-Jewish Assimilation Reassessed: A Review of the Recent Literature," *Judaica* 42 (Spring 1993): 134, 138, summarizing Simon Schwarzfuchs, *Du Juif à l'Israélite: Histoire d'une mutation*, 1770–1879 (Paris: Fayard, 1989).

43Frances Malino, *A Jew in the French Revolution: The Life of Zalkind Hourwitz* (Oxford: Blackwell, 1996), 145, quoting *Le Patriote Français*, 4 Prairial, An VI (24 May 1798).

44See *City of Boerne v Flores*, 117 S. Ct. 2157, 2172 (1997) Stevens, J., concurring).

45319 U.S. 624, 653 (1943).

46Isaac Kramnick and R. Laurence Moore, *The Godless Constitution: The Case against Religious Correctness* (New York: Norton, 1996), 15.

47*Lemon v Kurtzman*, 403 U.S. 602, 612 (1971). The Court has not relied on this test in recent years, but has refrained from overruling it.

48*Huns v McNair*, 413 U.S. 734, 743 (1973); *Roemer v Board of Public Works*, 426 U.S. 736, 752 (1976).

49*Employment Division v Smith*, 494 U.S. 872 (1990); see also *City of Boerne v Flores*, 117 S. Ct. 2157 (1997).

50Sherry, *Enlightening the Religion Clauses*, 477.

51For details about Sampson, and about the case, see Walter J. Walsh, *Religion, Ethnicity and History: Clues to the Cultural Construction of Law, in The New York Irish*, ed. R. Baylor and T. Meagher (Baltimore: Johns Hopkins University Press, 1996), 48:53–61.

52*People v Philips*, New York City Court of General Sessions (1813), published in W. Sampson, *The Catholic Question in America* (New York: Edward Gillespy, 1813; photo reprint, New York: Da Capo Press, 1974).

53Ibid., 85.

54*Stansbury v Marks*, 2 Dall. 213 (Pa. 1793).

[55]See Alasdair MacIntyre, *Three Rival Versions of Moral Enquiry* (Notre Dame, Ind.: University of Notre Dame Press, 1990).

[56]See *Lemon v Kurtzman*, 403 U.S. 602 (1971); *Committee for Public Education & Religious Liberty v Nyquist*, 413 U.S. 756 (1973).

[57]See *Rosenberger v Rector & Visitors of the University of Virginia*, 515 U.S. 819 (1995); *Witters v Washington Dept. of Services*, 474 U.S. 481 (1986).

[58]Charles L. Glenn, *Choice of Schools in Six Nations* (Washington, D.C.: Government Printing Office, 1989).

[59]See Charles Glenn, *The Myth of the Common School* (Amherst: University of Massachusetts Press, 1987); Diane Ravitch, *The Great School Wars, New York City 1805–1973: A History of the Public Schools as Battlefield of Social Change* (New York: Basic Books, 1974); Michael McConnell, *Multiculturalism, Majoritarianism, and Educational Choice: What Does Our Constitutional Tradition Have To Say?* 1991 U. Chi. Leg. For. 123, 134–39.

[60]W. S. Dutton, "The Proposed Substitution of Sectarian for Public Schools," *Common School Journal* (1 June 1848), 166–68, quoted in Glenn, *Myth*, 223.

[61]268 U.S. 510 (1925).

[62]Ibid., 535.

[63]Johnson, *History of the Jews*, 303.

[64]See Simon Schwarzfuchs, *Napoleon, the Jews and the Sanhedrin* (London: Routledge and Kegan Paul, 1979), 54.

CULTURE AND EQUALITY

An Egalitarian Critique of Multiculturalism

—*Brian Barry*—

EQUAL TREATMENT

The strategy of privatization entails a rather robust attitude towards cultural diversity. It says, in effect, 'Here are the rules which tell people what they are allowed to do. What they choose to do within those rules is up to them. But it has nothing to do with public policy.' A simple model of rational decision-making, but one adequate for the present purpose, would present the position as follows: the rules define a choice set, which is the same for everybody; within that choice set people pick a particular course of action by deciding what is best calculated to satisfy their underlying preferences for outcomes, given their beliefs about the way in which actions are connected to outcomes. From an egalitarian liberal standpoint, what matters are equal opportunities. If uniform rules create identical choice sets, then opportunities are equal. We may expect that people will make different choices from these identical choice sets, depending on their preferences for outcomes and their beliefs about the relation of actions to the satisfaction of their preferences. Some of these preferences and beliefs will be derived from aspects of a culture shared with others; some will be idiosyncratic. But this has no significance: either way it is irrelevant to any claims based on justice, since justice is guaranteed by equal opportunities.

None of this means, of course, that people will not in fact feel hard done by and complain that the system of uniform laws treats them unfairly. Many such complaints are, indeed, made. The question that has to be asked is what merit there is in these complaints. That will be the subject of the rest of the chapter. The main conclusion for which I shall argue is that a popular political response—and one that multiculturalists would like to see made more common—is actually very hard to justify in any particular case, even though it cannot be ruled out a priori. This is the approach that keeps the rule objected to for most of the population but allows members of cultural or religious minorities to opt out of the obligation to obey it. More precisely, I shall concede that this approach, which I shall call the rule-and-exemption approach, may sometimes be defensible on the basis of political prudence or an estimate of the balance of advantages. But I shall reject the characteristic case made by the supporters of multiculturalism, that a correct analysis would show exemptions for cultural minorities to be required in a great many cases by egalitarian liberal justice.

An example of the rule-and-exemption approach is the exemption from humane slaughter regulations that many countries have enacted to accommodate the beliefs of Jews and Muslims. Another is a family of exemptions from laws designed to reduce head injuries which have the effect of permitting turban-wearing Sikhs to ride motorcycles, work in the construction industry, and so on. I shall discuss both of these in the next section. Most, though not all, of these exemptions are claimed on the basis of religious belief. Indeed, Peter Jones has gone so far as to suggest that, if we leave aside the 'religious components of culture', there should be 'few, if any problems of mutual accommodation' arising from cultural diversity. We shall see in the course of this book how often demands for special treatment—by individuals and by organizations are based on religious belief. This is, perhaps, to be expected if we recognize the tendency for religious precepts to be experienced as more peremptory than norms that are supported only by custom.

We should at the same time, however, appreciate that claims based on religion are more likely to be sympathetically received by outsiders than claims based on custom, especially in largely Protestant (or ex-Protestant) countries, in which there is a traditional reluctance to 'force tender consciences'. This tendency is reinforced in the United States by the constitutional guarantee of 'freedom of religion', which encourages the packaging of custom as religion. The result is, for example, that wearing a *yarmulke* (skull cap) is presented as a religious obligation rather than as the traditional practice that it is for some Orthodox Jews. Even without this incentive, however, it is perceived as advantageous to press claims on the basis of religion wherever possible. Thus, it is questionable that the wearing of a turban is a religious obligation for Sikhs, as against a customary practice among some. In the parliamentary debate on the proposal to exempt turban-wearing Sikhs from the requirement that all motorcyclists must wear a crash helmet, those who favoured the exemption thought it important to insist on the religious standing of the turban, while those who were opposed to it argued for its customary status. There is, however, a countervailing force in Britain, as we shall see below: outside Northern Ireland, discrimination on the basis of religion is not illegal, but discrimination on the basis of race or ethnicity is. This means that there is an incentive to code what may plausibly be a religious obligation (e.g. the wearing of some kind of head-covering by Muslim women) as an ethnic cultural practice, so as to bring it within the scope of the Race Relations Act.

The strong claim made by many theorists of multiculturalism is that special arrangements to accommodate religious beliefs and cultural practices are demanded by justice. The argument is that failure to offer special treatment is in some circumstances itself a kind of unequal treatment. For, it is said, the same law may have a different impact on different people as a result of their religious beliefs or cultural practices. Thus, the liberal claim that equal treatment is generated by a system of uniform laws is invalid. What can be said of this argument? There can be no question that any given general law will have a different impact on different people. But is there anything inherently unfair about this? The essence of law is the protection of some interests at the expense of others when they come into conflict. Thus, the interests of women who do not want to be raped are given priority over the interests of potential rapists in the form of the law that prohibits rape. Similarly, the interests of children in not being interfered with sexually are given priority over the interests of potential paedophiles in the form of the law that prohibits their acting on their proclivities. These laws clearly have a much more severe impact on those who are strongly attracted to rape and paedophilia than on those who would not wish to engage in them even if there were no law against them. But it is absurd to suggest that this makes the laws prohibiting them unfair: they make a fair allocation of rights between the would-be rapist or paedophile and the potential victim.

The point is a completely general one. If we consider virtually any law, we shall find that it is much more burdensome to some people than to others. Speed limits inhibit only those who like to drive fast. Laws prohibiting drunk driving have no impact on teetotallers. Only smokers are stopped by prohibitions on smoking in public places. Only those who want to own a handgun are affected by a ban on them, and so on *ad infinitium*. This is simply how things are. The notion that inequality of impact is a sign of unfairness is not an insight derived from a more sophisticated conception of justice than that previously found in political philosophy. It is merely a mistake. This is not, of course, to deny that the unequal impact of a law may in some cases be an indication of its unfairness. It is simply to say that the charge will have to be substantiated in each case by showing exactly how the law is unfair. It is never enough to show no more than that it has a different impact on different people.

All of this bears on a line of thought in recent political philosophy according to which a legitimate claim for additional income can, in principle at least, be made by those with expensive tastes—people who have to eat plovers eggs and drink vintage claret (to take a famous example) if they are to achieve the same level of satisfaction as others can achieve with sausages and beer. The usual reaction to the idea that those with expensive tastes should get extra resources is that it is absurd, and such a reaction is perfectly sound. This is not simply because the proposal is unworkable: those who put forward the idea are usually quite willing to concede that. The error lies in thinking that, even as a matter of principle, fair treatment requires compensation for expensive tastes. To explain what is wrong with the idea, we have to invoke the fundamental premise that the subject of fairness is the distribution of rights, resources and opportunities. Thus, a fair share of income is a fair share of income: income is the stuff whose distribution is the subject of attributions of fairness. Suppose that you and I have an equal claim on society's resources, for whatever reason. Then it is simply not relevant that you will gain more satisfaction from using those resources than I will. What is fair is that our equal claim translates into equal purchasing power: what we do with it is our own business.

If we rule out the claim that equal treatment entails equal impact, there may still be other arguments for special arrangements to accommodate cultural practices or religious beliefs. But what are they? One natural recourse is to suggest that what I have said so far may be all very well for costs arising from preferences, but that costs arising from beliefs are a different kettle of fish. It is very hard to see why this proposition should be accepted, however confidently it is often advanced. Consider, for example, the way in which people's beliefs may make some job opportunities unattractive to them. Pacifists will presumably regard a career in the military as closed to them. Committed vegetarians are likely to feel the same about jobs in slaughterhouses or butchers' shops. Similarly, if legislation requires that animals should be stunned before being killed, those who cannot as a result of their religious beliefs cut such meat will have to give up eating meat altogether.

Faced with a meatless future, some Jews and Muslims may well decide that their faith needs to be reinterpreted so as to permit the consumption of humanely slaughtered animals. And indeed this has already happened. According to Peter Singer, 'in Sweden, Norway and Switzerland, for example, the rabbis have accepted legislation requiring the stunning [of animals prior to killing] with no exceptions for ritual slaughter'. The case for saying that humane slaughter regulations are not unfair does not, however, depend upon the claim that beliefs are a matter of choice, so that it is somehow people's own fault if they are incommoded by their beliefs. (That is not the point about expensive tastes either.) If we want to say, as Yael Tamir does, that people should be 'free to adhere to cultures and religions of their choice', that should be taken to mean only that they should not be penalized for changing their minds about the value of their current religious or cultural commitments. It should not be interpreted to mean that these commitments are the product of choice. It makes no sense to say that we can decide what to believe. Similarly, we can say if we like that people are responsible for their own beliefs, but that should be understood simply as a way of saying that they own them: their beliefs are not to be conceived of as some sort of alien affliction. (The same may, again, be said in general about preferences.) Talking, as Michael Sandel does, about people being 'encumbered' by their beliefs feeds this sense of alienation.

The position regarding preferences and beliefs is similar. We can try to cultivate certain tastes (by, for example, developing a familiarity or skill), and we can try to strengthen certain beliefs (by, for example, deliberately exposing ourselves to messages tending to confirm them), but in neither case is there any guarantee of success. Moreover, the decision to make the attempt must come from somewhere: we must already have a higher-order preference for developing the taste or a higher-order belief that it would be a good thing to strengthen the belief. Choice cannot, in either case, go all the way down. I suspect that one source of the idea that many preferences are easily changeable is a result of a tendency to muddle together preferences and choices. Suppose, for example, that I have a preference for vanilla over strawberry ice cream, other things being equal. That entails that, if other things are actually equal, I will choose vanilla. But this preference may be a weak one, which means that things do not have to be very unequal before my choice switches to strawberry. The weakness of my preference would be revealed by my willingness to pay only a little more for vanilla and my lack of reluctance to let somebody else have the last vanilla ice cream. Even so, the preference itself, even if weak, may be solidly based in physiology and almost impossible to change. The upshot is, then, that beliefs and preferences are in the same boat: we cannot change our beliefs by an act of will but the same can be said equally well of our preferences. It is false that the changeability of preferences is what makes it not unfair for them to give rise to unequal impact. It is therefore not true that the unchangeability of beliefs makes it unfair for them to give rise to unequal impacts.

Beliefs are not an encumbrance in anything like the way in which a physical disability is an encumbrance. Yet precisely this claim is sometimes made. Thus, Bhikhu Parekh argues that giving people special treatment on the basis of their beliefs 'is like two individuals who both enjoy the right to equal medical attention but who receive different treatments depending on the nature of their illness'. A disability—for example, a lack of physical mobility due to injury or disease—supports a strong prima facie claim to compensation because it limits the opportunity to engage in activities that others are able to engage in. In contrast, the effect of some distinctive belief or preference is to bring about a certain pattern of choices from among the set of opportunities that are available to all who are similarly placed physically or financially. The position of somebody who is unable to drive a car as a result of some physical disability is totally different from that of somebody who is unable to drive a car because doing so would be contrary to the tenets of his or her religion. To suggest that they are similarly situated is in fact offensive to both parties. Someone who needs a wheelchair to get around will be quite right to resent the suggestion that this need should be assimilated to an expensive taste. And somebody who freely embraces a religious belief that prohibits certain activities will rightly deny the imputation that this is to be seen as analogous to the unwelcome burden of a physical disability.

The critical distinction is between limits on the range of opportunities open to people and limits on the choices that they make from within a certain range of opportunities. Parekh deliberately blurs this distinction by writing that 'opportunity is a subject-dependent concept', so that 'a facility, a resource, or a course of action' does not constitute an opportunity for you, even if it is actually open to you, unless you have 'the cultural disposition . . . to take advantage of it'. This proposal actually destroys the meaning of the word opportunity, which originally related to Portunus, who was (and for anything I know to the contrary still is) the god who looks after harbours. When the wind and the tide were propitious, sailors had the opportunity to leave or enter the harbour. They did not have to do so if they did not want to, of course, but that did not mean (as Parekh's proposal would imply) that the opportunity then somehow disappeared. The existence of the opportunity was an objective state of affairs. That is not to say that opportunity could not be individualized: whether a certain conjunction of wind and tide created an opportunity for a particular ship might depend on its build and its rigging. But it did not depend on the 'cultural disposition' of the crew 'to take advantage of it'. They might, perhaps, have chosen not to sail because setting out on a voyage was contraindicated by a religious omen, but that simply meant that they had passed up the opportunity.

Lily Bart, the heroine of *The House of Mirth* (in the sense in which Becky Sharp is the heroine of Thackeray's *Vanity Fair*), spends a lot of time in the novel bemoaning the way in which the wealth of her relatives and friends provides them with opportunities—a word she uses several times in this context—that they do not take up because their horizons are limited by the stifling culture of upper-crust New York, and she reflects on the advantage she would be able to take of the same opportunities. If Parekh were right, we would have to convict Miss Bart and her creator, Edith Wharton, of committing a conceptual mistake. On Parekh's analysis, Lily Bart would have had to think that, if she had the wealth of her relatives and friends, she would have had a lot of opportunities that they did not have. But this would be, I submit, to lose the point of her complaint, which was precisely that they had the opportunities yet did not use them. Similarly, the opportunity to read a wide range of books is ensured by literacy plus access to a public library or (provided you have the money) a bookshop. If you belong to some Christian sect that teaches the sinfulness of reading any book except the Bible, you will choose not to avail yourself of this opportunity. But you still have exactly the same opportunity to read books as somebody who is similarly placed in all respects except for not having this particular belief.

The peculiar implications of Parekh's analysis are well illustrated by his treatment of one example of 'giving people special treatment on the basis of their beliefs'. At issue here is the exemption that Sikhs enjoy from the 'provisions designed to penalize those who carry knives and other sharply pointed objects' contained in the Criminal Justice Act of 1988, which 'specifically states that it is a defence for an accused to prove that he had the article with him in a public place "for religious reasons"', a provision that was 'introduced . . . to permit Sikhs to carry their *kirpans* (swords or daggers) in public places without fear of prosecution'. Parekh asks if non-Sikhs can 'legitimately complain of discrimination or unequal treatment' and replies that 'there is no discrimination involved both because their [i.e. non-Sikhs'] religious requirements are not ignored, and because they [i.e. non-Sikhs] do not suffer adversely as a result of the law respecting those [religious requirements] of the Sikhs'. However, the rationale of a law against the carrying of knives in public must be that unarmed citizens (pleonastically) 'suffer adversely' if some other people are going around carrying weapons. Unless a knife confers an advantage on its possessor, there is no point in having a law restricting the carrying of knives at all.

Assuming that the law's rationale is sound, it is absurd to deny that granting an exemption to it for members of one group inevitably reduces the personal security of all the rest of the population.

Parekh also argues that 'as for the complaint of inequality, there is a prima facie inequality of rights in the sense that Sikhs can do what others cannot. However the alleged inequality grows out of the requirements of the principle of equal respect for all, and it is not so much inequality as an appropriate translation of that principle in a different religious context. But the inequality of rights is not prima facie—it is real. The right to carry knives amidst a population none of whom can legally do the same is an inequality of rights, however we look at it. Whether or not it is a justifiable inequality is another matter. But it is playing with words to suggest that it is really a superior form of equality to the liberal one that says we have equal rights when we have the same ones.

I have argued so far that the differential impact of a general law cannot in itself found a claim that the law is unjust. But justice is not the only basis on which the argument for an exemption from the law might be made. If it is true that a law bears particularly harshly on some people, that is at the very least a reason for examining it to see if it might be modified so as to accommodate those who are affected by it in some special way. Prudence or generosity might support such a move. From a utilitarian point of view, we could pose the question by asking if it is worth giving up some of the benefits of the law in order to reduce the costs of complying with it. It does not follow, though, that the best approach is to keep the general rule unchanged and simply add an exemption for the members of some specific group. The alternative is to work out some less restrictive alternative form of the law that would adequately meet the objectives of the original one while offering the members of the religious or cultural minority whatever is most important to them. This avoids the invidiousness of having different rules for different people in the same society. In practice, however, it is the rule-and-exemption approach that is usually followed.

We can understand how this comes about if we think for a moment about the politics involved. Any open political system (not only one with formally representative political institutions) is inevitably subject to lobbying by minority groups with a special interest in some aspect of public policy. It very often happens that there is no similarly well-organized group on the other side. Governments and legislatures are naturally tempted, therefore, to take the path of least resistance and cave into these minority group demands. To a politician, the attractions of a general law with exemptions for members of specific groups are almost irresistible. No creative effort is required; and, while those who are concerned with the objective of the law may grumble at the special dispensations, they will at least be satisfied that they have achieved most of what they want. At the same time, the articulate special interests that are most opposed are bought off by permission to opt out. Sikhs, whose relatively small overall numbers in Britain are offset by their concentration in a small number of parliamentary constituencies, have been remarkably successful at playing this game, as we shall see.

Once we accept, however, that the case for exemptions must be based on the alleviation of hardship rather than the demands of justice, it seems to me much more problematic to make it out than is widely assumed. I do not wish to rule out the possibility that there will be cases in which both the general law and the exemption are defensible. Usually, though, either the case for the law (or some version of it) is strong enough to rule out exemptions, or the case that can be made for exemptions is strong enough to suggest that there should be no law anyway. Consider, for example, the claim that 'the core of Rastafarian religiosity resides in the revelatory dimensions induced by the sacramental use of *ganja* [cannabis], in which a new level of consciousness is attained. Adherents to the movement are enabled more easily to perceive Haile Selassie as the redeemer and to appreciate their own identities. It might perhaps be said of many other religious truths that they too would be more easy to believe in under the influence of mind-altering substances. However, there would obviously be insuperable practical problems in legalizing the use of cannabis for Rastafarians only, such as the difficulty of restricting its use to Rastafarian religious ceremonies, the absurdity of trying to distinguish 'genuine' from 'opportunistic' Rastafarians, and the virtual impossibility of preventing Rastafarian cannabis from 'leaking' into the general population. For the same reasons, claims for religiously based exemptions to laws prohibiting use of marijuana in the United States have been ruled out even by those Supreme Court judges sympathetic to such exemptions in general: 'the Ethiopian Zionist Coptic Church . . . teaches that marijuana is properly smoked "continually all day" ', and even if its use were officially prescribed only within the context of a religious ceremony, 'it would be difficult to grant a religious exemption without seriously compromising law enforcement efforts'. The best case for making cannabis legal for Rastafarians or members of the Ethiopian Zionist Coptic Church would be to argue that it is far less harmful than either alcohol or tobacco, both of which are legal. But this is an argument whose scope is not confined to Rastafarians. Rather, if it is valid, it constitutes a case for legalizing the consumption of cannabis by anybody.

THE RULE-AND-EXEMPTION APPROACH

Because it tastes better and is less likely to contain antibiotics or growth hormones, but also out of feelings of guilt (since I can see no answer to the moral case for vegetarianism), I try to buy only meat from animals that have been reared under conditions appropriate to them, fed only food that forms part of their natural diet, and have been slaughtered humanely. This is, literally, an expensive taste. A metaphorically expensive taste (since it might actually end up saving money) would be that of somebody who is a vegetarian out of moral conviction but misses the taste of meat and would still be buying it if they had not come across Peter Singer. A variant on this would be a vegetarian on religious grounds (a Brahmin, for example) or somebody whose religion forbade them to eat pork, such as an observant Jew or Muslim, if they hankered for what was not permitted. Provided we are prepared to extend the conception of 'expensive taste' to include costs that arise from moral convictions or religious beliefs, these are all cases of expensive tastes. They are also, I shall take it, all cases in which nobody would suggest that those with the expensive taste should be compensated out of public funds or granted some waiver from generally applicable laws.

I mentioned earlier that humane slaughter regulations will have the effect of ruling out the consumption of meat for Orthodox Jews and observant Muslims, unless their religious authorities declare that the traditional precepts do not have to be followed, as has occurred among Jews in Norway, Sweden, and Switzerland. These religious precepts may also be said to create an expensive taste, in conjunction with humane slaughter legislation, at any rate among those who would eat meat as long as it was kosher or halal. Unlike the previous cases, however, this is one in which the expensive taste is widely held to justify the demand that Jews and Muslims should be given special treatment in the form of an exemption from humane slaughter legislation so that they can go on eating meat consistently with their beliefs. Moreover, campaigns to secure such an exemption have been successful in almost all western countries, the exceptions being the three already listed. In Britain, for example, 'under the Slaughter of Poultry Act (1967) and the Slaughterhouses Act (1979) Jews and Muslims may slaughter poultry and animals in abattoirs according to their traditional methods'. 'Traditional methods' is a euphemism for bleeding animals to death while conscious, rather than stunning them prior to killing them, as is otherwise required.

There are two possible approaches to ritual slaughter that would not lead to the making of an exemption to a general rule. The first would be a libertarian one. It can be argued that, just as the decision to eat meat at all is currently left to the individual conscience, decisions about the way in which animals are killed should be left to the conscience of the consumer. In effect, the job of weighing animal welfare against human carnivorous tastes would be left for each person to perform. This argument is parallel to one used to oppose the prohibition of bloodsports to the effect that their moral acceptability should be left to the individual conscience. Alternatively, the case of ritual slaughter might be assimilated to the ban on cockfighting and dogfighting, customs in their time just as deep-rooted as hunting or hare-coursing but prohibited nonetheless on animal welfare grounds. Taking this line, the implication would be that there is a certain point beyond which cruelty to animals is a legitimate matter for collective decision-making, and that kosher/halal butchery is over that line.

The current situation in Britain is indefensible on libertarian grounds because it is fundamental to the libertarian position that consumers should have clear information on the basis of which to make choices. This condition is not met. There is no requirement that meat from animals killed while still conscious should be labelled to indicate this. Moreover, there is a conspiracy of silence maintained by government and retailers to conceal from consumers the fact that meat displayed on supermarket shelves may come from animals killed in this way. I have never seen this information provided at point of sale and my own informal survey indicates that it is a well-kept secret. In practice, 'a substantial proportion of meat produced by means of religious slaughter is marketed to the general public without any indication of its origins'. The reason for selling most of this meat (as much as two-thirds, according to Singer) on the general market is the cost of preparing meat that is to be sold as 'kosher'.

> For meat to be passed us 'kosher' by the Orthodox rabbis, it must, in addition to being from an animal killed while conscious, have had the forbidden tissues, such as veins, lymph nodes, and the sciatic nerve and its branches removed. Cutting these parts out of the hindquarters of an animal is a laborious business and so only the forequarters are sold as kosher meat.

Does this matter? I think it does. Already 'by 1983 a National Opinion Poll [in Britain] revealed that 77 per cent of respondents were altogether opposed to religious slaughter'. Since then, there is much evidence that public opinion has moved ahead of the politicians in concern about the welfare of farm animals. There has, for example, been a big swing away from purchase of eggs from hens in battery cages, and survey evidence suggests that more explicit labelling would have created a bigger swing still. It is therefore reasonable to assume that a very large proportion of the population would shun meat from animals killed by ritual slaughter if they were aware of its provenance.

At the opposite pole from the libertarian position is the proposal to require all animals to be stunned before death. This was advocated by the British government's own Farm Animal Welfare Council in its 1985 *Report on the Welfare of Livestock when Slaughtered by Religious Methods*. 'The Report's principal conclusion was that, although there was a dearth of scientific evidence to indicate at precisely what stage in the process of losing consciousness animals cease to feel pain, loss of consciousness following severance of the major blood vessels in the neck is not immediate. In their own words: 'The up-to-date scientific evidence available and our own observations leave no doubt in our minds that religious methods of slaughter, even when carried out under ideal conditions, must result in a degree of pain, suffering and distress which does not occur in the properly stunned animal.' On similar grounds, 'the Commission of the European Communities Scientific Veterinary Committee recommended to the European Parliament in 1990 that the legal exemptions from stunning should be abolished in all the Community's member states.'

In the face of this, it seems to me virtually impossible to provide an intellectually coherent rationale for the rule-plus-exemption strategy, even though it is easy enough to understand its political success. The libertarian line is that there should be no collective view about the demands of animal welfare. Individual consumers should be put in a position to make informed choices, according to their own religious beliefs, ideas about the importance of animal suffering, taste preferences, and anything else that comes into the equation. The alternative line is that there is a legitimate collective concern with the welfare of animals which underwrites the requirement that all animals be stunned prior to being killed.

What do we have to think in order to finish up with neither of these but rather with the notion that the general rule should be that stunning must take place yet at the same time that there should be a special exemption for religious slaughter? Clearly, we have to accept two things: first, that it is legitimate to take collective decisions in pursuit of animal welfare, and, second, that animal welfare is better served by stunning. (If we did not believe the second, there would be no point in having a restrictive policy that makes stunning the rule.) We then have to hold that an inferior method is nevertheless to be tolerated, so long as its practice is restricted to those for whom it has religious significance. A rough analogy would be to allow hunting but restrict it to those who could show that it was part of their culture. However, it is implausible that a fox would feel better about hunting if it knew that it was to be chased by the Duke of Beaufort than if it knew it was to be chased by Roger Scruton, whom it might regard as a parvenu unable to claim hunting as part of his ancestral way of life. Similarly, it is hard to see why some cows and sheep should have to suffer in ways that are unacceptable generally in order to enable people with certain religious beliefs to eat their carcasses. To withstand that objection, it is necessary to postulate that, although ritual slaughter is far from being best practice, it is nevertheless above some threshold of cruelty below which prohibition would be justified. This then has to be taken to legitimate some sort of collective decision about the relative weight of the interests involved in which those of the animals lose out. I would not be so bold as to say that nobody could in good faith maintain such a position. I do, however, wish to claim that it requires a capacity for mental gymnastics of an advanced order.

It is worth adding this: the rule-plus-exemption regime is predicated on the assumption that the total amount of suffering due to ritual slaughter is to be minimized—consistently with not prohibiting it, of course. But then it is inconsistent with that logic to permit the sale of any part of the carcass of an animal killed by ritual slaughter as anything except kosher meat. A requirement that all the meat must be marketed as kosher would cut in three the number of beasts killed without prior stunning if the demand for kosher meat remained the same. Since, however, the expense of removing the forbidden parts would have to be reflected in the price of kosher meat, there would presumably be some reduction in demand for it, so the total number of beasts killed under the exemption would decline even further. This kind of provision, which as far as I am aware has never been proposed, cannot reasonably be resisted by anyone who seriously accepts the premises that are required for the derivation of the rule-plus-exemption system.

Some will no doubt think that I have overlooked the most compelling argument in favour of an exemption, the argument from freedom of religion. Thus, Sebastian Poulter cites in support of the right to kill animals while conscious Article 9 (1) of the European Convention on Human Rights, which 'provides that everyone has a right to freedom of religion, including the right to manifest this religion in practice and observance', and Article 27 of the International Covenant on Civil and Political Rights, which says that members of minority groups 'shall not be denied the right . . . to profess and practise their own religion'. However, an appeal to religious liberty provides only spurious support for this and other similar exemptions, because the law does not restrict religious liberty, only the ability to eat meat.

However insubstantial it may be, the argument from religious liberty is often put forward in this kind of context and has been found persuasive by the British parliament.

> In 1976 Parliament enacted a special exemption for turbaned Sikhs from the statutory requirement that all motorcyclists must wear crash helmets. . . . Parliament voted in favour of the special exemption with little debate because it wished to safeguard the religious freedom of the Sikh community in Britain even though there was a strong counter-argument about the need for safety on the roads.

In the discussion within a Standing Committee of the House of Commons, 'the value of religious freedom was stressed by several speakers', so the question was conceived as one of 'whether the right to religious freedom should predominate over the principle of equal treatment in the enforcement of measures promoting road safety'.

The requirement that drivers and passengers should wear helmets was introduced in 1971 with no exemptions. This was challenged in court on the ground that 'the regulations [requiring a helmet] were null and void as being in contravention of the guarantee of freedom of religion enshrined in the European Convention of Human Rights'. Lord Widgery disposed of this claim with the crisp remark: 'No one is bound to ride a motorcycle. All that the law prescribes is that if you do ride a motorcycle you must wear a crash helmet.' The European Commission on Human Rights rejected a similar claim based on freedom of religion, saying that 'the compulsory wearing of crash helmets is a necessary safety measure for motorcyclists. The Commission is of the opinion therefore that any interference there may be with the applicant's freedom of religion was justified for the protection of health in accordance with article 9 (2).' If the regulations could be said to have interfered with freedom of religion, it was an interference justified by (as the judgement continued) 'the valid health considerations on which the regulations are based'. But the wording leaves it open whether or not the regulations could properly be counted as an interference at all. Lord Widgery's argument was that they did not, because the inability to ride a motorcycle does not prevent a Sikh from observing any demands of his religion. This is the right answer.

Lord Widgery continued by saying that Sikhs were 'prevented from riding a motorcycle, not because of the English law but by the requirements of their religion'. Poulter criticizes this by saying that he was 'transparently wrong in stating that their faith precluded the riding of motorcycles when it clearly did not. It was the provisions of English law which had this effect.' This is as silly as asking if it is the upper or lower blade of a pair of scissors that cuts the paper. The essential point is that the practice of their religion entails that turbaned Sikhs cannot ride a motorcycle without exposing themselves to a risk of preventable head injuries. The question is then whether or not they should nevertheless be allowed to assume that risk. The important point made by

Lord Widgery in this context is that if they are not given an exemption they are not discriminated against by the law, as they would be if there were a law that said 'No Sikh may ride a motorcycle.' To say, as Poulter does, that it is the law that precludes Sikhs from riding motorcycles assimilates a crash helmet law to this quite different kind of law, which could quite correctly be said to be discriminatory.

Once again we must insist on the crucial difference between a denial of equal opportunities to some group (for example, a law forbidding Sikhs to ride motorcycles) and a choice some people make out of that from a set of equal opportunities (for example, a choice not to ride a motorcycle) as a result of certain beliefs. Those who believe that, even with a crash helmet, riding a motorcycle is too dangerous to be a rational undertaking are (in exactly the same, misleading, sense) 'precluded' from riding one. We all constantly impose restrictions on ourselves in choosing among the options that are legally available to us according to our beliefs about what is right, polite, decent, prudent, professionally appropriate, and so on. Atheists are entitled to feel offended at the idea that the only restraints on self-gratification derive from religious belief.

It is interesting to note that, in the parliamentary debates, the ritual slaughter exemption was drawn on as an argument for the exemption of Sikhs from the requirement of wearing a crash helmet. We thus see how one dubious case is deployed to support another. The claim that exemptions for ritual slaughter are about religious freedom, as members of parliament seem to have believed, is just as bogus as in the crash helmet case, and for exactly the same reason: to adapt Lord Widgery's lapidary words, nobody is bound to eat meat. (Some Orthodox Jews are vegetarians.) Assuming that killing animals without prior stunning falls below the prevailing standards for the humane treatment of animals, the point is that those who are not prepared to eat meat from animals killed in any other way cannot eat meat without violating these minimum standards. It is not the law but the facts (assuming the facts bear it out) of neurophysiology that make this so. The law may condone the additional suffering of animals killed without prior stunning, but if it does we should be clear that what it is doing is accommodating the tastes of a subset of carnivores, not observing the demands of religious freedom.

As in the ritual slaughter case, it is hard to steer a path between the conclusion that wearing a crash helmet is so important that all motorcyclists should have to do it and the alternative of saying that this is a matter that people should be left free to decide for themselves. There is one argument for making turbans a special case that would be valid if its premises were true. However, the minor (factual) premise of the argument is not true. The major premise has been put forward by Parekh as follows: 'if another headgear served the purpose [of avoiding death and injury] equally well [as a crash helmet], there was no reason to disallow it.' This is undoubtedly true, and if turbans did serve this purpose equally well there would be no need to stipulate that the right to wear a turban instead of a crash helmet should be restricted to Sikh motorcyclists: the law could simply specify either a crash helmet or a turban. The minor premise consists in the claim that 'the turban largely satisfied that criterion' (that is to say, the criterion that whatever headgear was worn should avert death or injury as well as a crash helmet), and the conclusion is then drawn that, in virtue of this equivalence, the turban 'was accepted as legally equivalent to the helmet'. This is an imaginative reconstruction of the terms of the parliamentary debate, such as it was. In fact, the government's spokesman denied explicitly, on the basis of test results, 'that a properly tied turban in itself provides adequate protection in the event of an accident involving a blow to the head'. The choice was presented as one between 'road safety criteria' and 'religious tolerance', and this way of structuring the issue appears to have been generally accepted. Thus, Parekh's argument is invalidated by the falsity of its factual premise.

The relevance of the test results for the incidence of death and injury among motorcyclists could be challenged by suggesting that they assume no difference in behaviour between those wearing helmets and those not wearing them. Thus, if it said that 'by wearing a helmet the risk of death could be reduced by 40 per cent and the risk of serious injury by 10 per cent', the reply might be made that these figures translate into actual deaths and serious injuries only if those with and without helmets have accidents at exactly the same rate. Perhaps those lacking the protection of a helmet drive more safely, so that their rate of death and serious injury is no higher than that among those wearing helmets. If there is anything at all in this idea, it may be noted that it depends upon those who do not wear helmets being in possession of accurate information about their much greater exposure to death or serious injury from an accident of any given degree of gravity. Those who, like Parekh, propagate the myth that turbans are as safe as helmets will have a lot to answer for in this case.

Suppose, however, that people did have accurate information about risks and (consciously or unconsciously) adapted their behaviour to keep constant the level of risk of death or serious injury to which they exposed themselves. Then the conclusion would still not be that there should be a special exemption for turban-wearing Sikhs. Rather, it should be concluded that there is no point in imposing any safety measures that can be offset by changes in behaviour, because they are bound to be self-defeating. The hard-core version of this 'risk-budget' theory would suggest, indeed, that even safety measures that cannot be offset will fail to alter the death rate in the long run: if flying became less safe because airlines spent less money on maintenance, people would adapt (even if they flew as often as before) by being infinitesimally more cautious in overtaking or infinitesimally more careful when crossing the road so as to keep their 'risk budget' in balance. Quite apart from its limited a priori plausibility, this theory appears to be contradicted by the facts: in 1976, when the crash helmet law had been running for five years without any provision for an exemption, 'the Ministry of Transport estimated that compulsory helmets were saving around 200 fatal and serious casualties each year'—and this despite the fact that 80 per cent of motorcyclists had already been wearing crash helmets before the legislation became effective.

A more direct, and more defensible, argument against a compulsory crash helmet measure is that the legislation is paternalistic, and that if people choose not to wear crash helmets the resultant injuries are (literally) on their own heads. Libertarians may object on principle to having to adhere to such a law. Others may object not on general principle but on the ground that the thrill of riding a motorcycle at high speed is severely compromised by having to wear a crash helmet: a former colleague in North America once assured me that nothing matches riding a Harley-Davidson at full throttle down a deserted freeway, and that a bare head is essential to the value of the experience. These may add their voices to those of Sikhs in demanding to be allowed to decide for themselves what risks to take.

It is sometimes suggested that the case for a compulsory crash helmet measure can be made without appealing to paternalistic considerations. The argument is that the extra cost to the National Health Service arising from injuries that could have been avoided by wearing a helmet justifies the imposition of the rule. I strongly suspect that those who put forward this argument are for the most part actually moved by the paternalistic desire to reduce the toll of death and paralysis resulting from preventable head injuries but are deterred by the bogeyman of paternalism from saying so. In any case, the argument is superficial. If we really want to pursue the kind of macabre analysis proposed, we should bear in mind that a helmet is estimated as reducing deaths by 40 per cent but injuries by only 10 per cent. Deaths—provided they occur before arrival at the hospital—are cheap, involving only the cost of transport to the mortuary: in comparison, the last months of people who die of natural causes are often very expensive. Moreover, if we carry through this grisly calculus to the end, we have to reckon that healthy people who die suddenly in the prime of life are an excellent source of organ donation, thus saving other lives and also expense, since organ transplants are highly cost-effective in comparison with other forms of treatment. If we do the benefit-cost analysis right, it will perhaps turn out that crash helmets should be prohibited! If we do not believe that any such conclusion should be drawn, however the calculation comes out, then we cannot believe that the case for making crash helmets compulsory rests on benefit-cost considerations either.

Suppose we accept that it is a valid objective of public policy to reduce the number of head injuries to motorcyclists, and that this overrides the counter-argument from libertarian premises. Then it is hard to see how the validity of the objective somehow evaporates in the case of Sikhs and makes room for an exemption from the law requiring crash helmets. As in the ritual slaughter example, the argument for a general rule coupled with a specific exemption has to be made on balance-of-advantage grounds. Perhaps it is actually more plausible in this case, because the balance of gains and losses has Sikhs on both sides of the computation, rather than the desires of Orthodox Jews and Muslims on one side and the suffering of cows and sheep on the other. Nevertheless, it is still necessary to walk a fine line to make the desired answer emerge.

To finish up with a rule-plus-exemption regime, the injury-saving rationale of the law has to be conceded to be powerful enough to justify compulsion of the majority, while at the same time being deemed not powerful enough to outweigh the desire of the minority to ride a motorcycle without a crash helmet. From the other side, if we are too highly impressed by the point that those who choose to avail themselves of the exemption are not harming others but merely undertaking a self-imposed risk, we are liable to conclude that the same privilege should be available to all. Thus Poulter writes that *there is force in the argument that the people whose safety is principally put at risk are the turbaned Sikhs themselves. . . . If they decide that the practice of their religion outweighs the greater risk of physical injury, the values of a liberal democracy are hardly imperilled in the way in which they might be if a significant degree of harm was being inflicted upon others.*

But why should not anybody else make a similar claim? Religion appears to play no essential part in what is in essence a simple argument to the effect that people should be free to decide for themselves what risks of injury to accept. The case is thus analogous to the one involving the Rastafarians and cannabis discussed at the end of the previous section: if it is valid, the argument implies that the restrictive law should be repealed, not that it should be retained and some people allowed an exemption.

The persuasiveness of the balance-of-interests argument for exemption depends on the context. If not being able to ride a motorcycle ruled out a significant proportion of all the jobs in an area open to somebody with a certain level of trained ability, that would be relevant. But it does not. It would also be a matter of specific concern if the inability to ride a motorcycle prevented Sikhs from joining the police force, because it is important that the police should be open to all, and should in fact contain representatives of all minorities. This is not so much a matter of doing a favour to Sikhs as one of pursuing a benefit to all of us. But there is nothing to prevent police forces from organizing themselves so that Sikh members are not assigned to duties that entail riding a motorcycle. (The police already, quite rightly, permit Sikhs to wear turbans.)

Where turbans create a real employment problem is in the construction trade, which is the largest single source of employment for Sikhs, because 'the traditional occupation of the Ramgarhia "caste" was skilled work as artisans (carpenters, blacksmiths, bricklayers etc.)'. There is an extremely strong case based in industrial safety for requiring hard hats on construction sites, and 'the turban provides generally poor protection'. Even with a special exemption for Sikhs, the hard hat requirement reduced fatalities within two years of coming into operation from 26 to 15 per year and halved the number of major injuries from 140 to 70. The exemption for Sikhs from the hard hat regulation is, furthermore, in violation of a directive from the Council of the European Communities of 1989 which specifically mandated that 'helmets for head protection on building sites' were to be required for all workers by the end of 1992.

While the case for a universally applicable rule is strong, the particular circumstances make the balance-of-advantage argument for an exemption rather powerful. There is no official figure for the number of Sikhs in Britain but it is estimated at between 300,000 and 500,000. There are 'reckoned to be around 40,000' who are building workers. Assuming that Sikhs have now been settled long enough to have a more or less normal age and sex distribution and that the building workers are all males, this implies, if the lower figure for the total population is correct, that almost half of all male Sikhs of working age are engaged in construction work. Even the high figure for total numbers makes it over a quarter. Clearly, ending this employment for whatever (unknown) proportion of Sikh construction workers who wear turbans could be seriously disruptive socially, especially because Sikhs tend to live in geographically concentrated areas. Employment is important not only as a source of income but also as a means of social integration, so there is a strong argument against the sudden termination of the exemption. At the same time, it is hard to deny that the improvement in safety justified the compulsion of the 70 per cent of construction workers who were not wearing hard hats before the requirement was brought in. Perhaps the most sensible course would be to restrict the exemption to those already employed in the construction trade, and possibly in addition those already embarked on acquiring relevant qualifications. This would accept that those who have already availed themselves of the exemption have acquired a sort of vested interest in the job, while gradually phasing out the inherently dangerous business of working on a construction site with only the protection of a turban.

A PRAGMATIC CASE FOR EXEMPTIONS

My argument has been that there is a possible case for letting everybody do what they please and a possible case for constraining everyone alike, but that a great deal of finagling is needed in order to support a general rule with exemptions based on religious beliefs. In the cases considered here, I have made clear my own opinion that the case for having a restrictive law is a strong enough one to tip the balance in favour of universal constraint, apart from a continuation of the exemption from hard hat regulations for existing beneficiaries. Nothing turns on that as far as the validity of the general argument is concerned, and some readers may well think that in some cases the libertarian solution is the appropriate one. There is, however, one asymmetry between the two logically coherent positions. This involves the practical problems of moving from a currently anomalous situation to either of the internally consistent ones.

Anyone who believes that the case for having a restrictive law is strong enough to justify universal constraint is bound to believe, of course, that repealing a version of the law that contains exemptions so that there were no constraints at all would have bad consequences: more animal suffering, more tragic victims of motorcycling accidents, and so on. But it would not have bad effects on relations between members of different religious groups. It might even if anything have good effects in eliminating the cause of any resentment that the majority may feel about special privileges for minorities. In contrast, retaining the law but rescinding the exemptions would have good direct effects but would probably have bad effects on relations between different religious groups and would give an encouraging signal to racists who peddle nostalgic dreams of cultural homogeneity. At the same time, it would be widely regarded by members of religious minorities as representing some kind of attack on their position within the polity, and would thus increase the alienation that they already feel as a result of racially motivated harassment and job discrimination.

There is no need here to weigh the pros and cons to decide where the balance of advantage lies. Suppose, however, that the conclusion reached is that—at any rate in the current parlous state of race relations in Britain—rescinding the existing exemptions would over all do more harm than good. What then should be the position of those who nevertheless think that the constraints now enforced are valuable? The answer is surely that it is preferable to give up on consistency than abandon the advantages of the present legislation. The objectives are, after all, being met quite extensively, and these are not situations in which non-compliance with a general rule undermines the efforts of those who do comply. The good done is in direct proportion to the amount of compliance. If the current amount is the most that is desirable, taking account of side-effects, then the present state of affairs is the best attainable.

Does this mean that the entire argument up to now lacks any practical import? Not at all. For the way in which the existing exemptions are viewed has important policy implications. The usual context in which exemptions such as those discussed above are cited is as illustrations of some general principle mandating respect for religious differences. The suggestion is then made that following through this principle consistently would entail more exemptions for more groups. However, if (as I have maintained) there is no such principle, these cases are not the thin end of the wedge—they are the wedge itself. In other words, they are anomalies to be tolerated because the cure would be worse than the disease. But they provide no support for any extension to new cases. If the argument is made (as it surely will be) that it is inconsistent to have these exemptions and not others of a similar kind, the answer that can be given is that the current exemptions were a mistake that is awaiting rectification at an opportune time, so it would be absurd to add to their number in the meanwhile. Moreover, those that do exist should be limited as tightly as possible.

SUPREME COURT OF THE UNITED STATES

366 U.S. 599

BRAUNFELD V. BROWN

APPEAL FROM THE UNITED STATES DISTRICT COURT FOR THE EASTERN DISTRICT OF PENNSYLVANIA

No. 67 ARGUED: DECEMBER 8, 1960–DECIDED: MAY 29, 1961

[600] Mr. Chief Justice WARREN announced the judgment of the Court and an opinion in which Mr. Justice BLACK, Mr. Justice CLARK, and Mr. Justice WHITTAKER concur.

This case concerns the constitutional validity of the application to appellants of the Pennsylvania criminal statute,[1] enacted in 1959, which proscribes the Sunday retail sale of certain enumerated commodities. . . . [601] . . . [T]he only question for consideration is whether the statute interferes with the free exercise of appellants' religion.

Appellants are merchants in Philadelphia who engage in the retail sale of clothing and home furnishings within the proscription of the statute in issue. Each of the appellants is a member of the Orthodox Jewish faith, which requires the closing of their places of business and a total abstention from all manner of work from nightfall each Friday until nightfall each Saturday. They instituted a suit in the court below seeking a permanent injunction against the enforcement of the 1959 statute. Their complaint, as amended, alleged that appellants had previously kept their places of business open on Sunday; that each of appellants had done a substantial amount of business on Sunday, compensating somewhat for their closing on Saturday; that Sunday closing will result in impairing the ability of all appellants to earn a livelihood and will render appellant Braunfeld unable to continue in his business, thereby losing his capital investment; that the statute is unconstitutional for the reasons stated above. . . .

Appellants contend that the enforcement against them of the Pennsylvania statute will prohibit the free exercise [602] of their religion because, due to the statute's compulsion to close on Sunday, appellants will suffer substantial economic loss, to the benefit of their non-Sabbatarian competitors, if appellants also continue their Sabbath observance by closing their businesses on Saturday; that this result will either compel appellants to give up their Sabbath observance, a basic tenet of the Orthodox Jewish faith, or will put appellants at a serious economic disadvantage if they continue to adhere to their Sabbath. Appellants also assert that the statute will operate so as to hinder the Orthodox Jewish faith in gaining new adherents. And the corollary to these arguments is that if the free exercise of appellants' religion is impeded, that religion is being subjected to discriminatory treatment by the State.

In *McGowan v. Maryland*, 366 U.S. 420, 437–440 (1961), we noted the significance that this Court has attributed to the development of religious freedom in Virginia in determining the scope of the First Amendment's protection. We observed that when Virginia passed its Declaration of Rights in 1776, providing that "all men are equally entitled to the free exercise of religion," Virginia repealed its laws which in any way penalized 'maintaining any opinions in matters of religion, forbearing to repair to church, or the exercising any mode of worship whatsoever.' But Virginia retained its laws prohibiting Sunday labor.

We also took cognizance, in *McGowan*, of the evolution of Sunday Closing Laws from wholly religious sanctions to legislation concerned with the establishment of a day of community tranquillity, respite and recreation, a day when the atmosphere is one of calm and relaxation rather than one of commercialism, as it is during the other six days of the week . . . [603] . . .

Concededly, appellants and all other persons who wish to work on Sunday will be burdened economically by the State's day of rest mandate; and appellants point out that their religion requires them to refrain from work on Saturday as well. Our inquiry then is whether, in these circumstances, the First and Fourteenth Amendments forbid application of the Sunday Closing Law to appellants.

Certain aspects of religious exercise cannot, in any way, be restricted or burdened by either federal or state legislation. Compulsion by law of the acceptance of any creed or the practice of any form of worship is strictly forbidden. The freedom to hold religious beliefs and opinions is absolute. . . .

However, the freedom to act, even when the action is in accord with one's religious convictions, is not totally free from legislative restrictions. *Cantwell v. Connecticut*, 310 U.S. 296, 303–304, 306 (1940). As pointed out in *Reynolds v. United States*, 98 U.S. 145, 164 (1878), legislative power over mere opinion is forbidden but it may reach people's actions when they are found to be in violation of important social duties or subversive of good order, even when [604] the actions are demanded by one's religion. . . .

. . . [605] . . . .

Thus, in *Reynolds v. United States*, this Court upheld the polygamy conviction of a member of the Mormon faith despite the fact that an accepted doctrine of his church then imposed upon its male members the duty to practice polygamy. And, in *Prince v. Massachusetts*, 321 U.S. 158 (1944), this Court upheld a statute making it a crime for a girl under eighteen years of age to sell any newspapers, periodicals or merchandise in public places despite the fact that a child of the Jehovah's Witnesses faith believed that it was her religious duty to perform this work.

It is to be noted that, in the two cases just mentioned, the religious practices themselves conflicted with the public interest. In such cases, to make accommodation between the religious action and an exercise of state authority is a particularly delicate task, *id*. at 165, because resolution in favor of the State results in the choice to the individual of either abandoning his religious principle or facing criminal prosecution.

But, again, this is not the case before us because the statute at bar does not make unlawful any religious practices of appellants; the Sunday law simply regulates a secular activity and, as applied to appellants, operates so as to make the practice of their religious beliefs more expensive. Furthermore, the law's effect does not inconvenience all members of the Orthodox Jewish faith but only those who believe it necessary to work on Sunday. And even these are not faced with as serious a choice as forsaking their religious practices or subjecting themselves to criminal prosecution. Fully recognizing that the alternatives [606] open to appellants and others similarly situated—retaining their present occupations and incurring economic disadvantage or engaging in some other commercial activity which does not call for either Saturday or Sunday labor—may well result in some financial sacrifice in order to observe their religious beliefs, still the option is wholly different than when the legislation attempts to make a religious practice itself unlawful.

To strike down, without the most critical scrutiny, legislation which imposes only an indirect burden on the exercise of religion, i.e., legislation which does not make unlawful the religious practice itself, would radically restrict the operating latitude of the legislature. Statutes which tax income and limit the amount which may be deducted for religious contributions impose an indirect economic burden on the observance of the religion of the citizen whose religion requires him to donate a greater amount to his church; statutes which require the courts to be closed on Saturday and Sunday impose a similar indirect burden on the observance of the religion of the trial lawyer whose religion requires him to rest on a weekday. The list of legislation of this nature is nearly limitless.

Needless to say, when entering the area of religious freedom, we must be fully cognizant of the particular protection that the Constitution has accorded it. Abhorrence of religious persecution and intolerance is a basic part of our heritage. But we are a cosmopolitan nation made up of people of almost every conceivable religious preference. These denominations number almost three hundred. *Year Book of American Churches for 1958*, 257 *et seq.* Consequently, it cannot be expected, much less required, that legislators enact no law regulating conduct that may in some way result in an economic disadvantage to some religious sects and not to others because of the special practices of the various religions. We do not believe that such an effect is an absolute test [607] for determining whether the legislation violates the freedom of religion protected by the First Amendment.

Of course, to hold unassailable all legislation regulating conduct which imposes solely an indirect burden on the observance of religion would be a gross oversimplification. If the purpose or effect of a law is to impede the observance of one or all religions or is to discriminate invidiously between religions, that law is constitutionally invalid even though the burden may be characterized as being only indirect. But if the State regulates conduct by enacting a general law within its power, the purpose and effect of which is to advance the State's secular goals, the statute is valid despite its indirect burden on religious observance unless the State may accomplish its purpose by means which do not impose such a burden.

As we pointed out in *McGowan v. Maryland, supra*, at 444–45, we cannot find a State without power to provide a weekly respite from all labor and, at the same time, to set one day of the week apart from the others as a day of rest, repose, recreation and tranquillity—a day when the hectic tempo of everyday existence ceases and a more pleasant atmosphere is created, a day which all members of the family and community have the opportunity to spend and enjoy together, a day on which people may visit friends and relatives who are not available during working days, a day when the weekly laborer may best regenerate himself. This is particularly true in this day and age of increasing state concern with public welfare legislation.

[608] Also, in *McGowan*, we examined several suggested alternative means by which it was argued that the State might accomplish its secular goals without even remotely or incidentally affecting religious freedom. *Ante*, at 450–52. We found there that a State might well find that those alternatives would not accomplish bringing about a general day of rest. We need not examine them again here.

However, appellants advance yet another means at the State's disposal which they would find unobjectionable. They contend that the State should cut an exception from the Sunday labor proscription for those people who, because of religious conviction, observe a day of rest other than Sunday. By such regulation, appellants contend, the economic disadvantages imposed by the present system would be removed and the State's interest in having all people rest one day would be satisfied.

A number of States provide such an exemption, and this may well be the wiser solution to the problem. But our concern is not with the wisdom of legislation but with its constitutional limitation. Thus, reason and experience teach that to permit the exemption might well undermine the State's goal of providing a day that, as best possible, eliminates the atmosphere of commercial noise and activity. Although not dispositive of the issue, enforcement problems would be more difficult since there would be two or more days to police rather than one and it would be more difficult to observe whether violations were occurring.

Additional problems might also be presented by a regulation of this sort. To allow only people who rest on a day other than Sunday to keep their businesses open on that day might well provide these people with an economic advantage over their competitors who must [609] remain closed on that day; this might cause the Sunday-observers to complain that their religions are being discriminated against. With this competitive advantage existing, there could well be the temptation for some, in order to keep their businesses open on Sunday, to assert that they have religious convictions which compel them to close their businesses on what had formerly been their least profitable day. This might make necessary a state-conducted inquiry into the sincerity of the individual's religious beliefs, a practice which a State might believe would itself run afoul of the spirit of constitutionally protected religious guarantees. Finally, in order to keep the disruption of the day at a minimum, exempted employers would probably have to hire employees who themselves qualified for the exemption because of their own religious beliefs, a practice which a State might feel to be opposed to its general policy prohibiting religious discrimination in hiring. For all of these reasons, we cannot say that the Pennsylvania statute before us is invalid, either on its face or as applied.

Mr. Justice HARLAN concurs in the judgment. Mr. Justice BRENNAN and Mr. Justice STEWART concur in [610] our disposition of appellants' claims under the Establishment Clause and the Equal Protection Clause. Mr. Justice FRANKFURTER and Mr. Justice HARLAN have rejected appellants' claim under the Free Exercise Clause in a separate opinion.

Accordingly, the decision is *Affirmed*.

NOTE

[1]18 Purdon's Pa. Stat. Ann. (1960 Cum. Supp.) § 4699.10 provides: "Whoever engages on Sunday in the business of selling, or sells or offers for sale, on such day, at retail, clothing and wearing apparel, clothing accessories, furniture, housewares, home, business or office furnishings, household, business or office appliances, hardware, tools, paints, building and lumber supply materials, jewelry, silverware, watches, clocks, luggage, musical instruments and recordings, or toys, excluding novelties and souvenirs, shall, upon conviction thereof in a summary proceeding for the first offense, be sentenced to pay a fine of not exceeding one hundred dollars ($100), and for the second or any subsequent offense committed within one year after conviction for the first offense, be sentenced to pay a fine of not exceeding two hundred dollars ($200) or undergo imprisonment not exceeding thirty days in default thereof."

SUPREME COURT OF THE UNITED STATES

374 U.S. 398

SHERBERT V. VERNER

APPEAL FROM THE SUPREME COURT
OF SOUTH CAROLINA
NO. 526 ARGUED: APRIL 24, 1963–DECIDED: JUNE 17, 1963

OPINION: [399] MR. JUSTICE BRENNAN delivered the opinion of the Court.

Appellant, a member of the Seventh-day Adventist Church, was discharged by her South Carolina employer because she would not work on Saturday, the Sabbath Day of her faith. When she was unable to obtain other employment because, from conscientious scruples, she would not take Saturday work, she filed a claim for [400] unemployment compensation benefits under the South Carolina Unemployment Compensation Act. That law provides that, to be eligible for benefits, a claimant must be "able to work and . . . available for work"; and, further, [401] that a claimant is ineligible for benefits "[i]f . . . he has failed, without good cause . . . to accept available suitable work when offered him by the employment office or the employer. . . ." The appellee Employment Security Commission, in administrative proceedings under the statute, found that appellant's restriction upon her availability for Saturday work brought her within the provision disqualifying for benefits insured workers who fail, without good cause, to accept "suitable work when offered . . . by the employment office or the employer. . . ." The Commission's finding was sustained by the Court of Common Pleas for Spartanburg County. That court's judgment was, in turn, affirmed by the South Carolina Supreme Court, which rejected appellant's contention that, as applied to her, the disqualifying provisions of the South Carolina statute abridged her right to the free exercise of her religion secured under the Free Exercise Clause of the First Amendment through the Fourteenth Amendment. . . . [402] . . . We reverse the judgment of the South Carolina Supreme Court and remand for further proceedings not inconsistent with this opinion.

I

The door of the Free Exercise Clause stands tightly closed against any governmental regulation of religious beliefs as such, *Cantwell v. Connecticut*, 310 U.S. 296, 303 (1940). Government may neither compel affirmation of a repugnant belief, *Torcaso v. Watkins*, 367 U.S. 488 (1961); nor penalize or discriminate against individuals or groups because they hold religious views abhorrent to the authorities, *Fowler v. Rhode Island*, 345 U.S. 67 (1953); nor employ the taxing power to inhibit the dissemination of particular religious views, *Murdock v. Pennsylvania*, 319 U.S. 105 (1943); *Follett v. Town of McCormick*, 321 U.S. 573 (1944); *cf. Grosjean v. Am. Press Co.*, 297 U.S. 233 (1936). On the other hand, [403] the Court has rejected challenges under the Free

Exercise Clause to governmental regulation of certain overt acts prompted by religious beliefs or principles, for "even when the action is in accord with one's religious convictions, [it] is not totally free from legislative restrictions." *Braunfeld v. Brown*, 366 U.S. 599, 603 (1961). The conduct or actions so regulated have invariably posed some substantial threat to public safety, peace or order. *See, e.g., Reynolds v. United States*, 98 U.S. 145 (1878); *Jacobson v. Massachusetts*, 197 U.S. 11 (1905); *Prince v. Massachusetts*, 321 U.S. 158 (1944); *Cleveland v. United States*, 329 U.S. 14 (1946).

Plainly enough, appellant's conscientious objection to Saturday work constitutes no conduct prompted by religious principles of a kind within the reach of state legislation. If, therefore, the decision of the South Carolina Supreme Court is to withstand appellant's constitutional challenge, it must be either because her disqualification as a beneficiary represents no infringement by the State of her constitutional rights of free exercise, or because any incidental burden on the free exercise of appellant's religion may be justified by a "compelling state interest in the regulation of a subject within the State's constitutional power to regulate. . . ." *NAACP v. Button*, 371 U.S. 415, 438 (1963).

II

We turn first to the question whether the disqualification for benefits imposes any burden on the free exercise of appellant's religion. We think it is clear that it does. In a sense, the consequences of such a disqualification to religious principles and practices may be only an indirect result of welfare legislation within the State's general competence to enact; it is true that no criminal sanctions directly compel appellant to work a six-day week. But this is only the beginning, not the end, of our [404] inquiry. For "[i]f the purpose or effect of a law is to impede the observance of one or all religions or is to discriminate invidiously between religions, that law is constitutionally invalid even though the burden may be characterized as being only indirect." *Braunfeld v. Brown, supra*, at 607. Here, not only is it apparent that appellant's declared ineligibility for benefits derives solely from the practice of her religion, but the pressure upon her to forego that practice is unmistakable. The ruling forces her to choose between following the precepts of her religion and forfeiting benefits, on the one hand, and abandoning one of the precepts of her religion in order to accept work, on the other hand. Governmental imposition of such a choice puts the same kind of burden upon the free exercise of religion as would a fine imposed against appellant for her Saturday worship.   . . . [405–406] . . . .

III

We must next consider whether some compelling state interest enforced in the eligibility provisions of the South Carolina statute justifies the substantial infringement of appellant's First Amendment right. It is basic that no showing merely of a rational relationship to some colorable state interest would suffice; in this highly sensitive constitutional area, "[o]nly the gravest abuses, endangering paramount interests, give occasion for permissible limitation," *Thomas v. Collins*, 323 U.S. 516, 530 (1945). [407] No such abuse or danger has been advanced in the present case. The appellees suggest no more than a possibility that the filing of fraudulent claims by unscrupulous claimants feigning religious objections to Saturday work might not only dilute the unemployment compensation fund, but also hinder the scheduling by employers of necessary Saturday work. But that possibility is not apposite here, because no such objection appears to have been made before the South Carolina Supreme Court, and we are unwilling to assess the importance of an asserted state interest without the views of the state court. Nor, if the contention had been made below, would the record appear to sustain it; there is no proof whatever to warrant such fears of malingering or deceit as those which the respondents now advance. Even if consideration of such evidence is not foreclosed by the prohibition against judicial inquiry into the truth or falsity of religious beliefs, *United States v. Ballard*, 322 U.S. 78 (1944)—a question as to which we intimate no view, since it is not before us—it is highly doubtful whether such evidence would be sufficient to warrant a substantial infringement of religious liberties. For even if the possibility of spurious claims did threaten to dilute the fund and disrupt the scheduling of work, it would plainly be incumbent upon the appellees to demonstrate that no alternative forms of regulation would combat such abuses without infringing First Amendment rights. [408]

In these respects, then, the state interest asserted in the present case is wholly dissimilar to the interests which were found to justify the less direct burden upon religious practices in *Braunfeld v. Brown, supra*. The Court recognized that the Sunday closing law which that decision sustained undoubtedly served "to make the practice of [the Orthodox Jewish merchants'] . . . religious beliefs more expensive," 366 U.S. at 605. But the statute was nevertheless saved by a countervailing factor which finds no equivalent in the instant case—a strong state interest in providing one uniform day of rest for all workers. That secular objective could be achieved, the Court found, only by declaring Sunday to be that day of rest. Requiring exemptions for Sabbatarians, while theoretically possible, appeared to present an administrative [409] problem of such magnitude, or to afford the exempted class so great a competitive advantage, that such a requirement would have rendered the entire statutory scheme unworkable. In the present case, no such justifications underlie the determination of the state court that appellant's religion makes her ineligible to receive benefits.

IV

In holding as we do, plainly we are not fostering the "establishment" of the Seventh-day Adventist religion in South Carolina, for the extension of unemployment benefits to Sabbatarians in common with Sunday worshippers reflects nothing more than the governmental obligation of neutrality in the face of religious differences, and does not represent that involvement of religious with secular institutions which it is the object of the Establishment Clause to forestall. *See Sch. Dist. of Abington Twp. v. Schempp*, 374 U.S. 203 (1963). Nor does the recognition of the appellant's right to unemployment benefits under the state statute serve to abridge any other person's religious liberties. Nor do we, by our decision today, declare the existence of a constitutional right to unemployment benefits on the part [410] of all persons whose religious convictions are the cause of their unemployment. This is not a case in which an employee's religious convictions serve to make him a nonproductive member of society. Finally, nothing we say today constrains the States to adopt any particular form or scheme of unemployment compensation. Our holding today is only that South Carolina may not constitutionally apply the eligibility provisions so as to constrain a worker to abandon his religious convictions respecting the day of rest. This holding but reaffirms a principle that we announced a decade and a half ago, namely that no State may "exclude individual Catholics, Lutherans, Mohammedans, Baptists, Jews, Methodists, Non-believers, Presbyterians, or the members of any other faith, because of their faith, or lack of it, from receiving the benefits of public welfare legislation." *Everson v. Bd. of Educ.*, 330 U.S. 1, 16(1947).

In view of the result we have reached under the First and Fourteenth Amendments' guarantee of free exercise of religion, we have no occasion to consider appellant's claim that the denial of benefits also deprived her of the equal protection of the laws in violation of the Fourteenth Amendment.

The judgment of the South Carolina Supreme Court is reversed, and the case is remanded for further proceedings not inconsistent with this opinion.

It is so ordered.

SUPREME COURT OF THE UNITED STATES

406 U.S. 205

WISCONSIN V. YODER

CERTIORARI TO THE SUPREME COURT OF WISCONSIN
NO. 70-110 ARGUED: DECEMBER 8, 1971–DECIDED: MAY 15, 1972

OPINION: MR. CHIEF JUSTICE BURGER delivered the opinion of the Court.

On petition of the State of Wisconsin, we granted the writ of certiorari in this case to review a decision of the Wisconsin Supreme Court holding that respondents' convictions of violating the State's compulsory school attendance law were invalid under the Free Exercise Clause of the First Amendment to the United States Constitution, made applicable to the States by the Fourteenth Amendment. For the reasons hereafter stated, we affirm the judgment of the Supreme Court of Wisconsin.

Respondents Jonas Yoder and Wallace Miller are members of the Old Order Amish religion, and respondent Adin Yutzy is a member of the Conservative Amish Mennonite Church. They and their families are residents of Green County, Wisconsin. Wisconsin's compulsory school attendance law required them to cause their children to attend public or private school until reaching age 16, but the respondents declined to send their children, ages 14 and 15, to public school after they completed the eighth grade. The children were not enrolled in any private school, or within any recognized exception to the compulsory attendance law. . . . [208]

On complaint of the school district administrator for the public schools, respondents were charged, tried, and convicted of violating the compulsory attendance law in Green County Court, and were fined the sum of $5 each. Respondents defended on the ground that the application [209] of the compulsory attendance law violated their rights under the First and Fourteenth Amendments. The trial testimony showed that respondents believed, in accordance with the tenets of Old Order Amish communities generally, that their children's attendance at high school, public or private, was contrary to the Amish religion and way of life. They believed that, by sending their children to high school, they would not only expose themselves to the danger of the censure of the church community, but, as found by the county court, also endanger their own salvation and that of their children. . . .

In support of their position, respondents presented as expert witnesses scholars on religion and education whose testimony is uncontradicted. They expressed their opinions on the relationship of the Amish belief concerning school attendance to the more general tenets of their religion, and described the impact that compulsory high school attendance could have on the continued survival of Amish communities as they exist in the United States today. The history of the Amish [210] sect was given in some detail, beginning with the Swiss Anabaptists of the 16th century, who rejected institutionalized churches and sought to return to the early, simple, Christian life deemphasizing material success, rejecting the competitive spirit, and seeking to insulate themselves from the modern world. As a result of their common heritage, Old Order Amish communities today are characterized by a fundamental belief that salvation requires life in a church community separate and apart from the world and worldly influence. This concept of life aloof from the world and its values is central to their faith.

A related feature of Old Order Amish communities is their devotion to a life in harmony with nature and the soil, as exemplified by the simple life of the early Christian era that continued in America during much of our early national life. Amish beliefs require members of the community to make their living by farming or closely related activities. Broadly speaking, the Old Order Amish religion pervades and determines the entire mode of life of its adherents. . . .

Amish objection to formal education beyond the eighth grade is firmly grounded in these central religious concepts. They object to the high school, and higher education generally, because the values they teach [211] are in marked variance with Amish values and the Amish way of life; they view secondary school education as an impermissible exposure of their children to a "worldly" influence in conflict with their beliefs. The high school tends to emphasize intellectual and scientific accomplishments, self-distinction, competitiveness, worldly success, and social life with other students. Amish society emphasizes informal "learning through doing;" a life of "goodness," rather than a life of intellect; wisdom, rather than technical knowledge; community welfare, rather than competition; and separation from, rather than integration with, contemporary worldly society.

Formal high school education beyond the eighth grade is contrary to Amish beliefs not only because it places Amish children in an environment hostile to Amish beliefs, with increasing emphasis on competition in class work and sports and with pressure to conform to the styles, manners, and ways of the peer group, but also because it takes them away from their community, physically and emotionally, during the crucial and formative adolescent period of life. During this period, the children must acquire Amish attitudes favoring manual work and self-reliance and the specific skills needed to perform the adult role of an Amish farmer or housewife. They must learn to enjoy physical labor. Once a child has learned basic reading, writing, and elementary mathematics, these traits, skills, and attitudes admittedly fall within the category of those best learned through example and "doing," rather than in a classroom. And, at this time in life, the Amish child must also grow in his faith and his relationship to the Amish community if he is to be prepared to accept the heavy obligations imposed by adult baptism. In short, high school attendance with teachers who are not of the Amish faith— and may even be hostile to it—interposes a serious barrier to the integration of the Amish child into [212] the Amish religious community. . . .

On the basis of such considerations, Dr. Hostetler testified that compulsory high school attendance could not only result in great psychological harm to Amish children, because of the conflicts it would produce, but would also, in his opinion, ultimately result in the destruction of the Old Order Amish church community as it exists in the United States today. The testimony of Dr. Donald A. Erickson, an expert witness on education, also showed that the Amish succeed in preparing their high school age children to be productive members of the Amish community. . . . The evidence also showed that the Amish have an excellent [213] record as law-abiding and generally self-sufficient members of society. . . .

I

There is no doubt as to the power of a State, having a high responsibility for education of its citizens, to impose reasonable regulations for the control and duration of basic education. *See, e.g., Pierce v. Society of Sisters*, 268 U.S. 510, 534 (1925). Providing public schools ranks at the very apex of the function of a State. Yet even this paramount responsibility was, in *Pierce*, made to yield to the right of parents to provide an equivalent education in a privately operated system. . . . [214] . . .

It follows that, in order for Wisconsin to compel school attendance beyond the eighth grade against a claim that such attendance interferes with the practice of a legitimate religious belief, it must appear either that the State does not deny the free exercise of religious belief by its requirement or that there is a state interest of sufficient magnitude to override the interest claiming protection under the Free Exercise Clause. . . . [215] . . . .

II

We come then to the quality of the claims of the respondents concerning the alleged encroachment of Wisconsin's compulsory school attendance statute on their rights and the rights of their children to the free exercise of the religious beliefs they and their forebears have adhered to for almost three centuries. . . . .

. . .[W]e see that the record in this case abundantly supports the claim that the traditional way of life of the Amish is not merely a matter of personal preference, but one of deep religious conviction, shared by an organized group, and intimately related to daily living. . . . [217] . . . .

As the society around the Amish has become more populous, urban, industrialized, and complex, particularly in this century, government regulation of human affairs has correspondingly become more detailed and pervasive. The Amish mode of life has thus come into conflict increasingly with requirements of contemporary society exerting a hydraulic insistence on conformity to majoritarian standards. . . . As the record so strongly shows, the values and programs of the modern secondary school are in sharp conflict with the fundamental mode of life mandated by the Amish religion; modern laws requiring compulsory secondary education have accordingly engendered great concern and conflict. [218] The conclusion is inescapable that secondary schooling, by exposing Amish children to worldly influences in terms of attitudes, goals, and values contrary to beliefs, and by substantially interfering with the religious development of the Amish child and his integration into the way of life of the Amish faith community at the crucial adolescent stage of development, contravenes the basic religious tenets and practice of the Amish faith, both as to the parent and the child. . . .

[219] In sum, the unchallenged testimony of acknowledged experts in education and religious history, almost 300 years of consistent practice, and strong evidence of a sustained faith pervading and regulating respondents' entire mode of life support the claim that enforcement of the State's requirement of compulsory formal education after the eighth grade would gravely endanger, if not destroy, the free exercise of respondents' religious beliefs.

III

Neither the findings of the trial court nor the Amish claims as to the nature of their faith are challenged in this Court by the State of Wisconsin. Its position is that the State's interest in universal compulsory formal secondary education to age 16 is so great that it is paramount. . . .

. . . [220] . . . .

Nor can this case be disposed of on the grounds that Wisconsin's requirement for school attendance to age 16 applies uniformly to all citizens of the State and does not, on its face, discriminate against religions or a particular religion, or that it is motivated by legitimate secular concerns. A regulation neutral on its face may, in its application, nonetheless offend the constitutional requirement for governmental neutrality if it unduly burdens the free exercise of religion. *Sherbert v. Verner*, 374 U.S. 398 (1963). . . .

We turn, then, to the State's broader contention that its interest in its system of compulsory education is so compelling that even the established religious practices of the Amish must give way. . . .

The State advances two primary arguments in support of its system of compulsory education. It notes, as Thomas Jefferson pointed out early in our history, that some degree of education is necessary to prepare citizens to participate effectively and intelligently in our open political system if we are to preserve freedom and independence. Further, education prepares individuals to be self-reliant and self-sufficient participants in society. We accept these propositions.

[222] However, the evidence adduced by the Amish in this case is persuasively to the effect that an additional one or two years of formal high school for Amish children in place of their long-established program of informal vocational education would do little to serve those interests. Respondents' experts testified at trial, without challenge, that the value of all education must be assessed in terms of its capacity to prepare the child for life. It is one thing to say that compulsory education for a year or two beyond the eighth grade may be necessary when its goal is the preparation of the child for life in modern society as the majority live, but it is quite another if the goal of education be viewed as the preparation of the child for life in the separated agrarian community that is the keystone of the Amish faith. . . .

The State, attacks respondents' position as one fostering "ignorance" from which the child must be protected by the State. No one can question the State's duty to protect children from ignorance, but this argument does not square with the facts disclosed in the record. Whatever their idiosyncrasies as seen by the majority, this record strongly shows that the Amish community has been a highly successful social unit within our society, even if apart from the conventional "mainstream." Its members are productive and very law-abiding members of society; they reject public welfare in any of its usual modern forms.   . . . [223–24] . . . .

The State, however, supports its interest in providing an additional one or two years of compulsory high school education to Amish children because of the possibility that some such children will choose to leave the Amish community, and that, if this occurs, they will be ill-equipped for life. The State argues that, if Amish children leave their church, they should not be in the position of making their way in the world without the education available in the one or two additional years the State requires. However, on this record, that argument is highly speculative. There is no specific evidence of the loss of Amish adherents by attrition, nor is there any showing that, upon leaving the Amish community, Amish children, with their practical agricultural training and habits of industry and self-reliance, would become burdens on society because of educational shortcomings.   . . . [225] . . . .

. . . The Amish alternative to formal secondary school education has enabled them to function effectively in their day-to-day life under self-imposed limitations on relations with the world, and to survive and prosper in contemporary society as a separate, sharply identifiable and highly self-sufficient community for more than 200 years in this country. In itself, this is strong evidence that they are capable of fulfilling the social and political responsibilities of citizenship without compelled attendance beyond the eighth grade at the price of jeopardizing their free exercise of religious belief. . . . [226] . . .   . . . [227–29] . . . .

IV

Finally, the State, on authority of *Prince v. Massachusetts*, argues that a decision exempting Amish children from the State's requirement fails to recognize the substantive right of the Amish child to a secondary education, and fails to give due regard to the power of the State as parens patriae to extend the benefit of secondary education to children regardless of the wishes of their parents. Taken at its broadest sweep, the Court's language in *Prince* might be read to give support to the State's position. However, the Court was not confronted in *Prince* with a situation comparable to that of the Amish as revealed in this record; this is shown by the [230] Court's severe characterization of the evils that it thought the legislature could legitimately associate with child labor, even when performed in the company of an adult. 321 U.S. at 169–70. The Court later took great care to confine *Prince* to a narrow scope in *Sherbert v. Verner*, when it stated:

> On the other hand, the Court has rejected challenges under the Free Exercise Clause to governmental regulation of certain overt acts prompted by religious beliefs or principles, for "even when the action is in

accord with one's religious convictions, [it] is not totally free from legislative restrictions." Braunfeld v. Brown, 366 U.S. 599, 603. The conduct or actions so regulated have invariably posed some substantial threat to public safety, peace or order. . . . .

374 U.S. at 402–403.

This case, of course, is not one in which any harm to the physical or mental health of the child or to the public safety, peace, order, or welfare has been demonstrated or may be properly inferred. The record is to the contrary, and any reliance on that theory would find no support in the evidence.

Contrary to the suggestion of the dissenting opinion of MR. JUSTICE DOUGLAS, our holding today in no degree depends on the assertion of the religious interest of the child, as contrasted with that of the parents. It is the parents who are subject to prosecution here for failing to cause their children to attend school, and it [231] is their right of free exercise, not that of their children, that must determine Wisconsin's power to impose criminal penalties on the parent. The dissent argues that a child who expresses a desire to attend public high school in conflict with the wishes of his parents should not be prevented from doing so. There is no reason for the Court to consider that point, since it is not an issue in the case. The children are not parties to this litigation.   . . . [232] . . . .

Indeed, it seems clear that, if the State is empowered, as parens patriae, to "save" a child from himself or his Amish parents by requiring an additional two years of compulsory formal high school education, the State will, in large measure, influence, if not determine, the religious future of the child. . . .   . . . [233–34] . . . .

V

For the reasons stated we hold, with the Supreme Court of Wisconsin, that the First and Fourteenth Amendments prevent the State from compelling respondents to cause their children to attend formal high school to age 16. . . . [235–41] . . . .

DISSENT: MR. JUSTICE DOUGLAS, dissenting in part.

. . . The Court's analysis assumes that the only interests at stake in the case are those of the Amish parents, on the one hand, and those of the State, on the other. The difficulty with this approach is that, despite the Court's claim, the parents are seeking to vindicate not only their own free exercise claims, but also those of their high-school-age children.   . . . .

First, respondents' motion to dismiss in the trial court expressly asserts not only the religious liberty of the adults, but also that of the children, as a defense to the prosecutions. . . . [242] . . .

Second, it is essential to reach the question to decide the case not only because the question was squarely raised in the motion to dismiss, but also because no analysis of religious-liberty claims can take place in a vacuum. If the parents in this case are allowed a religious exemption, the inevitable effect is to impose the parents' notions of religious duty upon their children. Where the child is mature enough to express potentially conflicting desires, it would be an invasion of the child's rights to permit such an imposition without canvassing his views. As in *Prince v. Massachusetts*, 321 U.S. 158, it is an imposition resulting from this very litigation. As the child has no other effective forum, it is in this litigation that his rights should be considered. And if an Amish child desires to attend high school, and is mature enough to have that desire respected, the State may well be able to override the parents' religiously motivated objections.   [243] . . .

II

This issue has never been squarely presented before today. Our opinions are full of talk about the power of the parents over the child's education. *See Pierce v. Society of Sisters*, 268 U.S. 510; *Meyer v. Nebraska*, 262 U.S. 390. And we have in the past analyzed similar conflicts between parent and State with little regard for the views of the child. *See Prince v. Massachusetts, supra.* Recent cases, however, have clearly held that the children themselves have constitutionally protectible interests. . . . [244] . . . .

On this important and vital matter of education, I think the children should be entitled to be heard. While the parents, absent dissent, normally speak for the entire family, the education of the child is a matter on which the child will often have decided views. He may want to be a pianist or an astronaut or an oceanographer. [245] To do so he will have to break from the Amish tradition.

It is the future of the student, not the future of the parents, that is imperiled by today's decision. If a parent keeps his child out of school beyond the grade school, then the child will be forever barred from entry into the new and amazing world of diversity that we have today. The child may decide that that is the preferred course, or he may rebel. It is the student's judgment, not his parents', that is essential if we are to give full meaning to what we have said about the Bill of Rights and of the right of students to be masters of their own destiny. If he is harnessed to the Amish way of life [246] by those in authority over him, and if his education is truncated, his entire life may be stunted and deformed. The child, therefore, should be given an opportunity to be heard before the State gives the exemption which we honor today. . . . .

SUPREME COURT OF THE UNITED STATES

494 U.S. 872

EMPLOYMENT DIVISION, DEPARTMENT OF HUMAN RESOURCES OF OREGON V. SMITH

CERTIORARI TO THE SUPREME COURT OF OREGON
NO. 88-1213 ARGUED: NOV. 6, 1989–DECIDED: APRIL 17, 1990

[874] Justice SCALIA delivered the opinion of the Court.

. . . .

I

Oregon law prohibits the knowing or intentional possession of a "controlled substance" unless the substance has been prescribed by a medical practitioner. Or. Rev. Stat. § 475.992(4) (1987). The law defines "controlled substance" as a drug classified in Schedules I through V of the Federal Controlled Substances Act, 21 U.S.C. §§ 811-812 (1982 ed. and Supp. V). . . . Schedule I contains the drug peyote. . . .

Respondents Alfred Smith and Galen Black were fired from their jobs with a private drug rehabilitation organization because they ingested peyote for sacramental purposes at a ceremony of the Native American Church, of which both are members. When respondents applied to petitioner Employment Division for unemployment compensation, they were determined to be ineligible for benefits because they had been discharged for work-related "misconduct." . . .

[875–876] . . .

II

Respondents' claim for relief rests on our decisions in *Sherbert v. Verner*, 374 U.S. 398 (1963), *Thomas v. Review Board, Indiana Employment Security Division*, 450 U.S. 707 (1981), and *Hobbie v. Unemployment Appeals Commission of Florida*, 480 U.S. 136 (1987), in which we held that a State could not condition the availability of unemployment insurance on an individual's willingness to forgo conduct required by his religion. As we observed in *Employment Division, Department of Human Resources of Oregon v. Smith*, 485 U.S. 660, 670 (1988), however, the conduct at issue in those cases was not prohibited by law. We held that distinction to be critical, for "if Oregon does prohibit the religious use of peyote, and if that prohibition is consistent with the

Federal Constitution, there is no federal right to engage in that conduct in Oregon," and "the State is free to withhold unemployment compensation from respondents for engaging in work-related misconduct, despite its religious motivation." 485 U.S. at 672. Now that the Oregon Supreme Court has confirmed that Oregon does prohibit the religious use of peyote, we proceed to consider whether that prohibition is permissible under the Free Exercise Clause.

A

The Free Exercise Clause of the First Amendment, which has been made applicable to the States by incorporation into [877] the Fourteenth Amendment, see *Cantwell v. Connecticut*, 310 U.S. 296, 303 (1940), provides that "Congress shall make no law respecting an establishment of religion, or *prohibiting the free exercise thereof.* . . ." U.S. Const. amend. I (emphasis added). The free exercise of religion means, first and foremost, the right to believe and profess whatever religious doctrine one desires. Thus, the First Amendment obviously excludes all "governmental regulation of religious beliefs as such." *Sherbert v. Verner*, 374 U.S. at 402. The government may not compel affirmation of religious belief, *see Torcaso v. Watkins*, 367 U.S. 488 (1961), punish the expression of religious doctrines it believes to be false, *United States v. Ballard*, 322 U.S. 78, 86–88 (1944), impose special disabilities on the basis of religious views or religious status, *see McDaniel v. Paty*, 435 U.S. 618 (1978); *Fowler v. Rhode Island*, 345 U.S. 67, 69 (1953); *cf. Larson v. Valente*, 456 U.S. 228, 245 (1982), or lend its power to one or the other side in controversies over religious authority or dogma, see *Presbyterian Church v. Hull Church*, 393 U.S. 440, 445–452 (1969); *Kedroff v. St. Nicholas Cathedral*, 344 U.S. 94, 95–119 (1952); *Serbian Eastern Orthodox Diocese v. Milivojevich*, 426 U.S. 696, 708–725 (1976).

But the "exercise of religion" often involves not only belief and profession but the performance of (or abstention from) physical acts: assembling with others for a worship service, participating in sacramental use of bread and wine, proselytizing, abstaining from certain foods or certain modes of transportation. It would be true, we think (though no case of ours has involved the point), that a state would be "prohibiting the free exercise [of religion]" if it sought to ban such acts or abstentions only when they are engaged in for religious reasons, or only because of the religious belief that they display. It would doubtless be unconstitutional, for example, to ban the casting of "statues that are to be used [878] for worship purposes," or to prohibit bowing down before a golden calf.

Respondents in the present case, however, seek to carry the meaning of "prohibiting the free exercise [of religion]" one large step further. They contend that their religious motivation for using peyote places them beyond the reach of a criminal law that is not specifically directed at their religious practice, and that is concededly constitutional as applied to those who use the drug for other reasons. They assert, in other words, that "prohibiting the free exercise [of religion]" includes requiring any individual to observe a generally applicable law that requires (or forbids) the performance of an act that his religious belief forbids (or requires). As a textual matter, we do not think the words must be given that meaning. It is no more necessary to regard the collection of a general tax, for example, as "prohibiting the free exercise [of religion]" by those citizens who believe support of organized government to be sinful than it is to regard the same tax as "abridging the freedom . . . of the press" of those publishing companies that must pay the tax as a condition of staying in business. It is a permissible reading of the text, in the one case as in the other, to say that, if prohibiting the exercise of religion (or burdening the activity of printing) is not the object of the tax, but merely the incidental effect of a generally applicable and otherwise valid provision, the First Amendment has not been offended. . . .

Our decisions reveal that the latter reading is the correct one. We have never held that an individual's religious beliefs [879] excuse him from compliance with an otherwise valid law prohibiting conduct that the State is free to regulate. On the contrary, the record of more than a century of our free exercise jurisprudence contradicts that proposition. As described succinctly by Justice Frankfurter in *Minersville School Dist. Bd. of Educ. v. Gobitis*, 310 U.S. 586, 594–595 (1940):

> *Conscientious scruples have not, in the course of the long struggle for religious toleration, relieved the individual from obedience to a general law not aimed at the promotion or restriction of religious beliefs. The mere possession of religious convictions which contradict the relevant concerns of a political society does not relieve the citizen from the discharge of political responsibilities.*

(Footnote omitted.) We first had occasion to assert that principle in *Reynolds v. United States*, 98 U.S. 145 (1879), where we rejected the claim that criminal laws against polygamy could not be constitutionally applied to those whose religion commanded the practice. "Laws," we said,

> are made for the government of actions, and while they cannot interfere with mere religious belief and opinions, they may with practices. . . . Can a man excuse his practices to the contrary because of his religious belief? To permit this would be to make the professed doctrines of religious belief superior to the law of the land, and in effect to permit every citizen to become a law unto himself.

Id. at 166–167.

Subsequent decisions have consistently held that the right of free exercise does not relieve an individual of the obligation to comply with a "valid and neutral law of general applicability on the ground that the law proscribes (or prescribes) conduct that his religion prescribes (or proscribes)." *United States v. Lee*, 455 U.S. 252, 263, n.3 (1982) (STEVENS, J., concurring in judgment); *see Minersville School Dist. Bd. of Educ. v. Gobitis*, *supra*, 310 U.S. at 595 (collecting cases). In *Prince v. Massachusetts*, 321 U.S. 158 (1944), we held that a mother could be prosecuted under the child labor laws [880] for using her children to dispense literature in the streets, her religious motivation notwithstanding. We found no constitutional infirmity in "excluding [these children] from doing there what no other children may do." *Id.* at 171. In *Braunfeld v. Brown*, 366 U.S. 599 (1961) (plurality opinion), we upheld Sunday closing laws against the claim that they burdened the religious practices of persons whose religions compelled them to refrain from work on other days. . . .

[881] The only decisions in which we have held that the First Amendment bars application of a neutral, generally applicable law to religiously motivated action have involved not the Free Exercise Clause alone, but the Free Exercise Clause in conjunction with other constitutional protections, such as freedom of speech and of the press, *see Cantwell v. Connecticut*, 310 U.S. at 304, 307 (invalidating a licensing system for religious and charitable solicitations under which the administrator had discretion to deny a license to any cause he deemed nonreligious); *Murdock v. Pennsylvania*, 319 U.S. 105 (1943) (invalidating a flat tax on solicitation as applied to the dissemination of religious ideas); *Follett v. McCormick*, 321 U.S. 573 (1944) (same), or the right of parents, acknowledged in *Pierce v. Society of Sisters*, 268 U.S. 510 (1925), to direct the education of their children, *see Wisconsin v. Yoder*, 406 U.S. 205 (1972) (invalidating compulsory school attendance laws as applied to Amish parents who refused on religious grounds to send their children to school). [882] . . .

The present case does not present such a hybrid situation, but a free exercise claim unconnected with any communicative activity or parental right. Respondents urge us to hold, quite simply, that when otherwise prohibitable conduct is accompanied by religious convictions, not only the convictions but the conduct itself must be free from governmental regulation. We have never held that, and decline to do so now. There being no contention that Oregon's drug law represents an attempt to regulate religious beliefs, the communication of religious beliefs, or the raising of one's children in those beliefs, the rule to which we have adhered ever since Reynolds plainly controls. "Our cases do not at their farthest reach support the proposition that a stance of conscientious opposition relieves an objector from any colliding duty fixed by a democratic government." *Gillette v. United States*, *supra*, at 461.

B

Respondents argue that, even though exemption from generally applicable criminal laws need not automatically be extended to religiously motivated actors, at least the claim for a [883] religious exemption must be evaluated under the balancing test set forth in *Sherbert v. Verner*, 374 U.S. 398 (1963). Under the *Sherbert* test, governmental actions that substantially burden a religious practice must be justified by a compelling governmental interest. *See id.* at 402–403; *see also Hernandez v. Commissioner*, 490 U.S. at 699. Applying that test, we have, on three occasions, invalidated state unemployment compensation rules that conditioned the availability of benefits upon an applicant's willingness to work under conditions forbidden by his religion. *See Sherbert v. Verner*, *supra*; *Thomas v. Review Bd. of Indiana Employment Security Div.*, 450 U.S. 707 (1981); *Hobbie v. Unemployment Appeals Comm'n of Florida*, 480 U.S. 136 (1987). We have never invalidated any governmental action on the basis of the *Sherbert* test except the denial of unemployment compensation. Although we have sometimes purported to apply the *Sherbert* test in contexts other than that, we have always found the test satisfied, *see United States v. Lee*, 455 U.S. 252 (1982); *Gillette v. United States*, 401 U.S. 437 (1971). In recent years we have abstained from applying the Sherbert test (outside the unemployment compensation field) at all. In *Bowen v. Roy*, 476 U.S. 693 (1986), we declined to apply *Sherbert* analysis to a federal statutory scheme that required benefit applicants and recipients to provide their Social Security numbers. The plaintiffs in that case asserted that it would violate their religious beliefs to obtain and provide a Social Security number for their daughter. We held the statute's application to the plaintiffs valid regardless of whether it was necessary to effectuate a compelling interest. *See id.* at 699–701. In *Lyng v. Northwest Indian Cemetery Protective Assn.*, 485 U.S. 439 (1988), we declined to apply *Sherbert* analysis to the Government's logging and road construction activities on lands used for religious purposes by several Native American Tribes, even though it was undisputed that the activities "could have devastating effects on traditional Indian religious practices," 485 U.S. at 451. [884] In *Goldman v. Weinberger*, 475 U.S. 503 (1986), we rejected application of the *Sherbert* test to military dress regulations that forbade the wearing of yarmulkes. In *O'Lone v. Estate of Shabazz*, 482 U.S. 342 (1987), we sustained, without mentioning the *Sherbert* test, a prison's refusal to excuse inmates from work requirements to attend worship services.

Even if we were inclined to breathe into *Sherbert* some life beyond the unemployment compensation field, we would not apply it to require exemptions from a generally applicable criminal law. The *Sherbert* test, it must be recalled, was developed in a context that lent itself to individualized governmental assessment of the reasons for the relevant conduct. As a plurality of the Court noted in *Roy*, a distinctive feature of unemployment compensation programs is that their eligibility criteria invite consideration of the particular circumstances behind an applicant's unemployment: "The statutory conditions [in *Sherbert* and *Thomas*] provided that a person was not eligible for unemployment compensation benefits if, "without good cause," he had quit work or refused available work. The "good cause" standard created a mechanism for individualized exemptions." *Bowen v. Roy, supra*, 476 U.S. at 708 (opinion of Burger, C.J., joined by Powell and REHNQUIST, JJ.). See also *Sherbert, supra*, 374 U.S. at 401, n.4 (reading state unemployment compensation law as allowing benefits for unemployment caused by at least some "personal reasons"). As the plurality pointed out in *Roy*, our decisions in the unemployment cases stand for the proposition that where the State has in place a system of individual exemptions, it may not refuse to extend that system to cases of "religious hardship" without compelling reason. *Bowen v. Roy, supra*, 476 U.S. at 708.

Whether or not the decisions are that limited, they at least have nothing to do with an across-the-board criminal prohibition on a particular form of conduct. . . . [885] . . . . To make an individual's obligation to obey such a law contingent upon the law's coincidence with his religious beliefs, except where the State's interest is "compelling"—permitting him, by virtue of his beliefs, "to become a law unto himself," *Reynolds v. United States*, 98 U.S. at 167—contradicts both constitutional tradition and common sense.

The "compelling government interest" requirement seems benign, because it is familiar from other fields. But using it as the standard that must be met before the government may accord different treatment on the basis of race, *see, e.g.*, [886] *Palmore v. Sidoti*, 466 U.S. 429, 432 (1984), or before the government may regulate the content of speech, *see, e.g.*, *Sable Communications of California v. FCC*, 492 U.S. 115 (1989), is not remotely comparable to using it for the purpose asserted here. What it produces in those other fields—equality of treatment, and an unrestricted flow of contending speech—are constitutional norms; what it would produce here—a private right to ignore generally applicable laws—is a constitutional anomaly.

Nor is it possible to limit the impact of respondents' proposal by requiring a "compelling state interest" only when the conduct prohibited is "central" to the individual's religion. *Cf. Lyng v. Northwest Indian Cemetery Protective Assn., supra*, 485 U.S. at 474–476 (BRENNAN, J., dissenting). It is no [887] more appropriate for judges to determine the "centrality" of religious beliefs before applying a "compelling interest" test in the free exercise field than it would be for them to determine the "importance" of ideas before applying the "compelling interest" test in the free speech field. What principle of law or logic can be brought to bear to contradict a believer's assertion that a particular act is "central" to his personal faith? Judging the centrality of different religious practices is akin to the unacceptable "business of evaluating the relative merits of differing religious claims." *United States v. Lee*, 455 U.S. at 263 n.2 (STEVENS, J., concurring). As we reaffirmed only last Term, "[i]t is not within the judicial ken to question the centrality of particular beliefs or practices to a faith, or the validity of particular litigants' interpretation of those creeds." *Hernandez v. Commissioner*, 490 U.S. at 699. Repeatedly and in many different contexts, we have warned that courts must not presume to determine the place of a particular belief in a religion or the plausibility of a religious claim. *See, e.g., Thomas v. Review Bd. of Indiana Employment Security Div.*, 450 U.S. at 716; *Presbyterian Church v. Hull Church*, 393 U.S. at 450; *Jones v. Wolf*, 443 U.S. 595, 602–606 (1979); *United States v. Ballard*, 322 U.S. 78, 85–87 (1944).

[888] If the "compelling interest" test is to be applied at all, then, it must be applied across the board, to all actions thought to be religiously commanded. Moreover, if "compelling interest" really means what it says (and watering it down here would subvert its rigor in the other fields where it is applied), many laws will not meet the test. Any society adopting such a system would be courting anarchy, but that danger increases in direct proportion to the society's diversity of religious beliefs, and its determination to coerce or suppress none of them. Precisely because "we are a cosmopolitan nation made up of people of almost every conceivable religious preference," *Braunfeld v. Brown*, 366 U.S. at 606, and precisely because we value and protect that religious divergence, we cannot afford the luxury of deeming presumptively invalid, as applied to the religious objector, every regulation of conduct that does not protect an interest of the highest order. The rule respondents favor would open the prospect of constitutionally required religious exemptions from civic obligations of almost every conceivable kind—ranging from [889] compulsory military service, *see, e.g., Gillette v. United States*, 401 U.S. 437 (1971), to the payment of taxes, *see, e.g., United States v. Lee, supra*; to health and safety regulation such as manslaughter and child neglect laws, *see, e.g., Funkhouser v. State*, 763 P.2d 695 (Okla. Crim. App. 1988), compulsory vaccination laws, *see, e.g., Cude v. State*, 237 Ark. 927 (1964), drug laws, *see, e.g., Olsen v. Drug Enforcement Administration*, 878 F.2d 1458 (1989), and traffic laws, *see Cox v. New Hampshire*, 312 U.S. 569 (1941); to social welfare legislation such as minimum wage laws, *see Susan and Tony Alamo Foundation v. Secretary of Labor*, 471 U.S. 290 (1985), child labor laws, *see Prince v. Massachusetts*, 321 U.S. 158 (1944), animal cruelty laws, *see, e.g., Church of the Lukumi Babalu Aye Inc. v. City of Hialeah*, 723 F.Supp. 1467 (S.D. Fla. 1989), cf. *State v. Massey*, 229 N.C. 734, appeal dism'd, 336 U.S. 942 (1949), environmental protection laws, *see United States v. Little*, 638 F.Supp. 337 (Mont. 1986), and laws providing for equality of opportunity for the races, *see, e.g., Bob Jones University v. United States*, 461 U.S. 574, 603–604 (1983). The First Amendment's protection of religious liberty does not require this.

[890] Values that are protected against government interference through enshrinement in the Bill of Rights are not thereby banished from the political process. Just as a society that believes in the negative protection accorded to the press by the First Amendment is likely to enact laws that affirmatively foster the dissemination of the printed word, so also a society that believes in the negative protection accorded to religious belief can be expected to be solicitous of that value in its legislation as well. It is therefore not surprising that a number of States have made an exception to their drug laws for sacramental peyote use. See, e.g., Ariz. Rev. Stat. Ann. §§ 13-3402(B)(1)-(3) (1989); Colo. Rev. Stat. § 12-22-317(3) (1985); N.M. Stat. Ann. § 30-31-6(D) (Supp. 1989). But to say that a nondiscriminatory religious practice exemption is permitted, or even that it is desirable, is not to say that it is constitutionally required, and that the appropriate occasions for its creation can be discerned by the courts. It may fairly be said that leaving accommodation to the political process will place at a relative disadvantage those religious practices that are not widely engaged in; but that unavoidable consequence of democratic government must be preferred to a system in which each conscience is a law unto itself or in which judges weigh the social importance of all laws against the centrality of all religious beliefs.

* * * *

Because respondents' ingestion of peyote was prohibited under Oregon law, and because that prohibition is constitutional, Oregon may, consistent with the Free Exercise Clause, deny respondents unemployment compensation when their dismissal results from use of the drug. The decision of the Oregon Supreme Court is accordingly reversed.

It is so ordered.

[891] Justice O'CONNOR, with whom Justice BRENNAN, Justice MARSHALL, and Justice BLACKMUN join as to Parts I and II, concurring in the judgment.

Although I agree with the result the Court reaches in this case, I cannot join its opinion. In my view, today's holding dramatically departs from well settled First Amendment jurisprudence, appears unnecessary to resolve the question presented, and is incompatible with our Nation's fundamental commitment to individual religious liberty. . . . [892] . . .

II

The Court today extracts from our long history of free exercise precedents the single categorical rule that "if prohibiting the exercise of religion . . . is . . . merely the incidental effect of a generally applicable and otherwise valid provision, the First Amendment has not been offended." *Ante*, at 878 (citations omitted). Indeed, the Court holds that, where the law is a generally applicable criminal prohibition, our usual free exercise jurisprudence does not even apply. *Ante*, at 884. To reach this sweeping result, however, the Court must not only give a strained reading of the First Amendment but must also disregard our consistent application of free exercise doctrine to cases involving generally applicable regulations that burden religious conduct.

[893] A

The Free Exercise Clause of the First Amendment commands that "Congress shall make no law . . . prohibiting the free exercise [of religion]." In *Cantwell v. Connecticut*, 310 U.S. 296 (1940), we held that this prohibition applies to the States by incorporation into the Fourteenth Amendment and that it categorically forbids government regulation of religious beliefs. *Id.* at 303. As the Court recognizes, however, the "free exercise" of religion often, if not invariably, requires the performance of (or abstention from) certain acts. . . . Because the First Amendment does not distinguish between religious belief and religious conduct, conduct motivated by sincere religious belief, like the belief itself, must therefore be at least presumptively protected by the Free Exercise Clause.

The Court today, however, interprets the Clause to permit the government to prohibit, without justification, conduct mandated by an individual's religious beliefs, so long as that prohibition is generally applicable. *Ante*, at 878. But a law that prohibits certain conduct—conduct that happens to be an act of worship for someone—manifestly does prohibit that person's free exercise of his religion. A person who is barred from engaging in religiously motivated conduct is barred from freely exercising his religion. . . . It is difficult to deny that a law that prohibits [894] religiously motivated conduct, even if the law is generally applicable, does not at least implicate First Amendment concerns. . . .

To say that a person's right to free exercise has been burdened, of course, does not mean that he has an absolute right to engage in the conduct. Under our established First Amendment jurisprudence, we have recognized that the freedom to act, unlike the freedom to believe, cannot be absolute. *See, e.g., Cantwell, supra*, 310 U.S. at 304; *Reynolds v. United States*, 98 U.S. 145, 161–167. Instead, we have respected both the First Amendment's express textual mandate and the governmental interest in regulation of conduct by requiring the Government to justify any substantial burden on religiously motivated conduct by a compelling state interest and by means narrowly tailored to achieve that interest. See *Hernandez v. Commissioner*, 490 U.S. 680, 699 [895] (1989); *Hobbie, supra*, 480 U.S. at 141; *United States v. Lee*, 455 U.S. 252, 257–258 (1982); *Thomas v. Review Bd., Indiana Employment Security Div.*, 450 U.S. 707, 718 (1981); *McDaniel v. Paty*, 435 U.S. 618, 626–629 (1978) (plurality opinion); *Yoder, supra*, 406 U.S. at 215; *Gillette v. United States*, 401 U.S. 437, 462 (1971); *Sherbert v. Verner*, 374 U.S. 398, 403 (1963); *see also Bowen v. Roy, supra*, 476 U.S. at 732 (opinion concurring in part and dissenting in part); *West Virginia State Bd. of Educ. v. Barnette*, 319 U.S. 624, 639 (1943). The compelling interest test effectuates the First Amendment's command that religious liberty is an independent liberty, that it occupies a preferred position, and that the Court will not permit encroachments upon this liberty, whether direct or indirect, unless required by clear and compelling governmental interests "of the highest order," *Yoder, supra*, 406 U.S. at 215. . . . [896] . . .

The Court endeavors to escape from our decisions in *Cantwell* and *Yoder* by labeling them "hybrid" decisions, *ante*, at 892, but there is no denying that both cases expressly relied on the Free Exercise Clause, *see Cantwell*, 310 U.S. at 303–307; *Yoder*, 406 U.S. at 219–229, and that we have consistently regarded those cases as part of the mainstream of our free exercise jurisprudence. Moreover, in each of the other cases cited by the Court to support its categorical rule, *ante*, at 879–880, we rejected the particular constitutional claims before us only after carefully weighing the competing interests. *See Prince v. Massachusetts*, 321 U.S. 158, 168–170 (1944) (state interest in regulating children's activities justifies denial of religious exemption from child labor laws); *Braunfeld v. Brown*, 366 U.S. 599, 608–609 (1961) (plurality opinion) (state interest in uniform day of rest justifies denial of religious exemption from Sunday closing law); *Gillette, supra*, 401 U.S. at 462 (state interest in military affairs justifies denial of religious exemption from conscription laws); *Lee, supra*, 455 U.S. at 258–259 (state interest in comprehensive social security system justifies denial of religious exemption from mandatory participation requirement). That we rejected the free exercise [897] claims in those cases hardly calls into question the applicability of First Amendment doctrine in the first place. Indeed, it is surely unusual to judge the vitality of a constitutional doctrine by looking to the win-loss record of the plaintiffs who happen to come before us.

B

. . . . In my view, however, the essence of a free exercise claim is relief from a burden imposed by government on religious practices or beliefs, whether the burden is imposed directly through laws that prohibit or compel specific religious practices, or indirectly through laws that, in effect, make abandonment of one's own religion or conformity to the religious beliefs of others the price of an equal place in the civil community. As we explained in Thomas:

> *Where the state conditions receipt of an important benefit upon conduct proscribed by a religious faith, or where it denies such a benefit because of conduct mandated by religious belief, thereby putting substantial pressure on an adherent to modify his behavior and to violate his beliefs, a burden upon religion exists.*

450 U.S. at 717–718. [898] *See also Frazee v. Illinois Dept. of Employment Security*, 489 U.S. 829, 832 (1989); *Hobbie*, 480 U.S. at 141. A State that makes criminal an individual's religiously motivated conduct burdens that individual's free exercise of religion in the severest manner possible, for it "results in the choice to the individual of either abandoning his religious principle or facing criminal prosecution." *Braunfeld, supra*, 366 U.S. at 605. I would have thought it beyond argument that such laws implicate free exercise concerns. . . . [899] . . .

. . . Once it has been shown that a government regulation or criminal prohibition burdens the free exercise of religion, we have consistently asked the Government to demonstrate that unbending application of its regulation to the religious objector "is essential to accomplish an overriding governmental interest," *Lee, supra*, 455 U.S. at 257–258, or represents "the least restrictive means of achieving some compelling state interest," *Thomas*, 450 U.S. at 718. *See, e.g., Braunfeld, supra*, 366 U.S. at 607; *Sherbert, supra*, 374 U.S. at 406; *Yoder, supra*, 406 U.S. at 214–215; *Roy*, 476 U.S. at 728–732 (opinion concurring in part and dissenting in part). To me, the sounder approach—the approach more consistent with our role as judges to decide each case on its individual merits—is to apply this test in each case to determine whether the burden on the specific plaintiffs before us is constitutionally significant, and whether the particular criminal interest asserted by the State before us is compelling. Even if, as an empirical matter, a government's criminal laws might usually serve a compelling interest in health, safety, or public order, the First Amendment at least requires a case-by-case determination of the question, sensitive to the facts of each particular claim. . . . [900] . . . .

Similarly, the other cases cited by the Court for the proposition that we have rejected application of the *Sherbert* test outside the unemployment compensation field, *ante*, at 884, are distinguishable because they arose in the narrow, specialized contexts in which we have not traditionally required [901] the government to justify a burden on religious conduct by articulating a compelling interest. *See Goldman v. Weinberger*, 475 U.S. 503, 507 (1986) ("Our review of military regulations challenged on First Amendment grounds is far more deferential than constitutional review of similar laws or regulations designed for civilian society"); *O'Lone v. Estate of Shabazz*, 482 U.S. 342, 349 (1987) ("[P]rison regulations alleged to infringe constitutional rights are judged under a 'reasonableness' test less restrictive than that ordinarily applied to alleged infringements of fundamental constitutional rights") (citation omitted). That we did not apply the compelling interest test in these cases says nothing about whether the test should continue to apply in paradigm free exercise cases such as the one presented here.

The Court today gives no convincing reason to depart from settled First Amendment jurisprudence. There is nothing talismanic about neutral laws of general applicability or general criminal prohibitions, for laws neutral toward religion can coerce a person to violate his religious conscience or intrude upon his religious duties just as effectively as laws aimed at religion. Although the Court suggests that the compelling interest test, as applied to generally applicable laws, would result in a "constitutional anomaly," *ante*, at 886, the First Amendment unequivocally makes freedom of religion, like freedom from race discrimination and freedom of speech, a "constitutional nor[m]," not an "anomaly." *Ibid.* Nor would application of our established free exercise doctrine to this case necessarily be incompatible with our equal protection cases. *Cf. Rogers v. Lodge*, 458 U.S. 613, 618 (1982) (race-neutral law that "'bears more heavily on one race than another'" may violate equal protection) (citation omitted); *Castaneda v. Partida*, 430 U.S. 482, 492–495 (1977) (grand jury selection). . . . [902] . . . .

Finally, the Court today suggests that the disfavoring of minority religions is an "unavoidable consequence" under our system of government, and that accommodation of such religions must be left to the political process. *Ante*, at 890. In my view, however, the First Amendment was enacted precisely to protect the rights of those whose religious practices are not shared by the majority and may be viewed with hostility. . . .

SUPREME COURT OF THE UNITED STATES

403 U.S. 602

LEMON V. KURTZMAN

APPEAL FROM THE UNITED STATES DISTRICT COURT
FOR THE EASTERN DISTRICT OF PENNSYLVANIA

NO. 89 ARGUED: MARCH 3, 1971–DECIDED: JUNE 28, 1971

[606] MR. CHIEF JUSTICE BURGER delivered the opinion of the Court.

These two appeals raise questions as to Pennsylvania and Rhode Island statutes providing state aid to church-related elementary and secondary schools. Both statutes are challenged as violative of the Establishment and Free Exercise Clauses of the First Amendment and the Due Process Clause of the Fourteenth Amendment.

Pennsylvania has adopted a statutory program that provides financial support to nonpublic elementary and [607] secondary schools by way of reimbursement for the cost of teachers' salaries, textbooks, and instructional materials in specified secular subjects. Rhode Island has adopted a statute under which the State pays directly to teachers in nonpublic elementary schools a supplement of 15% of their annual salary. Under each statute, state aid has been given to church-related educational institutions. We hold that both statutes are unconstitutional.

... [608–611] ....

II

... [612] ....

The language of the Religion Clauses of the First Amendment is, at best, opaque, particularly when compared with other portions of the Amendment. Its authors did not simply prohibit the establishment of a state church or a state religion, an area history shows they regarded as very important and fraught with great dangers. Instead, they commanded that there should be "no law respecting an establishment of religion." . . . . A given law might not establish a state religion, but nevertheless be one "respecting" that end in the sense of being a step that could lead to such establishment, and hence offend the First Amendment.

In the absence of precisely stated constitutional prohibitions, we must draw lines with reference to the three main evils against which the Establishment Clause was intended to afford protection: "sponsorship, financial support, and active involvement of the sovereign in religious activity." *Walz v. Tax Commission*, 397 U.S. 664, 668 (1970).

Every analysis in this area must begin with consideration of the cumulative criteria developed by the Court over many years. Three such tests may be gleaned from our cases. First, the statute must have a secular legislative purpose; second, its principal or primary effect must be one that neither advances nor inhibits religion, *Board of Education v. Allen*, 392 U.S. 236, 243 (1968); [613] finally, the statute must not foster "an excessive government entanglement with religion." *Walz, supra*, at 674.

Inquiry into the legislative purposes of the Pennsylvania and Rhode Island statutes affords no basis for a conclusion that the legislative intent was to advance religion. On the contrary, the statutes themselves clearly state that they are intended to enhance the quality of the secular education in all schools covered by the compulsory attendance laws. There is no reason to believe the legislatures meant anything else. A State always has a legitimate concern for maintaining minimum standards in all schools it allows to operate. As in *Allen*, we find nothing here that undermines the stated legislative intent; it must therefore be accorded appropriate deference.

In *Allen*, the Court acknowledged that secular and religious teachings were not necessarily so intertwined that secular textbooks furnished to students by the State were, in fact, instrumental in the teaching of religion. 392 U.S. at 248. The legislatures of Rhode Island and Pennsylvania have concluded that secular and religious education are identifiable and separable. In the abstract, we have no quarrel with this conclusion.

The two legislatures, however, have also recognized that church-related elementary and secondary schools have a significant religious mission, and that a substantial portion of their activities is religiously oriented. They have therefore sought to create statutory restrictions designed to guarantee the separation between secular and religious educational functions, and to ensure that State financial aid supports only the former. All these provisions are precautions taken in candid recognition that these programs approached, even if they did not intrude upon, the forbidden areas under the Religion Clauses. We need not decide whether these legislative precautions restrict the principal or primary effect of the programs to the point where they do not offend the Religion [614] Clauses, for we conclude that the cumulative impact of the entire relationship arising under the statutes in each State involves excessive entanglement between government and religion.

III

In *Walz v. Tax Commission, supra*, the Court upheld state tax exemptions for real property owned by religious organizations and used for religious worship. That holding, however, tended to confine, rather than enlarge, the area of permissible state involvement with religious institutions by calling for close scrutiny of the degree of entanglement involved in the relationship. The objective is to prevent, as far as possible, the intrusion of either into the precincts of the other.

Our prior holdings do not call for total separation between church and state; total separation is not possible in an absolute sense. Some relationship between government and religious organizations is inevitable. *Zorach v. Clauson*, 343 U.S. 306, 312 (1952); *Sherbert v. Verner*, 374 U.S. 398, 422 (1963) (HARLAN, J., dissenting). Fire inspections, building and zoning regulations, and state requirements under compulsory school attendance laws are examples of necessary and permissible contacts. Indeed, under the statutory exemption before us in *Walz*, the State had a continuing burden to ascertain that the exempt property was, in fact, being used for religious worship. Judicial caveats against entanglement must recognize that the line of separation, far from being a "wall," is a blurred, indistinct, and variable barrier depending on all the circumstances of a particular relationship.   . . . .

[615] In order to determine whether the government entanglement with religion is excessive, we must examine the character and purposes of the institutions that are benefited, the nature of the aid that the State provides, and the resulting relationship between the government and the religious authority. MR. JUSTICE HARLAN, in a separate opinion in *Walz, supra*, echoed the classic warning as to "programs, whose very nature is apt to entangle the state in details of administration. . . ." *Id*. at 695. Here we find that both statues foster an impermissible degree of entanglement.

(a) Rhode Island Program

> ... [616] ....

The substantial religious character of these church-related schools gives rise to entangling church-state relationships of the kind the Religion Clauses sought to avoid. Although the District Court found that concern for religious values did not inevitably or necessarily intrude into the content of secular subjects, the considerable religious activities of these schools led the legislature to provide for careful governmental controls and surveillance by state authorities in order to ensure that state aid supports only secular education.

The dangers and corresponding entanglements are enhanced by the particular form of aid that the Rhode Island Act provides. Our decisions from *Everson* to *Allen* have permitted the States to provide church-related schools with secular, neutral, or nonideological services, facilities, or materials. Bus transportation, school lunches, public health services, and secular textbooks supplied in common to all students were not [617] thought to offend the Establishment Clause. We note that the dissenters in *Allen* seemed chiefly concerned with the pragmatic difficulties involved in ensuring the truly secular content of the textbooks provided at state expense.

In *Allen*, the Court refused to make assumptions, on a meager record, about the religious content of the textbooks that the State would be asked to provide. We cannot, however, refuse here to recognize that teachers have a substantially different ideological character from books. In terms of potential for involving some aspect of faith or morals in secular subjects, a textbook's content is ascertainable, but a teacher's handling of a subject is not. We cannot ignore the danger that a teacher under religious control and discipline poses to the separation of the religious from the purely secular aspects of pre-college education. The conflict of functions inheres in the situation.

> ... [618] ....

We do not assume, however, that parochial school teachers will be unsuccessful in their attempts to segregate their religious belief from their secular educational responsibilities. But the potential for impermissible fostering of religion is present. ... The State must be certain, given the Religion Clauses, that subsidized teachers do not inculcate religion—indeed, the State here has undertaken to do so. To ensure that no trespass occurs, the State has therefore carefully conditioned its aid with pervasive restrictions. An eligible recipient must teach only those courses that are offered in the public schools and use only those texts and materials that are found in the public schools. In addition, the teacher must not engage in teaching any course in religion.

A comprehensive, discriminating, and continuing state surveillance will inevitably be required to ensure that these restrictions are obeyed and the First Amendment otherwise respected. Unlike a book, a teacher cannot be inspected once so as to determine the extent and intent of his or her personal beliefs and subjective acceptance of the limitations imposed by the First Amendment. These prophylactic contacts will involve excessive and enduring entanglement between state and church.

[620] There is another area of entanglement in the Rhode Island program that gives concern. The statute excludes teachers employed by nonpublic schools whose average per-pupil expenditures on secular education equal or exceed the comparable figures for public schools. In the event that the total expenditures of an otherwise eligible school exceed this norm, the program requires the government to examine the school's records in order to determine how much of the total expenditures is attributable to secular education and how much to religious activity. This kind of state inspection and evaluation of the religious content of a religious organization is fraught with the sort of entanglement that the Constitution forbids. It is a relationship pregnant with dangers of excessive government direction of church schools, and hence of churches. ...

(b) Pennsylvania Program

The Pennsylvania statue also provides state aid to church-related schools for teachers' salaries. The complaint describes an educational system that is very similar to the one existing in Rhode Island. ...

As we noted earlier, the very restrictions and surveillance necessary to ensure that teachers play a strictly nonideological role give rise to entanglements between [621] church and state. The Pennsylvania statute, like that of Rhode Island, fosters this kind of relationship. Reimbursement is not only limited to courses offered in the public schools and materials approved by state officials, but the statute excludes "any subject matter expressing religious teaching, or the morals or forms of worship of any sect." In addition, schools seeking reimbursement must maintain accounting procedures that require the State to establish the cost of the secular, as distinguished from the religious, instruction.

The Pennsylvania statute, moreover, has the further defect of providing state financial aid directly to the church-related school. This factor distinguishes both *Everson* and *Allen*, for, in both those cases, the Court was careful to point out that state aid was provided to the student and his parents—not to the church-related school. *Board of Education v. Allen, supra*, at 243–244; *Everson v. Board of Education, supra*, at 18. In *Walz v. Tax Commission, supra*, at 675, the Court warned of the dangers of direct payments to religious organizations:

> "Obviously a direct money subsidy would be a relationship pregnant with involvement and, as with most governmental grant programs, could encompass sustained and detailed administrative relationships for enforcement of statutory or administrative standards. . . ."

The history of government grants of a continuing cash subsidy indicates that such programs have almost always been accompanied by varying measures of control and surveillance. The government cash grants before us now provide no basis for predicting that comprehensive measures of surveillance and controls will not follow. In particular, the government's post-audit power to inspect and evaluate a church-related school's financial records and to determine which expenditures are religious and [622] which are secular creates an intimate and continuing relationship between church and state.

IV

A broader base of entanglement of yet a different character is presented by the divisive political potential of these state programs. In a community where such a large number of pupils are served by church-related schools, it can be assumed that state assistance will entail considerable political activity. Partisans of parochial schools, understandably concerned with rising costs and sincerely dedicated to both the religious and secular educational missions of their schools, will inevitably champion this cause and promote political action to achieve their goals. Those who oppose state aid, whether for constitutional, religious, or fiscal reasons, will inevitably respond and employ all of the usual political campaign techniques to prevail. . . .

Ordinarily, political debate and division, however vigorous or even partisan, are normal and healthy manifestations of our democratic system of government, but political division along religious lines was one of the principal evils against which the First Amendment was intended to protect. . . . The potential divisiveness of such conflict is a threat to the normal political process. *Walz v. Tax Commission, supra*, at 695 (separate opinion of HARLAN, J.). *See also Board of Education v. Allen*, 392 U.S. at 249 (HARLAN, J., concurring); *Abington School District v. Schempp*, 374 U.S. 203, 307 (1963) (GOLDBERG, J., concurring). To have States or communities divide on the issues presented by state aid to parochial schools would tend to confuse [623] and obscure other issues of great urgency. We have an expanding array of vexing issues, local and national, domestic and international, to debate and divide on. It conflicts with our whole history and tradition to permit questions of the Religion Clauses to assume such importance in our legislatures and in our elections that they could divert attention from the myriad issues and problems that confront every level of government. . .   . . . [624] . . . .

V

In *Walz*, it was argued that a tax exemption for places of religious worship would prove to be the first step in an inevitable progression leading to the establishment of state churches and state religion. That claim could not stand up against more than 200 years of virtually universal practice imbedded in our colonial experience and continuing into the present.

The progression argument, however, is more persuasive here. We have no long history of state aid to church-related educational institutions comparable to 200 years of tax exemption for churches. Indeed, the state programs before us today represent something of an innovation. . . . Nor can we fail to see that, in constitutional adjudication, some steps which, when taken, were thought to approach "the verge" have become the platform for yet further steps. A certain momentum develops in constitutional theory, and it can be a "downhill thrust" easily set in motion but difficult to retard or stop. . . . [625] . . . .

. . . [N]othing we have said can be construed to disparage the role of church-related elementary and secondary schools in our national life. Their contribution has been and is enormous. . . .

The merit and benefits of these schools, however, are not the issue before us in these cases. The sole question is whether state aid to these schools can be squared with the dictates of the Religion Clauses. Under our system, the choice has been made that government is to be entirely excluded from the area of religious instruction, and churches excluded from the affairs of government.   . . . .

SUPREME COURT OF THE UNITED STATES

465 U.S. 668

LYNCH V. DONNELLY

CERTIORARI TO THE UNITED STATES COURT OF APPEALS FOR THE FIRST CIRCUIT

NO. 82-1256 ARGUED: OCTOBER 4, 1983–DECIDED: MARCH 5, 1984

SYLLABUS: The city of Pawtucket, R.I., annually erects a Christmas display in a park owned by a nonprofit organization and located in the heart of the city's shopping district. The display includes, in addition to such objects as a Santa Claus house, a Christmas tree, and a banner that reads "SEASONS GREETINGS," a creche or Nativity scene, which has been part of this annual display for 40 years or more. Respondents brought an action in Federal District Court, challenging the inclusion of the creche in the display on the ground that it violated the Establishment Clause of the First Amendment. . . .

Held: Notwithstanding the religious significance of the creche, Pawtucket has not violated the Establishment Clause.   . . . .

JUSTICE O'CONNOR, concurring.

I

The Establishment Clause prohibits government from making adherence to a religion relevant in any way to a person's standing in the political community. Government can run afoul of that prohibition in two principal ways. One is excessive [688] entanglement with religious institutions, which may interfere with the independence of the institutions, give the institutions access to government or governmental powers not fully shared by nonadherents of the religion, and foster the creation of political constituencies defined along religious lines. *E.g., Larkin v. Grendel's Den, Inc.*, 459 U.S. 116 (1982). The second and more direct infringement is government endorsement or disapproval of religion. Endorsement sends a message to nonadherents that they are outsiders, not full members of the political community, and an accompanying message to adherents that they are insiders, favored members of the political community. Disapproval sends the opposite message. *See generally Abington School District v. Schempp*, 374 U.S. 203 (1963).   . . . [689] . . . .

II

In this case, as even the District Court found, there is no institutional entanglement. Nevertheless, the respondents contend that the political divisiveness caused by Pawtucket's display of its creche violates the excessive entanglement prong of the *Lemon* test. . . . In my view, political divisiveness along religious lines should not be an independent test of constitutionality.

Although several of our cases have discussed political divisiveness under the entanglement prong of *Lemon, see, e.g., Committee for Public Education & Religious Liberty v. Nyquist,* 413 U.S. 756, 796 (1973); *Lemon v. Kurtzman, supra,* at 623, we have never relied on divisiveness as an independent ground for holding a government practice unconstitutional. Guessing the potential for political divisiveness inherent in a government practice is simply too speculative an enterprise, in part because the existence of the litigation, as this case illustrates, itself may affect the political response to the government practice. Political divisiveness is admittedly an evil addressed by the Establishment Clause. Its existence may be evidence that institutional entanglement is excessive or that a government practice is perceived as an endorsement of religion. But the constitutional inquiry should focus ultimately on the character of the government activity that might cause such divisiveness, not on the divisiveness itself. . . .

[690] III

The central issue in this case is whether Pawtucket has endorsed Christianity by its display of the creche. To answer that question, we must examine both what Pawtucket intended to communicate in displaying the creche and what message the city's display actually conveyed. The purpose and effect prongs of the *Lemon* test represent these two aspects of the meaning of the city's action.

The meaning of a statement to its audience depends both on the intention of the speaker and on the "objective" meaning of the statement in the community. Some listeners need not rely solely on the words themselves in discerning the speaker's intent: they can judge the intent by, for example, examining the context of the statement or asking questions of the speaker. Other listeners do not have or will not seek access to such evidence of intent. They will rely instead on the words themselves; for them, the message actually conveyed may be something not actually intended. If the audience is large, as it always is when government "speaks" by word or deed, some portion of the audience will inevitably receive a message determined by the "objective" content of the statement, and some portion will inevitably receive the intended message. Examination of both the subjective and the objective components of the message communicated by a government action is therefore necessary to determine whether the action carries a forbidden meaning.

The purpose prong of the *Lemon* test asks whether government's actual purpose is to endorse or disapprove of religion. The effect prong asks whether, irrespective of government's actual purpose, the practice under review in fact conveys a message of endorsement or disapproval. An affirmative answer to either question should render the challenged practice invalid.

A

The purpose prong of the *Lemon* test requires that a government activity have a secular purpose. That requirement [691] is not satisfied, however, by the mere existence of some secular purpose, however dominated by religious purposes. In *Stone v. Graham,* 449 U.S. 39 (1980), for example, the Court held that posting copies of the Ten Commandments in schools violated the purpose prong of the *Lemon* test, yet the State plainly had some secular objectives, such as instilling most of the values of the Ten Commandments and illustrating their connection to our legal system, *but see* 449 U.S. at 41. *See also Abington School District v. Schempp,* 374 U.S. at 223–224. The proper inquiry under the purpose prong of *Lemon,* I submit, is whether the government intends to convey a message of endorsement or disapproval of religion.

Applying that formulation to this case, I would find that Pawtucket did not intend to convey any message of endorsement of Christianity or disapproval of non-Christian religions. The evident purpose of including the creche in the larger display was not promotion of the religious content of the creche, but celebration of the public holiday through its traditional symbols. Celebration of public holidays, which have cultural significance even if they also have religious aspects, is a legitimate secular purpose.   . . . .

B

Focusing on the evil of government endorsement or disapproval of religion makes clear that the effect prong of the *Lemon* test is properly interpreted not to require invalidation of a government practice merely because it in fact causes, [692] even as a primary effect, advancement or inhibition of religion. The laws upheld in *Walz v. Tax Commission*, 397 U.S. 664 (1970) (tax exemption for religious, educational, and charitable organizations), in *McGowan v. Maryland*, 366 U.S. 420 (1961) (mandatory Sunday closing law), and in *Zorach v. Clauson*, 343 U.S. 306 (1952) (released time from school for off-campus religious instruction), had such effects, but they did not violate the Establishment Clause. What is crucial is that a government practice not have the effect of communicating a message of government endorsement or disapproval of religion. It is only practices having that effect, whether intentionally or unintentionally, that make religion relevant, in reality or public perception, to status in the political community.

Pawtucket's display of its creche, I believe, does not communicate a message that the government intends to endorse the Christian beliefs represented by the creche. Although the religious and indeed sectarian significance of the creche, as the District Court found, is not neutralized by the setting, the overall holiday setting changes what viewers may fairly understand to be the purpose of the display—as a typical museum setting, though not neutralizing the religious content of a religious painting, negates any message of endorsement of that content. The display celebrates a public holiday, and no one contends that declaration of that holiday is understood to be an endorsement of religion. The holiday itself has very strong secular components and traditions. Government celebration of the holiday, which is extremely common, generally is not understood to endorse the religious content of the holiday, just as government celebration of Thanksgiving is not so understood. The creche is a traditional symbol of the holiday that is very commonly displayed along with purely secular symbols, as it was in Pawtucket.

These features combine to make the government's display of the creche in this particular physical setting no more an endorsement of religion than such governmental "acknowledgments" [693] of religion as legislative prayers of the type approved in *Marsh v. Chambers*, 463 U.S. 783 (1983), government declaration of Thanksgiving as a public holiday, printing of "In God We Trust" on coins, and opening court sessions with "God save the United States and this honorable court." Those government acknowledgments of religion serve, in the only ways reasonably possible in our culture, the legitimate secular purposes of solemnizing public occasions, expressing confidence in the future, and encouraging the recognition of what is worthy of appreciation in society. For that reason, and because of their history and ubiquity, those practices are not understood as conveying government approval of particular religious beliefs. The display of the creche likewise serves a secular purpose—celebration of a public holiday with traditional symbols. It cannot fairly be understood to convey a message of government endorsement of religion. It is significant in this regard that the creche display apparently caused no political divisiveness prior to the filing of this lawsuit, although Pawtucket had incorporated the creche in its annual Christmas display for some years. For these reasons, I conclude that Pawtucket's display of the creche does not have the effect of communicating endorsement of Christianity.

SUPREME COURT OF THE UNITED STATES

515 U.S. 819

ROSENBERGER V. RECTOR AND VISITORS OF THE UNIVERSITY OF VIRGINIA

CERTIORARI TO THE UNITED STATES COURT OF APPEALS FOR THE FOURTH CIRCUIT

NO. 94-329 ARGUED: MARCH 1, 1995–DECIDED: JUNE 29, 1995

OPINION: JUSTICE KENNEDY delivered the opinion of the Court.

The University of Virginia, an instrumentality of the Commonwealth for which it is named and thus bound by the First and Fourteenth Amendments, authorizes the payment of outside contractors for the printing costs of a variety of student publications. It withheld any authorization for payments on behalf of petitioners for the sole reason that their student paper "primarily promotes or manifests a particular belie[f] in or about a deity or an ultimate reality." That the paper did promote or manifest views within the defined exclusion seems plain enough. The challenge is to the University's regulation and its denial of authorization, the case raising issues under the Speech and Establishment Clauses of the First Amendment.　　. . . [824–828] . . . .

II

It is axiomatic that the government may not regulate speech based on its substantive content or the message it conveys. . . . [829] . . . The government must abstain from regulating speech when the specific motivating ideology or the opinion or perspective of the speaker is the rationale for the restriction.

These principles provide the framework forbidding the State from exercising viewpoint discrimination, even when the limited public forum is one of its own creation. . . . [830] . . .

The SAF is a forum more in a metaphysical than in a spatial or geographic sense, but the same principles are applicable. . . .　　. . .[831–832] . . . .

The University's denial of WAP's request for third-party payments in the present case is based upon viewpoint discrimination. . . .　　. . . [833–837] . . . .

Based on the principles we have discussed, we hold that the regulation invoked to deny SAF support, both in its terms and in its application to these petitioners, is a denial of their right of free speech guaranteed by the First Amendment. It remains to be considered whether the violation following from the University's action is excused by the necessity of complying with the Constitution's prohibition against state establishment of religion. We turn to that question.

III   . . . [838] . . . .

If there is to be assurance that the Establishment Clause retains its force in guarding against those governmental actions it was intended to prohibit, we must in each case inquire [839] first into the purpose and object of the governmental action in question and then into the practical details of the program's operation. Before turning to these matters, however, we can set forth certain general principles that must bear upon our determination.

A central lesson of our decisions is that a significant factor in upholding governmental programs in the face of Establishment Clause attack is their neutrality towards religion. We have decided a series of cases addressing the receipt of government benefits where religion or religious views are implicated in some degree. The first case in our modern Establishment Clause jurisprudence was *Everson v. Board of Education of Ewing*, 330 U.S. 1 (1947). There we cautioned that in enforcing the prohibition against laws respecting establishment of religion, we must "be sure that we do not inadvertently prohibit [the government] from extending its general state law benefits to all its citizens without regard to their religious belief." *Id.* at 16. We have held that the guarantee of neutrality is respected, not offended, when the government, following neutral criteria and evenhanded policies, extends benefits to recipients whose ideologies and viewpoints, including religious ones, are broad and diverse. *See Bd. of Educ. of Kiryas Joel Vill. Sch. Dist. v. Grumet*, 512 U.S. 687, 704 (1994) (Souter, J.) ("[T]he principle is well grounded in our case law [and] we have frequently relied explicitly on the general availability of any benefit provided religious groups or individuals in turning aside Establishment Clause challenges"); *Witters v. Wash. Dept. of Servs. for Blind*, 474 U.S. 481, 487–88 (1986); *Mueller v. Allen*, 463 U.S. 388, 398–99 (1983); *Widmar v. Vincent*, 454 U.S. 263, 274–75 (1981). . . .

[840] The governmental program here is neutral toward religion. There is no suggestion that the University created it to advance religion or adopted some ingenious device with the purpose of aiding a religious cause. The object of the SAF is to open a forum for speech and to support various student enterprises, including the publication of newspapers, in recognition of the diversity and creativity of student life. The University's SAF Guidelines have a separate classification for, and do not make third-party payments on behalf of, "religious organizations," which are those "whose purpose is to practice a devotion to an acknowledged ultimate reality or deity." Pet. for Cert. 66a. The category of support here is for "student news, information, opinion, entertainment, or academic communications media groups," of which Wide Awake was 1 of 15 in the 1990 school year. . . .

The neutrality of the program distinguishes the student fees from a tax levied for the direct support of a church or group of churches. A tax of that sort, of course, would run contrary to Establishment Clause concerns dating from the earliest days of the Republic. The apprehensions of our predecessors involved the levying of taxes upon the public for the sole and exclusive purpose of establishing and supporting specific sects. The exaction here, by contrast, is a student activity fee designed to reflect the reality that student life in its many dimensions includes the necessity of wide-ranging speech and inquiry and that student expression is an integral part of the University's educational mission. . . . [841] . . . . [842] . . . .

It does not violate the Establishment Clause for a public university to grant access to its facilities on a religion-neutral basis to a wide spectrum of student groups, including groups which use meeting rooms for sectarian activities, accompanied by some devotional exercises. *See Widmar*, 454 U.S. at 269; *Bd. of Educ. of Westside Cmty. Sch. v. Mergens*, 496 U.S. 226, 252 (1990). This is so even where the upkeep, maintenance, and repair of the facilities [843] attributed to those uses is paid from a student activities fund to which students are required to contribute. *Widmar, supra*, at 265. The government usually acts by spending money. Even the provision of a meeting room, as in *Mergens* and *Widmar*, involved governmental expenditure, if only in the form of electricity and heating or cooling costs. The error made by the Court of Appeals, as well as by the dissent, lies in focusing on the money that is undoubtedly expended by the government, rather than on the nature of the benefit received by the recipient. If the expenditure of governmental funds is prohibited whenever those funds pay for a service that is, pursuant to a religion-neutral program, used by a group for sectarian purposes, then *Widmar, Mergens*, and *Lamb's Chapel* would have to be overruled. Given our holdings in these cases, it follows that a public university may maintain its own computer facility and give student groups access to that facility, including the use of the printers, on a religion neutral, say first-come-first-served, basis. If a religious student organization obtained access on that religion-neutral basis and used a computer to compose or a printer or copy machine to print speech with a religious content or viewpoint, the State's action in providing the group with access would no more violate the Establishment Clause than would giving those groups access to an assembly hall. *See Lamb's Chapel v. Ctr. Moriches Union Free Sch. Dist.*, 508 U.S. 384 (1993); *Widmar, supra*; *Mergens, supra*.   ... [844] ....

It is, of course, true that if the State pays a church's bills it is subsidizing it, and we must guard against this abuse. That is not a danger here, based on the considerations we have advanced and for the additional reason that the student publication is not a religious institution, at least in the usual sense of that term as used in our case law, and it is not a religious organization as used in the University's own regulations. It is instead a publication involved in a pure forum for the expression of ideas, ideas that would be both incomplete and chilled were the Constitution to be interpreted to require that state officials and courts scan the publication to ferret out views that principally manifest a belief in a divine being.   ... [845–846] ....

The judgment of the Court of Appeals must be, and is, reversed.

DISSENT: JUSTICE SOUTER, with whom JUSTICE STEVENS, JUSTICE GINSBURG and JUSTICE BREYER join, dissenting.

The Court today, for the first time, approves direct funding of core religious activities by an arm of the State. ... [864] ... I would hold that the University's refusal to support petitioners' religious activities is compelled by the Establishment Clause. ...

I

The central question in this case is whether a grant from the Student Activities Fund to pay Wide Awake's printing expenses would violate the Establishment Clause. ... The Court's principal reliance, however, is on an argument that providing religion with economically valuable services is permissible on the theory that services are economically indistinguishable from religious access to governmental speech forums, which sometimes is permissible. But this reasoning would commit the Court to approving direct religious aid beyond anything justifiable for the sake of access to speaking forums. ... [865] ...

A   ... [866–868] ....

Using public funds for the direct subsidization of preaching the word is categorically forbidden under the Establishment Clause, and if the Clause was meant to accomplish nothing else, it was meant to bar this use of public money. Evidence on the subject antedates even the Bill of Rights itself, as may be seen in the writings of Madison, whose authority on questions about the meaning of the Establishment Clause is well settled. Four years before the First Congress proposed the First Amendment, Madison gave his opinion on the legitimacy of using public funds for religious purposes, in the *Memorial and Remonstrance Against Religious Assessments*, which played the central role in ensuring the defeat of the Virginia tax assessment bill in 1786 and framed the debate upon which the Religion Clauses stand: "Who does not see that ... the same authority which can force a citizen to contribute three pence only of his property for the support of any one establishment, may force him to conform to any other establishment in all cases whatsoever?" James Madison, *Memorial and Remonstrance Against Religious Assessments* ¶3 (hereinafter Madison's *Remonstrance*), *reprinted in Everson v. Bd. of Educ. of Ewing, supra*, at 65–66 (appendix to dissent of Rutledge, J.).   [869–872] . . . .

[873] The principle against direct funding with public money is patently violated by the contested use of today's student activity fee. Like today's taxes generally, the fee is Madison's three pence. The University exercises the power of the State to compel a student to pay it, *see* Thomas Jefferson, *Preamble* to *A Bill for Establishing Religious Freedom, reprinted in* 5 *The Founder's Constitution* 84, 84 (Philip B. Kurland & Ralph Lerner eds., 1987), and the use of any part of it for the direct support of religious activity thus strikes at what we have repeatedly [874] held to be the heart of the prohibition on establishment. *Everson*, 330 U.S. at 15–16 ("The 'establishment of religion clause' . . . means at least this. . . . No tax in any amount, large or small, can be levied to support any religious activities or institutions, whatever they may be called, or whatever form they may adopt to teach or practice religion"); *see Sch. Dist. of Grand Rapids v. Ball*, 473 U.S. 373, 385 (1985) ("Although Establishment Clause jurisprudence is characterized by few absolutes, the Clause does absolutely prohibit government-financed or government-sponsored indoctrination into the beliefs of a particular religious faith"); *Comm. for Pub. Educ. v. Nyquist*, 413 U.S. 756, 780 (1973) ("In the absence of an effective means of guaranteeing that the state aid derived from public funds will be used exclusively for secular, neutral, and nonideological purposes, it is clear from our cases that direct aid in whatever form is invalid") . . . .

The Court, accordingly, has never before upheld direct state funding of the sort of proselytizing published in *Wide* [875] *Awake* and, in fact, has categorically condemned state programs directly aiding religious activity, *Sch. Dist. v. Ball, supra*, at 395 (striking programs providing secular instruction to nonpublic school students on nonpublic school premises because they are "indistinguishable from the provision of a direct cash subsidy to the religious school that is most clearly prohibited under the Establishment Clause") . . . .

Even when the Court has upheld aid to an institution performing both secular and sectarian functions, it has always made a searching enquiry to ensure that the institution kept the secular activities separate from its sectarian ones, with any direct aid flowing only to the former and never the latter. [876]   . . . .

B   . . . [877–878] . . .

In order to understand how the Court thus begins with sound rules but ends with an unsound result, it is necessary to explore those rules in greater detail than the Court does. . . . [T]he relationship between the prohibition on direct aid and the requirement of evenhandedness when affirmative government aid does result in some benefit to religion reflects the relationship between basic rule and marginal criterion. At the heart of the Establishment Clause stands the prohibition against direct public funding, but that prohibition does not answer the questions that occur at the margins of the Clause's application. Is any government activity that provides any incidental benefit to religion likewise unconstitutional? Would it be wrong to put out fires in burning churches, wrong to pay the bus fares of students on the way [879] to parochial schools, wrong to allow a grantee of special education funds to spend them at a religious college? These are the questions that call for drawing lines, and it is in drawing them that evenhandedness becomes important. However the Court may in the past have phrased its line-drawing test, the question whether such benefits are provided on an evenhanded basis has been relevant, for the question addresses one aspect of the issue whether a law is truly neutral with respect to religion (that is, whether the law either "advance[s] [or] inhibit[s] religion," *Allegheny County v. ACLU*, 492 U.S. 573, 592 (1989)). In *Widmar v. Vincent*, 454 U.S. 263, 274 (1981), for example, we noted that "[t]he provision of benefits to [a] broad . . . spectrum of [religious and nonreligious] groups is an important index of secular effect." *See also Bd. of Educ. of Kiryas Joel Vill. Sch. Dist. v. Grumet*, 512 U.S. 687, 702–705 (1994). In the doubtful cases (those not involving direct public funding), where there is initially room for argument about a law's effect, evenhandedness serves to weed out those laws that impermissibly advance religion by channeling aid to it exclusively. Evenhandedness is therefore a prerequisite to further enquiry into the constitutionality of a doubtful law, but evenhandedness goes no further. It does not guarantee success under Establishment Clause scrutiny.

Three cases permitting indirect aid to religion, *Mueller v. Allen*, 463 U.S. 388 (1983), *Witters v. Washington Department of Services for the Blind*, 474 U.S. 481 (1986), and *Zobrest v. Catalina Foothills School District*, 509 U.S. 1 (1993), are among the latest of those to illustrate this relevance of evenhandedness when advancement is not so obvious as to be patently unconstitutional. [880] Each case involved a program in which benefits given to individuals on a religion-neutral basis ultimately were used by the individuals, in one way or another, to support religious institutions. In each, the fact that aid was distributed generally and on a neutral basis was a necessary condition for upholding the program at issue. *Witters, supra,* at 487–488; *Mueller, supra,* at 397–399; *Zobrest, supra,* at 10–11. But the significance of evenhandedness stopped there. We did not, in any of these cases, hold that satisfying the condition was sufficient, or dispositive. Even more importantly, we never held that evenhandedness might be sufficient to render direct aid to religion constitutional. Quite the contrary. Critical to our decisions in these cases was the fact that the aid was indirect; it reached religious institutions "only as a result of the genuinely independent and private choices of aid recipients," *Witters, supra,* at 487; *see also Mueller, supra,* at 399–400; *Zobrest, supra,* at 10–13. In noting and relying on this particular feature of each of the programs at issue, we in fact reaffirmed the core prohibition on direct funding of religious activities. *See Zobrest, supra,* at 12–13; *Witters, supra,* at 487; *see also Mueller, supra,* at 399–400. Thus, our holdings in these cases were little more than extensions of the unremarkable proposition that "a State may issue a paycheck to one of its employees, who may then donate all or part of that paycheck to a religious institution, all without constitutional barrier. . . ." *Witters, supra,* at 486–487. . . . [881] . . .

[882] Evenhandedness as one element of a permissibly attenuated benefit is, of course, a far cry from evenhandedness as a sufficient condition of constitutionality for direct financial support of religious proselytization, and our cases have unsurprisingly repudiated any such attempt to cut the Establishment Clause down to a mere prohibition against unequal direct aid. . . .

. . . .

CHAPTER 3

Speech, Offense, and Threats

A THEORY OF FREEDOM OF EXPRESSION

—*Thomas Scanlon*—

I

. . . The doctrine of freedom of expression is generally thought to single out a class of "protected acts" which it holds to be immune from restrictions to which other acts are subject. In particular, on any very strong version of the doctrine there will be cases where protected acts are held to be immune from restriction despite the fact that they have as consequences harms which would normally be sufficient to justify the imposition of legal sanctions. It is the existence of such cases which makes freedom of expression a significant doctrine and which makes it appear, from a certain point of view, an irrational one. . . .

To answer this charge of irrationality is the main task of a philosophical defense of freedom of expression. Such an answer requires, first, a clear account of what the class of protected acts is, and then an explanation of the nature and grounds of its privilege. The most common defense of the doctrine of freedom of expression is a consequentialist one. This may take the form of arguing with respect to a certain class of acts, e.g., acts of speech, that the good consequences of allowing such acts to go unrestricted outweigh the bad. Alternatively, the boundaries of the class of protected acts may themselves be *defined* by balancing good consequences against bad, the question of whether a certain species of acts belongs to the privileged genus being decided in many if not all cases just by asking whether its inclusion would, on the whole, lead to more good consequences than bad. . . . Thus one thing which an adequate philosophical account of freedom of expression should do is to make clear in what way the definition of the class of protected acts and the justification for their privilege depend upon a balancing of competing goals or interests and to what extent they rest instead on rights or other absolute, i.e., nonconsequentialist, principles. . . .

II

. . . I want to begin by considering arguments which, like disclaimers of responsibility, have the effect of showing that what might at first seem to be reasons for restricting a class of acts cannot be taken as such reasons at all.

My main reason for beginning in this way is this: it is easier to say what the classic violations of freedom of expression have in common than it is to define the class of acts which is protected by that doctrine. What distinguishes these violations from innocent regulation of expression is not the character of the acts they interfere with but rather what they hope to achieve—for instance, the halting of the spread of heretical notions. This suggests that an important component of our intuitions about freedom of expression has to do not with the illegitimacy of certain restrictions but with the illegitimacy of certain justifications for restrictions. Very crudely, the intuition seems to be something like this: those justifications are illegitimate which appeal to the fact that it would be a bad thing if the view communicated by certain acts of expression were to become generally believed; justifications which are legitimate, though they may sometimes be overridden, are those that appeal to features of acts of expression (time, place, loudness) other than the views they communicate.

As a principle of freedom of expression this is obviously unsatisfactory as it stands. For one thing, it rests on a rather unclear notion of "the view communicated" by an act of expression; for another, it seems too restrictive, since, for example, it appears to rule out any justification for laws against defamation. In order to improve upon this crude formulation, I want to consider a number of different ways in which acts of expression can bring about harms, concentrating on cases where these harms clearly can be counted as reasons for restricting the acts that give rise to them. I will then try to formulate the principle in a way which accommodates these cases. I emphasize at the outset that I am not maintaining in any of these cases that the harms in question are always sufficient justification for restrictions on expression, but only that they can always be taken into account.

1. Like other acts, acts of expression can bring about injury or damage as a direct physical consequence. This is obviously true of the more bizarre forms of expression mentioned above, but no less true of more pedestrian forms: the sound of my voice can break glass, wake the sleeping, trigger an avalanche, or keep you from paying attention to something else you would rather hear. It seems clear that when harms brought about in this way are intended by the person performing an act of expression, or when he is reckless or negligent with respect to their occurrence, then no infringement of freedom of expression is involved in considering them as possible grounds for criminal penalty or civil action.

2. It is typical of the harms just considered that their production is in general quite independent of the view which the given act of expression is intended to communicate. This is not generally true of a second class of harms, an example of which is provided by the common law notion of assault. In at least one of the recognized senses of the term, an assault (as distinct from a battery) is committed when one person intentionally places another in apprehension of imminent bodily harm. Since assault in this sense involves an element of successful communication, instances of assault may necessarily involve expression. But assaults and related acts can also be part of larger acts of expression, as for example when a guerrilla theater production takes the form of a mock bank robbery which starts off looking like the real thing, or when a bomb scare is used to gain attention for a political cause. Assault is sometimes treated as inchoate battery, but it can also be viewed as a separate offense which consists in actually bringing about a specific kind of harm. Under this analysis, assault is only one of a large class of possible crimes which consist in the production in others of harmful or unpleasant states of mind, such as fear, shock, and perhaps certain kinds of offense. One may have doubts as to whether most of these harms are serious enough to be recognized by the law or whether standards of proof could be established for dealing with them in court. In principle, however, there seems to be no alternative to including them among the possible justifications for restrictions on expression.

3. Another way in which an act of expression can harm a person is by causing others to form an adverse opinion of him or by making him an object of public ridicule. Obvious examples of this are defamation and interference with the right to a fair trial.

4. As Justice Holmes said, "The most stringent protection of free speech would not protect a man in falsely shouting fire in a theater and causing a panic."[1]

5. One person may through an act of expression contribute to the production of a harmful act by someone else, and at least in some cases the harmful consequences of the latter act may justify making the former a crime as well. This seems to many people to be the case when the act of expression is the issuance of an order or the making of a threat or when it is a signal or other communication between confederates.

6. Suppose some misanthropic inventor were to discover a simple method whereby anyone could make nerve gas in his kitchen out of gasoline, table salt, and urine. It seems just as clear to me that he could be prohibited by law from passing out his recipe on handbills or broadcasting it on television as that he could be prohibited from passing out free samples of his product in aerosol cans or putting it on sale at

Abercrombie & Fitch. In either case his action would bring about a drastic decrease in the general level of personal safety by radically increasing the capacity of most citizens to inflict harm on each other. The fact that he does this in one case through an act of expression and in the other through some other form of action seems to me not to matter.

It might happen, however, that a comparable decrease in the general level of personal safety could be just as reliably predicted to result from the distribution of a particularly effective piece of political propaganda which would undermine the authority of the government, or from the publication of a theological tract which would lead to a schism and a bloody civil war. In these cases the matter seems to me to be entirely different, and the harmful consequence seems clearly not to be a justification for restricting the acts of expression.

What I conclude from this is that the distinction between expression and other forms of action is less important than the distinction between expression which moves others to act by pointing out what they take to be good reasons for action and expression which gives rise to action by others in other ways, e.g., by providing them with the means to do what they wanted to do anyway. This conclusion is supported, I think, by our normal views about legal responsibility.

If I were to say to you, an adult in full possession of your faculties "What you ought to do is rob a bank," and you were subsequently to act on this advice, I could not be held legally responsible for your act, nor could my act legitimately be made a separate crime. This remains true if I supplement my advice with a battery of arguments about why banks should be robbed or even about why a certain bank in particular should be robbed and why you in particular are entitled to rob it. It might become false—what I did might legitimately be made a crime—if certain further conditions held: for example, if you were a child, or so weak-minded as to be legally incompetent, and I knew this or ought to have known it; or if you were my subordinate in some organization and what I said to you was not advice but an order, backed by the discipline of the group; or if I went on to make further contributions to your act, such as aiding you in preparations or providing you with tools or giving you crucial information about the bank.

The explanation for these differences seems to me to be this. A person who acts on reasons he has acquired from another's act of expression acts on what *he* has come to believe and has judged to be a sufficient basis for action. The contribution to the genesis of his action made by the act of expression is, so to speak, superseded by the agent's own judgment. This is not true of the contribution made by an accomplice, or by a person who knowingly provides the agent with tools (the key to the bank) or with technical information (the combination of the safe) which he uses to achieve his ends. Nor would it be true of my contribution to your act if, instead of providing you with reasons for thinking bank robbery a good thing, I issued orders or commands backed by threats, thus changing your circumstances so as to *make* it a (comparatively) good thing for you to do. . . .

I will now state the principle of freedom of expression which was promised at the beginning of this section. The principle, which seems to me to be a natural extension of the thesis Mill defends in Chapter II of *On Liberty,* and which I will therefore call the Millian Principle, is the following:

> *There are certain harms which, although they would not occur but for certain acts of expression, nonetheless cannot be taken as part of a justification for legal restrictions on these acts. These harms are: (a) harms to certain individuals which consist in their coming to have false beliefs as a result of those acts of expression; (b) harmful consequences of acts performed as a result of those acts of expression, where the connection between the acts of expression and the subsequent harmful acts consists merely in the fact that the act of expression led the agents to believe (or increased their tendency to believe) these acts to be worth performing.*

I hope it is obvious that this principle is compatible with the examples of acceptable reasons for restricting expression presented in 1 through 6 above. (One case in which this may not be obvious, that of the man who falsely shouts "fire," will be discussed more fully below.) The preceding discussion, which appealed in part to intuitions about legal responsibility, was intended to make plausible the distinction on which the second part of the Millian Principle rests and, in general, to suggest how the principle could be reconciled with cases of the sort included in 5 and 6. But the principle itself goes beyond questions of responsibility. In order for a class of harms to provide a justification for restricting a person's act it is not necessary that he fulfill conditions for being legally responsible for any of the individual acts which actually produce those harms. In the nerve-gas case, for example, to claim that distribution of the recipe may be prevented one need not claim that a person who distributed it could be held legally responsible (even as an accessory) for any of the particular murders the gas is used to commit. Consequently, to explain why this case differs from sedition it would not be sufficient to claim that providing means involves responsibility while providing reasons does not.

I would like to believe that the general observance of the Millian Principle by governments would, in the long run, have more good consequences than bad. But my defense of the principle does not rest on this optimistic outlook. I will argue in the next section that the Millian Principle, as a general principle about how governmental restrictions on the liberty of citizens may be justified, is a consequence of the view, coming down to us from Kant and others, that a legitimate government is one whose authority citizens can recognize while still regarding themselves as equal, autonomous, rational agents. Thus, while it is not a principle about legal responsibility, the Millian Principle has its origins in a certain view of human agency from which many of our ideas about responsibility also derive.

Taken by itself, the Millian Principle obviously does not constitute an adequate theory of freedom of expression. Much more needs to be said about when the kinds of harmful consequences which the principle allows us to consider can be taken to be sufficient justification for restrictions on expression. Nonetheless, it seems to me fair to call the Millian Principle the basic principle of freedom of expression. This is so, first, because a successful defense of the principle would provide us with an answer to the charge of irrationality by explaining why certain of the most obvious consequences of acts of expression cannot be appealed to as a justification for legal restrictions against them. . . .

III

. . . To regard himself as autonomous in the sense I have in mind a person must see himself as sovereign in deciding what to believe and in weighing competing reasons for action. He must apply to these tasks his own canons of rationality, and must recognize the need to defend his beliefs and decisions in accordance with these canons. . . . An autonomous person cannot accept without independent consideration the judgment of others as to what he should believe or what he should do. He may rely on the judgment of others, but when he does so he must be prepared to advance independent reasons for thinking their judgment likely to be correct, and to weigh the evidential value of their opinion against contrary evidence.

The requirements of autonomy as I have so far described them are extremely weak. They are much weaker than the requirements Kant draws from essentially the same notion,[2] in that being autonomous in my sense (like being free in Hobbes's) is quite consistent with being subject to coercion with respect to one's actions. A coercer merely changes the considerations which militate for or against a certain course of action; weighing these conflicting considerations is still up to you.

An autonomous man may, if he believes the appropriate arguments, believe that the state has a distinctive right to command him. That is, he may believe that (within certain limits, perhaps) the fact that the law requires a certain action provides him with a very strong reason for performing that action, a reason which is quite independent of the consequences, for him or others, of his performing it or refraining. How strong this reason is—what, if anything, could override it—will depend on his view of the arguments for obedience to law. What is essential to the person's remaining autonomous is that in any given case his mere recognition that a certain action is required by law does not settle the question of whether he will do it. That question is settled only by his own decision, which may take into account his current assessment of the general case for obedience and the exceptions it admits, consideration of his other duties and obligations, and his estimate of the consequences of obedience and disobedience in this particular case.[3]

Thus, while it is not obviously inconsistent with being autonomous to recognize a special obligation to obey the commands of the state, there are limits on the *kind* of obligation which autonomous citizens could recognize. In particular, they could not regard themselves as being under an "obligation" to believe the decrees of the state to be correct, nor could they concede to the state the right to have its decrees obeyed without deliberation. The Millian Principle can be seen as a refinement of these limitations.

The apparent irrationality of the doctrine of freedom of expression derives from its apparent conflict with the principle that it is the prerogative of a state—indeed, part of its duty to its citizens—to decide when the threat of certain harms is great enough to warrant legal action, and when it is, to make laws adequate to meet this threat. (Thus Holmes's famous reference to "substantive evils that Congress has a right to prevent.")[4] Obviously this principle is not acceptable in the crude form in which I have just stated it; no one thinks that Congress can do *anything* it judges to be required to save us from "substantive evils." The Millian Principle specifies two ways in which this prerogative must be limited if the state is to be acceptable to autonomous subjects. The argument for the first part of the principle is as follows.

The harm of coming to have false beliefs is not one that an autonomous man could allow the state to protect him against through restrictions on expression. For a law to provide such protection it would have to be in effect and deterring potential misleaders while the potentially misled remained susceptible to persuasion by them. In order to be protected by such a law a person would thus have to concede to the state the right to decide that certain views were false and, once it had so decided, to prevent him from hearing them advocated even if he might wish to. The conflict between doing this and remaining autonomous would be direct if a person who authorized the state to protect him in this way necessarily also bound himself to accept the state's judgment about which views were false. The matter is not quite this simple, however, since it is conceivable that a person might authorize the state to act for him in this way while still reserving to himself the prerogative of deciding, on the basis of the arguments and evidence left available to him, where the truth was to be found. But such a person would be "deciding for himself" only in an empty sense, since in any case where the state exercised its prerogative he would be "deciding" on the basis of evidence preselected to include only that which supported one conclusion. While he would not be under an obligation to accept the state's judgment as correct, he would have conceded to the state the right to deprive him of grounds for making an independent judgment.

The argument for the second half of the Millian Principle is parallel to this one. What must be argued against is the view that the state, once it has declared certain conduct to be illegal, may when necessary move to prevent that conduct by outlawing its advocacy. The conflict between this thesis and the autonomy of citizens is, just as in the previous case, slightly oblique. Conceding to the state the right to use this means to secure compliance with its laws does not immediately involve conceding to it the right to require citizens to believe that what the law says ought not to be done ought not to be done. Nonetheless, it is a concession that autonomous citizens could not make, since it gives the state the right to deprive citizens of the grounds for arriving at an independent judgment as to whether the law should be obeyed.

These arguments both depend on the thesis that to defend a certain belief as reasonable a person must be prepared to defend the grounds of his belief as not obviously skewed or otherwise suspect. There is a clear parallel between this thesis and Mill's famous argument that if we are interested in having truth prevail we should allow all available arguments to be heard.[5] But the present argument does not depend, as Mill's may appear to, on an empirical claim that the truth is in fact more likely to win out if free discussion is allowed. Nor does it depend on the perhaps more plausible claim that, given the nature of people and governments, to concede to governments the power in question would be an outstandingly poor strategy for bringing about a situation in which true opinions prevail.

It is quite conceivable that a person who recognized in himself a fatal weakness for certain kinds of bad arguments might conclude that everyone would be better off if he were to rely entirely on the judgment of his friends in certain crucial matters. Acting on this conclusion, he might enter into an agreement, subject to periodic review by him, empowering them to shield him from any sources of information likely to divert him from their counsel on the matters in question. Such an agreement is not obviously irrational, nor, if it is entered into voluntarily, for a limited time, and on the basis of the person's own knowledge of himself and those he proposes to trust, does it appear to be inconsistent with his autonomy. The same would be true if the proposed trustees were in fact the authorities of the state. But the question we have been considering is quite different: Could an autonomous individual regard the state as having, not as part of a special voluntary agreement with him but as part of its normal powers qua state, the power to put such an arrangement into effect without his consent whenever *it* (i.e., the legislative authority) judged that to be advisable? The answer to this question seems to me to be quite clearly no. . . .

IV

The Millian Principle is obviously incapable of accounting for all of the cases that strike us as infringements of freedom of expression. On the basis of this principle alone we could raise no objection against a government that banned all parades or demonstrations (they interfere with traffic), outlawed posters and handbills (too messy), banned public meetings of more than ten people (likely to be unruly), and restricted newspaper publication to one page per week (to save trees). Yet such policies surely strike us as intolerable. That they so strike us is a reflection of our belief that free expression is a good which ranks above the maintenance of absolute peace and quiet, clean streets, smoothly flowing traffic, and rock-bottom taxes.

Thus there is a part of our intuitive view of freedom of expression which rests upon a balancing of competing goods. By contrast with the Millian Principle, which provides a single defense for all kinds of expression, here it does not seem to be a matter of the value to be placed on expression (in general) as opposed to other goods. The case seems to be different for, say, artistic expression than for the discussion of scientific matters, and different still for expression of political views.

Within certain limits, it seems clear that the value to be placed on having various kinds of expression flourish is something which should be subject to popular will in the society in question. The limits I have in mind here are, first, those imposed by considerations of distributive justice. Access to means of expression for whatever purposes one may have in mind is a good which can be fairly or unfairly distributed among the members of a society, and many cases which strike us as violations of freedom of expression are in fact instances of distributive injustice. This would be true of a case where, in an economically inegalitarian society, access to the principal means of expression was controlled by the government and auctioned off by it to the highest bidders, as is essentially the case with broadcasting licenses in the United States today. . . .

NOTES

[1] In *Schenck v. United States*, 249 U.S. 47 (1919).

[2] Kant's notion of autonomy goes beyond the one I employ in that for him there are special requirements regarding the reasons which an autonomous being can act on. (See the second and third sections of *Foundations of the Metaphysics of Morals*.) While his notion of autonomy is stronger than mine, Kant does not draw from it the same limitations on the authority of states (see *Metaphysical Elements of Justice*, sections 46–49).

[3] I am not certain whether I am here agreeing or disagreeing with Robert Paul Wolff (*In Defense of Anarchism* [New York, 1970]). At any rate I would not call what I am maintaining anarchism. The limitation on state power I have in mind is that described by John Rawls in the closing paragraphs of "The Justification of Civil Disobedience," in *Civil Disobedience: Theory and Practice*, ed. Hugo Bedau (New York, 1969).

[4] In *Schenck v. United States*.

[5] In chap. II of *On Liberty*.

LIMITS TO THE FREEDOM OF EXPRESSION

—Joel Feinberg—

. . . Despite the impressive case for complete liberty of expression, there are obvious instances where permitting a person to speak his mind freely will cause more harm than good all around. These instances have been lumped together in various distinct legal categories whose names have come to stand for torts or crimes and to suggest, by a powerful linguistic convention, unpermitted wrongdoing. Thus, there can be no more right to defame or to incite to riot than there can be a right way, in Aristotle's example,[1] to commit adultery. Underlying these linguistic conventions, however, is a settled residue of interest weightings as well as actual and hypothetical applications of the harm principle, often filled in or mediated in various ways by principles of other kinds. The various categories of excluded expressions are worth examining not only for the light they throw on the harm principle, but also for the conceptual and normative problems each raises on its own for political theory.

DEFAMATION AND "MALICIOUS TRUTH"

Defamatory statements are those that damage a person's reputation by their expression to third parties in a manner that "tends to diminish the esteem in which the plaintiff is held, or to excite adverse feelings or opinions against him."[2] The primary mode of discouraging defamers in countries adhering to the common law has been the threat of civil liability to a court-enforced order to pay cash to the injured party in compensation for the harm done his reputation. In cases of especially malicious defamation, the defendant may be ordered to pay a stiff fine ("punitive damages") to the plaintiff as well. Only in the most egregious cases (and rarely even then) has criminal liability been imposed for defamation, but nevertheless the threat of civil suit is sufficient to entitle us to say that our law does not leave citizens (generally) free to defame one another. Here then is one clear limit to our freedom of expression.

Not all expressions that harm another's reputation, of course, are legally forbidden. Even when damaging defamation has been proved by the plaintiff, the defendant may yet escape liability by establishing one of two kinds of defense. He may argue that his utterance or publication was "privileged," or simply that it is true. The former defense is established by showing either that the defendant, in virtue of his public office or his special relation to the plaintiff, has been granted an absolute immunity from liability for defamation (for example, he spoke in a judicial or legislative proceeding, or he had the prior consent of the plaintiff), or that he had a prior immunity contingent on the reasonableness of his conduct. Examples of this category of privilege are the immunity of a person protecting himself or another by a warning that someone is of poor character, or of a drama, literary, or political critic making "fair comment" of an extremely unfavorable kind about a performance, book, or policy. These immunities are still other

FEINBERG, Joel; *FREEDOM AND FULFILLMENT.* © 1992 Princeton University Press. Reprinted by permission of Princeton University Press.

examples of public policies that protect an interest (in this case, the interest in reputation) just to the point where the protection interferes with interests deemed more important—either to the public in general or to other private individuals. These policies imply that a person's reputation is a precious thing that deserves legal protection just as his life, health, and property do, but on the other hand, a certain amount of rough handling of reputations is to be expected in courtrooms, in the heated spontaneous debates of legislative chambers, in reviews of works presented to the public for critical comment, and in the rough-and-tumble competition among eminent persons for power or public acclaim. To withhold immunities in these special contexts would be to allow nervous inhibitions to keep hard truths out of law courts to the detriment of justice, or out of legislatures to the detriment of the laws themselves; or to make critics overly cautious, to the detriment of those who rely on their judgments; or to make political commentators overly deferential to power and authority, to the detriment of reform.

There is, however, no public interest in keeping those who are not in these special contexts uninhibited when they speak or write about others. Indeed, we should all be nervous when we make unfavorable comments, perhaps not on the ground that feelings and reputations will simply be damaged (there may be both justice and social gain in such damage), but at least on the ground that the unfavorable comment may be false. In a way, the rationale for the defamation action at law is the opposite of Mill's case for the free expression of opinion. The great public interest in possessing the truth in science, philosophy, politics, and so on, is best served by keeping everyone uninhibited in the expression of his views; but there are areas where there is a greater interest in avoiding falsehood than in acquiring truth, and here we are best served by keeping people very nervous indeed when they are tempted to speak their minds.

Once the plaintiff has proved that the defendant has published a defamatory statement about him, the defendant may avoid liability in another way, namely, by showing that the statement in question is true. "Out of a tender regard for reputations," writes William L. Prosser, "the law presumes in the first instance that all defamation is false, and the defendant has the burden of pleading and proving its truth."[3] In the large majority of American jurisdictions, truth is a "complete defense" that will relieve the defendant of liability even when he published his defamation merely out of spite, in the absence of any reasonable social purpose. One wonders why this should be. Is the public interest in "the truth" so great that it should always override a private person's interest in his own reputation? An affirmative answer, I should think, would require considerable argument.

Most of the historical rationales for the truth defense worked out in courts and legal treatises will not stand scrutiny. They all founder, I think, on the following kind of case. A New York girl supports her drug addiction by working as a prostitute in a seedy environment of crime and corruption. After a brief jail sentence, she decides to reform, and travels to the Far West to begin her life anew. She marries a respectable young man, becomes a leader in civic and church affairs, and rears a large and happy family. Then twenty years after her arrival in town, her neurotically jealous neighbor learns of her past, and publishes a lurid but accurate account of it for the eyes of the whole community. As a consequence, her "friends" and associates snub her; she is asked to resign her post as church leader; gossipmongers prattle ceaselessly about her; and obscene inscriptions appear on her property and in her mail. She dare not sue her neighbor for defamation since the defamatory report is wholly true. She has been wronged, but she has no legal remedy.

Applied to this case the leading rationales for the truth defense are altogether unconvincing. One argument claims that the true gravamen of the wrong in defamation is the deception practiced on the public in misrepresenting the truth, so that where there is no misrepresentation there is no injury—as if the injury to the reformed sinner is of no account. A variant of this argument holds the reformed sinner to be deserving of exposure on the ground that in covering up her past she deceives the public, thereby compounding the earlier delinquency. If this sort of "deception" is morally blameworthy, then so is every form of "covering up the truth," from cosmetics to window blinds! Others have argued that a delinquent plaintiff should not be allowed any standing in court because of his established bad character. A related contention is that "a person is in no position to complain of a reputation which is consistent with his actual character and behavior."[4] Both of these rationales apply well enough to the unrepentant sinner, but work nothing but injustice and suffering on the reformed person, on the plaintiff defamed in some way that does not reflect upon his character, or on the person whose "immoralities" have been wholly private and scrupulously kept from the public eye. It does not follow from the fact that a person's reputation is consistent with the truth that it is "deserved."

The most plausible kind of argument for the truth defense is that it serves some kind of overriding public interest. Some have argued that fear of eventual exposure can serve as effectively as the threat of punishment to deter wrongdoing. This argument justifies a kind of endless social penalty and is therefore more cruel than a system of criminal law, which usually permits a wrongdoer to wipe his slate clean. Others have claimed that exposure of character flaws and past sins protects the community by warning it of dangerous or untrustworthy persons. That argument is well put (but without endorsement) by Fowler V. Harper and Fleming James when they refer to "the social desirability as a general matter, of leaving individuals free to warn the public of antisocial members of the community, provided only that the person furnishing the information take the risk of its being false."[5] (William Blackstone went so far as to assert that the defendant who can show the truth of his defamatory remarks has rendered a public service in exposing the plaintiff and deserves the public's gratitude.[6]) This line of argument is convincing enough when restricted to public-spirited defamers and socially dangerous plaintiffs; but it lacks all plausibility when applied to the malicious and useless exposure of past misdeeds, or to non-moral failings and "moral" flaws of a wholly private and well-concealed kind.

How precious a thing, after all, is this thing denoted by the glittering abstract noun, the "Truth"? The truth in general is a great and noble cause, a kind of public treasury more important than any particular person's feelings; but the truth about a particular person may be of no great value at all except to that person. When the personal interest in reputation outweighs the dilute public interest in truth (and there is no doubt that this is sometimes the case) then it must be protected even at some cost to our general knowledge of the truth. The truth, like any other commodity, is not so valuable that it is a bargain at *any* cost. A growing number of American states have now modified the truth defense so that it applies only when the defamatory statement has been published with good motives, or is necessary for some reasonable public purpose, or (in some cases) both. The change is welcome.

In summary, the harm principle would permit all harmless statements about others whether true or false (harmless statements by definition are not defamatory), but it would impose liability for all defamatory false statements and all seriously defamatory true statements except those that serve (or seem likely to serve) some beneficial social purpose.

INVASIONS OF PRIVACY

Still other expressions are neither defamatory nor false, and yet they can unjustly wound the persons they describe all the same. These do not invade the interest in a good reputation so much as a special kind of interest in peace of mind, sometimes called a sense of dignity, sometimes the enjoyment of solitude, but most commonly termed the interest in personal privacy. As the legal "right to privacy" is now understood, it embraces a miscellany of things, protecting the right-holder not only from "physical intrusions upon his solitude" and "publicity given to his name or likeness or to private information about him" without his permission, but also from being placed "in a false light [but without defamation] in the public eye" and from the "commercial appropriation of elements of his personality."[7] (Some of these are really invasions of one's property rights through unpermitted commercial exploitation of one's name, image, personality, and so on. For that reason it has been urged that the invaded right in these cases be called "the right to publicity.") What concerns us here are statements conveying true and nondefamatory information about the plaintiff, of a very intimate and properly private kind, gathered and published without his consent, often to his shame and mortification. Business advantage and journalistic profit have become ever stronger motives for such statements, and the invention of tiny, very sensitive snooping devices has made the data easier than ever to come by.

Since the "invasion of privacy" tort has been recognized, plaintiffs have recovered damages from defendants who have shadowed them, looked into their windows, investigated their bank accounts, and tapped their telephone wires. In many of these cases, the court's judgment protected the plaintiff's interest in "being let alone," but in other cases the interest protected was not merely this, or not this at all, but rather the interest in *not being known about*. If there is a right not to be known about in some respects by anyone, than a fortiori there is a right not to be known about, in those respects, by nearly everyone. Privacy law has also protected the interests of those who do not want details of their lives called to the public's attention and made the subject of public wonder, amusement, discussion, analysis, or debate. Hence some plaintiffs have recovered from defendants who have published embarrassing details of their illness or physical deformity; their personal letters or unpublished notes, or inventories of their possessions; their photographs in a "good looks" popularity contest, or in a "before and after" advertisement for baldness or obesity cures, or on the labels of tomato cans; and from defendants who have published descriptions of the plaintiffs' sexual relations, hygienic habits, and other very personal matters. No life, of course, can be kept wholly private or immune from public inspection, even in some of its most personal aspects. "No one enjoys being stared at," Harper and James remind us, yet if a person "goes out on the street he [can have] no legal objection to people looking at him."[8] On the other hand, life would be hardly tolerable if there were no secrets we could keep (away from "the street"), no preserve of dignity, no guaranteed solitude.

There would probably be very little controversy over the existence of a right to privacy were it not the case that the interest in being let alone is frequently in conflict with other interests that seem at least equally deserving of protection. Even where the right is recognized by law, it is qualified by the recognition of very large classes of privileged expressions. First of all, like most other torts and crimes, the charge of invasion of privacy is completely defeated by proof that the plaintiff gave his consent to the defendant's conduct. Second, and more interesting, the right of privacy can conflict with the constitutionally guaranteed freedom of the press, which, according to Prosser, "justifies the publication of news and all other matters of legitimate public interest and concern."[9] For a court to adjudicate between a paper's right to publish and an individual's right to privacy, it must employ some standard for determining what is of legitimate public concern or, what amounts to the same thing, which news about a person is "fit to print." Such legal standards are always in the making, never finished, but the standard of "legitimate interest" has begun to take on a definite shape. American courts have decided, first of all, that "the person who intentionally puts himself in the public eye . . . has no right to complain of any publicity which reasonably bears on his activity."[10] The rationale for this judgment invokes the maxim that a person is not wronged by that to which he consents, or by that the risk of which he has freely assumed. The person who steps into the public spotlight ought to know what he is letting himself in for; hence the law presumes that he *does* know, and therefore that he is asking for it. Much the same kind of presumption lies behind the "fair comment" defense in defamation cases: The man who voluntarily publishes his own work is presumed to be inviting criticism and is therefore not entitled to complain when the criticism is adverse or harsh, providing only that it is relevant and not personally abusive. One can put oneself voluntarily into the public eye by running for or occupying public office; by becoming an actor, musician, entertainer, poet, or novelist; by inventing an interesting device or making a geographical or scientific discovery; or even by becoming wealthy. Once a person has become a public figure, he has sacrificed much of his right of privacy to the public's legitimate curiosity. Of course, one never forfeits *all* rights of privacy; even the public figure has a right to the privacy of his very most intimate affairs. (This may, however, be very small consolation to him.)

One cannot always escape the privilege of the press to invade one's privacy simply by avoiding public roles and offices, for the public spotlight can catch up with anyone. "Reluctant public characters" are nonetheless public and therefore, according to the courts, as legitimate objects of public curiosity as the voluntary public figures. Those unfortunates who attract attention unwillingly by becoming involved, even as victims, in accidents, or by being accused of crimes, or even as innocent bystanders to interesting events, have become "news," and therefore subject to the public's right to know. They maintain this unhappy status "until they have reverted to the lawful and unexciting life led by the great bulk of the community," but until then, "they are subject to the privileges which publishers have to satisfy the curiosity of the public as to their leaders, heroes, villains, and victims."[11] Again, the privilege to publish is not unlimited so that "the courts must somehow draw the distinction between conduct which outrages the common decencies and goes beyond what the public mores will tolerate, and that which the plaintiff must be expected in the circumstances to endure."[12]

When interests of quite different kinds head toward collisions, how can one determine which has the right of way? This problem, which lies behind the most puzzling questions about the grounds for liberty and coercion, tends to be concealed by broadly stated principles. The conflict between the personal interest in privacy and the public curiosity is one of the best illustrations of the problem, but it is hardly unique. In defamation cases, as we have seen, there is often a conflict between the public interest in truth and the plaintiff's interest in his own good name. In nuisance law, there is a conflict between the plaintiff's interest in the peaceful enjoyment of his land and the defendant's interest in keeping a hogpen, or a howling dog, or a small boiler factory. In suburban neighborhoods, the residents' interest in quiet often conflicts with motorcyclists' interest in cheap and speedy transportation. In buses and trains, one passenger's interest in privacy[13] can conflict with another's interest in listening to rock and roll music on a portable radio, or for that matter, with the interests of two nearby passengers in making unavoidably audible, but avoidably inane, conversation. The principle of "the more freedom the better" does not tell us whose freedom must give way in these competitive situations.

The invasion of privacy cases are among the very clearest examples of the inevitable clash of interests in populous modern communities. They are, moreover, examples that show that solving the problem is not just a matter of minimizing harm all around. Harm is the invasion of an interest, and invasions do differ in degree, but when interests of radically different kinds are invaded to the same degree, where is the greater harm? Perhaps we should say that some interests are more important than others in the sense that harm to them is likely to lead to greater damage to the whole economy of personal (or as the case may be, community) interests than harm to the lesser interest, just as harm to one's heart or brain will do more damage to one's bodily health than an "equal degree" of harm to less vital organs. Determining which interests are more "vital" in an analogous sense would be no easy task, but even if we could settle this matter, there would remain serious difficulties. In the first place, interests pile up and reinforce one another. My interest in peace and quiet may be more vital in my system than the motorcyclist's interests in speed, excitement, and economy are in his, but there is also the interest of the cyclist's employer in having workers efficiently transported to his factory, and the economic interest of the community in general (including me) in the flourishing of the factory owner's business; the interest of the motorcycle manufacturers in their own profits; the interest of the police and others (perhaps including me) in providing a relatively harmless outlet for adolescent exuberance, and in not having a difficult rule to enforce. There may be nowhere near so great a buildup of reinforcing interests, personal and public, in the quietude of my neighborhood.

There is still another kind of consideration that complicates the delicate task of interest-balancing. Interests differ not only in the extent to which they are thwarted, in their importance or "vitality," and the degree to which they are backed up by other interests, but also in their inherent moral quality. Some interests, simply by reason of their very natures, we might think better worth protecting than others. The interest in knowing the intimate details of Brigitte Bardot's married sex life (the subject of a sensational law suit in France) is a morally repugnant peeping tom's interest. The sadist's interest in having others suffer pain is a morbid interest. The interest in divulging a celebrity's private conversations is a busybody's interest. It is probably not conducive to the public good to encourage development of the character flaws from which these interests spring, but even if there were social advantage in the individual vices, there would be a case against protecting their spawned interests, based upon their inherent unworthiness. The interests in understanding, diagnosing, and simply being apprised of newsworthy events might well outbalance a given individual's reluctance to be known about, but photographs and descriptions with no plausible appeal except to the morbid and sensational can have very little weight in the scales.

CAUSING PANIC

Defamatory statements, "malicious truths," and statements that wrongfully invade privacy do harm to the persons they are about by conveying information or falsehood to third parties. Their publication tends to instill certain beliefs in others, and the very existence of those beliefs constitutes a harm to the person spoken or written about. Other classes of injurious expressions do harm in a rather different way, namely, by causing those who listen to them (or more rarely, those who read them) to act in violent or otherwise harmful ways. In these cases, the expressions need not be about any specifiable persons, or if they are about persons, those individuals are not necessarily the victims of the subsequent harm. When spoken words cause panic, breach the peace, or incite to crime or revolt, a variety of important interests, personal and social, will be seriously harmed. Such expressions, therefore, are typically proscribed by the criminal, and not merely the civil, law.

"The most stringent protection of free speech," wrote Holmes in his most celebrated opinion, "would not protect a man in falsely shouting fire in a theatre and causing a panic."[14] In some circumstances a person can cause even more harm by *truthfully* shouting "Fire!" in a crowded theater, for the flames and smoke might reinforce the tendency of his words to cause panic, and the fire itself might block exits, leading the hysterical crowds to push and trample. But we do not, and cannot fairly, hold the excited alarm-sounder criminally responsible for his warning when it was in fact true and shouted with good intentions. We can hardly demand on pain of punishment that persons pick their words carefully in emergencies, when emotions naturally run high and there is no time for judicious deliberation. A person's warning shout in such circumstances is hardly to be treated as a full-fledged voluntary act at all. Perhaps it can be condemned as negligent, but given the mitigating circumstances, such negligence hardly amounts to the gross and wanton kind that can be a basis of criminal liability. The law, then, can only punish harmful words of this class when they are spoken or written with the intention of causing the harm that in fact ensues, or when they are spoken or written in conscious disregard of a high and unreasonable risk that the harm will ensue. The practical joker in a crowded auditorium who whispers to his comrade, "Watch me start a panic," and then shouts, "Fire!" could be convicted for using words intentionally to cause a panic. The prankster who is willing to risk a general panic just for the fun of alarming one particular person in the audience could fairly be convicted for the grossly reckless use of dangerous words. Indeed, his recklessness is akin to that of the motorist who drives at an excessive speed just to frighten a timorous passenger.

Suppose, however, that the theater is virtually empty, and as the lights come on at the end of the film, our perverse or dim-witted jokester shouts, "Fire! Fire!" just for the sake of confusing the three or four other patrons and alarming the ushers. The ushers quickly see through the ruse and suffer only a few moments of anxiety, and the patrons walk quickly to the exits and depart. No harm to speak of has been done; nor could any have reasonably been anticipated. This example shows how very important are the surrounding circumstances of an utterance to the question of its permissibility. Given the presumptive case for liberty in general, and especially the powerful social interest in leaving persons free to use words as they see fit, there can be a countervailing case for suppression on the grounds of the words' dangerous tendency only when the danger in fact is great and the tendency immediate. These matters are determined not only by the particular words used, but by the objective character of the surrounding circumstances—what lawyers call "the time, place, and manner" of utterance.

The question of legal permissibility should not be confused with that of moral blameworthiness or even with civil liability. The practical joker, even in relatively harmless circumstances, is no moral paragon. But then neither are the liar, the vulgarian, the rude man, and the scandalmonger, most of whose faults are not fit subjects for penal legislation. We cannot make every instance of mendacity, rudeness, and malicious gossip criminal, but we can protect people from the serious injury that comes from fraud, battery, or defamation. Similarly, practical jokers should be blamed but not punished, unless their tricks reach the threshold of serious danger to others. On the other hand, almost all lies, bad tales, jokes, and tricks create some risk, and there is no injustice in making the perpetrator compensate (as opposed to being punished) even his unlikely victim. Thus, if a patron in the nearly empty theater described above sprains an ankle in hurrying toward an exit, there is no injustice in requiring the jokester to pay the medical expenses.

It is established in our law that when words did not in fact cause harm the speaker may nevertheless be punished for having uttered them only if there was high danger when they were spoken that serious harm would result. This condition of course could be satisfied even though the harm in fact was averted: Not everything probable becomes actual. Similarly, for a person rightly to be punished even for harm in fact caused by his words, the harm in its resultant magnitude must have been an objectively probable consequence of the spoken words in the circumstances; otherwise the speaker will be punished for an unforeseeable fluke. In either case, then, the clear and present danger that serious harm will follow a speaker's words is necessary if he is rightly to be punished.

As we have seen, punishment for the harm caused by words is proper only if the speaker caused the harm either *intentionally* or *recklessly*. Both of these "mental conditions" of guilt require the satisfaction of the clear and present danger formula, or something like it. Consider recklessness first. For there to be recklessness there must really be a substantial risk consciously and unreasonably run. A speaker is not being reckless if he utters words that have only a remote and speculative tendency to cause panics or riots.

Intentional harm-causing by words raises more complications. Suppose an evil-minded person wishes to cause a panic and believes what is false and wholly unsupported by any real evidence, namely, that his words will have that effect. Imagine that he attends a meeting of the Policemen's Benevolent Association and, at what he takes to be the strategic moment, he stands up and shrieks, "There's a mouse under my chair!" Perhaps these words would cause a panic at a meeting of boy scouts but it merely produces a round of contemptuous laughter here. Wanting a panic and sincerely believing that one is causing a panic by one's words, then, are not sufficient. Suppose, however, we complicate the story so that by some wholly unforeseeable fluke the spoken words do precipitate a panic. The story is hard to invent at this point, but let us imagine that one patrol officer laughs so hard that he tips over his chair causing another to drop his pipe, starting a fire, igniting live bullets, and so on. Now, in addition to evil desire and conscious belief in causal efficacy, we have a third important element: The words actually do initiate a causal process resulting in the desired panic. But these conditions still are not sufficient to permit us to say that the speaker *intentionally caused* a panic. Without the antecedent objective probability that a panic would follow these words in these circumstances, we have only a bizarre but tragic coincidence.

We would say much the same thing of a superstitious lady who "attempts" to start a riot by magical means. In an inconspicuous corner of a darkened theater, she sticks pins into a doll and mutters under her breath a magic incantation designed to produce a panic. Of course this does not work in the way intended, but a nearsighted and neurotic passerby observes her, takes the doll to be a real baby, and screams. The hoped-for panic then really follows. The evil lady cannot be found guilty of intentionally causing a panic, even though she intended to cause one and really did cause (or at least initiate a causal process that resulted in) one. She can be condemned for having very evil motives. But if people are sufficiently ignorant and impotent, the law, applying the harm principle, allows them to be as evil as they wish.

PROVOKING RETALIATORY VIOLENCE

Suppose a person utters words that have as their unhappy effects violence directed *at him* by his angry audience, counterviolence by his friends and protectors, and escalation into a riotous breach of the peace. This is still another way of causing harm by words. Should the speaker be punished? In almost every conceivable case, the answer should be No. There is a sense, of course, in which the speaker did not start the physical violence. He used only words, and while words can sting and infuriate, they are not instruments of violence in the same sense that fists, knives, guns, and clubs are. If the law suppresses public speech, either by withholding permits in advance or punishing afterwards, simply on the ground that the expressed views are so unpopular that some auditors can be expected to start fighting, then the law punishes some for the criminal proclivities of others. "A man does not become a criminal because someone else assaults him," writes Zechariah Chafee. Moreover, he continues, on any such theory, "a small number of intolerant men . . . can prevent *any kind* of meeting. . . . A gathering which expressed the sentiment of a majority of law-abiding citizens would become illegal because a small gang of hoodlums threatened to invade the hall."[15] When violent response to speech threatens, the obvious remedy is not suppression but rather increased police protection.

So much seems evident, but there may be some exceptions. Some words uttered in public places in the presence of many unwilling auditors may be so abusive or otherwise offensive as to be "reasonably considered a direct provocation to violence."[16] The captive auditor, after all, is not looking for trouble as he walks the public streets intent on his private errands. If he is forced to listen, as he walks past a street meeting, to speakers denouncing and ridiculing his religion, and forced to notice a banner with a large and abusive caricature of the pope,[17] his blood might reasonably be expected to boil. Antireligious and anticlerical opinions, of course, no matter how unpopular, are entitled to the full protection of the law. Even abusive, virulent, and mocking expressions of such views are entitled to full protection if uttered to private gatherings, in private or privately reserved places. Such expressions become provocative only when made in public places to captive auditors.

What makes an expression "provocative"? Surely, if words are to be suppressed on the ground that they are provocative of violence, they must be more than merely "provoking," else all unpopular opinions will be suppressed, to the great public loss. As far as I know, the concept of provocation has received thorough legal elaboration only in the law of homicide, where provocation reduces a charge of murder to that of manslaughter, thus functioning as a kind of mitigating consideration rather than as a justification or complete excuse. In the common law, for there to be sufficient provocation to mitigate: (1) The behavior of the victim must have been so aggravating that it would have produced "such excitement and passion as would obscure the reason of an ordinary man and induce him . . . to strike the blow."[18] (2) There must not have elapsed so much time between the provocation and the violence that a reasonable man's blood would have cooled. (3) But for the victim's provocation the violence would not have occurred. In short, provocation mitigates only when it in fact produces a reason-numbing rage in the attacker and is such that it could be expected to produce such a rage in any normal person in his circumstances. Nazi emblems might be expected to have this effect on a former inmate of a Nazi death camp, but the Democratic party line cannot be sufficiently provocative to excuse a violent Republican, and similarly the other way round. Indeed, in the law of homicide, *no mere words alone*, no matter how abusive or scurrilous, can be adequate provocation to justify or totally excuse killing as a response.

There would seem to be equally good reason not to consider mere words either as justifying or totally excusing nonlethal acts of violence. The "reasonable man" in a democracy must be presumed to have enough self-control to refrain from violent responses to odious words and doctrines. If he is followed, insulted, taunted, and challenged, he can get injunctive relief, or bring charges against his tormentor as a nuisance; if there is no time for this and he is backed to the wall he may be justified in using "reasonable force" in self-defense; or if he is followed to his own home, he can use the police to remove the nuisance. But if he is not personally harassed in these ways, he can turn on his heels and leave the provocation behind, and this is what the law, perhaps, should require of him.

Only when public speech satisfies stringent tests qualifying it as "direct provocation to violence" (if that is possible at all) will the harm principle justify its suppression. But there are many possible modes of suppression, and some are far more restrictive of liberty than others. Orders to cease and desist on pain of arrest are most economical, for they permit the speaker to continue to air his views in a nonprovocative way or else retire with his audience to a less public place. Lawful removal of the provocation (as a public nuisance) may be more satisfactory than permitting violent response to it, and is infinitely preferable to punishing the speaker. Nowhere in the law where provocation is considered as a defense do the rules deem the proven provoker (the victim) a criminal himself! At best his conduct mitigates the crime of his attacker, who is the only criminal.

One final point. While it is conceivable that some public speech can satisfy the common law test for provocation by being so aggravating that even a reasonable man could be expected to lose control of his reason when exposed to it, this can never be true of books. One can always escape the provocation of the printed word simply by declining to read it, and where escape from provocation is that easy, no "reasonable man" will succumb to it.

INCITEMENT TO CRIME OR INSURRECTION

In the criminal law, anyone who "counsels, commands, or encourages another to commit a crime" is himself guilty of the resultant crime as an "accessory before the fact." Counseling, commanding, and encouraging, however, must consist in more than merely uttering certain words in the presence of others. Surely there must also be serious (as opposed to playful) intent and some possibility at least of the words having their desired effect. It is not possible that these conditions can be satisfied if I tell my secretary that she should overthrow the U.S. government, or if a speaker tells an audience of bank presidents that they should practice embezzlement whenever they can. These situations are analogous to the efforts to start a panic by magical means or to panic police officers with words about mice.

The problem of interpreting the meaning of a rule making the counseling of crime itself a crime is similar, I should think, to that raised by a statute forbidding the planting of a certain kind of plant. One does not violate such a statute if he scatters the appropriate kind of seeds on asphalt pavement or in barren desert, even with evil intent. (Again, if you are stupid enough, the law—insofar as it derives from the harm principle—can allow you to be as evil as you wish.) To violate the statute, either one would have to dig a little hole in the appropriate sort of soil, deposit the appropriate seeds, cultivate, fertilize, allow for sufficient water, protect against winds, worms, and dogs; or one would have to find suitable conditions ready-made, where the soil is already receptive and merely dropping the seeds will create a substantial likelihood that plants will grow and thrive. By analogy, even words of advice, if they are to count as incitements to crime, must fall on reasonably receptive ears. The harm principle provides a ready rationale for this requirement. If we permit coercive repression of nondangerous words we will confer such abundant powers on the repressive organs of the state that they are certain to be abused. Moreover, we will so inhibit persons in their employment of language as to discourage both spontaneity and serious moral discussion, thus doing a great deal of harm and virtually no good at all. (The only "gain," if it is that, to be expected from looser standards of interpretation would be that nondangerous persons with evil motives could be scooped up in the state's tighter nets and punished.)

Counseling others to crime is not the only use of speech that can be described as incitement. We must also come to terms with instigating, egging on, and inflaming others to violence. Even Mill concedes that the opinion that "corn dealers are starvers of the poor," which deserves protection when published in the press, may nevertheless "justly incur punishment when delivered orally to an excited mob assembled before the house of a corn dealer."[19] The metaphor of planting seeds in receptive soil is perhaps less apt for this situation than the commonly employed "spark and tinder" analogy. Words that merely express legitimate though unpopular opinion in one context become "incendiary" when addressed to an already inflammable mob. As Chafee puts it: "Smoking is all right, but not in a powder magazine."[20] Of course the man who carries a cigar into a powder magazine may not know that the cigar he is carrying is lighted, or he may not know that he has entered a powder magazine. He may plead his lack of intention afterward (if he is still alive) as a defense. Similarly, the man who speaks his opinion to what he takes to be a calm audience, or an excited audience with different axes all ground fine, may plead his ignorance in good faith as a defense. But "the law" (as judges are fond of saying) "presumes that a person intends the natural and probable consequences of his actions," so that a defendant who denies that he intended to cause a riot may have the burden of proving his innocent intention to the jury.

In summary, there are two points to emphasize in connection with the punishment of inflammatory incitements. First, the audience must really be tinder, that is to say, not merely sullen, but angry to the point of frenzy, and so predisposed to violence. A left-wing radical should be permitted to deliver a revolutionary tirade before the ladies of the Daughters of the American Revolution, even if his final words are "to the barricades!" for that would be to light a match not in a powder magazine but in a Turkish steam bath. Second, no one should be punished for inciting others to violence unless he used words intentionally, or at least recklessly, with respect to that consequence. Otherwise at best a speaker will be punished for his mere negligence, and at worst he will be punished though perfectly innocent.

There is one further problem raised by the concept of incitement as a crime. It might well be asked how one person—the inciter—can be held criminally responsible for the free and deliberate actions of another person—the one who is incited by his words. This problem is common to both kinds of incitement, counseling and inflaming or egging on, but it seems especially puzzling in the case of advising and persuading; for the deliberate, thoughtful, unforced, and undeceived acceptance of the advice of another person is without question itself a voluntary act. Yet there may well be cases that are such that had not the advice been given, the crime would never have been perpetrated, so that the advisor can truly be said to have "got" the advisee to do something he might otherwise never have done. In this case, the initiative was the advisor's, and his advice was the crucial causal factor that led to the criminal act, so that it would be no abuse of usage to call it "the cause." And yet, for all of that, no one *forced* the advisee to act; he could have rejected the advice, but he did not.

If there is the appearance of paradox in this account, or in the very idea of one person's causing another to act voluntarily, it is no doubt the result of an unduly restrictive conception of what a cause is. There are, of course, a great many ways of causing another person to behave in a given way by the use of words. If we sneak up behind him and shout, "Boo!" we may startle him so that he jumps and shrieks. In this case our word functioned as a cause not in virtue of its meaning or the mediation of the other person's understanding, but simply as a noise, and the person's startled reaction to this physical stimulus was an involuntary as an eye-twitch or a knee-jerk. Some philosophers would restrict the notion of causing behavior to cases of this kind, but there is no good reason for such a restriction, and a strong case can be built against it based on both its capacity to breed paradox and common sense and usage. I can "get" an acquaintance to say "Good morning" by putting myself directly in his line of vision, smiling, and saying, "Good morning" to him. If I do these things and he predictably responds in the way I intended, I can surely say that my behavior was the cause, in those circumstances, of his behavior; for my conduct is not only a circumstance but for which his action would not have occurred, it is also a circumstance that, when added to those already present, made the difference between his speaking and remaining silent. Yet I did not force him to speak; I did not deceive him; I did not trick him. Rather I exploited those of his known policies and dispositions that made him antecedently "receptive" to my words. To deny that I caused him to act voluntarily, in short, is either to confuse causation with compulsion (an ancient philosophical mistake) or to regard one person's initiative as incompatible with another person's responsibility.[21]

In any case, where one person causes another to act voluntarily either by giving him advice or information or by otherwise capitalizing on his carefully studied dispositions and policies, there is no reason why *both* persons should not be held responsible for the act if it should be criminal. It is just as if the law made it criminal to contribute to a human explosion either by being human dynamite or by being a human spark: either by being predisposed by one's character to crime or by one's passions to violence, or else by providing the words or materials that could fully be anticipated to incite the violent or criminal conduct of others. It is surely no reasonable defense of the spark to say that but for the dynamite there would have been no explosion. Nor is it any more reasonable to defend the dynamite by arguing that but for the spark it should have remained forever quiescent.

There is probably even less reason for excluding from responsibility the speaker haranguing an inflammable mob on the grounds that the individuals in the throng are free adults capable of refraining from violence in the circumstances. A mob might well be understood as a kind of fictitious collective person whose passions are much more easily manipulated and whose actions more easily maneuvered than those of individual persons. If one looks at it this way, the caused behavior of an inflamed mob may be a good deal less than fully voluntary, even though the component individuals in it, being free adults, are all acting voluntarily on their own responsibility. . . .

NOTES

[1]Aristotle, *Nicomachean Ethics*, book 2, chapter 6, 1107a: "When a man commits adultery, there is no point in asking whether it was with the right woman or at the right time or in the right way, for to do anything like that is simply wrong."

[2]William L. Prosser, *Handbook of the Law of Torts*, 2d ed. (St. Paul: West, 1955), p. 584.

[3]Ibid., p. 631.

[4]Fowler V. Harper and Fleming James, Jr., *The Law of Torts* (Boston: Little, Brown, 1956), 1:416. The authors do not endorse this view.

[5]Ibid.

[6]William Blackstone, *Commentaries on the Laws of England* (1765, repr. Boston: Beacon, 1962), 3:125.

[7]Prosser, *Handbook*, p. 644.

[8]Harper and James, *Law of Torts*, p. 680.

[9]Prosser, *Handbook*, p. 642.

[10] Ibid.

[11] American Law Institute, *Restatement of the Law of Torts* (St. Paul: West, 1934), section 867, comment c.

[12] Prosser, *Handbook*, p. 644.

[13] "There are two aspects of the interest in seclusion. First, the interest in preventing others from seeing and hearing what one does and says. Second, *the interest in avoiding seeing and hearing what other people do and say*. . . . It may be as distasteful to suffer the intrusions of a garrulous and unwelcome guest as to discover an eavesdropper or peeper" (Harper and James, *Law of Torts*, p. 681; emphasis added).

[14] *Schenck v. United States*, 249 U.S. 47 (1919).

[15] Chafee, *Free Speech*, pp. 152, 161, 426. Cf. *Terminiello v. Chicago*, 337 U.S. 1 (1949).

[16] Chafee, *Free Speech*, p. 426.

[17] Ibid., p. 161.

[18] *Toler v. State*, 152 Tenn. 1, 13, 260 S.W. 134 (1923).

[19] Mill, *On Liberty*, pp. 67–68.

[20] Chafee, *Free Speech*, p. 397.

[21] For a more detailed exposition of this view, see my "Causing Voluntary Actions," in *Doing and Deserving* (Princeton, N.J.: Princeton University Press, 1970), p. 152.

SUPREME COURT OF THE UNITED STATES

403 U.S. 15

COHEN V. CALIFORNIA

APPEAL FROM THE COURT OF APPEAL OF CALIFORNIA, SECOND APPELLATE DISTRICT

NO. 299 ARGUED: FEBRUARY 22, 1971—DECIDED: JUNE 7, 1971

OPINION: [15] MR. JUSTICE HARLAN delivered the opinion of the Court.

This case may seem at first blush too inconsequential to find its way into our books, but the issue it presents is of no small constitutional significance.

[16] Appellant Paul Robert Cohen was convicted in the Los Angeles Municipal Court of violating that part of California Penal Code § 415 which prohibits "maliciously and willfully disturb[ing] the peace or quiet of any neighborhood or person . . . by . . . offensive conduct. . . ."[1] He was given 30 days' imprisonment. The facts upon which his conviction rests are detailed in the opinion of the Court of Appeal of California, Second Appellate District, as follows:

> "On April 26, 1968, the defendant was observed in the Los Angeles County Courthouse in the corridor outside of division 20 of the municipal court wearing a jacket bearing the words 'Fuck the Draft' which were plainly visible. There were women and children present in the corridor. The defendant was arrested. The defendant testified that he wore the jacket knowing that the words were on the jacket as a means of informing the public of the depth of his feelings against the Vietnam War and the draft.

> "The defendant did not engage in, nor threaten to engage in, nor did anyone as the result of his conduct [17] in fact commit or threaten to commit any act of violence. The defendant did not make any loud or unusual noise, nor was there any evidence that he uttered any sound prior to his arrest." 1 Cal. App. 3d 94, 97–98, 81 Cal. Rptr. 503, 505 (1969).

In affirming the conviction the Court of Appeal held that "offensive conduct" means "behavior which has a tendency to provoke *others* to acts of violence or to in turn disturb the peace," and that the State had proved this element because, on the facts of this case, "[i]t was certainly reasonably foreseeable that such conduct might cause others to rise up to commit a violent act against the person of the defendant or attempt to forceably remove his jacket." 1 Cal. App. 3d, at 99–100, 81 Cal. Rptr., at 506. The California Supreme Court declined review by a divided vote. We brought the case here, postponing the consideration of the question of our jurisdiction over this appeal to a hearing of the case on the merits. 399 U. S. 904. We now reverse. . . .

I

[18] In order to lay hands on the precise issue which this case involves, it is useful first to canvass various matters which this record does *not* present.

The conviction quite clearly rests upon the asserted offensiveness of the *words* Cohen used to convey his message to the public. The only "conduct" which the State sought to punish is the fact of communication. Thus, we deal here with a conviction resting solely upon "speech," cf. *Stromberg* v. *California*, 283 U. S. 359 (1931), not upon any separately identifiable conduct which allegedly was intended by Cohen to be perceived by others as expressive of particular views but which, on its face, does not necessarily convey any message and hence arguably could be regulated without effectively repressing Cohen's ability to express himself. Cf. *United States* v. *O'Brien*, 391 U. S. 367 (1968). Further, the State certainly lacks power to punish Cohen for the underlying content of the message the inscription conveyed. At least so long as there is no showing of an intent to incite disobedience to or disruption of the draft, Cohen could not, consistently with the First and Fourteenth Amendments, be punished for asserting the evident position on the inutility or immorality of the draft his jacket reflected. *Yates* v. *United States*, 354 U. S. 298 (1957).

[19] Appellant's conviction, then, rests squarely upon his exercise of the "freedom of speech" protected from arbitrary governmental interference by the Constitution and can be justified, if at all, only as a valid regulation of the manner in which he exercised that freedom, not as a permissible prohibition on the substantive message it conveys. This does not end the inquiry, of course, for the First and Fourteenth Amendments have never been thought to give absolute protection to every individual to speak whenever or wherever he pleases, or to use any form of address in any circumstances that he chooses. In this vein, too, however, we think it important to note that several issues typically associated with such problems are not presented here.

In the first place, Cohen was tried under a statute applicable throughout the entire State. Any attempt to support this conviction on the ground that the statute seeks to preserve an appropriately decorous atmosphere in the courthouse where Cohen was arrested must fail in the absence of any language in the statute that would have put appellant on notice that certain kinds of otherwise permissible speech or conduct would nevertheless, under California law, not be tolerated in certain places. See *Edwards* v. *South Carolina*, 372 U. S. 229, 236–237, and n. 11 (1963). Cf. *Adderley* v. *Florida*, 385 U. S. 39 (1966). No fair reading of the phrase "offensive conduct" can be said sufficiently to inform the ordinary person that distinctions between certain locations are thereby created.[2]

In the second place, as it comes to us, this case cannot be said to fall within those relatively few categories of [20] instances where prior decisions have established the power of government to deal more comprehensively with certain forms of individual expression simply upon a showing that such a form was employed. This is not, for example, an obscenity case. Whatever else may be necessary to give rise to the States' broader power to prohibit obscene expression, such expression must be, in some significant way, erotic. *Roth* v. *United States*, 354 U. S. 476 (1957). It cannot plausibly be maintained that this vulgar allusion to the Selective Service System would conjure up such psychic stimulation in anyone likely to be confronted with Cohen's crudely defaced jacket.

This Court has also held that the States are free to ban the simple use, without a demonstration of additional justifying circumstances, of so-called "fighting words," those personally abusive epithets which, when addressed to the ordinary citizen, are, as a matter of common knowledge, inherently likely to provoke violent reaction. *Chaplinsky* v. *New Hampshire*, 315 U. S. 568 (1942). While the four-letter word displayed by Cohen in relation to the draft is not uncommonly employed in a personally provocative fashion, in this instance it was clearly not "directed to the person of the hearer." *Cantwell* v. *Connecticut*, 310 U. S. 296, 309 (1940). No individual actually or likely to be present could reasonably have regarded the words on appellant's jacket as a direct personal insult. Nor do we have here an instance of the exercise of the State's police power to prevent a speaker from intentionally provoking a given group to hostile reaction. Cf. *Feiner* v. *New York*, 340 U. S. 315 (1951); *Terminiello* v. *Chicago*, 337 U. S. 1 (1949). There is, as noted above, no showing that anyone who saw Cohen was in fact violently aroused or that appellant intended such a result.

[21]Finally, in arguments before this Court much has been made of the claim that Cohen's distasteful mode of expression was thrust upon unwilling or unsuspecting viewers, and that the State might therefore legitimately act as it did in order to protect the sensitive from otherwise unavoidable exposure to appellant's crude form of protest. Of course, the mere presumed presence of unwitting listeners or viewers does not serve automatically to justify curtailing all speech capable of giving offense. See, e. g., *Organization for a Better Austin* v. *Keefe*, 402 U. S. 415 (1971). While this Court has recognized that government may properly act in many situations to prohibit intrusion into the privacy of the home of unwelcome views and ideas which cannot be totally banned from the public dialogue, e. g., *Rowan* v. *Post Office Dept.*, 397 U. S. 728 (1970), we have at the same time consistently stressed that "we are often 'captives' outside the sanctuary of the home and subject to objectionable speech." *Id.*, at 738. The ability of government, consonant with the Constitution, to shut off discourse solely to protect others from hearing it is, in other words, dependent upon a showing that substantial privacy interests are being invaded in an essentially intolerable manner. Any broader view of this authority would effectively empower a majority to silence dissidents simply as a matter of personal predilections.

In this regard, persons confronted with Cohen's jacket were in a quite different posture than, say, those subjected to the raucous emissions of sound trucks blaring outside their residences. Those in the Los Angeles courthouse could effectively avoid further bombardment of their sensibilities simply by averting their eyes. And, while it may be that one has a more substantial claim to a recognizable privacy interest when walking through a courthouse corridor than, for example, strolling through Central Park, surely it is nothing like the interest in [22] being free from unwanted expression in the confines of one's own home. Cf. *Keefe, supra.* Given the subtlety and complexity of the factors involved, if Cohen's "speech" was otherwise entitled to constitutional protection, we do not think the fact that some unwilling "listeners" in a public building may have been briefly exposed to it can serve to justify this breach of the peace conviction where, as here, there was no evidence that persons powerless to avoid appellant's conduct did in fact object to it, and where that portion of the statute upon which Cohen's conviction rests evinces no concern, either on its face or as construed by the California courts, with the special plight of the captive auditor, but, instead, indiscriminately sweeps within its prohibitions all "offensive conduct" that disturbs "any neighborhood or person." Cf. *Edwards* v. *South Carolina, supra.*[4]

II

Against this background, the issue flushed by this case stands out in bold relief. It is whether California can excise, as "offensive conduct," one particular scurrilous epithet from the public discourse, either upon the theory of the court below that its use is inherently likely to cause violent reaction or upon a more general assertion that the States, acting as guardians of public morality, [23] may properly remove this offensive word from the public vocabulary.

The rationale of the California court is plainly untenable. At most it reflects an "undifferentiated fear or apprehension of disturbance [which] is not enough to overcome the right to freedom of expression." *Tinker* v. *Des Moines Indep. Community School Dist.*, 393 U. S. 503, 508 (1969). We have been shown no evidence that substantial numbers of citizens are standing ready to strike out physically at whoever may assault their sensibilities with execrations like that uttered by Cohen. There may be some persons about with such lawless and violent proclivities, but that is an insufficient base upon which to erect, consistently with constitutional values, a governmental power to force persons who wish to ventilate their dissident views into avoiding particular forms of expression. The argument amounts to little more than the self-defeating proposition that to avoid physical censorship of one who has not sought to provoke such a response by a hypothetical coterie of the violent and lawless, the States may more appropriately effectuate that censorship themselves. Cf. *Ashton* v. *Kentucky*, 384 U. S. 195, 200 (1966); *Cox* v. *Louisiana*, 379 U. S. 536, 550–551 (1965).

Admittedly, it is not so obvious that the First and Fourteenth Amendments must be taken to disable the States from punishing public utterance of this unseemly expletive in order to maintain what they regard as a suitable level of discourse within the body politic. We [24] think, however, that examination and reflection will reveal the shortcomings of a contrary viewpoint.

At the outset, we cannot overemphasize that, in our judgment, most situations where the State has a justifiable interest in regulating speech will fall within one or more of the various established exceptions, discussed above but not applicable here, to the usual rule that governmental bodies may not prescribe the form or content of individual expression. Equally important to our conclusion is the constitutional backdrop against which our decision must be made. The constitutional right of free expression is powerful medicine in a society as diverse and populous as ours. It is designed and intended to remove governmental restraints from the arena of public discussion, putting the decision as to what views shall be voiced largely into the hands of each of us, in the hope that use of such freedom will ultimately produce a more capable citizenry and more perfect polity and in the belief that no other approach would comport with the premise of individual dignity and choice upon which our political system rests. See *Whitney* v. *California*, 274 U. S. 357, 375–377 (1927) (Brandeis, J., concurring).

To many, the immediate consequence of this freedom may often appear to be only verbal tumult, discord, and [25] even offensive utterance. These are, however, within established limits, in truth necessary side effects of the broader enduring values which the process of open debate permits us to achieve. That the air may at times seem filled with verbal cacophony is, in this sense not a sign of weakness but of strength. We cannot lose sight of the fact that, in what otherwise might seem a trifling and annoying instance of individual distasteful abuse of a privilege, these fundamental societal values are truly implicated. That is why "[w]holly neutral futilities . . . come under the protection of free speech as fully as do Keats' poems or Donne's sermons," *Winters* v. *New York*, 333 U. S. 507, 528 (1948) (Frankfurter, J., dissenting), and why "so long as the means are peaceful, the communication need not meet standards of acceptability," *Organization for a Better Austin* v. *Keefe*, 402 U. S. 415, 419 (1971).

Against this perception of the constitutional policies involved, we discern certain more particularized considerations that peculiarly call for reversal of this conviction. First, the principle contended for by the State seems inherently boundless. How is one to distinguish this from any other offensive word? Surely the State has no right to cleanse public debate to the point where it is grammatically palatable to the most squeamish among us. Yet no readily ascertainable general principle exists for stopping short of that result were we to affirm the judgment below. For, while the particular four-letter word being litigated here is perhaps more distasteful than most others of its genre, it is nevertheless often true that one man's vulgarity is another's lyric. Indeed, we think it is largely because governmental officials cannot make principled distinctions in this area that the Constitution leaves matters of taste and style so largely to the individual.

Additionally, we cannot overlook the fact, because it [26] is well illustrated by the episode involved here, that much linguistic expression serves a dual communicative function: it conveys not only ideas capable of relatively precise, detached explication, but otherwise inexpressible emotions as well. In fact, words are often chosen as much for their emotive as their cognitive force. We cannot sanction the view that the Constitution, while solicitous of the cognitive content of individual speech, has little or no regard for that emotive function which, practically speaking, may often be the more important element of the overall message sought to be communicated. Indeed, as Mr. Justice Frankfurter has said," [o]ne of the prerogatives of American citizenship is the right to criticize public men and measures—and that means not only informed and responsible criticism but the freedom to speak foolishly and without moderation." *Baumgartner* v. *United States*, 322 U. S. 665, 673–674 (1944).

Finally, and in the same vein, we cannot indulge the facile assumption that one can forbid particular words without also running a substantial risk of suppressing ideas in the process. Indeed, governments might soon seize upon the censorship of particular words as a convenient guise for banning the expression of unpopular views. We have been able, as noted above, to discern little social benefit that might result from running the risk of opening the door to such grave results.

It is, in sum, our judgment that, absent a more particularized and compelling reason for its actions, the State may not, consistently with the First and Fourteenth Amendments, make the simple public display here involved of this single four-letter expletive a criminal offense. Because that is the only arguably sustainable rationale for the conviction here at issue, the judgment below must be

Reversed.

[27] MR. JUSTICE BLACKMUN, with whom THE CHIEF JUSTICE and MR. JUSTICE BLACK join.

I dissent, and I do so for two reasons:

1. Cohen's absurd and immature antic, in my view, was mainly conduct and little speech. See *Street* v. *New York*, 394 U. S. 576 (1969); *Cox* v. *Louisiana*, 379 U. S. 536, 555 (1965); *Giboney* v. *Empire Storage Co.*, 336 U. S. 490, 502 (1949). The California Court of Appeal appears so to have described it, 1 Cal. App. 3d 94, 100, 81 Cal. Rptr. 503, 507, and I cannot characterize it otherwise. Further, the case appears to me to be well within the sphere of *Chaplinsky* v. *New Hampshire*, 315 U. S. 568 (1942), where Mr. Justice Murphy, a known champion of First Amendment freedoms, wrote for a unanimous bench. As a consequence, this Court's agonizing over First Amendment values seems misplaced and unnecessary.

2. I am not at all certain that the California Court of Appeal's construction of § 415 is now the authoritative California construction. . . .

NOTES

[1]The statute provides in full:

"Every person who maliciously and willfully disturbs the peace or quiet of any neighborhood or person, by loud or unusual noise, or by tumultuous or offensive conduct, or threatening, traducing, quarreling, challenging to fight, or fighting, or who, on the public streets of any unincorporated town, or upon the public highways in such unincorporated town, run any horse race, either for a wager or for amusement, or fire any gun or pistol in such unincorporated town, or use any vulgar, profane, or indecent language within the presence or hearing of women or children, in a loud and boisterous manner, is guilty of a misdemeanor, and upon conviction by any Court of competent jurisdiction shall be punished by fine not exceeding two hundred dollars, or by imprisonment in the County Jail for not more than ninety days, or by both fine and imprisonment, or either, at the discretion of the Court."

[2]It is illuminating to note what transpired when Cohen entered a courtroom in the building. He removed his jacket and stood with it folded over his arm. Meanwhile, a policeman sent the presiding judge a note suggesting that Cohen be held in contempt of court. The judge declined to do so and Cohen was arrested by the officer only after be emerged from the courtroom. App. 18–19.

SUPREME COURT OF ILLINOIS

69 III.2d 605

VILLAGE OF SKOKIE v. NATIONAL SOCIALIST PARTY OF AMERICA

No. 49769 FILED: JANUARY 27, 1978

[609] PER CURIAM:

Plaintiff, the village of Skokie, filed a complaint in the circuit court of Cook County seeking to enjoin defendants, the National Socialist Party of America (the American Nazi Party) and 10 individuals as "officers and members" of the party, from engaging in certain activities while conducting a demonstration within the village. The circuit court issued an order enjoining certain conduct during the planned demonstration. The appellate court modified the injunction order, and, as modified, defendants are enjoined from "[i]ntentionally displaying the swastika on or off their persons, in the course of a demonstration, march, or parade." (51 III. App. 3d 279, 295.) We allowed defendants' petition for leave to appeal.

The pleadings and the facts adduced at the hearing are fully set forth in the appellate court opinion, and only those matters necessary to the discussion of the issues will be repeated here. The facts are not disputed.

[610] It is alleged in plaintiff's complaint that the "uniform of the National Socialist Party of America consists of the storm trooper uniform of the German Nazi Party embellished with the Nazi swastika"; that the plaintiff village has a population of about 70,000 persons of which approximately 40,500 persons are of "Jewish religion or Jewish ancestry" and of this latter number 5,000 to 7,000 are survivors of German concentration camps; that the defendant organization is "dedicated to the incitation of racial and religious hatred directed principally against individuals of Jewish faith or ancestry and non-Caucasians"; and that its members "have patterned their conduct, their uniform, their slogan and their tactics along the pattern of the German Nazi Party."

Defendants moved to dismiss the complaint. In an affidavit attached to defendants' motion to dismiss, defendant Frank Collin, who testified that he was "party leader," stated that on or about March 20, 1977, he sent officials of the plaintiff village a letter stating that the party members and supporters would hold a peaceable, public assembly in the village on May 1, 1977, to protest the Skokie Park District's requirement that the party procure $350,000 of insurance prior to the party's use of the Skokie public parks for public assemblies. The demonstration was to begin at 3 p.m., last 20 to 30 minutes, and consist of 30 to 50 demonstrators marching in single file, back and forth, in front of the village hall. The marchers were to wear uniforms which include a swastika emblem or armband. They were to carry a party banner containing a swastika emblem and signs containing such statements as "White Free Speech," "Free Speech for the White Man," and "Free Speech for White America." The demonstrators would not distribute handbills, make any derogatory statements directed to any ethnic or religious group, or obstruct traffic. They would cooperate with any reasonable police instructions or requests.

[611] At the hearing on plaintiff's motion for an "emergency injunction" a resident of Skokie testified that he was a survivor of the Nazi holocaust. He further testified that the Jewish community in and around Skokie feels the purpose of the march in the "heart of the Jewish population" is to remind the two million survivors "that we are not through with you" and to show "that the Nazi threat is not over, it can happen again." Another resident of Skokie testified that as the result of defendants' announced intention to march in Skokie, 15 to 18 Jewish organizations, within the village and surrounding area, were called and a counterdemonstration of an estimated 12,000 to 15,000 people was scheduled for the same day. There was opinion evidence that defendants' planned demonstration in Skokie would result in violence.

The circuit court entered an order enjoining defendants from "marching, walking or parading in the uniform of the National Socialist Party of America; marching, walking or parading or otherwise displaying the swastika on or off their person; distributing pamphlets or displaying any materials which incite or promote hatred against persons of Jewish faith or ancestry or hatred against persons of any faith or ancestry, race or religion" within the village of Skokie. The appellate court, as earlier noted, modified the order so that defendants were enjoined only from intentional display of the swastika during the Skokie demonstration.

The appellate court opinion adequately discussed and properly decided those issues arising from the portions of the injunction order which enjoined defendants from marching, walking, or parading, from distributing pamphlets or displaying materials, and from wearing the uniform of the National Socialist Party of America. The only issue remaining before this court is whether the circuit court order enjoining defendants from displaying the swastika violates the first amendment rights of those defendants.

[612] In defining the constitutional rights of the parties who come before this court, we are, of course, bound by the pronouncements of the United States Supreme Court in its interpretation of the United States Constitution. (*Ableman v. Booth* (1859), 62 U.S. (21 How.) 506, 16 L.Ed. 169; *Cooper v. Aaron* (1958), 358 U.S. 1, 3 L.Ed.2d 1, 78 S.Ct. 1401.) The decisions of that court, particularly *Cohen v. California* (1971), 403 U.S. 15, 29 L.Ed.2d 284, 91 S.Ct. 1780, in our opinion compel us to permit the demonstration as proposed, including display of the swastika.

"It is firmly settled that under our Constitution the public expression of ideas may not be prohibited merely because the ideas are themselves offensive to some of their hearers" (*Bachellar v. Maryland* (1970), 397 U.S. 564, 567, 25 L.Ed.2d 570, 574, 90 S.Ct. 1312, 1315), and it is entirely clear that the wearing of distinctive clothing can be symbolic expression of a thought or philosophy. The symbolic expression of thought falls within the free speech clause of the first amendment (*Tinker v. Des Moines Independent Community School District* (1969), 393 U.S. 503, 21 L.Ed.2d 731, 89 S.Ct. 733), and the plaintiff village has the heavy burden of justifying the imposition of a prior restraint upon defendants' right to freedom of speech (*Carroll v. President of Princess Anne County* (1968), 393 U.S. 175, 21 L.Ed.2d 325, 89 S.Ct. 347; *Organization for a Better Austin v. Keefe* (1971), 402 U.S. 415, 29 L.Ed.2d 1, 91 S.Ct. 1575).

The village of Skokie seeks to meet this burden by application of the "fighting words" doctrine first enunciated in *Chaplinsky v. New Hampshire* (1942), 315 U.S. 568, 86 L.Ed. 1031, 62 S.Ct. 766. That doctrine was designed to permit punishment of extremely hostile personal communication likely to cause immediate physical response, "no words being 'forbidden except such as have a direct tendency to cause acts of violence by the [613] persons to whom, individually, the remark is addressed.'" (315 U.S. 568, 573, 86 L.Ed. 1031, 1036, 62 S.Ct. 766, 770.) In *Cohen* the Supreme Court restated the description of fighting words as "those personally abusive epithets which, when addressed to the ordinary citizen, are, as a matter of common knowledge, inherently likely to provoke violent reaction." (403 U.S. 15, 20, 29 L.Ed. 2d 284, 291, 91 S.Ct. 1780, 1785.) Plaintiff urges, and the appellate court has held, that the exhibition of the Nazi symbol, the swastika, addresses to ordinary citizens a message which is tantamount to fighting words. Plaintiff further asks this court to extend *Chaplinsky,* which upheld a statute punishing the use of such words, and hold that the fighting-words doctrine permits a prior restraint on defendants' symbolic speech. In our judgment we are precluded from doing so.

In *Cohen,* defendant's conviction stemmed from wearing a jacket bearing the words "Fuck the Draft" in a Los Angeles County courthouse corridor. The Supreme Court for reasons we believe applicable here refused to find that the jacket inscription constituted fighting words. That court stated:

> *"The constitutional right of free expression is powerful medicine in a society as diverse and populous as ours. It is designed and intended to remove governmental restraints from the arena of public discussion, putting the decision as to what views shall be voiced largely into the hands of each of us, in the hope that use of such freedom will ultimately produce a more capable citizenry and more perfect polity and in the belief that no other approach would comport with the premise of individual dignity and choice upon which our political system rests. See Whitney v. California, 274 U.S. 357, 375–377 (1927) (Brandeis, J., concurring).*

> *[614] To many, the immediate consequence of this freedom may often appear to be only verbal tumult, discord, and even offensive utterance. These are, however, within established limits, in truth necessary side effects of the broader enduring values which the process of open debate permits us to achieve. That the air may at times seem filled with verbal cacophony is, in this sense not a sign of weakness but of strength. We cannot lose sight of the fact that, in what otherwise might seem a trifling and annoying instance of individual distasteful abuse of a privilege, these fundamental societal values are truly implicated.*^{***} *'so long as the means are peaceful, the communication need not meet standards of acceptability,' Organization for a Better Austin v. Keefe, 402 U.S. 415, 419 (1971).*

> *Against this perception of the constitutional policies involved, we discern certain more particularized considerations that peculiarly call for reversal of this conviction. First, the principle contended for by the State seems inherently boundless. How is one to distinguish this from any other offensive word [emblem]? Surely the State has no right to cleanse public debate to the point where it is grammatically palatable to the most squeamish among us. Yet no readily ascertainable general principle exists for stopping short of that result were we to affirm the judgment below. For, while the particular four-letter word [emblem] being litigated here is perhaps more distasteful than most others of its genre, it is nevertheless often true that one man's vulgarity is another's lyric. Indeed, we think it is largely because governmental officials cannot make principled distinctions in this area that the Constitution [615] leaves matters of taste and style so largely to the individual.*

> * * *

> *Finally, and in the same vein, we cannot indulge the facile assumption that one can forbid particular words without also running a substantial risk of suppressing ideas in the process. Indeed, governments might soon seize upon the censorship of particular words [emblems] as a convenient guise for banning the expression of unpopular views. We have been able, as noted above, to discern little social benefit that might result from running the risk of opening the door to such grave results."* 403 U.S. 15, 24–26, 29 L.Ed.2d 284, 293–94, 91 S.Ct. 1780, 1787–88.

The display of the swastika, as offensive to the principles of a free nation as the memories it recalls may be, is symbolic political speech intended to convey to the public the beliefs of those who display it. It does not, in our opinion, fall within the definition of "fighting words," and that doctrine cannot be used here to overcome the heavy presumption against the constitutional validity of a prior restraint.

Nor can we find that the swastika, while not representing fighting words, is nevertheless so offensive and peace threatening to the public that its display can be enjoined. We do not doubt that the sight of this symbol is abhorrent to the Jewish citizens of Skokie, and that the survivors of the Nazi persecutions, tormented by their recollections, may have strong feelings regarding its display. Yet it is entirely clear that this factor does not justify enjoining defendants' speech. The *Cohen* court spoke to this subject:

> *"Finally, in arguments before this Court much has been made of the claim that Cohen's distasteful mode of expression was thrust upon [616] unwilling or unsuspecting viewers, and that the State might therefore*

legitimately act as it did in order to protect the sensitive from otherwise unavoidable exposure to appellant's crude form of protest. Of course, the mere presumed presence of unwitting listeners or viewers does not serve automatically to justify curtailing all speech capable of giving offense. See, e.g., Organization for a Better Austin v. Keefe, 402 U.S. 415 (1971). While this Court has recognized that government may properly act in many situations to prohibit intrusion into the privacy of the home of unwelcome views and ideas which cannot be totally banned from the public dialogue, e.g., Rowan v. Post Office Dept., 397 U.S. 728 (1970), we have at the same time consistently stressed that 'we are often "captives" outside the sanctuary of the home and subject to objectionable speech.' Id., at 738. The ability of government, consonant with the Constitution, to shut off discourse solely to protect others from hearing it is, in other words, dependent upon a showing that substantial privacy interests are being invaded in an essentially intolerable manner. Any broader view of this authority would effectively empower a majority to silence dissidents simply as a matter of personal predilections." 403 U.S. 15, 21, 29 L.Ed.2d 284, 291–92, 91 S.Ct. 1780, 1786.

See also *Kunz v. New York* (1951), 340 U.S. 290, 95 L.Ed. 280, 71 S.Ct. 312; *Street v. New York* (1969), 394 U.S. 576, 22 L.Ed.2d 572, 89 S.Ct. 1354.

Similarly, the Court of Appeals for the Seventh Circuit, in reversing the denial of defendant Collin's application for a permit to speak in Chicago's Marquette Park, noted that courts have consistently refused to ban speech because of the possibility of unlawful conduct by [617] those opposed to the speaker's philosophy.

"Starting with Terminiello v. City of Chicago, 337 U.S. 1, 69 S.Ct. 894, 93 L.Ed. 1131 (1949), and continuing to Gregory v. City of Chicago, 394 U.S. 111, 89 S.Ct. 946, 22 L.Ed. 134 (1969), it has become patent that a hostile audience is not a basis for restraining otherwise legal First Amendment activity. As with many of the cases cited herein, if the actual behavior is not sufficient to sustain a conviction under a statute, then certainly the anticipation of such events cannot sustain the burden necessary to justify a prior restraint." Collin v. Chicago Park District (7th Cir. 1972), 460 F.2d 746, 754.

Rockwell v. Morris (1961), 12 App. Div.2d 272, 211 N.Y.S.2d 25, *aff'd mem.* (1961), 10 N.Y.2d 721, 749, 219 N.Y.S.2d 268, 605, *cert. denied* (1961), 368 U.S. 913, 7 L.Ed.2d 131, 82 S.Ct. 194, also involved an American Nazi leader, George Lincoln Rockwell, who challenged a bar to his use of a New York City park to hold a public demonstration where anti-Semitic speeches would be made. Although approximately 2 1/2 million Jewish New Yorkers were hostile to Rockwell's message, the court ordered that a permit to speak be granted, stating:

"A community need not wait to be subverted by street riots and storm troopers; but, also, it cannot, by its policemen or commissioners, suppress a speaker, in prior restraint, on the basis of news reports, hysteria, or inference that what he did yesterday, he will do today. Thus, too, if the speaker incites others to immediate unlawful action he may be punished—in a proper case, stopped when disorder actually impends; but this is not to be confused with unlawful action from others who seek unlawfully to suppress or punish the speaker.

[618]So, the unpopularity of views, their shocking quality, their obnoxiousness, and even their alarming impact is not enough. Otherwise, the preacher of any strange doctrine could be stopped; the anti-racist himself could be suppressed, if he undertakes to speak in 'restricted' areas; and one who asks that public schools be open indiscriminately to all ethnic groups could be lawfully suppressed, if only he choose to speak where persuasion is needed most." 12 App. Div.2d 272, 281–82, 211 N.Y.S.2d 25, 35–36.

In summary, as we read the controlling Supreme Court opinions, use of the swastika is a symbolic form of free speech entitled to first amendment protections. Its display on uniforms or banners by those engaged in peaceful demonstrations cannot be totally precluded solely because that display may provoke a violent reaction by those who view it. Particularly is this true where, as here, there has been advance notice by the demonstrators of their plans so that they have become, as the complaint alleges, "common knowledge" and those to whom sight of the swastika banner or uniforms would be offensive are forewarned and need not view them. A speaker who gives prior notice of his message has not compelled a confrontation with those who voluntarily listen.

As to those who happen to be in a position to be involuntarily confronted with the swastika, the following observations from *Erznoznik v. City of Jacksonville* (1975), 422 U.S. 205, 45 L.Ed.2d 125, 95 S.Ct. 2268, are appropriate:

> "*The plain, if at all times disquieting, truth is that in our pluralistic society, constantly proliferating new and ingenious forms of expression, 'we are inescapably captive audiences for many purposes.' Rowan v. Post Office Dept., [397 U.S. 728,] 736. Much that we encounter offends our [619] esthetic, if not our political and moral, sensibilities. Nevertheless, the Constitution does not permit government to decide which types of otherwise protected speech are sufficiently offensive to require protection for the unwilling listener or viewer. Rather, absent the narrow circumstances described above [home intrusion or captive audience], the burden normally falls upon the viewer to 'avoid further bombardment of [his] sensibilities simply by averting [his] eyes.' Cohen v. California [403 U.S. 15,] 21.*" 422 U.S. 205, 210–11, 45 L.Ed.2d 125, 131–32, 95 S.Ct. 2268, 2273.

Thus by placing the burden upon the viewer to avoid further bombardment, the Supreme Court has permitted speakers to justify the initial intrusion into the citizen's sensibilities.

We accordingly, albeit reluctantly, conclude that the display of the swastika cannot be enjoined under the fighting-words exception to free speech, nor can anticipation of a hostile audience justify the prior restraint. Furthermore, *Cohen* and *Erznoznik* direct the citizens of Skokie that it is their burden to avoid the offensive symbol if they can do so without unreasonable inconvenience. Accordingly, we are constrained to reverse that part of the appellate court judgment enjoining the display of the swastika. That judgment is in all other respects affirmed.

Affirmed in part and reversed in part.

SUPREME COURT OF THE UNITED STATES

491 U.S. 397

TEXAS V. JOHNSON

CERTIORARI TO THE COURT OF CRIMINAL APPEALS OF TEXAS

NO. 88-155 ARGUED: MARCH 21, 1989—DECIDED: JUNE 21, 1989

OPINION: [399] JUSTICE BRENNAN delivered the opinion of the Court.

After publicly burning an American flag as a means of political protest, Gregory Lee Johnson was convicted of desecrating a flag in violation of Texas law. This case presents the question whether his conviction is consistent with the First Amendment. We hold that it is not.

I

While the Republican National Convention was taking place in Dallas in 1984, respondent Johnson participated in a political demonstration dubbed the "Republican War Chest Tour." As explained in literature distributed by the demonstrators and in speeches made by them, the purpose of this event was to protest the policies of the Reagan administration and of certain Dallas-based corporations. The demonstrators marched through the Dallas streets, chanting political slogans and stopping at several corporate locations to stage "die-ins" intended to dramatize the consequences of nuclear war. On several occasions they spray-painted the walls of buildings and overturned potted plants, but Johnson himself took no part in such activities. He did, however, accept an American flag handed to him by a fellow protestor who had taken it from a flagpole outside one of the targeted buildings.

The demonstration ended in front of Dallas City Hall, where Johnson unfurled the American flag, doused it with kerosene, and set it on fire. While the flag burned, the protestors chanted: "America, the red, white, and blue, we spit on you." After the demonstrators dispersed, a witness to the flag burning collected the flag's remains and buried them in his backyard. No one was physically injured or threatened with injury, though several witnesses testified that they had been seriously offended by the flag burning.

[400] Of the approximately 100 demonstrators, Johnson alone was charged with a crime. The only criminal offense with which he was charged was the desecration of a venerated object in violation of Tex. Penal Code Ann. §42.09(a)(3) (1989).[1] After a trial, he was convicted, sentenced to one year in prison, and fined $2,000. The Court of Appeals for the Fifth District of Texas at Dallas affirmed Johnson's conviction, 706 S. W. 2d 120

(1986), but the Texas Court of Criminal Appeals reversed, 755 S. W. 2d 92 (1988), holding that the State could not, consistent with the First Amendment, punish Johnson for burning the flag in these circumstances.

The Court of Criminal Appeals began by recognizing that Johnson's conduct was symbolic speech protected by the First Amendment: "Given the context of an organized demonstration, speeches, slogans, and the distribution of literature, anyone who observed appellant's act would have understood the message that appellant intended to convey. The act for which appellant was convicted was clearly 'speech' contemplated by the First Amendment." *Id.*, at 95. To justify Johnson's conviction for engaging in symbolic speech, the State asserted two interests: preserving the flag as a symbol of national unity and preventing breaches of the peace. The Court of Criminal Appeals held that neither interest supported his conviction.

[401] Acknowledging that this Court had not yet decided whether the Government may criminally sanction flag desecration in order to preserve the flag's symbolic value, the Texas court nevertheless concluded that our decision in *West Virginia Board of Education* v. *Barnette*, 319 U. S. 624 (1943), suggested that furthering this interest by curtailing speech was impermissible. "Recognizing that the right to differ is the centerpiece of our First Amendment freedoms," the court explained, "a government cannot mandate by fiat a feeling of unity in its citizens. Therefore, that very same government cannot carve out a symbol of unity and prescribe a set of approved messages to be associated with that symbol when it cannot mandate the status or feeling the symbol purports to represent." 755 S. W. 2d, at 97. Noting that the State had not shown that the flag was in "grave and immediate danger," *Barnette, supra*, at 639, of being stripped of its symbolic value, the Texas court also decided that the flag's special status was not endangered by Johnson's conduct. 755 S. W. 2d, at 97.

As to the State's goal of preventing breaches of the peace, the court concluded that the flag-desecration statute was not drawn narrowly enough to encompass only those flag burnings that were likely to result in a serious disturbance of the peace. And in fact, the court emphasized, the flag burning in this particular case did not threaten such a reaction. "'Serious offense' occurred," the court admitted, "but there was no breach of peace nor does the record reflect that the situation was potentially explosive. One cannot equate 'serious offense' with incitement to breach the peace." *Id.*, at 96. The court also stressed that another Texas statute, Tex. Penal Code Ann. §42.01 (1989), prohibited breaches of the peace. Citing *Boos* v. *Barry*, 485 U. S. 312 (1988), the court decided that § 42.01 demonstrated Texas' ability to prevent disturbances of the peace without punishing this flag desecration. 755 S. W. 2d, at 96.

[402] Because it reversed Johnson's conviction on the ground that § 42.09 was unconstitutional as applied to him, the state court did not address Johnson's argument that the statute was, on its face, unconstitutionally vague and overbroad. We granted certiorari, 488 U. S. 907 (1988), and now affirm.

II

Johnson was convicted of flag desecration for burning the flag rather than for uttering insulting words. This fact [403] somewhat complicates our consideration of his conviction under the First Amendment. We must first determine whether Johnson's burning of the flag constituted expressive conduct, permitting him to invoke the First Amendment in challenging his conviction. See, *e. g., Spence* v. *Washington*, 418 U. S. 405, 409–411 (1974). If his conduct was expressive, we next decide whether the State's regulation is related to the suppression of free expression. See, *e. g., United States* v. *O'Brien*, 391 U. S. 367, 377 (1968); *Spence, supra*, at 414, n. 8. If the State's regulation is not related to expression, then the less stringent standard we announced in *United States* v. *O'Brien* for regulations of noncommunicative conduct controls. See *O'Brien, supra*, at 377. If it is, then we are outside of *O'Brien*'s test, and we must ask whether this interest justifies Johnson's conviction under a more demanding standard.[2] See *Spence, supra*, at 411. A [404] third possibility is that the State's asserted interest is simply not implicated on these facts, and in that event the interest drops out of the picture. See 418 U. S., at 414, n. 8.

The First Amendment literally forbids the abridgment only of "speech," but we have long recognized that its protection does not end at the spoken or written word. While we have rejected "the view that an apparently limitless variety of conduct can be labeled 'speech' whenever the person engaging in the conduct intends thereby to express an idea," *United States* v. *O'Brien, supra*, at 376, we have acknowledged that conduct may be "sufficiently imbued with elements of communication to fall within the scope of the First and Fourteenth Amendments," *Spence, supra*, at 409.

In deciding whether particular conduct possesses sufficient communicative elements to bring the First Amendment into play, we have asked whether "[a]n intent to convey a particularized message was present, and [whether] the likelihood was great that the message would be understood by those who viewed it." 418 U. S., at 410–411. Hence, we have recognized the expressive nature of students' wearing of black armbands to protest American military involvement in Vietnam, *Tinker* v. *Des Moines Independent Community School Dist.*, 393 U. S. 503, 505 (1969); of a sit-in by blacks in a "whites only" area to protest segregation, *Brown* v. *Louisiana*, 383 U. S. 131, 141–142 (1966); of the wearing of American military uniforms in a dramatic presentation criticizing American involvement in Vietnam, *Schacht* v. *United States*, 398 U. S. 58 (1970); and of picketing about a wide variety of causes, see, *e. g., Food Employees* v. *Logan Valley Plaza, Inc.*, 391 U. S. 308, 313–314 (1968); *United States* v. *Grace*, 461 U. S. 171, 176 (1983).

Especially pertinent to this case are our decisions recognizing the communicative nature of conduct relating to flags. Attaching a peace sign to the flag, *Spence, supra*, at 409–410; refusing to salute the flag, *Barnette*, 319 U. S., at 632; and displaying a red flag, *Stromberg* v. *California*, 283 U. S. 359, [405] 368–369 (1931), we have held, all may find shelter under the First Amendment. See also *Smith* v. *Goguen*, 415 U. S. 566, 588 (1974) (WHITE, J., concurring in judgment) (treating flag "contemptuously" by wearing pants with small flag sewn into their seat is expressive conduct). That we have had little difficulty identifying an expressive element in conduct relating to flags should not be surprising. The very purpose of a national flag is to serve as a symbol of our country; it is, one might say, "the one visible manifestation of two hundred years of nationhood." *Id.*, at 603 (REHNQUIST, J., dissenting). Thus, we have observed:

> "[T]he flag salute is a form of utterance. Symbolism is a primitive but effective way of communicating ideas. The use of an emblem or flag to symbolize some system, idea, institution, or personality, is a short cut from mind to mind. Causes and nations, political parties, lodges and ecclesiastical groups seek to knit the loyalty of their followings to a flag or banner, a color or design." *Barnette, supra*, at 632.

Pregnant with expressive content, the flag as readily signifies this Nation as does the combination of letters found in "America."

We have not automatically concluded, however, that any action taken with respect to our flag is expressive. Instead, in characterizing such action for First Amendment purposes, we have considered the context in which it occurred. In *Spence*, for example, we emphasized that Spence's taping of a peace sign to his flag was "roughly simultaneous with and concededly triggered by the Cambodian incursion and the Kent State tragedy." 418 U. S., at 410. The State of Washington had conceded, in fact, that Spence's conduct was a form of communication, and we stated that "the State's concession is inevitable on this record." *Id.*, at 409.

The State of Texas conceded for purposes of its oral argument in this case that Johnson's conduct was expressive conduct, Tr. of Oral Arg. 4, and this concession seems to us as [406] prudent as was Washington's in *Spence*. Johnson burned an American flag as part—indeed, as the culmination—of a political demonstration that coincided with the convening of the Republican Party and its renomination of Ronald Reagan for President. The expressive, overtly political nature of this conduct was both intentional and overwhelmingly apparent. At his trial, Johnson explained his reasons for burning the flag as follows: "The American Flag was burned as Ronald Reagan was being renominated as President. And a more powerful statement of symbolic speech, whether you agree with it or not, couldn't have been made at that time. It's quite a just position [juxtaposition]. We had new patriotism and no patriotism." 5 Record 656. In these circumstances, Johnson's burning of the flag was conduct "sufficiently imbued with elements of communication," *Spence*, 418 U. S., at 409, to implicate the First Amendment.

III

The government generally has a freer hand in restricting expressive conduct than it has in restricting the written or spoken word. See *O'Brien*, 391 U. S. at 376–377; *Clark* v. *Community for Creative Non-Violence*, 468 U. S. 288, 293 (1984); *Dallas* v. *Stanglin*, 490 U. S. 19, 25 (1989). It may not, however, proscribe particular conduct *because* it has expressive elements. "[W]hat might be termed the more generalized guarantee of freedom of expression makes the communicative nature of conduct an inadequate *basis* for singling out that conduct for proscription. A law *directed at* the communicative nature of conduct must, like a law directed at speech itself, be justified by the substantial showing of need that the First Amendment requires." *Community for Creative Non-Violence* v. *Watt*, 227 U. S. App. D. C. 19, 55–56, 703 F. 2d 586, 622–623 (1983) (Scalia, J., dissenting) (emphasis in original), rev'd *sub nom. Clark* v. *Community for Creative Non-Violence, supra*. It is, in short, not simply the verbal or nonverbal nature of the expression, but the governmental [407] interest at stake, that helps to determine whether a restriction on that expression is valid.

Thus, although we have recognized that where " 'speech' and 'nonspeech' elements are combined in the same course of conduct, a sufficiently important governmental interest in regulating the nonspeech element can justify incidental limitations on First Amendment freedoms," *O'Brien, supra*, at 376, we have limited the applicability of *O'Brien's* relatively lenient standard to those cases in which "the governmental interest is unrelated to the suppression of free expression." *Id.*, at 377; see also *Spence, supra*, at 414, n. 8. In stating, moreover, that *O'Brien's* test "in the last analysis is little, if any, different from the standard applied to time, place, or manner restrictions," *Clark, supra*, at 298, we have highlighted the requirement that the governmental interest in question be unconnected to expression in order to come under *O'Brien's* less demanding rule.

In order to decide whether *O'Brien's* test applies here, therefore, we must decide whether Texas has asserted an interest in support of Johnson's conviction that is unrelated to the suppression of expression. If we find that an interest asserted by the State is simply not implicated on the facts before us, we need not ask whether *O'Brien's* test applies. See *Spence, supra*, at 414, n. 8. The State offers two separate interests to justify this conviction: preventing breaches of the peace and preserving the flag as a symbol of nationhood and national unity. We hold that the first interest is not implicated on this record and that the second is related to the suppression of expression.

A

Texas claims that its interest in preventing breaches of the peace justifies Johnson's conviction for flag desecration.[3] [408] However, no disturbance of the peace actually occurred or threatened to occur because of Johnson's burning of the flag. Although the State stresses the disruptive behavior of the protestors during their march toward City Hall, Brief for Petitioner 34–36, it admits that "no actual breach of the peace occurred at the time of the flagburning or in response to the flagburning." *Id.*, at 34. The State's emphasis on the protestors' disorderly actions prior to arriving at City Hall is not only somewhat surprising given that no charges were brought on the basis of this conduct, but it also fails to show that a disturbance of the peace was a likely reaction to Johnson's conduct. The only evidence offered by the State at trial to show the reaction to Johnson's actions was the testimony of several persons who had been seriously offended by the flag burning. *Id.*, at 6–7.

The State's position, therefore, amounts to a claim that an audience that takes serious offense at particular expression is necessarily likely to disturb the peace and that the expression may be prohibited on this basis.[4] Our precedents do not countenance such a presumption. On the contrary, they recognize that a principal "function of free speech under our system of government is to invite dispute. It may indeed best serve its high purpose when it induces a condition of unrest, creates dissatisfaction with conditions as they are, or [409] even stirs people to anger." *Terminiello* v. *Chicago*, 337 U. S. 1, 4 (1949). See also *Cox* v. *Louisiana*, 379 U. S. 536, 551 (1965); *Tinker* v. *Des Moines Independent Community School Dist.* 393 U. S., at 508–509; *Coates* v. *Cincinnati*, 402 U. S. 611, 615 (1971); *Hustler Magazine, Inc.* v. *Falwell*, 485 U. S. 46, 55–56 (1988). It would be odd indeed to conclude *both* that "if it is the speaker's opinion that gives offense, that consequence is a reason for according it constitutional protection," *FCC v. Pacifica Foundation*, 438 U. S. 726, 745 (1978) (opinion of STEVENS, J.), *and* that the government may ban the expression of certain disagreeable ideas on the unsupported presumption that their very disagreeableness will provoke violence.

Thus, we have not permitted the government to assume that every expression of a provocative idea will incite a riot, but have instead required careful consideration of the actual circumstances surrounding such expression, asking whether the expression "is directed to inciting or producing imminent lawless action and is likely to incite or produce such action." *Brandenburg* v. *Ohio*, 395 U. S. 444, 447 (1969) (reviewing circumstances surrounding rally and speeches by Ku Klux Klan). To accept Texas' arguments that it need only demonstrate "the potential for a breach of the peace," Brief for Petitioner 37, and that every flag burning necessarily possesses that potential, would be to eviscerate our holding in *Brandenburg*. This we decline to do.

Nor does Johnson's expressive conduct fall within that small class of "fighting words" that are "likely to provoke the average person to retaliation, and thereby cause a breach of the peace." *Chaplinsky* v. *New Hampshire*, 315 U. S. 568, 574 (1942). No reasonable onlooker would have regarded Johnson's generalized expression of dissatisfaction with the policies of the Federal Government as a direct personal insult or an invitation to exchange fisticuffs. See *id.*, at 572–573; *Cantwell* v. *Connecticut*, 310 U. S. 296, 309 (1940); *FCC* v. *Pacifica Foundation*, supra, at 745 (opinion of STEVENS, J.).

[410] We thus conclude that the State's interest in maintaining order is not implicated on these facts. The State need not worry that our holding will disable it from preserving the peace. We do not suggest that the First Amendment forbids a State to prevent "imminent lawless action." *Brandenburg, supra*, at 447. And, in fact, Texas already has a statute specifically prohibiting breaches of the peace, Tex. Penal Code Ann. §42.01 (1989), which tends to confirm that Texas need not punish this flag desecration in order to keep the peace. See *Boos* v. *Barry*, 485 U. S., at 327–329.

B

The State also asserts an interest in preserving the flag as a symbol of nationhood and national unity. In *Spence*, we acknowledged that the government's interest in preserving the flag's special symbolic value "is directly related to expression in the context of activity" such as affixing a peace symbol to a flag. 418 U. S., at 414, n. 8. We are equally persuaded that this interest is related to expression in the case of Johnson's burning of the flag. The State, apparently, is concerned that such conduct will lead people to believe either that the flag does not stand for nationhood and national unity, but instead reflects other, less positive concepts, or that the concepts reflected in the flag do not in fact exist, that is, that we do not enjoy unity as a Nation. These concerns blossom only when a person's treatment of the flag communicates some message, and thus are related "to the suppression of free expression" within the meaning of *O'Brien*. We are thus outside of *O'Brien's* test altogether.

IV

It remains to consider whether the State's interest in preserving the flag as a symbol of nationhood and national unity justifies Johnson's conviction.

As in *Spence*, "[w]e are confronted with a case of prosecution for the expression of an idea through activity," and "[a]ccordingly, we must examine with particular care the interests [411] advanced by [petitioner] to support its prosecution." 418 U. S., at 411. Johnson was not, we add, prosecuted for the expression of just any idea; he was prosecuted for his expression of dissatisfaction with the policies of this country, expression situated at the core of our First Amendment values. See, *e. g.*, *Boos* v. *Barry*, supra, at 318; *Frisby* v. *Schultz*, 487 U. S. 474, 479 (1988).

Moreover, Johnson was prosecuted because he knew that his politically charged expression would cause "serious offense." If he had burned the flag as a means of disposing of it because it was dirty or torn, he would not have been convicted of flag desecration under this Texas law: federal law designates burning as the preferred means of disposing of a flag "when it is in such condition that it is no longer a fitting emblem for display," 36 U. S. C. §176(k), and Texas has no quarrel with this means of disposal. Brief for Petitioner 45. The Texas law is thus not aimed at protecting the physical integrity of the flag in all circumstances, but is designed instead to protect it only against impairments that would cause serious offense to others. Texas concedes as much: "Section 42.09(b) reaches only those severe acts of physical abuse of the flag carried out in a way likely to be offensive. The statute mandates intentional or knowing abuse, that is, the kind of mistreatment that is not innocent, but rather is intentionally designed to seriously offend other individuals." *Id.*, at 44.

Whether Johnson's treatment of the flag violated Texas law thus depended on the likely communicative impact of his expressive conduct. Our decision in *Boos v. Barry, supra*, [412] tells us that this restriction on Johnson's expression is content based. In *Boos*, we considered the constitutionality of a law prohibiting "the display of any sign within 500 feet of a foreign embassy if that sign tends to bring that foreign government into 'public odium' or 'public disrepute.' " *Id.*, at 315. Rejecting the argument that the law was content neutral because it was justified by "our international law obligation to shield diplomats from speech that offends their dignity," *id.*, at 320, we held that "[t]he emotive impact of speech on its audience is not a 'secondary effect' " unrelated to the content of the expression itself. *Id.*, at 321 (plurality opinion); see also *id.*, at 334 (BRENNAN, J., concurring in part and concurring in judgment).

According to the principles announced in *Boos*, Johnson's political expression was restricted because of the content of the message he conveyed. We must therefore subject the State's asserted interest in preserving the special symbolic character of the flag to "the most exacting scrutiny." *Boos v. Barry, supra*, at 321.[8]

[413] Texas argues that its interest in preserving the flag as a symbol of nationhood and national unity survives this close analysis. Quoting extensively from the writings of this Court chronicling the flag's historic and symbolic role in our society, the State emphasizes the " 'special place' " reserved for the flag in our Nation. Brief for Petitioner 22, quoting *Smith v. Goguen*, 415 U. S., at 601 (REHNQUIST, J., dissenting). The State's argument is not that it has an interest simply in maintaining the flag as a symbol of *something*, no matter what it symbolizes; indeed, if that were the State's position, it would be difficult to see how that interest is endangered by highly symbolic conduct such as Johnson's. Rather, the State's claim is that it has an interest in preserving the flag as a symbol of *nationhood* and *national unity*, a symbol with a determinate range of meanings. Brief for Petitioner 20–24. According to Texas, if one physically treats the flag in a way that would tend to cast doubt on either the idea that nationhood and national unity are the flag's referents or that national unity actually exists, the message conveyed thereby is a harmful one and therefore may be prohibited.[5]

[414] If there is a bedrock principle underlying the First Amendment, it is that the government may not prohibit the expression of an idea simply because society finds the idea itself offensive or disagreeable. See, *e. g.*, *Hustler Magazine, Inc. v. Falwell*, 485 U. S., at 55–56; *City Council of Los Angeles v. Taxpayers for Vincent*, 466 U. S. 789, 804 (1984); *Bolger v. Youngs Drug Products Corp.*, 463 U. S. 60, 65, 72 (1983); *Carey v. Brown*, 447 U. S. 455, 462–463 (1980); *FCC v. Pacifica Foundation*, 438 U. S., at 745–746; *Young v. American Mini Theatres, Inc.*, 427 U. S. 50, 63–65, 67–68 (1976) (plurality opinion); *Buckley v. Valeo*, 424 U. S. 1, 16–17 (1976); *Grayned v. Rockford*, 408 U. S. 104, 115 (1972); *Police Dept. of Chicago v. Mosley*, 408 U. S. 92, 95 (1972); *Bachellar v. Maryland*, 397 U. S. 564, 567 (1970); *O'Brien*, 391 U. S., at 382; *Brown v. Louisiana*, 383 U. S., at 142–143; *Stromberg v. California*, 283 U. S., at 368–369.

We have not recognized an exception to this principle even where our flag has been involved. In *Street v. New York*, 394 U. S. 576 (1969), we held that a State may not criminally punish a person for uttering words critical of the flag. Rejecting the argument that the conviction could be sustained on the ground that Street had "failed to show the respect for our national symbol which may properly be demanded of every citizen," we concluded that "the constitutionally guaranteed "freedom to be intellectually . . . diverse or even contrary,' and the 'right to differ as to things that touch the heart of the existing order,' encompass the freedom to express publicly one's opinions about our flag, including those opinions which are defiant or contemptuous." *Id.*, at 593, quoting *Barnette*, 319 U. S., at 642. Nor may the government, we have held, compel conduct that would evince respect for the flag. "To sustain the compulsory flag salute we are required to say that a Bill of Rights which guards the individual's right to speak his own mind, left it open to public authorities to compel him to utter what is not in his mind." *Id.*, at 634.

[415] In holding in *Barnette* that the Constitution did not leave this course open to the government, Justice Jackson described one of our society's defining principles in words deserving of their frequent repetition: "If there is any fixed star in our constitutional constellation, it is that no official, high or petty, can prescribe what shall be orthodox in politics, nationalism, religion, or other matters of opinion or force citizens to confess by word or act their faith therein." *Id.*, at 642. In *Spence*, we held that the same interest asserted by Texas here was insufficient to support a criminal conviction under a flag-misuse statute for the taping of a peace sign to an American flag. "Given the protected character of [Spence's] expression and in light of the fact that no interest the State may have in preserving the physical integrity of a privately owned flag was significantly impaired on these facts," we held, "the conviction must be invalidated." 418 U. S., at 415. See also *Goguen*, *supra*, at 588 (WHITE, J., concurring in judgment) (to convict person who had sewn a flag onto the seat of his pants for "contemptuous" treatment of the flag would be "[t]o convict not to protect the physical integrity or to protect against acts interfering with the proper use of the flag, but to punish for communicating ideas unacceptable to the controlling majority in the legislature").

In short, nothing in our precedents suggests that a State may foster its own view of the flag by prohibiting expressive conduct relating to it. To bring its argument outside our [416] precedents, Texas attempts to convince us that even if its interest in preserving the flag's symbolic role does not allow it to prohibit words or some expressive conduct critical of the flag, it does permit it to forbid the outright destruction of the flag. The State's argument cannot depend here on the distinction between written or spoken words and nonverbal conduct. That distinction, we have shown, is of no moment where the nonverbal conduct is expressive, as it is here, and where the regulation of that conduct is related to expression, as it is here. See *supra*, at 402–403. In addition, both *Barnette* and *Spence* involved expressive conduct, not only verbal communication, and both found that conduct protected.

Texas' focus on the precise nature of Johnson's expression, moreover, misses the point of our prior decisions: their enduring lesson, that the government may not prohibit expression simply because it disagrees with its message, is not dependent on the particular mode in which one chooses to express an idea. If we were to hold that a State may forbid flag burning wherever it is likely to endanger the flag's symbolic role, but allow it wherever burning a flag promotes that role—as where, for example, a person ceremoniously burns a dirty flag — we would be saying that when it comes to impairing the flag's physical integrity, the flag itself may be used as [417] a symbol—as a substitute for the written or spoken word or a "short cut from mind to mind" —only in one direction. We would be permitting a State to "prescribe what shall be orthodox" by saying that one may burn the flag to convey one's attitude toward it and its referents only if one does not endanger the flag's representation of nationhood and national unity.

We never before have held that the Government may ensure that a symbol be used to express only one view of that symbol or its referents. Indeed, in *Schacht* v. *United States*, we invalidated a federal statute permitting an actor portraying a member of one of our Armed Forces to " 'wear the uniform of that armed force if the portrayal does not tend to discredit that armed force.' " 398 U. S., at 60, quoting 10 U. S. C. §772(f). This proviso, we held, "which leaves Americans free to praise the war in Vietnam but can send persons like Schacht to prison for opposing it, cannot survive in a country which has the First Amendment." *Id.*, at 63.

We perceive no basis on which to hold that the principle underlying our decision in *Schacht* does not apply to this case. To conclude that the government may permit designated symbols to be used to communicate only a limited set of messages would be to enter territory having no discernible or defensible boundaries. Could the government, on this theory, prohibit the burning of state flags? Of copies of the Presidential seal? Of the Constitution? In evaluating these choices under the First Amendment, how would we decide which symbols were sufficiently special to warrant this unique status? To do so, we would be forced to consult our own political preferences, and impose them on the citizenry, in the very way that the First Amendment forbids us to do. See *Carey* v. *Brown*, 447 U. S., at 466–467.

There is, moreover, no indication—either in the text of the Constitution or in our cases interpreting it—that a separate juridical category exists for the American flag alone. Indeed, we would not be surprised to learn that the persons [418] who framed our Constitution and wrote the Amendment that we now construe were not known for their reverence for the Union Jack. The First Amendment does not guarantee that other concepts virtually sacred to our Nation as a whole—such as the principle that discrimination on the basis of race is odious and destructive—will go unquestioned in the marketplace of ideas. See *Brandenburg* v. *Ohio*, 395 U. S. 444 (1969). We decline, therefore, to create for the flag an exception to the joust of principles protected by the First Amendment.

It is not the State's ends, but its means, to which we object. It cannot be gainsaid that there is a special place reserved for the flag in this Nation, and thus we do not doubt that the government has a legitimate interest in making efforts to "preserv[e] the national flag as an unalloyed symbol of our country." *Spence*, 418 U. S., at 412. We reject the suggestion, urged at oral argument by counsel for Johnson, that the government lacks "any state interest whatsoever" in regulating the manner in which the flag may be displayed. Tr. of Oral Arg. 38. Congress has, for example, enacted precatory regulations describing the proper treatment of the flag, see 36 U. S. C. §§ 173–177, and we cast no doubt on the legitimacy of its interest in making such recommendations. To say that the government has an interest in encouraging proper treatment of the flag, however, is not to say that it may criminally punish a person for burning a flag as a means of political protest. "National unity as an end which officials may foster by persuasion and example is not in question. The problem is whether under our Constitution compulsion as here employed is a permissible means for its achievement." *Barnette*, 319 U. S., at 640.

We are fortified in today's conclusion by our conviction that forbidding criminal punishment for conduct such as Johnson's will not endanger the special role played by our flag or the feelings it inspires. To paraphrase Justice Holmes, we submit that nobody can suppose that this one gesture of an unknown [419] man will change our Nation's attitude towards its flag. See *Abrams* v. *United States*, 250 U. S. 616, 628 (1919) (Holmes, J., dissenting). Indeed, Texas' argument that the burning of an American flag " 'is an act having a high likelihood to cause a breach of the peace,' " Brief for Petitioner 31, quoting *Sutherland* v. *DeWulf*, 323 F. Supp. 740, 745 (SD Ill. 1971) (citation omitted), and its statute's implicit assumption that physical mistreatment of the flag will lead to "serious offense," tend to confirm that the flag's special role is not in danger; if it were, no one would riot or take offense because a flag had been burned.

We are tempted to say, in fact, that the flag's deservedly cherished place in our community will be strengthened, not weakened, by our holding today. Our decision is a reaffirmation of the principles of freedom and inclusiveness that the flag best reflects, and of the conviction that our toleration of criticism such as Johnson's is a sign and source of our strength. Indeed, one of the proudest images of our flag, the one immortalized in our own national anthem, is of the bombardment it survived at Fort McHenry. It is the Nation's resilience, not its rigidity, that Texas sees reflected in the flag — and it is that resilience that we reassert today.

The way to preserve the flag's special role is not to punish those who feel differently about these matters. It is to persuade them that they are wrong. "To courageous, self-reliant men, with confidence in the power of free and fearless reasoning applied through the processes of popular government, no danger flowing from speech can be deemed clear and present, unless the incidence of the evil apprehended is so imminent that it may befall before there is opportunity for full discussion. If there be time to expose through discussion the falsehood and fallacies, to avert the evil by the processes of education, the remedy to be applied is more speech, not enforced silence." *Whitney* v. *California*, 274 U. S. 357, 377 (1927) (Brandeis, J., concurring). And, precisely because it is our flag that is involved, one's response to the flag [420A] burner may exploit the uniquely persuasive power of the flag itself. We can imagine no more appropriate response to burning a flag than waving one's own, no better way to counter a flag burner's message than by saluting the flag that burns, no surer means of preserving the dignity even of the flag that burned than by — as one witness here did — according its remains a respectful burial. We do not consecrate the flag by punishing its desecration, for in doing so we dilute the freedom that this cherished emblem represents.

V

Johnson was convicted for engaging in expressive conduct. The State's interest in preventing breaches of the peace does not support his conviction because Johnson's conduct did not threaten to disturb the peace. Nor does the State's interest in preserving the flag as a symbol of nationhood and national unity justify his criminal conviction for engaging in political expression. The judgment of the Texas Court of Criminal Appeals is therefore

Affirmed.

...[420B-439]...

NOTES

[1]Texas Penal Code Ann. §42.09 (1989) provides in full:

"§42.09. Desecration of Venerated Object

"(a) A person commits an offense if he intentionally or knowingly desecrates:

"(1) a public monument;

"(2) a place of worship or burial; or

"(3) a state or national flag.

"(b) For purposes of this section, 'desecrate' means deface, damage, or otherwise physically mistreat in a way that the actor knows will seriously offend one or more persons likely to observe or discover his action.

"(c) An offense under this section is a Class A misdemeanor."

[2]Although Johnson has raised a facial challenge to Texas' flag-desecration statute, we choose to resolve this case on the basis of his claim that the statute as applied to him violates the First Amendment. Section 42.09 regulates only physical conduct with respect to the flag, not the written or spoken word, and although one violates the statute only if one "knows" that one's physical treatment of the flag "will seriously offend one or more persons likely to observe or discover his action," Tex. Penal Code Ann. §42.09(b) (1989), this fact does not necessarily mean that the statute applies only to *expressive* conduct protected by the First Amendment. Cf. *Smith* v. *Goguen*, 415 U. S. 566, 588 (1974) (WHITE, J., concurring in judgment) (statute prohibiting "contemptuous" treatment of flag encompasses only expressive conduct). A tired person might, for example, drag a flag through the mud, knowing that this conduct is likely to offend others, and yet have no thought of expressing any idea; neither the language nor the Texas courts' interpretations of the statute precludes the possibility that such a person would be prosecuted for flag desecration. Because the prosecution of a person who had not engaged in expressive conduct would pose a different case, and because this case may be disposed of on narrower grounds, we address only Johnson's claim that § 42.09 as applied to political expression like his violates the First Amendment.

[3]Relying on our decision in *Boos* v. *Barry*, 485 U. S. 312 (1988), Johnson argues that this state interest is related to the suppression of free expression within the meaning of *United States* v. *O'Brien*, 391 U. S. 367 (1968). He reasons that the violent reaction to flag burnings feared by Texas would be the result of the message conveyed by them, and that this fact connects the State's interest to the suppression of expression. Brief for Respondent 12, n. 11. This view has found some favor in the lower courts. See *Monroe* v. *State Court of Fulton County*, 739 F. 2d 568, 574–575 (CA11 1984). Johnson's theory may overread *Boos* insofar as it suggests that a desire to prevent a violent audience reaction is "related to expression" in the same way that a desire to prevent an audience from being offended is "related to expression." Because we find that the State's interest in preventing breaches of the peace is not implicated on these facts, however, we need not venture further into this area.

[4]There is, of course, a tension between this argument and the State's claim that one need not actually cause serious offense in order to violate § 42.09. See Brief for Petitioner 44.

[5]Texas claims that "Texas is not endorsing, protecting, avowing or prohibiting any particular philosophy." Brief for Petitioner 29. If Texas means to suggest that its asserted interest does not prefer Democrats over Socialists, or Republicans over Democrats, for example, then it is beside the point, for Johnson does not rely on such an argument. He argues instead that the State's desire to maintain the flag as a symbol of nationhood and national unity assumes that there is only one proper view of the flag. Thus, if Texas means to argue that its interest does not prefer *any* viewpoint over another, it is mistaken; surely one's attitude toward the flag and its referents is a viewpoint.

SUPREME COURT OF THE UNITED STATES

31 U.S. 568

CHAPLINSKY V. NEW HAMPSHIRE

APPEAL FROM THE SUPREME COURT OF NEW HAMPSHIRE

NO. 255 ARGUED: FEBRUARY 5, 1942—DECIDED: MARCH 9, 1942

OPINION: [569] MR. JUSTICE MURPHY delivered the opinion of the Court.

Appellant, a member of the sect known as Jehovah's Witnesses, was convicted in the municipal court of Rochester, New Hampshire, for violation of Chapter 378, §2, of the Public Laws of New Hampshire:

"No person shall address any offensive, derisive or annoying word to any other person who is lawfully in any street or other public place, nor call him by any offensive or derisive name, nor make any noise or exclamation in his presence and hearing with intent to deride, offend or annoy him, or to prevent him from pursuing his lawful business or occupation."

The complaint charged that appellant, "with force and arms, in a certain public place in said city of Rochester, to wit, on the public sidewalk on the easterly side of Wakefield Street, near unto the entrance of the City Hall, did unlawfully repeat, the words following, addressed to the complainant, that is to say, 'You are a God damned racketeer' and 'a damned Fascist and the whole government of Rochester are Fascists or agents of Fascists,' the same being offensive, derisive and annoying words and names."

Upon appeal there was a trial *de novo* of appellant before a jury in the Superior Court. He was found guilty and the judgment of conviction was affirmed by the Supreme Court of the State. 91 N.H. 310, 18 A.2d 754....

There is no substantial dispute over the facts. Chaplinsky was distributing the literature of his sect on the streets [570] of Rochester on a busy Saturday afternoon. Members of the local citizenry complained to the City Marshal, Bowering, that Chaplinsky was denouncing all religion as a "racket." Bowering told them that Chaplinsky was lawfully engaged, and then warned Chaplinsky that the crowd was getting restless. Some time later, a disturbance occurred and the traffic officer on duty at the busy intersection started with Chaplinsky for the police station, but did not inform him that he was under arrest or that he was going to be arrested. On the way, they encountered Marshal Bowering, who had been advised that a riot was under way and was therefore hurrying to the scene. Bowering repeated his earlier warning to Chaplinsky, who then addressed to Bowering the words set forth in the complaint.

Chaplinsky's version of the affair was slightly different. He testified that, when he met Bowering, he asked him to arrest the ones responsible for the disturbance. In reply, Bowering cursed him and told him to come along. Appellant admitted that he said the words charged in the complaint, with the exception of the name of the Deity.

It is now clear that "Freedom of speech and freedom of the press, which are protected by the First Amendment from infringement by Congress, are among the fundamental personal rights and liberties which are protected by the Fourteenth Amendment from invasion by state [571] action." *Lovell* v. *Griffin*, 303 U.S. 444, 450. Freedom of worship is similarly sheltered. *Cantwell* v. *Connecticut*, 310 U.S. 296, 303.

Appellant assails the statute as a violation of all three freedoms, speech, press and worship, but only an attack on the basis of free speech is warranted. The spoken, not the written, word is involved. And we cannot conceive that cursing a public officer is the exercise of religion in any sense of the term. But even if the activities of the appellant which preceded the incident could be viewed as religious in character, and therefore entitled to the protection of the Fourteenth Amendment, they would not cloak him with immunity from the legal consequences for concomitant acts committed in violation of a valid criminal statute. We turn, therefore, to an examination of the statute itself.

Allowing the broadest scope to the language and purpose of the Fourteenth Amendment, it is well understood that the right of free speech is not absolute at all times and under all circumstances. There are certain well-defined and narrowly limited classes of speech, the prevention [572] and punishment of which have never been thought to raise any Constitutional problem. These include the lewd and obscene, the profane, the libelous, and the insulting or "fighting" words — those which by their very utterance inflict injury or tend to incite an immediate breach of the peace. It has been well observed that such utterances are no essential part of any exposition of ideas, and are of such slight social value as a step to truth that any benefit that may be derived from them is clearly outweighed by the social interest in order and morality. "Resort to epithets or personal abuse is not in any proper sense communication of information or opinion safeguarded by the Constitution, and its punishment as a criminal act would raise no question under that instrument." *Cantwell* v. *Connecticut*, 310 U.S. 296, 309–310.

The state statute here challenged comes to us authoritatively construed by the highest court of New Hampshire. It has two provisions — the first relates to words or names addressed to another in a public place; the second refers to noises and exclamations. The court said: "The two provisions are distinct. One may stand separately from the other. Assuming, without holding, that the second were unconstitutional, the first could stand if constitutional." We accept that construction of severability and limit our consideration to the first provision of the statute.

[573] On the authority of its earlier decisions, the state court declared that the statute's purpose was to preserve the public peace, no words being "forbidden except such as have a direct tendency to cause acts of violence by the persons to whom, individually, the remark is addressed." It was further said: "The word 'offensive' is not to be defined in terms of what a particular addressee thinks. . . . The test is what men of common intelligence would understand would be words likely to cause an average addressee to fight. . . . The English language has a number of words and expressions which by general consent are 'fighting words' when said without a disarming smile. . . . Such words, as ordinary men know, are likely to cause a fight. So are threatening, profane or obscene revilings. Derisive and annoying words can be taken as coming within the purview of the statute as heretofore interpreted only when they have this characteristic of plainly tending to excite the addressee to a breach of the peace. . . . The statute, as construed, does no more than prohibit the face-to-face words plainly likely to cause a breach of the peace by the addressee, words whose speaking constitutes a breach of the peace by the speaker—including 'classical fighting words', words in current use less 'classical' but equally likely to cause violence, and other disorderly words, including profanity, obscenity and threats."

We are unable to say that the limited scope of the statute as thus construed contravenes the Constitutional right of free expression. It is a statute narrowly drawn and limited to define and punish specific conduct lying within the domain of state power, the use in a public place of words likely to cause a breach of the peace. Cf. *Cantwell* v. *Connecticut*, 310 U.S. 296, 311; *Thornhill* v. *Alabama*, [574] 310 U.S. 88, 105. This conclusion necessarily disposes of appellant's contention that the statute is so vague and indefinite as to render a conviction thereunder a violation of due process. A statute punishing verbal acts, carefully drawn so as not unduly to impair liberty of expression, is not too vague for a criminal law. Cf. *Fox* v. *Washington*, 236 U.S. 273, 277.

Nor can we say that the application of the statute to the facts disclosed by the record substantially or unreasonably impinges upon the privilege of free speech. Argument is unnecessary to demonstrate that the appellations "damned racketeer" and "damned Fascist" are epithets likely to provoke the average person to retaliation, and thereby cause a breach of the peace.

The refusal of the state court to admit evidence of provocation and evidence bearing on the truth or falsity of the utterances, is open to no Constitutional objection. Whether the facts sought to be proved by such evidence constitute a defense to the charge, or may be shown in mitigation, are questions for the state court to determine. Our function is fulfilled by a determination that the challenged statute, on its face and as applied, does not contravene the Fourteenth Amendment.

Affirmed.

SUPREME COURT OF THE UNITED STATES

505 U.S. 377

R.A.V. v. City of St. Paul, Minnesota

CERTIORARI TO THE SUPREME COURT OF MINNESOTA

No. 90-5675 Argued: December 4, 1991—Decided: June 22, 1992

OPINION: [379] JUSTICE SCALIA delivered the opinion of the Court.

In the predawn hours of June 21, 1990, petitioner and several other teenagers allegedly assembled a crudely made cross by taping together broken chair legs. They then allegedly burned the cross inside the fenced yard of a black family that lived across the street from the house where petitioner was staying. Although this conduct could have been punished [380] under any of a number of laws, one of the two provisions under which respondent city of St. Paul chose to charge petitioner (then a juvenile) was the St. Paul Bias-Motivated Crime Ordinance, St. Paul, Minn., Legis. Code § 292.02 (1990), which provides:

> "Whoever places on public or private property a symbol, object, appellation, characterization or graffiti, including, but not limited to, a burning cross or Nazi swastika, which one knows or has reasonable grounds to know arouses anger, alarm or resentment in others on the basis of race, color, creed, religion or gender commits disorderly conduct and shall be guilty of a misdemeanor." Petitioner moved to dismiss this count on the ground that the St. Paul ordinance was substantially overbroad and impermissibly content based and therefore facially invalid under the First Amendment. The trial court granted this motion, but the Minnesota Supreme Court reversed. That court rejected petitioner's overbreadth claim because, as construed in prior Minnesota cases, see, e. g., In re Welfare of S. L. J., 263 N. W. 2d 412 (Minn. 1978), the modifying phrase "arouses anger, alarm or resentment in others" limited the reach of the ordinance to conduct that amounts to "fighting words," i. e., "conduct that itself inflicts injury or tends to incite immediate violence . . .," In re Welfare of R. A. V., 464 N. W. 2d 507, 510 (Minn. 1991) (citing Chaplin- [381] sky v. New Hampshire, 315 U. S. 568, 572 (1942)), and therefore the ordinance reached only expression "that the first amendment does not protect," 464 N. W. 2d, at 511. The court also concluded that the ordinance was not impermissibly content based because, in its view, "the ordinance is a narrowly tailored means toward accomplishing the compelling governmental interest in protecting the community against bias-motivated threats to public safety and order." Ibid. We granted certiorari, 501 U. S. 1204 (1991).

I

In construing the St. Paul ordinance, we are bound by the construction given to it by the Minnesota court. *Posadas de Puerto Rico Associates* v. *Tourism Co. of Puerto Rico*, 478 U. S. 328, 339 (1986); *New York* v. *Ferber*, 458 U. S. 747, 769, n. 24 (1982); *Terminiello* v. *Chicago*, 337 U. S. 1, 4 (1949). Accordingly, we accept the Minnesota Supreme Court's authoritative statement that the ordinance reaches only those expressions that constitute "fighting words" within the meaning of *Chaplinsky*. 464 N. W. 2d, at 510–511. Petitioner and his *amici* urge us to modify the scope of the *Chaplinsky* formulation, thereby invalidating the ordinance as "substantially overbroad," *Broadrick* v. *Oklahoma*, 413 U. S. 601, 610 (1973). We find it unnecessary to consider this issue. Assuming, *arguendo,* that all of the expression reached by the ordinance is proscribable under the "fighting words" doctrine, we nonetheless conclude that the ordinance is facially unconstitutional in that it prohibits otherwise permitted speech solely on the basis of the subjects the speech addresses.

[382] The First Amendment generally prevents government from proscribing speech, see, *e. g.,* *Cantwell* v. *Connecticut*, 310 U. S. 296, 309–311 (1940), or even expressive conduct, see, *e. g.,* *Texas* v. *Johnson*, 491 U. S. 397, 406 (1989), because of disapproval of the ideas expressed. Content-based regulations are presumptively invalid. *Simon & Schuster, Inc.* v. *Members of N. Y. State Crime Victims Bd.*, 502 U. S. 105, 115 (1991); *id.,* at 124 (Kennedy, J., concurring in judgment); *Consolidated Edison Co. of N. Y.* v. *Public Serv. Comm'n of N. Y.*, 447 U. S. 530, 536 (1980); *Police Dept. of Chicago* v. *Mosley*, 408 U. S. 92, 95 (1972). From 1791 to the present, however, our society, like other free but civilized societies, has permitted restrictions upon the content of speech in a [383] few limited areas, which are "of such slight social value as a step to truth that any benefit that may be derived from them is clearly outweighed by the social interest in order and morality." *Chaplinsky, supra,* at 572. We have recognized that "the freedom of speech" referred to by the First Amendment does not include a freedom to disregard these traditional limitations. See, *e. g., Roth* v. *United States*, 354 U. S. 476 (1957) (obscenity); *Beauharnais* v. *Illinois*, 343 U. S. 250 (1952) (defamation); *Chaplinsky* v. *New Hampshire, supra* ("'fighting' words"); see generally *Simon & Schuster, supra,* at 124 (Kennedy, J., concurring in judgment). Our decisions since the 1960's have narrowed the scope of the traditional categorical exceptions for defamation, see *New York Times Co.* v. *Sullivan*, 376 U. S. 254 (1964); *Gertz* v. *Robert Welch, Inc.*, 418 U. S. 323 (1974); see generally *Milkovich* v. *Lorain Journal Co.*, 497 U. S. 1, 13–17 (1990), and for obscenity, see *Miller* v. *California*, 413 U. S. 15 (1973), but a limited categorical approach has remained an important part of our First Amendment jurisprudence.

We have sometimes said that these categories of expression are "not within the area of constitutionally protected speech," *Roth, supra,* at 483; *Beauharnais, supra,* at 266; *Chaplinsky, supra,* at 571–572, or that the "protection of the First Amendment does not extend" to them, *Bose Corp.* v. *Consumers Union of United States, Inc.*, 466 U. S. 485, 504 (1984); *Sable Communications of Cal., Inc.* v. *FCC*, 492 U. S. 115, 124 (1989). Such statements must be taken in context, however, and are no more literally true than is the occasionally repeated shorthand characterizing obscenity "as not being speech at all," Sunstein, Pornography and the First Amendment, 1986 Duke L. J. 589, 615, n. 46. What they mean is that these areas of speech can, consistently with the First Amendment, be regulated *because of their constitutionally proscribable content* (obscenity, defamation, etc.)—not that they are categories of speech entirely invisible to the Constitution, so that they may be made the vehicles for [384] content discrimination unrelated to their distinctively proscribable content. Thus, the government may proscribe libel; but it may not make the further content discrimination of proscribing *only* libel critical of the government. We recently acknowledged this distinction in *Ferber*, 458 U. S., at 763, where, in upholding New York's child pornography law, we expressly recognized that there was no "question here of censoring a particular literary theme . . . ." See also *id.,* at 775 (O'Connor, J., concurring) ("As drafted, New York's statute does not attempt to suppress the communication of particular ideas").

Our cases surely do not establish the proposition that the First Amendment imposes no obstacle whatsoever to regulation of particular instances of such proscribable expression, so that the government "may regulate [them] freely," *post*, at 400 (White, J., concurring in judgment). That would mean that a city council could enact an ordinance prohibiting only those legally obscene works that contain criticism of the city government or, indeed, that do not include endorsement of the city government. Such a simplistic, all-or-nothing-at all approach to First Amendment protection is at odds with common sense and with our jurisprudence as well. It is [385] not true that "fighting words" have at most a "*de minimis*" expressive content, *ibid.*, or that their content is *in all respects* "worthless and undeserving of constitutional protection," *post,* at 401; sometimes they are quite expressive indeed. We have not said that they constitute "*no* part of the expression of ideas," but only that they constitute "no *essential* part of any exposition of ideas." *Chaplinsky, supra,* at 572 (emphasis added).

The proposition that a particular instance of speech can be proscribable on the basis of one feature (*e. g.,* obscenity) but not on the basis of another (*e. g.,* opposition to the city government) is commonplace and has found application in many contexts. We have long held, for example, that nonverbal expressive activity can be banned because of the action it entails, but not because of the ideas it expresses—so that burning a flag in violation of an ordinance against outdoor fires could be punishable, whereas burning a flag in violation of an ordinance against dishonoring the flag is not. See *Johnson,* 491 U. S., at 406–407. See also *Barnes* v. *Glen Theatre, Inc.,* 501 U. S. 560, 569–570 (1991) (plurality opinion); *id.,* at 573–574 (Scalia, J., concurring in judgment); *id.,* at 581–582 (Souter, J., concurring in judgment); *United* [386] *States* v. *O'Brien,* 391 U. S. 367, 376–377 (1968). Similarly, we have upheld reasonable "time, place, or manner" restrictions, but only if they are "justified without reference to the content of the regulated speech." *Ward* v. *Rock Against Racism,* 491 U. S. 781, 791 (1989) (internal quotation marks omitted); see also *Clark* v. *Community for Creative NonViolence,* 468 U. S. 288, 298 (1984) (noting that the *O'Brien* test differs little from the standard applied to time, place, or manner restrictions). And just as the power to proscribe particular speech on the basis of a noncontent element (*e. g.,* noise) does not entail the power to proscribe the same speech on the basis of a content element; so also, the power to proscribe it on the basis of *one* content element (*e. g.,* obscenity) does not entail the power to proscribe it on the basis of *other* content elements.

In other words, the exclusion of "fighting words" from the scope of the First Amendment simply means that, for purposes of that Amendment, the unprotected features of the words are, despite their verbal character, essentially a "nonspeech" element of communication. Fighting words are thus analogous to a noisy sound truck: Each is, as Justice Frankfurter recognized, a "mode of speech," *Niemotko* v. *Maryland,* 340 U. S. 268, 282 (1951) (opinion concurring in result); both can be used to convey an idea; but neither has, in and of itself, a claim upon the First Amendment. As with the sound truck, however, so also with fighting words: The government may not regulate use based on hostility—or favoritism—towards the underlying message expressed. Compare *Frisby* v. *Schultz,* 487 U. S. 474 (1988) (upholding, against facial challenge, a content-neutral ban on targeted residential picketing), with *Carey* v. *Brown,* 447 U. S. 455 (1980) (invalidating a ban on residential picketing that exempted labor picketing).

...[387]...

Even the prohibition against content discrimination that we assert the First Amendment requires is not absolute. It applies differently in the context of proscribable speech than in the area of fully protected speech. The rationale of the general prohibition, after all, is that content discrimination "raises the specter that the Government may effectively drive certain ideas or viewpoints from the marketplace," *Simon & Schuster,* 502 U. S., at 116; *Leathers* v. *Medlock,* 499 U. S. 439, 448 (1991); *FCC* v. *League of Women Voters of Cal.,* 468 U. S. 364, 383–384 (1984); *Consolidated Edison Co.,* 447 U. S., at 536; *Police Dept. of Chicago* v. *Mosley,* 408 U. S., [388] at 95–98. But content discrimination among various instances of a class of proscribable speech often does not pose this threat.

When the basis for the content discrimination consists entirely of the very reason the entire class of speech at issue is proscribable, no significant danger of idea or viewpoint discrimination exists. Such a reason, having been adjudged neutral enough to support exclusion of the entire class of speech from First Amendment protection, is also neutral enough to form the basis of distinction within the class. To illustrate: A State might choose to prohibit only that obscenity which is the most patently offensive *in its prurience* — *i. e.,* that which involves the most lascivious displays of sexual activity. But it may not prohibit, for example, only that obscenity which includes offensive *political* messages. See *Kucharek* v. *Hanaway,* 902 F. 2d 513, 517 (CA7 1990), cert. denied, 498 U. S. 1041 (1991). And the Federal Government can criminalize only those threats of violence that are directed against the President, see 18 U. S. C. §871—since the reasons why threats of violence are outside the First Amendment (protecting individuals from the fear of violence, from the disruption that fear engenders, and from the possibility that the threatened violence will occur) have special force when applied to the person of the President. See *Watts* v. *United States*, 394 U. S. 705, 707 (1969) (upholding the facial validity of § 871 because of the "overwhelmin[g] interest in protecting the safety of [the] Chief Executive and in allowing him to perform his duties without interference from threats of physical violence"). But the Federal Government may not criminalize only those threats against the President that mention his policy on aid to inner cities. And to take a final example (one mentioned by Justice Stevens, *post*, at 421–422), a State may choose to regulate price advertising in one industry but not in others, because the risk of fraud (one of the characteristics of commercial speech that justifies depriving it of full First Amendment protection, see *Virginia* [389] *State Bd. of Pharmacy* v. *Virginia Citizens Consumer Council, Inc.*, 425 U. S. 748, 771–772 (1976)) is in its view greater there. Cf. *Morales* v. *Trans World Airlines, Inc.*, 504 U. S. 374 (1992) (state regulation of airline advertising); *Ohralik* v. *Ohio State Bar Assn.*, 436 U. S. 447 (1978) (state regulation of lawyer advertising). But a State may not prohibit only that commercial advertising that depicts men in a demeaning fashion. See, *e. g.*, Los Angeles Times, Aug. 8, 1989, section 4, p. 6, col. 1.

Another valid for according differential treatment to even a content-defined subclass of proscribable speech is that the subclass happens to be associated with particular "secondary effects" of the speech, so that the regulation is "*justified* without reference to the content of the . . . speech," *Renton* v. *Playtime Theatres, Inc.*, 475 U. S. 41, 48 (1986) (quoting, with emphasis, *Virginia State Bd. of Pharmacy, supra*, at 771); see also *Young* v. *American Mini Theatres, Inc.*, 427 U. S. 50, 71, n. 34 (1976) (plurality opinion); *id.*, at 80–82 (Powell, J., concurring); *Barnes*, 501 U. S., at 586 (Souter, J., concurring in judgment). A State could, for example, permit all obscene live performances except those involving minors. Moreover, since words can in some circumstances violate laws directed not against speech but against conduct (a law against treason, for example, is violated by telling the enemy the Nation's defense secrets), a particular content-based subcategory of a proscribable class of speech can be swept up incidentally within the reach of a statute directed at conduct rather than speech. See *id.*, at 571 (plurality opinion); *id.*, at 577 (Scalia, J., concurring in judgment); *id.*, at 582 (Souter, J., concurring in judgment); *FTC* v. *Superior Court Trial Lawyers Assn.*, 493 U. S. 411, 425—432 (1990); *O'Brien*, 391 U. S., at 376–377. Thus, for example, sexually derogatory "fighting words," among other words, may produce a violation of Title VII's general prohibition against sexual discrimination in employment practices, 42 U. S. C. §2000e—2; 29 CFR § 1604.11 (1991). See also 18 [390] U. S. C. §242; 42 U. S. C. §§ 1981, 1982. Where the government does not target conduct on the basis of its expressive content, acts are not shielded from regulation merely because they express a discriminatory idea or philosophy. . . .

[391] II

Applying these principles to the St. Paul ordinance, we conclude that, even as narrowly construed by the Minnesota Supreme Court, the ordinance is facially unconstitutional. Although the phrase in the ordinance, "arouses anger, alarm or resentment in others," has been limited by the Minnesota Supreme Court's construction to reach only those symbols or displays that amount to "fighting words," the remaining, unmodified terms make clear that the ordinance applies only to "fighting words" that insult, or provoke violence, "on the basis of race, color, creed, religion or gender." Displays containing abusive invective, no matter how vicious or severe, are permissible unless they are addressed to one of the specified disfavored topics. Those who wish to use "fighting words" in connection with other ideas—to express hostility, for example, on the basis of political affiliation, union membership, or homosexuality—are not covered. The First Amendment does not permit St. Paul to impose special prohibitions on those speakers who express views on disfavored subjects. See *Simon & Schuster*, 502 U. S., at 116; *Arkansas Writers' Project, Inc.* v. *Ragland*, 481 U. S. 221, 229–230 (1987).

In its practical operation, moreover, the ordinance goes even beyond mere content discrimination, to actual viewpoint discrimination. Displays containing some words—odious racial epithets, for example—would be prohibited to proponents of all views. But "fighting words" that do not themselves invoke race, color, creed, religion, or gender—aspersions upon a person's mother, for example—would seemingly be usable *ad libitum* in the placards of those arguing *in favor* of racial, color, etc., tolerance and equality, but could not be used by those speakers' opponents. One could hold up a sign saying, for example, that all "anti- [392] Catholic bigots" are misbegotten; but not that all "papists" are, for that would insult and provoke violence "on the basis of religion." St. Paul has no such authority to license one side of a debate to fight freestyle, while requiring the other to follow Marquis of Queensberry rules.

What we have here, it must be emphasized, is not a prohibition of fighting words that are directed at certain persons or groups (which would be *facially* valid if it met the requirements of the Equal Protection Clause); but rather, a prohibition of fighting words that contain (as the Minnesota Supreme Court repeatedly emphasized) messages of "biasmotivated" hatred and in particular, as applied to this case, messages "based on virulent notions of racial supremacy." 464 N. W. 2d, at 508, 511. One must wholeheartedly agree with the Minnesota Supreme Court that "[i]t is the responsibility, even the obligation, of diverse communities to confront such notions in whatever form they appear," *id.*, at 508, but the manner of that confrontation cannot consist of selective limitations upon speech. St. Paul's brief asserts that a general "fighting words" law would not meet the city's needs because only a content-specific measure can communicate to minority groups that the "group hatred" aspect of such speech "is not condoned by the majority." Brief for Respondent 25. The point of the First Amendment is that majority preferences must be expressed in some fashion other than silencing speech on the basis of its content.

...[393]...

The content-based discrimination reflected in the St. Paul ordinance comes within neither any of the specific exceptions to the First Amendment prohibition we discussed earlier nor a more general exception for content discrimination that does not threaten censorship of ideas. It assuredly does not fall within the exception for content discrimination based on the very reasons why the particular class of speech at issue (here, fighting words) is proscribable. As explained earlier, see *supra*, at 386, the reason why fighting words are categorically excluded from the protection of the First Amendment is not that their content communicates any particular idea, but that their content embodies a particularly intolerable (and socially unnecessary) *mode* of expressing *whatever* idea the speaker wishes to convey. St. Paul has not singled out an especially offensive mode of expression—it has not, for example, selected for prohibition only those fighting words that communicate ideas in a threatening (as opposed to a merely obnoxious) manner. Rather, it has proscribed fighting [394] words of whatever manner that communicate messages of racial, gender, or religious intolerance. Selectivity of this sort creates the possibility that the city is seeking to handicap the expression of particular ideas. That possibility would alone be enough to render the ordinance presumptively invalid, but St. Paul's comments and concessions in this case elevate the possibility to a certainty.

St. Paul argues that the ordinance comes within another of the specific exceptions we mentioned, the one that allows content discrimination aimed only at the "secondary effects" of the speech, see *Renton* v. *Playtime Theatres, Inc.*, 475 U. S. 41 (1986). According to St. Paul, the ordinance is intended, "not to impact on [sic] the right of free expression of the accused," but rather to "protect against the victimization of a person or persons who are particularly vulnerable because of their membership in a group that historically has been discriminated against." Brief for Respondent 28. Even assuming that an ordinance that completely proscribes, rather than merely regulates, a specified category of speech can ever be considered to be directed only to the secondary effects of such speech, it is clear that the St. Paul ordinance is not directed to secondary effects within the meaning of *Renton*. As we said in *Boos* v. *Barry*, 485 U. S. 312 (1988). "Listeners' reactions to speech are not the type of 'secondary effects' we referred to in *Renton*." *Id.*, at 321. "The emotive impact of speech on its audience is not a 'secondary effect.'" *Ibid*. See also *id.*, at 334 (opinion of Brennan, J.).[1]

...[395-396]...

Let there be no mistake about our belief that burning a cross in someone's front yard is reprehensible. But St. Paul has sufficient means at its disposal to prevent such behavior without adding the First Amendment to the fire.

The judgment of the Minnesota Supreme Court is reversed, and the case is remanded for proceedings not inconsistent with this opinion.

It is so ordered.

...[397-436]...

NOTE

[1]St. Paul has not argued in this case that the ordinance merely regulates that subclass of fighting words which is most likely to provoke a violent response. But even if one assumes (as appears unlikely) that the categories selected may be so described, that would not justify selective regulation under a "secondary effects" theory. The only reason why such expressive conduct would be especially correlated with violence is that it conveys a particularly odious message; because the "chain of causation" thus necessarily "run[s] through the persuasive effect of the expressive component" of the conduct, Barnes v. Glen Theatre, Inc., 501 U. S. 560, 586 (1991) (Souter, J.,concurring in judgment), it is clear that the St. Paul ordinance regulates on the basis of the "primary" effect of the speech—i. e., its persuasive (or repellant) force.

SUPREME COURT OF THE UNITED STATES

538 U.S. 343

VIRGINIA V. BLACK

CERTIORARI TO THE SUPREME COURT OF VIRGINIA

NO. 01-1107 ARGUED: DECEMBER 11, 2002—DECIDED: APRIL 7, 2003

OPINION: [347] JUSTICE O'CONNOR announced the judgment of the Court and delivered the opinion of the Court with respect to Parts I, II, and III, and an opinion with respect to Parts IV and V, in which THE CHIEF JUSTICE, JUSTICE STEVENS, and JUSTICE BREYER join.

In this case we consider whether the Commonwealth of Virginia's statute banning cross burning with "an intent to intimidate a person or group of persons" violates the First Amendment. Va. Code Ann. §18.2–423 (1996). We conclude that while a State, consistent with the First Amendment, may ban cross burning carried out with the intent to intimidate, the provision in the Virginia statute treating any [348] cross burning as prima facie evidence of intent to intimidate renders the statute unconstitutional in its current form.

I

Respondents Barry Black, Richard Elliott, and Jonathan O'Mara were convicted separately of violating Virginia's cross-burning statute, §18.2–423. That statute provides:

> "It shall be unlawful for any person or persons, with the intent of intimidating any person or group of persons, to burn, or cause to be burned, a cross on the property of another, a highway or other public place. Any person who shall violate any provision of this section shall be guilty of a Class 6 felony. "Any such burning of a cross shall be prima facie evidence of an intent to intimidate a person or group of persons."

On August 22, 1998, Barry Black led a Ku Klux Klan rally in Carroll County, Virginia. Twenty-five to thirty people attended this gathering, which occurred on private property with the permission of the owner, who was in attendance. The property was located on an open field just off Brushy Fork Road (State Highway 690) in Cana, Virginia.

When the sheriff of Carroll County learned that a Klan rally was occurring in his county, he went to observe it from the side of the road. During the approximately one hour that the sheriff was present, about 40 to 50 cars passed the site, a "few" of which stopped to ask the sheriff what was happening on the property. App. 71. Eight to ten houses were located in the vicinity of the rally. Rebecca Sechrist, who was related to the owner of the property where the rally took place, "sat and watched to see wha[t] [was] going on" from the lawn of her in-laws' house. She looked on as the Klan prepared for the gathering and subsequently conducted the rally itself. *Id.*, at 103.

During the rally, Sechrist heard Klan members speak about "what they were" and "what they believed in." *Id.*, [349] at 106. The speakers "talked real bad about the blacks and the Mexicans." *Id.*, at 109. One speaker told the assembled gathering that "he would love to take a .30/.30 and just random[ly] shoot the blacks." *Ibid.* The speakers also talked about "President Clinton and Hillary Clinton," and about how their tax money "goes to . . . the black people." *Ibid.* Sechrist testified that this language made her "very . . . scared." *Id.*, at 110.

At the conclusion of the rally, the crowd circled around a 25- to 30-foot cross. The cross was between 300 and 350 yards away from the road. According to the sheriff, the cross "then all of a sudden . . . went up in a flame." *Id.*, at 71. As the cross burned, the Klan played Amazing Grace over the loudspeakers. Sechrist stated that the cross burning made her feel "awful" and "terrible." *Id.*, at 110.

When the sheriff observed the cross burning, he informed his deputy that they needed to "find out who's responsible and explain to them that they cannot do this in the State of Virginia." *Id.*, at 72. The sheriff then went down the driveway, entered the rally, and asked "who was responsible for burning the cross." *Id.*, at 74. Black responded, "I guess I am because I'm the head of the rally." *Ibid.* The sheriff then told Black, "[T]here's a law in the State of Virginia that you cannot burn a cross and I'll have to place you under arrest for this." *Ibid.*

Black was charged with burning a cross with the intent of intimidating a person or group of persons, in violation of § 18.2–423. At his trial, the jury was instructed that "intent to intimidate means the motivation to intentionally put a person or a group of persons in fear of bodily harm. Such fear must arise from the willful conduct of the accused rather than from some mere temperamental timidity of the victim." *Id.*, at 146. The trial court also instructed the jury that "the burning of a cross by itself is sufficient evidence from which you may infer the required intent." *Ibid.* When Black objected to this last instruction on First Amendment grounds, [350] the prosecutor responded that the instruction was "taken straight out of the [Virginia] Model Instructions." *Id.*, at 134. The jury found Black guilty, and fined him $2,500. The Court of Appeals of Virginia affirmed Black's conviction. Rec. No. 1581-99-3 (Va. App., Dec. 19, 2000), App. 201.

On May 2, 1998, respondents Richard Elliott and Jonathan O'Mara, as well as a third individual, attempted to burn a cross on the yard of James Jubilee. Jubilee, an African-American, was Elliott's next-door neighbor in Virginia Beach, Virginia. Four months prior to the incident, Jubilee and his family had moved from California to Virginia Beach. Before the cross burning, Jubilee spoke to Elliott's mother to inquire about shots being fired from behind the Elliott home. Elliott's mother explained to Jubilee that her son shot firearms as a hobby, and that he used the backyard as a firing range.

On the night of May 2, respondents drove a truck onto Jubilee's property, planted a cross, and set it on fire. Their apparent motive was to "get back" at Jubilee for complaining about the shooting in the backyard. *Id.*, at 241. Respondents were not affiliated with the Klan. The next morning, as Jubilee was pulling his car out of the driveway, he noticed the partially burned cross approximately 20 feet from his house. After seeing the cross, Jubilee was "very nervous" because he "didn't know what would be the next phase," and because "a cross burned in your yard . . . tells you that it's just the first round." *Id.*, at 231.

Elliott and O'Mara were charged with attempted cross burning and conspiracy to commit cross burning. O'Mara pleaded guilty to both counts, reserving the right to challenge the constitutionality of the cross-burning statute. The judge sentenced O'Mara to 90 days in jail and fined him $2,500. The judge also suspended 45 days of the sentence and $1,000 of the fine.

At Elliott's trial, the judge originally ruled that the jury would be instructed "that the burning of a cross by itself is [351] sufficient evidence from which you may infer the required intent." *Id.*, at 221–222. At trial, however, the court instructed the jury that the Commonwealth must prove that "the defendant intended to commit cross burning," that "the defendant did a direct act toward the commission of the cross burning," and that "the defendant had the intent of intimidating any person or group of persons." *Id.*, at 250. The court did not instruct the jury on the meaning of the word "intimidate," nor on the prima facie evidence provision of § 18.2–423. The jury found Elliott guilty of attempted cross burning and acquitted him of conspiracy to commit cross burning. It sentenced Elliott to 90 days in jail and a $2,500 fine. The Court of Appeals of Virginia affirmed the convictions of both Elliott and O'Mara. *O'Mara* v. *Commonwealth*, 33 Va. App. 525, 535 S. E. 2d 175 (2000).

Each respondent appealed to the Supreme Court of Virginia, arguing that § 18.2–423 is facially unconstitutional. The Supreme Court of Virginia consolidated all three cases, and held that the statute is unconstitutional on its face. 262 Va. 764, 553 S. E. 2d 738 (2001). It held that the Virginia cross-burning statute "is analytically indistinguishable from the ordinance found unconstitutional in *R. A. V.* [v. *St. Paul*, 505 U. S. 377 (1992)]." *Id.*, at 772, 553 S. E. 2d, at 742. The Virginia statute, the court held, discriminates on the basis of content since it "selectively chooses only cross burning because of its distinctive message." *Id.*, at 774, 553 S. E. 2d, at 744. The court also held that the prima facie evidence provision renders the statute overbroad because "[t]he enhanced probability of prosecution under the statute chills the expression of protected speech." *Id.*, at 777, 553 S. E. 2d, at 746.

...[352]...

II

. . . Burning a cross in the United States is inextricably intertwined with the history of the Ku Klux Klan.

The first Ku Klux Klan began in Pulaski, Tennessee, in the spring of 1866. Although the Ku Klux Klan started as a social club, it soon changed into something far different. The Klan fought Reconstruction and the corresponding drive to allow freed blacks to participate in the political process. [353] Soon the Klan imposed "a veritable reign of terror" throughout the South. S. Kennedy, Southern Exposure 31 (1991) (hereinafter Kennedy). The Klan employed tactics such as whipping, threatening to burn people at the stake, and murder. W. Wade, The Fiery Cross: The Ku Klux Klan in America 48–49 (1987) (hereinafter Wade). The Klan's victims included blacks, southern whites who disagreed with the Klan, and "carpetbagger" northern whites.

The activities of the Ku Klux Klan prompted legislative action at the national level. In 1871, "President Grant sent a message to Congress indicating that the Klan's reign of terror in the Southern States had rendered life and property insecure." *Jett* v. *Dallas Independent School Dist.*, 491 U. S. 701, 722 (1989) (internal quotation marks and alterations omitted). In response, Congress passed what is now known as the Ku Klux Klan Act. See "An Act to enforce the Provisions of the Fourteenth Amendment to the Constitution of the United States, and for other Purposes," 17 Stat. 13 (now codified at 42 U. S. C. §§ 1983, 1985, and 1986). President Grant used these new powers to suppress the Klan in South Carolina, the effect of which severely curtailed the Klan in other States as well. By the end of Reconstruction in 1877, the first Klan no longer existed.

The genesis of the second Klan began in 1905, with the publication of Thomas Dixon's The Clansmen: An Historical Romance of the Ku Klux Klan. Dixon's book was a sympathetic portrait of the first Klan, depicting the Klan as a group of heroes "saving" the South from blacks and the "horrors" of Reconstruction. Although the first Klan never actually practiced cross burning, Dixon's book depicted the Klan burning crosses to celebrate the execution of former slaves. *Id.*, at 324–326; see also *Capitol Square Review and Advisory Bd.* v. *Pinette*, 515 U. S. 753, 770–771 (1995) (THOMAS, J., concurring). Cross burning thereby became associated with the first Ku Klux Klan. When D. W. Griffith turned Dixon's book into the movie The Birth of a Nation in 1915, [354] the association between cross burning and the Klan became indelible. In addition to the cross burnings in the movie, a poster advertising the film displayed a hooded Klansman riding a hooded horse, with his left hand holding the reins of the horse and his right hand holding a burning cross above his head. Wade 127. Soon thereafter, in November 1915, the second Klan began.

From the inception of the second Klan, cross burnings have been used to communicate both threats of violence and messages of shared ideology. The first initiation ceremony occurred on Stone Mountain near Atlanta, Georgia. While a 40-foot cross burned on the mountain, the Klan members took their oaths of loyalty. See Kennedy 163. This cross burning was the second recorded instance in the United States. The first known cross burning in the country had occurred a little over one month before the Klan initiation, when a

Georgia mob celebrated the lynching of Leo Frank by burning a "gigantic cross" on Stone Mountain that was "visible throughout" Atlanta. Wade 144 (internal quotation marks omitted).

The new Klan's ideology did not differ much from that of the first Klan. As one Klan publication emphasized, "We avow the distinction between [the] races, . . . and we shall ever be true to the faithful maintenance of White Supremacy and will strenuously oppose any compromise thereof in any and all things." *Id.*, at 147–148 (internal quotation marks omitted). Violence was also an elemental part of this new Klan. By September 1921, the New York World newspaper documented 152 acts of Klan violence, including 4 murders, 41 floggings, and 27 tar-and-featherings. Wade 160.

Often, the Klan used cross burnings as a tool of intimidation and a threat of impending violence. For example, in 1939 and 1940, the Klan burned crosses in front of synagogues and churches. See Kennedy 175. After one cross burning at a synagogue, a Klan member noted that if the cross burning did not "shut the Jews up, we'll cut a few [355] throats and see what happens." *Ibid.* (internal quotation marks omitted). In Miami in 1941, the Klan burned four crosses in front of a proposed housing project, declaring, "We are here to keep niggers out of your town. . . . When the law fails you, call on us." *Id.*, at 176 (internal quotation marks omitted). And in Alabama in 1942, in "a whirlwind climax to weeks of flogging and terror," the Klan burned crosses in front of a union hall and in front of a union leader's home on the eve of a labor election. *Id.*, at 180. These cross burnings embodied threats to people whom the Klan deemed antithetical to its goals. And these threats had special force given the long history of Klan violence.

. . .[356]. . .

Throughout the history of the Klan, cross burnings have also remained potent symbols of shared group identity and ideology. The burning cross became a symbol of the Klan itself and a central feature of Klan gatherings. According to the Klan constitution (called the kloran), the "fiery cross" was the "emblem of that sincere, unselfish devotedness of all klansmen to the sacred purpose and principles we have espoused." The Ku Klux Klan Hearings before the House Committee on Rules, 67th Cong., 1st Sess., 114, Exh. G (1921); see also Wade 419. And the Klan has often published its newsletters and magazines under the name The Fiery Cross. See *Id.*, at 226, 489.

At Klan gatherings across the country, cross burning became the climax of the rally or the initiation. Posters advertising an upcoming Klan rally often featured a Klan member holding a cross. See N. MacLean, Behind the Mask of Chivalry: The Making of the Second Ku Klux Klan 142–143 (1994). Typically, a cross burning would start with a prayer by the "Klavern" minister, followed by the singing of Onward Christian Soldiers. The Klan would then light the cross on fire, as the members raised their left arm toward the burning cross and sang The Old Rugged Cross. Wade 185. Throughout the Klan's history, the Klan continued to use the burning cross in their ritual ceremonies.

For its own members, the cross was a sign of celebration and ceremony. During a joint Nazi-Klan rally in 1940, the proceeding concluded with the wedding of two Klan members who "were married in full Klan regalia beneath a blazing cross." *Id.*, at 271. In response to antimasking bills introduced in state legislatures after World War II, the Klan burned crosses in protest. See Chalmers 340. On March 26, 1960, the Klan engaged in rallies and cross burnings throughout the South in an attempt to recruit 10 million members. See Wade 305. Later in 1960, the Klan became [357] an issue in the third debate between Richard Nixon and John Kennedy, with both candidates renouncing the Klan. After this debate, the Klan reiterated its support for Nixon by burning crosses. See *id.*, at 309. And cross burnings featured prominently in Klan rallies when the Klan attempted to move toward more nonviolent tactics to stop integration. See *id.*, at 323; cf. Chalmers 368–369, 371–372, 380, 384. In short, a burning cross has remained a symbol of Klan ideology and of Klan unity.

To this day, regardless of whether the message is a political one or whether the message is also meant to intimidate, the burning of a cross is a "symbol of hate." *Capitol Square Review and Advisory Bd.* v. *Pinette*, 515 U. S., at 771 (THOMAS, J., concurring). And while cross burning sometimes carries no intimidating message, at other times the intimidating message is the *only* message conveyed. For example, when a cross burning is directed at a particular person not affiliated with the Klan, the burning cross often serves as a message of intimidation, designed to inspire in the victim a fear of bodily harm. Moreover, the history of violence associated with the Klan shows that the possibility of injury or death is not just hypothetical. The person who burns a cross directed at a particular person often is making a serious threat, meant to coerce the victim to comply with the Klan's wishes unless the victim is willing to risk the wrath of the Klan. Indeed, as the cases of respondents Elliott and O'Mara indicate, individuals without Klan affiliation who wish to threaten or menace another person sometimes use cross burning because of this association between a burning cross and violence.

In sum, while a burning cross does not inevitably convey a message of intimidation, often the cross burner intends that the recipients of the message fear for their lives. And when a cross burning is used to intimidate, few if any messages are more powerful.

...[358-360]...

III B

The Supreme Court of Virginia ruled that in light of *R. A. V. v. City of St. Paul, supra,* even if it is constitutional to ban cross burning in a content-neutral manner, the Virginia cross-burning statute is unconstitutional because it discriminates on the basis of content and viewpoint. 262 Va., at 771–776, 553 S. E. 2d, at 742–745. It is true, as the Supreme Court of Virginia held, that the burning of a cross is symbolic expression. The reason why the Klan burns a cross at its rallies, or individuals place a burning cross on someone else's lawn, is that the burning cross represents the message that the speaker wishes to communicate. Individuals burn crosses as opposed to other means of communication because cross burning carries a message in an effective and dramatic manner.

[361] The fact that cross burning is symbolic expression, however, does not resolve the constitutional question. The Supreme Court of Virginia relied upon *R. A. V.* v. *City of St. Paul, supra,* to conclude that once a statute discriminates on the basis of this type of content, the law is unconstitutional. We disagree.

In *R. A. V.,* we held that a local ordinance that banned certain symbolic conduct, including cross burning, when done with the knowledge that such conduct would " 'arouse anger, alarm or resentment in others on the basis of race, color, creed, religion or gender' " was unconstitutional. *Id.,* at 380 (quoting the St. Paul Bias-Motivated Crime Ordinance, St. Paul, Minn., Legis. Code § 292.02 (1990)). We held that the ordinance did not pass constitutional muster because it discriminated on the basis of content by targeting only those individuals who "provoke violence" on a basis specified in the law. 505 U. S., at 391. The ordinance did not cover "[t]hose who wish to use "fighting words' in connection with other ideas — to express hostility, for example, on the basis of political affiliation, union membership, or homosexuality." *Ibid.* This content-based discrimination was unconstitutional because it allowed the city "to impose special prohibitions on those speakers who express views on disfavored subjects." *Ibid.*

We did not hold in *R. A. V.* that the First Amendment prohibits *all* forms of content-based discrimination within a proscribable area of speech. Rather, we specifically stated that some types of content discrimination did not violate the First Amendment:

> *"When the basis for the content discrimination consists entirely of the very reason the entire class of speech at issue is proscribable, no significant danger of idea or [362] viewpoint discrimination exists. Such a reason, having been adjudged neutral enough to support exclusion of the entire class of speech from First Amendment protection, is also neutral enough to form the basis of distinction within the class." Id., at 388.*

Indeed, we noted that it would be constitutional to ban only a particular type of threat: "[T]he Federal Government can criminalize only those threats of violence that are directed against the President . . . since the reasons why threats of violence are outside the First Amendment . . . have special force when applied to the person of the President." *Ibid.* And a State may "choose to prohibit only that obscenity which is the most patently offensive *in its prurience* — *i. e.,* that which involves the most lascivious displays of sexual activity." *Ibid.* (emphasis in original). Consequently, while the holding of *R. A. V.* does not permit a State to ban only obscenity based on "offensive *political* messages," *ibid.,* or "only those threats against the President that mention his policy on aid to inner cities," *ibid.,* the First Amendment permits content discrimination "based on the very reasons why the particular class of speech at issue . . . is proscribable," *id.,* at 393.

Similarly, Virginia's statute does not run afoul of the First Amendment insofar as it bans cross burning with intent to intimidate. Unlike the statute at issue in *R. A. V.*, the Virginia statute does not single out for opprobrium only that speech directed toward "one of the specified disfavored topics." *Id.*, at 391. It does not matter whether an individual burns a cross with intent to intimidate because of the victim's race, gender, or religion, or because of the victim's "political affiliation, union membership, or homosexuality." *Ibid.* Moreover, as a factual matter it is not true that cross burners direct their intimidating conduct solely to racial or religious minorities. See, *e. g., supra*, at 355 (noting the instances of cross burnings directed at union members); *State v. Miller*, 6 Kan. App. 2d 432, 629 P. 2d 748 (1981) (describing [363] the case of a defendant who burned a cross in the yard of the lawyer who had previously represented him and who was currently prosecuting him). Indeed, in the case of Elliott and O'Mara, it is at least unclear whether the respondents burned a cross due to racial animus. See 262 Va., at 791, 553 S. E. 2d, at 753 (Hassell, J., dissenting) (noting that "these defendants burned a cross because they were angry that their neighbor had complained about the presence of a firearm shooting range in the Elliott's yard, not because of any racial animus").

The First Amendment permits Virginia to outlaw cross burnings done with the intent to intimidate because burning a cross is a particularly virulent form of intimidation. Instead of prohibiting all intimidating messages, Virginia may choose to regulate this subset of intimidating messages in light of cross burning's long and pernicious history as a signal of impending violence. Thus, just as a State may regulate only that obscenity which is the most obscene due to its prurient content, so too may a State choose to prohibit only those forms of intimidation that are most likely to inspire fear of bodily harm. A ban on cross burning carried out with the intent to intimidate is fully consistent with our holding in *R. A. V.* and is proscribable under the First Amendment.

IV

The Supreme Court of Virginia ruled in the alternative that Virginia's cross-burning statute was unconstitutionally overbroad due to its provision stating that "[a]ny such burning of a cross shall be prima facie evidence of an intent to intimidate a person or group of persons." Va. Code Ann. §18.2–423 (1996). The Commonwealth added the prima facie provision to the statute in 1968. The court below did not reach whether this provision is severable from the rest of the cross-burning statute under Virginia law. See § 1–17.1 ("The provisions of all statutes are severable unless . . . it is [364] apparent that two or more statutes or provisions must operate in accord with one another"). In this Court, as in the Supreme Court of Virginia, respondents do not argue that the prima facie evidence provision is unconstitutional as applied to any one of them. Rather, they contend that the provision is unconstitutional on its face.

The Supreme Court of Virginia has not ruled on the meaning of the prima facie evidence provision. It has, however, stated that "the act of burning a cross alone, with no evidence of intent to intimidate, will nonetheless suffice for arrest and prosecution and will insulate the Commonwealth from a motion to strike the evidence at the end of its case-in-chief." 262 Va., at 778, 553 S. E. 2d, at 746. The jury in the case of Richard Elliott did not receive any instruction on the prima facie evidence provision, and the provision was not an issue in the case of Jonathan O'Mara because he pleaded guilty. The court in Barry Black's case, however, instructed the jury that the provision means: "The burning of a cross, by itself, is sufficient evidence from which you may infer the required intent." App. 196. This jury instruction is the same as the Model Jury Instruction in the Commonwealth of Virginia. See Virginia Model Jury Instructions, Criminal, Instruction No. 10.250 (1998 and Supp. 2001).

The prima facie evidence provision, as interpreted by the jury instruction, renders the statute unconstitutional.

...[365]...

The act of burning a cross may mean that a person is engaging in constitutionally proscribable intimidation. But that same act may mean only that the person is engaged in core political speech. The prima facie evidence provision in this statute blurs the line between these two meanings of a burning cross. As interpreted by the jury instruction, the provision chills constitutionally protected political speech because of the possibility that the Commonwealth will prosecute — and potentially convict — somebody engaging only in lawful political speech at the core of what the First Amendment is designed to protect.

As the history of cross burning indicates, a burning cross is not always intended to intimidate. Rather, sometimes the cross burning is a statement of ideology, a symbol of group [366] solidarity. It is a ritual used at Klan gatherings, and it is used to represent the Klan itself. Thus, "[b]urning a cross at a political rally would almost certainly be protected expression." *R. A. V.* v. *St. Paul*, 505 U. S., at 402, n. 4 (White, J., concurring in judgment) (citing *Brandenburg* v. *Ohio*, 395 U. S., at 445). Cf. *National Socialist Party of America* v. *Skokie*, 432 U. S. 43 (1977) *(per curiam)*. Indeed, occasionally a person who burns a cross does not intend to express either a statement of ideology or intimidation. Cross burnings have appeared in movies such as Mississippi Burning, and in plays such as the stage adaptation of Sir Walter Scott's The Lady of the Lake.

The prima facie provision makes no effort to distinguish among these different types of cross burnings. It does not distinguish between a cross burning done with the purpose of creating anger or resentment and a cross burning done with the purpose of threatening or intimidating a victim. It does not distinguish between a cross burning at a public rally or a cross burning on a neighbor's lawn. It does not treat the cross burning directed at an individual differently from the cross burning directed at a group of like-minded believers. It allows a jury to treat a cross burning on the property of another with the owner's acquiescence in the same manner as a cross burning on the property of another without the owner's permission. To this extent I agree with JUSTICE SOUTER that the prima facie evidence provision can "skew jury deliberations toward conviction in cases where the evidence of intent to intimidate is relatively weak and arguably consistent with a solely ideological reason for burning." *Post*, at 385 (opinion concurring in judgment in part and dissenting in part).

It may be true that a cross burning, even at a political rally, arouses a sense of anger or hatred among the vast majority of citizens who see a burning cross. But this sense of anger or hatred is not sufficient to ban all cross burnings. As Gerald Gunther has stated, "The lesson I have drawn [367] from my childhood in Nazi Germany and my happier adult life in this country is the need to walk the sometimes difficult path of denouncing the bigot's hateful ideas with all my power, yet at the same time challenging any community's attempt to suppress hateful ideas by force of law." Casper, Gerry, 55 Stan. L. Rev. 647, 649 (2002) (internal quotation marks omitted). The prima facie evidence provision in this case ignores all of the contextual factors that are necessary to decide whether a particular cross burning is intended to intimidate. The First Amendment does not permit such a shortcut.

For these reasons, the prima facie evidence provision, as interpreted through the jury instruction and as applied in Barry Black's case, is unconstitutional on its face. We recognize that the Supreme Court of Virginia has not authoritatively interpreted the meaning of the prima facie evidence provision. Unlike JUSTICE SCALIA, we refuse to speculate on whether *any* interpretation of the prima facie evidence provision would satisfy the First Amendment. Rather, all we hold is that because of the interpretation of the prima facie evidence provision given by the jury instruction, the provision makes the statute facially invalid at this point. We also recognize the theoretical possibility that the court, on remand, could interpret the provision in a manner different from that so far set forth in order to avoid the constitutional objections we have described. We leave open that possibility. We also leave open the possibility that the provision is severable, and if so, whether Elliott and O'Mara could be retried under § 18.2–423.

V

With respect to Barry Black, we agree with the Supreme Court of Virginia that his conviction cannot stand, and we affirm the judgment of the Supreme Court of Virginia. With respect to Elliott and O'Mara, we vacate the judgment [368] of the Supreme Court of Virginia, and remand the case for further proceedings.

It is so ordered.

CHAPTER 4

Race, Racism, and Equality under the Law

REPRODUCING
THE STATE

—Jacqueline Stevens—

Rather than distinguishing race as a concept whose reality is more tenuous than that of other identities, I want to propose an alternative understanding, one that follows from the work of W.E.B. Du Bois, and also portions of writings by Appiah, David Goldberg, and others who regularly point out the salience of stories of origins for race and also the role of geography in its manifestations. Ultimately, what makes someone Black, for example, at least in the United States, is that we understand that at some point she had ancestors in Africa; what makes someone White is that we understand that at some point she had ancestors in Europe. This also accounts for how it is that someone may "look" White and yet "be" Black (and vice versa), depending on the story one wants to tell. So, out of the tensions in the meanings of "race" as a folk concept, supplemented by a recognition of the importance of geography to regulating our ideas about phenotypical differences as specifically racial, a definition of race can emerge: a subpopulation of human beings with observed or imagined physical characteristics understood to correspond with a geographical territory of origins. Presently the geographical territory of racial origins is understood as a continent. At times the equally artificial boundaries of the state-nation are also imagined as outlining territories of "origin"al differences in bodily appearance. This definition recognizes the importance of imputed visible differences attached to a story of origins from a geographical territory.

The phrase "geographical territory of origins" captures the concern with origins that underlies stories of ancestry. To be "originally" from a place implies that one has ancestors who lived in a particular place. At the same time, the emphasis on geography denotes the fixed and contingent character of representations of race better than more vague phenomenologies of familial ancestry or genes alone. This also makes the story of race seem fairly essentialist. From Africa: Black. From Europe: White.

According to the *Dictionary of Human Geography* 'Caucasoid' refers to "one of the primary races of people, found in Europe, N. America, and from the Middle East to northern India. It is the most variable in physical appearance of all the great races." The entry then goes on to describe skin color, eye color, and hair colors and textures of the Caucasoid.[1] 'Mongoloid' is defined as the "peoples of Southeast, East and Central Asia and the American Indians." A physical description follows.[2] Finally, 'Negroid' is defined first by physical characteristics, and then by place of origins: "The majority of Negroids have their origins in Africa.[3] From these entries it seems that "race" refers to a set of physical characteristics attached to one's ties to ancestors from places like Europe, Asia, and Africa.

Africa, Europe, and Asia are geographical places that are naturalized by their correspondence with geologically formed regions of the earth. Insofar as Asia seems natural, it is only natural, given variations in climate and terrain, that groups of people from different geographical regions will differ amongst themselves, supposedly making them racially distinct. But if the story were that simple, then the fetishisms associated specifically with race would be random. With no further explanation it is indeed nonsensical for us to assign arbitrary phenotype and genotype configurations to adaptations made to "geography"—constructing the rubric of race—and not to mutations and adaptations of flat-footedness. What makes Asians? The answer—whatever made Asia—does not lead in the essentialist justification of racial classifications that it first appears. The notion that *geographical* differences lead to differences among people is not the same is saying that "race" is the outcome of *geological* difference.

Clinal differences among selected pairings of genotype and phenotype are clustered into races by the contingency of national borders and by geography—our synthetic graphics of the earth—not geology, or what we see when we understand the earth does not change all that much and all that quickly, that relative to an individual's life-span the earth is more or less immutable.[4] The geographical determination underlying the use of "race" rests on another category that is actually far more naturalized (and with far less reason) than race. What is Africa? A continent. What is a continent? According to the *Dictionary of Geography*, a 'continent' is "one of the earth's major constituent land masses," "Africa," "North America," "Central and South America," "Asia," "Europe," "Australia," or "Antarctica," each of which occupy so many millions of square miles, depending on whether or not one includes the former USSR. Calculations are offered for Europe and Asia with and without the USSR, which alone should prompt us to wonder about the natural status of the continents.[5] From the *Dictionary of Geography* we have learned that Africa is a continent. A continent is Africa. . . .

Custom, not nature, makes continents. According to an 1835 speech by Rep. Trimble, a staunch believer in Manifest Destiny, although God had given the world "natural boundaries," societies had not accepted them:

> Man, in his made career of glory, his thirst for dominion, had rejected as useless the great and permanent boundaries of nature, and sought out ideal, perishable limits of his own condition.[6]

Historian Albert Weinberg, considering this speech, writes "The principle of the natural barrier is thus concerned not with the unifying territorial features, but with those which clearly and securely separate peoples.[7] Rivers and mountains do not separate peoples. Governments do. People do not gain their identity from the land. Rather, the land gains its identity from the people who occupy it. "Germany" exists because that is the place where "Germans" live. Borders do not arise from the land, but from the identities of the occupying nations. When Rep. Ingersoll, another believer in Manifest Destiny, referred to political sovereignty as a consequence of the "natural boundaries between the Anglo-Saxon and Mauritanian races[8] he was making the point that the Anglo-Saxons and Mauritanians make geography (according to where they live), and not the other way around.

Herodotus, in his many descriptions of parts of the world, defines a territory according to the group of people that occupy it. He writes, "I cannot help but laugh at the absurdity of all the map-makers—there are plenty of them—who show Ocean running like a river round a perfectly circular earth with Asia and Europe of the same size.[9] He then offers to straighten out the misconceptions as to what the earth looks like:

> Let me spend a few words in giving a proper notion of the size and shape of these two continents. Persian territory extends southward to the Red Sea, as it is called; north of them are the Medes, and then the Saspires, then the Colchians, who go as far as the northern sea, where the mouth of the Phasis is. These four nations [ethnoi] fill the area between the Black sea and the Persian gulf. Thence run westward two great continental promontories, one of which stretches from the Phasis on the north along the Black Sea and the Hellespont to the Mediterranean at Sigeum in the Troad, and again, in the south, along the Mediterranean coast from the Myriandric gulf, near Phoenicia, to Cape Triopium. This branch of the continent contains thirty nations.[10]

A continent is what has nations. A specific continent is such by virtue of the nations there. Asia looks different, depending on what we think about whether it includes the former Soviet Union, not certain rivers and mountains. A continent is also literally named by state-nations. Antarctica exists by an agreement not among the scientists who work there, but the state-nations in which they have citizenship. (A committee of representatives of state-nations designated "Antarctica" a place and stipulated the terms of research and commerce possible there.)[11]

RACE AND MARRIAGE

Just as the existence of continents is determined by political societies, within political societies racial forms of being are determined by the government. One of the major sites where the government—acting in the name of the state as a membership organization—has intervened to define the meaning of race as well as specific racial identities has been marriage law. Current governmental racial classifications all follow from the legal history of racial classifications. The state does not treat racial identity as amenable to synchronic reassessments. Rather, one's race is the race of one's ancestors, which is always what the state announces was the race of one's ancestors.

Just as the form of political societies is a constitutive unit in the aggregation of the geographical space that race entails, the state constitutes racially specific marriage forms. In the United States courts have construed the correct and hence legal marriage form as simultaneously "Christian" and "European." This collapsed racial/religious rubric articulates the marital relation specific to this state-nation. One of the most famous marriage cases, *Reynolds v. United States* 8 S. Ct. 145 (1878), upholds penalties for polygamous marriage against Mormon assertions of the First Amendment's Free Exercise Clause: "Polygamy has always been odious among the northern and western nations of Europe, and, until the establishment of the Mormon Church, was almost exclusively a feature of the life of Asiatic and of African people."[12] In this opinion, Europe is conflated with northern and western Europe, as a racialized experience in contrast with those of "Asiatic and of African people." Obviously the category is confused. Of interest are not the details or logic of the classification, but the formal articulation of a specifically national marriage structure within a framework of a racialized religion. The state's association of marriage with nationality, race, and religion binds the last three in a manner constitutive of a particular kinship form. The form, i.e., the rules and prohibitions for the right kind of marriage follows from an overdetermined nexus of principles imputed to affiliations of a specific religion (Christianity) and a specific race (European), and not utilitarian principles of good child-rearing practices, or deontological arguments about the single most rational marriage form.

The twentieth century anxiety over illegitimacy in the United States is, in part, a consequence of marriage laws with racial overtones. Patriarchal monogamy is not viewed simply as preferable to other marriage arrangements, but as specifically European, while anything else is regarded by the state as Asian or African. Why is the state so invested in marriage? If the state is formally committed to sex equality and has no interest in favoring one inheritance practice over another, one would expect the state to recede from legislating in this area. What is it to the state whether a father is married to the mother of his child, or whether, relatedly, kinship is matrilocal or even matriarchal? In his still-influential *Report on the Negro Family* (1967) Patrick Moynihan admitted the political motives for favoring a patriarchal family:

> There is, presumably, no special reason why a society in which males are dominant in family relationships is to be preferred to a matriarchal arrangement. However, it is clearly a disadvantage for a minority group to be operating on one principle, while the great majority of the population, and the one with the most advantages to begin with, is operating on another. This is the present situation of the Negro. Ours [i.e., White society] is a society which presumes male leadership in private and public affairs.[13]

That is, most people in this country are White; Whites have power over Blacks; Whites have patriarchal values; therefore, African-Americans should be more patriarchal as well.[14] The explanation is illuminating, especially when pragmatic arguments against the consequences of matrilocal households as well as illegitimacy fail.

In Europe the countries with the lowest rates of marriage and the highest proportions of illegitimate children perform better than those with high rates of marriage and low rates of illegitimacy, on a wide array of quality-of-life indicators. In the United States out-of-wedlock births were at 21 percent in 1990. In Sweden and in Denmark, the figures were 46.4 percent and 41.9 percent, respectively. In Austria 21.5 percent of children were born out of wedlock. These countries outperform the United States in average levels of education and income per capita. They have lower rates of infant mortality and violent crime. Among the countries with far lower rates of out-of-wedlock births are those with largely Catholic populations, including Ireland (7.8 percent), Italy (4.4 percent), and Spain (3.9 percent). These countries fare worse than the United States when it comes to levels of education, income per capita, and rates of infant mortality. They have more violent crimes than do the European countries with high rates of out-of-wedlock births, but not as many as in the United States.[15] The inference is not that marriage or illegitimacy has obvious economic consequences, but that both interact with other practices in ways that stymie simplistic utilitarian inferences about the institution.

In addition to the form of marriage being specifically racialized, the rules of marriage have also been relied on by the state to reproduce racial identities. In an early decision allowing a railroad to have "separate but equal" seating, the Court relied on "the Creator's" thoughts on marriage in particular, to prove it appropriate for the state to recognize racial differences:

> Conceding equality, with natures as perfect and rights as sacred, yet God has made them dissimilar, with those natural instincts and feelings which He always imparts to His creatures when He intends that they shall not overstep the natural boundaries He has assigned to them. The natural law which forbids their intermarriage and that social amalgamation which leads to a corruption of races, is as clearly divine as that which imparted to them different natures . . . From social amalgamation [sitting next to someone of a different race on a train] it is but a step to illicit intercourse, and but another to intermarriage.[16]

Importantly, *intermarriage*, not illicit sex, is the furthest one might stray from a Christian God's intention. Children of interracial parents had to be classified as having a father of the same race as the mother, or the parents would be punished.[17] That marriage was a factor in the reproduction of racial affiliations was a point Tocqueville made, when he wrote that "whites and emancipated Negroes face each other like two foreign peoples on the same soil." Tocqueville maintained that "there are only two possibilities for the future: the Negroes and whites must either mingle completely, or they must part." Elaborating on "mingling" he explained that "it is the mulatto who forms the bridge between black and white; everywhere where there are a great number of mulattoes, the fusion of the two races are not impossible.[18] It was, of course, the 'mulatto' that marriage law annihilated—a legal eradication that was reinforced in the "one drop" rule, making 'mulattoes' Colored or White. Current debate over the proposal of a "multiracial" category on the Census and other government documents is the legacy of *Loving v. Virginia* (1967), the United States Supreme Court case that overturned miscegenation laws. Only after the legal prohibitions on interracial marriage are eliminated is it possible to see significant increases in the numbers of "inter-racial" children.

Anti-miscegenation laws prohibited so-called interracial marriage in this country until 1967.[19] The purpose of these laws was to regulate the "Whiteness" of the country. Marriage regulation was a proxy for physical restraints against interracial heterosexual intercourse, to wit: "Free persons and slaves are incapable of contracting marriage together; the celebration of such marriages is forbidden, and the marriage is void; it is the same with respect to the marriages contracted by free white persons with free people of color.[20] Hence relatively few children were reported as being the offspring of interracial couples, even where the actual identities of the parents were known. With "miscegenation" and "fornication" both against the law, interracial children were either legal nonentities or evidence of a crime.

canterbury Tales

Another consequence of these laws was that these illegitimate children could not inherit: "Bastard, adulterous or incestuous children shall not enjoy the right of inheriting the estates of their natural father or mother, in any of the cases above mentioned, the law allowing them nothing more than a mere alimony.[21] This law helps explain disparities in the wealth of Blacks and Whites. Legitimate Black children would be the descendants of slaves; illegitimate Black children were precluded from inheritance. States still distinguish between the claims of legitimate and illegitimate children against their parents estates. Parents currently can, of course, will their estates to whomever they please. But the state-issued classifications establish a grammar that produces "illegitimate" and "legitimate" children and hence the norms of attachment and obligation associated with these different classes of children: "Although these code articles do not openly differentiate rights to inherit by race or color, they effectively protect the estate of white families from being passed on to colored relatives.[22] With laws regulating both miscegenation and legitimacy in effect until the 1970s, the disparity in family wealth between Whites and Blacks is completely predictable.

RACE AND BIRTH CERTIFICATES

States list one's parents "race" on one's birth certificate and hence have sole control over the criteria for determining what counts as one's own race. The consequences of these birth certificates extend beyond the life of the individual, as subsequent generations have their race determined through ancestry, and the mark of one's racial ancestry is indicated on the earlier birth certificates. The federal forms used to register births require the recording of the race of both parents. The possible designations are: Other Asian or Pacific Islander, White,

Black, Indian (includes Aleuts and Eskimos), Chinese, Japanese, Hawaiian (includes part Hawaiian), other non-White, Filipino. The list raises many questions. Why designations for "other Asian" and "other White" but not "other Black"? Why so many national designations for "Asians"? Despite the idiosyncrasy of these categories, the state is adamant on its prerogative to maintain them.

In 1985 the United States Supreme Court let stand a lower-court decision allowing Louisiana state officials to classify their citizens racially.[23] But even if the plaintiff had succeeded, she would not be considered, from the point of view of the state, indubitably White. The procedure for changing birth certificates in Louisiana is to cross out the old designation and then write the new designation in red ink. This means that the old designation is not obliterated but remains in a manner that will continue to raise questions about one's true identity. A crossed-out "Negro" might still be regarded as being Negro, or so thought the plaintiffs who filed suits to have Louisiana issue them "clean" birth certificates when their racial designations had changed.

In one case a previously "White" family had their classification changed, unbeknownst to them:

> Gerard H. Cline Sr. requested a birth certificate for his son, Gerard H. Cline, Jr., for use in enrolling him in school. At that time, he was informed that the boy's race had been changed from white to Negro, and also that the same change was made on the birth certificates of his wife, Elaine Mary Dejean, her sister, Marguerite Estelle Dejean Rosenbohm, their brother, Sidney Dejean, Jr., their children, Lionel Rosenbohm, Jr., Charmain Rosenbohm, Kathleen Rosenbohm, and Sidney Dejean, III, and the birth and death certificates of the children's grandfather, Sidney Joseph Dejean, Sr. The alterations were made by drawing lines through the word "White" which appeared on the original certificates and the word Negro was written in ink to designate their race. These alterations occurred without the knowledge of any of the plaintiffs, and the person who made the changes and the reason therefor are both unknown.[24]

The family was not satisfied when the redesignation was crossed out, but desired new birth certificates, because the alterations, by law, are seen as alterations, prompting them to be interrogated in ways that racial designations on clean birth certificates are not. The law says that "Except for delayed or altered certificates, every original certificate on file in the division of public health statistics is prima facie evidence of the facts therein stated.[25] The court and the law acknowledge that the state wants to keep records that will call into question changed designations. Because Cline convinced them that there was no question concerning his family's race, they were issued new records.

In another case, the crossed-out version of the birth certificate was upheld. The plaintiff wanted to have his birth registration changed by

> showing him to be white instead of colored and to change his name from Larry Lille Toledano to Larry Lille Muller. He alleged that he was born to Idyl D Hall on March 4, 1937, seventy-eight days after his mother's marriage to Chester J. Toledano. He alleged that he was of the white race; that his father is Edwin J. Mullet, who was married to his mother at the time of his conception; that his mother married Chester J. Toledano on January 11, 1937, and that she obtained a divorce from Edwin J. Mullet on December 16, 1953 (obviously the pleader meant 1936 . . .).[26]

In several places in the opinion the Court expressed some doubt about the authenticity of the records Toledano had produced. While not accusing him of lying outright, the judge held that the crossed-out designation of Toledano as "colored" was an accurate portrait of Toledano's race: "It is our opinion that no amount of obliteration or erasure on the birth certificate will erase or change the fact that the plaintiff was registered at birth as colored. . . . To effectively wipe out all evidence of the error, it would be necessary to expunge the records of this case.[27] The state's doubt must remain in the records.

For purposes of recording information on birth certificates, most states now ask hospitals to indicate the parents' race and do not record the child's race, although this is reported for purposes of more detailed records not printed on the actual certificate.[28] But even here the state's role in racial classifications is substantial. Because it is impossible to change the racial designation on a birth certificate, one is at the mercy of one's parents for racial identity. Further, the identification of the parents discussed above is done by hospital employees, not the parents, and may be used to question racial identities at marriage or death. Finally, the classificatory possibilities are predetermined by the state—Asian, Black, Japanese, for instance—based on ideas about physical traits associated with political territories. One may engage in long debates over one's own racial form of being, but the only definition that has force is that of the state birth certificate, and its criteria depend on political-geographical boundaries, not personal, subjective affinities.

RACE AND THE GOVERNMENT

The United States federal government provides the following definitions of various races, for purposes of entitlement programs and affirmative action policies:

1. Black, not of Hispanic Origin: A person having origins in any of the black racial groups of Africa.

2. Hispanic: A person of Mexican, Puerto Rican, Cuban, Central or South American or other Spanish culture or origin, regardless of race.

3. Asian or Pacific Islander: A person having origins in any of the original peoples of the Far East, Southeast Asia, the Indian Subcontinent, or the Pacific Islands. This area includes, for example, China, Japan, Korea, the Philippine Islands, and Samoa.

4. American Indian or Alaskan Native. A person having origins in any of the original people of North America, and who maintain cultural identification through tribal affiliation or community recognition.

5. White, not of Hispanic Origin. A person having origins in any of the original people of Europe, North Africa, or the Middle East. Additional subcategories based on national origin or primary language spoken may be used where appropriate, on either a national or a regional basis.[29]

These classifications are consistent with the use of national boundaries to equate continents with races. One is Asian if one has "origins" in China, Japan, or Korea for instance. What does it mean to have "origins" in a country? Normally we think of 'origins' as a beginning. To be a member of categories 3 through 5 requires one to have "origins" in an "original people." What is an "original people"? How does one come to have an origin in a nation or a continent? One's parents give one an origin, but they might give one that origin in one place or another, and they might have had their beginning in one place or another and then just move. So it is one's "origins" in contrast to a place of birth that determine race. That covers the immigrants from Europe who have children in Asia, ensuring their children will not be classified as "Asian." How original must the original people be? If it is correct that the human species itself began in what we call Africa, then based on the above definition we are all African.[30] If no one has "origins" in Europe, then no person can, following government classifications, be labeled White.

The U.S. government seems to recognize the problem of original origins in its tautological first definition: A "Black" person is a person who is of a "black racial group" in Africa. This appears necessary so that one does not count Whites born in South Africa, for instance, as Black, insofar as they have their origins in Africa.[31] In this case the "Africa" qualification of who is Black is useless, irrelevant. Either everyone with origins at some point in Africa is Black (the definition does not stipulate a time period), which would include everyone; or "Black" refers to skin color alone, in which case the invocation of "Africa" is entirely irrelevant.

These federal classificatory schemes are also challenged by groups who want to readjust categories for the purpose of aggregate data collection, as well as by individuals who feel wronged by the present system. Mustafa Hefny brought a lawsuit against the OMB on the grounds that he was misclassified as White because he immigrated from Egypt: "Hefny says that as a Nubian, his hair is kinkier, his complexion darker and his features more African than blacks such as Detroit Mayor Dennis Archer and retired Gen. Colin Powell.[32] Hefney's challenge relies on a political society to assign race. He simply is redefining his political society of origins. "Nubian" is not a physiological description. A Nubian is a descendant of the Nubians, "an ancient kingdom in Northeast Africa, in what is now Egypt and Sudan.[33] The geographical designation of the ancient kingdom Nubia (a political society and geographical territory) is one Hefny associates with certain physical characteristics ("kinky hair") he thinks mark him Black.

These classifications have changed in the past, and they will, no doubt, change again.[34] Reflecting the tautologies that permeate the system, one study called for "all blacks to be identified as blacks—not just those whose origins are from the black racial groups of Africa.[35] It is ironic that the discipline that gave us scientific understandings of "race," namely that of anthropology, is now the one telling us that race does not exist, and that insofar as the concept does exist, it is primarily a matter of political organizations and boundaries. Of racial classifications in the Arctic, anthropologist Debra Schindler writes: "'Race' is a sociological phenomenon associated with oppression by the state, not a physiological boundary defined by specific biochemical criteria."[36] A response states: "It would be productive . . . to focus research upon features suitable for verification of polity differences in the past, beginning with polities indicated in primary Russian data and Aleut folklore."[37] So, while political scientists are busy studying "races" based on illogical typologies that have been repudiated by the people who developed them, anthropologists are deciding that political communities might have something to do with what we call 'race'.

WHAT RACE IS (NOT)—II

The account of racial taxonomies offered is not definite about the content of any particular race but is very specific as to the form taken by race. Such specificity challenges the notion that race is a diffuse concept, that "racism appeals either to inherent superiority or to differences. These putative differences may be strictly physical, intellectual, linguistic, or cultural."[38] David Goldberg also notes: "It should be obvious from all I have said that race cannot be a static, fixed entity, indeed is not an entity in any objective sense at all. I am tempted to say that race is whatever anyone in using that term or its cognates conceives of collective social relations."[39] Goldberg refers to the "complexity" of the concept of race. Sometimes it is one thing and sometimes something else, depending perhaps on the self-identification of the individual."[40] This is a highly unsatisfying theoretical position, no more appropriate for a scholarly definition of race than for those of freedom, justice, or anything else.

Goldberg attempts to demonstrate the slippery qualities of the concepts of race, religion, ethnicity, and nationality by asking "What is a Jew?"[41] But the possibility of assigning all of these designations to Jews does not mean these concepts are contingent or vague. Imagine a chair in my living room. "What's that?" is asked by an insurance agent, an interior decorator, and a three year old. The replies: 1) "It's worth about $100"; 2) "A family heirloom that I must hold onto." 3) "That? That's a chair." Goldberg asks "What is a Jew?" notices a variety of answers, and claims this a function of the ambiguity of all of them—race, nation, ethnicity, religion, and so on. This does not follow any more than it follows that because "cost" is one among several possible ways of conceptualizing a response, that "cost," "heirlooms," and "furniture" are ambiguous words or concepts. Each of these is a perfectly clear concept, relevant in different contexts.

Also, it matters that certain answers to "What's that?" won't do. If the response were "Oh, that's the hallway," the interlocutor would know she had been misunderstood, that this reply could not possibly refer to the chair, on the one hand. On the other hand the "heirloom" response could indicate an ostensive mistake, with the respondent thinking that the decorator had been asking about an old chest of drawers directly behind the chair. 'Chair' and 'chest' have something in common that 'chair' and 'hallway' do not share: the possibility of being both furniture.

The same holds for uses of 'race', 'nationality', 'ethnicity', and 'religion'. Races may be located either by reference to individual nations or aggregations of nations, so that the same group may be named as a nation or a race. 'Japanese' or 'Asians' may be thought races. But no racial designation exists independent of the political-geographical designation of both Japan and Asia. This means that 'Japanese' may be a national designation, depending on whether or not physical attributes are associated with the form of being. This is what prompts Goldberg to attribute an insurmountable vagueness to what counts as racial exclusions.[42] Returning to his example, Jews are a *race* when they are a people who are thought to have certain *physical differences* associated with a geographical territory of origins. In this case, the biblically described lands of the "Israelites" count as the place of origins. ('Israelites', not Jews, is the translation of the designation in the Hebrew Bible.)[43] Jews are a *nation* when conceptualized as members of a specific political society; they are Israelites by ancestry, but not necessarily physically distinct from other groups.[44] Jews are an *ethnicity* when considered as a potential national group within the borders of some place that is not Israel, not their "original" nation.[45] Finally, Jews are a *religious* group when described as a membership organization that distinguishes in particular ways between the sacred and profane. Likewise, Blacks are a racial group when thought of in terms of physical differences associated with a territory of origins, i.e., Africa; and likewise Whites are a racial group when conceptualized as having physical differences associated with origins in Europe.

Are Blacks an ethnic group? When Jesse Jackson organized to have "Blacks" identify as "African-American," he was calling for African-Americans to be just another ethnic group. Ethnic groups designate a people associated with a nation that exists elsewhere. Africa is not a nation, but an aggregation of nations. It is only because Africa has some of the political instruments associated with a nation that the label African-American is even conceivable. The numerous Pan-African conventions, organizations, and agreements[46] consolidate Africa as a political space that makes possible a sense of ancestral ties to that region and not simply one's tribe. However, it is the incommensurability of these African institutions with those of actual state-nations that makes the use of this "ethnic" label both possible and awkward.

NOTES

[1]Brian Goodall, *Dictionary of Human Geography* (Middlesex and New York: Penguin, 1987), p. 157.

[2]Ibid., p. 310.

[3]Ibid., p. 320. For purposes of my analysis it is irrelevant that this definition indicates a majority" and not all "Negroids" are from Africa. Here I simply want to show the use of geographical designations in definitions of race.

[4]Geological maps are also contingent. Their taxonomic devices change depending on the interests of the scientists or those who commission their work.

[5]F. J. Monkhouse, *A Dictionary of Geography* (Chicago: Aldine Publishing Company, 1970).

[6]Quoted in Albert Weinberg, *Manifest Destiny: A study of nationalist expansion in American history* (Gloucester: P. Smith, 1958), p. 55. I use this quotation here because, as we shall see below, the doctrine of Manifest Destiny was important to the consolidation of the national identity of the United States much later in the century as well. It is relevant, then, to note the theory as being located in a very statist understanding of geography.

[7]Ibid.

[8]Ibid. It is telling that Ingersoll notes this boundary in particular, since contemporary U.S. law treats those from Algeria and Morocco (formerly Mauritanian territory) as White.

[9]Herodotus, *Histories*, Book IV.36.

[10]Ibid., Book IV.37–38.

[11]"On Map of Antarctica, What Isn't in a Name?" *New York Times*, January 12, 1997, p. A7.

[12]*Reynolds* 165. Current court opinions continue to support a particular form of marriage in the name of "enlightened nations" and "our traditions," so that the cultural specificity of this marriage form is recognized and privileged, but without naming the specific other compared to which "ours" is enlightened. See, for example, *Singer v. Hara, 522* P.2d 1197 (1974); the current marriage form is justified due to the "prevailing mores and moral concepts of this age," which the court finds rooted in "scriptural, canonical, and civil law," in *Adams v. Howerton* 486 F. Supp. 1119, 1123 (1980); polygamy is a "blot on our civilization" and "contrary to the spirit of Christianity and of the civilization which Christianity has produced in the Western world" in *Morman Church v. U.S.* 136 U.S. 149 (1889); *Moore v. East Cleveland* 431 U.S. 495, 503 (1976); *Cabers v. Mohammed* 441 U.S. 397. On the Constitutional status of the specifically Christian form of marriage in this country, Carol Weisbrod writes that "co-option of the state by the church must now be justified by the state in entirely secular terms" ("Family, Church, and State: An Essay on Constitutionalism and Religious Authority," *Journal of Family Law* 26 [1987–88], p. 765). The Supreme Court does not follow this practice consistently, as in the references to Leviticus in *Bowers v. Hardwick* 478 U.S. [191] (1986); and a still influential federal court decision against same-sex marriage holds that the exclusive validity of different sex marriages is as "old as the book of Genesis" (*Baker v. Nelson* 191 N.W. 2d at 186).

[13]The Negro Family: The Case for National Action" in *The Moynihan Report and the Politics of Controversy*, Lee Rainwater and William Yancey, eds. (Cambridge and London: MIT Press, 1967), p. 75, emphasis added.

[14]For an affirmative statement about this difference, see Karen Sacks, *Sisters and Wives* (Westport: Greenwood Press, 1977).

[15]Source: Michael Wolff, Peter Rutte, and Albert F. Bayers, *Where We Stand* (New York, Toronto, and London: Bantam Books, 1992).

[16]*West Chester and Philadelphia Railroad Co. v. Miles* Penn. S. Ct., 211 (1867).

[17]Paul Lombardo writes: "Administrative enforcement by minor state bureaucracies also perpetuated the accepted mythologies, especially those involving the miscegenation taboo." He then describes a twenty-year racist correspondence between Virginia's head of the Registrar of Vital Statistics and John Powell, founder of the Anglo-Saxon Clubs of America (ASCA), which began in the early 1920s. "Miscegenation, Eugenics, and Racism: Footnotes to *Loving v. Virginia*," *University of California Davis Law Review* 21 (Winter, 1988), p. 427. See also Robert Sickels, *Race, Marriage, and the Law* (Albuquerque: University of New Mexico Press, 1972), and Raymond Diamond and Robert Control, "Codifying Caste: Los Angeles' Racial Classification Scheme and the Fourteenth Amendment," *Loyola Law Review* 29 (Spring, 1983), pp. 255–85.

[18]*Democracy in America*, tr. George Lawrence (New York: Anchor, 1969), pp. 355, 356.

[19]In another telling portrait of the multiple layers of marriage politics, colonial law in Virginia prohibited "fornication" between "Negroes" and "Christians," again suggesting that religion, race, gender, nationality, and sexuality are always politically intertwined. Nancy Cott, "Giving Character to Our Whole Civil Polity: Marriage and the Public Order . . . ," in *United States History as Women's History*, ed. Linda Kerber et al. (Chapel Hill and London: University of North Carolina Press, 1995), p. 388, note 45.

[20]Louisiana Civil Code 1808, page 24, article 8, quoted in Domínguez, *White by Definition*, p. 25.

[21]Louisiana, Article 920 (revised Civil Code of 1870), quoted in ibid., p. 63.

[22]Ibid., p. 73.

[23]La. App. 4 Cir. 1985. *Dot v. State*, 479 So.2d 369, writ denied 485 So. 2d, appeal dismissed 107 S. Ct. 638.

[24]*Cline v. City of New Orleans* La., 207 So, 2d 856, 858 (1968).

[25]Louisiana Revised Statute 40:266, quoted in *Cline* (above, note 84), at 859.

[26]*Toledano v. Drake*, 161 So.2d 339, 340 (1964).

[27]*Toldedano*, 311.

[28]Dominguez, *White by Definition*, p. 3.

[29]Paragraph 42.402 Definitions, Subpart F—Coordination of Enforcement of Non-discrimination in Federally Assisted Programs, 28 CFR Ch 1 (7-1-92 edition), p. 692.

[30]Rebecca Cann, Mark Storekin, Allan Wilson, "Mitochondrial DNA and Human Evolution," *Nature 325*, 1 (January, 1, 1987), pp. 31–36. This article was popularized as the one with the story about an African woman who, between 100,000 and 140,000 years ago, supposedly was the mother of the entire *homo sapiens* species. The basis of this claim is a study of the DNA from 150 placentas from around the world. The authors invoke the statistical principle of parsimony to claim that "[a]ll present-day humans are descendants of that African population," insofar as this hypothesis minimizes the "number of intercontinental migrations needed to account for the geographical distribution of mtDNA types" (pp. 35, 33).

[31]This also speaks to the problem of the "African-American" appellation, rather than "Black." Presumably a light-skinned person from a Dutch-born family who had emigrated to the United States from South Africa would count as an "African-American," which may not be a bad thing, insofar as it causes us to understand the contingency of these supposedly natural classifications.

[32]John Hughes, "Man Sues to Change Federal definitions," *Detroit Free Press*, June 5, 1997, 17A.

[33]Ibid.

[34]The 2000 census will provide people the opportunity of checking more than one box under the heading of "race."

[35]Hughes, "Man Sues."

[36]Schindler, "Anthropology in the Arctic," *Current Anthropology* 26, 4 (August/October 1985), p. 483.

[37]Ibid., p. 484. Schindler's essay argues against those anthropologists of the Arctic who persist in using racial typologies. But one of the more striking aspects of this article and the responses to it is the extent to which Schindler is taken to task by these specialists for constructing "straw men," based on the fact that few archaeologists or anthropologists in her field use racial typologies in their work. Only one of the approximately dozen responses actually defends racial typologies, and his defense is a qualified one (Kenneth Weiss, "Discussion," *Current Anthropology* 26, 4 [August/October, 1985], pp. 490–91).

[38]Goldberg, *Racist Culture* (Cambridge: Blackwell, 1993), p. 56.

[39]Ibid., p. 81.

[40]Ibid., pp. 101–3, 86.

[41]Ibid., p. 101.

[42]Ibid., p. 103.

[43]"Jews" are named as such by the Romans, a point discussed in Chapter 6.

[44]Israelites were patrilineal until the Mishnaic period, at which point it is recorded in the Talmud: "Your son by an Israelite mother is called your son, but your son by a heathen woman is not called your son" (*Qiddusbin*: 68b. From "Patrilineal Descent," in *Oxford Dictionary of the Jewish Religion*, R. J. Werblowsky and Geoffrey Wigoder, ed. [New York and Oxford: Oxford University Press, 1997]).

[45]It is also true that "ethnicity" is often experienced as a category of exoticism, such as when people refer to "ethnic" food or dress. I want to emphasize the importance of the fact that the underlying reference groups for all of these invocations are forms parasitic on political organizations, and not just any kind of difference. The Beatniks, for instance, inspired the formation of a sub-culture that was exotic vis-à-vis mainstream 1950s United States. But those who associated with Jack Kerouac were not considered to be part of an "ethnic" group. 'Punk', 'queer', 'stock car race fans' and even 'neo-Nazi' name particular sub-cultures in the United States, but they are not idiomatically called 'ethnic'. Again, the taxonomy I have in mind does not require that the political society actually exist, only that it is thought to have existed in the past or aspires to exist as a political society in the future. Insofar as continents are also a function of political societies, an 'ethnic' invocation vis-à-vis Africa or Asia is consistent with my definition. In the latter case, it is the addition of certain state-nations into a continent that forms this political society.

[46]And see Appiah, *In My Father's House*, p. 180.

ARTICLES AND AMENDMENTS PERTAINING TO RACE AND EQUALITY

—U.S. Constitution—

ARTICLES PERTAINING TO SLAVERY AND INDIANS

Article I, Sec. 2: The House of Representatives shall be composed of Members chosen every second Year by the People of the several States, and the Electors in each State shall have the Qualifications requisite for Electors of the most numerous Branch of the State Legislature . . .

Representatives and direct Taxes shall be apportioned among the several States which may be included within this Union, according to their respective Numbers, which shall be determined by adding to the whole Number of free Persons, including those bound to Service for a Term of Years, and excluding Indians not taxed, three fifths of all other Persons.

[The notorious "3/5ths" provision for "other persons"—i.e., slaves—was a compromise between slave states, which wanted their whole populations to be counted for purposes of determining the number of representatives they could send to the House, and free states, which wanted to dilute the representative power of the slave states by allowing only their free populations to count.]

Section 8. The Congress shall have Power To lay and collect Taxes, Duties, Imposts and Excises, to pay the Debts and provide for the common Defence and general Welfare of the United States; . . .

To regulate Commerce with foreign Nations, and among the several States, and with the Indian Tribes;

[Here the Constitution implicitly recognizes the distinct sovereignty of Indian Tribes, who have a distinct legal status to this day.]

Section 9. The Migration or Importation of such Persons as any of the States now existing shall think proper to admit, shall not be prohibited by the Congress prior to the Year one thousand eight hundred and eight, but a Tax or duty may be imposed on such Importation, not exceeding ten dollars for each Person.

[This provision ensured the right of slave states to import slaves until 1808.]

Article IV, Section 2. No Person held to Service or Labour in one State, under the Laws thereof, escaping into another, shall, in Consequence of any Law or Regulation therein, be discharged from such Service or Labour, but shall be delivered up on Claim of the Party to whom such Service or Labour may be due.

[This provision required free states to deliver escaped slaves back to their owners. Together with the Section 9 provision for the importation of slaves, this section was cited by the Supreme Court in the notorious Scott v. Sandford 60 U.S. (19 How.) 393, 411 (1857) to establish that slaves and their descendents—i.e., blacks—were not citizens

under the Constitution. The 14th Amendment voids this decision, and the 13th Amendment voids its bases by making slavery unconstitutional.]

AMENDMENTS EXPANDING THE SCOPE OF EQUALITY

Amendment 13. (1865) Section 1. Neither slavery nor involuntary servitude, except as a punishment for crime whereof the party shall have been duly convicted, shall exist within the United States, or any place subject to their jurisdiction. Section 2. Congress shall have power to enforce this article by appropriate legislation.

[The Court has interpreted this provision to empower Congress not merely to abolish forced labor, but to prohibit the imposition of "the badges and the incidents of slavery"—a potentially far-reaching power to prohibit stigmatizing acts by the states or even individuals. However, in the post-Reconstruction era, the potentially radical implications of this amendment were undercut by the Civil Rights Cases *109 U.S. 3, 22 (1883) (refusing to view segregated public accommodations as a badge of servitude) and* Hodges v. U.S. *203 U.S. 1 (1906) (refusing to view private coercion of blacks with the intent of driving them out of employment as inflicting a badge of inferiority).* Jones v. Alfred H. Mayer Co., *392 U.S. 409, 441 n.78 (1968) overruled* Hodges, *thereby recognizing a Congressional power under the 13th Amendment to prohibit private discrimination in public accommodations and contracts.]*

Amendment 14. (1868) Section. 1. All persons born or naturalized in the United States and subject to the jurisdiction thereof, are citizens of the United States and of the State wherein they reside. No State shall make or enforce any law which shall abridge the privileges or immunities of citizens of the United States; nor shall any State deprive any person of life, liberty, or property, without due process of law; nor deny to any person within its jurisdiction the equal protection of the laws. *reversing slavery*

Section. 2. Representatives shall be apportioned among the several States according to their respective numbers, counting the whole number of persons in each State, excluding Indians not taxed. But when the right to vote at any election for the choice of electors for President and Vice President of the United States, Representatives in Congress, the Executive and Judicial officers of a State, or the members of the Legislature thereof, is denied to any of the male inhabitants of such State, being twenty-one years of age, and citizens of the United States, or in any way abridged, except for participation in rebellion, or other crime, the basis of representation therein shall be reduced in the proportion which the number of such male citizens shall bear to the whole number of male citizens twenty-one years of age in such State. *reversing 3/5*

Section. 3. No person shall be a Senator or Representative in Congress, or elector of President and Vice President, or hold any office, civil or military, under the United States, or under any State, who, having previously taken an oath, as a member of Congress, or as an officer of the United States, or as a member of any State legislature, or as an executive or judicial officer of any State, to support the Constitution of the United States, shall have engaged in insurrection or rebellion against the same, or given aid or comfort to the enemies thereof. But Congress may by a vote of two-thirds of each House, remove such disability.

Section. 4. The validity of the public debt of the United States, authorized by law, including debts incurred for payment of pensions and bounties for services in suppressing insurrection or rebellion, shall not be questioned. But neither the United States nor any State shall assume or pay any debt or obligation incurred in aid of insurrection or rebellion against the United States, or any claim for the loss or emancipation of any slave; but all such debts, obligations and claims shall be held illegal and void.

Section. 5. The Congress shall have power to enforce, by appropriate legislation, the provisions of this article.

Amendment 15. (1870) Section. 1. The right of citizens of the United States to vote shall not be denied or abridged by the United States or by any State on account of race, color, or previous condition of servitude.

Section. 2. The Congress shall have power to enforce this article by appropriate legislation.

Amendment 19. (1920) The right of citizens of the United States to vote shall not be denied or abridged by the United States or by any State on account of sex. Congress shall have power to enforce this article by appropriate legislation.

Amendment 23. (1961) Section. 1. The District constituting the seat of Government of the United States shall appoint in such manner as the Congress may direct: A number of electors of President and Vice President equal to the whole number of Senators and Representatives in Congress to which the District would be entitled if it were a State, but in no event more than the least populous State; they shall be in addition to those appointed by the States, but they shall be considered, for the purposes of the election of President and Vice President, to be electors appointed by a State; and they shall meet in the District and perform such duties as provided by the twelfth article of amendment. Sec. 2. The Congress shall have power to enforce this article by appropriate legislation.

[This Amendment enfranchised the residents of Washington, D.C. for the purpose of electing the President and V.P. of the U.S. Residents still have no voting representative in Congress, despite the fact that in 1961, Washington D.C. had a larger population than 13 of the States.]

Amendment 24. (1964) Section. 1. The right of citizens of the United States to vote in any primary or other election for President or Vice President, for electors for President or Vice President, or for Senator or Representative in Congress, shall not be denied or abridged by the United States or any State by reason of failure to pay any poll tax or other tax. Section. 2. The Congress shall have power to enforce this article by appropriate legislation.

[The poll tax was widely used in the South to prevent blacks from voting.]

Amendment 26. (1971) Section. 1. The right of citizens of the United States, who are eighteen years of age or older, to vote shall not be denied or abridged by the United States or by any State on account of age. Section. 2. The Congress shall have power to enforce this article by appropriate legislation.

SPECIAL LEGAL DOCTRINES USED BY THE UNITED STATES TO RESTRICT THE RIGHT OF INDIAN PEOPLES TO OWN LAND AND BE SELF-GOVERNING

—*James E. Falkowski*—

CASE LAW

Except for the provisions mentioned earlier, the rights of indigenous peoples were ignored by the international legal system. Instead, their rights were determined by the domestic law of the overland European colonizers. A survey of the case law and policy of the United States will, therefore, be instructive for a number of reasons. First, the following cases illustrate the restrictions placed on the collective right of Indians to own land more fully than does the U.S. response to the questionnaire sent to the special rapporteur on the Study of the Problem of Discrimination against Indigenous Populations.[1] These cases, especially the cases developing the domestic trust, are also relevant to the civil and political rights of Indians, in particular their right to self-government.[2] Second, because the case law of the United States is the most highly developed body of law on indigenous peoples,[3] these cases are followed in other countries, including Australia,[4] Canada,[5] and New Zealand.[6] Therefore, they reflect state practice or customary international law.

Third, the United States has rejected assimilation policies in favor of a policy called self-determination. This has created a dilemma because prior case law is founded on assumptions leading to assimilation and not to self-determination. This case law must be reexamined before its relevance to the current self-determination policy can be fully understood, since "the judicial process is by nature evolutionary, building on what has gone before."[7] This also parallels the dilemma the United Nations faces in considering the rejection of the assimilation policy of the ILO and the emerging agenda of the Working Group on Indigenous Populations.

The first case addressing the nature of the right of Indians to own land was *Fletcher v. Peck*.[8] It was also the first case involving an interpretation of the contract clause of the federal Constitution, and it arose out of one of the largest land frauds perpetrated during the early years of the American Republic.[9] Additionally, it set the precedent of deciding Indian rights in cases to which they are not a party.

The facts of the case are as follows: In 1795 the Georgia legislature passed legislation enabling the state of Georgia to sell the right to buy Indian land to speculating land companies.[10] In 1796 a new legislature repealed the 1795 enabling legislation.[11] A "feigned" diversity suit was brought for the recovery of money paid, because of a breach of warranty of title over land conveyed to Fletcher by Peck.[12] In his deed to Fletcher, Peck covenanted

> that the state of Georgia aforesaid was, at the time of the passing of the act of the legislature thereof, (entitled as aforesaid,) legally seised in fee of the soil thereof, subject only to the extinguishment of part of the Indian title thereon. And that the legislature of the said state at the time of passing the act of sale aforesaid; had good right to sell and dispose of the same in manner pointed out by the said act. . . . And further, that the title to the premises so conveyed by the State of Georgia, and finally vested in the said Peck, has been in no way constitutionally or legally impaired by virtue of any subsequent act of any subsequent legislature of the said state of Georgia.[13]

The U.S. Supreme Court's decision, written by Chief Justice John Marshall, found for Peck because Georgia's first grant was a legal contract and its repeal violated the contract clause.[14]

The nature of Indian title arose tangentially, because Fletcher argued that Peck breached the covenant in the deed that the state of Georgia had a right to sell fee title to the land that was in the possession of the Indians.[15] Peck argued that the covenant was not breached because the state could sell its right to buy the land subject to Indian title.[16] Peck cited Vattel's *Law of Nations* to support his argument:

> What is the Indian title? It is mere occupancy for the purpose of hunting. It is not like our tenures; they have no idea of a title to the soil itself. It is overrun by them, rather than inhabited. It is not a true and legal possession.[17]

Chief Justice Marshall found that the state of Georgia had the right to sell the Indian land. Therefore, the covenant was not breached.[18] Not only did Georgia have a right to sell Indian land, but Marshall—who was forced to use this language because of the words used in the covenant—described Georgia's title as "seisin in fee" subject to Indian title.[19] Marshall even noted that the use of this language implied that a grantee could maintain an action of ejectment against the Indians.[20]

Justice Johnson's dissent strongly disagreed with Marshall's use of language in the majority opinion:

> Can, then, one nation be said to be seised of a fee-simple in lands, the right of soil of which is in another nation? It is awkward to apply the technical idea of fee-simple to the interests of a nation, but I must consider an absolute right of soil as an estate to them and their heirs. A fee-simple estate may be held in reversion, but our law will not admit the idea of its being limited after a fee-simple. In fact, if the Indian nations be the absolute proprietors of their soil, no other nation can be said to have the same interest in it. What, then, practically, is the interest of the states in the soil of the Indians within their boundaries? Unaffected by particular treaties, it is nothing more than what was assumed at the first settlement of the country, to wit, a right of conquest or of purchase, exclusively of all competitors within certain defined limits.[21]

Subsequent case law demonstrates that the misuse of words with precise legal meanings has resulted not only in a great deal of confusion, but also in a loss of Indian rights.[22] There have been two interpretations given to Marshall's language. One interpretation describes Indian title "as sacred as the fee-simple of the whites."[23] However, another, more recent interpretation describes "aboriginal title" as "not a property right but a 'mere possessory right' subject to the whim of the sovereign."[24]

The nature of Indian title next came before the Supreme Court in *Johnson v. McIntosh*.[25] Once again, Indians were not a party to the controversy, so the issues were framed without any consideration of their interests.[26] The plaintiffs claimed land under grants made to them, via a private individual, by the Illinois and Piankeshaw

Indian nations in 1773 and 1775.[27] The defendant claimed the same land under grants made to him by the U.S. government, which bought the land from the same Indians in 1795.[28]

The issue in the case was whether the courts of the United States were bound to recognize the plaintiffs' title.[29] The plaintiffs argued that since both parties claimed from the same source, it would be "unnecessary, and merely speculative, to discuss the question respecting the sort of title or ownership, which may be thought to belong to savage tribes, in the lands on which they live."[30] Therefore, the only issue was whether individuals could buy land from the Indians or whether that was the exclusive prerogative of the United States.[31]

The plaintiffs also argued that individuals had the right to purchase Indian lands since they were not prohibited from doing so when the purchases were made in 1773 and 1775.[32] Further, the plaintiffs argued that a statute passed by Virginia in 1779 asserting that the state had "the exclusive right of pre-emption from the Indians" was not competent to take away vested rights.[33] The fact that Indians held their land in common "did not affect the strength of their title by occupancy."[34]

The defendant argued that the Indians had no right to sell their land to a private individual because "the civilized powers of Europe and of this continent . . . have uniformly disregarded their supposed right to the territory included within the jurisdictional limits of those powers."[35] The foundation of title was the doctrine of discovery by which the United States acquired sovereignty and dominion and that "overlooks all proprietary rights in the natives."[36] Accordingly, Indians "remain in a state of nature, and have never been admitted into the general society of nations."[37] "The Statutes of Virginia, and of all the other colonies, and of the United States, treat them as an inferior race of people, without the privileges of citizens and under the perpetual protection and pupilage of the government."[38]

According to the defendant, Indian title was "a mere right of usufruct and habitation, without power of alienation."[39] Since the Indians owned their land collectively, they

> could have acquired no proprietary interest in the vast tracts of territory which they wandered over; and their right to the lands on which they hunted could not be considered as superior to that which is acquired to the sea by fishing in it. The use in the one case, as well the other, is not exclusive. According to every theory of property, the Indians had no individual rights to land; nor had they any collectively, or in their national capacity; for the lands occupied by each tribe were not used by them in such a manner as to prevent their being appropriated by a people of cultivators. All the proprietary rights of civilized nations on this continent are founded upon this principle.[40]

Chief Justice Marshall, writing for the majority, found for the defendant, and built further on the unfortunate choice of language that he had used in *Fletcher*.[41] *Fletcher* found that whites held fee title subject to Indian title.[42] *Johnson* found Indian title to be a mere "right of occupancy."[43] Marshall justified this diminution of the right of Indians to own land to a mere possessory interest based on the doctrine of discovery. The doctrine of discovery was "confined to countries 'then unknown to all Christian people.' . . . Thus [it] assert[s] a right to take possession notwithstanding the occupancy of the natives, who were heathens."[44]

As far as Chief Justice Marshall was concerned, the "character and religion" of the Indians "afforded an apology for considering them as a people over whom the superior genius of Europe might claim an ascendancy."[45] In exchange for unlimited independence, Christian-European states "made ample compensation to the inhabitants of the new [world] by bestowing on them civilization and Christianity."[46] In other words, according to U.S. Supreme Court Chief Justice John Marshall, Indians could not own land because they were uncivilized heathens. Thus, "discovery gave an exclusive right to extinguish the Indian title of occupancy, either by purchase or conquest; and gave also a right to such a degree of sovereignty as the circumstances of the people would allow them to exercise."[47] Supreme Court Justice Story, in his *Commentaries*, recognized that *Johnson* was in conflict with the laws of nature,[48] but he rationalized Marshall's reasoning as follows:

> European nations . . . claimed an absolute dominion over the whole territories afterwards occupied by them, not in virtue of any conquest of or cession by, the Indian natives, but as a right acquired by discovery. Some of them, indeed, obtained a sort of confirmatory grant from the papal authority. But as between

themselves they treated the dominion and title of territory as resulting from priority of discovery; and that European power which had first discovered the country and set up marks of possession was deemed to have gained the right, though it had not yet formed a regular colony there. We have also seen that the title of the Indians was not treated as a right of propriety and dominion, but as a mere right of occupancy. As infidels, heathens, and savages, they were not allowed to possess the prerogatives belonging to absolute, sovereign, and independent nations. The territory over which they wandered and which they used for their temporary and fugitive purposes, was, in respect to Christians, deemed as if it were inhabited only by brute animals.[49]

Chief Justice Marshall also was aware that his decision was "opposed to natural right, and to the usages of civilized nations."[50] It was opposed to natural right because the decision hinged on distinctions that failed to recognize the inherent equality of all human beings.[51] Marshall had already developed some expertise in finessing racial issues by couching them in less than totally candid language. Through the use of neutral principles of property law, Marshall had upheld chattel slavery.[52] The decision was opposed to the usages of civilized nations because Marshall confined the usages of civilized nations to Christian-European nations, with special legal doctrines applying to "wandering hordes" of Indians.[53]

An alternative analysis that was not opposed to natural law or the usages of civilized nations was only briefly considered by Marshall. International law recognized that when Indian nations ceded land to the United States by treaty, a plaintiff's interest in the land was governed by the land tenure system of the new sovereign.[54] Rights acquired before the cession were lost unless reserved by the treaty or guaranteed by the new sovereign.[55] In the plaintiff's case, since neither was done, the only recourse would be against the Indian nation that originally sold him the land. When the plaintiff bought the land from the Indians he incorporated himself with them and his rights were governed exclusively by the law of these Indians.[56] The situation would be the same today if an American citizen were to purchase land in Canada.

A great deal of confusion has been caused by the following language used in *Johnson*:

That law which regulated, and ought to regulate in general, the relations between the conqueror and conquered, was incapable of application to a people under such circumstances. The resort of some new and different rule, better adapted to the actual state of things, was unavoidable. Every rule which can be suggested will be found to be attended with great difficulty.

However extravagant the pretension of converting the discovery of an inhabited country into conquest may appear; if the principle has been asserted in the first instance, and afterwards sustained; if a country has been acquired and held under it; if the property of the great mass of the community originates in it, it becomes the law of the land, and cannot be questioned.[57]

In this passage, Marshall recognized that the doctrine of conquest did not apply to the Indians.[58] Rather, Marshall was converting the doctrine of discovery into the doctrine of conquest "by judicial fiat."[59] Only by pretending that Indian nations were conquered nations could Marshall justify his decision. The Supreme Court recognized that it was making no distinction between vacant land and land occupied by Indians.[60]

Thus, in this passage, Marshall invented a self-conscious legal fiction—the "myth of conquest"—to overlook the territorial integrity and political independence of Indian nations.[61] It should also be noted that language in this passage is totally unnecessary to the holding of the decision (*obiter dicta*), since the land at issue had been sold by the Indians. *Johnson*, with very few exceptions, "has been the basis of all subsequent determinations of Indian rights."[62]

The next important case, which not only reaffirmed the nature of Indian title as defined in *Johnson* but also established the domestic U.S. version of the sacred trust of civilization, was *Cherokee Nation v. Georgia*.[63] The rules developed in *Johnson* and *Cherokee Nation* are fundamental to understanding the unique legal doctrines that the U.S. courts apply only to Indians.

The facts of *Cherokee Nation v. Georgia* are as follows: The Cherokee Nation of Indians was having a dispute with the state of Georgia. The Cherokee Nation of Indians sought original jurisdiction before the Supreme

Court of the United States under Article III of the U.S. Constitution.[64] Article III gives the Supreme Court original jurisdiction to hear disputes between states of the Union and "foreign States."[65] The Supreme Court held that the Cherokee nation was a foreign state within the meaning of international law:

> Is the Cherokee nation a foreign state, in the sense in which that term is used in the constitution? The counsel for the plaintiffs have maintained the affirmative of this proposition with great earnestness and ability. So much of the argument as was intended to prove the character of the Cherokees as a state, as a distinct political society, separated from others, capable of managing its own affairs and governing itself, has, in the opinion of a majority of the judges, been completely successful. They have been uniformly treated as a state, from the settlement of our country. The numerous treaties made with them by the United States, recognize them as a people capable of maintaining the relations of peace and war, of being responsible in their political character for any violation of their engagements, or for any aggression committed on the citizens of the United States, by any individual of their community. Laws have been enacted in the spirit of these treaties. The acts of our government plainly recognize the Cherokee nation as a state, and the courts are bound by those acts.[66]

However, the Supreme Court ruled that "an Indian tribe or nation within the United States" was not a foreign state within the meaning of Article III.[67]

There were three major reasons given by the Supreme Court to support inventing this distinction.[68] First, the Supreme Court seized on the language used in the commerce clause of the Constitution to distinguish an Indian nation from a foreign nation. The Commerce clause gives Congress the power to "regulate commerce with foreign Nations, and among the several States, and with the Indian Tribes."[69] In the majority opinion, Marshall wrote: "We perceive plainly that the constitution, in this article, does not comprehend Indian tribes in the general term 'foreign nations'; not, we presume, because a tribe may not be a nation, but because it is not foreign to the United States."[70]

Second, and the point for which the case is most often cited, Marshall created the domestic trust relationship by interpreting the protection language of the Treaty of Holstein as making the Cherokee nation—and by analogy, all other Indian nations—"domestic dependent nations."[71] Marshall viewed Indians as being "in a state of pupilage; their relations to the United States resembles that of a ward to his guardian."[72] Although Marshall cited no authority for this analogy, he apparently derived this language from the writings of Victoria[73] and Burke.[74] These are the same sources from which the international trust developed.[75] However, the objectives of the domestic and international trusts are diametrically opposed. The ultimate objective of the international trust is the development of self-government, while the ultimate objective of the domestic trust is the destruction of self-government.[76]

Third, and a point that is often overlooked, is the fact that the guardianship notion was founded on the rule established in *Johnson* that did not recognize the right of Indians to own land. Based on this rule, Indian enclaves were placed "a grade below" the enclaves of Europe.[77] Marshall wrote that "the Indian territory is admitted to compose a part of the United States . . . [and] the Indians . . . occupy a territory to which we assert a title independent of their will."[78] Thus, Indian nations were not foreign nations because Marshall did not consider their land to be foreign. Rather, the Supreme Court regarded the land of this vanishing race as a "certain future acquisition."[79] This is how Marshall found an "aggregate of aliens composing a state" not to be a foreign state.[80]

Cherokee Nation's companion case, and the leading case to reject the *Johnson–Cherokee Nation* doctrine on the nature of the rights of Indians to own land and be self-governing, is *Worcester v. Georgia*.[81] Although *Worcester* is no longer "good law," it does provide a point of contrast against which the development of all subsequent domestic Indian law ought to be viewed. *Worcester* incorporates much of the dissenting opinion of *Cherokee Nation*, which found the Cherokees to be a foreign nation within the meaning of both international law and Article III.[82]

Worcester was a test case challenging the constitutionality of laws passed by the state of Georgia that extended their jurisdiction over the Cherokees.[83] Reverend Worcester had been residing on Cherokee territory and preaching the Christian gospel, with the permission of the Cherokees but in violation of a Georgia law that "forbade the residence of whites in Cherokee country without an oath of allegiance to the state and a license to remain."[84] Reverend Worcester was sentenced by a Georgia trial court to serve four years in jail, and he lost an appeal of this decision before the Georgia Supreme Court.[85]

The case was then appealed to the U.S. Supreme Court. Reverend Worcester argued that the laws passed by Georgia were unconstitutional as they were repugnant to the treaties between the Cherokee Nation and the federal government.[86] The U.S. Supreme Court held that the Georgia laws were void and that all "intercourse" with the Indians was to be carried on exclusively by the federal government.[87]

However, in reaching this decision, Chief Justice Marshall took a radically different view of the nature of Indian title. Marshall set the stage for his rejection of the theories of Vattel when he wrote:

> *America, separated from Europe by a wide ocean, was inhabited by a distinct people, divided into separate nations, independent of each other and of the rest of the world, having institutions of their own, and governing themselves by their own laws. It is difficult to comprehend the proposition, that the inhabitants of either quarter of the globe could have rightful original claims of dominion over the inhabitants of the other, or over the lands they occupied; or that the discovery of either by the other should give the discoverer rights in the country discovered, which annulled the pre-existing rights of its ancient possessors.*
>
> *After lying concealed for a series of ages, the enterprise of Europe, guided by nautical science, conducted some of her adventurous sons into this western world. They found it in the possession of a people who had made small progress in agriculture or manufactures, and whose general employment was war, hunting, and fishing.*
>
> *Did these adventurers, by sailing along the coast, and occasionally landing on it, acquire for the several governments to whom they belonged, or by whom they were commissioned, a rightful property in the soil, from the Atlantic to the Pacific; or rightful dominion over the numerous people who occupied it? Or has nature, or the great Creator of all things, conferred these rights over hunters and fishermen, on agriculturists and manufacturers?[88]*

In rejection of the principles set forth in *Johnson* and *Cherokee Nation*, the rights of both Indians and whites to own land were recognized as being equal with one exception. This exception was the belief that discovery gave the discovering European nation the exclusive right to purchase Indian land should the Indians choose to sell it.[89] Although discovery gave the discovering European nation the exclusive right to purchase, it did not "found that right on a denial of the possessor to sell."[90] Discovery "asserted a title against Europeans only, and [was] considered as blank paper so far as the rights of the natives were concerned."[91]

Further, the existence of the Cherokee Indians as a nation and their right to self-government and territorial integrity were explicitly recognized by treaty:

> *This treaty, thus explicitly recognizing the national character of the Cherokees, and their right of self government; thus guarantying their lands; assuming the duty of protection, and of course pledging the faith of the United States for that protection has been frequently renewed, and is now in full force. . . . From the commencement of our government, congress has passed acts to regulate trade and intercourse with the Indians. . . . All of these acts, and especially that of 1802, which is still in force, manifestly consider the several Indian nations as distinct political communities, having territorial boundaries, within which their authority is exclusive, and having a right to all the lands within those boundaries, which is not only acknowledged, but guaranteed by the United States. . . .*
>
> *The treaties and laws of the United States contemplated the Indian territory as completely separated from that of the states; and provide that all intercourse with them shall be carried on exclusively by the government of the union . . . the articles so often repeated in Indian treaties; extending to them, first, the protection of Great Britain, and afterwards that of the United States. These articles are associated with others, recognizing their title to self government. The very fact of repeated treaties with them recognizes it; and the settled doctrine of the law of nations is, that a weaker power does not surrender its independence—its right to self government, by associating with a stronger, and taking its protection. A weak state in order to provide for its safety, may place itself under the protection of one more powerful, without stripping itself of the right of government, and ceasing to be a state. Examples of this kind are not wanting in Europe. "Tributary and feudatory states," says Vattel, "do not thereby cease to be sovereign and independent states, so long as self government and sovereign and independent authority are left in the administration of the state."[92]*

Thus, not only was the state of Georgia preempted from exercising any jurisdiction within Cherokee territory, but the Indians' authority within their own territorial boundaries was also exclusive.[93] The only legitimate power of either the federal or state governments over Indians was based on consent as expressed in treaties.[94] No other rule would recognize the inherent right of all peoples to self-government. The situation would be the same today if New York State passed the same law asserting jurisdiction over Canada.

In recognizing the human rights and treaty rights of the Cherokee Nation of Indians, the seventy-seven-year-old Marshall knew that he would have a confrontation with President Andrew Jackson, who was an old Indian fighter and an advocate of the removal of Indians. Jackson is reported to have said, "John Marshall has made his decision, now let him enforce it."[95] Since Marshall had no power to enforce the decision, Reverend Worcester continued to languish in the Georgia jail.

Before *Worcester*, Marshall knew that he would go down in history as the inventor of a body of law that applied special legal doctrines to Indians that were different from the laws applied to whites. *Worcester* has been viewed by some as Marshall's attempt to right the wrongs that he had perpetrated on Indian peoples in his prior decisions.[96] After *Worcester*, the institution of the U.S. Supreme Court was shaken to its roots by being so rudely confronted with the reality of the limits of its powers. As a result of this decision, neither Marshall nor the Supreme Court ever again confronted the other branches of government with a decision that applied the same rules to Indians and whites alike. To understand American Indian law, it is important to understand the two opposing views of the nature of Indian rights, mentioned above. Unfortunately, contemporary cases have rejected the *Worcester* view of Indian title in favor of the *Johnson–Cherokee Nation* view. Contemporary analysis rejects *Worcester* as being based on "platonic [*sic*] notions of Indian sovereignty"[97] and allows both the states and the federal government to assert jurisdiction over Indian land without Indian consent.

Federal interference is based on a perversion of the guardianship notion first mentioned in *Cherokee Nation*. The trust ought to be limited to a duty of protection in the best interests of the Indians and an obligation to encourage their self-government.[98] Instead, the domestic trust presumes that Indians are incompetent to govern their own affairs, and the federal government in its self-appointed role as guardian has asserted plenary power to steal Indian land and destroy Indian self-government.[99] In the leading case of *Lone Wolf v. Hitchcock*, the Supreme Court upheld the federal government's power to unilaterally abrogate treaties with Indians and take their land,[100] although such abrogations violate the most fundamental principles of international and trust law.[101] Furthermore, the Supreme Court, which established the domestic trust relationship, has refused to provide remedies for breaches of trust duties.[102] One leading authority found that "the net result is the creation of a new power, a power to regulate Indians."[103]

Not only has the federal government failed to protect Indians from itself, it has also failed to protect them from state governments. In early cases, the U.S. Supreme Court protected Indians from state governments because the Indians "owe no allegiance to the States, and receive from them no protection. Because of the local ill feeling, the people of the States where they are found are often their deadliest enemies."[104] More recently, in addition to expressly delegating authority over Indians to state governments,[105] the federal government has also recognized certain "inherent" limitations on the authority of Indians over their land vis-à-vis state governments.[106] The federal courts have also reversed the presumption in *Worcester* that state governments have no jurisdiction over Indians in favor of "creating a presumption of state jurisdiction."[107]

Under current analysis, state jurisdiction is not preempted by the federal government unless the Indians can show that tribal self-government would be impaired by it. In *Williams v. Lee*, the Supreme Court reversed earlier cases that protected Indians from state governments when it found that "absent governing Acts of Congress, the question has always been whether the state action infringed on the right of reservation Indians to make their own laws and be ruled by them."[108] This standard invites litigation, and it has been an enormous financial drain on the Indians, who are the poorest segment of the population. Federal courts have also upheld state jurisdiction in numerous other cases despite the fact that treaties are often involved and that "[i]mplicit in these treaty terms . . . was the understanding that the internal affairs of the Indians remained exclusively within the jurisdiction of whatever tribal government existed."[109]

All these assertions of power over Indians are based on the doctrines of discovery and wardship which apply only to Indians. These doctrines are derived from the nature of the right of Indians to own land as defined in

Johnson. Using these doctrines, any interference with Indian self-government can be easily rationalized. If the Indians' land does not really belong to them,[110] or if they can be treated as a race of incompetents,[111] then their consent does not need to be obtained. Rather than follow any of the limitations that should have been placed on these doctrines, the U.S. Supreme Court has been further expanding on the *Johnson* view of Indian title and Indian rights.

The best example is *Tee-Hit-Ton Indians v. United States.*[112] In 1955, the Tee-Hit-Ton Indians of Alaska sued the United States for taking timber from land "claimed, occupied, and used" by the Tee-Hit-Ton Indians "from time immemorial."[113] The federal government—demonstrating the inherent conflict of interest it faces as the Indians' "guardian"—argued that

> the Tee-Hit-Tons' property interest, if any, is merely that of the right to use the land at the Government's will; [and] that Congress has never recognized any legal interest of petitioner in the land and therefore without such recognition, no compensation is due the petitioner for a taking by the United States.[114]

The U.S. Supreme Court decided the case on "the rule derived from *Johnson v. McIntosh* that the taking by the United States of unrecognized Indian title is not compensable under the Fifth Amendment."[115] The Supreme Court described the "nature of aboriginal interest in land" as "original Indian title or *permission from the whites to occupy.*"[116] Thus, such Indian land can be taken without due process or just compensation.[117]

The Supreme Court also gave its traditional allusion to the "myth of conquest":

> Every American schoolboy knows that the savage tribes of this continent were deprived of their ancestral ranges by force and that, even when the Indians ceded millions of acres by treaty in return for blankets, food and trinkets, it was not a sale but the conquerors' will that deprived them of their land.[118]

Once again, the doctrine of conquest was totally inapplicable to the Tee-Hit-Tons, or any other Indians in Alaska, because there were never any hostilities between whites and Indians in the entire state.[119]

In addition to what "every American schoolboy" knows about the savage tribes of this continent, the Supreme Court cited Wheaton as an authority.[120] Wheaton's position is enlightening:

> The Spaniards and Portuguese took the lead among the nations of Europe, in the splendid maritime discoveries in the East and the West, during the fifteenth and sixteenth centuries. According to the European ideas of that age, the heathen nations of the other quarters of the globe were the lawful spoil and prey of their civilized conquerors, and as between the Christian powers themselves, the Sovereign Pontiff was the supreme arbiter of conflicting claims. Hence the famous bull, issued by Pope Alexander VI, in 1493, by which he granted to the united crowns of Castile and Arragon all lands discovered, and to be discovered, beyond a line drawn from pole to pole, one hundred leagues west from the Azores, or Western Islands, under which Spain has since claimed to exclude all other European nations from the possession and use, not only of the lands but of the seas in the New World west of that line. . . . On the other hand, Great Britain, France, and Holland, disregarded the pretended authority of the Papal See, and pushed their discoveries, conquests, and settlements, both in the East and West Indies; until conflicting with the paramount claims of Spain and Portugal, they produced bloody and destructive wars between the different maritime powers of Europe. But there was one thing in which they all agreed, that of almost entirely disregarding the right of the native inhabitants of these regions. Thus the bull of Pope Alexander VI reserved from the grant to Spain all lands which had been previously occupied by any Christian nation. . . . It thus became a maxim of policy and law, that the right of the native Indians was subordinate to that of the first Christian discoverer, whose paramount claim excluded that of every other civilized nation, and gradually extinguished that of the natives.[121]

Not only did Wheaton ignore Pope Paul III's bull, he also gave the grants of the English monarchs equal dignity with the bull of Pope Alexander VI. This was a rather creative way of not recognizing the right of Alaskan Indians to own land. The Russians "discovered" Alaska and sold the right of preemption to the United States.[122] Therefore, what the Spanish or English governments did was of questionable relevance to Alaska.

However, in *Tee-Hit-Ton*, the Supreme Court even went beyond the expansive interpretation that Marshall gave to Vattel's theories in *Johnson.* The description of Indian title as "permission from the whites to occupy" implies that Indians are "tenants at will": If the whites revoked their "permission," the Indians would be trespassing on their own land![123]

The real reason for the Supreme Court's decision was buried in a footnote. Somehow the government got into evidence the fact that if the Supreme Court gave just compensation for the taking of unrecognized Indian title, estimated pending claims would be worth $9 billion.[124] This compares to the $800 million paid for all the land purchased from the Indians in the United States.[125] Really, this was a purely economic decision.

The decision also has a macabre twist. The Supreme Court failed to cite or distinguish as authority a law review article written by Felix S. Cohen (who had died two years earlier) that would have reached the opposite result.[126] Clearly the judges were aware of the article written in 1947 because they plagiarized one of its key phrases—"every American schoolboy"—out of context. Cohen wrote:

> Every American schoolboy is taught to believe that the lands of the United States were acquired by purchase or treaty from Britain, Spain, France, Mexico, and Russia, and that for all the continental lands so purchased we paid about 50 million dollars out of the Federal Treasury. Most of us believe this story as unquestioningly as we believe in electricity or corporations. We have seen little maps of the United States in our history books and big maps in our geography books showing the vast area that Napoleon sold us in 1803 for 15 million dollars and the various other cessions that make up the story of our national expansion. As for the original Indian owners of the continent, the common impression is that we took the land from them by force and proceeded to lock them up in concentration camps called reservations.
>
> Notwithstanding this prevailing mythology, the historic fact is that practically all of the real estate acquired by the United States since 1776 was purchased not from Napoleon or any other emperor or czar but from its original Indian owners.[127]

Compare this language to the opinion of the Supreme Court that "every American schoolboy" knows the continent was taken from the Indians by conquest.[128] This followed the Supreme Court's tradition of creating mythology in Indian law cases rather than following historical fact.

The Supreme Court's position was based on what Cohen referred to as the "menagerie" theory of Indian title. According to this theory; "Indians are less than human and . . . their relations to their lands is not the human relation of ownership but rather something similar to the relation that animals bear to the areas in which they may be temporarily confined."[129] As to the origins of this theory, Cohen wrote:

> The sources of this "menagerie" theory are many and varied and sometimes elegantly pedigreed. There is the feudal doctrine, which has seldom been heard in this country for a century or so except in Indian cases, that ultimate dominion over land rests in the sovereign. . . . There are other subtler sources of the "menagerie" theory of Indian reservations which are seldom set forth in legal briefs but exert a deep influence on public administration. One of the most insidious of these is the doctrine that the only good Indian is a dead Indian, when it follows, by frontier logic, that the only good Indian title is one that has been extinguished, through transfer to a white man or a white man's government. And finally there is the more respectable metaphysical doctrine that since government is the source of all rights there are no rights against the Government, from which it may be deduced that Indians who have been deprived of their possessions by governmental action are without redress. All these doctrines, it may be hoped, have been finally consigned to the dust bins of history by the course of decisions of the Supreme Court that culminates in the Alcea case.[130]

However, the Supreme Court does not find the body of law treating Indians as less than human to be invidious racial discrimination. In the leading case of *Morton v. Mancari*, the Court upheld an Indian hiring preference statute.[131] Although a higher standard of review is applied to other racial classifications (the strict scrutiny test), a lower standard of review is applied to an "Indian" classification ("reasonably and directly related to a legitimate, nonracially based goal").[132] The Court was concerned that if it applied the same standard of review to an "Indian" classification, "an entire Title of the United States Code (25 U.S.C.)" would be declared unconstitutional.[133]

The Court reasoned, in a footnote, that the term "Indian" was not a racial classification because it only dealt with federally recognized Indians.[134] In other words, a subclassification of a racial group does not constitute a racial classification. Additionally, it is the federal government that determines whether someone is a member of the subclassification. Moreover, on its face, the statute applies to all members of the racial group "Indians" and is not limited to "federally recognized Indians."[135] The same reasoning could have been used to uphold black slavery as nonracial on the grounds that some black people were not slaves.

This review establishes the fact that the U.S. Supreme Court that laid the foundation for domestic Indian law was a racist institution.[136] Not only did it uphold chattel slavery, but it also relied on the racist line of writers of international law as authority for its denial of the rights of Indians to own land and be self-governing. The Supreme Court still follows the same line of cases although it omits some of the most offensive language. In 1883, the Supreme Court found that the whites were "superiors of a different race."[137] When the current chief justice of the Supreme Court, William Rehnquist, cited this language as authority in 1978, he omitted the offensive language "superiors of" and wrote, "a different race."[138]

FEDERAL INDIAN POLICY

Federal Indian policy, although often couched in language that claims to help or protect Indians, has often been used as a pretext for taking or controlling Indian land.[139] The ultimate objective of the domestic trust has been the coerced assimilation of Indians into mainstream American society at the expense of Indian land ownership and self-government. One author has noted, "We sometimes fail to realize that the formulation of all Indian policies in American history; even the most just, has been based on certain attitudes that could best be described as racial."[140]

After the Revolutionary War, the United States continued to follow many of the precedents set by the British government in dealing with the Indians. The first policy statement made by Congress was the Northwest Ordinance of 1787, which read:

> The utmost good faith shall always be observed towards the Indians, their lands and property shall never be taken from them without their consent; and in their property rights and liberty, they never shall be invaded or disturbed, unless in just and lawful wars authorized by Congress; but laws founded in justice and humanity shall from time to time be made, for preventing wrongs being done to them, and for preserving peace and friendship with them.[141]

The policy was built on the themes first set forth by Victoria and Pope Paul III recognizing the human rights of indigenous peoples.[142] However, this policy has rarely been carried out in practice.

In these early years, the federal government's major concerns were with the regulation of trade and land cessions with the Indians.[143] A federal monopoly was established in both areas. In 1790, the first Nonintercourse Act was passed. In addition to regulating trade with Indians, this act forbid the conveyance of Indian lands without the consent of the federal government.[144] The legal status of the Indians was described as follows:

> From the earliest times the Indians, though treated as subject to the sovereignty first of the foreign colonizing powers, then of the colonies or States, and finally, of the United States, have been considered not as citizens or subjects, that is, as members of the various bodies politic within whose midst they have lived, but, from the constitutional viewpoint, as aliens, and their tribes as foreign nations to be dealt with as such, namely, by treaties and agreements rather than by statutes.[145]

Despite the First Amendment's express prohibition against the establishment of religion, this did not apply to the Indians. Congress began appropriating funds to missionaries to Christianize and civilize the Indians.[146] The government would often authorize a large number of missionaries from different Protestant denominations to convert the Indians on a single reservation.

Within fifty years of becoming the first state in the Western Hemisphere to be recognized as a member of the Family of Nations, in 1823 the United States developed the Monroe Doctrine. This policy was based on the "'doctrine of two spheres' which assumed that the nations of the 'New World' and those of the 'Old World' were essentially different in political and economic terms."[147] This rule of American international law recognized existing European colonies and the independence of former European colonies. It also continued the nonrecognition of indigenous nations and established the legitimacy of the overland colonization of indigenous nations free from international reproach.

In the development of Indian policy, one author noted five basic alternatives:

Alternative 1: destroy the status quo: violate, or render inoperative, treaty guarantees; destroy tribal integrity; kill or remove Indians, or wait for them to die off.

Alternative 2: maintain the status quo: support existing treaty guarantees, tribal integrity, and the right of tribes to hold land in common; protect the individual Indian against white aggression.

Alternative 3: change the status quo by voluntary agreement of tribes, leading gradually to individual allotment of lands and adoption of "civilized" ways.

Alternative 4: change the status quo by involuntary means by destroying tribal autonomy, and forcing Indians rapidly into individual allotment of lands, subjection to the white man's law, and mandatory citizenship.

Alternative 5: any of the above alternatives, but with the addition of benefits to white farmers greedy for Indian land, to white miners eager to exploit Indian mineral wealth, and to railroad companies anxious for Indian land and rights-of-way.[148]

The federal government adopted a combination of the first, fourth, and fifth alternatives.

In the 1830s the federal government initiated the Removal policy.[149] Under this policy, land-hungry whites took the Indians' eastern lands in exchange for land west of the Mississippi River. This area was known as the Great American Desert, and it "was then considered to be uninhabitable by white people."[150] The justification for this policy was that "only if the Indians were removed beyond contact with whites could the slow process of education, civilization and Christianization take place."[151] This exchange of land was a way to "avoid dealing with the more difficult and more basic political conflicts of interest inherent in allowing a 'sovereign nation' to exist within a state without being incorporated into the federal system."[152]

The already educated, civilized, and Christianized Cherokees were among those eastern Indians removed to the western lands. This episode in Cherokee history is known as the "Trail of Tears" because about one-fifth of the Cherokees died when they were removed by the United States in the middle of winter.[153] New treaties were made with the Cherokee Nation of Indians, and they were promised

a permanent home, . . . which shall, under the most solemn guarantee of the United States, be, and remain, theirs forever—a home that shall never, in all future time, be embarrassed by having extended around it the lines, or placed over it the jurisdiction of a Territory or State, nor be pressed upon by the extension, in any way, of any of the limits of any existing Territory or State.[154]

In 1871, in a rider attached to an appropriation bill, Congress passed a law providing:

No Indian nation or tribe within the territory of the United States shall be acknowledged or recognized as an independent nation, tribe, or power with whom the United States may contract by treaty; but no obligation of any treaty lawfully made and ratified with any such Indian nation or tribe prior to March 3, 1871 shall be hereby invalidated or impaired.[155]

"By this section, the policy of the government, maintained for nearly 100 years of entering into treaties with the various tribes of Indians within the geographical limits of the United States as with a foreign nation was changed."[156] Although existing treaty rights were not intended to be impaired and Indians were still supposed to be dealt with on the basis of consent, Congress began passing legislation affecting Indians without the Indians' consent.[157]

The U.S. Supreme Court upheld such legislation based on a perversion of the trust concept. Indians were regarded as incompetent wards, and the federal government was presumed to be acting in their best interest.[158] In fact, the leading case upheld the sale of Indian lands to non-Indians by the federal government without Indian consent.[159] This is how consent is dispensed with in a country where all just government is supposed to be based on the consent of the governed.[160] Although the 1871 act appears on its face to be racially discriminatory and a violation of the separation of powers clause, it has not been declared unconstitutional.[161]

In 1887 the General Allotment policy was initiated even though previous experiments with allotments had disastrous effects on Indians.[162] The Allotment Act was supposed to make the entire race of Indian people into farmers in twenty-five years by allotting each Indian an individually owned parcel of land out of the communally held Indian lands, most of which were guaranteed to them by treaty. During the twenty-five-year trust period, the federal government was to hold trust title to the Indian land. After the twenty-five-year period was over, the Indian allottee, if declared competent, would be given fee title to the land. This would make the Indian an American citizen, without his or her consent, and the jurisdiction of the Indian nation over that plot of land would come to an end.[163]

After the allotments were made to Indians, the "surplus" Indian land was sold to non-Indians.[164] This was the real reason for the policy, and was well known at the time. During the debates on this legislation, a small minority of congressmen spoke out against the legislation in the following terms:

> The main purpose of this bill is not to help the Indian, or solve the Indian problem, or provide a method for getting out of our Indian troubles so much as it is to provide a method for getting at the valuable Indian lands and opening them up to white settlement. The main object of the bill is in the last sections of it, not in the first. The sting of this animal is in its tail. . . . The provisions for the apparent benefit of the Indian are but the pretext to get at his lands and occupy them. With that accomplished, we have securely paved the way for the extermination of the Indian races upon this part of the continent.[165]

Even the sponsor of the bill, Senator Henry L. Dawes (R-Mass.), acknowledged that the act was a "violation of treaties" and a "flagrant disregard of inalienable rights."[166]

Under the Allotment Act, almost two-thirds of the remaining Indian land passed into the hands of the whites.[167] The numbers are staggering. For various reasons, 20 million acres of Indian land were spared from the Allotment Act. The remaining 118 million acres of land held by Indians in 1887 had been reduced to 28 million acres by 1934. Additionally, most of the land taken by the whites was the best farming land, and most of the land remaining with the Indians is desert or semidesert. This transparent land theft scheme has been called an "orgy of plunder and exploitation unparalleled in American history."[168]

When this policy was finally repudiated by the federal government and the trust period was extended, the Indians' "right of occupancy" was subject to the further restriction that the federal government held trust title to their land. "Equally important with the outright loss of land is the effect of the allotment system in making such lands as remain in Indian ownership unusable."[169] After the original Indian allottee died, the allotted land was divided up among that person's heirs, resulting in small parcels of land that were not economically feasible units. In this way, the federal government obtained control over the leasing and management of much of the remaining Indian land.[170] This policy is responsible for the poverty in which many Indian peoples live today.

With respect to the Cherokees, the United States unilaterally allotted their lands in 1906. The Cherokee Indians were declared to be citizens, and they were forced to incorporate within the state of Oklahoma, in violation of the promises made to them when they were forcibly removed from their traditional lands in the eastern part of the United States.[171]

"From the first settlement of the American colonies the Indians were treated as alien peoples outside of the control of domestic laws."[172] In 1924, without Indian consent, Congress unilaterally declared all Indians born in the United States to be U.S. citizens.[173] Although this was done under the pretext of giving Indians rights—especially the right to vote—in effect, it took away the Indians' right to be citizens of their own indigenous nations without interference from the United States.[174] It reduces Indians from what ought to be a people with the right to control their remaining land to a small, insignificant minority in a majority rule system. One example is the Navajo Indians, who have a 25,000-square-mile reservation and a population of 200,000. Although this reservation is larger than forty UN member states, the Navajo are not allowed any representation in the U.S. Senate, and their potential congressional voting strength is split between four states of the Union.[175]

In 1934, after the allotment policy was acknowledged to be a failure, Congress passed the Indian Reorganization Act.[176] The Indian Reorganization Act stopped allotments, but only if the Indians would accept a constitution written by the federal government. The Indian Reorganization Act constitutions, among other things, imposed a separation of church and state on the Indians' traditional theocratic governments.[177] The legitimacy of these governments is often called into question in view of the known Indian tradition of not attending meetings or participating in elections with which they did not agree. Such governments were often voted in by a nontraditionalist, Christian minority, and the United States no longer recognizes the authority of the traditional Indian governments with whom they previously had negotiated treaties.[178]

The ultimate solution to the "Indian Problem" was the Termination policy, initiated in the 1950s.[179] The goal of the Termination policy was the complete integration of Indians "into the mass of the population as full, tax-paying citizens."[180] Under this policy, the federal government withdrew recognition of all special Indian rights (treaty, executive order, statutory, and aboriginal). Indian land was divided into individual parcels, and this land again soon passed into the hands of the white population. Over one hundred Indian groups were terminated. Although the Termination policy has been rejected as "morally and legally unacceptable," only one terminated Indian group has been reinstated.[181]

The final reversal of federal Indian policy to date occurred in 1970 with the initiation of the Self-Determination policy.[182] The name of this policy is very misleading. It has almost nothing to do with the meaning of self-determination under international law. This domestic policy only gives Indians very limited control over some of their educational programs.

As this review of domestic Indian policy has shown, it can be changed at any time. Only a constitutional amendment requiring Indian consent would be adequate to really protect the right of Indians to self-government.[183] It is also clear that the United States still regards Indian rights to be only temporary.[184]

NOTES

[1]The response of the U.S. Government was so misleading and incomplete that an American Indian rebuttal was made. United States' Response to the Study of the Problem of Discrimination of Indigenous Populations, 7 American Indian Law Newsletter, no. 11, special issue (1974).

[2]*Id.* at 75.

[3]G. Bennett, Aboriginal Title in the Common Law: A Stony Path Through Feudal Doctrine, 27 Buf. L. Rev. 617 (1978).

[4]*Millirrpummy, Nabalco Pty. Ltd.* (1971) 17 F.L.R. 141; *see also* P. Biskup, Not Slaves, Not Citizens: The Aboriginal Problem in Western Australia 1898–1954 (1973); S. Haas, An Outward Sign of an Inward Struggle: The Fight for Human Rights of the Australian Aborigine, 5 Fla. Int'l. L.J. 81 (Fall 1989).

[5]L. Green, Trusteeship and Canada's Indians, 3 Dalhousie L.J. 104 (1976); *see also* Native Rights in Canada (P. A. Cumming & N. H. Mickenberg eds. 1972); M. Asch, Home and Native Land: Aboriginal Rights and the Canadian Constitution (1984); B. H. Wildsmith, Aboriginal Peoples and Section 25 of the Canadian Charter of Rights and Freedoms (1988); B. Slattery, Ancestral Lands: Alien Laws: Judicial Perspectives on Aboriginal Title (1983); Pathways to Self-Determination: Canadian Indians and the Canadian Constitution (L. Little Bear, M. Boldt & J. A. Long eds. 1984).

[6]N. Smith, Maori Land Law (1960); *see also* R. Falk, The Role of Domestic Courts in the International Legal Order (1964); I. H. Kawharu, Waitangi, Maori and Pukeha Perspectives on the Treaty of Waitangi 98–99 (1989).

[7]R. Ericson & D. R. Snow, The Indian Battle for Self-Determination, 58 Ca. L. Rev. 445, 486 (1970).

[8]10 U.S. (6 Cranch.) 87 (1812).

[9]C. Haines, The Role of the Supreme Court in American Government and Politics 1789–1835, at 309 (1960).

[10]10 U.S. (6 Cranch.) 87, 88 (1812).

[11]*Id.* at 89.

[12]C. Haines, *supra* note 9, at 314; *see also* J. Norgren, Protection of What Rights They Have: Original Principles of Federal Indian Law, 64 N.D.L. Rev. 73, 83 (1988); G. T. Dunne, Justice Joseph Story and the Rise of the Supreme Court 70–76 (1970).

[13]10 U.S. (6 Cranch.) 87, 88 (1812).

[14]*Id.* at 139.

[15]*Id.* at 124.

[16]*Id.* at 121.

[17]*Id.*

[18]*Id.* at 142.

[19]*Id.* at 142–43; *see also* R. L. Barsh and J. Y. Henderson, The Road: Indian Tribes and Political Liberty 38 (1980).

[20]*Id.* at 142.

Ejectment is an action to restore possession of property to the person entitled to it. Not only must the plaintiff establish a right to possession in himself, but he must also show that the defendant is in wrongful possession. If the defendant has only trespassed on the land, the action is for trespass (i.e. damages).

Black's Law Dictionary 464 (1979).

[21]Black's Law Dictionary, *supra* note 20, at 147.

[22]H. Berman, The Concept of Aboriginal Rights in the Early Legal History of the United States, 27 Buf. L. Rev. 637, 638 (1978); *see also* Veeder, Greed and Bigotry: Hallmark of American Indian Law, 3 Am. Ind. J., no. 12, at 2, 8 (1977).

[23]*Mitchell v. United States*, 34 U.S. (9 Pet.) 711, 746 (1835).

[24]N. J. Newton, At the Whim of the Sovereign: Aboriginal Title Reconsidered, 31 Hast. L.J. 1215 (1980).

[25]21 U.S. (8 Wheat.) 543 (1823).

[26]N. J. Newton, *supra* note 24, at 1221–22.

[27]21 U.S. (8 Wheat.) 543, 553–55 (1823).

[28]*Id.* at 572.

[29]*Id.*

[30]*Id.* at 562–63.

[31]*Id.* at 563.

[32]*Id.* at 563.

[33]*Id.* at 565 n.a.

[34]*Id.* at 563.

[35]*Id.* at 567.

[36]*Id.*

[37]*Id.*

[38]*Id.* at 569.

[39]*Id.*

[40]*Id.* at 569–70.

[41]*Id.* at 592.

[42]*Fletcher v. Peck, supra* note 8, at 142–43.

[43]*Johnson v. McIntosh, supra* note 25, at 574, 591.

[44]*Id.* at 576–77.

[45]*Id.* at 573.

[46]*Id.* at 573.

[47]*Id.* at 587.

[48]J. Story, 1 Commentaries on the Constitution of the United States 4 (1858).

[49]*Id.* at 106 (footnotes omitted). *Cf.* J. Story, A Discourse Pronounced at the Request of the Essex Historical Society 71 (1928): "If, abstractly considered, mere discovery could confer any title, the natives already possessed it by such prior discovery." *See also*

D. Getches, D. Rosenfelt & C. Wilkinson, Cases and Materials on Federal Indian Law 297 (1979); Sir James McIntosh, Progress of Ethical Philosophy 49–50 (Philadelphia ed. 1832). "A state is also distinguishable from an unsettled horde of wandering savages not yet formed into civil society": J. B. Moore, A Digest of International Law 15 (1906).

[50] 21 U.S. 543, 591 (1823).

[51] H. Berman, *supra* note 22, at 651.

[52] D. M. Roper, In Quest of Judicial Objectivity: The Marshall Court and the Legitimation of Slavery, 21 Stan. L. Rev. 532 (1969).

[53] *Cherokee Nation v. Georgia*, 30 U.S. (5 Pet.) 1, 27 (1831).

[54] R. Barsh and J. Henderson, *supra* note 19, at 45–46.

[55] *Id.* at 46.

[56] *Id.*

[57] 21 U.S. 543, 591 (1823).

[58] See also H. Berman, *supra* note 22, at 691: F. S. Cohen, Handbook of Federal Indian Law 282 n. 20 (1942).

[59] H. Berman, *supra* note 22, at 648.

[60] 21 U.S. 453, 596 (1823).

[61] H. Berman, *supra* note 22, at 647; *see also* R. Barsh and J. Henderson, *supra* note 19, at 48, 143 n 24, 278; F. Jennings, The Invasion of America: Indians, Colonialism, and the Cant of Conquest 15–16, 32 (1975); R. A. Williams, Jr., The American Indian in Western Legal Thought: The Discourses of Conquest 315, 330–33 n. 14 (1990); *cf.* J. Y. Henderson, Unraveling the Riddle of Aboriginal Title, 5 Am. Ind. L. Rev. 75, 92 (1977).

[62] Indian Tribes, A Report of the United States Commission of Civil Rights 16–17 (June 1981).

[63] 30 U.S. (5 Pet.) 1 (1831).

[64] *Id.* at 15.

[65] U.S. Const. art. 3, sect. 2.

[66] 30 U.S. 1, 15 (1831).

[67] *Id.* at 19.

[68] See N. J. Newton, *supra* note 24, at 1224.

[69] U.S. Const. art. 1, sect. 8.

[70] 30 U.S. 1, at 18 (1831).

[71] *Id.* at 17; *see also* F. S. Cohen, *supra* note 38, at 46–48.

[72] *Id.*; *see also* R. L. Barsh & J. Y. Henderson, *supra* note 19, at 55.

[73] J. B. Scott, The Spanish Origin of International Law 78 (1934); *see also* J. Norgren, Protection of What Rights They Have: Original Principles of Federal Indian Law 64 N. D. L. Rev. 73, 77 nn. 12–17 (1988); R. A. Williams, Jr., The Medieval and Renaissance Origins of the Status of the American Indian in Western Legal Thought, 57 So. Cal. L. Rev. 1, 68 (1983); Rethinking the Trust Doctrine in Federal Indian Law, 98 Harv. L. Rev. 422, 424 (1984); H. Frieger, Principles of the Indian Law and the Act of June 18, 1934, in 3 Geo. Wash. L. Rev. 279, 288 (1935); F. S. Cohen, The Spanish Origin of Indian Rights in the Law of the United States, 31 Geo. L. Rev. 1, 17 (1942).

[74] C. Toussaint, Trusteeship System of the United Nations (1956); *see also* Rethinking the Trust Doctrine in Federal Indian Law, 98 Harv. L. Rev. 422, 425 (1984); A. Beverridge, The Life of John Marshall 10–12 (1919); Who Was Who in America, Historical Volume 1607–1896, at 404 (rev. ed. 1967).

[75] *Id.*; *see also* Y. El-Ayouty, The United Nations and Decolonization (1971); E. Sady, The United Nations and Dependent Peoples (1956).

[76] The domestic trust relationship in the Western Hemisphere has deviated from the trust relationship first envisaged by Victoria. It now appears to be modeled after the regime of tutelage derived from Roman law (ST/HR/SER.A/11, at 6). Under Roman law, "children were things for their father, and he was in legal possession of them": S. W. Dyde, Hegel's Philosophy of Right 50 (1890). The treatment of Indians as incompetent wards is one of the aspects of the domestic trust that Indians are trying to have changed: *see* U.N. Doc. E/CN.4/Sub. 2/NGO/98, reprinted in 13 Akwesasne Notes, no. 4, at 21–22 (Autumn 1981); Felix S. Cohen, writing in 1942, found this wardship language to be susceptible to over a thousand different meanings: F. S. Cohen, *supra* note 58, at 170 n. 289.

[77] 30 U.S. 1, 26 (1831).

[78]*Id.* at 17.

[79]*Id.* at 25.

[80]*Id.* at 15.

[81]31 U.S. (6 Pet.) 315 (1832).

[82]*Cherokee Nation v. Georgia*, 30 U.S. (5 Pet.) 1, 49 (1831).

[83]J. Burke, The Cherokee Cases: A Study In Law, Politics, and Morality, 21 Stan. L. Rev. 500, 510 (1969), *see also* U. B. Phillips, Georgia and State Rights 66–68 (1968).

[84]F. S. Cohen, *supra* note 58, at 55.

[85]31 U.S. (6 Pet.) 515, 536 (1132).

[86]*Id.* at 538.

[87]*Id.* at 560.

[88]*Id.* at 542–43.

[89]*Id.* at 559.

[90]*Id.* at 544.

[91]*Id.* at 546.

[92]*Id.* at 556–61.

[93]*Id.* at 556.

[94]*Id.* at 557.

[95]J. P. Kinney, A Continent Lost—A Civilization Won 71 (1975); *see also* A. M. Josephy, Red Power: The American Indians Fight for Freedom 32 (1971); *cf.* R. N. Satz, American Indian Policy in the Jacksonian Era 60 n. 31 (1975); S. P. McSloy, American Indians and the Constitution: An Argument for Nationhood, 14 Am. Ind. L. Rev. 139 (1989).

[96]R. L. Barsh & J. Y. Henderson, *supra* note 19, at 60–61.

[97]*McClanahan v. Arizona State Tax Commission*, 411 U.S. 164; *see also* W. Walters, Review Essay: Preemption, Tribal Sovereignty, and *Worcester v. Georgia*, 62 Ore. L. Rev. 127 (1983).

[98]*See* Appendix 2; *see also* Rethinking the Trust Doctrine in Federal Indian Law, 98 Harv. L. Rev. 422, 429, 439 (1984).

[99]Indian Tribes, *supra* note 62, at 27–28, *see also* N. Carter, Race and Power Politics as Aspects of Federal Guardianship over American Indians: Land Related Cases 1887–1924, 4 Am. Ind. L. Rev. 197 (1976).

[100]*Lone Wolf v. Hitchcock*, 187 U.S. 553 (1903).

Treaties with Indians were viewed as ruses, and violated with complete unscrupulousness . . . United States policy . . . drifted in the middle of the nineteenth century to a policy of the destruction of all Indian organisation. . . . It became—and was actually called officially—a policy of liquidation applied to Indian properties and Indian life.

J. Collier, America's Colonial Record 31 (1947), cited in Sir Alan Burns, In Defence of Colonies: British Colonial Territories in International Affairs 30 n. 4 (1957). *Cf.* J. Cranford, The Creation of States in International Law 182 (1979).

[101]All treaty law is based on the principle of *pacta sunt servanda*, or the belief that it is binding on the parties to it and must be performed by them in good faith: Vienna Convention on the Law of Treaties, art. 26 (1969).

[102]*United States v. Mitchell*, 445 U.S. 535 (1980); *cf. Tito v. Waddell*, 2 W.L.R. 496 (1977).

[103]W. G. Rice, Jr., The Position of the American Indian in the Law of the United States, 16 J. Comp. Leg., ser. III, at 78, 81 (1934), cited in F. S. Cohen, *supra* note 58, at 89; *see also* M. Savage, Native Americans and the Constitution: The Original Understanding, 16 Am. Ind. L. Rev. 57 (1991).

[104]*United States v. Kagama*, 118 U.S. 375, 384 (1886).

[105]18 U.S.C. sect. 1162 *et seq.*

[106]*United States v. McBratney*, 104 U.S. 621 (1881); *Oliphant v. Suquamish Indian Tribe*, 435 U.S. 191 (1978); Indigenous Law and the State (B. W. Morse & G. R. Woodman eds. 1988).

[107]D. Getches, D. Rosenfelt & C. Wilkinson, *supra* note 49, at 299.

[108]*Williams v. Lee*, 358 U.S. 217 (1959); *see also* C. F. Wilkinson, American Indians, Time, and the Law (1987).

[109]*Id.* at 221–22.

[110]"The True basis of guardianship as revealed by the cases between 1887 and 1924, was nothing more than raw power applied to a subjugated people who were considered to be racially inferior": N. Carter, *supra* note 99, at 225.

[111]Indian Tribes, *supra* note 99, at 33–35; R. L. Barsh & J. Y. Henderson, *supra* note 19, at 185–86.

[112]348 U.S. 272 (1955); *see also* R. T. Coulter, The Denial of Legal Remedies to Indian Nations under U.S. Law, 13 Am. Ind. J. 5, 7 (1987).

[113]*Id.* at 277.

[114]*Id.*; *see also* E. S. Cahn, Our Brother's Keeper. The Indian in White America 156–62 (1969); American Indian Policy Review Commission Final Report, submitted to Congress 129 (May 17, 1977) (re conflict of interest).

[115]*Id.* at 289.

[116]*Id.* at 279. Emphasis added.

[117]R. T. Coulter, *supra* note 112, at 5, 7.

[118]348 U.S. 272, 89–90 (1955).

[119]N. J. Newton, *supra* note 24, at 1242–44; *see also* K. Kickingbird & K. Ducheneaux, One Hundred Million Acres 34 (1973); J. Youngblood Henderson, Unraveling the Riddle of Aboriginal Title, 5 Am. Ind. L. Rev. 75, 15–16 (1977) (noting that conquest generally extinguishes external sovereignty only and not rights to private property); The Aggressions of Civilization: Federal Indian Policy since the 1880's, at 194–95 (S. Cadwalader & V. DeLoria, Jr., eds. 1984).

[120]F. S. Cohen, Original Indian Title, 32 Minn. L. Rev. 28, 34–35 (1948); *see also* N. J. Newton, *supra* note 24, at 1215 n. 1.

[121]H. Wheaton, Elements of International Law (W. B. Lawrence ed. 1866).

[122]348 U.S. 272, 275; *see also* J. C. Wise & V. DeLoria, Jr., The Red Man in the New World Drama: A Politico-Legal Study with a Pageantry of American Indian History 35–44 (1971).

[123]A. K. Weinberg, Manifest Destiny 34, 97 (1935).

[124]*Tee-Hit-Ton Indians v. United States, supra* note 112 at 283 n. 17.

[125]F. S. Cohen, *supra* note 120, at 28, 46.

[126]*Id.*

[127]*Id.* at 34–35; Cohen cites Jefferson as his authority:

That the lands of his country were taken from them by conquest, is not so general a truth as is supposed. I find in our historians and records, repeated proofs of purchase, which cover a considerable part of the lower country; and many more would doubtless be found on further search. The upper country, we know, has been acquired altogether by purchases made in the most unexceptional form.

T. Jefferson, Notes on the State of Virginia, 1781–1785, repr. in P. Padover, The Complete Jefferson 632 (1943).

[128]See *supra* text accompanying note 118.

[129]F. S. Cohen, *supra* note 58, at 288.

[130]F. S. Cohen, *supra* note 120, at 58; *Referring to Alcea Band of Tillamooks v. United States* 341 U.S. 48, 71 Ct. 552, 95 L. Ed. 738 (1951).

[131]417 U.S. 535 (1974).

[132]*Id.* at 554.

[133]*Id.* at 552.

[134]*Id.* at 553 n. 24.

[135]Section 12 of the Indian Reorganization Act, 25 U.S.C., section 472, provides:

The Secretary of the Interior is directed to establish standards of health, age, character, experience, knowledge, and ability for Indians who may be appointed, without regard to civil-service laws to the various positions maintained. How or hereafter, by the Indian office, in the administration of functions or services affecting any Indian tribe. Such qualified Indians shall hereafter have the preference to appointment to vacancies in any such positions.

[136]United States Supreme Court cases indicate a "virulently racist attitude": Rethinking the Trust Doctrine, *supra* note 98, at 426. "Slaves and Indians were those unfortunate men essentially outside of America's civil society, but ruled by it": R. K. Faulkner, The Jurisprudence of John Marshall 58 (1968). "Their position demanded the strictest interpretation of the legal definition of Indians as 'wards of the nation,' and of the racialist characterization of the Indians as permanent inferiors": R. Slotkin, The Fatal Environment: The Myth of the Frontier in the Age of Industrialization 1800–1890, at 320–21 (1985). *See also* I. Harvey, Constitutional Law: Congressional Plenary Power over Indian Affairs—A Doctrine Rooted in Prejudice, 10 Am. Ind. L. Rev. 117 (1982); J. Burke, The Cherokee Cases: A Study in Law, Politics, and Morality, 21 Stan. L. Rev. 500 (1969); R. F. Weston, Racism in U.S. Imperialism (1972); W. Washburn, The Moral and Legal Justification for Dispossessing the Indians (1959).

[137]*Ex parte Crow Dog*, 109 U.S. 556, 557 (1883); *see also* S. L. Harring Crow Dog's Case: A Chapter in the History of Tribal Sovereignty, 14 Am. Ind. L. Rev. 191 (1989).

[138]*Oliphant v. Suquamish Indian Tribe* 435 U.S. 191, 211 (1978); *see also* R. A. Williams, Jr., The Algebra of Federal Indian Law: The Hard Trail of Decolonizing and Americanizing the White Man's Indian Jurisprudence, 1986 Wis. L. Rev. 219, 266–74 (1986).

[139]Indian Tribes, *supra* note 99, at 16–17; *see also* F. Prucha, The Indians in American Society from the Revolutionary War to the Present 2–4 (1984); F. Prucha, Indian Policy in the United States: Historical Essays (1981).

[140]R. A. Trennert, Alternatives to Extinction 1 (1975); *see also* M. B. Hooker, Legal Pluralism: An Introduction to Colonial and Neo-Colonial Laws 312–31 (1957).

[141]Northwest Ordinance, July 13, 1787, ch. 8, 1 Stat. 50, art. III.

[142]F. S. Cohen, *supra* note 73, at 12; *see also* J. Norgren, Protection of What Rights They Have Original Principles of Federal Indian Law, 64 N. Dak. L. Rev. 73, 80–81 (1988).

[143]F. Prucha, American Policy in the Formative Years: Indian Trade and Intercourse Acts, 1790–1834 (1962); J. M. Sosin, The Revolutionary Frontier 1763–1783, at 82 (1967).

[144]25 U.S.C. section 177.

[145]W. Willoughby, The Constitutional Law of the United States 294–95 (1910).

[146]Indian Tribes, *supra* note 99, at 19; L. Priest, Uncle Sam's Stepchildren 28 (1942); R. H. Keller, American Protestantism and United States Indian Policy 149 (1983); R. Berkhofer, Jr., The White Man's Indian 149–51 (1978); R. Berkhofer, Jr., Salvation and the Savage: An Analysis of Protestant Missions and American Indian Response 1787–1862 (1972) R. Pierce Beaver, Church, State, and the American Indians: Two and a Half Centuries of Partnership in Missions between Protestant Churches and Government (1966).

[147]7 Encyclopedia of Public International Law, Monroe Doctrine 339 (1984); *see also* M. Kryzanek, U.S.-Latin American Relations (1990); A. Thomas & A. Thomas, Jr., The Organization of American States and the Monroe Doctrine—Legal Implications, 30 La. L. Rev. 541 (1969–70). The Monroe Doctrine was mentioned in Article 21 of the League of Nations Covenant: M. F. Lindley, The Acquisition and Government of Backward Territory in International Law, Being a Treatise on the Law and Practice Relating to Colonial Expansion 77–79 (1926). The Monroe Doctrine "implied or carried with it, an assumption of superiority, and of a right to exercise some kind of protectorate over the countries to whose territory that doctrine applies": E. Dickson, The Equality of States in International law 178 (1920, repr. 1977).

[148]W. Washburn, The Assault on Indian Tribalism: The General Allotment Law (Dawes Act) of 1887, at 4–5 (1975).

[149]R. Berkhofer, Salvation and the Savage (1967).

[150]Indian Tribes, *supra* note 99, at 18.

[151]F. Prucha, *supra* note 143, at 224.

[152]R. Ericson & D. R. Snow, The Indian Battle for Self-Determination, 58 Ca. L. Rev. 445 (1970).

[153]L. French, The Death of a Nation, 4 Am. Ind. J., no. 6, at 6 (1978); A. Debo, And Still the Waters Run: The Betrayal of the Five Civilized Tribes (1940).

[154]F. S. Cohen, *supra* note 58, at 45–46.

[155]25 U.S.C. section 71.

[156]*In re Heff*, 197 U.S. 488 (1905); *see also* R. T. Devlin, The Treaty Power under the Constitution of the United States, Chapter XII Treaties with Indians 404–19 (1908).

[157]F. S. Cohen, *supra* note 58, at 67; *United States v. Sante Fe Pac. R. Co.*, 317, U.S. 329 (C.C.A. 1940).

[158]U.S. Congress, 1 American Indian Policy Review Commission, Final Report Submitted to Congress 3 (1977).

[159]*Lone Wolf v. Hitchcock*, 187 U.S. 553 (1903).

[160]C. Scott, Administrative Law: Self-Determination and the Consent Power: The Role of the Government in Indian Decisions, 5 Am. Ind. L. Rev. 195 (1977); U.S. Congress, *supra* note 158, at 59–60.

[161]E. McGimpsey, Indian Tribal Sovereignty, in 2 Studies in American Indian Law 14–15 (Johnson ed. 1971); G. W. Rice, Indian Rights: 25 U.S.C. Section 71: The End of Indian Sovereignty or a Self-Limitation of Contractual Ability? 5 Am. Ind. L. Rev. 239, 246 (1977).

[162]25 U.S.C. section 331, *et seq.*; *see also* F. E. Leupp, The Indian and His Problem 61 (1910); H. Pritz, The Movement for Indian Assimilation 1860–1890 (1963); L. Priest, Uncle Sam's Stepchildren 177 (1942); P. Gates, Indian Allotments Preceding the Dawes Act (1971).

[163]W. Willoughby, *supra* note 145, at 310.

[164]25 U.S.C. section 348 (1970).

[165]W. Washburn, *supra* note 248, at 39 (dissenting opinion of Representatives R. Errett, C. Hooker, and T. Gunter).

[166]*Id.* at 47.

[167]F. S. Cohen, *supra* note 58, at 216.

[168]A. Debo, *supra* note 153, at 91; *see also* W. Washburn, *supra* note 148; J. Kinney, A Continent Lost—A Civilization Won (1975).

After the passage of the Dawes Act in 1887, the agricultural affairs of the Indians rapidly deteriorated. The allotment of individual land-holdings was a travesty of justice, because the vast majority of Indian lands were located in the semiarid Great Plains and the arid West. There, allotments of 160 acres or fewer were totally inadequate to enable the Indians to become self-sufficient farmers.

R. Hurt, Indian Agriculture in America 231 (1987).

[169]John Collier, Memorandum, Hearing on H.R. 7920 before the House Commission on Indian Affairs, 73d Cong., 2d Sess., 16–18 (1934), cited in D. Getches, D. Rosenfelt & C. Wilkinson, *supra* note 49, at 74; *see also* K. Kickingbird & K. Ducheneaux, *supra* note 119, at 14–31.

[170]D. Getches, D. Rosenfelt & C. Wilkinson, *supra* note 49, at 72–77.

[171]W. Willoughby, *supra* note 145, at 317–18; A. Debo, *supra* note 153.

[172]W. Willoughby, *supra* note 145, at 296.

[173]8 U.S.C. section 1401(a)(2); *see also* F. S. Cohen, *supra* note 58, at 153.

[174]F. S. Cohen, *supra* note 58, at 153–59; V. DeLoria, Jr., Behind the Trial of Broken Treaties, An Indian Declaration of Independence 166–68 (1974).

[175]T. Wyckoff, The Navajo Nation Tomorrow—51st State, Commonwealth, or . . .? 5 Am. Ind. L. Rev. 267 (1977); *see also* The Navajo Nation: An American Colony, A Report of the United States Commission on Civil Rights (September 1975).

[176]Tribal Self-Government and the Indian Reorganization Act of 1934, 70 Mich. L. Rev. 955 (1972).

[177]25 U.S.C. section 476.

[178]The Jury's Report: Report of the Fourth Russell Tribunal on the Rights of the Indians of the America's November 1980, 12 Akwesasne Notes, no. 5, at 31–35 (Winter 1980); *see also* Communication to the United Nations Commission on Human Rights and Sub-Commission On Prevention of Discrimination and Protection of Minorities, Violations of the Human Rights of the Mohawk People by the United States of America. The Right to Self-Determination, March 11, 1980; *Id.* Violations of the Human Rights of the Hopi People by the United States of America, The Right of Self-Determination and the Right to Own Land, March 11, 1980 (submitted by the Indian Law Resources Center).

[179]C. F. Wilkinson, The Evolution of the Termination Policy, 5 Am. Ind. L. Rev. 139 (1977).

[180]D. Getches, D. Rosenfelt & C. Wilkinson, *supra* note 49, at 86.

[181]*Id.* at 107; *see also* J. F. Preloznik & S. A. Feisenthal, The Menominee Struggle to Maintain Their Tribal Assets and Protect Their Treaty Rights Following Termination, 51 N.D.L. Rev. 53 (1974); The American Indian Policy Review Commission has recommended that Congress adopt legislation permitting the restoration of all terminated tribes: *See* U.S. Congress, *supra* note 158, ch. 13.

[182]25 U.S.C. section 450 *et seq.*

[183]E. McGimpsey, *supra* note 161, at 36; R. Barsh & J. Henderson, *supra* note 19, at 280. As a matter of American constitutional law, Indians not taxed are still excluded from some constitutional protections: U.S. Const., art. I, section 2. *See also* J. White, Taxing Those They Found Here (1972); U.S. Census Bureau, Report on Indians Taxed and Indians Not Taxed in the United States (except Alaska) at the Eleventh Census: 1890 (1894).

[184]United States' Response to the Study of the Problem of Discrimination against Indigenous Populations, *supra* note 1, at 12.

THE PROXIMATE CAUSES OF EMPLOYMENT DISCRIMINATION*

—Barbara F. Reskin—

High on the agenda of sociology is to understand the origins and consequences of inequality. This understanding is potentially one of our important contributions to public policy. Examples of such sociological research topics include access to quality education, welfare "reform" and poverty, and the amount of job competition between immigrants and native-born low-wage workers. In this essay, which focuses on gender and race/ethnic discrimination in the workplace, I argue that the standard sociological approaches to explaining workplace discrimination have not been very fruitful in producing knowledge that can be used to eradicate job discrimination. If sociological research is to contribute to the battle against injustice, we need to direct more attention to how inequality is produced. In the following pages, I suggest that research findings from our sister discipline, social psychology, can help us understand both the original and the proximate causes of employment discrimination. This (sometimes interdisciplinary) approach that distinguishes original and proximate causes may be useful and even necessary in other specialty areas where sociologists seek to create a more just society.

In the twentieth century, most sociologists concerned with reducing employment discrimination assumed that once we demonstrated that discrimination persisted, our evidence would find its way to policy makers who would eradicate this discrimination. Thus, sociologists and other social scientists developed a variety of innovative techniques to assess the extent of employment discrimination. Researchers conducted sophisticated analyses establishing race and gender disparities in various employment outcomes, net of qualifications; confirmed through surveys employers' aversion to hiring people of color (Kirschenman and Neckerman 1991; Bobo, Oliver, Valenzuela, and Johnson 2000); and designed ingenious ways to estimate the prevalence of discriminatory treatment (Fix and Struyk 1993; Blumrosen, Bendick, Miller, and Blumrosen 1998). In terms of our policy impact, however, we might have spent our time better in counseling labor market entrants or working as human resource specialists. If we want to use sociology to reduce discrimination in the twenty-first century, we need to move beyond demonstrating that employment discrimination exists, and investigate why it persists in work organizations. To do this, we need to expand our conceptualization of discrimination to recognize that it occurs as a result of nonconscious cognitive processes, as well as from the deliberate negative treatment of people of color and white women.

The prominent sociological explanations for discrimination at the beginning of the new century are grounded in conflict theory (e.g., Blumer 1958; Blalock 1967, 1982; Reskin 1988; Martin 1992; Jackman 1994; Tomaskovic-Devey 1993; Tilly 1998). According to a conflict-theory perspective, the beneficiaries of systems of inequality pro-

*These ideas benefited from the comments of Lowell Hargens and William Bielby and of the *Contemporary Sociology* editors and editorial board members. I was also helped by talking with Marilynn Brewer. Any logical or factual errors are entirely my responsibility.

tect their privileges by using the resources they control to exclude members of subordinate groups. Thus, these theories explain discrimination in terms of the strategic, self-interested actions by members of privileged groups who intentionally exclude and exploit subordinate-group members to protect or advance their own interests. However, conflict-theoretic approaches to discrimination are deficient in important respects. Most important, they do not identify the specific processes through which group motives give rise to outcomes that preserve group interests, and they cannot explain the variation in employment discrimination across contemporary workplaces.[1] As a result, they have not proven fruitful in identifying remedying mechanisms.

I should note that most of my past research assumes that intergroup competition prompts dominant groups to discriminate against members of subordinate groups. I remain convinced that this theoretical perspective accurately characterizes the behavior of some people. But intergroup conflict is not the only source of discrimination, or even the most important one. By conceptualizing discrimination as the result of conflict-based behavior, we cannot identify the proximate causes of discrimination that results from other processes. In sum, I argue that the theoretical approach that many sociologists embrace intellectually has not generated explanatory models of the causes of employment discrimination. If our goal in studying discrimination is to discover how to reduce it, conflict theories are not particularly fruitful in helping us to understand *why* discrimination occurs regularly in tens of thousands of work organizations.

In this essay, I argue that we should turn our attention to *how* as well as *why* discrimination occurs, and I propose that social cognition theory can answer both these questions. I make two claims. First, although some employment discrimination results from people pursuing their group-based interests or prejudices, much discrimination stems from normal cognitive processes (the subject of social cognition theory) that occur regardless of individuals' motives.[2] Second, the *proximate cause* of most discrimination is whether and how personnel practices in work organizations constrain the biasing effects of these automatic cognitive processes.

In brief, social cognition theory holds that people automatically categorize others into ingroups and outgroups. The visibility and cultural importance of sex and race and their role as core bases of stratification make them almost automatic bases of categorization.[3] Having categorized others, people tend to automatically "feel, think, and behave toward [particular members of the category] the same way they . . . feel, think, and behave toward members of that social category more generally" (Fiske, Lin, and Neuberg 1999). Importantly, categorization is accompanied by stereotyping, attribution bias, and evaluation bias. These, in turn, introduce sex, race, and ethnic biases into our perceptions, interpretations, recollections, and evaluations of others. These biases are cognitive rather than motivational; in other words, they occur independently of decision makers' group interests or their conscious desire to favor or harm others (Krieger 1995: 1188).

The expected outcomes of these habitual cognitive processes are race and sex discrimination. But discrimination is not inevitable. Organizational arrangements can activate or suppress social psychological and cognitive processes (Baron and Pfeffer 1994: 191). We cannot rid work organizations of discrimination until we recognize both that much employment discrimination originates in automatic cognitive processes, and that it occurs because of work organizations' personnel practices. Sociologists' knowledge of social and organizational behavior qualifies us for this task. After summarizing the cognitive processes that produce employment discrimination, I propose that sociology in the twenty-first century should examine how employment practices mediate whether these processes give rise to discriminatory outcomes.

SOCIAL COGNITION PROCESSES AS THE EXOGENOUS CAUSES OF DISCRIMINATION

A large body of research in cognitive psychology suggests that to cope in a complex and demanding environment, people are "cognitive misers" who economize through categorization, ingroup preference, stereotyping, and attribution bias (Fiske 1998: 362). These processes, sometimes characterized as cognitive "shortcuts," occur regardless of people's feelings toward other groups or their desires to protect or improve their own status (Fiske 1998: 364).[4] If unchecked, they can produce outcomes that "perpetrators" neither intend nor recognize.

SOCIAL CATEGORIZATION

The categorization of people into ingroups and outgroups is a rapid, automatic, nonconscious process. By conserving cognitive resources, automatic categorization helps people manage an enormous volume of incoming stimuli (Fiske 1998: 364, 375). In keeping with cognitive impulses toward efficiency, categorization into in- and outgroups often is based on sex and race because of their widespread availability as "master statuses" that have long been the bases for differential treatment (Hughes 1945).[5] However, I propose that it is primarily through categorization and its concomitants that sex and race are bases for unequal treatment.

Inherent in the categorization of people into in- and outgroups is the tendency to exaggerate between-group differences, while minimizing within-group differences, especially among members of the outgroup. (An example of this is the phenomenon: "I know an X [outgroup category] said it, but I can't remember which X" [Fiske 1998: 372]). Conceptually, social categorization resembles the sociological concept of differentiation, but each plays a different role in theoretical accounts of discrimination. While a social psychological perspective sees categorization as automatic and not necessarily group-serving, sociologists view differentiation as a fundamental mechanism of stratification through which dominant groups preserve their privileged position (e.g., to divide and conquer [Edwards 1979], or to justify unequal treatment [Reskin 1988]).

INGROUP PREFERENCE

Categorization is more than a data-reduction device that our brains use to deal with the barrage of stimuli to which they are exposed. Classifying people into ingroups and outgroups leads more or less automatically to distorted perceptions and biased evaluation of ingroup and outgroup members, and hence to discrimination (Brewer and Brown 1998). In- versus outgroup membership defines the pool of others to whom people are attracted, with whom they seek equal treatment, and who serve as their reference group (Baron and Pfeffer 1994). In general, people are more comfortable with, have more trust in, hold more positive views of, and feel more obligated to members of their own group (Perdue, Dovidio, Gurtman, and Tyler 1990). As a result, people try to avoid outgroup members, and they favor ingroup members in evaluations and rewards (Brewer and Brown 1998: 567; Fiske 1998: 361). Thus, at least in the lab, the unequal treatment associated with group membership results more often from ingroup preference than outgroup antipathy.

Given white men's predominance in many workplaces, minorities' and white women's status as outgroup members probably contributes to the devaluation of jobs that are predominantly female and predominantly minority. This account of devaluation suggests that we should observe the overvaluation of men's and whites' activities in settings in which men and whites are the ingroup as a job-level phenomenon.

STEREOTYPING

Stereotypes are unconscious habits of thought that link personal attributes to group membership. Stereotyping is an inevitable concomitant of categorization: As soon as an observer notices that a "target" belongs to a stereotyped group (especially an outgroup), characteristics that are stereotypically linked to the group are activated in the observer's mind, *even among people who consciously reject the stereotypes* (Bodenhausen, Macrae, and Garst 1998). To appreciate the importance of stereotyping for discriminatory outcomes, it is helpful to distinguish descriptive and prescriptive stereotypes.

Descriptive stereotypes, which characterize how group members *are*, influence how we perceive others and interpret their behavior. Descriptive stereotyping can precipitate discrimination because it predisposes observers toward interpretations that conform to stereotypes and blinds them to disconfirming possibilities (Fiske 1998: 367), especially when the behavior that observers must make sense of is subject to multiple interpretations (e.g., she worked late because women are helpful, rather than she worked late because she wants a promotion). Thus, descriptive stereotypes distort observers' impressions of the behavior of members of stereotyped groups.

Prescriptive stereotypes are generalizations about how members of a group *are supposed to be*, based usually on descriptive stereotypes of how they are. These normative stereotypes serve as standards against which observers evaluate others' behavior. Both descriptive and prescriptive stereotypes influence what we remember about others and the inferences we draw about their behavior (Heilman 1995: 6). Thus, stereotypes serve as "implicit theories, biasing in predictable ways the perception, interpretation, encoding, retention, and recall of information about other people" (Krieger 1995: 1188).

The cognitive processes involved in stereotyping make stereotypes tenacious. People unconsciously pursue, prefer, and remember "information" that supports their stereotypes (including remembering events that did not occur), and ignore, discount, and forget information that challenges them (Fiske 1998). From the standpoint of social cognition theory, stereotypes are adaptive: People process information that conforms to their stereotypes more quickly than inconsistent information, and they are more likely to stereotype when they are under time pressure, partly because stereotyping conserves mental resources (Fiske 1998: 366; Fiske et al. 1999: 244). Research on people's efforts to suppress stereotypes is relevant.[6] In one study, subjects instructed to avoid sexist statements in a sentence-completion task could comply when they had enough time, but when they had to act quickly the statements they constructed were more sexist than those of subjects who had not been told to avoid making sexist statements. And according to a comparison of subjects who were and were not instructed to suppress stereotypes, the former could refrain from expressing stereotypes, but in a "rebound effect," they expressed stronger stereotypes in subsequent judgments than did subjects who had not tried to suppress their stereotypes in the first place (Bodenhausen et al. 1998: 326).

EVALUATION BIAS AND ATTRIBUTION BIAS

Stereotype-based expectations and ingroup favoritism act as distorting lenses through which observers assess others' performance and account for their successes and failures (Crocker, Major, and Steele 1998: 539). Descriptive stereotypes affect observers' expectations and hence the explanations they construct. When the actions of others conform to our expectations, we tend to attribute their behavior to *stable, internal* propensities (e.g., ability), while we attribute actions that are inconsistent with our stereotype-based expectations to *situational* (i.e., external) or *transient* factors (e.g., task difficulty, luck, or effort). In this way, stereotype-based expectations give rise to biased attributions. For example, given the stereotype that men are good at customarily male tasks, competent performance by men doesn't require an explanation; men's failures do, however, and observers tend to attribute these unexpected outcomes to situational factors such as bad luck or lack of effort, none of which predict future failure. In contrast, women are stereotypically not expected to do well at customarily male endeavors, so explaining their failure is easy: They lack the requisite ability (an internal trait) and hence are likely to fail in the future. In contrast, their successes are unexpected, so they must have resulted from situational factors that do not predict future success (Swim and Sanna 1996; Brewer and Brown 1998: 560).

Ingroup preference and outgroup derogation lead to similar attribution processes. Because observers expect ingroup members to succeed and outgroup members to fail, they attribute ingroup success and outgroup failure to internal factors, and ingroup failure and outgroup success to situational factors. Observers also tend to characterize behavior that is consistent with their expectations in abstract terms and unexpected behavior in concrete terms. For example, given the same act—arriving late for a meeting—an observer would recall that an ingroup member was delayed, but that an outgroup member is a tardy person. Once a behavior has been interpreted and encoded into memory, it is the interpretation, not the initial behavior, to which people have ready access (Krieger 1995: 1203). Thus, observers would predict that the outgroup member, but not the ingroup member, would be tardy in the future.

POWER AND COGNITIVE BIASES

Up to this point, I have treated discrimination motivated by status politics or antipathy and discrimination that results automatically from unconscious cognitive processes as if they were mutually exclusive. Although cognition researchers have given relatively little attention to their relationship, a handful of experimental studies indicate that power differentials condition these cognitive processes. These studies have shown that although the propensity to categorize is universal, occupying a position of power may prompt people to invest extra effort into categorizing others (Goodwin, Operario, and Fiske 1998). In addition, power affects the degree to which people act on the propensity to stereotype. People can't afford to stereotype others on whom they depend because they need to assess them accurately, but they can afford to stereotype subordinate groups and are more likely do so than subordinate group members are to stereotype members of dominant groups (Fiske et al. 1999: 241). In addition, under conditions of perceived threat, the more stake observers have in the status quo, and hence the more to lose, the more likely they are to stereotype out-groups (Operario, Goodwin, and Fiske 1998: 168). The sense of entitlement that accompanies dominant-group status is likely to give dominant group members particular confidence in their stereotypes. This propensity is reinforced by the fact that powerful observers actively seek information that confirms their stereotypes and disregard disconfirming information. However, priming the powerful with egalitarian values leads them to pay closer attention to information that contradicts outgroup stereotypes (Operario et al. 1998: 172–73). Finally, members of high-status ingroups show more bias in favor of ingroup members than do members of low-status ingroups (Brewer and Brown 1998: 570).

THE PROXIMATE CAUSES OF DISCRIMINATION

According to social cognition theory, bias and discrimination result from the individual-level cognitive processes summarized above. Cognitive psychologists agree, however, that these biases can be controlled (Fiske 1998: 375). Thus, the proximate causes of discrimination are the contextual factors that permit or counter the effects of these habits of the brain. The course I urge for sociology in the twenty-first century is to investigate how organizational practices can check these factors. Experimental research on contextual factors that appear to minimize the likelihood of stereotyping and its biasing effects provides a starting point for this enterprise. These factors include constructing heterogeneous groups, creating interdependence among ingroup and outgroup members, minimizing the salience of ascribed status dimensions in personnel decisions, replacing subjective data with objective data, and making decision makers accountable for their decisions.

Of course, organizations' ability to apply the findings from experimental research to the exogenous causes of discrimination depends on the external validity of the experimental results described above. Work organizations are vastly more complex than laboratory experiments. In particular, work organizations are hothouses that nurture power and status differences. Thus, the first task for sociologists—perhaps in collaboration with social psychologists—is to determine whether the cognitive processes that I have reviewed operate the same way in work organizations as they do in the lab.[7] If they do, the next step is to investigate the proximate causes of employment discrimination: the social, contextual, and organizational mechanisms that suppress or exacerbate these exogenous causes. Below I summarize the experimental research. I hope readers view this summary as a set of propositions that specify how organizations can prevent nonconscious cognitive processes from culminating in employment discrimination.

HETEROGENEITY OF WORK GROUPS

Categorization is too fundamental to cognitive processing to be prevented, and ingroup favoritism is remarkably hard to eradicate, even for people with a material stake in ending it (Brewer and Brown 1998: 566). But organizations can discourage the categorization of people based on their sex, race, and ethnicity, and thus reduce sex and race discrimination. Creating work groups and decision-making groups that are heterogeneous with respect to these ascriptive characteristics should suppress ingroup preference and outgroup derogation, stereotyping, and concomitant bias personnel decisions. (In addition, if neither ingroup nor outgroup members numerically dominate decision-making groups, personnel outcomes are less likely to be linked to group membership.)

Of course, organizations whose work groups are well integrated by sex and race are not the ones in which discrimination is a serious problem. Organizations in which work groups are segregated may be able to create superordinate identities (i.e., more inclusive ingroups) that are independent of sex and race (Brewer and Brown 1998: 583). In laboratory experiments, researchers can artificially create categories to which subjects become attached, even on the most trivial basis, so workers should be receptive to recategorization based on characteristics that are contextually salient (Fiske 1998: 361). Organizations may be able to create such categories by using existing functional categories that are relevant and hence cognitively available to workers, or they may be able to create new categories that supplant ascriptively defined categories as the basis for the cognitive processes discussed here. Among possible bases of categorization are teams, divisions or branches, job groups, and the organization itself.[8] With respect to the last of these, the more organizations emphasize organizational culture, the easier it should be to expand the ingroup to encompass all employees. Organizations can maximize the impact of heterogeneous groupings by reinforcing ingroup identification through task interdependence, job rotation, and other collective activities. Sociology should place high on its agenda for the twenty-first century a study of organizations' ability to minimize ascriptively based categorization by emphasizing other categories and the impact of such re-engineered groups on stereotypes and attribution bias.

INTERDEPENDENCE

Intergroup contact that exposes people to individuating information about outgroup members challenges outgroup stereotypes, and hence should reduce bias. But for intergroup contact to change ingroup members' perceptions, the latter must attend to information about outgroup members (Goodwin et al. 1998: 681). The conditions that should foster such attention are enumerated in the contact hypothesis. This hypothesis argues that intergroup contact alters ingroup members' attitudes only if the groups come together with a common goal, have institutional support for their joint enterprise, and have close and sustained contact in equal-status positions (Brewer and Brown 1998: 576–78).

The logic of the contact hypothesis assumes that ingroup members' interdependence with outgroup members encourages the former to notice counterstereotypic information about the latter and thus to form more individuated and accurate impressions.[9] By the same logic, ingroup members' dependence on outgroup members should motivate the former to seek accurate information about the latter. Based on this expected association, Goodwin and his colleagues (1998: 694) contended that supervisors who know that their salaries depend on their subordinates' productivity or evaluations will judge their subordinates more accurately. *yeah no bias here*

Intergroup competition based on status characteristics is counterproductive because it encourages each group to stereotype the other. Fiske and her colleagues (1999: 241–42) speculated that this happens because group members devote most of their available cognitive resources to obtaining accurate information about their teammates, rather than about their opponents.[10] Thus, cooperative interdependence can reduce stereotyping, while competitive interdependence increases it.

SALIENCE

Anything that focuses observers' attention on a stereotyped category "primes" stereotyping, and it does so without the observer's awareness (Heilman 1995; Fiske 1998: 366). For example, men who were primed with stereotypic statements about women were more likely to ask a female job applicant "sexist" questions and exhibit sexualized behavior (and it took them longer than nonprimed men to recognize non-sexist words; Fiske et al. 1999). Thus, a comment about pregnancy, a sex discrimination lawsuit, or diversity immediately before a committee evaluates a female job candidate is likely to exacerbate sex stereotyping in the evaluation (Heilman 1995). The process of priming may mean that injunctions to a search committee to look closely at female or minority candidates can backfire, tainting the evaluations of women and minorities. Similarly, when women and men are interacting and gender is relevant to purpose of the interaction, cultural gender stereotypes become "effectively salient" (Ridgeway 1997: 221).[11] Organizational contexts can also make category membership salient. A highly skewed sex or race composition in a work group is likely to activate stereotypes (Bodenhausen et al. 1998: 317).

how the hell could that be measured

FORMALIZED EVALUATION SYSTEMS

Stereotyping and its concomitants distort how we interpret the behavior of outgroups, and the vaguer the information to which we are responding, the more subject it is to misinterpretation. In work settings, this means that recollections and evaluations that are based on unstructured observations are particularly vulnerable to race or sex bias (Fiske, Bersoff, Borgida, Deaux, and Heilman 1991). Organizations should be able to minimize race and sex bias in personnel decisions by using objective, reliable, and timely information that is directly relevant to job performance (Heilman 1995). For objective measures to minimize intergroup bias, organizations must provide a detailed specification of all performance criteria along with precise information for each candidate for each criterion (Krieger 1995: 1246). Employers should further reduce attribution errors by routinely collecting concrete performance data and implementing evaluation procedures in which evaluators rely exclusively on these data *without attributions* explaining them.

ACCOUNTABILITY

The biasing effects of stereotypes and other cognitive distortions on evaluative judgments are reduced when decision makers know that they will be held accountable for the criteria they use to make decisions and for the accuracy of the information upon which they base their decisions (Salancik and Pfeffer 1978; Tetlock 1992; Tetlock and Lerner 1999).[12] If evaluators know that they will be held accountable for their judgments before being exposed to the information on which they will base their judgment, accountability not only reduces the expression of biases, it also reduces bias in nonconscious cognitive processes, such as the encoding of information (Tetlock 1992). The benefits of accountability vanish under time pressure, however (Tetlock and Lerner 1999). Indeed, time pressure, mental "busyness," and information overload—all common in contemporary work organizations—exacerbate the effects of stereotypes on judgment and memory (Bodenhausen et al. 1998: 319).

The processes underlying the importance of accountability no doubt help explain how antidiscrimination and affirmative action laws and regulations increase job access for people of color and white women. Goals, timetables, and monitoring—all effective affirmative action mechanisms—hold organizations responsible for sex- and race-balanced hiring and the sex and race composition of their job assignments (Reskin 1998). Hypothetically, organizations can achieve similar results through programs that make decision makers at all levels responsible for ensuring that their decisions are not tainted by ingroup preference and for the outcomes of those decisions.

CONCLUSIONS

All common social scientific theories of discrimination, as well as the dominant legal approach to discrimination (Krieger 1995, 1998), locate its source in intrapsychic processes such as prejudice, ignorance, the sense of threat, and the desire to maintain or improve one's position. They differ, however, in whether they view the consequences of intrapsychic processes as motivated or automatic. Theories that assume that discrimination is motivated by antipathy toward or fear of another group view discrimination as an aberration within a generally fair reward system (Black 1989). According to social cognition theory, in contrast, the basic cognitive processes through which everyone's brain sorts through data distort all our perceptions, bias all our attributions, and induce all of us to favor ingroup members. *Laissez-faire* decision making in work organizations—and other domains, including schools, voluntary organizations, and the family—transforms these biases into discrimination against outgroup members. If the cognitive processes that lead to discrimination are universal, as experimental evidence suggests, then they cause a huge amount of employment discrimination that is neither intended nor motivated by conscious negative feelings toward outgroups. And the organizational practices that determine how the input of individuals contribute to personnel decisions, and hence precipitate, permit, or prevent the activation of cognitive biases, are the proximate causes of most employment discrimination.

Although I and others suspect that most employment discrimination originates in the cognitive processes I have summarized, we should not lose sight of the fact that discrimination also results from conscious actions that are motivated by ignorance, prejudice, or the deliberate efforts by dominant group members to preserve their privileged status. Twentieth-century sociology has focused on these conscious processes of exploitation and exclusion, as well as on structures that preserve a discriminatory status quo.[13] This approach assumes that dominant group members intentionally create work structures and organizational arrangements whose purpose is to preserve or enhance their position. Among many examples I could offer is the widespread and deliberate exclusion of minorities and women from police and fire departments (Chetkovich 1997; also see Reskin 2000). When people's group position motivates them to discriminate, exclusionary organizational practices are *superficial* causes of discrimination, and they require different interventions.[14] Organizations, I have argued, can reduce discrimination issuing from nonconscious cognitive processes. Remedying discrimination that results from dominant group members' deliberate construction of exclusionary personnel practices will require race- and gender-conscious interventions, including formal charges of sex-/race-based discrimination, collective action organized on the basis of status groups,[15] or intervention by regulatory agencies, including sex- and race-conscious remedial affirmative action.

The same characteristics—sex, race, ethnicity—are the primary bases of both automatic cognitive categorization and social stratification; indeed, their centrality in each process reinforces them in the other process. Moreover, automatic cognitive categorization and race- or sex-based social stratification have the same result: privileging ingroup members who are usually white males of European ancestry. Moreover, both cognitive-based and conflict-group-based processes comprise "countless small acts by a changing cast of characters, . . . that incrementally and consistently limit the employment prospects of one group of workers compared with those of another" (Nelson and Bridges 1999: 243). Individually, either process leads to the accumulation of advantages and disadvantages. Sometimes both cognitive biases and prejudice- or conflict-based discrimination are at work, with reinforcing effects. Ridgeway's (1997: 227) analysis illustrates this with respect to gender: "Only occasionally will gender be so salient in the situation that men will act self-consciously as men to preserve their interests[, but] the repeated background activation of gender status over many workplace interactions, biasing behavior in subtle or more substantial degrees, produces the effect of men acting in their gender interest, even when many men feel no special loyalty to their sex."

As I said above, some members of the dominant group actively discriminate against people based on their race, sex, national origin, as well as other characteristics such as age, sexual orientation, weight, and religion. Here I have questioned the assumption that I and many other sociologists brought to the study of workplace inequality in the twentieth century: that most discrimination results from the purposive actions by dominant group members who seek to preserve and expand their privileges. While dominant group members benefit from such discrimination, the salience of race and sex in contemporary society and in cognitive processes such as categorization and stereotyping allows most dominant group members to benefit without their having to take any action. By assuming that discrimination is largely the result of purposive action, we are on the wrong track for reducing discrimination. Plaintiffs routinely lose discrimination lawsuits because they cannot prove that their employer intended to discriminate against them (for examples, see Krieger 1995; Reskin 2000).[16] And employers, who share our view that discrimination involves deliberate attempts to harm people because of their status, find discrimination charges implausible and reject them out of hand. The recognition that discrimination often stems from universal cognitive processes may make organizations less resistant to charges of discrimination and more receptive to modifying their employment practices to remove the effect of cognitive biases against people of color and white women.

Sociology's history of trying to expose, understand, and reduce discrimination is to our discipline's credit. Most of our progress in the last several decades of the twentieth century has been in documenting discrimination's extent and persistence. We have made less headway in understanding its persistence and very little in figuring out how to reduce it because we have not correctly theorized how or why discrimination occurs. I have argued that much of it results from nonconscious cognitive processes. If I'm right, then its proximate cause is the organizational practices that permit or prevent it. Exactly how and when organizations contain the effects of cognitive biases should be high on the discipline's agenda for the twenty-first century.

REFERENCES

Baron, James N. and Jeffrey Pfeffer. 1994. "The Social Psychology of Organizations and Inequality." *Social Psychology Quarterly 57*: 190–209.

Bielby, William T. 2000. "How to Minimize Workplace Gender and Racial Bias." *Contemporary Sociology* 29: 120–29.

Black, Donald. 1989. *Sociological Justice*. New York: Oxford University Press.

Blalock, Hubert M. 1967. *Toward a Theory of Minority-Group Relations*. New York: Wiley.

———. 1982. *Race and Ethnic Relations*. Englewood Cliffs, NJ: Prentice Hall.

Blumer, Herbert. 1958. "Race Prejudice as a Sense of Group Position." *Pacific Sociological Review* 1: 3–7.

Blumrosen, Alfred W., Marc Bendick, John J. Miller, and Ruth Blumrosen. 1998. "Employment Discrimination against Women in Washington State, 1997." Employment Discrimination Project Report Number 3. Newark, NJ: Rutgers University School of Law.

Bobo, Larry D., Melvin L. Oliver, A. Valenzuela, and J. H. Johnson. 2000. *Prismatic Metropolis: Race, Segregation and Inequality in Los Angeles*. New York: Russell Sage Foundation.

Bodenhausen, Galen V., C. Neil Macrae, and Jennifer Garst. 1998. "Stereotypes in Thought and Deed: Social-Cognitive Origins of Intergroup Discrimination." Pp. 311–35 in *Intergroup Cognition and Intergroup Behavior*, edited by Constantine Sedikides, John Schopler, and Chester A. Insko. Mahwah, NJ: Lawrence Erlbaum Associates.

Brewer, Marilyn B. and Rupert J. Brown. 1998. "Intergroup Relations." Pp. 554–94 in *Handbook of Social Psychology*, edited by D. T. Gilbert, S. T. Fiske, and G. Lindzey. New York: McGraw-Hill.

Chetkovich, C. 1997. *Real Heat: Gender and Race in the Urban Fire Service*. New Brunswick, NJ: Rutgers University Press.

Crocker, Jennifer, Brenda Major, and Claude Steele. 1998. "Social Stigma." Pp. 504–53 in *Handbook of Social Psychology*, edited by D. T. Gilbert, S. T. Fiske, and G. Lindzey. New York: McGraw-Hill.

DiTomaso, Nancy. 1993. Notes on Xerox Case: Balanced Work Force at Xerox. Unpublished.

Edwards, Richard. 1979. *Contested Terrain*. New York: Basic Books.

Fiske, Susan T. 1998. "Stereotyping, Prejudice and Discrimination." Pp. 357–411 in *Handbook of Social Psychology*, edited by D. T. Gilbert, S. T. Fiske, and G. Lindzey. New York: McGraw-Hill.

Fiske, Susan T., Donald N. Bersoff, Eugene Borgida, Kay Deaux, and Madeline E. Heilman. 1991. "Social Science Research on Trial. Use of Sex Stereotyping Research in Price Waterhouse v. Hopkins." *American Psychologist* 46: 1049–60.

Fiske, Susan T., Monica Lin, and Steven L. Neuberg. 1999. "The Continuum Model: Ten Years Later." Pp. 231–54 in *Dual Process Theories in Social Psychology*, edited by Shelly Chaiken and Yaacov Trope. New York: Guilford Press.

Fix, Michael and Raymond J. Struyk, eds. 1993. *Clear and Convincing Evidence. Measurement of Discrimination in America*. Washington, DC: Urban Institute.

Goodwin, Stephanie A., Don Operario, and Susan T. Fiske. 1998. "Situational Power and Interpersonal Dominance Facilitate Bias and Inequality." *Journal of Social Issues* 54: 677–98.

Greenwald, Anthony and Mahzarin Banaji. 1999. "Implicit Association Test." www.yale.edu\ implicit\.

Heilman, M. E. 1995. "Sex Stereotypes and Their Effects in the Workplace: What We Know and What We Don't Know." *Journal of Social Issues* 10: 3–26.

Hughes, Everett C. 1945. "Dilemmas and Contradictions of Status." *American Journal of Sociology* 50: 353–59.

Jackman, Mary R. 1994. *The Velvet Glove*. Berkeley: University of California Press.

Kirschenman, Joleen and Kathryn M. Neckerman. 1991. "'We'd Love to Hire Them but . . . .': The Meaning of Race for Employers." Pp. 203–34 in *The Urban Underclass*, edited by Christopher Jencks and Paul Peterson. Washington, DC: Brookings Institution.

Krieger, Linda Hamilton. 1995. "The Contents of Our Categories: A Cognitive Bias Approach to Discrimination and Equal Employment Opportunity." *Stanford Law Review* 47: 1161–248.

_____. 1998. "Civil Rights Perestroika: Intergroup Relations after Affirmative Action." *California Law Review* 86: 1253–1333.

Lieberson, Stanley. 1985. *Making It Count*. Berkeley: University of California Press.

Martin, Patricia Yancey. 1992. "Gender Interaction and Inequality in Organizations." Pp. 208–31 in *Gender Interaction and Inequality*, edited by Cecilia Ridgeway. New York: Springer-Verlag.

Nelson, Robert L. and William P. Bridges. 1999. *Legalizing Gender Inequality: Courts, Markets, and Unequal Pay for Women in America*. Cambridge: Cambridge University Press.

Operario, Don, Stephanie A. Goodwin, and Susan T. Fiske. 1998. "Power Is Everywhere: Social Control and Personal Control Both Operate at Stereotype Activation, Interpretation, and Inhibition." Pp. 163–75 in *Stereotype Activation and Inhibition*, edited by Robert S. Wyer. Mahway, NJ: Lawrence Erlbaum Associates.

Perdue, C. W., J. F. Dovidio, M. B. Gurtman, and R. B. Tyler. 1990. "'Us' and 'Them': Social Categorization and the Process of Intergroup Bias." *Journal of Personality and Social Psychology* 59: 475–86.

Reskin, Barbara F. 1988. "Bringing the Men Back In: Sex Differentiation and the Devaluation of Women's Work." *Gender & Society* 2: 58–81.

_____. 1998. *The Realities of Affirmative Action*. Washington, DC: American Sociological Association.

_____. 2000. "Employment Discrimination and Its Remedies." Forthcoming in *Handbook on Labor Market Research*, edited by Ivar Berg and Arne Kalleberg. New York: Plenum.

Ridgeway, Cecilia. 1997. "Interaction and the Conservation of Gender Inequality." *American Sociological Review* 62: 218–35.

Salancik, Gerald R. and Jeffrey Pfeffer. 1978. "Uncertainty, Secrecy, and the Choice of Similar Others." *Social Psychology* 41: 246–55.

Swim, Janet K. and Lawrence J. Sanna. 1996. "He's Skilled, She's Lucky: A Meta-Analysis of Observers' Attributions for Women's and Men's Successes and Failures." *Personality and Social Psychology Bulletin* 22: 507–19.

Tetlock, Phillip E. 1992. "The Impact of Accountability on Judgment and Choice: Toward a Social Contingency Model." *Advances in Experimental Social Psychology* 25: 331–76.

Tetlock, Phillip E. and Jennifer S. Lerner. 1999. "The Social Contingency Model: Identifying Empirical and Normative Boundary Conditions on the Error-and-Bias Portrait of Human Nature." Pp. 571–85 in *Dual Process Theories in Social Psychology*, edited by Shelly Chaiken and Yaacov Trope. New York: Guilford Press.

Tilly, Charles. 1998. *Durable Inequality*. Berkeley: University of California Press.

Tomaskovic-Devey, Donald. 1993. *Gender and Racial Inequality at Work: The Sources and Consequences of Job Segregation*. Ithaca, NY: ILR Press.

Watkins, Steve. 1993. "Racism du jour at Shoney's *The Nation*, October 18.

NOTES

[1] In addition, they do not generate research hypotheses that are falsifiable.

[2] In describing these processes as "normal," I mean only that normal mental functioning requires cognitive simplification.

[3] In this essay I use the term *race* as shorthand for race, color, ethnicity, and national origin.

[4] For a demonstration, take the Implicit Association Tests for racism, sexism, and ageism at www.yale.edu/implicit/ (Greenwald and Banaji 1999).

[5] Ridgeway (1997) offers a related analysis. While she concurs with the psychologists whose work I cite on the importance of categorization, she construes categorization as an emergent property of interaction. Although she does not address the effect of sex categorization except through interactional processes, her conclusions on the consequences of categorization resemble some of those reviewed here. She also provides a useful account of the effect of gender categorization on gender status beliefs.

[6] When "attentional resources" are limited, stereotyping increases (Fiske et al. 1999. 237).

[7] Bielby (2000) believes they should be even stronger in work organizations than in laboratory experiments.

[8] Of course, for these categories to supplant sex- and race-based categorization, category membership cannot be associated with sex or race.

[9]Workers may initially resist these collective arrangements, however. In addition, when the context changes, the former groupings are likely to re-emerge (Brewer and Brown 1998: 582–83). In other words, intergroup contact is not a quick fix; it makes a difference only when it occurs through a permanent transformation of the workplace.

[10]Interpersonal (i.e., one-on-one) competition reduces stereotyping, because competitors' success depends on having accurate information about their opponent.

[11]As Ridgeway (1997: 221) observed, the diffuse nature of sex stereotypes makes them relevant in many situations.

[12]See DiTomaso (1993) for a description of Xerox's successful use of accountability.

[13]At least one social psychological theory, "realistic group conflict" theory, attributes discrimination to group conflict (Brewer and Brown 1998: 565).

[14]For discussion of superficial causes, see Lieberson (1985) or Reskin (1988).

[15]For example, in challenging intentional, bias-based racial discrimination by Shoney's Restaurants, the NAACP Legal Defense Fund publicized an 800 number for complaints against Shoney's, generating both the basis for a class action lawsuit and supporting evidence from white supervisory employees who supported the lawsuit (Watkins 1993).

[16]For a discussion of the legal limitations associated with the standard conception of discrimination as actions intended to harm people based on their sex, race, or color, see Krieger (1995).

THE ANATOMY
RACIAL INEQUA

—Glenn C. Loury—

I rely heavily in this book on the elementary observation that, in the first instance, "race" is a mode of percep-tual categorization people use to navigate their way through a murky, uncertain social world. I want us to think about people as being hungry for information, constantly seeking to better understand the social environment in which they are embedded, searching always for markers, guideposts, clues that can equip them to make wiser choices on matters of consequence. This is a *cognitive*, not a *normative* activity. Information-hungry human agents—in making pragmatic judgments, to be sure, but also as a necessity for survival—will notice visible, physical traits presented by those whom they encounter in society: their skin color, hair texture, facial bone structure, and so forth. There is neither shame nor mystery in this. The practice of grouping people together on the basis of their common possession of visible bodily marks is a universal aspect of the human condition. One of the ways that we generate and store social information is to classify the persons we encounter—that is, form broad categories between which contrasts can be drawn and about which generaliza-tions can be made—so we can better know what is to be expected from those with whom we must deal, but about whom all too little can be discerned. So I would like to begin with a few observations about the act of "racial classification."

RACIAL CLASSIFICATION AS A COGNITIVE ACT

As befits an economist, I employ the concept of classification in the decision-theoretic sense: Decision-makers (*agents*) act in ways that affect others (*subjects*) on the basis of what can be observed about those toward whom their actions are directed. An employer hires, a banker lends, a landlord rents, a neighbor moves, a suitor woos, or not, and so on. As a purely cognitive matter, agents, surveying the field of human subjects, endeavor to discern relevant distinctions among subjects in that field in order to refine their actions, that those actions may better serve their ends. To make a distinction of this kind is to engage in an act of "classification" in the sense that I intend here. When distinctions are based in some way on a subject's "race," then we are deal-ing with an act of "racial classification."

Two things should be obvious straightaway: First, whether "race" is a part of the calculation or not, classifying human subjects in this general way is a universal practice, one that lies at the root of all social-cognitive behav-ior. There can only be the question of how, not whether, human agents will classify those subject to their actions. Second, at this level of generality, the normative status of even a race-based classification cannot be definitively assessed absent some consideration of the purposes on behalf of which the classifying act has been undertaken. That is, the simple fact that a person classifies others (or herself, for that matter) in terms of "race" is in itself neither a good nor a bad thing. Normative judgment must, at the very least, entail some analysis of the goals of classifying agents.

this last point because it has apparently eluded some commentators on race relations in American life argue that, since no exact biological taxonomy can vindicate the "race" idea, any use of this category for ssificatory purposes is, *ipso facto*, morally dubious. But that cannot be correct. Even the current U.S. Supreme Court, in its doctrine of "strict scrutiny," recognizes that whether or not the reasons for a racial classification are *compelling* should constitute one of the tests to determine if it passes muster in constitutional terms. Yet the point is much more general. For both the racist employer (bent on holding blacks down) and the diligent public servant (intent on enforcing the laws against discrimination) will alike and necessarily be "guilty" of classifying the field of human subjects in racial terms as they carry forward their respective, diametrically opposed projects. It follows that the cognitive act of so classifying is insufficient, by itself, to allow a normative judgment....

WHAT IS RACE?

I want now to say more formally what I intend by the term "race". In this book I use that term to refer to *a cluster of inheritable bodily markings carried by a largely endogamous group of individuals, markings that can be observed by others with ease, that can be changed or misrepresented only with great difficulty, and that have come to be invested in a particular society at a given historical moment with social meaning*. This definition has three aspects: ease of identification, relative immutability, and social signification. While physical markings on the human body are central to my notion of "race," I stress (in keeping with Axiom 1) that nothing turns on the underlying biological factors that may engender those markings. I only require that the pertinent physical traits are passed on across generations, are easily discerned, and are not readily disguised. Moreover, *what is "essential" here is that these physical traits are taken to signify something of import within an historical context*. "Race," on my account, is all about embodied social signification. As such, much depends on the processes through which powerful meanings come to be associated with particular bodily marks. Obviously, these will have to be historically specific, culturally mediated processes....

SELF-CONFIRMING RACIAL STEREOTYPES

A "self-confirming stereotype" is a statistical generalization about some class of persons regarding what is taken *with reason* to be true about them as a class, but cannot be readily determined as true or false for a given member of the class. Furthermore, this generalization is "reasonable" in the specific sense that it is *self-confirming*: Observers, by acting on the generalization, set in motion a sequence of events that has the effect of reinforcing their initial judgment. And so a "self-confirming racial stereotype" is simply a generalization of this kind about a class of persons defined in part or altogether on the basis of whatever categories of racial classification happen to be operative in observers' minds. I wish to consider the rationality, durability, efficiency, and fairness of self-confirming racial stereotypes.

Obviously, a generalization about some group can be supported by evidence without that evidence having in any way been influenced by the actions of those making the generalization. Thus not all "reasonable" stereotypes will be self-confirming. However, I am interested here in the special circumstance in which those making a surmise about some group of persons have within their power the ability to act so as to influence the population being observed. For reasons that will become clear, I see this particular circumstance as being highly relevant to the task of understanding and evaluating the social problem of persistent racial inequality in the United States.

I acknowledge that this use of the term "stereotype" diverges from common parlance. *Webster's New World Dictionary* defines "stereotype" as "A fixed idea or popular conception about how a certain type of person looks, acts, etc." One senses a connotation of "unreasonableness" in that definition—the stereotype being a false or too simplistic surmise about some group: "blacks are lazy," "Jews are cunning," and so on. While I do not dispute that this crude overgeneralizing behavior occurs, it is not my subject here. Rather, my model of stereotypes is designed to show the limited sense in which even "reasonable" generalizations, those for which ample supporting evidence can be found, are fully "rational." I argue that such generalizations often represent instances of what I will refer to as "biased social cognition."

The self-confirming property of stereotypes as defined here is, therefore, crucial to my argument. I will be positing situations in which stereotypic thinking seems plausible, so I can go on to show that, even then, where race is involved things may not be quite as they appear.

To illustrate, if agents hold a negative stereotype about blacks they may think (correctly) that, on the average and all else equal, commercial loans to blacks pose a greater risk of default or black residential neighborhoods are more likely to decline. But this can hardly be the end of the story. What about the possibility that race conveys this information only because agents expect it to, and then act in ways that lead to the confirmation of their expectations? What if blacks have trouble getting further extensions of credit in the face of a crisis, and so default more often? Or what if nonblack residents panic at the arrival of blacks, selling their homes too quickly and below the market value to lower-income buyers, thereby promoting neighborhood decline?

If under such circumstances observers attribute racially disparate behaviors to inherent limitations of the stereotyped group—thinking, say, that blacks do not repay their loans or take care of their property because they are just less responsible people on average—these agents might well be mistaken. Yet, given that their surmise about blacks is supported by hard evidence, they might well persist in the error. Now, notice one thing: This mistake would be of great *political* moment. For attributing an endogenous difference (a difference produced within a system of interactions) to an exogenous cause (a cause located outside that system) leaves one less interested in working for systemic reform. *This* is the effect I am after with the models to be elaborated below, and this is why I am willing to employ an apparently loaded phrase like "biased social cognition": *It is a politically consequential cognitive distortion to ascribe the disadvantage to be observed among a group of people to qualities thought to be intrinsic to that group when, in fact, that disadvantage is the product of a system of social interactions.* My contention is that in American society, when the group in question is blacks, the risk of this kind of causal misattribution is especially great.

THE LOGIC OF SELF-CONFIRMING STEREOTYPES

Now, whether race is involved or not, the logic of self-confirming stereotypes as I conceive them entails three key components:

1. *rational statistical inference in the presence of limited information* (an employer, for example, wants to know how reliably and skillfully a prospective employee will work, if hired, and draws conclusions based on the data at hand—say, the employee's performance during a probationary period);

2. *feedback effects on the behavior of individuals* due to their anticipation that such inferences will be made about them (a worker, in the example, decides whether or not to acquire certain skills partly on the basis of what this worker thinks employers will conclude about him when he seeks work); and

3. *a resulting convention (economists call this an "equilibrium")* in which mutually confirming beliefs and behaviors emerge out of this interaction (the employer's surmise about his workers and the workers' decisions about skill acquisition are mutually consistent).

How can we relate this abstract way of thinking to the subject at hand? In the broadest terms, this stereotype-logic provides an analytic template to illustrate how the cognizance of race comes into existence and is reproduced through time in society. This logic, in other words, provides insight into how and why observers use *racial* categories for their classifying purposes. The point is that the inferential, self-confirming logic just outlined can easily be contingent on the *racial* characteristics of subjects, such that altogether different outcomes occur for subjects belonging to different races—that is, distinguishable by observable bodily marks. Although these race-markers may be of no intrinsic significance, they nevertheless can serve as useful indices around which human agents organize their expectations.

One way to think about race conventions, then, is to see them as the equilibria that emerge when subjects and agents in the habit of noticing certain racial markers interact with one another on matters of consequence under conditions of limited information. It becomes "rational" for agents to classify a subject using functionally irrelevant (racial) markers because this allows them more accurately to assess that subject's functionally relevant but unobservable traits. Physical traits matter because observers (correctly) expect them to matter. This expectation induces agents to interact with subjects in a manner that depends on race, thereby creating different incentives for subjects in racially distinct population subgroups. Responding to these incentives, subjects adapt according to how they expect to be perceived, which is to say, they adapt differently depending on their race. In the equilibrium, this race-varying behavior by subjects is consistent (on the average) with observing agents' initial beliefs, confirming the agents' supposition that a subject's race would be informative. Race conventions emerge as by-products of the happenstance of observable morphological variability in human populations. Put differently, race matters "in the equilibrium" (as we economists would say) as a result of the inexorable logic of self-confirming feedback loops.

At this (admittedly high) level of generality, a "race" could be constructed around any cluster of inheritable physical markers shared by a largely endogamous human subpopulation that are easy for observers accurately to assess and that can be misrepresented only with difficulty. Observers, doing the best they can under trying circumstances, end up partitioning the field of human subjects in such a way that a person's hard-to-observe but functionally relevant (say, economic) traits can be effectively estimated by conditioning on that person's evidently informative though functionally irrelevant (racial) traits.

This, then, is my "model" of self-confirming racial stereotypes.

SOME ILLUSTRATIONS

We are clearly in need of examples at this point. A few thought experiments will illustrate the logic just outlined.

Imagine a group of employers who harbor the a priori belief that blacks are more likely than others to be low-effort trainees. Suppose they observe the number of mistakes any employee makes on the job, but not the effort exerted by that employee during the training period. Let employers have the option of terminating a worker during the training period, and suppose they find it much more difficult to do so later on. Then employers will set a lower threshold for blacks than for other employees on the number of mistakes needed to trigger dismissal, since, given their prior beliefs, they will be quicker to infer that a black worker has not put in enough effort to learn the job. Mistakes by black workers early in their tenure will provide evidence of the employers' worst fears, more so than an equal number of mistakes by other workers. Employers will, therefore, be less willing to extend the benefit of the doubt to blacks during the training period.

But how will black workers respond to such behavior by employers? It is costly to exert effort during the training period, and the reward for doing so can only be realized if an employee escapes termination. Knowing they are more likely to be fired if they make a few mistakes, an outcome over which they cannot exert full control, more black than other workers may find that exerting high effort during the training period is, on net, a losing proposition for them. If so, fewer of them will elect to exert themselves. But this will only confirm the employers' initial beliefs, thereby bringing about a convention in which the employers' racial stereotype—"blacks tend to be low-effort trainees"—will (seem to) be entirely reasonable.

Alternatively, suppose most taxi drivers refuse to stop for young black men after a certain hour because they fear being robbed, though a few drivers will stop for anyone. Let there be two types of young men—those merely trying to get home late at night and those intent on robbery—and let us suppose that the relative number of the two types does not depend on race. Now, for most young men, anticipating a long wait will discourage dependence on taxi transportation. They may arrange to ride with friends, take public transport, or bring a car, and this is especially so if a young man is simply trying to get home. But a person bent on robbery will not be so easily deterred. Even though he knows most cabs are unlikely to stop, he only needs one to do so to get in his night's work. Given that taxi drivers treat blacks differently, stopping less frequently for them, and that robbers are less easily deterred than are the law abiding, the drivers' reluctance to stop will discourage relatively more of the law abiding than of the robbers among blacks from relying on taxi transportation. This effect will not be present for nonblacks, since drivers are quite willing to stop for them. Hence, through a process that economists call "adverse selection," the set of young black men actually seen to be hailing taxis after dark may well come to contain a noticeably larger than average fraction of robbers, precisely the circumstance presumed by the drivers in the first place.

Notice what is happening here: The drivers' own behaviors have created the facts on which their pessimistic expectations are grounded. Indeed, in the context of this thought experiment, were most drivers as willing to stop for young black men as for others, the set of blacks hailing cabs would be no more threatening than the overall population average. But then it would be reasonable for drivers to pay no heed to race when deciding whether or not to stop! So is it "rational," or not, for drivers to use race as a signifier of danger? Clearly, once a convention employing the self-confirming stereotype has been established, the drivers' beliefs and actions are defensible on the basis of reason. And yet the deeper conclusion—that there is an intrinsic connection between race and crime—is altogether unjustified. I think it is safe to assume that this subtle distinction will elude most cab drivers, politicians, Op-Ed writers, and not a few social scientists!

Consider another example. Suppose automobile dealers think black buyers have higher reservation prices than whites—prices above which they will simply walk away rather than haggle further. On this belief, dealers will be tougher when bargaining with blacks, more reluctant to offer low prices, more eager to foist on them expensive accessories, and so on. Now, given that such race-based behavior by dealers is common, blacks will come to expect tough dealer bargaining as the norm when they shop for cars. As such, a black buyer who contemplates walking away will have to anticipate less favorable alternative opportunities and higher search costs than will a white buyer who entertains that option. And so the typical black buyer may find it rational to accept a price rather than continue searching elsewhere, even though the typical white may reject that same price. Yet this racial difference in typical behavior by buyers is precisely what justified the view among dealers that a customer's race would predict bargaining behavior. Thus, even if there are no intrinsic differences in bargaining ability between the two populations, a convention can emerge in which the dealers' rule of thumb, "be tougher with blacks," is all too clearly justified by the facts.

Here is a final example. Suppose black and white students apply for admission to a group of professional schools, and that the schools are keen to admit what they think of as an adequate number of blacks. Suppose further that, in the experience of the admissions officers at these schools, there is a substantial disparity in the academic merit of black and white applicants, on the average, and that the use of a uniform standard for the two racial groups would not yield an adequate number of black admissions. Accordingly, in order to meet their racial diversity goals, these admissions officers are convinced that they must accept some blacks with test scores and/or grades that would lead to rejection if submitted by a white applicant. Let most schools follow this policy, and consider the incentives for achievement that will have been created in the racially distinct student populations. Blacks will (correctly) anticipate that the level of performance sufficient for them to gain admission is lower than the level (correctly) presumed necessary by whites. If students are, at least to some extent, responsive to these differing incentives, then those anticipating tougher standards may (on average) exert greater effort than those anticipating more relaxed admission standards. If this is so, the initial belief by admissions officers—that different standards were necessary to achieve enough diversity—may have been a self-fulfilling prophecy: There may have been no difference in the underlying tendency of the two groups of students to achieve high test scores and grades. Using race-dependent admissions standards may have set in motion a sequence of events that, in the end, confirmed in the officers' minds that their preferential handling of black applicants was required. Had the officers steadfastly stuck to racially uniform standards, they might thereby have created a factual circumstance in which their diversity goals could be met without any use of race in the admissions process.

SOME GOOD QUESTIONS

At this point, a reader may be asking some questions, such as:

1. If the racial markers are truly arbitrary, then why are the blacks so often on the short end of this process? (I will call this. Good Question #1.)

2. If the association between payoff-irrelevant markers and payoff-relevant traits is not intrinsic, but is engendered by the nature of agent-subject interaction, then shouldn't somebody learn what is going on and intervene to short-circuit the feedback loop producing this inequality? (Good Question #2.)

3. If knowing about unobserved traits is really so important, why don't observing agents invest in identifying other, nonracial, markers that may be equally or more informative but less racially invidious? (Good Question #3.)

4. Doesn't this kind of classificatory behavior, however reasonable or even necessary in certain circumstances, have very different effects on people who may share the same physical markers but are otherwise quite dissimilar? (Good Question #4.)

These questions go to the heart of the matter, and dealing with them leads naturally into a discussion of racial stigma. Before going further, however, I wish to make two observations.

First, I want to declare that I do not see the feedback mechanism just illustrated as the be-all and end-all of race-based behavior in society. As will become evident, I believe people attend to racial markers because they convey *social meanings*, and not just *social information*. Still, I think that to study conventional stereotyping is an empirically relevant and analytically useful exercise. It yields insight into how racially disparate outcomes can be understood without recourse to essentialist assumptions of innate racial difference. It shows how acquired differences in capabilities between members of different racial groups—due for instance to unequal access to resources critical for human development—can be magnified into even larger differences in social outcomes. It clarifies why "The data bear me out when I say 'those people' are really less productive" is no good answer to the complaint that widely disparate group outcomes should be a cause of concern for anyone interested in social justice. This way of thinking at least hints at how great the cost may be—for members of a racially marked group, to be sure, but for the entire society as well—when widely held negative stereotypes about a visibly distinct subset of the population are allowed to persist indefinitely. And it shows why broad-based, system-wide interventions may be the only way to break into the causal chain that perpetuates racial inequality over time.

Second, I want to discourage any rush to moral judgment about the behavior of observing agents (the employers, cab drivers, automobile dealers, or admissions officers) in the examples just offered. As I see it, we are dealing with deep-seated cognitive behavior here. There is no getting around classification—it is the way of the world. People will classify when the stakes are high enough. Thus, our imaginary taxi driver stands to gain $10 from a law-abiding fare but to lose, say, $10,000 on average if he stops for a robber (allowing for possible loss of life or limb). With those stakes, even if the probability of robbery is on the order of one chance in a thousand, a small difference in the behavior of racial groups may shift a driver's cost-benefit calculus from a "stop" to a "do not stop" decision. With the stakes so high, with information so limited, and given that a real correlation between "race" and "chance of robbery" is there to be observed, why should we condemn this taxi driver?

However, consider a traffic cop sitting in a $50,000 cruiser, who has received $100,000 worth of training, is backed by a big bureaucracy, and has a computer at his fingertips that allows him, by simply reading a license plate, to instantly generate reams of information. This is an observer with no excuse for allowing his behavior to be driven by racial generalizations. So my purpose here is to *analyze*, not *moralize*. I am arguing neither "for" nor "against" stereotypes. I seek merely to grasp their consequences; to fathom how racial stereotyping creates the facts that are its own justification; to understand how reasonable people, who base their surmises on hard evidence, can nonetheless hold the pernicious idea that blacks are different from others in some deeper (than race) way that accounts for their lowly status. The social production of such outcomes must first be understood. Only then, it seems to me, will it be possible to engage in effective social criticism.

But what about those good questions? I will address them in turn.

The self-confirming feedback process just illustrated treated each instance in isolation from the others, made no mention of history, and ignored factors like *prejudice* and *misinformation*—indeed, willful misinformation. Nor did it allow for any interaction between, on the one hand, reasonable information-based distinctions and, on the other hand, maltreatment of persons due to old-fashioned, unreasoning racial antipathy. And crucially, it did not ask whether persons subject to marker-based discrimination would have their ideas about their own worth or that of others with the same markers affected in any way. It is clear that, in the case of African Americans, all of these are counterfactual omissions. Taking such factors into account would, I submit, go some way toward answering Good Question #1.

Now, consider Good Question #2, which might be expanded as follows: Why don't people learn about the self-confirming feedback mechanism and intervene so as to break the production of racial stereotypes, or disrupt their reproduction through time? Why doesn't somebody do something about the entrenchment and reification of this way of thinking? If race-based classification is a human product—a social construction—then shouldn't humans be able to control it? This question goes to the core of my concerns in this book, so I will take it up at some length.

LEARNING ABOUT FEEDBACK EFFECTS

To aid in this reflection, consider the key distinction between "competitive" and "monopolistic" observing situations. A competitive situation is one in which there are a large number of observing agents, each encountering subjects from an even larger, common population, each taking actions in relation to these subjects but knowing that, owing to their relatively insignificant size, no action they can take will affect the population's characteristics. A monopolistic situation is one in which a single observing agent (or a quite small number) acts on a population of subjects. Examples of competitive observing situations include the taxi drivers encountering prospective fares and deciding whether or not to stop on the basis of their estimates of the likelihood of being robbed, and the low-wage labor market of a big city where many small employers hire from a common labor pool and use "race" as an indicator of likely worker reliability. Examples of monopolistic observing situations include a police department setting policy about how its officers should conduct traffic surveillance, the labor market in a small city where one or a few big employers dominate the hiring, and a huge bureaucracy like the military that deals with millions of people on a national scale.

Now, a monopolistic observer might upon reflection become aware of how his behavior (the use of racial markers to formulate race-dependent estimates of subjects' hard-to-observe traits) produces feedback effects in the distinct populations in a way that ends up confirming his initial beliefs. That is, a monopolistic observer might try to take into account the incentive effects sketched earlier so as to improve the equity and the efficiency of the subject-observer interactions. But this would not be possible for a competitive observer. Even if a small employer or a taxi driver learned or was told about such feedback effects, there would be nothing to be done because, in a competitive situation, an individual's action has so little impact on the overall observing environment. So Good Question #2 is most relevant in monopolistic observing situations.

This terminology—referring to "monopolistic" and "competitive" observing situations—is borrowed from economics in analogy with the distinction between sellers who do and those who do not have the power to set market prices. The analogy can be taken one step further: Even when sellers lack market power they can still act in concert, with the aid of government regulations, to set and enforce a minimum price. Likewise, in my model, even though competitive agents cannot influence the observing environment on their own, their collective action via government remains a possibility. So Good Question #2 may still be relevant in competitive observing situations, once allowance is made for the possibility of a coordinated response implemented through public policy. In any event, the question is certainly relevant in monopolistic observing situations, and these are numerous enough. So why, we must ask, do those observers who have "the power to create facts" not learn and intervene?

To venture an answer, and to hint further at the role of racial stigma in my overall argument, suppose this observer can credit two qualitative causal accounts of what produces his data. The first is the story just told, in which "race" predicts behavior only because, thinking it will do so, the observer uses the race-marker to discriminate, thereby inducing a statistical association between functionally irrelevant though easily observable marker and functionally relevant but unobservable trait. The second account posits that the marker itself is intrinsically relevant in some way. That is, the second account credits to some extent the view (racial essentialism) that I explicitly rejected in Axiom 2. Now, if a monopolistic observer believes mainly the first account, he will see the racially disparate outcome as being anomalous or surprising. He may therefore find it to be *in his own self-interest* to experiment, so as to learn about the structure that is generating his observations. He may be led in this way to reduce his reliance on the racial marker and, in so doing, to unmake the factual circumstance that initially justified its use.

However, if this monopolistic observer credits mainly the second, essentialist account, he will not see much of a benefit to be garnered from experimentation. (We need not assume that the observer wholly believes one story or the other; he may think either possible. My argument works so long as the essentialist account is given sufficient weight.) In this case, the observer's experience does more than simply confirm his beliefs; it comports with his inchoate sense of the natural order of things. "Those people just don't make good workers," he will conclude, and he will continue to view them with the skepticism that, on the unsurprising (and uninspiring) evidence at hand, they seem so richly to deserve, looking down on their feeble and ineffective strivings, to borrow a phrase from W. E. B. Du Bois, with "amused contempt and pity."

Now, a rationalistic account could be developed in which an agent experiments even though with current beliefs this seems unlikely to pay, because the agent thinks those beliefs may be wrong and realizes that experimentation may uncover the error. This, for instance, is one way that scientific communities function so as to advance the frontiers of knowledge. However, as Thomas Kuhn observed long ago, experimentation of this kind generally requires an observer to encounter events that are anomalous, challenging previously taken-for-granted understandings (Kuhn 1962). And whereas the incentives facing scientific investigators are structured precisely so as to encourage this "anomaly hunting," it is something of an understatement to observe that the incentives facing those who employ low-skilled workers or who run police departments are not so structured.

The key point here, and the answer I have for Good Question #2, is this: Learning to discard an erroneous or incomplete causal explanation in matters of race is generally not a straightforward undertaking. If, on Kuhn's account, highly disciplined scientific communities have trouble abandoning an outmoded paradigm, we may be sure that less formal social aggregates will as well. Revision of beliefs may well be a cognitive activity, but that cognition is always rooted in a social context and influenced by the taken-for-granted suppositions that agents hold. As a result, if a racial disparity does not strike a powerful observer as being disturbing, anomalous, contrary to his unexamined and perhaps not even consciously espoused presumptions about the nature of his social world, then he may make no special effort to uncover a deeper (than race) cause of the disparity. Certainly, the possibility that his own behavior has helped to engender the problem will be unlikely to occur to him. However reasonable (that is, nonarbitrary, grounded in evidence) his beliefs may be, the process through which he arrives at and holds on to those beliefs need not, and generally will not, be "rational" at all. . . .

RACE AND SOCIAL COGNITION

Barry Barnes makes a good point that applies far beyond the confines of a nursery or a playpen: We cannot hope to explain all of human behavior with a cost-benefit calculus. Specifically, when we ask how people acquire the mechanisms of symbolic expression peculiar to the communities in which they are embedded, we must consider the meaning of their relations with others. Plausibly, much social learning will come about as a by-product of social activity undertaken for its own sake: One wants to get along in the world, in this community, with other people. So one undertakes to see the world as others do—not because the benefit of doing so outweighs the cost, but because that is the way of being in the world with these people. This kind of thinking suggests that it is futile to look for "rationality" at the foundation of all social action.

But although Barnes's critique is powerful, we need not adopt so comprehensive a view to appreciate a key point. We can stick with a more or less rational account of learning, and simply observe that people have to take a "cognitive leap of faith" with respect to how they specify the environment in which their learning is to take place. That choice of specification, plausibly, cannot be a fully rational act. Intuitively, the cognition underlying it is more a "pattern recognition" than a "deductive" type of cognition. It is as if the agent is thinking: "This fits. This feels about right. I think this framing of the problem is more or less accurate. Now, having so framed, I will go on to make a deductive calculation about whether this or that alternative hypothesis, seen from within my adopted frame of reference, makes sense."

I admit that this is far from a rigorous social-psychological argument. I am aware that, by advancing it, I step rather far out on the proverbial limb. But as the force of Good Question #2 makes clear, some speculation of this sort is warranted, given the stakes. For if agents do not learn about mechanisms within their control that reproduce racial inequality through time, the results may be tragic. Consider the possibility that learning about the ultimate (not proximate) causes of a group disparity fails to occur for one division of the population (black/white) because, when told that the blacks are lagging, people's sense is: "They are about where we expected them to be." But learning does take place for a different division of the population (male/female) because, upon hearing that the girls are lagging, people instinctively harbor the thought: "Something must be dreadfully wrong."

This is no simple accusation of "racism." Nor am I charging the American people with caring more about gender inequality than about racial inequality—though it may be that they do so. Rather, I am making what I take to be a pertinent observation about the cognitive-adaptive possibilities implicit in various social situations, in which observers try to discern how the facts on which they base their decisions have been generated.

Specifically, I want to distinguish two cognitive acts required to process social information—*specification* and *inference*. An observer first adopts a *specification*, within the framework of which an *inference* is subsequently drawn. Specification refers to the *qualitative* framework guiding an agent's data processing. Inference refers to the *quantitative* calculation of parameters from available data. The language is borrowed from statistics but is intended to apply to the cognitive assessments of ordinary persons, not statisticians.

Now, I assert that the mental processes underlying these cognitive acts are fundamentally different, and that while inference may be well conceived as a fully rational enterprise, specification is best thought of as an intuitive, instinctual, pattern-recognition type of activity. The cognition underlying the self-confirming feedback loops that lead to racial stereotypes, as illustrated in the foregoing thought experiments, is an instance of *inference*. But the questioning of long-held beliefs, and the willingness to experiment for the sake of learning though this might seem not to pay—these are instances of *specification*. We should expect nonrational factors—in particular, the taken-for-granted meanings that may be unreflectively associated with certain racial markers—to exert a significant influence on the latter type of cognitive behavior.

Here, then, is my final answer to Good Question #2: "Race" may be a human product, but, because it is a social convention that emerges out of the complex interactions of myriad, autonomous decision-makers, it is not readily subjected to human agency. Between us reflective agents and our social artifacts stand mechanisms of social intercourse that are anything but transparent. Because we filter social experience through racial categories, and given the ancillary meanings with which those categories are freighted, we can be led to interpret our data in such a way that the arbitrariness of the race convention remains hidden from our view, leaving us "cognitive prisoners" inside a symbolic world of our own unwitting construction.

BECOMING "STREETWISE"

I conclude this chapter by considering Good Questions #3 and #4. Why don't observers look for nonracial markers to solve their inference problems? And what ensues when people who happen to share some markers are, willy-nilly, grouped into a single racial category, and yet those so grouped are objectively very different persons? Obviously, these two questions are closely related: The more heterogeneous is a racial group, the greater is the gain to an observer from using nonracial markers.

But we have already discussed this problem; looking for nonracial markers is merely another way of experimenting with one's specification of the process generating one's data. It is, in the colloquialism made famous by the University of Pennsylvania sociologist Elijah Anderson, a way of being "streetwise" (Anderson 1990). I will employ Anderson's framework to make a final point about racial stereotypes.

Adapting the theory first elaborated by Erving Goffman (1959), Anderson uses the streets of the racially mixed West Philadelphia neighborhoods near the campus of the University of Pennsylvania as a laboratory. He studies the problem of "decoding" which all social actors must solve when meeting others in public. One cannot be entirely certain of the character or intent of "the other"; it is necessary to process such information as may be gleaned from an examination of the external self-presentation of those being encountered. The context of the meeting—time of day, physical setting, whether the individual is alone or in a group, and so on—will affect how these external clues are read. As an encounter unfolds, communication between the parties, ranging from a meeting of eyes (or the avoidance of same) to an exchange of greetings, permits further inferences to be drawn. Race—an easily and instantly ascertainable characteristic—may, as I have suggested, be expected to play a large role in this game of inference. Social class—as conveyed by dress, manner, occupation, and speech—may also be quite important. (In fact, as Anderson's account makes clear, these two indicia of social identity interact in subtle and complex ways.) An individual's experience of the social environment is strongly influenced by how he and those he encounters in public negotiate such meetings.

Anderson describes in elegant detail the rules of public etiquette, norms of mutual expectation, conventions of deference, methods of self-protection, strategies of turf-claiming, signals of intention, deciphering of cues, mistakes, biases, bluffs, threats, and self-fulfilling prophecies that are implicit in the interactions he observes. His ethnography is a wonderful illustration (indeed, a *vindication*) of the theoretical approach I am promoting in this book. He identifies social roles, public routines, and behavioral devices common to the encounters he chronicles. And he suggests compelling explanations for many puzzling features of life on the streets of the communities he has studied.

Anderson's core concept in this work is the notion of becoming "streetwise," meaning adept at subtly decoding the markers presented to one in the streets. At the crudest level, a resident uses race, or possibly race combined with class, as a key indicator of danger (or of opportunity, depending on what the observer is on the lookout for). But on Anderson's account streetwise persons advance beyond this crude level, becoming shrewder at navigating the streets, thereby enabling themselves to sustain deeper and more meaningful relationships across the racial divide. An observer becomes streetwise by experimenting with nonracial markers, or perhaps more accurately, by supplementing racial markers with a wide array of nonracial ones that refine the discriminatory practice and permit more nuance in the treatment of those bearing a negative racial marker. Thus the white lady who runs into her apartment as soon as she sees a black kid approaching from across the street, clutching her bag close, looking furtively over her shoulder, is not "streetwise." She hasn't bothered to take any note of the signs: Is the kid carrying a book under his arm? How is he dressed? What are his gait and demeanor? She hasn't learned about other, nonracial information that might be powerfully informative in that particular situation. "Street wisdom" is just a generalization of that remark.

This behavior—acquiring street wisdom—is surely commendable, one would think. We might all hope (and pray?) that those authorized to use deadly force on America's city streets will soon acquire greater wisdom in this regard. But notice one thing. By eschewing stereotype-driven behavior and using a more refined set of indices to guide their discrimination, observers encourage the production of those very indices of differentiation by better-off members of the negatively stereotyped group, because they are the ones who gain most by separating themselves from the masses. I do not say here that this is necessarily a bad thing, though I can easily imagine circumstances in which it would be.

The strategies of social identity manipulation used by racially marked people to inhibit being stereotyped—their methods of "partial passing"—are endless: affectations of speech; dressing up to shop at a downtown store; writing more equations on the blackboard than needed, to show a skeptical audience that one does indeed have complete command of the discipline's technical apparatus; "whistling Vivaldi" while walking along a city's mean streets so as not to be mistaken for a thug—most generally, adopting styles of self-presentation that aim to communicate "I'm not one of THEM; I'm one of YOU!" Such differentiating behavior can undermine a pernicious equilibrium in which the use of an intrinsically irrelevant racial trait has become institutionalized as a social convention.

But such strategies can also be a way to undermine solidarity in the race-marked population, and to encourage the selective out-migration (through subtle forms of "partial passing") of the most talented. And they can promote a fractured ego, an insider's own-group antipathy—"if only THEY would get their acts together, then people like ME wouldn't have such a problem"—which is anything but pretty. When this process results in the pursuit of social mobility in a racially marked group by means of directed marriage patterns intended to preserve lightened skin tones over the generations (a commonplace of African-American society in years gone by which has yet to fully dissipate, and which can be found in Brazilian society even today); or when the better-off classes of the racially marked indulge themselves by preening obsessively over minute symbols of their relatively superior status (as the sociologist E. Franklin Frazier described nearly a half-century ago; Frazier 1957), the nature of the problem becomes apparent.

I wish to avoid misunderstanding. I do not intend these remarks to be an attack on the act of "partial passing" as such. Nor do I see that act as some kind of immoral betrayal. But neither can I celebrate it blithely as a glorious exercise in individual liberty, or as a god-sent mechanism for subverting an otherwise oppressive racial order. To the contrary, the tragedy of the selective out-migration of a relative few from the marked population through partial passing is that it places the burden of reforming a racially stereotypic order on those with little leverage to alter underlying social structures (letting our monopolistic observers off the hook). And, perhaps more importantly though certainly more speculatively, it promotes a liberal individualist ideology of personal achievement that reinforces, rather than challenges, an order in which the scourge of racial stigma can flourish. . . .

LOOKING AHEAD

With these speculations in view, the key role that racial stigma plays in my argument should now be easier to see. In the next chapter I propose that durable racial inequality be understood as the outgrowth of a series of "vicious circles of cumulative causation." The story goes something like this: The "social meaning of race"— that is, the tacit understandings associated with "blackness" in the public's imagination, especially the negative connotations—biases the social cognitions and distorts the specifications of observing agents, inducing them to make causal misattributions detrimental to blacks. Observers have difficulty identifying with the plight of a people whom they mistakenly assume simply to be "reaping what they have sown." This lack of empathy undermines public enthusiasm for egalitarian racial reform, thus encouraging the reproduction through time of racial inequality. Yet, absent such reforms, the low social conditions of (some) blacks persist, the negative social meanings ascribed to blackness are thereby reinforced, and so the racially biased social-cognitive processes are reproduced, completing the circle. As they navigate through the epistemological fog, observing agents find their cognitive sensibilities being influenced by history and culture, by social conditions, and by the continuing construction and transmission of civic narrative. Groping along, these observers—acting in varied roles, from that of economic agent to that of public citizen—"create facts" about race, even as they remain blind to their ability to unmake those facts and oblivious to the moral implications of their handiwork.

Calling this behavior racism, while doing little violence to the language, also fails to produce much insight. How, we should ask, will this self-reinforcing process be contested? Epithets are unlikely to be of much help. Subtle dynamics underlie racially biased social cognition—dynamics that are not much illuminated when conceived as some form of anti-black enmity. Note, for instance, that the argument to this point has made no reference to the race of the observer. Whereas a theory grounded in racial enmity would have trouble explaining anti-black sentiments held by other blacks, nothing in my theory prevents a black from succumbing to the same cognitive biases as anyone else, when drawing inferences about the underlying causes of racial inequality. Nor would I dismiss the possibility that perceptions by blacks of the larger society—of the opportunities available to them for upward mobility, for instance—might be distorted by racially conditioned causal misattributions on their part.

Here is yet another reason to resist the temptation to moralize when discussing these issues. *I hold that it is more fruitful to focus on the cognitive rather than the normative aspects of this problem, attending to how people—often unreflectively—think about social information.* So, anyway, I hope to persuade the reader with the argument to follow.

SUPREME COURT OF THE UNITED STATES

426 U.S. 229

WASHINGTON V. DAVIS

CERTIORARI TO THE UNITED STATES COURT OF APPEALS
FOR THE DISTRICT OF COLUMBIA CIRCUIT

NO. 74-1492 ARGUED: MARCH 1, 1976–DECIDED:
JUNE 7, 1976

SYLLABUS: Respondents Harley and Sellers, both Negroes (hereinafter respondents), whose applications to become police officers in the District of Columbia had been rejected, in an action against District of Columbia officials (petitioners) and others, claimed that the Police Department's recruiting procedures, including a written personnel test (Test 21), were racially discriminatory and violated the Due Process Clause of the Fifth Amendment, 42 U.S.C. § 1981 and D.C. Code § 1-320 (1973). Test 21 is administered generally to prospective Government employees to determine whether applicants have acquired a particular level of verbal skill. Respondents contended that the test bore no relationship to job performance, and excluded a disproportionately high number of Negro applicants. . . . The Court of Appeals . . . directed summary judgment in favor of respondents, having applied to the constitutional issue the statutory standards enunciated in *Griggs v. Duke Power Co.*, 401 U.S. 424 (1971), which held that Title VII of the Civil Rights Act of 1964, as amended, prohibits the use of tests that operate to exclude members of minority groups unless the employer demonstrates that the procedures are substantially related to job performance. The court held that the lack of discriminatory intent in the enactment and administration of Test 21 was irrelevant; that the critical fact was that four times as many blacks as whites failed the test; and that such disproportionate impact sufficed to establish a constitutional violation, absent any proof by petitioners that the test adequately measured job performance.

Held:

1. The Court of Appeals erred in resolving the Fifth Amendment issue by applying standards applicable to Title VII cases. Pp. 238–248.

(a) Though the Due Process Clause of the Fifth Amendment contains an equal protection component prohibiting the Government from invidious discrimination, it does not follow that a law or other official act is unconstitutional solely because it has a racially disproportionate impact regardless of whether it reflects a racially discriminatory purpose. Pp. 239–245.

. . . [231] . . . .

OPINION: [232] MR. JUSTICE WHITE delivered the opinion of the Court.

This case involves the validity of a qualifying test administered to applicants for positions as police officers in the District of Columbia Metropolitan Police Department. The test was sustained by the District Court but invalidated by the Court of Appeals. We are in agreement with the District Court, and hence reverse the judgment of the Court of Appeals.   . . . [233–237] . . . .

[238] II

Because the Court of Appeals erroneously applied the legal standards applicable to Title VII cases in resolving the constitutional issue before it, we reverse its judgment in respondents' favor. . . .

As the Court of Appeals understood Title VII, employees or applicants proceeding under it need not concern themselves with the employer's possibly discriminatory purpose, but instead may focus solely on the racially differential impact of the challenged hiring or promotion [239] practices. This is not the constitutional rule. We have never held that the constitutional standard for adjudicating claims of invidious racial discrimination is identical to the standards applicable under Title VII, and we decline to do so today.

The central purpose of the Equal Protection Clause of the Fourteenth Amendment is the prevention of official conduct discriminating on the basis of race. It is also true that the Due Process Clause of the Fifth Amendment contains an equal protection component prohibiting the United States from invidiously discriminating between individuals or groups. *Bolling v. Sharpe*, 347 U.S. 497 (1954). But our cases have not embraced the proposition that a law or other official act, without regard to whether it reflects a racially discriminatory purpose, is unconstitutional solely because it has a racially disproportionate impact.

. . . [240] . . . .

The school desegregation cases have also adhered to the basic equal protection principle that the invidious quality of a law claimed to be racially discriminatory must ultimately be traced to a racially discriminatory purpose. That there are both predominantly black and predominantly white schools in a community is not, alone, violative of the Equal Protection Clause. The essential element of de jure segregation is "a current condition of segregation resulting from intentional state action." *Keyes v. Sch. Dist. No. 1*, 413 U.S. 189, 205 (1973). "The differentiating factor between de jure segregation and so-called de facto segregation . . . is purpose or intent to segregate." *Id.* at 208. . . . [241] . . .

This is not to say that the necessary discriminatory racial purpose must be express or appear on the face of the statute, or that a law's disproportionate impact is irrelevant in cases involving Constitution-based claims of racial discrimination. A statute, otherwise neutral on its face, must not be applied so as invidiously to discriminate on the basis of race. *Yick Wo v. Hopkins*, 118 U.S. 356 (1886). It is also clear from the cases dealing with racial discrimination in the selection of juries that the systematic exclusion of Negroes is itself such an "unequal application of the law . . . as to show intentional discrimination." *Akins v. Texas*, 325 U.S. 398, 404 (1945). *Smith v. Texas*, 311 U.S. 128 (1940); *Pierre v. Louisiana*, 306 U.S. 354 (1939); *Neal v. Delaware*, 103 U.S. 370 (1881). A prima facie case of discriminatory purpose may be proved as well by the absence of Negroes on a particular jury combined with the failure of the jury commissioners to be informed of eligible Negro jurors in a community, *Hill v. Texas*, 316 U.S. 400, 404 (1942), or with racially nonneutral selection procedures, *Alexander v. Louisiana*, 405 U.S. 625 (1972); *Avery v. Georgia*, 345 U.S. 559 (1953); *Whitus v. Georgia*, 385 U.S. 545 (1967). With a prima facie case made out, "the burden of proof shifts to the State to rebut the presumption of unconstitutional action by showing that permissible racially neutral selection criteria and procedures have produced the monochromatic result." *Alexander, supra*, at 632.

[242] Necessarily, an invidious discriminatory purpose may often be inferred from the totality of the relevant facts, including the fact, if it is true, that the law bears more heavily on one race than another. It is also not infrequently true that the discriminatory impact—in the jury cases, for example, the total or seriously disproportionate exclusion of Negroes from jury venires—may for all practical purposes demonstrate

unconstitutionality because, in various circumstances, the discrimination is very difficult to explain on nonracial grounds. Nevertheless, we have not held that a law, neutral on its face and serving ends otherwise within the power of government to pursue, is invalid under the Equal Protection Clause simply because it may affect a greater proportion of one race than of another. Disproportionate impact is not irrelevant, but it is not the sole touchstone of an invidious racial discrimination forbidden by the Constitution. Standing alone, it does not trigger the rule, *McLaughlin v. Florida*, 379 U.S. 184 (1964), that racial classifications are to be subjected to the strictest scrutiny, and are justifiable only by the weightiest of considerations.   . . . [243–246] . . . .

Nor, on the facts of the case before us, would the disproportionate impact of Test 21 warrant the conclusion that it is a purposeful device to discriminate against Negroes, and hence an infringement of the constitutional rights of respondents, as well as other black applicants. As we have said, the test is neutral on its face, and rationally may be said to serve a purpose the Government is constitutionally empowered to pursue. Even agreeing with the District Court that the differential racial effect of Test 21 called for further inquiry, we think the District Court correctly held that the affirmative efforts of the Metropolitan Police Department to recruit black officers, the changing racial composition of the recruit classes and of the force in general, and the relationship of the test to the training program negated any inference that the Department discriminated on the basis of race or that "a police officer qualifies on the color of his skin, rather than ability." 348 F. Supp. at 18.

Under Title VII, Congress provided that, when hiring [247] and promotion practices disqualifying substantially disproportionate numbers of blacks are challenged, discriminatory purpose need not be proved, and that it is an insufficient response to demonstrate some rational basis for the challenged practices. It is necessary, in addition, that they be "validated" in terms of job performance in any one of several ways, perhaps by ascertaining the minimum skill, ability, or potential necessary for the position at issue and determining whether the qualifying tests are appropriate for the selection of qualified applicants for the job in question. However this process proceeds, it involves a more probing judicial review of, and less deference to, the seemingly reasonable acts of administrators and executives than is appropriate under the Constitution where special racial impact, without discriminatory purpose, is claimed. We are not disposed to adopt this more rigorous standard for the purposes [248] of applying the Fifth and the Fourteenth Amendments in cases such as this.

A rule that a statute designed to serve neutral ends is nevertheless invalid, absent compelling justification, if in practice it benefits or burdens one race more than another would be far reaching and would raise serious questions about, and perhaps invalidate, a whole range of tax, welfare, public service, regulatory, and licensing statutes that may be more burdensome to the poor and to the average black than to the more affluent white.

Given that rule, such consequences would perhaps be likely to follow. However, in our view, extension of the rule beyond those areas where it is already applicable by reason of statute, such as in the field of public employment, should await legislative prescription. . . . .

SUPREME COURT OF THE UNITED STATES

401 U.S. 424

GRIGGS v. DUKE POWER CO.

CERTIORARI TO THE UNITED STATES COURT OF APPEALS FOR THE FOURTH CIRCUIT

NO. 124 ARGUED: DECEMBER 14, 1970–DECIDED: MARCH 8, 1971

JUDGES: BURGER, C.J., delivered the opinion of the Court, in which all members joined except BRENNAN, J., who took no part in the consideration or decision of the case.

OPINION: [425] MR. CHIEF JUSTICE BURGER delivered the opinion of the Court.

We granted the writ in this case to resolve the question whether an employer is prohibited by the Civil Rights Act of 1964, Title VII, from requiring a high school education [426] or passing of a standardized general intelligence test as a condition of employment in or transfer to jobs when (a) neither standard is shown to be significantly related to successful job performance, (b) both requirements operate to disqualify Negroes at a substantially higher rate than white applicants, and (c) the jobs in question formerly had been filled only by white employees as part of a longstanding practice of giving preference to whites.

Congress provided, in Title VII of the Civil Rights Act of 1964, for class actions for enforcement of provisions of the Act, and this proceeding was brought by a group of incumbent Negro employees against Duke Power Company. All the petitioners are employed at the Company's Dan River Steam Station, a power generating facility located at Draper, North Carolina. At the time this action was instituted, the Company had 95 employees at the Dan River Station, 14 of whom were Negroes; 13 of these are petitioners here.

The District Court found that, prior to July 2, 1965, the effective date of the Civil Rights Act of 1964, the [427] Company openly discriminated on the basis of race in the hiring and assigning of employees at its Dan River plant. The plant was organized into five operating departments: (1) Labor, (2) Coal Handling, (3) Operations, (4) Maintenance, and (5) Laboratory and Test.

Negroes were employed only in the Labor Department, where the highest paying jobs paid less than the lowest paying jobs in the other four "operating" departments, in which only whites were employed. Promotions were normally made within each department on the basis of job seniority. Transferees into a department usually began in the lowest position.

In 1955, the Company instituted a policy of requiring a high school education for initial assignment to any department except Labor, and for transfer from the Coal Handling to any "inside" department (Operations,

Maintenance, or Laboratory). When the Company abandoned its policy of restricting Negroes to the Labor Department in 1965, completion of high school also was made a prerequisite to transfer from Labor to any other department. From the time the high school requirement was instituted to the time of trial, however, white employees hired before the time of the high school education requirement continued to perform satisfactorily and achieve promotions in the "operating" departments. Findings on this score are not challenged.

The Company added a further requirement for new employees on July 2, 1965, the date on which Title VII became effective. To qualify for placement in any but the Labor Department, it became necessary to register satisfactory scores on two professionally prepared aptitude [428] tests, as well as to have a high school education. Completion of high school alone continued to render employees eligible for transfer to the four desirable departments from which Negroes had been excluded if the incumbent had been employed prior to the time of the new requirement. In September, 1965, the Company began to permit incumbent employees who lacked a high school education to qualify for transfer from Labor or Coal Handling to an "inside" job by passing two tests—the Wonderlic Personnel Test, which purports to measure general intelligence, and the Bennett Mechanical Comprehension Test. Neither was directed or intended to measure the ability to learn to perform a particular job or category of jobs. The requisite scores used for both initial hiring and transfer approximated the national median for high school graduates.

The District Court had found that, while the Company previously followed a policy of overt racial discrimination in a period prior to the Act, such conduct had ceased. The District Court also concluded that Title VII was intended to be prospective only, and, consequently, the impact of prior inequities was beyond the reach of corrective action authorized by the Act.

The Court of Appeals was confronted with a question of first impression, as are we, concerning the meaning of Title VII. After careful analysis, a majority of that court concluded that a subjective test of the employer's intent should govern, particularly in a close case, and that, in this case, there was no showing of a discriminatory purpose in the adoption of the diploma and test requirements. On this basis, the Court of Appeals concluded there was no violation of the Act.

[429] . . . .

The objective of Congress in the enactment of Title VII is plain from the language of the statute. It was to achieve equality of employment opportunities and remove [430] barriers that have operated in the past to favor an identifiable group of white employees over other employees. Under the Act, practices, procedures, or tests neutral on their face, and even neutral in terms of intent, cannot be maintained if they operate to "freeze" the status quo of prior discriminatory employment practices.

The Court of Appeals' opinion, and the partial dissent, agreed that, on the record in the present case, "whites register far better on the Company's alternative requirements" than Negroes. 420 F.2d 1225, 1239 n.6. This consequence would appear to be directly traceable to race. Basic intelligence must have the means of articulation to manifest itself fairly in a testing process. Because they are Negroes, petitioners have long received inferior education in segregated schools, and this Court expressly recognized these differences in *Gaston County v. United States*, 395 U.S. 285 (1969). There, because of the inferior education received by Negroes in North Carolina, this Court barred the institution of a literacy test for voter registration on the ground that the test would abridge the right to vote indirectly on account of race. Congress did not intend by Title VII, however, to guarantee a job to every person regardless of qualifications. In short, the Act does not command that any [431] person be hired simply because he was formerly the subject of discrimination, or because he is a member of a minority group. Discriminatory preference for any group, minority or majority, is precisely and only what Congress has proscribed. What is required by Congress is the removal of artificial, arbitrary, and unnecessary barriers to employment when the barriers operate invidiously to discriminate on the basis of racial or other impermissible classification.

Congress has now provided that tests or criteria for employment or promotion may not provide equality of opportunity merely in the sense of the fabled offer of milk to the stork and the fox. On the contrary, Congress has now required that the posture and condition of the job seeker be taken into account. It has—to resort again to the fable—provided that the vessel in which the milk is proffered be one all seekers can use. The Act proscribes not only overt discrimination, but also practices that are fair in form, but discriminatory in operation. The touchstone is business necessity. If an employment practice which operates to exclude Negroes cannot be shown to be related to job performance, the practice is prohibited.

On the record before us, neither the high school completion requirement nor the general intelligence test is shown to bear a demonstrable relationship to successful performance of the jobs for which it was used. Both were adopted, as the Court of Appeals noted, without meaningful study of their relationship to job performance ability. Rather, a vice-president of the Company testified, the requirements were instituted on the Company's judgment that they generally would improve the overall quality of the workforce.

The evidence, however, shows that employees who have not completed high school or taken the tests have continued to perform satisfactorily, and make progress in departments for which the high school and test criteria [432] are now used. The promotion record of present employees who would not be able to meet the new criteria thus suggests the possibility that the requirements may not be needed even for the limited purpose of preserving the avowed policy of advancement within the Company. In the context of this case, it is unnecessary to reach the question whether testing requirements that take into account capability for the next succeeding position or related future promotion might be utilized upon a showing that such long-range requirements fulfill a genuine business need. In the present case, the Company has made no such showing.

The Court of Appeals held that the Company had adopted the diploma and test requirements without any "intention to discriminate against Negro employees." 420 F.2d at 1232. We do not suggest that either the District Court or the Court of Appeals erred in examining the employer's intent; but good intent or absence of discriminatory intent does not redeem employment procedures or testing mechanisms that operate as "built-in headwinds" for minority groups and are unrelated to measuring job capability.

The Company's lack of discriminatory intent is suggested by special efforts to help the undereducated employees through Company financing of two-thirds the cost of tuition for high school training. But Congress directed the thrust of the Act to the consequences of employment practices, not simply the motivation. More than that, Congress has placed on the employer the burden of showing that any given requirement must have a manifest relationship to the employment in question.

[433] The facts of this case demonstrate the inadequacy of broad and general testing devices, as well as the infirmity of using diplomas or degrees as fixed measures of capability. History is filled with examples of men and women who rendered highly effective performance without the conventional badges of accomplishment in terms of certificates, diplomas, or degrees. Diplomas and tests are useful servants, but Congress has mandated the common sense proposition that they are not to become masters of reality.

The Company contends that its general intelligence tests are specifically permitted by § 703(h) of the Act. That section authorizes the use of "any professionally developed ability test" that is not "designed, intended *or used* to discriminate because of race. . . ." (Emphasis added.)

The Equal Employment Opportunity Commission, having enforcement responsibility, has issued guidelines interpreting § 703(h) to permit only the use of job-related tests.[5] The administrative interpretation of the [434] Act by the enforcing agency is entitled to great deference. *See, e.g., United States v. City of Chicago*, 400 U.S. 8 (1970); *Udall v. Tallman*, 380 U.S. 1 (1965); *Power Reactor Co. v. Electricians*, 367 U.S. 396 (1961). Since the Act and its legislative history support the Commission's construction, this affords good reason to treat the guidelines as expressing the will of Congress.

Section 703(h) was not contained in the House version of the Civil Rights Act, but was added in the Senate during extended debate. For a period, debate revolved around claims that the bill, as proposed, would prohibit all testing and force employers to hire unqualified persons simply because they were part of a group formerly subject to job discrimination. Proponents of Title VII sought throughout the debate to assure the critics that the Act would have no effect on job-related tests. Senators Case of New Jersey and Clark of Pennsylvania, comanagers of the bill on the Senate floor, issued a memorandum explaining that the proposed Title VII "expressly protects the employer's right to insist that any prospective applicant, Negro or white, *must meet the applicable job qualifications*. Indeed, the very purpose of Title VII is to promote hiring on the basis of job qualifications, rather than on the basis of race or color." 110 Cong. Rec. 7247. (Emphasis added.) Despite [435] these assurances, Senator Tower of Texas introduced an amendment authorizing "professionally developed ability tests." Proponents of Title VII opposed the amendment because, as written, it would permit an employer to give any test "whether it was a good test or not, so long as it was professionally designed. Discrimination could actually exist under the guise of compliance with the statute." 110 Cong. Rec. 13504 (remarks of Sen. Case).

The amendment was defeated, and, two days later, Senator Tower offered a substitute amendment which was adopted verbatim, and is now the testing provision of § 703(h). . . . From the sum of the legislative history relevant in this case, the conclusion is inescapable that the EEOC's construction of § 703(h) to require that employment tests be job-related comports with congressional intent.

Nothing in the Act precludes the use of testing or measuring procedures; obviously they are useful. What Congress has forbidden is giving these devices and mechanisms controlling force unless they are demonstrably a reasonable measure of job performance. Congress has not commanded that the less qualified be preferred over the better qualified simply because of minority origins. Far from disparaging job qualifications as such, Congress has made such qualifications the controlling factor, so that race, religion, nationality, and sex become irrelevant. What Congress has commanded is that any tests used must measure the person for the job, and not the person in the abstract.

The judgment of the Court of Appeals is, as to that portion of the judgment appealed from, reversed.

NOTES

[5]EEOC Guidelines on Employment Testing Procedures, issued August 24, 1966, provide:

> The Commission accordingly interprets 'professionally developed ability test' to mean a test which fairly measures the knowledge or skills required by the particular job or class of jobs which the applicant seeks, or which fairly affords the employer a chance to measure the applicant's ability to perform a particular job or class of jobs. The fact that a test was prepared by an individual or organization claiming expertise in test preparation does not, without more, justify its use within the meaning of Title VII.

The EEOC position has been elaborated in the new Guidelines on Employee Selection Procedures, 29 C.F.R. § 1607, 35 Fed. Reg. 12333 (Aug. 1, 1970). These guidelines demand that employers using tests have available "data demonstrating that the test is predictive of or significantly correlated with important elements of work behavior which comprise or are relevant to the job or jobs for which candidates are being evaluated." *Id.* at § 1607.4(c).

SUPREME COURT OF THE UNITED STATES

469 U.S. 287

ALEXANDER V. CHOATE

CERTIORARI TO THE UNITED STATES COURT OF APPEALS FOR THE SIXTH CIRCUIT

NO. 83-727 ARGUED: OCT. 1, 1984–DECIDED: JAN. 9, 1985

OPINION: [289] JUSTICE MARSHALL delivered the opinion of the Court.

In 1980, Tennessee proposed reducing the number of annual days of inpatient hospital care covered by its state Medicaid program. The question presented is whether the effect upon the handicapped that this reduction will have is cognizable under § 504 of the Rehabilitation Act of 1973 or its implementing regulations. We hold that it is not.

I

Faced in 1980–1981 with projected state Medicaid costs of $42 million more than the State's Medicaid budget of $388 million, the directors of the Tennessee Medicaid program decided to institute a variety of cost-saving measures. Among these changes was a reduction from 20 to 14 in the number of inpatient hospital days per fiscal year that Tennessee Medicaid would pay hospitals on behalf of a Medicaid recipient. Before the new measures took effect, respondents, Tennessee Medicaid recipients, brought a class action for declaratory and injunctive relief in which they alleged, inter alia, that the proposed 14-day limitation on inpatient coverage would have a discriminatory effect on the handicapped. Statistical evidence, which petitioners do not [290] dispute, indicated that in the 1979–1980 fiscal year, 27.4% of all handicapped users of hospital services who received Medicaid required more than 14 days of care, while only 7.8% of nonhandicapped users required more than 14 days of inpatient care.

Based on this evidence, respondents asserted that the reduction would violate § 504 of the Rehabilitation Act of 1973, 87 Stat. 394, as amended, 29 U.S.C. § 794, and its implementing regulations. Section 504 provides: "No otherwise qualified handicapped individual . . . shall, solely by reason of his handicap, be excluded from the participation in, be denied the benefits of, or be subjected to discrimination under any program or activity receiving Federal financial assistance. . . ." 29 U.S.C. § 794.

Respondents' position was twofold. First, they argued that the change from 20 to 14 days of coverage would have a disproportionate effect on the handicapped and hence was discriminatory.[1] The second, and major, thrust of respondents' attack was directed at the use of *any* annual limitation on the number of inpatient days covered, for respondents acknowledged that, given the special needs of the handicapped for medical care, any such limitation was likely to disadvantage the handicapped disproportionately. Respondents noted, however, that federal law does not require States to impose any annual durational limitation on inpatient coverage, [291] and that the Medicaid programs of only 10 States impose such restrictions. Respondents therefore suggested that Tennessee follow these other States and do away with any limitation on the number of annual inpatient days covered. Instead, argued respondents, the State could limit the number of days of hospital coverage on a per-stay basis, with the number of covered days to vary depending on the recipient's illness (for example, fixing the number of days covered for an appendectomy); the period to be covered for each illness could then be set at a level that would keep Tennessee's Medicaid program as a whole within its budget. The State's refusal to adopt this plan was said to result in the imposition of gratuitous costs on the handicapped and thus to constitute discrimination under § 504. . . .

[292] . . . .

II

The first question the parties urge on the Court is whether proof of discriminatory animus is always required to establish a violation of § 504 and its implementing regulations, or whether federal law also reaches action by a recipient of federal funding that discriminates against the handicapped by effect rather than by design. The State of Tennessee argues that § 504 reaches only purposeful discrimination against the handicapped. As support for this position, the State relies heavily on our recent decision in *Guardians Assn. v. Civil Service Commission of New York City*, 463 U.S. 582 (1983).

In *Guardians*, we confronted the question whether Title VI of the Civil Rights Act of 1964, 42 U.S.C. § 2000d *et seq.*, which prohibits discrimination against racial and ethnic minorities in programs receiving federal aid, reaches both [293] intentional and disparate-impact discrimination. No opinion commanded a majority in *Guardians*, and Members of the Court offered widely varying interpretations of Title VI. Nonetheless, a two-pronged holding on the nature of the discrimination proscribed by Title VI emerged in that case. First, the Court held that Title VI itself directly reached only instances of intentional discrimination. Second, the Court held that actions having an unjustifiable disparate impact on minorities could be redressed through agency regulations designed to implement the purposes of Title VI. In essence, then, we held that Title VI had delegated to the agencies in the first instance the complex determination of what sorts of disparate impacts upon minorities constituted sufficiently significant social problems, and were readily [294] enough remediable, to warrant altering the practices of the federal grantees that had produced those impacts.

Guardians, therefore, does not support petitioners' blanket proposition that federal law proscribes only intentional discrimination against the handicapped. Indeed, to the extent our holding in *Guardians* is relevant to the interpretation of § 504, *Guardians* suggests that the regulations implementing § 504, upon which respondents in part rely, could make actionable the disparate impact challenged in this case. Moreover, there are reasons to pause before too quickly extending even the first prong of *Guardians* to § 504. *Cf. Consol. Rail Corp. v. Darrone*, 465 U.S. 624, 632–33 & n. 13 (1984) (recognizing distinctions between Title VI and § 504).

[295] Discrimination against the handicapped was perceived by Congress to be most often the product, not of invidious animus, but rather of thoughtlessness and indifference—of benign neglect. Thus, Representative Vanik, introducing the predecessor to § 504 in the House, described the treatment [296] of the handicapped as one of the country's "shameful oversights," which caused the handicapped to live among society "shunted aside, hidden, and ignored." 117 Cong. Rec. 45974 (1971). Similarly, Senator Humphrey, who introduced a companion measure in the Senate, asserted that "we can no longer tolerate the invisibility of the handicapped in America . . . ." 118 Cong. Rec. 525–26 (1972). And Senator Cranston, the Acting Chairman of the Subcommittee that drafted § 504, described the Act as a response to "previous societal neglect." 119 Cong. Rec. 5880, 5883

(1973). *See also* 118 Cong. Rec. 526 (1972) (statement of cosponsor Sen. Percy) (describing the legislation leading to the 1973 Act as a national commitment to eliminate the "glaring neglect" of the handicapped). Federal agencies and commentators on the plight of the handicapped similarly have found that discrimination against the handicapped is primarily the result of apathetic attitudes rather than affirmative animus.

In addition, much of the conduct that Congress sought to alter in passing the Rehabilitation Act would be difficult if [297] not impossible to reach were the Act construed to proscribe only conduct fueled by a discriminatory intent. For example, elimination of architectural barriers was one of the central aims of the Act, *see, e.g.*, S. Rep. No. 93-318, p. 4 (1973), yet such barriers were clearly not erected with the aim or intent of excluding the handicapped. Similarly, Senator Williams, the chairman of the Labor and Public Welfare Committee that reported out § 504, asserted that the handicapped were the victims of "[d]iscrimination in access to public transportation" and "[d]iscrimination because they do not have the simplest forms of special educational and rehabilitation services they need. . . ." 118 Cong. Rec. 3320 (1972). And Senator Humphrey, again in introducing the proposal that later became § 504, listed, among the instances of discrimination that the section would prohibit, the use of "transportation and architectural barriers," the "discriminatory effect of job qualification . . . procedures," and the denial of "special educational assistance" for handicapped children. *Id.* at 525–26. These statements would ring hollow if the resulting legislation could not rectify the harms resulting from action that discriminated by effect as well as by design.

[298] At the same time, the position urged by respondents—that we interpret § 504 to reach all action disparately affecting the handicapped—is also troubling. Because the handicapped typically are not similarly situated to the nonhandicapped, respondents' position would in essence require each recipient of federal funds first to evaluate the effect on the handicapped of every proposed action that might touch the interests of the handicapped, and then to consider alternatives for achieving the same objectives with less severe disadvantage to the handicapped. The formalization and policing of this process could lead to a wholly unwieldy administrative and adjudicative burden. *See* Note, *Employment Discrimination Against the Handicapped and Section 504 of the Rehabilitation Act: An Essay on Legal Evasiveness*, 97 Harv. L. Rev. 997, 1008 (1984) (describing problems with pure disparate-impact model in context of employment discrimination against the handicapped). Had Congress intended § 504 to be a National Environmental Policy Act for the handicapped, requiring the preparation of "Handicapped Impact [299] Statements" before any action was taken by a grantee that affected the handicapped, we would expect some indication of that purpose in the statute or its legislative history. Yet there is nothing to suggest that such was Congress' purpose. Thus, just as there is reason to question whether Congress intended § 504 to reach only intentional discrimination, there is similarly reason to question whether Congress intended § 504 to embrace all claims of disparate-impact discrimination.

Any interpretation of § 504 must therefore be responsive to two powerful but countervailing considerations—the need to give effect to the statutory objectives and the desire to keep § 504 within manageable bounds. Given the legitimacy of both of these goals and the tension between them, we decline the parties' invitation to decide today that one of these goals so overshadows the other as to eclipse it. While we reject the boundless notion that all disparate-impact showings constitute prima facie cases under § 504, we assume without deciding that § 504 reaches at least some conduct that has an unjustifiable disparate impact upon the handicapped. On that assumption, we must then determine whether the disparate effect of which respondents complain is the sort of disparate impact that federal law might recognize.

III

. . . [300] . . . .

[301] The balance struck in *Davis* requires that an otherwise qualified handicapped individual must be provided with meaningful access to the benefit that the grantee offers. The benefit itself, of course, cannot be defined in a way that effectively denies otherwise qualified handicapped individuals the meaningful access to which they are entitled; to assure meaningful access, reasonable accommodations in the grantee's program or benefit may have to be made. In this [302] case, respondents argue that the 14-day rule, or any annual

durational limitation, denies meaningful access to Medicaid services in Tennessee. We examine each of these arguments in turn.

The 14-day limitation will not deny respondents meaningful access to Tennessee Medicaid services or exclude them from those services. . . .

[303–309] . . .

IV

The 14-day rule challenged in this case is neutral on its face, is not alleged to rest on a discriminatory motive, and does not deny the handicapped access to or exclude them from the particular package of Medicaid services Tennessee has chosen to provide. The State has made the same benefit—14 days of coverage equally accessible to both handicapped and nonhandicapped persons, and the State is not required to assure the handicapped "adequate health care" by providing them with more coverage than the nonhandicapped. In addition, the State is not obligated to modify its Medicaid program by abandoning reliance on annual durational limitations on inpatient coverage. Assuming, then, that § 504 or its implementing regulations reach some claims of disparate-impact discrimination, the effect of Tennessee's reduction in annual inpatient coverage is not among them. For that reason, the Court of Appeals erred in holding that respondents had established a prima facie violation of § 504. The judgment below is accordingly reversed.

It is so ordered.

NOTE

[1]The evidence indicated that, if 19 days of coverage were provided, 16.9% of the handicapped, as compared to 4.2% of the nonhandicapped, would not have their needs for inpatient care met.

SUPREME COURT OF THE UNITED STATES

443 U.S. 193

United Steelworkers v. Weber

Certiorari to the United States Court of Appeals for the Fifth Circuit

No. 78-432 Argued: March 28, 1979–Decided: June 27, 1979

[Note: In this case, the Supreme Court upheld a race-based affirmative action program for entry into a training program for skilled steelworkers, notwithstanding Title VII's prohibition of racial discrimination. Two rationales for this were articulated, one by Justice Brennan and the other by Justice Blackman. Excerpts from their opinions follow.]

SYLLABUS: In 1974, petitioners United Steelworkers of America (USWA) and Kaiser Aluminum Chemical Corp. (Kaiser) entered into a master collective bargaining agreement covering terms and conditions of employment at 15 Kaiser plants. The agreement included an affirmative action plan designed to eliminate conspicuous racial imbalances in Kaiser's then almost exclusively white craft work forces by reserving for black employees 50% of the openings in in-plant craft training programs until the percentage of black craft workers in a plant is commensurate with the percentage of blacks in the local labor force. This litigation arose from the operation of the affirmative action plan at one of Kaiser's plants where, prior to 1974, only 1.83% of the skilled craft workers were black, even though the local workforce was approximately 39% black. Pursuant to the national agreement, Kaiser, rather than continuing its practice of hiring trained outsiders, established a training program to train its production workers to fill craft openings, selecting trainees on the basis of seniority, with the proviso that at least 50% of the trainees were to be black until the percentage of black skilled craft workers in the plant approximated the percentage of blacks in the local labor force. During the plan's first year of operation, seven black and six white craft trainees were selected from the plant's production workforce, with the most senior black trainee having less seniority than several white production workers whose bids for admission were rejected. Thereafter, respondent Weber, one of those white production workers, instituted this class action in Federal District Court, alleging that, because the affirmative action program had resulted in junior black employees' receiving training in preference to senior white employees, respondent and other similarly situated white employees had been discriminated against in violation of the provisions of §§ 703(a) and (d) of Title VII of the Civil Rights Act of 1964 that make it unlawful to "discriminate . . . because [194] of . . . race" in hiring and in the selection of apprentices for training programs. The District Court held that the affirmative action plan violated Title VII, entered judgment in favor of the plaintiff class, and granted injunctive relief. The Court of Appeals affirmed, holding that all employment preferences based upon race, including those preferences incidental to bona fide affirmative action plans, violated Title VII's prohibition against racial discrimination in employment.

Held:

1. Title VII's prohibition in §§ 703(a) and (d) against racial discrimination does not condemn all private, voluntary, race-conscious affirmative action plans. Pp. 200–208. [195] . . . .

OPINION: [197] MR. JUSTICE BRENNAN delivered the opinion of the Court. . . . [198–201]

Respondent argues that Congress intended in Title VII to prohibit all race-conscious affirmative action plans. Respondent's argument rests upon a literal interpretation of §§ 703(a) and (d) of the Act. Those sections make it unlawful to "discriminate . . . because of . . . race" in hiring and in the selection of apprentices for training programs. . . .

Respondent's argument is not without force. But it overlooks the significance of the fact that the Kaiser-USWA plan is an affirmative action plan voluntarily adopted by private parties to eliminate traditional patterns of racial segregation. In this context, respondent's reliance upon a literal construction of §§ 703(a) and (d) and upon *McDonald* is misplaced. *See McDonald v. Santa Fe Trail Transp. Co., supra,* at 281 n.8. It is a "familiar rule, that a thing may be within the letter of the statute and yet not within the statute, because not within its spirit, nor within the intention of its makers." *Holy Trinity Church v. United States,* 143 U.S. 457, 459 (1892). The prohibition against racial discrimination in §§ 703(a) and (d) of Title VII must therefore be read against the background of the legislative history of Title VII and the historical context from which the Act arose. *See Train v. Colo. Pub. Interest Research Group,* 426 U.S. 1, 10 (1976); *Nat'l Woodwork Mfrs. Assn. v. NLRB,* 386 U.S. 612, 620 (1967); *United States v. Am. Trucking Assns.,* 310 U.S. 534, 543–44 (1940). Examination of those sources makes [202] clear that an interpretation of the sections that forbade all race-conscious affirmative action would "bring about an end completely at variance with the purpose of the statute," and must be rejected. *United States v. Pub. Utils. Comm'n,* 345 U.S. 295, 315 (1953). [add'l cit. omitted].

Congress' primary concern in enacting the prohibition against racial discrimination in Title VII of the Civil Rights Act of 1964 was with "the plight of the Negro in our economy." 110 Cong. Rec. 6548 (1964) (remarks of Sen. Humphrey). Before 1964, blacks were largely relegated to "unskilled and semi-skilled jobs." *Ibid.* (remarks of Sen. Humphrey); *id.* at 7204 (remarks of Sen. Clark); *id.* at 7379–7380 (remarks of Sen. Kennedy). Because of automation, the number of such jobs was rapidly decreasing. *See id.* at 6548 (remarks of Sen. Humphrey); *id.* at 7204 (remarks of Sen. Clark). As a consequence, "the relative position of the Negro worker [was] steadily worsening. In 1947, the nonwhite unemployment rate was only 64 percent higher than the white rate; in 1962, it was 124 percent higher." *Id.* at 6547 (remarks of Sen. Humphrey). *See also id.* at 7204 (remarks of Sen. Clark). . . . Congress feared that the goals of the Civil Rights Act—the integration of blacks into the mainstream of American society—could not be achieved unless this trend were reversed. And Congress recognized that that would not be possible [203] unless blacks were able to secure jobs "which have a future." *Id.* at 7204 (remarks of Sen. Clark). *See also id.* at 7379–80 (remarks of Sen. Kennedy). As Senator Humphrey explained to the Senate:

> *What good does it do a Negro to be able to eat in a fine restaurant if he cannot afford to pay the bill? What good does it do him to be accepted in a hotel that is too expensive for his modest income? How can a Negro child be motivated to take full advantage of integrated educational facilities if he has no hope of getting a job where he can use that education?*

Id. at 6547.

> *Without a job, one cannot afford public convenience and accommodations. Income from employment may be necessary to further a man's education, or that of his children. If his children have no hope of getting a good job, what will motivate them to take advantage of educational opportunities?*

Id. at 6552. . . .

Accordingly, it was clear to Congress that "[t]he crux of the problem [was] to open employment opportunities for Negroes in occupations which have been traditionally closed to them," 110 Cong. Rec. 6548 (1964) (remarks of Sen. Humphrey), and it was to this problem that Title VII's prohibition against racial discrimination in employment was primarily addressed.

It plainly appears from the House Report accompanying the Civil Rights Act that Congress did not intend wholly to prohibit private and voluntary affirmative action efforts as one method of solving this problem. The Report provides:

> No bill can or should lay claim to eliminating all of [204] the causes and consequences of racial and other types of discrimination against minorities. There is reason to believe, however, that national leadership provided by the enactment of Federal legislation dealing with the most troublesome problems will create an atmosphere conducive to voluntary or local resolution of other forms of discrimination.

H.R. Rep. No. 914, 88th Cong., 1st Sess., pt. 1, p. 18 (1963). (Emphasis supplied.)

Given this legislative history, we cannot agree with respondent that Congress intended to prohibit the private sector from taking effective steps to accomplish the goal that Congress designed Title VII to achieve. The very statutory words intended as a spur or catalyst to cause "employers and unions to self-examine and to self-evaluate their employment practices and to endeavor to eliminate, so far as possible, the last vestiges of an unfortunate and ignominious page in this country's history," *Albemarle Paper Co. v. Moody*, 422 U.S. 405, 418 (1975), cannot be interpreted as an absolute prohibition against all private, voluntary, race-conscious affirmative action efforts to hasten the elimination of such vestiges. It would be ironic indeed if a law triggered by a Nation's concern over centuries of racial injustice and intended to improve the lot of those who had "been excluded from the American dream for so long," 110 Cong. Rec. 6552 (1964) (remarks of Sen. Humphrey), constituted the first legislative prohibition of all voluntary, private, race-conscious efforts to abolish traditional patterns of racial segregation and hierarchy.

. . . [205–207]. . . .

[208] We therefore hold that Title VII's prohibition in § 703(a) and (d) against racial discrimination does not condemn all private, voluntary, race-conscious affirmative action plans.

III

We need not today define in detail the line of demarcation between permissible and impermissible affirmative action plans. It suffices to hold that the challenged Kaiser-USWA affirmative action plan falls on the permissible side of the line. The purposes of the plan mirror those of the statute. Both were designed to break down old patterns of racial segregation and hierarchy. Both were structured to "open employment opportunities for Negroes in occupations which have been traditionally closed to them." 110 Cong. Rec. 6548 (1964) (remarks of Sen. Humphrey).

At the same time, the plan does not unnecessarily trammel the interests of the white employees. The plan does not require the discharge of white workers and their replacement with new black hirees. *Cf. McDonald v. Santa Fe Trail Transp. Co.*, 427 U.S. 273 (1976). Nor does the plan create an absolute bar to the advancement of white employees; half of those trained in the program will be white. Moreover, the plan is a temporary measure; it is not intended to maintain racial balance, but simply to eliminate a manifest racial imbalance. Preferential selection of craft trainees at the Gramercy plant will end as soon as the percentage of black skilled craft workers in the Gramercy plant approximates the [209] percentage of blacks in the local labor force. *See* 415 F. Supp. at 763.

We conclude, therefore, that the adoption of the Kaiser-USWA plan for the Gramercy plant falls within the area of discretion left by Title VII to the private sector voluntarily to adopt affirmative action plans designed to eliminate conspicuous racial imbalance in traditionally segregated job categories. Accordingly, the judgment of the Court of Appeals for the Fifth Circuit is *Reversed*.

. . . .

MR. JUSTICE BLACKMUN, concurring.   . . . .

I

In his dissent from the decision of the United States Court of Appeals for the Fifth Circuit, Judge Wisdom pointed out that this litigation arises from a practical problem in the administration of Title VII. The broad prohibition against discrimination places the employer and the union on what he accurately [210] described as a "high tightrope without a net beneath them." 563 F.2d 216, 230. If Title VII is read literally, on the one hand they face liability for past discrimination against blacks, and on the other they face liability to whites for any voluntary preferences adopted to mitigate the effects of prior discrimination against blacks.

In this litigation, Kaiser denies prior discrimination, but concedes that its past hiring practices may be subject to question. Although the labor force in the Gramercy area was approximately 39% black, Kaiser's workforce was less than 15% black, and its craft workforce was less than 2% black. Kaiser had made some effort to recruit black painters, carpenters, insulators, and other craftsmen, but it continued to insist that those hired have five years' prior industrial experience, a requirement that arguably was not sufficiently job-related to justify under Title VII any discriminatory impact it may have had. *See Parson v. Kaiser Aluminum & Chem. Corp.*, 575 F.2d 1374, 1389 (5th Cir. 1978), *cert. denied sub nom. Steelworkers v. Parson*, 441 U.S. 968 (1979). The parties dispute the extent to which black craftsmen were available in the local labor market. They agree, however, that after critical reviews from the Office of Federal Contract Compliance, Kaiser and the Steelworkers established the training program in question here and modeled it along the lines of a Title VII consent decree later entered for the steel industry. *See United States v. Allegheny-Ludlum Indus., Inc.*, 517 F.2d 826 (5th Cir. 1975). Yet when they did this, respondent Weber sued, alleging that Title VII prohibited the program because it discriminated against him as a white person and it was not supported by a prior judicial finding of discrimination against blacks.

Respondent Weber's reading of Title VII, endorsed by the Court of Appeals, places voluntary compliance with Title VII in profound jeopardy. The only way for the employer and the union to keep their footing on the "tightrope" it creates would be to eschew all forms of voluntary affirmative action. Even [211] a whisper of emphasis on minority recruiting would be forbidden. Because Congress intended to encourage private efforts to come into compliance with Title VII, *see Alexander v. Gardner-Denver Co.*, 415 U.S. 36, 44 (1974), Judge Wisdom concluded that employers and unions who had committed "arguable violations" of Title VII should be free to make reasonable responses without fear of liability to whites. 563 F.2d at 230. Preferential hiring along the lines of the Kaiser program is a reasonable response for the employer, whether or not a court, on these facts, could order the same step as a remedy. The company is able to avoid identifying victims of past discrimination, and so avoids claims for backpay that would inevitably follow a response limited to such victims. If past victims should be benefited by the program, however, the company mitigates its liability to those persons. Also, to the extent that Title VII liability is predicated on the "disparate effect" of an employer's past hiring practices, the program makes it less likely that such an effect could be demonstrated. *Cf. County of Los Angeles v. Davis*, 440 U.S. 625, 633–34 (1979) (hiring could moot a past Title VII claim). And the Court has recently held that work-force statistics resulting from private affirmative action were probative of benign intent in a "disparate treatment" case. *Furnco Constr. Corp. v. Waters*, 438 U.S. 567, 579–80 (1978).

The "arguable violation" theory has a number of advantages. It responds to a practical problem in the administration of Title VII not anticipated by Congress. It draws predictability from the outline of present law and closely effectuates the purpose of the Act. Both Kaiser and the United States urge its adoption here. Because I agree that it is the soundest way to approach this case, my preference would be to resolve this litigation by applying it and holding that Kaiser's craft training program meets the requirement that voluntary affirmative action be a reasonable response to an "arguable violation" of Title VII.

[212] II

The Court, however, declines to consider the narrow "arguable violation" approach, and adheres instead to an interpretation of Title VII that permits affirmative action by an employer whenever the job category in question is "traditionally segregated." *Ante* at 209 & n.9. The sources cited suggest that the Court considers a job category to be "traditionally segregated" when there has been a societal history of purposeful exclusion of blacks from the job category, resulting in a persistent disparity between the proportion of blacks in the labor force and the proportion of blacks among those who hold jobs within the category.

"Traditionally segregated job categories," where they exist, sweep far more broadly than the class of "arguable violations" of Title VII. The Court's expansive approach is somewhat [213] disturbing for me because, as MR. JUSTICE REHNQUIST points out, the Congress that passed Title VII probably thought it was adopting a principle of nondiscrimination that would apply to blacks and whites alike. While setting aside that principle can be justified where necessary to advance statutory policy by encouraging reasonable responses as a form of voluntary compliance that mitigates "arguable violations," discarding the principle of nondiscrimination where no countervailing statutory policy exists appears to be at odds with the bargain struck when Title VII was enacted.

A closer look at the problem, however, reveals that, in each of the principal ways in which the Court's "traditionally segregated job categories" approach expands on the "arguable violations" theory, still other considerations point in favor of the broad standard adopted by the Court, and make it possible for me to conclude that the Court's reading of the statute is an acceptable one.

A. The first point at which the Court departs from the "arguable violations" approach is that it measures an individual employer's capacity for affirmative action solely in terms of a statistical disparity. The individual employer need not have engaged in discriminatory practices in the past. While, under Title VII, a mere disparity may provide the basis for a prima facie case against an employer, *Dothard v. Rawlinson*, 433 U.S. 321, 329–31 (1977), it would not conclusively prove a violation of the Act. *Teamsters v. United States*, 431 U.S. 324, 339–40 n.20 (1977); *see* § 703(j), 42 U.S.C. § 2000e-2(j). As a practical matter, however, this difference may not be that great. While the "arguable violation" standard is conceptually satisfying in practice, the emphasis would be on "arguable," rather than on "violation." The great difficulty in the District Court was that no one had any incentive to prove that Kaiser had violated the Act. Neither Kaiser nor the Steelworkers wanted to establish a past violation, nor did Weber. The blacks harmed had never sued, and so had no established representative. The Equal Employment Opportunity [214] Commission declined to intervene, and cannot be expected to intervene in every case of this nature. To make the "arguable violation" standard work, it would have to be set low enough to permit the employer to prove it without obligating himself to pay a damages award. The inevitable tendency would be to avoid hairsplitting litigation by simply concluding that a mere disparity between the racial composition of the employer's workforce and the composition of the qualified local labor force would be an "arguable violation," even though actual liability could not be established on that basis alone. *See* Note, 57 N.C.L. Rev. 695, 714–19 (1979).

B. The Court also departs from the "arguable violation" approach by permitting an employer to redress discrimination that lies wholly outside the bounds of Title VII. For example, Title VII provides no remedy for pre-Act discrimination, *Hazelwood Sch. Dist. v. United States*, 433 U.S. 299, 309–10 (1977); yet the purposeful discrimination that creates a "traditionally segregated job category" may have entirely predated the Act. More subtly, in assessing a prima facie case of Title VII liability, the composition of the employer's workforce is compared to the composition of the pool of workers who meet valid job qualifications. *Hazelwood*, 433 U.S. at 308 & n.13; *Teamsters v. United States*, 431 U.S. at 339–40 & n.20. When a "job category" is traditionally segregated, however, that pool will reflect the effects of segregation, and the Court's approach goes further and permits a comparison with the composition of the labor force as a whole, in which minorities are more heavily represented. Strong considerations of equity support an interpretation of Title VII that would permit private affirmative action to reach where Title VII itself does not. The bargain struck in 1964 with the passage of Title VII guaranteed equal opportunity for white and black alike, but where Title VII provides no remedy for blacks, it should not be construed to foreclose private affirmative action from supplying relief. It seems unfair for respondent Weber to argue, as he does, that the [215] asserted scarcity of black craftsmen in Louisiana, the product of historic discrimination, makes Kaiser's training program illegal because it ostensibly absolves Kaiser of all Title VII liability. Brief for Respondents 60. Absent compelling evidence of legislative intent, I would not interpret Title VII itself as a means of "locking in" the effects of segregation for which Title VII provides no remedy. Such a construction, as the Court points out, *ante* at 204, would be "ironic," given the broad remedial purposes of Title VII. . . .

SUPREME COURT OF THE UNITED STATES

488 U.S. 469

CITY OF RICHMOND V. J.A. CROSON CO. (O'CONNOR)

APPEAL FROM THE UNITED STATES COURT OF APPEALS FOR THE FOURTH CIRCUIT

NO. 87-998 ARGUED: OCTOBER 5, 1988–DECIDED JANUARY 23, 1989

[Note: This opinion rejected the City of Richmond's set-aside of 30% of contracting dollars to minority-owned business enterprises, mainly on the ground that the City had not provided evidence that discrimination against minority businesses was a continuing problem in Richmond. Justice O'Connor wrote Part II, joined by the Chief Justice and Justice White.]

II

. . . . In *Fullilove v. Klutznick*, 448 U.S. 448 (1980), we upheld the minority set-aside contained in § 103(f)(2) of the Public Works Employment Act of 1977 . . . against a challenge based on the equal protection component of the Due Process Clause. The Act authorized a $4 billion appropriation for federal grants to state and local governments for use in public works projects. . . . The Act also contained the following requirement: "'Except to the extent the Secretary [487] determines otherwise, no grant shall be made under this Act . . . unless the applicant gives satisfactory assurance to the Secretary that at least 10 per centum of the amount of each grant shall be expended for minority business enterprises.'" *Fullilove*, 448 U.S. at 454 (quoting 91 Stat. 116, 42 U.S.C. § 6705(f)(2)). . . . [488] . . . .

In reviewing the legislative history behind the Act, the principal opinion focused on the evidence before Congress that a nationwide history of past discrimination had reduced minority participation in federal construction grants. *Id.* at 458–467. . . . The Chief Justice concluded that "Congress had abundant historical basis from which it could conclude that traditional procurement practices, when applied to minority businesses, could perpetuate the effects of prior discrimination." *Id.* at 478. . . [478–91] . . . .

It would seem equally clear, however, that a state or local subdivision (if delegated the authority from the State) has the authority to eradicate the effects of private discrimination [492] within its own legislative jurisdiction.

This authority must, of course, be exercised within the constraints of § 1 of the Fourteenth Amendment. . . . As a matter of state law, the city of Richmond has legislative authority over its procurement policies, and can use its spending powers to remedy private discrimination, if it identifies that discrimination with the particularity required by the Fourteenth Amendment. . . .

Thus, if the city could show that it had essentially become a "passive participant" in a system of racial exclusion practiced by elements of the local construction industry, we think it clear that the city could take affirmative steps to dismantle such a system. It is beyond dispute that any public entity, state or federal, has a compelling interest in assuring that public dollars, drawn from the tax contributions of all citizens, do not serve to finance the evil of private prejudice. *Cf. Norwood v. Harrison*, 413 U.S. 455, 465 (1973) ("Racial discrimination in state-operated schools is barred by the Constitution and [i]t is also axiomatic that a state may not induce, [493] encourage or promote private persons to accomplish what it is constitutionally forbidden to accomplish").

SUPREME COURT OF THE UNITED STATES

539 U.S. 306

GRUTTER V. BOLLINGER

CERTIORARI TO THE UNITED STATES COURT
OF APPEALS FOR THE SIXTH CIRCUIT

NO. 02-241 ARGUED: APRIL 1, 2003–DECIDED:
JUNE 23, 2003

[311] JUSTICE O'CONNOR delivered the opinion of the Court.

This case requires us to decide whether the use of race as a factor in student admissions by the University of Michigan Law School (Law School) is unlawful.

[312–322] . . .

We last addressed the use of race in public higher education over 25 years ago. In the landmark *Bakke* case, we reviewed a racial set-aside program that reserved 16 out of 100 seats in a medical school class for members of certain minority groups. 438 U.S. 265 (1978). The decision produced six separate opinions, none of which commanded a majority of the Court. . . . The only holding for the Court in *Bakke* was that a "State has a substantial interest that legitimately may be served by a properly devised admissions program involving [323] the competitive consideration of race and ethnic origin." *Id.* at 320. Thus, we reversed that part of the lower court's judgment that enjoined the university "from any consideration of the race of any applicant." *Ibid.*

Since this Court's splintered decision in *Bakke*, Justice Powell's opinion announcing the judgment of the Court has served as the touchstone for constitutional analysis of race-conscious admissions policies. Public and private universities across the Nation have modeled their own admissions programs on Justice Powell's views on permissible race-conscious policies. . . .

. . . [324] . . .

Justice Powell approved the university's use of race to further only one interest: "the attainment of a diverse student body." *Id.* at 311. With the important proviso that "constitutional limitations protecting individual rights may not be disregarded," Justice Powell grounded his analysis in the academic freedom that "long has been viewed as a special concern of the First Amendment." *Id.* at 312, 314. Justice Powell emphasized that nothing less than the "'nation's future depends upon leaders trained through wide exposure' to the ideas and mores of students as diverse as this Nation of many peoples." *Id.* at 313 (quoting *Keyishian v. Board of Regents of Univ. of State of N.Y.*, 385 U.S. 589, 603 (1967)). In seeking the "right to select those students who will contribute the most to the 'robust exchange of ideas,'" a university seeks "to achieve a goal that is of paramount importance in the fulfillment of its mission." 438 U.S. at 313. Both "tradition and experience lend support to the view that the contribution of diversity is substantial." *Ibid.*

Justice Powell was, however, careful to emphasize that in his view race "is only one element in a range of factors a university properly may consider in attaining the goal of a heterogeneous student body." *Id.* at 314. For Justice Powell, "it is not an interest in simple ethnic diversity, in which a specified percentage of the student body is in effect guaranteed to be members of selected ethnic groups," that [325] can justify the use of race. *Id.* at 315. Rather, "the diversity that furthers a compelling state interest encompasses a far broader array of qualifications and characteristics of which racial or ethnic origin is but a single though important element." *Ibid.*

. . . [326–327] . . .

. . . Before this Court, as they have [328] throughout this litigation, respondents assert only one justification for their use of race in the admissions process: obtaining "the educational benefits that flow from a diverse student body." Brief for Respondents Bollinger et al. i. In other words, the Law School asks us to recognize, in the context of higher education, a compelling state interest in student body diversity.

. . . .

The Law School's educational judgment that such diversity is essential to its educational mission is one to which we defer. The Law School's assessment that diversity will, in fact, yield educational benefits is substantiated by respondents and their amici. Our scrutiny of the interest asserted by the Law School is no less strict for taking into account complex educational judgments in an area that lies primarily within the expertise of the university. Our holding today is in keeping with our tradition of giving a degree of deference to a university's academic decisions, within constitutionally prescribed limits. *See Regents of Univ. of Mich. v. Ewing*, 474 U.S. 214, 225 (1985); *Board of Curators of Univ. of Mo.* [329] *v. Horowitz*, 435 U.S. 78, 96, n.6 (1978); *Bakke*, 438 U.S. at 319, n.53 (opinion of Powell, J.).

We have long recognized that, given the important purpose of public education and the expansive freedoms of speech and thought associated with the university environment, universities occupy a special niche in our constitutional tradition. *See, e.g., Wieman v. Updegraff*, 344 U.S. 183, 195 (1952) (Frankfurter, J., concurring); *Sweezy v. New Hampshire*, 354 U.S. 234, 250 (1957); *Shelton v. Tucker*, 364 U.S. 479, 487 (1960); *Keyishian v. Board of Regents of Univ. of State of N.Y.*, 385 U.S. at 603. In announcing the principle of student body diversity as a compelling state interest, Justice Powell invoked our cases recognizing a constitutional dimension, grounded in the First Amendment, of educational autonomy: "The freedom of a university to make its own judgments as to education includes the selection of its student body." *Bakke, supra*, at 312. From this premise, Justice Powell reasoned that by claiming "the right to select those students who will contribute the most to the 'robust exchange of ideas,'" a university "seek[s] to achieve a goal that is of paramount importance in the fulfillment of its mission." 438 U.S. at 313 (quoting *Keyishian v. Board of Regents of Univ. of State of N.Y., supra*, at 603). Our conclusion that the Law School has a compelling interest in a diverse student body is informed by our view that attaining a diverse student body is at the heart of the Law School's proper institutional mission, and that "good faith" on the part of a university is "presumed" absent "a showing to the contrary." 438 U.S. at 318–319.

As part of its goal of "assembling a class that is both exceptionally academically qualified and broadly diverse," the Law School seeks to "enroll a 'critical mass' of minority students." Brief for Respondents Bollinger et al. 13. The Law School's interest is not simply "to assure within its student body some specified percentage of a particular group merely because of its race or ethnic origin." *Bakke*, 438 U.S. at [330] 307 (opinion of Powell, J.). That would amount to outright racial balancing, which is patently unconstitutional. *Ibid.; Freeman v. Pitts*, 503 U.S. 467, 494 (1992) ("Racial balance is not to be achieved for its own sake"); *Richmond v. J.A. Croson Co.*, 488 U.S. at 507. Rather, the Law School's concept of critical mass is defined by reference to the educational benefits that diversity is designed to produce.

These benefits are substantial. As the District Court emphasized, the Law School's admissions policy promotes "cross-racial understanding," helps to [2340] break down racial stereotypes, and "enables [students] to better understand persons of different races." App. to Pet. for Cert. 246a. These benefits are "important and laudable," because "classroom discussion is livelier, more spirited, and simply more enlightening and interesting" when the students have "the greatest possible variety of backgrounds." *Id.* at 246a, 244a.

The Law School's claim of a compelling interest is further bolstered by its amici, who point to the educational benefits that flow from student body diversity. In addition to the expert studies and reports entered into evidence at trial, numerous studies show that student body diversity promotes learning outcomes, and "better prepares students for an increasingly diverse workforce and society, and better prepares them as professionals." Brief for American Educational Research Association et al. as Amici Curiae 3; *see, e.g.,* W. Bowen & D. Bok, *The Shape of the River* (1998); *Diversity Challenged: Evidence on the Impact of Affirmative Action* (G. Orfield & M. Kurlaender eds., 2001); *Compelling Interest: Examining the Evidence on Racial Dynamics in Colleges and Universities* (M. Chang, D. Witt, J. Jones, & K. Hakuta eds., 2003).

These benefits are not theoretical but real, as major American businesses have made clear that the skills needed in today's increasingly global marketplace can only be developed through exposure to widely diverse people, cultures, ideas, and viewpoints. Brief for 3M et al. as Amici Curiae [331] 5; Brief for General Motors Corp. as Amicus Curiae 3–4. What is more, highranking retired officers and civilian leaders of the United States military assert that, "[b]ased on [their] decades of experience," a "highly qualified, racially diverse officer corps . . . is essential to the military's ability to fulfill its principle [sic] mission to provide national security." Brief for Julius W. Becton, Jr. et al. as Amici Curiae 27. The primary sources for the Nation's officer corps are the service academies and the Reserve Officers Training Corps (ROTC), the latter comprising students already admitted to participating colleges and universities. *Id.* at 5. At present, "the military cannot achieve an officer corps that is *both* highly qualified *and* racially diverse unless the service academies and the ROTC used limited race-conscious recruiting and admissions policies." *Ibid.* (emphasis in original). To fulfill its mission, the military "must be selective in admissions for training and education for the officer corps, *and* it must train and educate a highly qualified, racially diverse officer corps in a racially diverse setting." *Id.* at 29 (emphasis in original). We agree that "[i]t requires only a small step from this analysis to conclude that our country's other most selective institutions must remain both diverse and selective." *Ibid.*

We have repeatedly acknowledged the overriding importance of preparing students for work and citizenship, describing education as pivotal to "sustaining our political and cultural heritage" with a fundamental role in maintaining the fabric of society. *Plyler v. Doe,* 457 U.S. 202, 221 (1982). This Court has long recognized that "education . . . is the very foundation of good citizenship." *Brown v. Board of Education,* 347 U.S. 483, 493 (1954). For this reason, the diffusion of knowledge and opportunity through public institutions of higher education must be accessible to all individuals regardless of race or ethnicity. The United States, as amicus curiae, affirms that "[e]nsuring that public institutions are open and available to all segments of American [332] society, including people of all races and ethnicities, represents a paramount government objective." Brief for United States as Amicus Curiae 13. And, "[n]owhere is the importance of such openness more acute than in the context of higher education." *Ibid.* Effective participation by members of all racial and ethnic groups in the civic life of our Nation is [2341] essential if the dream of one Nation, indivisible, is to be realized.

Moreover, universities, and in particular, law schools, represent the training ground for a large number of our Nation's leaders. *Sweatt v. Painter,* 339 U.S. 629, 634 (1950) (describing law school as a "proving ground for legal learning and practice"). Individuals with law degrees occupy roughly half the state governorships, more than half the seats in the United States Senate, and more than a third of the seats in the United States House of Representatives. *See* Brief for Association of American Law Schools as Amicus Curiae 5–6. The pattern is even more striking when it comes to highly selective law schools. A handful of these schools accounts for 25 of the 100 United States Senators, 74 United States Courts of Appeals judges, and nearly 200 of the more than 600 United States District Court judges. *Id.* at 6.

In order to cultivate a set of leaders with legitimacy in the eyes of the citizenry, it is necessary that the path to leadership be visibly open to talented and qualified individuals of every race and ethnicity. All members of our heterogeneous society must have confidence in the openess and integrity of the educational institutions that provide this training. As we have recognized, law schools "cannot be effective in isolation from the individuals and institutions with which the law interacts." *See Sweatt v. Painter, supra,* at 634. Access to legal education (and thus the legal profession) must be inclusive of talented and qualified individuals of every race and ethnicity, so that all members of our heterogeneous society [333] may participate in the educational institutions that provide the training and education necessary to succeed in America.

The Law School does not premise its need for critical mass on "any belief that minority students always (or even consistently) express some characteristic minority viewpoint on any issue." Brief for Respondent Bollinger et al. 30. To the contrary, diminishing the force of such stereotypes is both a crucial part of the Law School's mission, and one that it cannot accomplish with only token numbers of minority students. Just as growing up in a particular region or having particular professional experiences is likely to affect an individual's views, so too is one's own, unique experience of being a racial minority in a society, like our own, in which race unfortunately still matters. The Law School has determined, based on its experience and expertise, that a "critical mass" of underrepresented minorities is necessary to further its compelling interest in securing the educational benefits of a diverse student body.

. . . .

INTRODUCTION: AFTER *BAKKE*

—Robert Post—

Democracy and public education have long been regarded as inseparably complementary. Democracy is the practice of collective self-determination; public education is an investment by the state to disseminate the training and knowledge prerequisite for that practice. The question I wish to analyze concerns the distinctive contribution of public higher education to democratic practice. The question will, I hope, illuminate what I regard as the second great strength of Powell's opinion in *Bakke*, which is its accommodation of affirmative action within a justificatory framework that unsettles the slide toward group rights and entitlements.

"The essence of democracy," writes Jean Piaget, "resides in its attitude towards law as a product of collective will, and not as something emanating from a transcendent will or from the authority established by divine right. It is therefore the essence of democracy to replace the unilateral respect of authority by the mutual respect of autonomous wills." Democracy, we might more precisely say, entails the perpetual process of reconciling the self-determination of autonomous wills with the *collective* self-determination of a polity. This process, which is perennially open-ended, occurs through the medium of a public discourse sustained by a public culture.

Two consequences flow from this formulation. First, there is a strong affiliation between democracy and individualism, because the autonomous wills of individuals are conceptualized as politically prior to and constitutive of the rights of groups. If this were not the case, if the self-determination of individuals were to be subordinated to the identities and norms of particular groups, the possibilities of collective self-determination would to that precise extent be circumscribed.

Second, because of this political individualism, democratic public culture must also be understood as distinct from the cultures of particular groups and communities. Even though we know that in actuality the identities of individuals are formed through socialization into the mores of specific and historical groups and communities, the ideal of self-determination requires that public culture always maintain the possibility of citizens imagining themselves as something other than what they in fact are. Public culture must be large enough to encompass this possibility and therefore to embrace all possible groups and communities. Public culture is, as Thomas Keenan writes, the "realm . . . of others, of all that is other to—and in— the subject itself."

Historically and sociologically, public culture typically evolves from "cultural differentiation"; it functions, as the sociologists tell us, as a "universe of discourse" within which distinct communities can nevertheless come together to form a single democratic polity. Public culture appears as a site of difference, in which communication occurs between those who do not share the identity and assumptions that define distinctive communities. Successful participation in public culture therefore requires a special form of cultural capital: the ability to interact in a "critical" manner that establishes distance from local certitudes and thereby creates the possibility of spanning the boundaries between disparate groups.

Institutions of higher education are today a primary source of that cultural capital. They aspire to cultivate the remarkable and difficult capacity to regard oneself from the perspective of the other, which is the foundation of the critical interaction necessary for active and effective citizenship. The cultivation of this capacity is especially important for public universities, for they are in part created to educate generations of future citizens so as to maintain the legitimacy of democratic self-government. Public universities have the educational obligation to dispense the cultural capital at their disposal in a manner that accounts for the health of public culture.

There are many dimensions to this obligation, but certainly one aspect entails facilitating participation in public culture by members of politically salient communities. A political culture without such participation would be neither democratic nor healthy, but merely repressive. In the United States, and especially in California, racial and ethnic identities mark lines of intense political division. If the racial and ethnic rifts that divide us are to be transcended by a democratic state that is legitimate to all sides, there must be articulate participation in public culture that concomitantly spans the lines of these controversies. I would argue, therefore, that the educational mission of the University of California ought to include the obligation to promote this participation.

If "normal" admission standards, by which I mean admission standards formulated to achieve other educational goals of the university, would in effect operate so as to exclude members of politically salient racial and ethnic communities, then the university's obligation to encourage a flourishing public culture may well require standards of admission that explicitly recognize racial and ethnic identity. The justification of these standards would not depend on any theory of group rights or entitlements; it would not reflect the extrinsic goal of compensating for past wrongs or oppression; it would not rely upon any pedagogical theory of the heuristic value of diversity. It would flow instead from the educational goal of fostering the public culture on which rests the success of democratic self-governance. It would follow from the perception that in the United States today democratic legitimacy very much depends on the active participation of an educated and critical citizenry that spans existing racial and ethnic differences.

Because this goal would conceptualize university applicants as potential citizens who are capable of transcending local attachments and identities, it would entail admission standards that, like those proposed by Powell in *Bakke*, ideologically privilege the individuality of applicants. This means that racial and ethnic identity would be relevant, but not determinative. An admissions policy based on the goal of nurturing public culture would thus retain Powell's pragmatic accommodation between a symbolic commitment to individualism and a practically effective response to social dislocation.

It is uncertain whether this justification for affirmative action, if candidly expressed, would pass constitutional muster. But the primary purpose of this volume is to think frankly among ourselves, rather than to speculate about the constitutional interpretation of nine justices. Our fundamental challenge is to decide what we wish to accomplish politically and how we wish to accomplish it, and we may hope that in the end constitutional law will follow the lead of informed judgment.

RACISM AND JUSTICE

THE CASE FOR AFFIRMATIVE ACTION

—Gertrude Ezorsky—

THE TIES OF RACE-NEUTRAL PROCEDURES TO OVERT RACISM

Overt racism, past and present, contributes to social and residential segregation, thereby isolating blacks at every income level from white society. Because of such isolation, blacks are vulnerable, by exclusion, to selection by personal connections. The negative impact of qualification standards in employment is sustained by racially biased funding of education and training resources and by the cumulative racist impact of such practices as tracking in schools. Blacks suffer the adverse effects of seniority-based promotion and layoff because of past racist hiring of whites ahead of blacks.

Institutional racism also reinforces future racism by contributing to the disproportionate presence of blacks at the bottom of employment—a presence that helps perpetuate the racist attitude that blacks are inherently inferior. White notions of black people have been formed in a social world where blacks visibly predominate at these bottom levels. Thus they have labored—and continue to labor—as maids and porters, at "hot, heavy, and dirty" jobs in the foundries and paint pits of the auto plants, the boiler rooms of utilities, the dusty basements of tobacco factories, and in the murderous heat of the steel mills' coke ovens.

Today, while some blacks have moved on up, it is still true that the more disagreeable the job, the greater the chance of finding a high proportion of blacks doing it. In 1984, Herman Schwartz, a legal scholar, noted that blacks constitute over 50 percent of the nation's maids and garbage collectors, but only 4 percent of its managers and 3 percent of its physicians and lawyers.

The racially exclusionary impact of race-neutral policies on employment also contributes to the official black unemployment rate as perpetually double that of whites, thereby reenforcing the racist view of blacks as unwilling to work. Thus these race-neutral policies function as social mechanisms through which the victimizing effects of overt racism, past and present, continue to keep blacks at the bottom levels of employment. . . .

REMEDIES FOR RACISM

In assessing the remedies for racism, I will be concerned not with legal issues (e.g., whether these remedies are compatible with the Constitution) but rather with their practical effectiveness and moral acceptability. The development of legal remedies in the 1960s and 1970s, in conformity with the 1964 Civil Rights Act and a federal executive order, provides an instructive context for such assessment.

The Complaint Remedy for Overt Discrimination

Actions taken to remedy overt discrimination against identifiable individuals may be referred to, broadly speaking, as complaints. These complaints can be lodged in a court or administrative agency under Title 7 of the 1964 Civil Rights Act, which prohibits such discrimination, and may be pursued against a firm or a union on behalf of an identifiable individual or group. A class-action suit claiming salary or promotion discrimination against all class members, such as all minority workers in a firm, exemplifies a group complaint. If overt hiring or promotion discrimination is proved, the employer is required to remedy the violation, usually by hiring or promoting the complainant or, in the case of salary discrimination, by awarding back pay.

While complaint remedies satisfy a reasonable claim for restitution, they are deficient in a number of ways. First, they are often not practical even in obvious cases of racial bias. Victims are frequently reluctant to complain because workers who assert their rights are labeled troublemakers. (Many of the rights we now take for granted were won by troublemakers.) That label can damage a person—especially a black person—for her entire working life. A realistic assessment of such damage to themselves and the families they support often stops black people from initiating justified complaints.

Second, the blacks who do file complaints must prove that their employer acted out of racial bias. Such bias appears evident when no alternative explanation for racially unequal pay is plausible, but in other situations management frequently has effective strategies for covering up racial bias.

How does a black applicant know whether the job has really "just been filled"? How can an experienced black worker demonstrate that the announcement of a managerial opening was canceled because the employer learned that she—a *black* employee—was clearly the best-qualified candidate? Also, firms can enlist the cooperation of employment agencies in concealing behind-the-scenes discrimination. The difficulty of proving bias, when employers often have the power to conceal such prejudice, reduces the effectiveness of the complaint remedy.

A similar problem confronts a black person who seeks housing in white areas where jobs are available. Landlords and realtors, like employers, have effective strategies for defeating complaints of racial prejudice. Does a black apartment-seeker have proof—or the time to assemble proof—that a landlord's excuses ("The apartment isn't available because it needs repair") are conjured up to exclude blacks, or that a real estate agent is steering black clients away from white neighborhoods?

Since the complaint remedy requires proof of bias, it does not apply to institutional race-neutral policies. Yet qualification standards can be manipulated by prejudiced employers to exclude blacks, especially, as we have seen, vague personality standards. Decisive proof of bias is frequently not obtainable in such cases.

Where employers hire by personal connections, blacks isolated by segregation from white society are unaware of job openings. Having never applied, these segregated blacks have no grounds for filing a discrimination complaint. Hence segregation contributes to the inadequacy of the complaint remedy.

The complaint remedy is also irrelevant to the racist impact of impartially applied qualification standards that sustain the victimizing effects of past racism, such as the underfunding of segregated black schools and the refusal of employers and unions to hire and train black workers. Absent racism, there would have been, statistically speaking, a racial redistribution of workers; *some* blacks moving up, *some* whites moving down. But those blacks and those whites cannot be identified as individuals. Yet the blacks, so victimized, are out there in the world of work, real persons still suffering the effects of racist injury.

While complaints are an inadequate tool for overcoming racism, especially institutional racism, they nevertheless can be financially burdensome to employers because they require payment of legal fees and, in some cases, back-pay settlements. These costs increase when back pay is awarded to a group of employees who have brought a class-action suit. As we shall see in the next section, an employer strategy for preventing such suits turned out to be the remedy for institutional discrimination—affirmative action.

My analysis of affirmative action focuses primarily on its practice before 1980; after this time, as we shall see, the federal government's impetus to enforce and sustain affirmative action declined substantially.

Broadly speaking, affirmative action (hereafter AA) consists not merely of passive nondiscrimination but of active measures to increase significantly the recruitment and upgrading of minorities. Blacks are not required, as in the complaint remedy, to prove an employer's overt discrimination against them; hence a crucial weakness of the complaint remedy is eliminated.

Both before and after the federal government initiated AA requirements, civil rights organizations pursued hoycotts, picketing, wild cat strikes, and demonstrations that brought direct pressure on employers and unions for recruiting, training, and upgrading more blacks. Among these groups were People United to Serve Humanity (OPERATION PUSH), the Committee on Racial Equality (CORE), the Dodge Revolutionary Union Movement (DRUM), a Detroit-based, militant, and sometimes violence-prone black auto-worker group, and the United Construction Workers' Association (UCWA), a Seattle-based black-worker organization.

In 1964 the A&P made an agreement with CORE, stating that 90 percent of its new employees for the following year would be nonwhite. In 1968, DRUM called for the hiring of additional black foremen in auto plants. In 1972, after a court ordered Seattle craft unions to increase their black apprentices, UCWA closed down construction projects to speed up compliance with the court order. No doubt such activity by the civil rights movement contributed to the development of government-sanctioned AA in the 1960s and early 1970s.

AA was targeted to reduce the adverse effects in employment of past and present racist practices. As we have seen, such practices include segregated education, housing discrimination in areas of available employment, the last-hired, first-fired policies of employers which deprived blacks of seniority and work experience, the exclusion of blacks from white society where personal connections to jobs are made, and the refusal of unions and firms to train black youths. The effects of such racist practices show up in the statistical overrepresentation of blacks at the bottom of the occupational ladder and among the unemployed. AA aimed to diminish these effects by moving the black work force toward approximate statistical parity—that is, to achieve occupational integration throughout the hierarchy of employment. It is true that, absent a racist past, such statistical parity might not now exist everywhere in employment. But although a past without racism cannot be reconstructed, we do know that when occupational integration is finally achieved, the significant effects in employment of that invidious history will in large part be gone. Moreover, persons who mature in a society where the upper employment levels are racially integrated will be less likely to assume that blacks belong at the bottom.

Some courts and government civil rights agencies, construing statistical underrepresentation of blacks in sectors of employment as the continuing effect of a racist past, have perceived AA recruitment as a means of eradicating such underrepresentation. They also became aware, however, that such efforts to hire and upgrade minorities were consistently blocked by the adverse racial impact of neutral selection practices which continued to preserve white predominance, especially in desirable positions. Hence, as a number of government agencies and courts have recognized, increased recruitment of blacks requires that reasonable strategies be devised to reduce institutional discrimination, that is, to lessen the racist impact of employment neutrals: selection by personal connections, qualification requirements, and seniority status. A 1984 report by the Citizens' Commission on Civil Rights sums up that story: "[These AA remedies] grew out of the persistent use of practices such as word-of-mouth recruiting, 'old boy' networks, aptitude and other tests not related to job performance which continued to prevent the employment of minorities and women even after overt practices of discrimination had ended."

Thus, while employment neutrals have functioned as social mechanisms that perpetuate the victimizing effects of past and present racist injury, AA in employment has become the social remedy that is designed to reduce that racist impact in the workplace. Let us examine AA from that perspective.

Unspecific vs. Specific AA: Good Faith vs. Numerical Goals

As we have seen, selection by personal connections tends to favor whites at the expense of blacks. Outreach to minority candidates seemed an obvious way to remedy the racist impact of such selection. It is important to distinguish two ways in which such outreach can be conducted: First, there are "good faith" efforts to recruit blacks, made without numerical goals or timetables for hiring them. This method exemplifies *unspecific* AA. Second, there are good faith efforts capped by definite, dated numerical targets. The second illustrates *specific* AA.

Unspecific outreach efforts include advertising positions and recruitment visits to black schools. Such visits to minorities exemplify a *purely racial* remedy since they benefit only minorities. Advertising positions, however, is a *quasi-racial* remedy since it also benefits those whites who, excluded from behind-the-scenes hiring networks, learn about job openings through such advertising.

The seriousness of unspecific outreach, uncapped by dated numerical targets, depends on the determination of the employer or surrogate—such as a referral union—to direct jobs toward blacks, hence away from whites. Without pressure for recruiting a definite number of blacks, however, the employer can go through the motions of AA and hire only a token number or none at all. The fact is that unspecific outreach is simply insufficient. Resistance to breaking comfortable recruitment habits that substantially benefit one's friends, family, and so forth is predictable.

The need for specific AA in academia—where the traditional "old boy" system draws graduate-school friends into one's department family—was noted in 1975 by Harold C. Fleming, president of the Potomac Institute: "A high degree of specificity . . . is the only way affirmative action can . . . be meaningfully monitored. . . . It is no indictment of the morality of professors to suggest that they share our common human frailty in finding it difficult to change old habits and ingrained practices without pressure from, and accountability to, authority outside our own comfortable peer group.

Generally speaking, where resistance is expected or extra effort required—as when a person plans to save money or a firm decides to increase production—the effectiveness of definite, dated goals is recognized. In collective bargaining, unions demand not vague employer promises to try to raise wages but definite, contractually binding pay increases.

In firms where desirable positions have formerly been filled by personal connections, effective AA can divert good jobs from one's white contacts and give them to blacks. In such situations, vague outreach efforts without definite numerical goals are bound to be inadequate. Such efforts will also be insufficient in situations where hiring procedures—whatever they are—can be manipulated by prejudiced personnel officers. Lack of specificity invites evasion. Moreover, even impartial employers find unspecific outreach requirements difficult to administer. Without definite numerical targets, they have no standard of reasonable progress in the recruitment of minorities.

The practical necessity for dated numerical targets became obvious to federal investigators monitoring the AA efforts of government contractors in the 1960s and 1970s. They found that entrenched habits of dispensing positions, especially desirable ones, to personal connections often paralyzed minority outreach.

For example, the Kaiser Aluminum and Chemical Company, located in a 39-percent black Louisiana area, had an only 9-percent-black work force. A "white pipeline" had worked to exclude blacks from the relatively well-paid positions in this United Steelworkers—organized plant. A significant breakthrough for blacks was made, however, in the early 1970s by the implementation of a 50-percent-minority hiring goal for production workers and in 1974 by the establishment of a 50-percent-minority craft training program.

In the building trades, craft-union members' preference for their white personal contacts for top-paying apprenticeships was virtually automatic until AA was introduced in the late 1960s and 1970s. A case indicating the need for numerical goals involved the Los Angeles Steam Fitters Local #250. Not a single nonwhite held a card in this union of three thousand members. The local made no serious move to bring in black apprentices until 1972, when the Justice Department insisted on dated numerical goals. The three previous years of "good faith" efforts had accomplished nothing.

In the Philadelphia area in 1969, after eight years of supposed commitment during the 1960s to equal opportunity with little result, government construction contractors were ordered by the U.S. Department of Labor to set minority numerical goals. The Philadelphia Plan, which incorporated these goals, had national repercussions for the construction industry, as legal scholar William B. Gould describes: "The winds of Philadephia were being felt throughout the land. The belief that the unions and contractors had obligations to recruit minorities, obligations which could be effected only if 'goals' and 'timetables' for minority hiring were established, was reflected both in the acceleration of black demands and in a new-found inclination by the white building trades and contractors to negotiate plans. For the first time, a climate which favored meaningful efforts to alleviate employment discrimination was beginning to develop."

These cases illustrate the need for numerical remedies in firms and industries where recruitment by personal connections had been practiced. Numerical targets also act as a powerful deterrent against overt racism. A racist employer under pressure to hire a definite number of blacks will hesitate before victimizing a black applicant. When we appraise AA remedies for neutral selection practices, the importance of goals and timetables will again he evident.

Government civil rights agencies and the courts have played a major role in developing numerical remedies. Their authority for establishing such remedies derives mainly from two sources: First, Executive Order 11246 guidelines (1971) require that dated numerical targets for hiring, training, and promoting minorities be set by firms that hold government contracts but have underutilized minorities, that is, have employed fewer than "would reasonably be expected by their availability." Employers who fail to meet their numerical goals but can demonstrate "good faith" efforts are not subject to loss of government contracts. Second, Title 7 of the 1964 Civil Rights Act empowers the courts to order such "affirmative action as may be appropriate" for relief of past discrimination. Consequently, courts have issued powerful judicial decrees, such as the AT&T consent decree and the Steel Industry Settlement, mandating numerical targets for reducing minority underutilization. Because courts have construed such reduction by employers as evidence that past discrimination is being remedied, firms seeking to prevent costly Title 7 suits have, as voluntary affirmative action, established numerical goals.

In some situations where blacks are notoriously scarce, the courts have approved "set-asides," which unlike goals, reserve a specific number of positions for minorities only. Whites are excluded from competing for such positions. A 10-percent government contract set-aside for minority-owned firms was upheld by the Supreme Court in *Fullilove* v. *Klutznick* (1980). In black-owned firms hiring by personal connections tends to benefit blacks. Hence government contract set-asides for minority firms are bound to increase black employment.

While the moral problems raised by AA will be discussed in Part II, it will he useful at this point to clarify one issue concerning numerical remedies which has moral import. Some analysts refer to numerical remedies as "quotas"; however, that label should be avoided. It is true that a numerical goal (or set-aside) does not differ, semantically speaking, from a numerical quota. Nevertheless, tagging AA numerical remedies as "quotas" is misleading, for that label suggests that such AA measures are relevantly similar to the old quotas that decades ago excluded many Jews from professional schools. But the old exclusionary quotas against Jews were motivated by a false, derogatory notion of their social inferiority, a notion that defined Jews as pushy, vulgar, and mercenary. Those quotas aimed to maintain a professional society restricted by such immoral bias—a society dominated by Christian gentlemen. In contrast, an important purpose of AA numerical remedies is occupational integration, a work-place society where biased stereotypes of blacks as inferior have largely been dissipated. To tag such AA measures as quotas falsely suggests that they, like yesterday's quotas, serve an immoral end.

Presumably, AA critics who use the quota label pejoratively believe that numerical remedies serve an immoral purpose. That conclusion requires demonstration by argument, and the quota label is not a substitute for such argument.

SUPREME COURT OF THE UNITED STATES

515 U.S. 200

ADARAND CONSTRUCTORS, INC.
V. PENA

CERTIORARI TO THE UNITED STATES COURT OF APPEALS FOR THE TENTH CIRCUIT

NO. 93-1841 ARGUED: JANUARY 17, 1995–DECIDED: JUNE 12, 1995

[Note: In this opinion, the Supreme Court held that all state uses of racial classifications, whether at the state or the Federal level, are subject to "strict scrutiny": they must (a) be for a compelling purpose and (b) the means used must be narrowly tailored to serve that purpose. The author of the Court's opinion, Justice O'Connor, allowed that some race-based affirmative action programs could, in principle, satisfy this standard of scrutiny. Here, Justice Thomas, while concurring with the Court's judgment that strict scrutiny is the appropriate standard of review, rejects O'Connor's view that the state may use racial preferences to remedy discrimination. Justice Scalia agrees.]

CONCURRENCE: [240] JUSTICE THOMAS, concurring in part and concurring in the judgment.

I agree with the majority's conclusion that strict scrutiny applies to *all* government classifications based on race. I write separately, however, to express my disagreement with the premise underlying Justice Stevens' and Justice Ginsburg's dissents: that there is a racial paternalism exception to the principle of equal protection. I believe that there is a "moral [and] constitutional equivalence," *post* at 243 (Stevens, J., dissenting), between laws designed to subjugate a race and those that distribute benefits on the basis of race in order to foster some current notion of equality. Government cannot make us equal; it can only recognize, respect, and protect us as equal before the law.

That these programs may have been motivated, in part, by good intentions cannot provide refuge from the principle that under our Constitution, the government may not make distinctions on the basis of race. As far as the Constitution is concerned, it is irrelevant whether a government's racial classifications are drawn by those who wish to oppress a race or by those who have a sincere desire to help those thought to be disadvantaged. There can be no doubt that the paternalism that appears to lie at the heart of this program is at war with the principle of inherent equality that underlies and infuses our Constitution. *See Declaration of Independence* ("We hold these truths to be self-evident, that all men are created equal, that they are endowed by their Creator with certain unalienable Rights, that among these are Life, Liberty, and the pursuit of Happiness").

These programs not only raise grave constitutional questions, they also undermine the moral basis of the equal protection principle. Purchased at the price of immeasurable human suffering, the equal protection principle reflects our Nation's understanding that such classifications ultimately have a destructive impact on the individual and our society. Unquestionably, "[i]nvidious [racial] discrimination is an engine [241] of oppression," *post* at 243. It is also true that "[r]emedial" racial preferences may reflect "a desire to foster equality in society," *ibid*. But there can be no doubt that racial paternalism and its unintended consequences can be as poisonous and pernicious as any other form of discrimination. So-called "benign" discrimination teaches many that because of chronic and apparently immutable handicaps, minorities cannot compete with them without their patronizing indulgence. Inevitably, such programs engender attitudes of superiority or, alternatively, provoke resentment among those who believe that they have been wronged by the government's use of race. These programs stamp minorities with a badge of inferiority and may cause them to develop dependencies or to adopt an attitude that they are "entitled" to preferences. Indeed, Justice Stevens once recognized the real harms stemming from seemingly "benign" discrimination. *See Fullilove v. Klutznick*, 448 U.S. 448, 545 (1980) (Stevens, J., dissenting) (noting that "remedial" race legislation "is perceived by many as resting on an assumption that those who are granted this special preference are less qualified in some respect that is identified purely by their race").

In my mind, government-sponsored racial discrimination based on benign prejudice is just as noxious as discrimination inspired by malicious prejudice. In each instance, it is racial discrimination, plain and simple.

[239]. . . .

CONCURRENCE: JUSTICE SCALIA, concurring in part and concurring in the judgment.

I join the opinion of the Court, except Part III-C, and except insofar as it may be inconsistent with the following: in my view, government can never have a "compelling interest" in discriminating on the basis of race in order to "make up" for past racial discrimination in the opposite direction. *See Richmond v. J.A. Croson Co.*, 488 U.S. 469, 520 (1989) (Scalia, J., concurring in judgment). Individuals who have been wronged by unlawful racial discrimination should be made whole, but, under our Constitution, there can be no such thing as either a creditor or a debtor race. That concept is alien to the Constitution's focus upon the individual, *see* amend. XIV, § 1 ("[N]or shall any State . . . deny *to any person*" the equal protection of the laws) (emphasis added), and its rejection of dispositions based on race, *see* amend. 15, § 1 (prohibiting abridgment of the right to vote "on account of race") or based on blood, *see* art. III, § 3 ("[N]o Attainder of Treason shall work Corruption of Blood"); art. I, § 9 ("No Title of Nobility shall be granted by the United States"). To pursue the concept of racial entitlement—even for the most admirable and benign of purposes—is to reinforce and preserve for future mischief the way of thinking that produced race slavery, race privilege and race hatred. In the eyes of government, we are just one race here. It is American.

. . . .

SUPREME COURT OF THE UNITED STATES

488 U.S. 469

CITY OF RICHMOND V. J.A. CROSON CO.
(SCALIA)

APPEAL FROM THE UNITED STATES COURT OF APPEALS FOR THE FOURTH CIRCUIT

NO. 87-998 ARGUED: OCTOBER 5, 1988–DECIDED: JANUARY 23, 1989

[Note: This opinion rejected the City of Richmond's set-aside of 30% of contracting dollars to minority-owned business enterprises, mainly on the ground that the City had not provided evidence that discrimination against minority businesses was a continuing problem in Richmond. In this excerpt, Justice Scalia objects to Justice O'Connor's view that the state may use racial classifications to remedy the effects of private sector discrimination.]

CONCURRENCE: JUSTICE SCALIA, concurring in the judgment.

I agree with much of the Court's opinion, and, in particular, with Justice O'Connor's conclusion that strict scrutiny must be applied to all governmental classification by race, whether or not its asserted purpose is "remedial" or "benign." *Ante* at 493, 495. I do not agree, however, with Justice O'Connor's dictum suggesting that, despite the Fourteenth Amendment, state and local governments may in some circumstances discriminate on the basis of race in order (in a broad sense) "to ameliorate the effects of past discrimination." *Ante* at 476–77. The benign purpose of compensating for social disadvantages, whether they have been acquired by reason of prior discrimination or otherwise, can no more be pursued by the illegitimate means of racial discrimination than can other assertedly benign purposes we have repeatedly rejected. *See, e.g., Wygant v. Jackson Board of Education*, 476 U.S. 267, 274–76 (1986) (plurality opinion) (discrimination in teacher assignments to provide "role models" for minority students); *Palmore v. Sidoti*, 466 U.S. 429, 433 (1984) (awarding custody of child to father, after divorced mother entered an interracial remarriage, in order to spare child social "pressures and stresses"); *Lee v. Washington*, 390 U.S. 333 (1968) (per curiam) (permanent racial segregation of all prison inmates, presumably to reduce possibility of racial conflict). The difficulty of overcoming the effects of past discrimination is as nothing compared with the difficulty of eradicating from our society the source of those effects, which is the tendency—fatal to a Nation such as ours—to classify and judge men and women on the basis of their country of origin or the color of their skin. A solution [521] to the first problem that aggravates the second is no solution at all. I share the view expressed by Alexander Bickel that "[t]he lesson of the great decisions of the Supreme Court and the lesson of contemporary history have been the same for at least a generation: discrimination on the basis of race is illegal, immoral, unconstitutional, inherently wrong, and destructive of democractic society." A. Bickel, *The Morality of Consent* 133 (1975). At least where state or local action is at issue, only a social emergency rising to the level of imminent danger to life and limb— for example, a prison race riot, requiring temporary segregation of inmates, *cf. Lee v. Washington, supra*— can justify an exception to the principle embodied in the Fourteenth Amendment that "[o]ur Constitution is colorblind, and neither knows nor tolerates classes among citizens," *Plessy v. Ferguson*, 163 U.S. 537, 559 (1896) (Harlan, J., dissenting); *accord, Ex parte Virginia*, 100 U.S. 339, 345 (1880). . . . [522–24]. . . .

In my view, there is only one circumstance in which the States may act *by race* to "undo the effects of past discrimination:" where that is necessary to eliminate their own maintenance of a system of unlawful racial classification. If, for example, a state agency has a discriminatory pay scale compensating black employees in all positions at 20% less than their nonblack counterparts, it may assuredly promulgate an order raising the salaries of "all black employees" to eliminate the differential. *Cf. Bazemore v. Friday*, 478 U.S. 385, 395–396 (1986). This distinction explains our school desegregation cases, in which we have made plain that States and localities sometimes have an obligation to adopt race-conscious remedies. While there is no doubt that those cases have taken into account the continuing "effects" of previously mandated racial school assignment, we have held those effects to justify a race-conscious remedy only because we have concluded, in that context, that they perpetuate a "dual school system." We have stressed each school district's constitutional "duty to *dismantle* its dual system," and have found that "[e]ach instance of a failure or refusal to fulfill this affirmative duty *continues the violation* of the Fourteenth Amendment." *Columbus Bd. of Educ. v. Penick*, 443 U.S. 449, 458–59 (1979) (emphasis added). Concluding in this context that race-neutral efforts at "dismantling the state-imposed dual system" were so ineffective that they might "indicate a lack of good faith," *Green v. New Kent County Sch. Bd.*, 391 U.S. 430, 439 (1968); *see also* [525] *Raney v. Bd. of Educ. of Gould Sch. Dist.*, 391 U.S. 443 (1968), we have permitted, as part of the local authorities' "affirmative duty to disestablish the dual school system[s]," such voluntary (that is, non-court-ordered) measures as attendance zones drawn to achieve greater racial balance, and out-of-zone assignment by race for the same purpose. *McDaniel v. Barresi*, 402 U.S. 39, 40–41 (1971). While thus permitting the use of race to declassify racially classified students, teachers, and educational resources, however, we have also made it clear that the remedial power extends no further than the scope of the continuing constitutional violation. *See, e.g., Columbus Bd. of Educ. v. Penick, supra*, at 465; *Dayton Bd. of Educ. v. Brinkman*, 433 U.S. 406, 420 (1977); *Milliken v. Bradley*, 418 U.S. 717, 744 (1974); *Keyes v. Sch. Dist. No. 1, Denver, Colo.*, 413 U.S. 189, 213 (1973). And it is implicit in our cases that after the dual school system has been completely disestablished, the States may no longer assign students by race. *Cf. Pasadena City Bd. of Educ. v. Spangler*, 427 U.S. 424 (1976) (federal court may not require racial assignment in such circumstances). . . .

[526] A State can, of course, act "to undo the effects of past discrimination" in many permissible ways that do not involve classification by race. In the particular field of state contracting, for example, it may adopt a preference for small businesses, or even for new businesses—which would make it easier for those previously excluded by discrimination to enter the field. Such programs may well have racially disproportionate impact, but they are not based on race. And, of course, a State may "undo the effects of past discrimination" in the sense of giving the identified victim of state discrimination that which it wrongfully denied him—for example, giving to a previously rejected black applicant the job that, by reason of discrimination, had been awarded to a white applicant, even if this means terminating the latter's employment. In such a context, the white job-holder is not being selected for disadvantageous treatment because of his race, but because he was wrongfully awarded a job to which another is entitled. That is worlds apart from the system here, in which those to be disadvantaged are identified solely by race.

I agree with the Court's dictum that a fundamental distinction must be drawn between the effects of "societal" discrimination and the effects of "identified" discrimination, and that the situation would be different if Richmond's plan were "tailored" to identify those particular bidders who "suffered from the effects of past discrimination by the city or prime contractors." *Ante* at 507–508. In my view, however, the reason that would make a difference is not, as the Court states, that it would justify race-conscious action—*see, e.g., ante* at 504–506, 507–508—but rather that it would enable race-neutral remediation. Nothing prevents Richmond from according a contracting preference to identified victims of discrimination. While most of the beneficiaries might be black, neither the beneficiaries nor those disadvantaged by the preference would be identified *on the basis of their race.* In other words, far from justifying racial classification, identification [527] of actual victims of discrimination makes it less supportable than ever, because more obviously unneeded.

In his final book, Professor Bickel wrote:

> *[A] racial quota derogates the human dignity and individuality of all to whom it is applied; it is invidious in principle as well as in practice. Moreover, it can easily be turned against those it purports to help. The history of the racial quota is a history of subjugation, not beneficence. Its evil lies not in its name, but in its effects: a quota is a divider of society, a creator of castes, and it is all the worse for its racial base, especially in a society desperately striving for an equality that will make race irrelevant.*

Bickel, *The Morality of Consent*, at 133. Those statements are true and increasingly prophetic. Apart from their societal effects, however, which are "in the aggregate disastrous," *id.* at 134, it is important not to lose sight of the fact that even "benign" racial quotas have individual victims, whose very real injustice we ignore whenever we deny them enforcement of their right not to be disadvantaged on the basis of race. *Johnson v. Transportation Agency, Santa Clara County*, 480 U.S. 616, 677 (1987) (Scalia, J., dissenting). As Justice Douglas observed:

> *A DeFunis who is white is entitled to no advantage by virtue of that fact; nor is he subject to any disability, no matter what his race or color. Whatever his race, he had a constitutional right to have his application considered on its individual merits in a racially neutral manner.*

DeFunis v. Odegaard, 416 U.S. 312, 337 (1974) (dissenting opinion). When we depart from this American principle, we play with fire, and much more than an occasional DeFunis, Johnson, or Croson burns.

It is plainly true that, in our society, blacks have suffered discrimination immeasurably greater than any directed at other racial groups. But those who believe that racial preferences can help to "even the score" display, and reinforce, a manner of thinking by race that was the source of the injustice and that will, if it endures within our society, be the [528] source of more injustice still. The relevant proposition is not that it was blacks, or Jews, or Irish who were discriminated against, but that it was individual men and women, "created equal," who were discriminated against. And the relevant resolve is that that should never happen again. Racial preferences appear to "even the score" (in some small degree) only if one embraces the proposition that our society is appropriately viewed as divided into races, making it right that an injustice rendered in the past to a black man should be compensated for by discriminating against a white. Nothing is worth that embrace. Since blacks have been disproportionately disadvantaged by racial discrimination, any race-neutral remedial program aimed at the disadvantaged *as such* will have a disproportionately beneficial impact on blacks. Only such a program, and not one that operates on the basis of race, is in accord with the letter and the spirit of our Constitution.

SUPREME COURT OF THE UNITED STATES

551 U.S. 701

PARENTS INVOLVED IN COMMUNITY SCHOOLS
v. SEATTLE SCHOOL DISTRICT, NO. 1

CERTIORARI TO THE UNITED STATES COURT
OF APPEALS FOR THE NINTH CIRCUIT

MEREDITH EX REL. MCDONALD V. JEFFERSON COUNTY
BOARD OF EDUCATION

CERTIORARI TO THE UNITED STATES COURT
OF APPEALS FOR THE SIXTH CIRCUIT

NO. 05-908; NO. 05-915 ARGUED: DECEMBER 4,
2006–DECIDED: JUNE 28, 2007

[Note: in this decision, the Court rejected two school districts' use of race alone as a "tiebreaking" factor in allocating students to schools, when students' voluntary choices would lead to relatively racially homogeneous schools. The opinion of the Court, authored by Chief Justice Roberts, rejected the schools' use of race to promote diversity on narrow grounds, arguing that if promoting the educational goods of diversity is the goal, then a constitutionally valid plan must include other factors in addition to race to advance that goal. It thus did not exclude the use of race as a diversity factor in public schools' plans, but rejected the exclusive use of race as not narrowly tailored to the compelling educational interest of diversity. Roberts himself also rejected diversity as a state interest compelling enough to justify the use of race, but this part of his opinion was not joined by a majority of justices and hence does not constitute the Court's opinion. In this concurring opinion, Justice Thomas goes further than the opinion of the Court, asserting a near-absolute principle of color-blindness as a fundamental constitutional norm.]

Justice Thomas, concurring.

Today, the Court holds that state entities may not experiment with race-based means to achieve ends they deem socially desirable. I wholly concur in The Chief Justice's opinion. I write separately to address several of the contentions in Justice Breyer's dissent [hereinafter the dissent]. Contrary to the dissent's arguments, resegregation is not occurring in Seattle or Louisville; these school boards have no present interest in remedying past segregation; and these race-based student-assignment programs do not serve any compelling state interest. Accordingly, the plans are unconstitutional. Disfavoring a color-blind interpretation of the Constitution, the dissent would give school boards a free hand to make decisions on the basis of race—an approach reminiscent of that advocated by the segregationists in *Brown v. Board of Education*, 347 U.S. 483 (1954). This approach is just as wrong today as it was a half-century ago. . . .

. . . .

III

Most of the dissent's criticisms of today's result can be traced to its rejection of the color-blind Constitution. *See post* at 29. The dissent attempts to marginalize the notion of a color-blind Constitution by consigning it to me and Members of today's plurality. *See ibid.; see also post* at 61. But I am quite comfortable in the company I keep. My view of the Constitution is Justice Harlan's view in *Plessy*: "Our Constitution is color-blind, and neither knows nor tolerates classes among citizens." *Plessy v. Ferguson*, 163 U.S. 537, 559 (1896) (dissenting opinion). And my view was the rallying cry for the lawyers who litigated *Brown*. *See, e.g.*, Brief for Appellants in *Brown v. Board of Education*, O.T. 1953, Nos. 1, 2, and 4, p. 65 ("That the Constitution is color blind is our dedicated belief"); Brief for Appellants in *Brown v. Board of Education*, O.T. 1952, No. 1, p. 5 ("The Fourteenth Amendment precludes a state from imposing distinctions or classifications based upon race and color alone"); *see also In Memoriam: Honorable Thurgood Marshall*, Proceedings of the Bar and Officers of the Supreme Court of the United States X (1993) (remarks of Judge Motley) ("Marshall had a 'Bible' to which he turned during his most depressed moments. The 'Bible' would be known in the legal community as the first Mr. Justice Harlan's dissent in *Plessy v. Ferguson*, 163 U.S. 537, 552 (1896). I do not know of any opinion which buoyed Marshall more in his pre-Brown days . . .").

The dissent appears to pin its interpretation of the Equal Protection Clause to current societal practice and expectations, deference to local officials, likely practical consequences, and reliance on previous statements from this and other courts. Such a view was ascendant in this Court's jurisprudence for several decades. It first appeared in *Plessy*, where the Court asked whether a state law providing for segregated railway cars was "a reasonable regulation." 163 U.S. at 550. The Court deferred to local authorities in making its determination, noting that in inquiring into reasonableness "there must necessarily be a large discretion on the part of the legislature." *Ibid.* The Court likewise paid heed to societal practices, local expectations, and practical consequences by looking to "the established usages, customs and traditions of the people, and with a view to the promotion of their comfort, and the preservation of the public peace and good order." *Ibid.* Guided by these principles, the Court concluded: "[W]e cannot say that a law which authorizes or even requires the separation of the two races in public conveyances is unreasonable, or more obnoxious to the Fourteenth Amendment than the acts of Congress requiring separate schools for colored children in the District of Columbia." *Id.* at 550–551.

The segregationists in *Brown* embraced the arguments the Court endorsed in *Plessy*. Though *Brown* decisively rejected those arguments, today's dissent replicates them to a distressing extent. Thus, the dissent argues that "[e]ach plan embodies the results of local experience and community consultation." *Post* at 47. Similarly, the segregationists made repeated appeals to societal practice and expectation. *See, e.g.*, Brief for Appellees on Reargument in *Briggs v. Elliott*, O.T. 1953, No. 2, p. 76 ("[A] State has power to establish a school system which is capable of efficient administration, taking into account local problems and conditions"). The dissent argues that "weight [must be given] to a local school board's knowledge, expertise, and concerns," *post* at 48, and with equal vigor, the segregationists argued for deference to local authorities. *See, e.g.*, Brief for Kansas on Reargument in *Brown v. Board of Education*, O.T. 1953, No. 1, p. 14 ("We advocate only a concept of constitutional law that permits determinations of state and local policy to be made on state and local levels. We defend only the validity of the statute that enables the Topeka Board of Education to determine its own course"). The dissent argues that today's decision "threatens to substitute for present calm a disruptive round of race-related litigation," *post* at 2, and claims that today's decision "risks serious harm to the law and for the Nation," *post* at 65. The segregationists also relied upon the likely practical consequences of ending the state-imposed system of racial separation. *See, e.g.*, Brief for Appellees on Reargument in *Davis v. County School Board*, O.T. 1953, No. 3, p. 37 ("Yet a holding that school segregation by race violates the Constitution will result in upheaval in all of those places not now subject to Federal judicial scrutiny. This Court has made many decisions of widespread effect; none would affect more people more directly in more fundamental interests and, in fact, cause more chaos in local government than a reversal of the decision in this case"). And foreshadowing today's dissent, the segregationists most heavily relied upon judicial precedent. *See, e.g.*, Brief for Appellees on Reargument in *Briggs v. Elliott*, O.T. 1953, No. 2, p. 59 ("[I]t would be difficult indeed to find a case so favored by precedent as is the case for South Carolina here").

The similarities between the dissent's arguments and the segregationists' arguments do not stop there. Like the dissent, the segregationists repeatedly cautioned the Court to consider practicalities and not to embrace too theoretical a view of the Fourteenth Amendment. And just as the dissent argues that the need for these programs will lessen over time, the segregationists claimed that reliance on segregation was lessening and might eventually end.

What was wrong in 1954 cannot be right today. Whatever else the Court's rejection of the segregationists' arguments in *Brown* might have established, it certainly made clear that state and local governments cannot take from the Constitution a right to make decisions on the basis of race by adverse possession. The fact that state and local governments had been discriminating on the basis of race for a long time was irrelevant to the *Brown* Court. The fact that racial discrimination was preferable to the relevant communities was irrelevant to the *Brown* Court. And the fact that the state and local governments had relied on statements in this Court's opinions was irrelevant to the *Brown* Court. The same principles guide today's decision. None of the considerations trumpeted by the dissent is relevant to the constitutionality of the school boards' race-based plans because no contextual detail—or collection of contextual details, *post* at 2–22—can "provide refuge from the principle that under our Constitution, the government may not make distinctions on the basis of race." *Adarand*, 515 U.S. at 240 (Thomas, J., concurring in part and concurring in judgment).

In place of the color-blind Constitution, the dissent would permit measures to keep the races together and proscribe measures to keep the races apart. See *post* at 28–34, 64–65. Although no such distinction is apparent in the Fourteenth Amendment, the dissent would constitutionalize today's faddish social theories that embrace that distinction. The Constitution is not that malleable. Even if current social theories favor classroom racial engineering as necessary to "solve the problems at hand," *post* at 21, the Constitution enshrines principles independent of social theories. *See Plessy*, 163 U.S. at 559 (Harlan, J., dissenting) ("The white race deems itself to be the dominant race in this country. And so it is, in prestige, in achievements, in education, in wealth and in power. So, I doubt not, it will continue to be for all time. . . . But in view of the Constitution, in the eye of the law, there is in this country no superior, dominant, ruling class of citizens. . . . Our Constitution is color-blind, and neither knows nor tolerates classes among citizens"). Indeed, if our history has taught us anything, it has taught us to beware of elites bearing racial theories. *See, e.g.*, *Dred Scott v. Sandford*, 60 U.S. (19 How.) 393, 407 (1857) ("[T]hey [members of the "negro African race"] had no rights which the white man was bound to respect"). Can we really be sure that the racial theories that motivated *Dred Scott* and *Plessy* are a relic of the past or that future theories will be nothing but beneficent and progressive? That is a gamble I am unwilling to take, and it is one the Constitution does not allow.

* * *

The plans before us base school assignment decisions on students' race. Because "[o]ur Constitution is color-blind, and neither knows nor tolerates classes among citizens," such race based decisionmaking is unconstitutional. *Plessy*, *supra* at 559 (Harlan, J., dissenting). I concur in the Chief Justice's opinion so holding.

THE MORAL STATUS OF AFFIRMATIVE ACTION

—*Louis P. Pojman*—

"*A ruler who appoints any man to an office, when there is in his dominion another man better qualified for it, sins against God and against the State.*" (The Koran).

"[Affirmative action] is the meagerest recompense for centuries of unrelieved oppression." (Quoted by Shelby Steele as the justification for affirmative action.) . . .

DEFINITIONS

First let me define my terms:

Discrimination is simply judging one thing to differ from another on the basis of some criterion. "Discrimination" is essentially a good quality, having reference to our ability to make distinctions. As rational and moral agents we need to make proper distinctions. To be rational is to discriminate between good and bad arguments, and to think morally is to discriminate between reasons based on valid principles and those based on invalid ones. What needs to be distinguished is the difference between rational and moral discrimination on the one hand, and irrational and immoral discrimination on the other hand.

Prejudice is a discrimination based on irrelevant grounds. It may simply be an attitude which never surfaces in action, or it may cause prejudicial actions. A prejudicial discrimination in action is immoral if it denies someone a fair deal. So discrimination on the basis of race or sex where these are not relevant for job performance is unfair. Likewise, one may act prejudicially in applying a relevant criterion on insufficient grounds, as in the case where I apply the criterion of being a hard worker but then assume, on insufficient evidence, that the black man who applies for the job is not a hard worker.

There is a difference between *prejudice* and *bias*. Bias signifies a tendency towards one thing rather than another where the evidence is incomplete or based on non-moral factors. For example, you may have a bias towards blondes and I towards redheads. But prejudice is an attitude (or action) where unfairness is present—where one *should* know or do better, as in the case where I give people jobs simply because they are redheads. Bias implies ignorance or incomplete knowledge, whereas prejudice is deeper, involving a moral failure—usually a failure to pay attention to the evidence. But note that calling people racist or sexist without good evidence is also an act of prejudice. I call this form of prejudice "defamism," for it unfairly defames the victim. It is a contemporary version of McCarthyism.

From *Public Affairs Quarterly*, Vol. 6.2, April 1992 by Louis P. Pojman. Copyright © 1998 by North American Philosophical Publications. Reprinted by permission.

Equal opportunity is offering everyone a fair chance at the best positions that society has at its disposal. Only native aptitude and effort should be decisive in the outcome, not factors of race, sex, or special favors.

Affirmative action is the effort to rectify the injustice of the past by special policies. Put this way, it is Janus-faced or ambiguous, having both a backward-looking and a forward-looking feature. The backward-looking feature is its attempt to correct and compensate for past injustice. This aspect of affirmative action is strictly deontological. The forward-looking feature is its implicit ideal of a society free from prejudice; this is both deontological and utilitarian.

When we look at a social problem from a backward-looking perspective we need to determine who has committed or benefited from a wrongful or prejudicial act and to determine who deserves compensation for that act.

When we look at a social problem from a forward-looking perspective we need to determine what a just society (one free from prejudice) would look like and how to obtain that kind of society. The forward-looking aspect of affirmative action is paradoxically race-conscious, since it uses race to bring about a society which is not race-conscious, which is color-blind (in the morally relevant sense of this term).

It is also useful to distinguish two versions of affirmative action. *Weak affirmative action* involves such measures as the elimination of segregation (namely the idea of "separate but equal"), widespread advertisement to groups not previously represented in certain privileged positions, special scholarships for the disadvantaged classes (e.g., all the poor), using under-representation or a history of past discrimination as a tie breaker when candidates are relatively equal, and the like.

Strong affirmative action involves more positive steps to eliminate past injustice, such as reverse discrimination, hiring candidates on the basis of race and gender in order to reach equal or near equal results, proportionate representation in each area of society.

A BRIEF HISTORY OF AFFIRMATIVE ACTION

1. After a long legacy of egregious racial discrimination the forces of civil justice came to a head during the decade of 1954–1964. In the 1954 U.S. Supreme Court decision, *Brown v. Board of Education*, racial segregation was declared inherently and unjustly discriminatory, a violation of the constitutional right to equal protection, and in 1964 Congress passed the Civil Rights Act which banned all forms of racial discrimination.

During this time the goal of the Civil Rights Movement was equal opportunity. The thinking was that if only we could remove the hindrances to progress, invidious segregation, discriminatory laws, and irrational prejudice against blacks, we could free our country from the evils of past injustice and usher in a just society in which the grandchildren of the slave could play together and compete with the grandchildren of the slave owner. We were after a color-blind society in which every child had an equal chance to attain the highest positions based not on his skin color but on the quality of his credentials. In the early 60s when the idea of reverse discrimination was mentioned in civil rights groups, it was usually rejected as a new racism. The Executive Director of the NAACP, Roy Wilkins, stated this position unequivocally during congressional consideration of the 1964 civil rights law. "Our association has never been in favor of a quota system. We believe the quota system is unfair whether it is used for [blacks] or against [blacks]...[We] feel people ought to be hired because of their ability, irrespective of their color.... We want equality, equality of opportunity and employment on the basis of ability.

So the Civil Rights Act of 1964 was passed outlawing discrimination on the basis of race or sex.

> *Title VII, Section 703(a) Civil Rights Act of 1964: It shall be an unlawful practice for an employer (1) to fail or refuse to hire or to discharge any individual or otherwise to discriminate against any individual with respect to his compensation, terms, conditions, or privileges of employment, because of such individual's race, color, sex, or national origin; or*
>
> *(2) to limit, segregate, or classify his employees or applicants for employment in any way which would deprive or tend to deprive any individual of employment opportunities or otherwise adversely affect his status as an employee because of such individual's race, color, religion, sex, or national origin. [42 U.S.C.2000e-2(a)]*

. . . Nothing contained in this title shall be interpreted to require any employer to grant preferential treatment to any individual or to any group on account of an imbalance which may exist with respect to the total numbers or percentage of persons of any race . . . employed by any employer . . . in comparison with the total or percentage of persons of such race . . . in any community, State, section, or other areas, or in the available work force in any community, State, section, or other area. [42 U.S.C.2000e-2(j)]

The Civil Rights Act of 1964 espouses a meritocratic philosophy, calling for equal opportunity and prohibiting reverse discrimination as just another form of prejudice. The Voting Rights Act (1965) was passed and Jim Crow laws throughout the South were overturned. Schools were integrated and public accommodations opened to all. Branch Rickey's promotion of Jackie Robinson from the minor leagues in 1947 to play for the Brooklyn Dodgers was seen as the paradigm case of this kind of equal opportunity—the successful recruiting of a deserving person.

2. But it was soon noticed that the elimination of discriminatory laws was not producing the fully integrated society that leaders of the civil rights movement had envisioned. Eager to improve the situation, in 1965 President Johnson went beyond equal opportunity to affirmative action. He issued the famous Executive Order 11246 in which the Department of Labor was enjoined to issue government contracts with construction companies on the basis of race. That is, it would engage in reverse discrimination in order to make up for the evils of the past. He explained the act in terms of the shackled runner analogy.

Imagine a hundred yard dash in which one of the two runners has his legs shackled together. He has progressed ten yards, while the unshackled runner has gone fifty yards. How do they rectify the situation? Do they merely remove the shackles and allow the race to proceed? Then they could say that "equal opportunity" now prevailed. But one of the runners would still be forty yards ahead of the other. Would it not be the better part of justice to allow the previously shackled runner to make up the forty-yard gap; or to start the race all over again? That would be affirmative action towards equality. (President Lyndon Johnson, 1965, inaugurating the affirmative action policy of Executive Order 11246).

In 1967 President Johnson issued Executive Order 11375 extending affirmative action (henceforth "AA") to women. Note here that AA originates in the executive branch of government. Until the Kennedy-Hawkins Civil Rights Act of 1990, AA policy was never put to a vote or passed by Congress. Gradually, the benefits of AA were extended to Hispanics, native Americans, Asians, and handicapped people.

The phrase "An Equal Opportunity/Affirmative Action Employer" ("AA/EO") began to appear as official public policy. But few noticed an ambiguity in the notion of "AA" which could lead to a contradiction in juxtaposing it with "EO," for there are two types of AA. At first AA was interpreted as, what I have called, "weak affirmative action," in line with equal opportunity, signifying wider advertisement of positions, announcements that applications from blacks would be welcomed, active recruitment and hiring blacks (and women) over *equally* qualified men. While few liberals objected to these measures, some expressed fears of an impending slippery slope towards reverse discrimination.

However, except in professional sports—including those sponsored by universities—weak affirmative action was not working, so in the late 60s and early 70s a stronger version of affirmative action was embarked upon—one aimed at equal results, quotas (or "goals"—a euphemism for "quotas"). In *Swann v. Charlotte-Mecklenburg* (1971), regarding the busing of children out of their neighborhood . . . to promote integration, the Court, led by Justice Brennan, held that affirmative action was implied in *Brown* and was consistent with the Civil Rights Act of 1964. The NAACP now began to support reverse discrimination.

Thus began the search for minimally qualified blacks in college recruitment, hiring, and the like. Competence and excellence began to recede into second place as the quest for racial, ethnic, and gender diversity became the dominant goals. The slogan "We have to become race conscious in order to eliminate race consciousness" became the paradoxical justification for reverse discrimination.

3. In 1968 the Department of Labor ordered employers to engage in utilization studies as part of its policy of eliminating discrimination in the workplace. The office of Federal Contract Compliance of the U.S. Department of Labor (Executive Order 11246) stated that employers with a history of *underutilization* of

minorities and women were required to institute programs that went beyond passive nondiscrimination through deliberate efforts to identify people of "affected classes" for the purpose of advancing their employment. Many employers found it wise to adopt policies of preferential hiring in order to preempt expensive government suits.

Employers were to engage in "utilization analysis" of their present work force in order to develop "specific and result-oriented procedures": to which the employer commits *every good-faith effort* in order to provide "relief for members of an '*affected class*', who by virtue of past *discrimination* continue to suffer the present effects of that discrimination." This self-analysis is supposed to discover areas in which such affected classes are underused, considering their availability and skills. "*Goals and timetables* are to be developed to guide efforts to correct deficiencies in the employment of affected classes of people in each level and segment of the work force." Affirmative action also calls for "rigorous examination" of standards and criteria for job performance, not so as to "dilute necessary standards" but in order to ensure that "arbitrary and discriminatory employment practices are eliminated" and to eliminate unnecessary criteria which "have had the effect of eliminating women and minorities" either from selection or promotion.

4. In 1969 two important events occurred. (a) The Philadelphia Plan—The Department of Labor called for "goals and timetables" for recruiting minority workers. In Philadelphia area construction industries, where these companies were all-white, family-run businesses, the contractor's union took the case to court on the grounds that Title VII of the Civil Rights Act prohibits quotas. The Third Circuit Court of Appeals upheld the Labor Department, and the Supreme Court refused to hear it. This case became the basis of the EEOC's aggressive pursuit of "goals and timetables" in other business situations.

(b) In the Spring of 1969 James Forman disrupted the service of Riverside Church in New York City and issued the Black Manifesto to the American Churches, demanding that they pay blacks $500,000,000 in reparations. The argument of the Black Manifesto was that for three and a half centuries blacks in America have been "exploited and degraded, brutalized, killed and persecuted" by whites; that this was part of the persistent institutional patterns of first, legal slavery and then, legal discrimination and forced segregation: and that through slavery and discrimination whites had procured enormous wealth from black labor with little return to blacks. These facts were said to constitute grounds for reparations on a massive scale. The American churches were but the first institutions to be asked for reparations.

5. The Department of Labor issued guidelines in 1970 calling for hiring representatives of *underutilized* groups. "*Nondiscrimination* requires the elimination of all existing discriminatory conditions, whether purposeful or inadvertent. . . . Affirmative action requires . . . the employer to make additional efforts to recruit, employ and promote qualified members of groups formerly excluded" (HEW Executive Order 22346, 1972). In December of 1971 Guidelines were issued to eliminate underutilization of minorities, aiming at realignment of the job force at every level of society.

6. In *Griggs v. Duke Power Company* (1971) the Supreme Court interpreted Title VII of the Civil Rights Act as forbidding use of aptitude tests and high school diplomas in hiring personnel. These tests were deemed presumptively discriminatory, employers having the burden of proving such tests relevant to performance. The notion of *sufficiency* replaced that of excellence or best qualified, as it was realized (though not explicitly stated) that the goal of racial diversity required compromising the standards of competence.

7. In 1977, the EEOC called for and *expected* proportional representation of minorities in every area of work (including universities).

8. In 1978 the Supreme Court addressed the Bakke case. Alan Bakke had been denied admission to the University of California at Davis Medical School even though his test scores were higher than the sixteen blacks who were admitted under the affirmative action quota program. He sued the University of California and the U.S. Supreme Court ruled (*University of California v. Bakke*, July 28, 1978) in a 5 to 4 vote that reverse discrimination and quotas are illegal except (as Justice Powell put it) when engaged in for purposes of promoting diversity (interpreted as a means to extend free speech under the First Amendment) and restoring a situation where an institution has had a history of prejudicial discrimination. The decision was greeted with applause

from anti-AA quarters and dismay from pro-AA quarters. Ken Tollett lamented, "The affirmance of Bakke would mean the reversal of affirmative action: it would be an officially sanctioned signal to turn against blacks in this country.... Opposition to special minority admissions programs and affirmative action is anti-black.

But Tollett was wrong. The Bakke case only shifted the rhetoric from "quota" language to "goals and timetables" and "diversity" language. In the '80s affirmative action was alive and well, with preferential hiring, minority scholarships, and race norming prevailing in all walks of life. No other white who has been excluded from admission to college because of his race has ever won his case. In fact only a year later, Justice Brennan was to write in *U.S. Steel v. Weber* that prohibition of racial discrimination against "any individual" in Title VII of the Civil Rights Act did not apply to discrimination against whites.

9. Perhaps the last step in the drive towards equal results took place in the institutionalization of grading applicants by group-related standards, race norming. Race norming is widely practiced but most of the public is unaware of it, so let me explain it.

Imagine that four men come into a state employment office in order to apply for a job. One is black, one Hispanic, one Asian, and one white. They take the standard test (a version of the General Aptitude Test Battery or VG-GATB). All get a composite score of 300. None of them will ever see that score. Instead the numbers will be fed into a computer and the applicants' percentile ranking emerges. The scores are group-weighted. Blacks are measured against blacks, whites against whites, Hispanics against Hispanics. Since blacks characteristically do less well than other groups, the effect is to favor blacks. For example, a score of 300 as an accountant will give the black a percentile score of 87, a Hispanic a percentile score of 74 and a white or oriental a score of 47. The black will get the job as the accountant.

This is known as race norming. Until an anonymous governmental employee recently blew the whistle, this practice was kept a secret in several state employment services. Prof. Linda Gottfredson of the University of Delaware, one of the social scientists to expose this practice, has since had her funding cut off. In a recent letter to the *New York Times* she writes:

> One of America's best-kept secrets is that the Employment Service of the Department of Labor has unabashedly promulgated quotas. In 1981 the service recommended that state employment agencies adopt a race-conscious battery to avoid adverse impact when referring job applicants to employers.
>
> ... The score adjustments are not trivial. An unadjusted score that places a job applicant at the 15th percentile among whites would, after race-norming, typically place a black near the white 50th percentile. Likewise, unadjusted scores at the white 50th percentile would, after race-norming, typically place a black near the 85th percentile for white job applicants. ...[I]ts use by 40 states in the last decade belies the claim that Griggs did not lead to quotas. ...

ARGUMENTS FOR AFFIRMATIVE ACTION

Let us now survey the main arguments typically cited in the debate over affirmative action. I will briefly discuss seven arguments on each side of this issue.

1. Need for Role Models

This argument is straightforward. We all have need of role models, and it helps to know that others like us can be successful. We learn and are encouraged to strive for excellence by emulating our heroes and role models.

However, it is doubtful whether role models of one's own racial or sexual type are necessary for success. One of my heroes was Gandhi, an Indian Hindu, another was my grade school science teacher, one Miss DeVoe, and another was Martin Luther King. More important than having role models of one's own type is having genuinely good people, of whatever race or gender, to emulate. Furthermore, even if it is of some help to people with low self-esteem to gain encouragement from seeing others of their particular kind in leadership roles, it is doubtful whether this need is a sufficient condition to justify preferential hiring or reverse discrimination. What good is a role model who is inferior to other professors or business personnel? Excellence will rise to the top in a system of fair opportunity. Natural development of role models will come more slowly and more surely. Proponents of preferential policies simply lack the patience to let history take its own course.

2. The Need of Breaking the Stereotypes

Society may simply need to know that there are talented blacks and women, so that it does not automatically assign them lesser respect or status. We need to have unjustified stereotype beliefs replaced with more accurate ones about the talents of blacks and women. So we need to engage in preferential hiring of qualified minorities even when they are not the most qualified.

Again, the response is that hiring the less qualified is neither fair to those better qualified who are passed over nor an effective way of removing inaccurate stereotypes. If competence is accepted as the criterion for hiring, then it is unjust to override it for purposes of social engineering. Furthermore, if blacks or women are known to hold high positions simply because of reverse discrimination, then they will still lack the respect due to those of their rank. In New York City there is a saying among doctors, "Never go to a black physician under 40," referring to the fact that AA has affected the medical system during the past fifteen years. The police use "Quota Cops" and "Welfare Sergeants" to refer to those hired without passing the standardized tests. (In 1985 180 black and Hispanic policemen, who had failed a promotion test, were promoted anyway to the rank of sergeant.) The destruction of false stereotypes will come naturally as qualified blacks rise naturally in fair competition (or if it does not—then the stereotypes may be justified). Reverse discrimination sends the message home that the stereotypes are deserved—otherwise, why do these minorities need so much extra help?

3. Equal Results Argument

Some philosophers and social scientists hold that human nature is roughly identical, so that on a fair playing field the same proportion from every race and gender and ethnic group would attain to the highest positions in every area of endeavor. It would follow that any inequality of results itself is evidence for inequality of opportunity. John Arthur, in discussing an intelligence test, Test 21, puts the case this way.

> History is important when considering governmental rules like Test 21 because low scores by blacks can be traced in large measure to the legacy of slavery and racism: Segregation, poor schooling, exclusion from trade unions, malnutrition, and poverty have all played their roles. Unless one assumes that blacks are naturally less able to pass the test, the conclusion must be that the results are themselves socially and legally constructed, not a mere given for which law and society can claim no responsibility.

> The conclusion seems to be that genuine equality requires equal results. Obviously blacks have been treated unequally throughout U.S. history, and just as obviously the economic and psychological effects of that inequality linger to this day, showing up in lower income and poorer performance in school and on tests than whites achieve. Since we have no reason to believe that differences in performance can be explained by factors other than history, equal results are a good benchmark by which to measure progress made toward genuine equality.

The result of a just society should be equal numbers in proportion to each group in the work force.

However, Arthur fails even to consider studies that suggest that there are innate differences between races, sexes, and groups. If there are genetic differences in intelligence and temperament within families, why should we not expect such differences between racial groups and the two genders? Why should the evidence for this be completely discounted?

Perhaps some race or one gender is more intelligent in one way than another. At present we have only limited knowledge about genetic differences, but what we do have suggests some difference besides the obvious physiological traits. The proper use of this evidence is not to promote discriminatory policies but to be open to the possibility that innate differences may have led to an overrepresentation of certain groups in certain areas of endeavor. It seems that on average blacks have genetic endowments favoring them in the development of skills necessary for excellence in basketball.

Furthermore, on Arthur's logic, we should take aggressive AA against Asians and Jews since they are overrepresented in science, technology, and medicine. So that each group receives its fair share, we should ensure that 12 percent of U.S. philosophers are black, reduce the percentage of Jews from an estimated 15 percent to 2 percent—firing about 1,300 Jewish philosophers. The fact that Asians are producing 50 percent of Ph.D.'s in science and math and blacks less than 1 percent clearly shows, on this reasoning, that we are providing special secret advantages to Asians.

But why does society have to enter into this results game in the first place? Why do we have to decide whether all difference is environmental or genetic? Perhaps we should simply admit that we lack sufficient evidence to pronounce on these issues with any certainty—but if so, should we not be more modest in insisting on equal results? Here is a thought experiment. Take two families of different racial groups, Green and Blue. The Greens decide to have only two children, to spend all their resources on them, to give them the best education. The two Green kids respond well and end up with achievement test scores in the 99th percentile. The Blues fail to practice family planning. They have fifteen children. They can only afford two children, but lack of ability or whatever prevents them from keeping their family down. Now they need help for their large family. Why does society have to step in and help them? Society did not force them to have fifteen children. Suppose that the achievement scores of the fifteen children fall below the 25th percentile. They cannot compete with the Greens. But now enters AA. It says that it is society's fault that the Blue children are not as able as the Greens and that the Greens must pay extra taxes to enable the Blues to compete. No restraints are put on the Blues regarding family size. This seems unfair to the Greens. Should the Green children be made to bear responsibility for the consequences of the Blues' voluntary behavior?

My point is simply that Arthur needs to cast his net wider and recognize that demographics and childbearing and -rearing practices are crucial factors in achievement. People have to take some responsibility for their actions. The equal results argument (or axiom) misses a greater part of the picture.

4. The Compensation Argument

The argument goes like this: Blacks have been wronged and severely harmed by whites. Therefore white society should compensate blacks for the injury caused them. Reverse discrimination in terms of preferential hiring, contracts, and scholarships is a fitting way to compensate for the past wrongs.

This argument actually involves a distorted notion of compensation. Normally, we think of compensation as owed by a specific person A to another person B whom A has wronged in a specific way C. For example, if I have stolen your car and used it for a period of time to make business profits that would have gone to you, it is not enough that I return you car. I must pay you an amount reflecting your loss and my ability to pay. If I have only made $5,000 and only have $10,000 in assets, it would not be possible for you to collect $20,000 in damages—even though that is the amount of loss you have incurred.

Sometimes compensation is extended to groups of people who have been unjustly harmed by the greater society. For example, the U.S. government has compensated Japanese-Americans who were interred during the Second World War, and the West German government has paid reparations to the survivors of Nazi concentration camps. But here a specific people have been identified who were wronged in an identifiable way by the government of the nation in question.

On the face of it the demand by blacks for compensation does not fit the usual pattern. Perhaps Southern states with Jim Crow laws could be accused of unjustly harming blacks, but it is hard to see that the U.S. government was involved in doing so. Furthermore, it is not clear that all blacks were harmed in the same way or whether some were *unjustly* harmed or harmed more than poor whites and others (e.g., short people). Finally, even if identifiable blacks were harmed by identifiable social practices, it is not clear that most forms of affirmative action are appropriate to restore the situation. The usual practice of a financial payment seems more appropriate than giving a high-level job to someone unqualified or only minimally qualified, who, speculatively, might have been better qualified had he not been subject to racial discrimination. If John is the star tailback of our college team with a promising professional future, and I accidentally (but culpably) drive my pick-up truck over his legs, and so cripple him, John may be due compensation, but he is not due the tailback spot on the football team.

Still, there may be something intuitively compelling about compensating members of an oppressed group who are minimally qualified. Suppose that the Hatfields and the McCoys are enemy clans and some youths from the Hatfields go over and steal diamonds and gold from the McCoys, distributing it within the Hatfield economy. Even though we do not know which Hatfield youths did the stealing, we would want to restore the wealth, as far as possible, to the McCoys. One way might be to tax the Hatfields, but another might be to give preferential treatment in terms of scholarships and training programs and hiring to the McCoys.

This is perhaps the strongest argument for affirmative action, and it may well justify some weak versions of AA, but it is doubtful whether it is sufficient to justify strong versions with quotas and goals and timetables in skilled positions. There are at least two reasons for this. First, we have no way of knowing how many people of group G would have been at competence level L had the world been different. Secondly, the normal criterion of competence is a strong prima facie consideration when the most important positions are at stake. There are two reasons for this: (1) Society has given people expectations that if they attain certain levels of excellence they will be awarded appropriately and (2) filling the most important positions with the best qualified is the best way to insure efficiency in job-related areas and in society in general. These reasons are not absolutes. They can be overridden. But there is a strong presumption in their favor so that a burden of proof rests with those who would override them.

At this point we get into the problem of whether innocent non-blacks should have to pay a penalty in terms of preferential hiring of blacks. We turn to that argument.

5. Compensation from Those Who Innocently Benefited from Past Injustice

White males as innocent beneficiaries of unjust discrimination of blacks and women have no grounds for complaint when society seeks to rectify the tilted field. White males may be innocent of oppressing blacks and minorities (and women), but they have unjustly benefited from that oppression or discrimination. So it is perfectly proper that less qualified women and blacks be hired before them.

The operative principle is: He who knowingly and willingly benefits from a wrong must help pay for the wrong. Judith Jarvis Thomson puts it this way. "Many [white males] have been direct beneficiaries of policies which have downgraded blacks and women . . . and even those who did not directly benefit . . . had, at any rate, the advantage in the competition which comes of the confidence in one's full membership [in the community], and of one's right being recognized as a matter of course." That is, white males obtain advantages in self-respect and self-confidence deriving from a racist system that denies these to blacks and women.

Objection. As I noted in the previous section, compensation is normally individual and specific. If A harms B regarding x, B has a right to compensation from A in regards to x. If A steals B's car and wrecks it, A has an obligation to compensate B for the stolen car, but A's son has no obligation to compensate B. Furthermore, if A dies or disappears B has no moral right to claim that society compensate him for the stolen car—though if he has insurance, he can make such a claim to the insurance company. Sometimes a wrong cannot be compensated, and we just have to make the best of an imperfect world.

Suppose my parents, divining that I would grow up to have an unsurpassable desire to be a basketball player, bought an expensive growth hormone for me. Unfortunately, a neighbor stole it and gave it to little Lew Alcindor, who gained the extra 18 inches—my 18 inches—and shot up to an enviable 7 feet 2 inches. Alias Kareem Abdul Jabbar, he excelled in basketball, as I would have done had I had my proper dose.

Do I have a right to the millions of dollars that Jabbar made as a professional basketball player—the unjustly innocent beneficiary of my growth hormone? I have a right to something from the neighbor who stole the hormone, and it might be kind of Jabbar to give me free tickets to the Laker basketball games, and perhaps I should be remembered in his will. As far as I can see, however, he does not *owe* me anything, either legally or morally.

Suppose further that Lew Alcindor and I are in high school together and we are both qualified to play basketball, only he is far better than I. Do I deserve to start in his position because I would have been as good as he is had someone not cheated me as a child? Again, I think not. But if being the lucky beneficiary of wrongdoing does not entail that Alcindor (or the coach) owes me anything in regards to basketball, why should it be a reason to engage in preferential hiring in academic positions or highly coveted jobs? If minimal qualifications are not adequate to override excellence in basketball, even when the minimality is a consequence of wrongdoing, why should they be adequate in other areas?

6. The Diversity Argument

It is important that we learn to live in a pluralistic world, learning to get along with other races and cultures, so we should have fully integrated schools and employment situations. Diversity is an important symbol and educative device. Thus preferential treatment is warranted to perform this role in society.

But, again, while we can admit the value of diversity, it hardly seems adequate to override considerations of merit and efficiency. Diversity for diversity's sake is moral promiscuity, since it obfuscates rational distinctions, and unless those hired are highly qualified the diversity factor threatens to become a fetish. At least at the higher levels of business and the professions, competence far outweighs considerations of diversity. I do not care whether the group of surgeons operating on me reflect racial or gender balance, but I do care that they are highly qualified. And likewise with airplane pilots, military leaders, business executives, and, may I say it, teachers and professors. Moreover, there are other ways of learning about other cultures besides engaging in reverse discrimination.

7. Anti-Meritocratic (Desert) Argument to Justify Reverse Discrimination: "No One Deserves His Talents"

According to this argument, the competent do not deserve their intelligence, their superior character, their industriousness, or their discipline: thus they have no right to the best positions in society; therefore society is not unjust in giving these positions to less (but still minimally) qualified blacks and women. In one form this argument holds that since no one deserves anything, society may use any criteria it pleases to distribute goods. The criterion most often designated is social utility. Versions of this argument are found in the writings of John Arthur, John Rawls, Bernard Boxill, Michael Kinsley, Ronald Dworkin, and Richard Wasserstrom. Rawls writes, "No one deserves his place in the distribution of native endowments, any more than one deserves one's initial starting place in society. The assertion that a man deserves the superior character that enables him to make the effort to cultivate his abilities is equally problematic; for his character depends in large part upon fortunate family and social circumstances for which he can claim no credit. The notion of desert seems not to apply to these cases." Michael Kinsley is even more adamant:

> Opponents of affirmative action are hung up on a distinction that seems more profoundly irrelevant: treating individuals versus treating groups. What is the moral difference between dispensing favors to people on their "Merits" as individuals and passing out society's benefits on the basis of group identification?

> Group identifications like race and sex are, of course, immutable. They have nothing to do with a person's moral worth. But the same is true of most of what comes under the label "merit." The tools you need for getting ahead in a meritocratic society—not all of them but most: talent, education, instilled cultural values such as ambition—are distributed just as arbitrarily as skin color. They are fate. The notion that people somehow "deserve" the advantages of these characteristics in a way they don't "deserve" the advantage of their race is powerful, but illogical.

It will help to put the argument in outline form.

1. Society may award jobs and positions as it sees fit as long as individuals have no claim to these positions.

2. To have a claim to something means that one has earned it or deserves it.

3. But no one has earned or deserves his intelligence, talent, education or cultural values which produce superior qualifications.

4. If a person does not deserve what produces something, he does not deserve its products.

5. Therefore better qualified people do not deserve their qualifications.

6. Therefore, society may override their qualifications in awarding jobs and positions as it sees fit (for social utility or to compensate for previous wrongs).

So it is permissible if a minimally qualified black or woman is admitted to law or medical school ahead of a white male with excellent credentials or if a less qualified person from an "underutilized" group gets a professorship ahead of a far better qualified white male. Sufficiency and underutilization together outweigh excellence.

Objection. Premise 4 is false. To see this, reflect just because I do not deserve the money that I have been given as a gift (for instance) does not mean that I am not entitled to what I get with that money. If you and I both get with that money. If you and I both get a gift of $100 and I bury mine in the sand for five years while you invest yours wisely and double its value at the end of five years, I cannot complain that you should split the increase 50/50 since neither of us deserved the original gift. If we accept the notion of responsibility at all, we must hold that persons deserve the fruits of their labor and conscious choices. Of course, we might want to distinguish moral from legal desert and argue that, morally speaking, effort is more important than outcome, whereas, legally speaking, outcome may be more important. Nevertheless, there are good reasons in terms of efficiency, motivation, and rough justice for holding a strong prima facie principle of giving scarce high positions to those most competent.

The attack on moral desert is perhaps the most radical move that egalitarians like Rawls and company have made against meritocracy, but the ramifications of their attack are farreaching. The following are some of its implications. Since I do not deserve my two good eyes or two good kidneys, the social engineers may take one of each from me to give to those needing an eye or a kidney—even if they have damaged their organs by their own voluntary actions. Since no one deserves anything, we do not deserve pay for our labors or praise for a job well done or first prize in the race we win. The notion of moral responsibility vanishes in a system of leveling.

But there is not good reason to accept the argument against desert. We do act freely and, as such, we are responsible for our actions. We deserve the fruits of our labor, reward for our noble feats and punishment for our misbehavior.

We have considered seven arguments for affirmative action and have found no compelling case for strong AA and only one plausible argument (a version of the compensation argument) for weak AA. We must now turn to the arguments against affirmative action to see whether they fare any better.

ARGUMENTS AGAINST AFFIRMATIVE ACTION

1. Affirmative Action Requires Discrimination Against a Different Group

Weak affirmative action weakly discriminates against new minorities, mostly innocent young white males, and strong affirmative action strongly discriminates against these new minorities. . . . this discrimination is unwarranted, since, even if some compensation to blacks were indicated, it would be unfair to make innocent white males bear the whole brunt of the payments. In fact, it is poor white youth who become the new pariahs on the job market. The children of the wealthy have no trouble getting into the best private grammar schools and, on the basis of superior early education, into the best universities, graduate schools, managerial and professional positions. Affirmative action simply shifts injustice, setting blacks and women against young white males, especially ethnic and poor white males. It does little to rectify the goal of providing equal opportunity to all. If the goal is a society where everyone has a fair chance, then it would be better to concentrate on support for families and early education and decide the matter of university admissions and job hiring on the basis of traditional standards of competence.

2. Affirmative Action Perpetuates the Victimization Syndrome

Shelby Steele admits that affirmative action may seem "the meagerest recompense for centuries of unrelieved oppression" and that it helps promote diversity. At the same time, though, notes Steele, affirmative action reinforces the spirit of victimization by telling blacks that they can gain more by emphasizing their suffering, degradation, and helplessness than by discipline and work. This message holds the danger of blacks becoming permanently handicapped by a need for special treatment. It also sends to society at large the message that blacks cannot make it on their own.

Leon Wieseltier sums up the problem this way.

> *The memory of oppression is a pillar and a strut of the identity of every people oppressed. It is no ordinary marker of difference. It is unusually stiffening. It instructs the individual and the group about what to expect of the world, imparts an isolating sense of aptness. . . . Don't be fooled, it teaches, there is only repetition. For that reason, the collective memory of an oppressed people is not only a treasure but a trap.*

> *In the memory of oppression, oppression outlives itself. The scar does the work for the wound. That is the real tragedy: that injustice obtains the power to distort long after it has ceased to be real. It is a posthumous victory for the oppressors, when pain becomes a tradition. And yet the atrocities of the past must never be forgotten. This is the unfairly difficult dilemma of the newly emancipated and the newly enfranchised: An honorable life is not possible if they remember too little and a normal life is not possible if they remember too much.*

With the eye of recollection, which does not "remember too much," Steele recommends a policy that offers "educational and economic development of disadvantaged people regardless of race and the eradication from our society—through close monitoring and severe sanctions—of racial and gender discrimination.

3. Affirmative Action Encourages Mediocrity and Incompetence

Last spring Jesse Jackson joined protesters at Harvard Law School in demanding that the Law School faculty hire black women. Jackson dismissed Dean of the Law School Robert C. Clark's standard of choosing the best qualified person for the job as "cultural anemia." "We cannot just define who is qualified in the most narrow vertical, academic terms," he said. "Most people in the world are yellow, brown, black, poor, non-Christian and don't speak English, and they can't wait for some white males with archaic rules to appraise them." It might be noted that if Jackson is correct about the depth of cultural decadence at Harvard, blacks might be well advised to form and support their own more vital law schools and leave places like Harvard to their archaism.

At several universities, the administrations have forced departments to hire members of minorities even when far superior candidates were available. Shortly after obtaining my Ph.D in the late 70s I was mistakenly identified as a black philosopher (I had a civil rights record and was once a black studies major) and was flown to a major university, only to be rejected for a more qualified candidate when it [was] discovered that I was white.

Stories of the bad effects of affirmative action abound. The philosopher Sidney Hook writes that "At one Ivy League university, representatives of the Regional HEW demanded an explanation of why there were no women or minority students in the Graduate Department of Religious Studies. They were told that a reading knowledge of Hebrew and Greek was presupposed. Whereupon the representatives of HEW advised orally: 'Then end those old-fashioned programs that require irrelevant languages. And start up programs on relevant things which minority group students can study without learning languages.'"

Nicholas Capaldi notes that the staff of HEW itself was one-half women, three-fifths members of minorities, and one-half black—a clear case of racial over-representation.

In 1972 officials at Stanford University discovered a proposal for the government to monitor curriculum in higher education: the "Summary Statement . . . Sex Discrimination Proposed HEW Regulation to Effectuate Title IX of the Education Amendment of 1972" to "establish and use internal procedure for reviewing curricula, designed both to ensure that they do not reflect discrimination on the basis of sex and to resolve complaints concerning allegations of such discrimination, pursuant to procedural standards to be prescribed by the Director of the office of Civil Rights." Fortunately, Secretary of HEW Caspar Weinberger, when alerted to the intrusion, assured Stanford University that he would never approve of it.

Government programs of enforced preferential treatment tend to appeal to the lowest possible common denominator. Witness the 1974 HEW Revised Order No. 14 on Affirmative Action expectations for preferential hiring: "Neither minorities nor female employees should be required to possess higher qualifications than those of the lowest qualified incumbents."

Furthermore, no tests may be given to candidates unless it is *proved* to be relevant to the job.

> *No standard or criteria which have, by intent or effect, worked to exclude women or minorities as a class can be utilized, unless the institution can demonstrate the necessity of such standard to the performance of the job in question.*

> *Whenever a validity study is called for . . . an investigation of suitable selection procedures and suitable alternative methods of using the selection procedure which have as little adverse impact as possible. . . . Whenever the user is shown an alternative selection procedure with evidence of less adverse impact and substantial evidence of validity for the same job in similar circumstances, the user should investigate it to determine the appropriateness of using or validating it in accord with these guidelines.*

At the same time Americans are wondering why standards in our country are falling and the Japanese are getting ahead. Affirmative action with its twin idols, Sufficiency and Diversity, is the enemy of excellence. I will develop this thought below (IV.6.).

4. Affirmative Action Policies Unjustly Shift the Burden of Proof

Affirmative action legislation tends to place the burden of proof on the employer who does not have an "adequate" representation of "underutilized" groups in his work force. He is guilty until proven innocent. I have already recounted how in the mid-80s the Supreme Court shifted the burden of proof back onto the plaintiff, while Congress is now attempting to shift the burden back to the employer. Those in favor of deeming disproportional representation "guilty until proven innocent" argue that it is easy for employers to discriminate against minorities by various subterfuges, and I agree that steps should be taken to monitor against prejudicial treatment. But being prejudiced against employers is not the way to attain a just solution to discrimination. The principle: Innocent until proven guilty applies to employers as well as criminals. Indeed, it is clearly special pleading to reject this basic principle of Anglo-American law in this case of discrimination while adhering to it everywhere else.

5. An Argument from Merit

Traditionally, we have believed that the highest positions in society should be awarded to those who are best qualified—as the Koran states in the quotation at the beginning of this paper. Rewarding excellence both seems just to the individuals in the competition and makes for efficiency. Note that one of the most successful acts of integration, the recruitment of Jackie Robinson in the late 40s, was done in just this way, according to merit. If Robinson had been brought into the major league as a mediocre player or had batted .200 he would have been scorned and sent back to the minors where he belonged.

Merit is not an absolute value. There are times when it may be overridden for social goals, but there is a strong prima facie reason for awarding positions on its basis, and it should enjoy a weighty presumption in our social practices.

In a celebrated article Ronald Dworkin says that "Bakke had no case" because society did not owe Bakke anything. That may be, but then why does it owe anyone anything? Dworkin puts the matter in Utility terms, but if that is the case, society may owe Bakke a place at the University of California at Davis, for it seems a reasonable rule-utilitarian principle that achievement should be rewarded in society. We generally want the best to have the best positions, the best qualified candidate to win the political office, the most brilliant and competent scientist to be chosen for the most challenging research project, the best qualified pilots to become commercial pilots, only the best soldiers to become generals. Only when little is at stake do we weaken the standards and content ourselves with sufficiency (rather than excellence)—there are plenty of jobs where "sufficiency" rather than excellence is required. Perhaps we now feel that medicine or law or university professorships are so routine that they can be performed by minimally qualified people—in which case AA has a place.

But note, no one is calling for quotas or proportional representation of *underutilized* groups in the National Basketball Association where blacks make up 80 percent of the players. But if merit and merit alone reigns in sports, should it not be valued at least as much in education and industry?

6. The Slippery Slope

Even if strong AA or reverse discrimination could meet the other objections, it would face a tough question: Once you embark on this project, how do you limit it? Who should be excluded from reverse discrimination? Asians and Jews are over-represented, so if we give blacks positive quotas, should we place negative quotas on these other groups? Since white males, "WMs," are a minority which is suffering from reverse discrimination, will we need a new affirmative action policy in the twenty-first century to compensate for the discrimination against WMs in the late twentieth century?

Furthermore, affirmative action has stigmatized the *young* white male. Assuming that we accept reverse discrimination, the fair way to make sacrifices would be to retire *older* white males who are more likely to have benefited from a favored status. Probably the least guilty of any harm to minority groups is the young white male—usually a liberal who has been required to bear the brunt of ages of past injustice. Justice Brennan's announcement that the Civil Rights Act did not apply to discrimination against whites shows how the clearest language can be bent to serve the ideology of the moment.

7. The Mounting Evidence Against the Success of Affirmative Action

Thomas Sowell of the Hoover Institute has shown in his book *Preferential Policies: An International Perspective* that preferential hiring almost never solves social problems. It generally builds in mediocrity or incompetence and causes deep resentment. It is a short-term solution which lacks serious grounding in social realities.

For instance, Sowell cites some disturbing statistics on education. Although twice as many blacks as Asian students took the nationwide Scholastic Aptitude Test in 1983, approximately fifteen times as many Asian students scored above 700 (out of a possible 800) on the mathematics half of the SAT. The percentage of Asians who scored above 700 in math was also more than six times higher than the percentage of American Indians and more than ten times higher than that of Mexican Americans—as well as more than double the percentage of whites. As Sowell points out, in all countries studied, "intergroup performance disparities are huge"(108).

> There are dozens of American colleges and universities where the median combined verbal SAT score and mathematics SAT score total 1200 or above. As of 1983 there were fewer than 600 black students in the entire U.S. with combined SAT scores of 1200. This meant that, despite widespread attempts to get a black student "representation" comparable to the black percentage of the population (about 11 percent), there were not enough black students in the entire country for the Ivy League alone to have such a "representation" without going beyond the pool—even if the entire pool went to the eight Ivy League colleges.

Often it is claimed that a cultural bias is the cause of the poor performance of blacks on SATs (or IQ tests), but Sowell shows that these test scores are actually a better predictor of college performance for blacks than for Asians and whites. He also shows the harmfulness of the effect on blacks of preferential acceptance. At the University of California, Berkeley, where the freshman class closely reflects the actual ethnic distribution of California high school students, more than 70 percent of blacks fail to graduate. All 312 black students entering Berkeley in 1987 were admitted under "affirmative action" criteria rather than by meeting standard academic criteria. So were 480 out of 507 Hispanic students. In 1986 the median SAT score for blacks at Berkeley was 952, for Mexican Americans 1,014, for American Indians 1,082, and for Asian Americans 1,254. (The average SAT for all students was 1,181.)

The result of this mismatching is that blacks who might do well if they went to a second-tier or third-tier school where their test scores would indicate they belong, actually are harmed by preferential treatment. They cannot compete in the institutions where high abilities are necessary.

Sowell also points out that affirmative action policies have mainly assisted middle-class blacks, those who have suffered least from discrimination. "Black couples in which both husband and wife are college educated overtook white couples of the same description back in the early 1970s and continued to at least hold their own in the 1980s" (115).

Sowell's conclusion is that similar patterns of results obtained from India to the United States wherever preferential policies exist. "In education, preferential admissions policies have led to high attrition rates and substandard performances for those preferred students . . . who survived to graduate." In all countries the preferred tended to concentrate in less difficult subjects which lead to less remunerative careers. "In the employment market, both blacks and untouchables at the higher levels have advanced substantially while those at the lower levels show no such advancement and even some signs of retrogression. These patterns are also broadly consistent with patterns found in countries in which majorities have created preferences for themselves . . ." (116).

The tendency has been to focus at the high-level end of education and employment rather than on the lower level of family structure and early education. But if we really want to help the worst off improve, we need to concentrate on the family and early education. It is foolish to expect equal results when we begin with grossly unequal starting points—and discriminating against young white males is no more just than discriminating against women, blacks or anyone else.

CONCLUSION

Let me sum up. The goal of the Civil Rights movement and of moral people everywhere has been equal opportunity. The question is: How best to get there? Civil Rights legislation removed the legal barriers to equal opportunity, but did not tackle the deeper causes that produced differential results. Weak affirmative action aims at encouraging minorities in striving for the highest positions without unduly jeopardizing the rights of majorities, but the problem of weak affirmative action is that it easily slides into strong affirmative action where quotas, "goals," and equal results are forced into groups, thus promoting mediocrity, inefficiency, and resentment. Furthermore, affirmative action aims at the higher levels of society—universities and skilled jobs—yet if we want to improve our society, the best way to do it is to concentrate on families, children, early education, and the like. Affirmative action is, on the one hand, too much, too soon and on the other hand, too little, too late.

Martin Luther said that humanity is like a man mounting a horse who always tends to fall off on the other side of the horse. This seems to be the case with affirmative action. Attempting to redress the discriminatory iniquities of our history, our well-intentioned social engineers engage in new forms of discriminatory iniquity and thereby think that they have successfully mounted the horse of racial harmony. They have only fallen off on the other side of the issue.

CHAPTER 5

Sex Equality, Liberty, and the Law

SUPREME COURT OF THE UNITED STATES

477 U.S. 57

Meritor Savings Bank v. Vinson

Certiorari to the United States Court of Appeals for the District of Columbia Circuit

No. 84-1979 Argued: March 25, 1986–Decided: June 19, 1986

OPINION: [59] JUSTICE REHNQUIST delivered the opinion of the Court.

This case presents important questions concerning claims of workplace "sexual harassment" brought under Title VII of the Civil Rights Act of 1964, 78 Stat. 253, *as amended*, 42 U.S.C. § 2000e *et seq.*

I

In 1974, respondent Mechelle Vinson met Sidney Taylor, a vice-president of what is now petitioner Meritor Savings Bank (bank) and manager of one of its branch offices. When respondent asked whether she might obtain employment at the bank, Taylor gave her an application, which she completed and returned the next day; later that same day, Taylor called her to say that she had been hired. With Taylor as her supervisor, respondent started as a teller-trainee, and thereafter was promoted to teller, head teller, and assistant [60] branch manager. She worked at the same branch for four years, and it is undisputed that her advancement there was based on merit alone. In September, 1978, respondent notified Taylor that she was taking sick leave for an indefinite period. On November 1, 1978, the bank discharged her for excessive use of that leave.

Respondent brought this action against Taylor and the bank, claiming that, during her four years at the bank, she had "constantly been subjected to sexual harassment" by Taylor in violation of Title VII. She sought injunctive relief, compensatory and punitive damages against Taylor and the bank, and attorney's fees.

At the 11-day bench trial, the parties presented conflicting testimony about Taylor's behavior during respondent's employment. Respondent testified that, during her probationary period as a teller-trainee, Taylor treated her in a fatherly way and made no sexual advances. Shortly thereafter, however, he invited her out to dinner and, during the course of the meal, suggested that they go to a motel to have sexual relations. At first she refused, but out of what she described as fear of losing her job, she eventually agreed. According to respondent, Taylor thereafter made repeated demands upon her for sexual favors, usually at the branch, both during and after business hours; she estimated that over the next several years she had intercourse with him some 40 or 50 times. In addition, respondent testified that Taylor fondled her in front of other employees, followed her into the women's restroom when she went there alone, exposed himself to her, and even forcibly raped her on several occasions. These activities ceased after 1977, respondent stated, when she started going with a steady boyfriend.

Respondent also testified that Taylor touched and fondled other women employees of the bank, and she attempted to [61] call witnesses to support this charge. But while some supporting testimony apparently was admitted without objection, the District Court did not allow her "to present wholesale evidence of a pattern and practice relating to sexual advances to other female employees in her case in chief, but advised her that she might well be able to present such evidence in rebuttal to the defendants' cases." *Vinson v. Taylor*, 22 EPD ¶ 30,708, p. 14,693 n.1, 23 FEP Cases 37, 38–39 n.1 (DC 1980). Respondent did not offer such evidence in rebuttal. Finally, respondent testified that, because she was afraid of Taylor, she never reported his harassment to any of his supervisors and never attempted to use the bank's complaint procedure.

Taylor denied respondent's allegations of sexual activity.... The bank also denied respondent's allegations, and asserted that any sexual harassment by Taylor was unknown to the bank and engaged in without its consent or approval.

The District Court denied relief, but did not resolve the conflicting testimony about the existence of a sexual relationship between respondent and Taylor. It found instead that "[i]f [respondent] and Taylor did engage in an intimate or sexual relationship during the time of [respondent's] employment with [the bank], that relationship was a voluntary one having nothing to do with her continued employment at [the bank] or her advancement or promotions at that institution." *Id.* at 14,692, 23 FEP Cases at 42 (footnote omitted). The court ultimately found that respondent "was not the victim of sexual harassment and was not the victim of sexual discrimination" while employed at the bank. *Ibid.*, 23 FEP Cases at 43.

[62] . . . .

The Court of Appeals for the District of Columbia Circuit reversed. 243 U.S. App. D.C. 323, 753 F.2d 141 (1985). Relying on its earlier holding in *Bundy v. Jackson*, 205 U.S. App. D.C. 444, 641 F.2d 934 (1981), decided after the trial in this case, the court stated that a violation of Title VII may be predicated on either of two types of sexual harassment: harassment that involves the conditioning of concrete employment benefits on sexual favors, and harassment that, while not affecting economic benefits, creates a hostile or offensive working environment. The court drew additional support for this position from the Equal Employment Opportunity Commission's Guidelines on Discrimination Because of Sex, 29 C.F.R. § 1604.11(a) (1985), which set out these two types of sexual harassment claims. Believing that "Vinson's grievance was clearly of the [hostile environment] type," 243 U.S. App. D.C. at 327, 753 F.2d at 145, and that the District Court had not considered whether a violation of this type had occurred, the court concluded that a remand was necessary.   . . . [63] . . . .

II

Title VII of the Civil Rights Act of 1964 makes it "an unlawful employment practice for an employer . . . to discriminate against any individual with respect to his compensation, terms, conditions, or privileges of employment, because of such individual's race, color, religion, sex, or national origin." 42 U.S.C. § 2000e-2(a)(1). The prohibition against discrimination based on sex was added to Title VII at the last minute on the floor of the House of Representatives. 110 *Cong. Rec.* 2577–2584 (1964). . . . [T]he bill quickly passed as amended, and we are left with little legislative history to guide us in interpreting the Act's prohibition against discrimination based on "sex."

Respondent argues, and the Court of Appeals held, that unwelcome sexual advances that create an offensive or hostile working environment violate Title VII. Without question, when a supervisor sexually harasses a subordinate because of the subordinate's sex, that supervisor "discriminate[s]" on the basis of sex. Petitioner apparently does not challenge this proposition. It contends instead that, in prohibiting discrimination with respect to "compensation, terms, conditions, or privileges" of employment, Congress was concerned with what petitioner describes as "tangible loss" of "an economic character," not "purely psychological aspects of the workplace environment." Brief for Petitioner 30–31, 34. In support of this claim petitioner observes that, in both the legislative history of Title VII and this Court's Title VII decisions, the focus has been on tangible, economic barriers erected by discrimination.

We reject petitioner's view. First, the language of Title VII is not limited to "economic" or "tangible" discrimination. The phrase "terms, conditions, or privileges of employment" evinces a congressional intent " 'to strike at the entire spectrum of disparate treatment of men and women' " in employment. *Los Angeles Dept. of Water and Power v. Manhart*, 435 U.S. 702, 707 n.13 (1978), *quoting Sprogis v. United Air Lines, Inc.*, 444 F.2d 1194, 1198 (7th Cir. 1971). Petitioner has pointed to nothing in the Act to suggest that Congress contemplated the limitation urged here.

[65] Second, in 1980 the EEOC issued Guidelines specifying that "sexual harassment," as there defined, is a form of sex discrimination prohibited by Title VII. As an "administrative interpretation of the Act by the enforcing agency," *Griggs v. Duke Power Co.*, 401 U.S. 424, 433–434 (1971), these Guidelines, " 'while not controlling upon the courts by reason of their authority, do constitute a body of experience and informed judgment to which courts and litigants may properly resort for guidance,' " *General Electric Co. v. Gilbert*, 429 U.S. 125, 141–142 (1976), *quoting Skidmore v. Swift & Co.*, 323 U.S. 134, 140 (1944). The EEOC Guidelines fully support the view that harassment leading to noneconomic injury can violate Title VII.

In defining "sexual harassment," the Guidelines first describe the kinds of workplace conduct that may be actionable under Title VII. These include "[u]nwelcome sexual advances, requests for sexual favors, and other verbal or physical conduct of a sexual nature." 29 C.F.R. § 1604.11(a) (1985). Relevant to the charges at issue in this case, the Guidelines provide that such sexual misconduct constitutes prohibited "sexual harassment," whether or not it is directly linked to the grant or denial of an economic quid pro quo, where "such conduct has the purpose or effect of unreasonably interfering with an individual's work performance or creating an intimidating, hostile, or offensive working environment." § 1604.11(a)(3).

In concluding that so-called "hostile environment" (i.e., non quid pro quo) harassment violates Title VII, the EEOC drew upon a substantial body of judicial decisions and EEOC precedent holding that Title VII affords employees the right to work in an environment free from discriminatory intimidation, ridicule, and insult. *See generally* 45 Fed. Reg. 74676 (1980). *Rogers v. EEOC*, 454 F.2d 234 (5th Cir. 1971), *cert. denied*, 406 U.S. 957 (1972), was apparently the first case to recognize a cause of action based upon a discriminatory work environment. In *Rogers*, the Court of Appeals for the Fifth [66] Circuit held that a Hispanic complainant could establish a Title VII violation by demonstrating that her employer created an offensive work environment for employees by giving discriminatory service to its Hispanic clientele. The court explained that an employee's protections under Title VII extend beyond the economic aspects of employment:

> [T]he phrase "terms, conditions or privileges of employment" in [Title VII] is an expansive concept which sweeps within its protective ambit the practice of creating a working environment heavily charged with ethnic or racial discrimination. . . . One can readily envision working environments so heavily polluted with discrimination as to destroy completely the emotional and psychological stability of minority group workers. . . .

454 F.2d at 238. Courts applied this principle to harassment based on race, *e.g., Firefighters Inst. for Racial Equal. v. St. Louis*, 549 F.2d 506, 514–515 (8th Cir.), *cert. denied sub nom. Banta v. United States*, 434 U.S. 819 (1977); *Gray v. Greyhound Lines, East*, 178 U.S. App. D.C. 91, 98, 545 F.2d 169, 176 (1976), religion, *e.g., Compston v. Borden, Inc.*, 424 F. Supp. 157 (S.D. Ohio 1976), and national origin, *e.g., Cariddi v. Kansas City Chiefs Football Club*, 568 F.2d 87, 88 (8th Cir. 1977). Nothing in Title VII suggests that a hostile environment based on discriminatory sexual harassment should not be likewise prohibited. The Guidelines thus appropriately drew from, and were fully consistent with, the existing case law.

Since the Guidelines were issued, courts have uniformly held, and we agree, that a plaintiff may establish a violation of Title VII by proving that discrimination based on sex has created a hostile or abusive work environment. As the Court of Appeals for the Eleventh Circuit wrote in *Henson v. Dundee*, 682 F.2d 897, 902 (1982):

[67]   *Sexual harassment which creates a hostile or offensive environment for members of one sex is every bit the arbitrary barrier to sexual equality at the workplace that racial harassment is to racial equality. Surely, a requirement that a man or woman run a gauntlet of sexual abuse in return for the privilege of being allowed to work and make a living can be as demeaning and disconcerting as the harshest of racial epithets.*

Accord, *Katz v. Dole*, 709 F.2d 251, 254–255 (4th Cir. 1983); *Bundy v. Jackson*, 205 U.S. App. D.C. at 444–454, 641 F.2d at 934–944; *Zabkowicz v. W. Bend Co.*, 589 F. Supp. 780 (E.D. Wis. 1984).

Of course, as the courts in both *Rogers* and *Henson* recognized, not all workplace conduct that may be described as "harassment" affects a "term, condition, or privilege" of employment within the meaning of Title VII. See *Rogers v. EEOC*, *supra*, at 238 ("mere utterance of an ethnic or racial epithet which engenders offensive feelings in an employee" would not affect the conditions of employment to sufficiently significant degree to violate Title VII); *Henson*, 682 F.2d at 904 (quoting same). For sexual harassment to be actionable, it must be sufficiently severe or pervasive "to alter the conditions of [the victim's] employment and create an abusive working environment." *Ibid.* Respondent's allegations in this case—which include not only pervasive harassment but also criminal conduct of the most serious nature—are plainly sufficient to state a claim for "hostile environment" sexual harassment.

The question remains, however, whether the District Court's ultimate finding that respondent "was not the victim of sexual harassment," 22 EPD ¶ 30,708, at 14,692–14,693, 23 FEP Cases at 43, effectively disposed of respondent's claim. The Court of Appeals recognized, we think correctly, that this ultimate finding was likely based on one or both of two erroneous views of the law. First, the District Court apparently believed that a claim for sexual harassment will not lie [68] absent an *economic* effect on the complainant's employment. See *ibid.* ("It is without question that sexual harassment of female employees in which they are asked or required to submit to sexual demands as a *condition to obtain employment or to maintain employment or to obtain promotions* falls within protection of Title VII") (emphasis added). Since it appears that the District Court made its findings without ever considering the "hostile environment" theory of sexual harassment, the Court of Appeals' decision to remand was correct.

Second, the District Court's conclusion that no actionable harassment occurred might have rested on its earlier "finding" that "[i]f [respondent] and Taylor did engage in an intimate or sexual relationship . . . that relationship was a voluntary one." *Id.* at 14,692, 23 FEP Cases at 42. But the fact that sex-related conduct was "voluntary," in the sense that the complainant was not forced to participate against her will, is not a defense to a sexual harassment suit brought under Title VII. The gravamen of any sexual harassment claim is that the alleged sexual advances were "unwelcome." 29 C.F.R. § 1604.11(a) (1985). . . . The correct inquiry is whether respondent, by her conduct, indicated that the alleged sexual advances were unwelcome, not whether her actual participation in sexual intercourse was voluntary.

Petitioner contends that even if this case must be remanded to the District Court, the Court of Appeals erred in one of the terms of its remand. Specifically, the Court of Appeals stated that testimony about respondent's "dress and personal fantasies," 243 U.S. App. D.C. at 328 n.36, 753 F.2d at 146 n.36, which the District Court apparently admitted [69] into evidence, "had no place in this litigation." *Ibid.* The apparent ground for this conclusion was that respondent's voluntariness vel non in submitting to Taylor's advances was immaterial to her sexual harassment claim. While "voluntariness" in the sense of consent is not a defense to such a claim, it does not follow that a complainant's sexually provocative speech or dress is irrelevant as a matter of law in determining whether he or she found particular sexual advances unwelcome. To the contrary, such evidence is obviously relevant. The EEOC Guidelines emphasize that the trier of fact must determine the existence of sexual harassment in light of "the record as a whole" and "the totality of circumstances, such as the nature of the sexual advances and the context in which the alleged incidents occurred." 29 C.F.R. § 1604.11(b) (1985). . . . While the District Court must carefully weigh the applicable considerations in deciding whether to admit evidence of this kind, there is no per se rule against its admissibility.

. . . [70–73] . . . .

IV

In sum, we hold that a claim of "hostile environment" sex discrimination is actionable under Title VII, that the District Court's findings were insufficient to dispose of respondent's hostile environment claim, and that the District Court did not err in admitting testimony about respondent's sexually provocative speech and dress. As to employer liability, we conclude that the Court of Appeals was wrong to entirely disregard agency principles and impose absolute liability on employers for the acts of their supervisors, regardless of the circumstances of a particular case.

Accordingly, the judgment of the Court of Appeals reversing the judgment of the District Court is affirmed, and the case is remanded for further proceedings consistent with this opinion.

It is so ordered.

SEXUAL HARASSMENT OF WORKING WOMEN

A CASE OF SEX DISCRIMINATION

—*Catharine A. MacKinnon*—

SEXUAL HARASSMENT AS SEX DISCRIMINATION: AN INEQUALITY ARGUMENT

Practices which express and reinforce the social inequality of women to men are clear cases of sex-based discrimination in the *inequality* approach. Sexual harassment of working women is argued to be employment discrimination based on gender where gender is defined as the social meaning of sexual biology. Women are sexually harassed by men because they are women, that is, because of the social meaning of female sexuality, here, in the employment context. Three kinds of arguments support and illustrate this position: first, the exchange of sex for survival has historically assured women's economic dependence and inferiority as well as sexual availability to men. Second, sexual harassment expresses the male sex-role pattern of coercive sexual initiation toward women, often in vicious and unwanted ways. Third, women's sexuality largely defines women as women in this society, so violations of it are abuses of women as women.

Tradition

Sexual harassment perpetuates the interlocked structure by which women have been kept sexually in thrall to men and at the bottom of the labor market. Two forces of American society converge: men's control over women's sexuality and capital's control over employees' work lives. Women historically have been required to exchange sexual services for material survival, in one form or another. Prostitution and marriage as well as sexual harassment in different ways institutionalize this arrangement.

The impact of these forces, which affect all women, often varies by class. Exclusion of moderately well-off women (that is, women attached to moderately well-off men) from most gainful occupations was often excused by fears that virtuous women would fall victim to sexual predators if they were allowed to work. This exclusion, however, insured their dependence for survival upon bartering attractiveness and sexuality for subsistence, only from different men. Deprived of education and training in marketable skills, excluded from most professions, and disdaining as unsuitable the menial work reserved for their lower-class sisters, such women's adequacy was traditionally measured in large part by sexual allure. As they entered the paid labor force in increasing numbers, the sexual standard they were judged by accompanied them; the class status they held as adjuncts to middle-class men did not. Working-class and poor women did not have the choice between the home and the workplace. And they have always maintained an even more precarious hold on jobs than their male counterparts, with chronically lower wages, and usually without security or the requisites to claim advancement. Because they were women, these factors put them at the mercy of the employer sexually as well as economically. Once in the work force, usually in women's jobs, the class distinctions among women were qualified by their common circumstance, which was sex defined. "Sometimes the employer's son, or the master himself, or the senior stablehand, would have taken them. Men didn't always use brute force, the physical coercion or the threat of it that is the standard definition of rape. Often the threat of dismissal was sufficient." . . .

The generality of "women" and "men" must be qualified by recognizing the distinctive effect of race. Racism does not allow black men to share white men's dominance of economic resources. Black women have not tended to be economically dependent upon black men to the degree white women have been upon white men. To the extent black women are employed by white men, as most have been from slavery until the present, the foregoing analysis applies directly to them, intensified, not undercut, by race. . . .

Similar to the way in which the status of American blacks of both sexes encompasses personal and economic exploitation, sexual harassment deprives women of personhood by relegating them to subservience through jointly exploiting their sexuality and their work. As women begin to achieve the minimum material conditions under which equality with men can concretely be envisioned, and increasingly consider their skills worth a wage and their dignity worth defending, the necessity to exchange sex for support becomes increasingly intolerable. It is a reminder of that image of a deprived reality in which sexuality and attractiveness to men were all a woman had to offer—and she had very little control over either. The history of the role of sexuality in enforcing women's second-class economic status, sketched only very briefly here, makes sexual requirements of work "uniquely disturbing to women."

> It is a reminder, a badge or indicia [sic] of the servile status she suffered . . . and which she is now trying to shake off. . . . To make her advancement on the job depend on her sexual performance is to resurrect her former status as man's property or plaything.

But is such status really a thing of the past? The sexual harassment cases and evidence suggest that it is not. . . .

A guarantee against discrimination "because of sex" has little meaning if a major traditional dynamic of enforcement and expression of inferior sex status is allowed to persist untouched. A guarantee of equal access to job training, education, and skills has little substance if a requirement of equality in hiring, promotion, and pay can legally be withheld if a woman refuses to grant sexual favors. A man who is allowed to measure a woman's work by sexual standards cannot be said to employ her on the basis of merit. If a woman must grant sexual consideration to her boss in exchange for employment benefits, her material status still depends upon her sexual performance, and the legal promise of equality for women is an illusion.

Sex Roles

In *Stanton v. Stanton*, the Supreme Court spoke of the "role-typing society has long imposed" on the basis of sex. Congress effectively recognized the unsuitability of sex-based social role distinctions as they deprive women of economic opportunities in the original enactment and later extension and strengthening of Title VII, the federal contract compliance provisions, and in the Congressional passage of the Equal Pay Act and Equal Rights Amendment. No difference between the sexes was considered to justify the inferior economic status women were found to occupy throughout the economy, a status which sexual harassment exploits and promotes. In the vast and growing scholarly literature investigating social role differentiation by sex in America, dominance and aggressiveness are found to characterize the ideal of "masculinity" in general and in sexual relations. Women's sex roles define the feminine ideal in general and in-sex as submissive, passive, and receptive to male initiative. A major substantive element in the social meaning of masculinity, what men learn makes them "a man," is sexual conquest of women; in turn, women's femininity is defined in terms of acquiescence to male sexual advances. Social expectations, backed by a variety of sanctions ranging from rape to job reprisals to guilt manipulation, enforce these models by which both sexes learn to act out, and thereby become, the sex they are assigned. The inequality in the description is apparent: women are conditioned to become, and to think of themselves as, the proper subordinates of men, who learn to define their male identity partly in terms of their prowess in sexually dominating women. Some men are beginning to consider that this aspect of male identity not only systematically oppresses women, but, as it aggrandizes men's power, restricts their humanity.

Sexual harassment is discrimination "based on sex" within the social meaning of sex, as the concept is socially incarnated in sex roles. Pervasive and "accepted" as they are, these rigid roles have no place in the allocation of social and economic resources. If they are allowed to persist in these spheres, economic equality for women is impossible. The "sex stereotype" comes the closest to capturing the sex role argument in legal form. In the sexual harassment cases, some plaintiffs' attorneys have urged it as a theory for prohibiting sexual harassment under Title VII. Difficult as it is to criticize one of the few concepts available, the sex stereotype is ill-suited to the requisite analysis of sexual harassment.

A claim that a practice is discriminatory because it is based upon a sex stereotype is grounded either upon an argument that the stereotype is not, in general, true (hence practices based upon it are arbitrary), or upon an individual woman's claim to be an exception or potential exception to what *is* generally true of women. The concept essentially addresses the use of false images of women in employment. Accordingly, it is useful for attacking sexualized job descriptions and work-related conceptions. It also helps to rebut the misconception that women enjoy sexual harassment, were a kind of "consent" defense to arise. In a sense, a sex stereotype is present in the male attitude, expressed through sexual harassment, that women are sexual beings whose privacy and integrity can be invaded at will, beings who exist for men's sexual stimulation or gratification. The strength of the argument is that it allows men to be considered sincere, if wrong, in their treatment of women according to long accepted, if inappropriate, norms. But as an affirmative argument—that is, that sexual harassment is treatment based on sex because it is treatment based upon a sex stereotype—the argument is unfortunately incomplete.

The sex stereotype concept locates the overgeneralization, the distortion which is the substance of the injury of stereotyping, on the level of *image*, when the injury of sexual harassment is both on the level of image and on the level of reality. In the context of employment, sexual harassment is plainly an arbitrary practice. But it is not only or even fundamentally arbitrariness—in the sense of a divergence between a reality and a behavior purported to be based upon it—that is damaging to women about the practice. To the extent sexual harassment converges with, and mirrors, the accepted social reality of sexual relations, it corresponds to the real social meaning of the sex difference. It does not diverge from or distort this reality. To the extent sexual harassment reflects real social differences between the sexes, it is not arbitrary. If the social meaning of sexuality is accepted, sexual harassment can be seen as a differentiation in treatment due to the social realities of sex.

That is, it is the social reality of sexual relations, as expressed in sexual harassment, that "normally" and every day sexually oppresses women in order to affirm male sexual identity, as socially defined. This reality of treatment, which is the reference point for the argument of stereotyping that the practice is sex-based, is no false picture or illusion. These social relations themselves are shaped by an arguably false but, nevertheless, socially controlling image of relations between women and men. Thus, sexual harassment forms an integral part of the social stereotyping of all women as sexual objects and each individual grievant is but one example of it. So how does the practice lack a "factual basis"? To what true generalization about women is a sexually harassed woman "an exception"? For a heterosexual male so inclined, it is true, not illusory, that only a woman qualifies as the object of sexual harassment, just as for a white racist only a black qualifies as the object of racial harassment. This is true not because of a stereotype from which an exceptional woman might except herself, but because of the pervasively stereotyped social reality women live in.

Diaz v. Pan American World Airways, the leading confrontation between the BFOQ and the sex stereotype, reveals the structure and limitations of the approach. In *Diaz*, a male applicant for a flight attendant position was rejected because the airlines considered only women. They had found women were, on the average, better at performing "the non-mechanical aspects of the job." Passengers preferred being served by women; women were better at reassuring anxious passengers in the flight cabin environment; sex was found the best predictor of these occupational qualities. Sex was therefore, the airlines argued, a BFOQ. The Court of Appeals disagreed. Passenger preference, if as alleged, exemplified "to a large extent, [the] very prejudices the Act was meant to overcome." Only when customer preference is based upon "the company's inability to perform the primary function or service it offers," here safely transporting passengers from one place to another, can it ground a BFOQ. Pan American could not fail to consider all males simply because most males may not adequately reassure passengers. Moreover, "we do not agree that in this case 'all or substantially all men' have been shown to be inadequate." While the ability of individuals to perform the nonmechanical functions of the job could be taken into consideration, sex averaging was not allowed. Presumably, if some abilities were job-related and more women than men applicants exhibited them through a validated predictor, and were therefore hired, a "disparate impact" by sex would be allowed.

One imagines the real situation in *Diaz* as follows. Due to social conditioning, women as a group probably are more supportive toward anxious others; both sexes have learned to accept nurturance and support more readily from women than from men. More basically, stewardesses were preferred because of their sex appeal to male customers who command the financial power to enforce their preferences. That this is economic reality makes it no less sexist, especially since women's corresponding lack of economic power gives them little choice. Stewardesses were originally conceived in part for their qualities as sex objects. Until recently, they had to be unmarried, meet height and weight requirements, and could not wear glasses. These requirements, along with the often provocative dress required, primarily "reassure" men of women's sexual attractiveness to them. The airline did not openly argue that an inseparable part of the stewardess job definition was to look sexy. Would this have presented a sex stereotype in the sense of lacking "factual basis," or would it have been a reality, based upon the fact that women's sexual attractiveness sells tickets in a market within which airlines otherwise lack distinguishing characteristics? What if, in the *Harvard Law Review*'s felicitous legalism, it is argued that "the function of sexual allure cannot be separated from the nonsexual functions of the position without substantial loss of effectiveness." Is sex then a BFOQ?

What would have been the result if a woman with appropriate qualifications who applied for any job with the airlines complained of sex discrimination because she was trained as a stewardess instead of as a pilot? Suppose the airlines claimed sex as a BFOQ for both positions: men are more reassuring to passengers as pilots, women are more reassuring as stewardesses; the more mechanical aspects of the pilot's job utilize male advantages while the nonmechanical aspects give women advantages as stewardesses. There is no sex discrimination. Pan American provides jobs for both sexes—just different jobs, the jobs for which the social experience of each sex best qualifies them. This is merely an extension to the question of justification of the "separate but equal" picture of actuarial selection in *Gilbert*, although the results are just as dramatically unequal. The parallel would be even closer if the airlines argued that the cockpits and instrument panels of planes were arranged according to the size of the average man, and it would cost too much to change them to accommodate the smaller height and length of extremities of the average woman. Even the solution of hiring only those women who fit planes built to male specifications, a solution for a few, only serves to highlight which sex sets the standard.

Sexuality

Sexual harassment is discrimination "based on sex" in the inequality approach because women are socially defined as women largely in sexual terms. The behaviors to which women are subjected in sexual harassment are behaviors specifically defined and directed toward the characteristics which define women's sexuality: secondary sex characteristics and sex-role behavior. It is no accident that the English language uses the term *sex* ambiguously to refer both to gender status (as in "the female sex") and to the activity of intercourse (as in "to have sex"). The term *sexual* is used in both senses. . . .

As a critical convergence of the physiological, psychological, social, economic, cultural and aesthetic, and political forces, sexuality is overburdened with determinants. Gender itself is largely defined in terms of sexuality in that heterosexuality is closely bound up with the social conceptions of maleness and femaleness.

Woman's sexuality is a major medium through which gender identity and gender status are socially expressed and experienced. An attack upon sexuality is an attack upon womanhood. A deprivation in employment worked through women's sexuality is a deprivation in employment because one is a woman, through one of the closest referents by which women are socially identified as such, by themselves and by men. Only women, and (as is not the case with pregnancy) all women possess female sexuality,* the focus, occasion, and vehicle for this form of employment deprivation. Few men would maintain that they would have found a given woman just as ready or appropriate a target for sexual advances if she had been sexually male. Indeed, the close association between sexuality and gender identity makes it hard to imagine that a woman would be sexually the same if male. If any practice could be said to happen to a woman because she is a woman, sexual harassment should be one of the more straightforward examples of it.

How the law will conceptualize sexuality on closer consideration is an open question. The question is whether a gender comparison requires that sex characteristics be equivalent or whether it is sufficient that they are analogous. That is, must the sexes possess the same characteristic in order to be considered comparable, or is it enough that each has a corresponding version of its own? Presuming the law's narrow definition of "sex" as "gender," with the implicit heterosexual referent in practice, at least three possible legal approaches come to mind. First, the sexuality of women vis-à-vis men could be considered an aspect of "gender *per se.*" Discrimination "because of sexuality" would be merged with, and subsumed under, discrimination "because of sex." This could be more or less a social or a biological conception, depending upon the understanding of the determinants of sexuality and gender. Second, sexuality could be construed analytically as a variable "other than gender *per se*" as to which the sexes could be compared. Women and men each possess sexuality, so differential treatment with regard to sexuality could be sex discrimination. In a closely related argument, sexuality as in sexual harassment might be considered "other than gender *per se,*" but a "practice," not a status. This approach allows a "pattern or practice" concerning sexuality, as for any other variable, to be alleged to be discriminatory on the basis of the conformity of the practice with gender categories. Such a disparity by gender would produce discrimination "in effect" in that sexual harassment, if allowed, would have a disparate impact upon women as a gender/sexual group. Third, sexuality could be deemed an aspect of "gender *per se,*" but the sexuality of males and females could be considered unique to each sex, as pregnancy was unique to women in the *Gilbert* case. Adverse judgments based upon sexuality would not, in this approach, be sex discrimination because no comparison of unique attributes is possible.

Courts' treatment of women's sexuality in a discrimination context, although rare and backhanded, provides glimpses of some judicial preconceptions and hints at possible resolutions. Women's sexuality has occasionally, if implicitly, been used in attempts to exclude women as a gender group from employment opportunities. In *Eslinger v. Thomas,* the plaintiff successfully challenged an attempt to restrict women's access to jobs by presuming that women might be thought to be sexually used on those jobs. The South Carolina Senate did not hire women as pages. Citing the "public image" of the Senate and its members as the reason, the Senate resolved that the duties of pages—running personal errands, chauffeuring, packing bags, cashing checks, etc.—were "not suitable under existing circumstances for young ladies and may give rise to the appearance of impropriety." The senators' brief argued that the exclusion of women fostered "public confidence" and "avoided placing its employees in a conceivably damaging position, protecting itself from appearing to the public that an innocent relationship is not so innocent."

The Court of Appeals found no fair and substantial relation between the object of the legislation—combatting the appearance of impropriety—and the ground of difference—sex—upon which the classification rested. It adopted an analysis that captured the sexualization of women as a gender:

> On the one hand, the female is viewed as a pure, delicate and vulnerable creature who must be protected from exposure to criminal influences; and on the other, as a brazen temptress, from whose seductive blandishments the innocent male must be protected. Every woman is either Eve or Little Eva—and either way, she loses.

Reaching a contrasting result, the Supreme Court in *Dothard* (1978) held that male sex was a BFOQ for the prisoner contact positions at the male penitentiary. The violent, overcrowded, understaffed "jungle atmosphere" and "rampant violence" in Alabama prisons was given as the reason. The State Commissioner of

---

*Transsexuals and transvestites would probably be considered legally female for this purpose.

Corrections had testified that the reason a woman with the same height and weight as a man could not perform all the duties at an all-male correctional institution (a view not adopted) was:

> The innate intention between a male and a female. The physical capabilities, the emotions that go into the psychic make-up of a female vs. the psychic make-up of a male. The attitude of the rural type inmate we have vs. that of a woman. The superior feeling that a man has historically, over that of a female.

The Court's gesture of protection repeated the historical pattern of excluding women from job opportunities, foreclosing women's choices by deciding what risks they will run.

Women's sexuality disqualified *all* women—as a gender—for the job, not just sexy or sexually provocative or attractive women. The majority held that women may be disqualified from employment as prison guards because of the "likelihood that inmates would assault a woman because she was a woman." It is taken for granted that sexual assault is assault "because she was a woman." The rationale for the exclusion of all women from employment on sexual grounds is described as "[t]he employee's very womanhood." In the context of the BFOQ, which makes male sex a bona fide job qualification, it is clear beyond cavil that women are disqualified because of their sexuality, which is equated with their gender. For purposes of women's exclusion, it sufficed to show that the employment treatment was based on gender to suggest that a woman would be treated as a sex object. Incarcerated criminals would *see* a woman guard as a woman, which would provoke misbehavior and upset prison discipline. Justice Marshall's critical response is worth quoting at length:

> In short, the fundamental justification for the decision is that women as guards will generate sexual assaults. . . . With all respect, this rationale regrettably perpetuates one of the most insidious of the old myths about women—that women, wittingly or not are seductive sex objects. The effect of the decision, made, I am sure, with the best of intentions, is to punish women because their very presence might provoke sexual assaults. It is women who are made to pay the price in lost job opportunities for the threat of depraved conduct by prison inmates. . . . The proper response to inevitable attacks on both female and male guards is not to limit the employment opportunities of law-abiding women who wish to contribute to their community, but to take swift and punitive action against inmate offenders. Presumably, one of the goals of the Alabama prison system is the eradication of inmates' antisocial behavior patterns so that prisoners will be able to live one day in free society. Sex offenders can begin this process by learning to relate to women guards in a socially acceptable manner. To deprive women of job opportunities because of the threatened behavior of convicted criminals is to turn our social priorities upside down.

Sexual harassment of women prison guards by male prisoners became the reason they should not occupy the job at all. If the extent of sexual assault in all kinds of jobs were known, would women be banished from the workplace entirely? The fact that the Supreme Court conformed women's job opportunities to the behavior patterns of convicted criminals suggests that they may impute sexual harassment to the presence of women's "very womanhood," rather than to men's failure to restrain themselves. To allow sexual violence to be so much a condition of women's work that it keeps women out of workplaces altogether seems to presuppose that male sexual violence is somehow inevitable or unchangeable (perhaps natural?), even in this most controlled of environments. Permitting the normally sexist offender to define the conditions of women's work poses women's sexuality as the threat to prison discipline, when it is the men's attitudes toward women's sexuality that is threatening. When male guards are considered, by contrast, it is not their presence but the prisoners' attitudes and structural relationship to them (as evidenced by assaults, which are common) that are considered threats to discipline. To Justice Marshall, "the only matter of innate recognition is that the incidence of sexually motivated attacks on guards will be minute compared to the 'likelihood that inmates will assault' a *guard* because he or she is a guard." Few would conclude, at least from this, that there should be no guards.

The argument that imposing a sexual condition upon employment is discrimination "by sexual condition," not by sex-as-gender—what might be termed the "sex plus sex" approach—can now be criticized. To separate verbally what is not separated socially by distinguishing a requirement of "sexuality" (or, in a narrow conception of sexuality, genitality) from a gender-based practice cannot eliminate the fact that it is women who are the victims of it. It can only momentarily obscure the doctrinal basis for challenging it.

This argument contrasts with the approach to sex discrimination taken in the *Gilbert* and *Geduldig* cases. An examination of the logic of these cases reveals the deep cleavage over the meaning and purpose of antidiscrimination law that animates the two approaches and their divergent implications for the issue of sexual harassment. In those cases, excluding pregnancy from a disability plan was held not sex discrimination because the differentiation was not sex-based. The reasons were, first, under both California's and General Electric's plans, "There is no risk from which men are protected and women are not. Likewise, there is no risk from which women are protected and men are not." Second, not all women get pregnant, so there is a lack of "identity between the excluded disability and gender as such" requisite for a differentiation to be legally cognizable as sex-based: "The program divides potential recipients into pregnant women and nonpregnant persons. While the first group is exclusively female, the second includes members of both sexes." Third, the intention of the exclusion was not to harm women, but to avoid the cost of covering their pregnancy disabilities. So the policy was not contaminated by a sex-based motive and, in this sense, was not "based on sex."

Gilbert and *Geduldig* exemplify this approach to what is "sex-based," which any argument that sexual harassment is sex discrimination should confront, although all the litigation of the issue has evaded it thus far. The first approach to sex-basis suffers from an ellipsis termed, in formal logic, the fallacy of the undistributed middle. The proper mediate term supplied, what is apparently meant is that there is no risk "*to which both sexes are biologically subject*" for which one is covered while the other is not. The "arbitrariness" to which such a test would be addressed is a refusal, for example, to insure women's broken bones while insuring those of men. Without the middle supplied, statements like the following can be logically deduced: under California's plan, women are protected equally with men from the attendant expenses of prostatitis and circumcision. In fact, the only medical contingency not covered by the plan is pregnancy—neither men's nor women's.

Under *Gilbert*, the requirement for discriminatory insurance coverage seems to be that either one sex is potentially affected by a disability and covered, while the other is potentially affected and not covered, or that only one sex is potentially affected and not covered, with all members of that sex in that position. But the standard set by those disabilities actually covered by both plans is not this standard. There is no disability unique to men which is not covered. The plans do not require all men to be potentially affected by a disability for men's sex-specific ailments to be covered. The class of those with prostatitis includes no women, but the class of those without the disease will include all women and some men. Yet the impossibility of women contracting prostatitis is symmetrical to the impossibility of men getting pregnant. Under the Court's rules, a company is not prevented on sex discrimination grounds from excluding (together with pregnancy-related disabilities) disabilities due to breast cancer or hysterectomy, while covering prostatitis and circumcisions, because these disabilities specific to women do not affect all women. It is plain that the Court allowed these plans to choose to cover all disabilities which affect some men but no women, while excluding a disability which affects many women but no men. Further, although under the Court's rules prostate coverage could be excluded, it is not—and that fact remains, for the *Gilbert* court, itself noncomparable to the pregnancy exclusion. Clearly, if one is in the realm of "sex-specific disabilities," pregnancy and prostate trouble are comparable. But in the realm of "female disabilities" and "male disabilities" presumptive comparisons belie the fact that the categories are divided by a difference: the sex difference. The Court did not compare the standard set by those disabilities included with those excluded to see if sex made the difference.

The hidden requirement of sex-comparability is revealed: before differential treatment will be considered sex-based, both sexes have to be potentially so treated. By this test, pregnancy cannot give rise to a sex-based difference in *treatment* because pregnancy is a risk to which only one sex is subject. Apparently, no exclusion of risk, or anything else that is exclusive to one sex because of sex, could be found discriminatory under this standard. Short of this, it is even open to question whether a factor that *varies* by sex, whether because of sex or sexism, could be challenged when it becomes the basis for variant detrimental treatment of one sex.

The *Dothard* result clearly diverges from this, yet it vindicates—or at least does not pose facts that require a challenge to—the comparability requirement. Height and weight, which vary by sex, were not allowed to be used to exclude women from employment opportunities. Real differences were not allowed to justify unequal outcomes. But women's height and weight can reasonably be compared with men's, so comparison of the underlying variable posed no difficulty. Similarly, in *Manhart*, the fact that women live longer than men was not allowed to justify unequal contributions to the pension plan, to women's disadvantage. The common factor that made comparison seem reasonable was human mortality. These cases restrict the sphere of application of the *Gilbert* approach without really undercutting the approach itself. They do not provide a context for confronting the question of why the sexes should have to be comparable in order for differential treatment of women to be discriminatory. Nor do they clarify the reasons why some factors, such as women's greater longevity and smaller size, are placed in a context which makes them comparable to men's, while other factors, such as pregnancy—both sexes do have temporary disabilities—are conceptualized as unique.

As is to be expected, the *Gilbert/Geduldig* approach to sex discrimination has arisen in the sexual harassment context. In *Williams*, the defendant argued that

> since the primary variable in the claimed class is willingness vel non *[or not] to furnish sexual consideration, rather than gender, the sex discrimination proscriptions of the act [Title VII] are not invoked. Plaintiff was allegedly denied employment enhancement not because she was a woman, but rather because she decided not to furnish the sexual consideration claimed to have been demanded. Therefore, plaintiff is in no different class from other employees, regardless of their gender or sexual orientation, who are made subject to such carnal demands.*

Sexual harassment is argued to be a matter of sexuality, not gender, so it cannot be sex discrimination. The district court in *Barnes* made the same distinction between discrimination "because she was a woman" and discrimination "because she refused to engage in a sexual affair with her supervisor." As the reply brief for defendant in *Corne* stated it: "Plaintiffs do not allege disparate treatment because of sex, but merely the context of advances from a man to a woman."

The "sexuality, not sex" argument ignores the substance of the social meaning of being of the female sex, in which one is largely defined as a female in terms of one's sexuality. Sexual harassment makes of women's sexuality a badge of female servitude. To say that a woman is fired not because she is a woman but because she refuses to have sex with her male superiors is like saying that a black man was fired not because he was black but because he refused to shuffle for his white superiors. (The EEOC, in fact, found it unlawful to discharge a black worker because white co-workers disliked him for being self-confident instead of submissive. The issue of his manner or the dislike it generated was not considered so "personal" as not to be race discrimination but as the form that racism took between the perpetrators and the victim.) To say that sexual harassment is based on sexuality, not sex, is as if an employer defended a charge of racial discrimination against a black by saying the underlying variable was skin color, not race. Perhaps it was to avoid similar pretexts that discrimination on the basis of "color," sometimes a visible index of race, is prohibited, together with race. Will it be necessary legislatively to add "sexuality" to sex discrimination statutes to make the point that female sexuality is part of female sex?*

A combination of "blame the victim" disposition with a presumptive sex symmetry underlies the "sexuality, not sex" formulation. Just as rich and poor alike can sleep under bridges at night and go to jail for stealing bread, men equally with women can be fired for their refusal to engage in a sexual affair with their (male, heterosexual) supervisor. To say that job reprisals occurred because the women declined the invitation, which was her choice, is to conclude from the facts that she was a woman, about which she had no choice, and that she was sexually propositioned, about which she had no choice, that the law should leave her no choice but to submit—or else. An employment standard is proposed which the other sex would rarely be (and is not in most cases alleged to be) required to meet. The plaintiff is then told that it is her failure to meet the standard that caused the job difficulties. Meaning: if only she had engaged in the sexual affair with her supervisor, none of this would have happened. Further meaning: if she does not cooperate as a woman, she will just have to take the consequences as an employee. If only she had not been a woman, she probably would not have been asked. . . .

---

*Adding "sexuality" to legislative prohibitions of discrimination based on sex might be a good idea in any case. It might have the added effect, depending upon how the term was interpreted, of expanding gay rights.

SEXUAL HARASSMENT AS SEX DISCRIMINATION: A DIFFERENCES ARGUMENT

The basic question the differences approach poses is: how can you tell that this happened because one is a woman, rather than to a person who just happens to be a woman? The basic answer, which presupposes sex comparability, is: a man in her position would not be or was not so treated. A presumptive sex equality underlies the placing of one sex in the other's position. This is the sex reversal that forms the basis for the inference of differentiation. The central conceptual difficulty (which often occurs as a difficulty of proof) arises because of the necessity to infer from a context, a frequency distribution, a single event, or proximate circumstances that a given discrimination is sex-specific, without deeply investigating the concrete social meaning of gender status. To take the differences approach requires temporary suspension of the fact that the sexes are substantively unequal, not just different, a fact which calls into question the appropriateness of presuming equality in order to measure disparity.

An argument under the differences approach can, nonetheless, be made against sexual harassment. The Supreme Court distinguishes between disparate treatment, in which "the employer simply treats some people less favorably than others because of their race, color, religion, sex, or national origin," and disparate impact, which "involves employment practices that are facially neutral in their treatment of different groups but that in fact fall more harshly on one group than another and cannot be justified by business necessity." In the disparate treatment case, "proof of discriminatory motive is critical, although it can in some situations be inferred from the mere fact of differences in treatment." "Proof of discriminatory motive . . . is not required under a disparate impact theory." The discussion here is accordingly divided into arguments that support each of these theories.

Disparate Treatment

As a practice, sexual harassment singles out a gender-defined group, women, for special treatment in a way which adversely affects and burdens their status as employees. Sexual harassment limits women in a way men are not limited. It deprives them of opportunities that are available to male employees without sexual conditions. In so doing, it creates two employment standards: one for women that includes sexual requirements, one for men that does not. From preliminary indications, large numbers of working women, regardless of characteristics which distinguish them from each other, report being sexually harassed. Most sexually harassed people are women. These facts indicate that the incidents are something more than "personal" and "unique" and have some connection to the female condition as a whole.

To argue that sexual harassment is an "arbitrary" practice based on sex, it is necessary either to explain why the differences approach to gender classification need not apply to the sexual harassment situation or to meet its requirements. As we have repeatedly seen, disability benefits for pregnancy provided a critical test for the conflict between two conceptions of sex discrimination. Pregnancy disability posed a "real" difference between the sexes as the basis for an employment practice by means of which only women were disadvantaged. Sexual harassment also poses a "real" difference between the sexes, together with an employment practice based upon it, most victims of which are women. But the differences between the *Gilbert* and *Geduldig* facts and situations of sexual harassment, in relation to the applicable doctrine, are several and striking. The most basic is that, unlike pregnancy, the treatment of women and men in employment can be compared on the underlying variable: sexuality. Sexuality is not unique to women. Women have female sexuality, men have male sexuality. Both sexes can be victims of the practice. When one gender is the victim of a practice as to which the treatment of the sexes can be compared, the practice can be considered sex-based.

Sexual harassment can be further distinguished from the *Gilbert* pregnancy disability conceptualization. First, sexual harassment is a precondition of employment or a condition of work, not a discretionary benefit. There is no employer choice not to have working conditions or employment criteria at all, an option that was thought important in the case of temporary disability insurance. Since the sphere for the discrimination cannot be cast as employer largesse in the first place, the argument that no arbitrary differentiation should exist within it is strengthened. Second, the impact of sexual harassment upon women's work provides a measure of the detrimental effect of the challenged practice, rather than a reason the distinction may be felt to be proper in employment, consistent with the profit motive. Pregnant women leave work and seek compensation; sexually harassed women cannot work well or at all and seek relief.

Third, in *Gilbert*, the dimension along which women and men arguably could be compared—temporary disability coverage—militated against a finding of discrimination, since aggregate benefits were found to be distributed roughly equally by sex, pregnancy excluded. Even if all employees were paid more instead of provided benefits, the ultimate cost of coverage for pregnancy would have been higher. By no measure does sexual harassment, in general, fall equally upon women and men. If it does, that is a defense. Sexual harassment makes the employment experience as a whole more injurious, more stressful, more insecure, and less economically beneficial for women than for men, for reasons having nothing legitimately to do with the job or with women's work performance. Fourth, unlike pregnancy, there is nothing about unwanted sexual solicitation and pressure that, even within social values as they are, arguably "contributes to the well-being" of the woman, once the incidents are distinguished from good clean fun. Especially when women decline or reject the advances, their participation cannot be said to be voluntary. Even when they comply with or ignore the advances, voluntariness, under the circumstances, is a question of fact.

Specific contextual factors have supported findings of sex-based discrimination in situations analogous to, and highly suggestive for, sexual harassment. In a Commission Precedent Decision, the EEOC found "sex-based intimidation" under circumstances in which an employer demoted a recently promoted female employee from her supervisory position because her male inferiors harassed her and refused to assist her in performing job tasks which required teamwork. The only evidence in the opinion that the practices occurred because of sex was that the supervisor was a woman and the harassing workers were men. Perhaps the EEOC understood that a woman supervising men was in a socially unusual and exposed position. A man who failed to elicit cooperation from female inferiors might, by this logic, simply be considered an ineffective supervisor. It was not argued, apparently, that if a man were not assisted by male or female co-workers it would not have been sex discrimination, so, therefore, should not be here. The treatment might arguably have been "intimidation" to either sex, but a man in her position would not have been and was not so treated.

Focusing upon the "sexual" rather than the "harassment" aspect, another EEOC decision involved a female employee who was discharged for having a sexual affair with a male employee, while the male employee was only "talked to" about it. The EEOC held that at least part of the reason the female employee was disciplined more severely than the male was that she was female. "Where similarly placed persons of different sexes receive dissimilar treatment, it is reasonable to infer that sex was a factor in the dissimilar treatment." Without agonizing about the place of "sexuality" in gender, the EEOC simply found that women's sexuality and men's sexuality were differently treated while the sexes were similarly situated.

Ignoring the factor of the woman's apparent consent, this case parallels a common situation of sexual harassment in which the offending superior is "talked to" while the woman loses her job. Perhaps due to a common assumption that men are generically "human" while women are defined by sexuality, men are not usually thought to be sexually defined in these situations in a way that bears comparison with women. For whatever reason, no sexual harassment case has relied upon the theory of differential employer treatment of the perpetrator and the victim on the basis of sex, due to such handling of a sexual incident.

Sexual harassment, in most cases, is an employment practice that would not have occurred if the victim's sex had been different. Some difficulties in proving that the practice is not individual affinity but sex-based arise when women who sexually comply are benefited on the job. This does not mean that sexual harassment as a practice is not sex-based. The woman who complies is in a different legal position from the woman who resists, but she is still a victim of the practice. Should women have no recourse from sexual exactions because, due to their lack of recourse, they have been forced to submit? Having allowed employers to require women sexually to submit as the price of a job, can the law use the fact of women's sexual submission as a reason they are not injured by such a requirement? When women perform sexually because they must, should their compliance exonerate the employer who requires it? Men have required that women act sexy in order to get jobs and perform sexual services in order to keep or advance in them. Having been reduced to submissive sex objects on the job, had their economic desperation exploited, having been forced into sexual subservience through threats of material retaliation, women are then criticized for acting sexy, being submissively dependent, and complying sexually. Having been forced into a position in which their employment goals can sometimes be achieved (if at all, and then precariously) only by sexual means, women are branded as unworthy of a legal prohibition on these exactions because they have complied. The so-called benefits of sexual compliance, the scraps thrown the "good nigger" as the reward for apparently voluntary submission, are considered the reason such requirements should be allowed. In this logic, women are first excluded from employment opportunities free of sexual extortion and then stigmatized by having the behavior that the context produced in them (that is, their survival skill), singled out as the reason they are unfit for the guarantees of equality. Their degradation is further mocked when the situation is considered a net benefit. This resembles the white supremacist logic of depriving blacks of the tools of an education, calling them nonintellectual and ignorant when they challenge the system of unequal educational opportunities, and concluding that they must be happy that way when they are defeated.

If sexual compliance is required *in addition* to all the job-related standards the women involved must meet, as is most often the case, the practice can be attacked by any victim, whether she complied or not, although the victim who rejected the advances has the better legal case. Having to meet a sexual standard is an injury in itself, whether or not another employment interest was consequentially damaged. If sexual compliance is required of women *in lieu of* meeting job-related standards, which seems to be much less usual, it is open to clearest attack by men, who are not given an equal opportunity to meet the real requirements of the job, which depend upon female sexuality. It is also open to attack by arguably qualified women who were never sexually approached, as well as by noncompliant women who refused. The fact the latter were approached with a promise of employment benefits in exchange for sex suggests that these women met the employer's *other* requirements for the job, whatever they were. These situations represent the furthest reach of the concept, probably beyond the currently imaginable reach of most courts. Otherwise non-qualified benefited women, by contrast, may be casualties of the sex war, but they are not in a good position to charge sex discrimination. The factual difficulty arises in distinguishing among benefited women between the qualified and the nonqualified when sexual harassment intervenes as a substitute selection procedure. So long as this is kept properly a question of fact, women will at least have a chance to argue their qualifications. At last, the ugly suspicion will be exposed that whatever women achieve is due to the extraordinary power of their sexuality, and whenever women fail it is due to the ordinary deficiencies of their gender.

Women need not be compliant to reap the benefits of misogyny, nor does a benefit given to another woman automatically mean that a practice is not sex-based. One federal district judge has held that if one woman benefits from a practice whereby another woman is disadvantaged, that fact in itself does not defeat a conclusion that Title VII sex discrimination has occurred. In *Skelton v. Balzano*, a supervisor reneged on a promise to advance one woman and instead advanced another, with the intent (which the judge found credible) that the two women would develop conflicts and "devour" each other. Rejecting the defense that as a matter of law there can be no sex discrimination when one woman is advanced over another, the court held: "It is enough to show by a preponderance of the evidence *that if plaintiff had been a man she would not have been treated in the same manner*, and at the very least would have been afforded genuine opportunity to advance."

SUPREME COURT OF THE UNITED STATES

523 U.S. 75

ONCALE V. SUNDOWNER OFFSHORE SERVICES

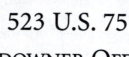

CERTIORARI TO THE UNITED STATES COURT
OF APPEALS FOR THE FIFTH CIRCUIT

No. 96-568 ARGUED: DECEMBER 3, 1997–DECIDED: MARCH 4, 1998

OPINION: JUSTICE SCALIA delivered the opinion of the Court.

This case presents the question whether workplace harassment can violate Title VII's prohibition against "discriminat[ion] . . . because of . . . sex," 42 U.S.C. § 2000e-2(a)(1), when the harasser and the harassed employee are of the same sex.

I

The District Court having granted summary judgment for respondent, we must assume the facts to be as alleged by petitioner Joseph Oncale. The precise details are irrelevant to the legal point we must decide, and in the interest of both brevity and dignity we shall describe them only generally. In late October 1991, Oncale was working for respondent Sundowner Offshore Services on a Chevron U.S.A., Inc., oil platform in the Gulf of Mexico. He was employed as a roustabout on an eight-man crew which included respondents John Lyons, Danny Pippen, and Brandon Johnson. Lyons, the crane operator, and Pippen, the driller, had supervisory authority, App. 41, 77, 43. On several occasions, Oncale was forcibly subjected to sex-related, humiliating actions against him by Lyons, Pippen and Johnson in the presence of the rest of the crew. Pippen and Lyons also physically assaulted Oncale in a sexual manner, and Lyons threatened him with rape.

Oncale's complaints to supervisory personnel produced no remedial action; in fact, the company's Safety Compliance Clerk, Valent Hohen, told Oncale that Lyons and Pippen "picked [on] him all the time too," and called him a name suggesting homosexuality. *Id.* at 77. Oncale eventually quit—asking that his pink slip reflect that he "voluntarily left due to sexual harassment and verbal abuse." *Id.* at 79. When asked at his deposition why he left Sundowner, Oncale stated "I felt that if I didn't leave my job, that I would be raped or forced to have sex." *Id.* at 71.

Oncale filed a complaint against Sundowner in the United States District Court for the Eastern District of Louisiana, alleging that he was discriminated against in his employment because of his sex. Relying on the

Fifth Circuit's decision in *Garcia v. Elf Atochem North America*, 28 F.3d 446, 451–452 (5th Cir. 1994), the district court held that "Mr. Oncale, a male, has no cause of action under Title VII for harassment by male co-workers." App. 106. On appeal, a panel of the Fifth Circuit concluded that *Garcia* was binding Circuit precedent, and affirmed. 83 F.3d 118 (1996). We granted certiorari. 520 U.S. 1263 (1997). [78]

II

Title VII of the Civil Rights Act of 1964 provides, in relevant part, that "[i]t shall be an unlawful employment practice for an employer . . . to discriminate against any individual with respect to his compensation, terms, conditions, or privileges of employment, because of such individual's race, color, religion, sex, or national origin." 78 Stat. 255, as amended, 42 U.S.C. § 2000e–2(a)(1). We have held that this not only covers "terms" and "conditions" in the narrow contractual sense, but "evinces a congressional intent to strike at the entire spectrum of disparate treatment of men and women in employment." *Meritor Savings Bank, FSB v. Vinson*, 477 U.S. 57, 64 (1986) (citations and internal quotation marks omitted). "When the workplace is permeated with discriminatory intimidation, ridicule, and insult that is sufficiently severe or pervasive to alter the conditions of the victim's employment and create an abusive working environment, Title VII is violated." *Harris v. Forklift Systems, Inc.*, 510 U.S. 17, 21 (1993) (citations and internal quotation marks omitted).

Title VII's prohibition of discrimination "because of . . . sex" protects men as well as women, *Newport News Shipbuilding & Dry Dock Co. v. EEOC*, 462 U.S. 669, 682 (1983), and in the related context of racial discrimination in the workplace we have rejected any conclusive presumption that an employer will not discriminate against members of his own race. "Because of the many facets of human motivation, it would be unwise to presume as a matter of law that human beings of one definable group will not discriminate against other members of that group." *Castaneda v. Partida*, 430 U.S. 482, 499 (1977). See also *id.* at 515–516 n.6 (Powell, J., joined by Burger, C.J., and Rehnquist, J., dissenting). . . . [79] . . . If our precedents leave any doubt on the question, we hold today that nothing in Title VII necessarily bars a claim of discrimination "because of . . . sex" merely because the plaintiff and the defendant (or the person charged with acting on behalf of the defendant) are of the same sex.

. . . .

We see no justification in the statutory language or our precedents for a categorical rule excluding same-sex harassment claims from the coverage of Title VII. As some courts have observed, male-on-male sexual harassment in the workplace was assuredly not the principal evil Congress was concerned with when it enacted Title VII. But statutory prohibitions often go beyond the principal evil to cover reasonably comparable evils, and it is ultimately the provisions of our laws rather than the principal concerns of our legislators by which we are governed. Title VII prohibits "discriminat[ion] [80] . . . because of . . . sex" in the "terms" or "conditions" of employment. Our holding that this includes sexual harassment must extend to sexual harassment of any kind that meets the statutory requirements.

Respondents and their amici contend that recognizing liability for same-sex harassment will transform Title VII into a general civility code for the American workplace. But that risk is no greater for same-sex than for opposite-sex harassment, and is adequately met by careful attention to the requirements of the statute. Title VII does not prohibit all verbal or physical harassment in the workplace; it is directed only at "*discriminat[ion] . . . because of . . . sex*." We have never held that workplace harassment, even harassment between men and women, is automatically discrimination because of sex merely because the words used have sexual content or connotations. "The critical issue, Title VII's text indicates, is whether members of one sex are exposed to disadvantageous terms or conditions of employment to which members of the other sex are not exposed." *Harris, supra*, at 25 (Ginsburg, J., concurring).

Courts and juries have found the inference of discrimination easy to draw in most male-female sexual harassment situations, because the challenged conduct typically involves explicit or implicit proposals of sexual activity; it is reasonable to assume those proposals would not have been made to someone of the same sex. The same chain of inference would be available to a plaintiff alleging same-sex harassment, if there were credible evidence that the harasser was homosexual. But harassing conduct need not be motivated by sexual desire to support an inference of discrimination on the basis of sex. A trier of fact might reasonably find such discrimination, for example, if a female victim is harassed in such sex-specific and derogatory terms by another woman as to make it clear that the harasser is motivated by general hostility to the presence of women in the workplace. A same-sex harassment plaintiff may also, of course, offer direct [81] comparative evidence about how the alleged harasser treated members of both sexes in a mixed-sex workplace. Whatever evidentiary route the plaintiff chooses to follow, he or she must always prove that the conduct at issue was not merely tinged with offensive sexual connotations, but actually constituted "*discrimina[tion]* . . . because of . . . sex."

And there is another requirement that prevents Title VII from expanding into a general civility code: As we emphasized in *Meritor* and *Harris*, the statute does not reach genuine but innocuous differences in the ways men and women routinely interact with members of the same sex and of the opposite sex. The prohibition of harassment on the basis of sex requires neither asexuality nor androgyny in the workplace; it forbids only behavior so objectively offensive as to alter the "conditions" of the victim's employment. "Conduct that is not severe or pervasive enough to create an objectively hostile or abusive work environment—an environment that a reasonable person would find hostile or abusive—is beyond Title VII's purview." *Harris*, 510 U.S. at 21, *citing Meritor*, 477 U.S. at 67. We have always regarded that requirement as crucial, and as sufficient to ensure that courts and juries do not mistake ordinary socializing in the workplace—such as male-on-male horseplay or intersexual flirtation—for discriminatory "conditions of employment."

We have emphasized, moreover, that the objective severity of harassment should be judged from the perspective of a reasonable person in the plaintiff's position, considering "all the circumstances." *Harris, supra*, at 23. In same-sex (as in all) harassment cases, that inquiry requires careful consideration of the social context in which particular behavior occurs and is experienced by its target. A professional football player's working environment is not severely or pervasively abusive, for example, if the coach smacks him on the buttocks as he heads onto the field—even if the same behavior would reasonably be experienced as abusive by the coach's secretary (male or female) back at the office. The [82] real social impact of workplace behavior often depends on a constellation of surrounding circumstances, expectations, and relationships which are not fully captured by a simple recitation of the words used or the physical acts performed. Common sense, and an appropriate sensitivity to social context, will enable courts and juries to distinguish between simple teasing or roughhousing among members of the same sex, and conduct which a reasonable person in the plaintiff's position would find severely hostile or abusive.

III

Because we conclude that sex discrimination consisting of same-sex sexual harassment is actionable under Title VII, the judgment of the Court of Appeals for the Fifth Circuit is reversed, and the case is remanded for further proceedings consistent with this opinion.

It is so ordered.

THE SILENCED WORKPLACE

EMPLOYER CENSORSHIP UNDER TITLE VII

—Kingsley R. Browne—

For the past two decades, and especially since the Supreme Court's 1986 decision in *Meritor Savings Bank v. Vinson*, employers have engaged in extensive censorship of their employees' speech because of fear of liability for hostile-environment harassment. To date, there has been only a little judicial recognition that requiring employers to engage in such censorship raises serious First Amendment issues.

The definition of hostile-environment harassment under which employers must operate is both broad and vague. It includes "verbal or physical conduct" that is "sufficiently severe or pervasive to alter the conditions of [the victim's] employment and create an abusive working environment." Under this standard, courts have held that there is no requirement of intent on the part of the alleged harasser or that statements be specifically directed at the plaintiff. Indeed, some courts have allowed plaintiffs to rely on speech that they heard about only indirectly.

Although defenders of the current system typically justify regulation by invoking the most extreme cases of obscene and abusive speech by employees, harassment regulation reaches far beyond the egregious cases. Not only do obscene sexual propositions count as sexual harassment, nonobscene propositions may as well. Indeed, the Ninth Circuit has suggested that even "well-intentioned compliments" may constitute harassment. Moreover, sexual material that does not constitute an advance—such as pin-ups, calendars, and sexual cartoons—may likewise be deemed harassment. Sexism, like sexuality, is also regulated, so that suggestions that women do not belong in the workplace or in particular jobs may support a finding of liability, as may terms of reference deemed disrespectful of women, such as "honey," "sweetie," and "babe." While such expression is typically not enough by itself to justify a finding of liability, the fact that it is considered in the hostile-environment inquiry has substantial First Amendment implications.

It is the thesis of this essay that the current regulatory scheme mandates rampant employer censorship that is inconsistent with established First Amendment principles. Two aspects of harassment regulation raise especially grave First Amendment issues. First, speech is often targeted for sanctions on the basis of its viewpoint; and second, the standard for liability is so vague that employers are unsure about what they must censor and are therefore forced into overcensorship.

THE FIRST AMENDMENT APPLIES TO HOSTILE-ENVIRONMENT REGULATION

Title VII requires employers to prevent their employees from harassing other employees. When harassment takes the form of speech, as it often does, the employer's obligation is therefore to prevent its employees from speaking. This governmentally imposed obligation to restrict speech raises serious First Amendment concerns.

Although the First Amendment restricts only governmental power to regulate speech, the necessary state action exists in the dictates of Title VII and its enforcement by the courts. Just as regulations of the Federal Railway Administration that required private railroads to test employees for drugs were subject to Fourth Amendment challenge, regulations requiring private (and public) employers to regulate speech are subject to First Amendment challenge. In either case, when the employer complies with its obligations, it "does so by compulsion of sovereign authority."

Elsewhere I have detailed the doctrinal argument that hostile-environment regulation cannot be justified under current law, and I will not recapitulate that discussion. It is appropriate, however, to address arguments made by other contributors to this volume that the First Amendment lacks application in the workplace or at least that it does not apply in the same way that it applies outside the workplace.

Frederick Schauer has argued that regulation of workplace speech does not even plausibly raise a First Amendment issue. His argument is not that the speech, because of its content, falls into some category that the Supreme Court has labeled "not speech," such as obscenity or fighting words, but rather that the workplace is not a First Amendment domain.

The notion that the First Amendment has no application in workplace harassment cases is far-fetched. In a line of cases beginning with *Pickering v. Board of Education*, the Court has held that the speech of *public* employees is protected by the First Amendment. Under these cases, the government has a substantial burden if it seeks to punish an employee's speech on a matter of public concern, and "[e]ven where a public employee's speech does not touch upon a matter of public concern, that speech is not 'totally beyond the protection of the First Amendment.'"

The power of the government to regulate public employee speech is based upon the fact that "the government as employer . . . has far broader powers than does the government as sovereign" because its "interest in achieving its goals as effectively and efficiently as possible is elevated from a relatively subordinate interest when it acts as sovereign to a significant one when it acts as employer." Thus, if the First Amendment limits the government when it acts as employer, it cannot limit the government less when it acts as regulator.

Acceptance of the argument that the First Amendment provides no protection to the speech of private-sector employees would lead to the paradoxical result that the government as regulator may engage in greater speech regulation than the government as employer. As a descriptive matter, that has in fact been the consequence of the lack of attention courts have paid to the First Amendment rights of private employees; however, this result is due more to oversight than to principle. For example, in *Rankin v. McPherson*, the Court held that a county constable was prohibited by the First Amendment from discharging a black employee who, after hearing of an attempt on the life of President Reagan, stated "if they go for him again, I hope they get him." In contrast, the government *as regulator* was effectively entitled to *require* punishment of a white employee for the statement that "niggers ought to be shot like [Vernon Jordan] was." Similarly, vulgar criticism of racial preferences by a public employee has been held to be constitutionally protected, yet criticism of racial preferences by a private employee may contribute to a hostile-environment finding. It is hard to understand why the government in its regulatory capacity can compel a private employer to punish speech that a public employer acting in its capacity as an employer would be constitutionally prohibited from restricting.

Robert Post has argued that full-blown protection for speech exists only in the domain of "public discourse," a term he has defined "as encompassing the communicative processes necessary for the formation of public opinion, whether or not that opinion is directed toward specific government personnel, decision, or policies." Although his definition appears to be directed toward the content of the speech, rather than its location, Post rejects the notion that much public discourse occurs in the workplace. He asserts that in the workplace "an image of dialogue among autonomous self-governing citizens would be patently out of place." Yet it is not clear why this should be so. Referring to the notion that a clear split exists between work life and private life, sociologist Beth Schneider has observed: "Although this set of ideas still permeates sociological and everyday thought, it is not necessarily consistent with either individuals' opinions or the reality of their daily work or sexual lives. For generations, sociologists have found that work relationships are far from simply task-oriented, but the source of friendship and informal social ties with consequences for workers as well as their workplaces." For many people, the workplace is the primary venue for discussions of social and political issues; what is on the news at night is grist for the mill the next day at work. Excluding the workplace from constitutional protection deprives millions of workers of a valuable opportunity to express themselves without fear of governmentally required sanctions. . . .

HOSTILE-ENVIRONMENT REGULATION VIOLATES FIRST AMENDMENT STANDARDS

The Regulation is Not Viewpoint Neutral

A central principle of First Amendment doctrine is that viewpoint-based restrictions on speech are impermissible absent compelling circumstances. According to the Supreme Court, "[i]t is axiomatic that the government may not regulate speech based on its substantive content or the message it conveys" and that "[w]hen the government targets not subject matter, but particular views taken by speakers on a subject, the violation of the First Amendment is all the more blatant." Courts and commentators have identified a number of viewpoint-related reasons for prohibiting expression deemed harassing. In *Robinson v. Jacksonville Shipyards, Inc.*, for example, the court justified employer liability that was based in large part on the presence of sexually suggestive materials as follows:

> *Pornography on an employer's wall or desk communicates a message about the way he views women, a view strikingly at odds with the way women wish to be viewed in the workplace. Depending on the material in question, it may communicate that women should be objects of sexual aggression, that they are submissive slaves to male desires, or that their most salient and desirable attributes are sexual. Any of these images may communicate to male coworkers that it is acceptable to view women in a predominantly sexual way.*

Thus, sexual expression may send a message that women should be viewed as sexual creatures.

Often the message that is being punished in harassment cases is not that women should be viewed sexually, but rather that they do not belong in the workplace or in particular jobs. For example, suggestions that women should not be police officers or physicians have been held to support hostile-environment findings. In the racial-harassment context, reference to minorities as "tokens," posters stating that "The KKK is still alive," and the wearing of "Wallace for President" buttons have also contributed to a hostile-environment finding. While it is true that in some cases such expression may make it harder for women and minorities to do their job because of their reaction to it, that does not mean that regulation of the expression on that basis is viewpoint-neutral. The Supreme Court has repeatedly emphasized that the impact of speech on its audience is not a content-neutral basis for regulation.

In the cases just described, and there are many more, liability was imposed for statements that were deemed impermissible precisely because of their viewpoint. Statements that women's primary attributes are sexual and that they should not hold certain positions may be actionable; statements expressing the opposite view would not be. Statements suggesting that blacks hired through affirmative-action plans are not qualified may be actionable; statements expressing the opposite view would not be. Yet these are clearly opinions, and for the government to allow expression of one set of opinions but prohibit their opposites violates its obligation, when exercising regulatory power, to remain neutral in the marketplace of ideas.

Courts have not been reluctant to acknowledge just what they are requiring of employers. The Sixth Circuit has stated: "Title VII . . . require[s] that an employer take prompt action to prevent . . . bigots from expressing their opinions in a way that abuses or offends their co-workers. By informing people that the expression of racist or sexist attitudes in public is unacceptable, people may eventually learn that such views are undesirable in private, as well. Thus, Title VII may advance the goal of eliminating prejudices and biases in our society." Thus, not only does the law require the employer to monitor employee speech for bigotry, its explicit justification is to harness the power of the government to censor speech in the Orwellian hope that changing the way people speak will change the way they think.

The Hostile-Environment Standard is Hopelessly Vague and Effectively Mandates Overcensorship by Employers

Some of the expression regulated by harassment rules is entitled to little First Amendment protection. Some may be obscene; some may constitute "fighting words." Such speech is freely regulable by appropriately tailored rules, at least as long as the regulation is not viewpoint based. However, regulation of speech through harassment law goes far beyond these clearly regulable forms of speech, and the standard that separates the permissible from the impermissible is hopelessly vague.

The Supreme Court has repeatedly held that speech regulations must be sufficiently clear that they not create a "chilling effect" on speech, causing prudent persons to steer far wide of a line they cannot clearly see. The hostile-environment standard does not satisfy this First Amendment notice requirement. Its proscription of "verbal or physical conduct of a sexual nature [that] creat[es] an intimidating, hostile, or offensive work environment" gives employers little notice of what speech they must prohibit and what they may allow. As Justice Scalia observed in his concurrence in *Harris v. Forklift Systems, Inc.,* this standard lets "virtually unguided juries decide whether sex-related conduct engaged in (or permitted by) an employer is egregious enough to warrant an award of damages." While such a "standardless standard" may not violate the requirements of due process when applied to nonexpressive behavior, the First Amendment requires greater specificity.

Any vague regulation of speech can create a chilling effect, as potential speakers weigh the risks of speaking. The chilling effect of harassment regulation, however, is greatly exacerbated by two features of the liability regime: employer liability and the totality-of-the-circumstances standard.

The system of holding employers, rather than harassing employees, liable substantially increases the amount of speech that is suppressed. When an individual's speech is directly punishable, the speaker's desire for self-expression counterbalances to an extent his desire to avoid punishment. The speaker may thus take a chance and test the limits of the regulation. Yet when a third party is responsible for regulating the speech and is also subject to a substantial penalty for underregulation, the incentives are far less symmetrical. The employer gains little gratification from the speech of its employees but is exposed to financial risk by it, leaving the incentives overwhelmingly on the side of restriction. Overregulation is thus relatively cheap for the employer, and underregulation is potentially very expensive.

The totality-of-the-circumstances test also heightens the incentive for over-regulation. An employer cannot know whether a given expression is ultimately going to form a basis for liability without knowing what else will be said by the particular speaker and by all other coworkers. The employer must deal with speech one incident at a time, asking itself not whether the speech at issue would by itself create liability, but rather whether it might, when combined with other speech that may not yet have occurred, ultimately contribute to a hostile-environment finding.

Imagine, for example, that an employer knew that a particular expression would not be deemed "sufficiently severe or pervasive" unless it was spoken five times. A male employee makes the statement once to a female coworker, and she complains to her supervisor. Does the rational supervisor tell the male employee that he can make the statement three more times and then he must quit, or does he tell him not to say it again? The answer is obvious. Since in any ensuing litigation the employer will be faced with all speech that the plaintiff was exposed to—and the employer will be judged by the adequacy of its response—the predictable response by the employer is to silence the employee. And that is the advice that lawyers give to their clients. The much-vaunted "zero tolerance" policies adopted by employers make perfect sense given the liability rules, and it is hard to fault employers for adopting them or lawyers for recommending them.

THE REACTION OF EMPLOYERS TO THE LIABILITY REGIME

Most commentators who have argued against the First Amendment defense have focused on decided cases, arguing that judges and juries can distinguish between egregious and nonegregious cases. Moreover, they argue, many cases involve not just speech but often other offensive conduct such as sexual touching. Thus, they contend, hostile-environment law does not result in any substantial amount of inappropriate censorship.

Judging the effects of a rule by who wins and loses in litigation is a common but misguided tendency of lawyers, who think that if the right people are winning, then the law is working properly. However, law in general, and harassment law in particular, is aimed primarily at shaping conduct outside the courtroom, and it is out there—in the workplace—that one must look to see its results.

In placing its imprimatur on the hostile-environment theory, the Supreme Court in *Meritor Savings* suggested that an effective sexual harassment policy may confer some protection on employers. Since *Meritor*, lawyers have routinely counseled their clients to adopt and enforce strict harassment policies, and most employers, at least large employers, have followed this advice.

While it is true that the most visible effects of harassment law are the litigated harassment cases, these are merely the tip of the iceberg. Reported cases are a misleading indicator of the law's effects, however, involving as they often do either the breakdown of an employer's sexual harassment policy or an employer who lacks a strong interest in complying with the law. A more relevant form of data, and one that is often ignored, is the behavior of employers who seek to comply with the law. That requires an analysis of the actual enforcement of employer harassment policies.

Application of employer harassment policies is for the most part invisible to the legal system. In the vast majority of cases, employees simply comply with the instructions they have been given. When there is an arguable violation, the offending employee is counseled not to do it again and he complies with the instruction, leaving no public record of the event.

Reported cases involving application of employer sexual harassment policies are largely limited to employees having some sort of just-cause protection, since at-will employees generally have no remedy for discipline or discharge for alleged violations of such policies. There have been a few lawsuits brought by employees discharged for violating their employer's sexual harassment policies. There have also been many arbitrations pursued on behalf of unionized employees who were disciplined or discharged for violating such policies, and there have been administrative proceedings initiated by disciplined or discharged civil service employees. The employer attitude displayed in all of these reported cases is consistent with the legal advice that they receive: when it comes to avoiding sexual harassment liability, it is better to be safe than sorry, and being safe means censoring a lot of speech. Consider the following cases:

- A Miller Brewing Company executive recounted in the workplace an episode of *Seinfeld*, in which the protagonist could not recall the name of a woman he was going out with; all he could remember was that her name rhymed with a female sexual anatomical part. It turned out that the woman's name was Dolores. When a woman in the office did not understand the joke, the executive showed her a dictionary page containing the word "clitoris" (obviously, the rhyme was a bit off). The woman filed an internal sexual harassment charge, and the man was discharged.

- An Arizona police officer, upon learning that he scored well on the sergeant's exam, e-mailed a friend of his, a civilian woman in the department, "Now that I am on the Sergeant's List will you sleep with me?" His friend was amused and not at all offended but unfortunately for him mentioned the message to someone who reported it to a supervisor. The officer's name was then removed from the Sergeant's List.

- A computer operator brought a copy of *National Lampoon* magazine to work. It was found by a female employee who gave it to a manager. The manager decided that the pictures of scantily clad women in the magazine violated the company's sexual harassment policy, and the employee was discharged.

- A leadman at an Oregon manufacturing plant along with several other male employees looked unobtrusively at a copy of *Penthouse* magazine containing pictures of local celebrity Tonya Harding. One of the employees later mentioned the magazine to a female coworker, who in turn notified management. The employee was suspended for three days.

- A Hispanic woman wore an African print scarf on her head. Some black employees were offended that she would wear an African scarf and complained. She was told to remove it because it offended her co-employees, and when she refused, she was discharged for insubordination.

- A superintendent of station branch operations of the United States Postal Service addressed a subordinate "on more than one occasion" as "sweet thing." He was demoted to the position of letter carrier.

- A machinist foreman, while on an errand to the area in which a female apprentice was working, engaged her in a conversation in which he told her such things as that he was from the "old school" and did not believe that women had any place in the shipyards, that the apprentice program was a "joke," and that she should have gotten a "typewriter" job. Although the foreman was not her supervisor, he was demoted to a nonsupervisory machinist position.

- Just before Halloween, an air traffic controller found a piece of rope in a construction area of the Indianapolis control tower and tied it in a hangman's noose and hung it over the curtain rod that cordoned off the construction area. Apparently, no one saw it, but he admitted he had done it after a second noose (which he had nothing to do with) appeared and caused a furor among black employees. Although there was no allegation that he had any racial motivation (and an arbitrator subsequently found that he clearly did not), the employee was suspended for two days.

- A warehouse worker foreman in a unit that performed heavy manual labor made statements on approximately ten occasions during a four-year period "that he believed that women in general were incapable of performing work in the [warehouse] and that he would never hire a woman." Although there were no findings that he had ever engaged in any discriminatory acts, he was demoted to the position of aircraft freight loader for violation of the agency's discrimination and harassment policy.

A common feature of the above cases is that the expression for which the employee was disciplined or discharged was clearly not egregious enough by itself to support a finding of employer liability for harassment, yet the expression was interpreted to be a policy violation. That fact has led some to argue that such cases cannot be characterized as an effect of harassment law; instead, they are aberrant responses—"overreaction" by paranoid employers. That argument assumes that an employer should not discipline an employee until offensive speech is so severe or pervasive that it violates the law. But that is surely an unrealistic view of the situation facing the employer. The totality-of-the-circumstances standard effectively requires the employer to act before an employee's speech reaches the "severe or pervasive" threshold, not only because of uncertainty about just where the threshold lies, but also because the employer will be called upon to defend against not just that employee's speech but also the speech of all other employees. This fact has caused courts and administrative agencies to conclude that employers appropriately respond well before Title VII has been violated. As the Merit Systems Protection Board has observed, while one "isolated incident" of "sexist" harassment does not violate Title VII, "[S]uch conduct by one of its supervisory employees cannot go unchecked by the agency, lest the agency be said to condone such remarks by its employees. Furthermore, if such conduct were not to be held actionable, a course of conduct or pattern of discriminatory behavior could emerge wherein the agency as employer could ultimately be held liable under Title VII." Of course, employers dealing with at-will employees need not even persuade an administrative agency or arbitrator that acting prior to reaching the legal standard for harassment is justified, since even clear overreaction to the threat of harassment liability poses little legal risk.

If the cases described above do reflect overreaction, it is largely in the sanction imposed by the employer rather than in the censorship itself. That is, while one might believe that the employers overreacted in the amount of discipline imposed, it is unlikely that any employment lawyer would think that counseling the employees not to repeat their transgressions constituted overreaction. In today's climate, no competent counsel would advise employers that they are free to allow employees to engage in "shop talk" or tell sexual, racial, and ethnic jokes as long as they are not grossly offensive; nor would competent counsel advise employers that employees should be permitted to express controversial views on racial and sexual matters. As a pamphlet issued by the Maryland Commission on Human Relations puts it, "Because the legal boundaries are so poorly marked, the best course of action is to avoid all sexually offensive conduct in the workplace."

POTENTIAL MODIFICATIONS THAT WOULD REDUCE FIRST AMENDMENT PROBLEMS

Given that current hostile-environment standards cannot withstand First Amendment scrutiny, the question remains whether there are some incremental modifications in Title VII doctrine that could cure the problem or whether more dramatic measures must be taken. It appears that incremental changes would not help very much.

Directly Targeted Speech

Some commentators have conceded that current harassment standards unduly restrict expression, but that the problems that I have identified can be avoided by requiring that speech be "targeted" toward a particular victim in order to be actionable. Thus, a plaintiff could not rely on overheard jokes or objectionable displays that are exhibited for all to see. Such a standard would unquestionably be an improvement over the current standard. It would eliminate liability for "harassment in the air," and it would cut down substantially on the number of "undeserving" plaintiffs who prevail in litigation. But faith in this revised standard reflects the outlook previously described—the view that a law is working appropriately if the right parties are prevailing in the litigated cases. The relevant question, however, is whether a "targeted" standard would substantially reduce the core problem of hostile-environment regulation, which is censorship by employers because of fear of liability. The answer appears to be in the negative.

Under any sensible interpretation of a "targeted" standard, statements that were intentionally made in the plaintiff's presence would qualify even if they were not formally directed toward her. That is, if a woman overhears sexist jokes or remarks and asserts that they were made because of her presence, it would presumably be a jury question whether the statements were in fact "targeted." Similarly, if a woman argues that suggestive pictures were posted specifically to offend her, she may be able to get to a jury on her claim. Of course, if the picture predated her employment in that location, such a claim would be hard to make. However, if she complained about the first picture after she entered the workplace and then additional pictures were posted, she might reasonably argue that the later pictures were directed at her in retaliation for her earlier complaints.

A "targeted" standard would simply not provide the employer the tools for distinguishing between the speech it must regulate and the speech it may allow. Many of the cases described in the prior section could plausibly be characterized as involving "targeted" speech. While not sufficient by itself to create liability, the speech in each of those cases could potentially be aggregated with other speech to support a hostile-environment finding. Thus, the employer would still experience pressure to censor the speech, and even a "targeted" standard would still require the employer to impose viewpoint-based speech restrictions.

Individual Liability

No reasonably likely system of employer liability under Title VII will substantially reduce the problem of employer overcensorship. The pressure to overcensor is inherent in a third-party liability system that is coupled with an inherently vague standard. The point is not that no system of employer liability will be perfect; rather, it is that no system of employer liability can avoid the suppression of far more speech than the First Amendment can tolerate.

It may be that a better way of regulating harassment—at least harassment taking the form of speech—would be to eliminate employer liability under Title VII and rely on tort law, under which individual offending employees could be held directly liable for their actions, perhaps under the theory of intentional infliction of emotional distress. Even this standard—which requires "outrageous conduct" on the part of the defendant—raises substantial First Amendment problems. In *Hustler Magazine, Inc. v. Falwell*—admittedly a "public figure" case—the Supreme Court rejected the "outrageousness" standard precisely because of its lack of objective content.

Remaining First Amendment difficulties notwithstanding, an individual-liability system would eliminate some of the chief evils of the current regime. It would reduce the pressure on employers to impose draconian speech codes. No longer would the censor of the speech be someone different from the speaker, and no longer would a single party be responsible for the aggregate of speech by numerous speakers. An individual-liability system would also have the salutary effect of imposing liability on the primary malefactor. This may, in turn, create greater disincentives for individual employees to engage in egregious harassing behavior, when they know that their houses—and not just their jobs—may be on the line.

Although one might argue that the proper remedy would be simply to add an individual-liability component to Title VII, there are several reasons why that would not be a good idea. First, individual liability under Title VII would be merely an adjunct to employer liability; if employers could still be liable, all the pressures for overcensorship would remain. Second, because a regime of individual liability under Title VII would presumably hold liable not just the harassers but also the supervisors who failed to take adequate steps to counteract the harassment, the pressure to overcensor would actually increase. Instead of the supervisor's risking his employer's money if he decides not to censor speech, now he would be risking his own money. Since the supervisor personally captures very little of the benefit of whatever enhanced morale might flow from declining to sanction every silly sexist statement, the situation would likely be worse than it is today.

An individual-liability tort regime would likely cause juries to view harassment cases in a more speech-protective light. Such a regime may reduce the pro-plaintiff bias of juries in sexual harassment cases, because the jury would have flesh-and-blood parties on both sides of the case, rather than having a sympathetic plaintiff on one side and a deep-pocket corporate employer on the other. Diminishing the lottery-like aspect of filing sexual harassment claims can only be a good thing. The likelihood of liability based upon offensive, but not egregious, language would be reduced, as may be the likelihood that liability would be based on any viewpoint expressed as opposed to the manner of its expression.

Some will argue that this is exactly the wrong thing to do. Employer liability places pressure on the party most able to control the workplace. While that might have been a good argument at the outset of our experiment with sexual-harassment liability, experience has shown that employer liability causes substantial overcensorship. The power to control, coupled with substantial liability for inadequate control, has led to a regime that cannot be countenanced under the First Amendment.

Eliminating employer liability would not destroy employers' incentives to prevent egregious harassment. The majority of employers will prevent the most egregious speech out of concern for efficient operation of the workplace. However, employers would probably be less hypersensitive and draw the line between what is permissible and impermissible in a different place than they are forced to draw it now.

Some take the fact that a small minority of employers tolerate truly outrageous conduct even under today's law as evidence that the law, rather than going too far, does not go far enough. Consequently, they would argue, this is no time for retrenchment. While it is true that even under today's system of employer liability some employers permit highly obnoxious behavior, that does not tell us a great deal about the incentive effects of the law, because some employers do not appear to be particularly sensitive to the governing rules.

It seems to be axiomatic for many that the continued existence of any discrimination or harassment is an argument for increasing the levels of regulation, enforcement, and sanctions. But we seem strangely selective in our insistence on a "zero tolerance" standard. Most people view murder as being worse than sexual harassment, but no one argues that the fact that the murder rate is well above zero is reflective of inadequate laws against murder or inadequate enforcement of existing laws. Why not? Probably because people understand that although murder is a bad thing, there is something in human nature that makes it inevitable. We devote substantial resources to combating crime and are pleased when crime rates go down, but each new report of a murder or robbery does not result in an outcry for more regulation. On the other hand, the assumption seems to be that phenomena such as sexual harassment and discrimination can be entirely eliminated with a little education and "attitude adjustment." Yet it is probably the case that sexual harassment, no less than any number of other forms of antisocial behavior, is a product of built-in predispositions rather than merely a lack of education. If that is so, complete elimination of sexual harassment and discrimination may be no more achievable a goal than complete elimination of crime.

CONCLUSION

Concerns about suppression of speech by harassment law have so far been largely overshadowed by concerns about equality. Labeling speech "discriminatory" has been viewed as a sufficient basis for suppression. But if the First Amendment means anything, it means that some speech that people think is bad is beyond the reach of the law. Unfortunately, the First Amendment is too seldom viewed as a real constraint on policy choices. Rather, the analysis seems to go: "Is this a good policy? If so, then it must not violate the First Amendment." Needless to say, such an approach leads to the same results that would be reached in the absence of a First Amendment.

Proponents of speech regulation always believe that the world would be a better place without the speech they wish to censor, and they often argue that the speech they seek to censor is somehow *sui generis*, so that allowing regulation in this instance will not justify censoring other speech that they think should not be censored. But it is time to recognize that harassment regulation under the present scheme of employer liability exacts far too high a cost in suppressed expression.

FREE SPEECH AND HOSTILE ENVIRONMENTS

—*Jack M. Balkin*—

Does sexual harassment law conflict with the First Amendment? A number of commentators now argue that it does.[1] Generally, these objections focus on employer liability for hostile environments. Virtually no one finds fault with regulating quid pro quo sexual harassment: employers who tell employees to "sleep with me or you're fired" make threats that are not protected by the First Amendment.

Hostile environments, however, do not always involve threats. They stem from individual acts of discriminatory speech and other conduct by all the persons who inhabit a workplace, including managers, employees, and even occasionally clients and customers. A hostile environment exists when "the workplace is permeated with 'discriminatory intimidation, ridicule, and insult' that is 'sufficiently severe or pervasive to alter the conditions of the victim's employment and create an abusive working environment.'"[2] Some of this behavior may be directed at particular employees; other elements may be directed at no one in particular but may help foster an abusive environment. Even if individual acts do not constitute a hostile environment separately, they can be actionable when taken together. The test is whether the conduct, taken as a whole, would lead to an environment that the employee reasonably perceives as abusive.[3]

Employers can be liable for maintaining a hostile work environment even if management did not personally engage in any of the predicate acts. In *Burlington Industries, Inc. v. Ellerth*[4] and *Faragher v. City of Boca Raton*,[5] the Supreme Court held that employers are liable for harassment by supervisory personnel, subject to affirmative defenses when the harassment did not result in a tangible employment action like firing or demotion.[6] The degree of vicarious liability for nonsupervisory personnel (such as coworkers) is still contested, but currently most courts hold an employer liable if the employer knew or should have known of the harassment and did not take prompt corrective action.[7]

Employers who want to minimize hostile environment liability cannot merely prohibit individual instances of harassing conduct. They must also limit conduct that might, in combination with other conduct, contribute to a hostile environment. Hence employers are tempted to create prophylactic rules against all the potential components of a hostile environment. Some of these will be unwelcome physical advances, assaults, and forms of abuse. Others will be largely verbal: sexual jokes and innuendo, taunts and threats, sexually oriented cartoons, pictures, and pornography. Some of this verbal abuse may even be couched in political or factual terms; for example, coworkers might oppose affirmative action programs for women or quote scientific studies arguing that women are less competent at certain jobs. Because employers have no general interest in preserving employee speech rights unrelated to efficiency, they will impose regulations as broad as they think necessary to insulate themselves from liability.[8] The most important complaints about the constitutionality of sexual harassment law stem from these incentives to censor employee speech that might contribute to a hostile environment.

THE APPARENT PROBLEM: COLLATERAL CENSORSHIP

The concern that sexual harassment law produces employee censorship is actually an instance of a more general problem in free speech law—*collateral censorship*.[9] Collateral censorship occurs when private party A has the power to control speech by another private party B, the government threatens to hold A liable based on what B says, and A then censors B's speech to avoid liability. The offending speech may be defamatory, obscene, fraudulent, or a violation of copyright. In most situations A has greater incentives to censor B than B has to self-censor. Hence A can be expected to censor B collaterally with little regard for the value of B's speech to B or to society at large.

It is tempting but incorrect to argue that collateral censorship is never unconstitutional because there is no state action. In fact, there is state action in every case of collateral censorship, because the government has created incentives for private parties to censor each other, and expects censorship to be the result.

Even so, collateral censorship is not necessarily unconstitutional. For example, editors and publishers, driven by fear of defamation suits, may refuse to run stories by their reporters, or may severely edit them, even when the story involves core political speech, and even when the reporter insists that a story is accurate. Reporters who insist on writing what the editor or publisher forbids may be disciplined or even fired. Yet these limitations on employee speech do not violate the First Amendment. Cases like *New York Times Co. v. Sullivan*[10] and *Gertz v. Robert Welch, Inc.*[11] limit publishers' liability for defamation to prevent valuable speech from being chilled. But they do not distinguish between the rights of editors and their employees. In fact, in *Cantrell v. Forest City Publishing Co.*, the Court approved a jury charge that allowed the jury to hold the publisher liable for knowing falsehoods written by its staff writer even if the publisher was otherwise blameless.[12] Vicarious liability clearly gives a publisher strong incentives to censor employee speech, yet the Court found no constitutional problem.

In like fashion, federal securities laws require investment houses, brokerage firms, investment advisers, and even corporate officials to avoid making misleading statements about company profits, securities, and related investments. Companies are strictly regulated concerning what they may say about these matters, particularly in highly regulated procedures like proxy contests.[13] Statements made by their employees, even politically motivated statements, may subject them to liability. Thus, rational companies will often severely limit the kinds of public statements their employees may make, and discipline or terminate employees who disobey. But these rules do not violate the First Amendment because they specifically chill *employee* speech.

In both the defamation and the securities fraud cases, collateral censorship is permissible because it makes sense, given the purposes of the regulatory regime, to treat the private censor and the private speaker as the "same speaker" for purposes of First Amendment law. In both cases the private censor (the employer) has the *right to control* the content of the speaker's (the employee's) speech and is properly *responsible* for the harmful effects of that speech.

Why might it be permissible to hold one speaker liable for the harms of another? One reason is that the private censor and speaker are part of the same enterprise that produces the harm in question: they either collectively produce a single product that causes harm (a libelous publication), or their collective efforts create a harm or a risk of harm (misleading or fraudulent information about investments). Another reason is that the private censor is in the best position to avoid the harm. That might be so if the private censor is particularly good at distinguishing protected from unprotected harmful speech, can avoid harms more easily and effectively than the speaker, or has better information than the speaker.

Thus, we can identify three factors that justify treating the private censor and speaker as "the same speaker": (1) the private censor's right to control the private speaker's speech, (2) the joint or collective production of a harm or danger of harm, and (3) the private censor's superior ability to avoid the harm. Not surprisingly, these reasons resemble the traditional justifications for vicarious liability, in which courts treat employer and employee as the "same tort-feasor" for purposes of liability.[14] (They also suggest why the Court found little difficulty with holding publishers liable for reporters' speech in *Cantrell*, even though that rule clearly chills the speech of reporters.)

It is easy to see why the justifications for vicarious liability are relevant to the constitutionality of collateral censorship. If we hold the private censor responsible for the private speaker's harmful speech, it is reasonable to expect the private censor to censor. Conversely, if we don't want to encourage the private censor to censor (because we value the free flow of ideas), we should ensure that the private censor is not held responsible for the private speaker's harmful speech. Thus, collateral censorship is most acceptable from a First Amendment standpoint when vicarious liability is most acceptable, and it is least acceptable from a First Amendment standpoint when vicarious liability is least acceptable.

This reasoning also explains why collateral censorship is permissible even when the censor and speaker are not employer and employee, or part of the same business enterprise. For example, book publishers often demand that authors rewrite or even omit potentially defamatory passages as a condition of publication. No one doubts that these practices affect authors' practical ability to speak. But this collateral censorship does not violate their First Amendment rights, even when they engage in explicitly political speech. Like newspaper editors, book publishers have the right to editorial control over authors as a condition of publication and that is why they are liable for their authors' defamatory statements.

Conversely, collateral censorship is most problematic when vicarious liability makes the least sense. A good example is when liability is imposed on a distributor, a common carrier, or some other conduit that is not part of the same business enterprise as the censored speaker, lacks the right to exercise editorial control, and lacks information about the nature of the content flowing through its channels. . . .

Defamation law recognizes the problem of collateral censorship through what is called the distributor's privilege. Usually someone who repeats a defamatory statement is as liable for publishing it as the original speaker (assuming the person also acts with the requisite degree of fault).[15] However, a distributor of information, like a newsstand or a bookstore, is generally not held to this standard unless the distributor knows of the publication's defamatory content.[16] The fear is that if distributors were held to be publishers, distributors might restrict the kinds of books and magazines they sold, greatly reducing the public's access to protected expression.

To receive the common law privilege, a distributor does not have to be a common carrier, which must take on all customers without oversight. Although distributors make some content-based judgments—for example, in choosing what books or magazines to stock—their editorial control is very different from and much more limited than that of the book publisher or magazine editor.

In the telecommunications industry, collateral censorship is a recurrent constitutional problem: cable companies and Internet service providers regularly act as conduits for the speech of unrelated parties. Treating them like publishers or editors would have the same sorts of effects that the Court was worried about in *Smith v. California*. Thus, in the Telecommunications Act of 1996, Congress extended a special privilege to Internet service providers whose customers post indecent, obscene, or "otherwise objectionable" matter in cyberspace, declaring that, as a matter of law, they should not be considered the publishers of such material.[17]

Hostile environment law surely produces collateral censorship. But it does not involve a distributor or conduit relationship. The employer who censors employees for fear of creating a hostile environment is more like the employer who censors employees out of fear of liability for defamation or securities fraud, and less like the Internet service provider who censors its customers, or the bookstore owner who refuses to stock certain books in order to avoid liability.

Unlike the case of the bookstore owner and the book author, the employer and employee in a hostile environment case are part of the same business enterprise. The employer has the contractual right to control the employee's speech and conduct. Perhaps more important, the law has good reasons to hold the employer accountable for the acts of its employees.

First, the employer is better able to see the larger picture about what conduct might contribute to sex discrimination. Hostile environments emerge from a combination of behaviors that not all employees may have knowledge of.

Second, the employer is better able than individual employees to prevent hostile environments from emerging, especially when they result from collective actions that no individual employee may be able or willing to prevent.

Third, precisely because the creation of a hostile environment does not stem from any single act, but from many acts taken together, it makes sense to treat the harm to equal opportunity in the workplace as a single harm. Collective action problems may reduce the incentives of individual employees to prevent hostile environments. Thus it may make even more sense to treat employer and employees as a "single speaker" engaged in a single harm than it does in the case of defamation or securities fraud.[18]

Fourth, the employer faces incentives to acquiesce in hostile environments that have no analogue in defamation or securities fraud situations. This makes the case for employer liability—and the need for incentives to police employees—even stronger. Sexual harassment is a form of sex discrimination. It helps keep jobs and employment opportunities sex-segregated according to traditional gender roles—for example, by keeping women out of higher-paying construction positions and in lower-paying secretarial positions, or by imposing obstacles to advancement for women even in integrated workforces. Employers may accept (or ignore) sex discrimination by their male employees (including sexual harassment) in order to avoid labor disruption and preserve esprit de corps and loyalty among a particular class of valuable (male) workers. In theory, employers could save money by staffing jobs with less well paid women rather than with men, but this might produce enormous labor disruptions, even with nonunionized workers. Under these conditions, acquiescence is a second-best solution for maximizing profits. Employers will accept a sex-segregated workforce with only a few token women in "male" positions (enforced by many different forms of sex discrimination, including employee harassment) as a compromise with existing male employees who want to maintain higher wages and workplace status.[19] In short, the different incentives of employers and employees may push them toward a common strategy, producing a workplace culture that distributes job opportunities by sex and enforces this result through subtle and not-so-subtle forms of discrimination and harassment.

Congress has a right to prevent this result. Title VII gives women and minorities an equal right to pursue work and an equal right to workplace opportunities. Through Title VII, Congress and the courts have imposed on all employers an obligation to guarantee their employees a workplace free from sexual discrimination and harassment, whether caused by managers or by coworkers—just as OSHA regulations require employers to guarantee a workplace free from defective health and safety conditions caused by management or by coworkers. In effect, Congress has required employers to produce a certain kind of business culture in the workplace. The Supreme Court's decisions in *Ellerth* and *Faragher* confirm this: employers are strongly encouraged to create antiharassment policies and compliance procedures.[20] The speech and behavior of individual employees is integral to the production of workplace culture, and the employer is in the best position to manage that culture, just as employers always managed business culture before the application of antidiscrimination laws.

In sum, collateral censorship is a problem only when vicarious liability for employee conduct is unjustified. Because there are abundant good reasons to hold employers liable for employees' creation of a hostile environment, the collateral censorship produced by Title VII does not offend the First Amendment.

THE REAL PROBLEM: CAPTIVE AUDIENCES

Critics can still raise other First Amendment objections, which fall into three categories. First, the courts' standard of abusive conduct is unduly vague. Second, sexual harassment doctrines are overbroad because they prohibit speech that would clearly be protected outside the workplace. Third, sexual harassment doctrines make distinctions on the basis of content and viewpoint. On closer inspection, however, none of these objections proves fatal.

The vagueness argument proves entirely too much: it applies equally to most judge-made communications torts. For example, speech is defamatory "if it tends . . . to lower [an individual] in the estimation of the community or to deter third persons from associating or dealing with him."[21] Intentional infliction of emotional distress requires words or conduct "so outrageous in character, and so extreme in degree, as to go beyond all possible bounds of decency, and to be regarded as atrocious, and utterly intolerable in a civilized community . . . [where] recitation of the facts to an average member of the community would arouse his resentment against the actor, and lead him to exclaim, 'Outrageous!' "[22] A judicial standard of sexual harassment that requires severe or pervasive intimidation, ridicule, insult, and abuse does not seem unduly vague in comparison with these torts. In fact, much of the objection to the vagueness of hostile environment doctrine seems directed at the worry that employers will collaterally censor employees. Collateral censorship will certainly occur, but it does not make hostile environment law unconstitutional, any more than it makes defamation or securities fraud law unconstitutional.

The second argument—that harassing speech would be protected outside of the workplace—is more promising. But it, too, proves unavailing. Speech that would be protected in the public square often becomes unprotected when it occurs in special social situations involving special social roles. If a White House intern sleeps with the President and falsely denies it at a press conference, her false statement is protected. However, if she repeats the same denial in an affidavit or on the witness stand, she can be prosecuted for perjury. The same words inserted into a new social context create different responsibilities and different degrees of First Amendment protection.

Sexually harassing speech that would be protected outside of the workplace becomes unprotected within it because it occurs in a relationship of economic and social dependence—the employment relation—and because it involves a form of sex discrimination that (1) materially alters the terms and conditions of employment for women, (2) reinforces the lower status of women in employment relationships, and (3) preserves gender stratification in employment markets. In short, speech used to create a hostile working environment is unprotected not because of its content, but because in the social context in which it occurs, it is a method of employment discrimination.

Employment discrimination law prevents harms to material or economic interests like salary and working conditions. But it is also concerned with the social status of women, blacks, and other minorities. It attempts to dismantle unjust forms of social stratification based on race or sex that get visited on individual employees in the workplace. Title VII protects against both material- and status-based harms because material and status elements are inextricably intertwined in the workplace, and cannot easily be separated. This should not be surprising: common sense tells us that people with large corner offices do not receive lower salaries and reduced authority as a trade-off, and people in cubicles don't get juicier work assignments as compensation. Rather, people with high status and esteem also usually enjoy better salaries and working conditions. Conversely, people lower in the hierarchy of the workplace usually enjoy less pleasant working conditions and lower compensation.

Because material benefits and social status are so deeply interconnected in the workplace, harms to people's group status that significantly impair their working conditions constitute employment discrimination under Title VII. That is why there is nothing particularly unusual or special about hostile environment liability. Hostile environment situations are just a special case of ordinary disparate treatment discrimination: they are harms to employees' group status—imposed on account of their membership in the group—that materially alter their working conditions as individuals.

Racist and misogynist speech outside the workplace can also reproduce group status distinctions and impose status harms. But the First Amendment does not generally permit recovery for harms to one's group status.[23] It allows recovery for defamation, but primarily for injury to individual reputation.[24] In the special context of the workplace, however, the First Amendment does permit people to recover for harms to group status when (and only when) these status-based harms so materially alter their working conditions that they constitute employment discrimination under Title VII. As explained in *Harris v. Forklift Systems* and *Meritor Savings Bank v. Vinson*, the plaintiff must face a workplace "permeated with 'discriminatory intimidation, ridicule, and insult' that is 'sufficiently severe or pervasive to alter the conditions of the victim's employment and create an abusive working environment' " as judged by a reasonable person.[25] Just as false speech before a jury is punishable not merely because it is false but because false speech in this setting is perjury, status-based harms in the workplace are sanctionable not merely because they are offensive but because in this setting these harms are mechanisms of employment discrimination. They are forms of disparate treatment that help sustain job segregation in the workplace.

Workers in hostile environments are surrounded by an abusive environment they cannot easily escape. First Amendment doctrines permit content-based regulation to protect "captive audiences." Simply put, a person trapped in a hostile work environment is a "captive audience" for First Amendment purposes with respect to the speech and conduct that produce the discrimination. Hostile environments do the work of job segregation by making workers captive audiences. Although courts created the captive audience doctrine for other situations, it actually makes better sense in the context of the workplace.[26]

Generally speaking, people are captive audiences when they are unavoidably and unfairly coerced into listening. According to the Supreme Court, the paradigmatic case of a captive audience involves assaultive speech directed at the home.[27] The Court's other major example has been people riding on public buses who cannot avoid looking at political advertisements.[28]

Read too broadly, captive audience doctrine would give the state enormous power to silence people based on vague notions of captivity.[29] Thus, it is not surprising that First Amendment scholars have tried to limit the doctrine to speech aimed at the home, where courts view privacy concerns as at their highest. So understood, the "captive audience" doctrine is not about captive *audiences* at all, but about the special nature of particular *places* like the home.

This view of captive audience doctrine is mistaken. It is both over- and underinclusive. People are not captive audiences simply because they are at home. They can throw away junk mailings, change the dial, activate v-chips, operate the channel blocking capabilities of cable boxes, install filtering software, or, if all else fails, disconnect the cable service, turn off the television, and stop subscribing to an Internet service provider.

Nor is the home an unalloyed example of "privacy." In the information age, we increasingly receive information in our homes rather than outside them. New technologies like the Internet redraw and even collapse the boundaries between public and private spaces. People can participate in public discourse and public deliberation on the Internet while sitting at home in their underwear. In most cases the protection of children is a much better justification for content regulation than captive audience doctrine.[30]

Conversely, limiting captive audience situations to the home misses the point of the metaphor of *captivity*—that a person must listen to speech because he or she is practically unable to leave. Children may be subject to discipline in the home, but for most adults, the place they are most subject to the discipline of others, and least free to leave, is at work. Economic coercion leaves many workers unable to avoid exposure to harassing speech. Employees are a much better example of a captive audience than the so-called paradigm case of people sitting in their homes who suddenly come across indecent speech on television.

Being "captive" is a matter of practicality rather than necessity. It is about the right not to have to flee rather than the inability to flee. The Supreme Court has suggested that people riding in buses subjected to political advertisements were a captive audience; but surely these people could have chosen other forms of transportation, albeit at greater expense and inconvenience. Even people in their homes are not physically prevented from leaving them. The point of captive audience doctrine, however, is that they should not have to be put to such a choice. The coercion brought upon them is unfair. In like fashion, minimum wage workers may have to move from job to job to avoid harassment. But the question is not whether there is another equally low-paying job available. The question is whether they should have to leave a job to avoid being sexually harassed.[31] It would undermine the central purpose of Title VII to argue that it gave workers no right to stay in a job free from sexual harassment. Moreover, as noted before, the kind of employment discrimination at issue here promotes gender segregation in job opportunities precisely by surrounding the plaintiff in a hostile environment of speech and conduct. If the plaintiff's only remedy is to leave, the mechanisms of job segregation will simply proceed unabated.

Captive audience doctrine should not focus on particular *spaces* like the home. Rather, it should regulate particular *situations* where people are particularly subject to unjust and intolerable harassment and coercion. Captive audience doctrine, like the doctrines of Fourth Amendment privacy, should protect people in coercive situations, not places.[32] "The workplace" is not a place; it is a set of social relations of power and privilege, which may or may not have a distinct geographical nexus. If a male supervisor makes an obscene phone call from his home to a female subordinate in a hotel room, this unwelcome behavior can and should contribute to a hostile work environment, even though both supervisor and subordinate are miles away from the office.

The practical necessities of earning a living and the economic coercion inherent in social relations in the workplace create captive audience situations; but this does not mean that the workplace should be treated as a First Amendment-free zone. In fact, the workplace should be an arena of special, not lessened, free speech protection. Precisely because people spend so much of their lives at work, the workplace is an important site of public discourse.[33] Much employee speech in the workplace is not, nor should it be considered, exclusively "managerial," "instrumental," or "private." We may talk more about public matters, sports, gossip, politics, and the affairs of the day at work than we do at home. The problem with existing employment law is that it gives employers too much power to control the speech of employees on every subject, not simply on matters of sex and sexuality.

One way to justify sexual harassment liability in the workplace would be to make a categorical distinction between the world of public discourse and the world of the workplace. Thus, one might argue that "there are good reasons for the law to regard persons as autonomous within the context of political deliberation, but there are equally good reasons for the law to regard persons as dependent within the workplace.[34] However, because the workplace is also an important site of public discourse, the law cannot simply insist that workers are to be regarded as dependent in all their speech interactions in the workplace. Otherwise, Congress could regulate virtually all workplace speech. Put in the language of captive audience doctrine, workers would be captive audiences for all purposes.

That is why it is important to remember that the basis of captive audience doctrine is social relations rather than geographical places. Sexual harassment helps maintain sexual stratification of the workplace using the economic dependency of workers as a powerful form of leverage. Therefore the law may regard workers as dependent and not autonomous with respect to speech that helps maintain such stratification, but not with respect to other speech.

Critics of hostile environment liability miss this point, I think, when they argue that "[h]arassment law, if viewed as an attempt to protect a captive audience, is . . . underinclusive" because it applies only to speech that "creates a hostile environment based on race, sex, religion or national origin."[35] The point is precisely that people are almost never captive audiences for every purpose, even in the workplace. They are captive audiences only with respect to certain forms of unjust coercion that use the employee's economic dependence as a springboard. Sex discrimination is one of those situations. Another is the use of economic coercion to prevent or hinder decisions about unionization, as illustrated in labor cases like *NLRB v. Gissel Packing Co.*[36]

In *Gissel* the Supreme Court upheld an NLRB order that required an employer to bargain with a union that had lost an election. The election was held to be tainted by the employer's (truthful) statements that election of a union could lead to closing of the employer's plant or, if the union called a strike, to a transfer of operations. Kingsley Browne, a critic of hostile environment liability, insists that "[t]he reasoning of *Gissel* does not support a general governmental right to regulate speech in the workplace."[37] I quite agree. *Gissel* holds that when unfair employment practices take advantage of the coercion already inherent in the employment relationship, the government may step in to regulate workplace speech in order to promote equality values and protect employees' right to bargain freely. Similarly, captive audience doctrine applies only to situations where speech and conduct together will help perpetuate job segregation or other forms of employment discrimination.

In short, we should not confuse the economic dependence of employees with their ability to participate in public discourse about the things that matter to them. Precisely because workers are economically dependent within the workplace, but engage in public discourse there, Congress might want to make them *more* autonomous within the workplace by guaranteeing them certain speech rights against their employers. This means, for example, that employee political speech that is directed to issues of public concern should be exempted as a basis for hostile environment liability as a matter of statutory construction and that Congress might even want to take positive steps to protect political speech from retribution by employers.

Clearly some political speech can contribute to sexual stratification in the workplace, at least at the margins. But it is unlikely that in most cases it is the major contributor. Working through the facts of actual cases, one is more likely to find pranks, taunts, sexual suggestions, and personal invective than political agitation as the basic technology for creating hostile environments. Because political speech is valuable, and because it contributes only marginally to sexual stratification, courts should exempt it.[38]

Some commentators have argued for a distinction between directed and nondirected speech: only speech specifically directed at a particular individual or set of individuals (such as face-to-face insults) would form the basis of hostile environment liability, while nondirected speech would be exempt. I think a better distinction is between "open" and "hidden" speech. The former is speech that openly contributes to preserving sexual stratification—that is, putting women in their place. The latter is speech relegated to private consumption by willing participants or to private conversation among willing listeners. Take the case of pornography, the classic example of nondirected speech. We should distinguish employees who keep pornography in their desk drawers out of sight from those employees who keep pornography prominently displayed around the workplace where coworkers are likely to see it. We should treat male employees who tell each other dirty jokes not intended to be overheard by female coworkers differently than employees who do so openly in order to distress and offend their female counterparts. Some speech is not intended for general consumption, particularly speech that occurs out of public view and away from other coworkers. Employees can avoid exposure to this speech with relatively little effort and the burden should be on them to do so. Thus, as a matter of statutory construction, courts should not consider "hidden" or "nonpublic" speech between willing participants as constituting a hostile environment, even if it is not overtly political in character. The same should apply to "after-hours" speech and gossip between willing participants that is not intended to be overheard by coworkers.[39]

The open/hidden distinction is superior to the directed/nondirected distinction because it is more consistent with the purposes of hostile environment liability. By itself an individual employee's comment or expression may not constitute a hostile environment, but many different acts taken together can. From the perspective of the female or black employee, the hostility of environment is experienced as a whole, not in isolated bits. It is the environment as a whole—and the felt sense that women or minorities are poorly regarded or unwelcome in the workplace—that preserves or maintains sexual or racial stratification. The open/hidden distinction imagines the cumulative effect of expression from the perspective of the victim of the hostile environment, who experiences it as a gestalt. By contrast, the directed/nondirected distinction looks at the issue of hostile environment from the perspective of the individual perpetrator, who may well not understand how his or her nondirected expression contributes to an overall feeling of unwelcomeness or second-class citizenship.

The final constitutional objection to hostile environment law is that its judge-made doctrines are content- and viewpoint-based. Once again, this proves too much: the same charge could be leveled against defamation, fraud, and most other communications torts. Juries in defamation cases are required to make content-based judgments about what kinds of statements would hold people up to shame or ridicule in the community and to assess damages based on the degree of injury to reputation. Moreover, liability for defamation necessarily depends on viewpoint. If a defendant falsely says, "Smith is a crook," she may be subject to liability, but not if she falsely says, "Smith is an honest man."

Title VII protects workers from a limited class of status-based harms in order to guarantee equality in the workplace. As in the case of defamation, if status-based harms are to be protected at all, some content-based and even viewpoint-based distinctions are inevitable. Thus, it makes perfect sense that a sign saying "Sarah is Employee of the Month" would ordinarily not give rise to liability, while a sign reading "Sarah is a dumb-ass woman."[40] might form part of a hostile environment case. Such content-based distinctions are adapted to the very reasons why employment discrimination law protects workers from status-based or dignitary injury.[41]

THE DEEPER ISSUE: EMPLOYER CONTROL

There is some irony in libertarian complaints about employees' freedom of speech. In America the state has generally offered very little protection for employee speech. The traditional common law rule has been that employees can be fired at will absent a contractual provision to the contrary. Unless employees have sufficient bargaining power to demand "just cause" provisions in their contract, the employer can sanction or fire them for virtually any reason, including displeasure with their speech, even their political speech.[42] The common law regime is still the default rule today, and it provides employers with one of their most potent weapons for shaping the culture of the workplace and the behavior of their employees. American law stands in marked contrast with that of many other countries. In Europe, for example, employees often enjoy more substantial rights against arbitrary discharge.[43]

Thus, sexual harassment doctrines do not pose a simple conflict between some employees' liberty and other employees' equality. The question is not whether employees will have freedom of speech, but *how* employers will control employee speech—whether they will do so in response to the incentives produced by Title VII or for their own purposes.

Blaming employee censorship on Title VII diverts our attention from a larger issue: employers exercise considerable and sometimes tyrannical control over the speech and behavior of their employees. Throughout history American employers often have been deeply interested in control over the culture of the workplace. They are no less interested than the government in inculcating social norms of appropriate speech and behavior. Often they go even further, imposing elaborate dress codes and rules of social etiquette. In fact, the most important counterweights to the employer's power to shape workplace culture through hiring and firing decisions are antidiscrimination laws. Without the incentives created by sexual harassment law, employees are simply remitted to the economic and social control of employers. In other words, First Amendment challenges to sexual harassment law are a defense of employer prerogatives presented in the guise of worker liberties.

In the long run, employers will not necessarily lose much control over the workplace because of sexual harassment law. To the contrary, compliance with government regulation is often not a danger but an opportunity. Employers will use sexual harassment law as a new device for controlling their subordinates, by combining legal compliance with other bureaucratic and economic goals. Many tales of unjust compliance practices can be understood in precisely this way. The excuse of sexual harassment liability allows employers to impose ever new controls on employee behavior during an age when employees are spending more and more time at work and tend to rely more and more on the workplace to meet their partners.

When First Amendment challenges are raised to sexual harassment law, civil libertarians should not be diverted from the deeper issues of employer control and employee freedom. We can protect the First Amendment best by following the law as it is written—by awarding damages only in cases where severe or pervasive abuse materially alters employment conditions. But we should also not forget to protect employees—all employees—by working for greater speech rights against their employers than American law has seen fit to give them. For many employees, those are the speech rights that really count.

NOTES

[1] *See, e.g.,* Kingsley R. Browne, "Title VII as Censorship: Hostile-Environment Harassment and the First Amendment," 52 *Ohio State Law Journal* 481, 548 (1991); Eugene Volokh, "Freedom of Speech and Workplace Harassment," 39 *UCLA Law Review* 1791, 1846 (1992); Eugene Volokh, "How Harassment Law Restricts Free Speech," 47 *Rutgers Law Review* 563, 567 (1995); Eugene Volokh, "What Speech Does 'Hostile Work Environment' Harassment Law Restrict?" 85 *Georgetown Law Journal* 627, 647 (1997).

[2] *Harris v. Forklift Systems, Inc.,* 510 U.S. 17, 21 (1993) (quoting *Meritor Savings Bank v. Vinson,* 477 U.S. 57, 65, 67 (1986)).

[3] *Harris,* 510 U.S. at 21, 21–23.

[4] 524 U.S. 742 (1998).

[5] 524 U.S. 775 (1998).

[6]*See Burlington Industries, Inc. v. Ellerth*, 524 U.S. 742, 765 (1998).

[7]*See* Sexual Harassment, 29 C.F.R. § 1604.11(d) (1996). *See also Faragher v. City of Boca Raton*, 524 U.S. 775, 799–800 (1998) (collecting cases).

[8]Employers are not completely free to censor employee speech, of course: they are also constrained by wrongful discharge law, union rules, and civil service regulations.

[9]I borrow this term from Michael I. Meyerson, "Authors, Editors, and Uncommon Carriers: Identifying the 'Speaker' Within the New Media," 71 *Notre Dame Law Review* 79, 116, 118 (1995).

[10]376 U.S. 254, 283 (1964).

[11]418 U.S. 323, 350 (1974).

[12]419 U.S. 245, 253–54 (1974).

[13]For a general discussion, *see* Burt Neuborne, "The First Amendment and Government Regulation of Capital Markets," 55 *Brooklyn Law Review* 5 (1989).

[14]*See* W. Page Keeton et al., *Prosser and Keeton on the Law of Torts* 69, at 499–501 (5th ed. 1984) (describing standard justifications for vicarious liability).

[15]*See Restatement (Second) of Torts* § 578 (1977) ("Except as to those who only deliver or transmit defamation published by a third person, one who repeats or otherwise republishes defamatory matter is subject to liability as if he had originally published it").

[16]*See id.* § 581 ("One who . . . delivers or transmits defamatory matter published by a third person is subject to liability if, but only if, he knows or has reason to know of its defamatory character").

[17]47 U.S.C. § 230(c)(1); *see Blumenthal v. Drudge*, 992 F. Supp. 44, 49–52 (D.D.C. 1998). In fact, the 1996 act gives Internet service providers more protection than the traditional distributor's privilege, because knowledge of defamatory content is not sufficient to subject them to liability. *See Zeran v. America Online*, 129 F.3d 327, 331–32 (4th Cir. 1997), cert. denied, 524 U.S. 937 (1998).

[18]The argument for the constitutionality of collateral censorship in hostile environment cases is in some ways even stronger than in defamation and securities fraud cases because most courts currently hold the employer liable only if the employer knows or should have known of the harassment and does not take prompt corrective action. In other words, employers are not held strictly liable for employee speech (as in other vicarious liability situations) but are only liable when they fail to exercise due care in rooting out and remedying hostile environments. Hence the degree of collateral censorship should, in theory, be less in these cases.

[19]I am indebted to Vicki Schultz for this argument.

[20]*Ellertb*, 524 U.S. at 763–64; *Faragher*, 524 U.S. at 807.

[21]*Restatement (Second) of Torts* § 559 (1977).

[22]*Id.* § 46 cmt. d.

[23]*See R.A.V. v. City of St. Paul*, 505 U.S. 377, 391–92 (1992); *Texas v. Johnson*, 491 U.S. 397, 414 (1989). The First Amendment may permit recovery for "fighting words," or for intentional infliction of emotional distress, *see Chaplinsky v. New Hampshire*, 315 U.S. 568, 571–72 (1942), but these categories are very limited and do not include all or even most racist or misogynist speech.

[24]Compare *Gertz v. Robert Welch, Inc.*, 418 U.S. 323, 341 (1974) (discussing compelling interest in protecting individual reputation), with *Beauharnais v. Illinois*, 343 U.S. 250, 263–64 (1952) (upholding group libel statute). *Beauharnais* has never been overruled but its precedential value is generally thought doubtful, especially after *New York Times* Co. v. *Sullivan*, 376 U.S. 254 (1964), and *R.A.V. v. City of St. Paul*, 505 U.S. 377 (1992). *See* Laurence H. Tribe, American Constitutional Law § 12–12, at 861 n.2, § 12–17, at 921 n.9, § 12–17, at 926–27 (2d ed. 1988).

[25]*Harris*, 510 U.S. at 21 (quoting *Vinson*, 477 U.S. at 65, 67).

[26]*See* J. M. Balkin, "Some Realism About Pluralism: Legal Realist Approaches to the First Amendment," 1990 *Duke Law Journal* 375, 424 (1990).

[27]*See, e.g., Frisby v. Schultz*, 487 U.S. 474, 487 (1988) (upholding ban on residential picketing directed at a single house); *cf. Kovacs v. Cooper*, 336 U.S. 77, 87 (1949) (upholding ban on sound trucks to protect residents).

[28]*See Lehman v. City of Shaker Heights*, 418 U.S. 298, 301–4 (1974) (plurality opinion) (upholding ban of political advertising on public buses on grounds that passengers are a "captive audience").

[29]*Cohen v. California*, 403 U.S. 15, 21 (1971).

[30]*See* J. M. Balkin, "Media Filters, the V-Chip, and the Foundations of Broadcast Regulation," 45 *Duke Law Journal* 1131, 1137–39 (1996).

[31]Vicki Schultz has described the "revolving door" phenomenon of women in low-paying jobs who are continually forced to change jobs because of sex discrimination or harassment. *See* Vicki Schultz, "Telling Stories About Women and Work: Judicial Interpretations of Sex Segregation in the Workplace in Title VII Cases Raising the Lack of Interest Argument," 103 *Harvard Law Review* 1749, 1826, 1839 (1990). These women find themselves in a perpetual exodus from jobs that are "a dime a dozen." But the phenomenon of these forced exits is not an argument against the application of captive audience doctrine to harassment law; it is an argument for it.

[32]*Cf. Katz v. United States*, 389 U.S. 347, 351 (1967) (holding that the Fourth Amendment "protects people, not places").

[33]*See* Cynthia Estlund, "Freedom of Expression in the Workplace and the Problem of Discriminatory Harassment," 75 *Texas Law Review* 687, 717–18 (1997). Indeed, Kent Greenawalt argues that workers are "captive speakers," because they may have few other places to express themselves, and because "[w]hen people are working, the only place they can express themselves is within the workplace." Kent Greenawalt, *Fighting Words* 86 (1995) (emphasis omitted).

[34]Robert C. Post, "The Perils of Conceptualism: A Response to Professor Fallon," 103 *Harvard Law Review* 1744, 1746 (1990).

[35]Volokh, "Freedom of Speech," *supra* note 1 at 1843.

[36]395 U.S. 575 (1969).

[37]Browne, *supra* note 1 at 514.

[38]*Cf.* Richard H. Fallon, Jr., "Sexual Harassment, Content Neutrality, and the First Amendment Dog That Didn't Bark," 1994 *Supreme Court Review* 1, 47 (arguing for a somewhat narrower exemption for speech "'reasonably designed or intended to contribute to reasoned debate on issues of public concern'") (citing Harvard Law School's draft Guidelines Concerning Sexual Harassment).

[39]Nevertheless, such speech might be evidence of sex discrimination, or of other speech or conduct that would constitute a hostile environment.

[40]*See Harris*, 510 U.S. at 19.

[41]*Cf. R.A.V. v. City of St. Paul*, 505 U.S. 377, 389 (1992) (holding that content-based discrimination within a category of unprotected speech is justified when it furthers the purpose for which the speech is unprotected). Not surprisingly, even Eugene Volokh drops his objections to content- and viewpoint-based restrictions on harassment when the harassment is directed at a particular person. *See* Volokh, "Freedom of Speech," *supra* note 1 at 1866–67.

Note, moreover, that under the logic of *R.A.V.*, one may not argue that Title VII is unconstitutionally content-based because it does not cover harassment on all subjects, but only on the basis of race, sex, national origin, and religion. Congress is permitted to decide that discrimination on those grounds is more unjust, inflicts greater or more distinctive harms on its victims, or causes greater social problems than other forms of discrimination which it has chosen not to prohibit. *See Wisconsin v. Mitchell*, 508 U.S. 476, 487–88 (1993).

[42]*See* Cynthia L. Estlund, "Free Speech and Due Process in the Workplace," 71 *Indiana Law Review* 101, 116–17 (1995).

[43]*See, e.g.*, Frances Raday, "Individual and Collective Dismissal—A Job Security Dichotomy," 10 *Comparative Labor Law Journal* 121 (1989).

CHAPTER 6

The Justification of Punishment

THE EXPRESSIVE FUNCTION OF PUNISHMENT

—*Joel Feinberg*—

It might well appear to a moral philosopher absorbed in the classical literature of his discipline, or to a moralist sensitive to injustice and suffering, that recent philosophical discussions of the problem of punishment have somehow missed the point of his interest. Recent influential articles[1] have quite sensibly distinguished between questions of definition and justification, between justifying general rules and particular decisions, between moral and legal guilt. So much is all to the good. When these articles go on to *define* "punishment," however, it seems to many that they leave out of their ken altogether the very element that makes punishment theoretically puzzling and morally disquieting. Punishment is defined in effect as the infliction of hard treatment by an authority on a person for his prior failing in some respect (usually an infraction of a rule or command).[2] There may be a very general sense of the word "punishment" which is well expressed by this definition; but even if that is so, we can distinguish a narrower, more emphatic sense that slips through its meshes. Imprisonment at hard labor for committing a felony is a clear case of punishment in the emphatic sense. But I think we would be less willing to apply that term to parking tickets, offside penalties, sackings, flunkings, and disqualifications. Examples of the latter sort I propose to call *penalties* (merely), so that I may inquire further what distinguishes punishment, in the strict and narrow sense that interests the moralist, from other kinds of penalties.[3]

One method of answering this question is to focus one's attention on the class of nonpunitive penalties in an effort to discover some clearly identifiable characteristic common to them all, and absent from all punishments, on which the distinction between the two might be grounded. The hypotheses yielded by this approach, however, are not likely to survive close scrutiny. One might conclude, for example, that mere penalties are less severe than punishments, but although this is generally true, it is not necessarily and universally so. Again, we might be tempted to interpret penalties as mere "pricetags" attached to certain types of behavior that are generally undesirable, so that only those with especially strong motivation will be willing to pay the price.[4] In this way deliberate efforts on the part of some Western states to keep roads from urban centers to wilderness areas few in number and poor in quality would be viewed as essentially no different from various parking fines and football penalties. In each case a certain kind of conduct is discouraged without being absolutely prohibited: anyone who desires strongly enough to get to the wilderness (or park overtime, or interfere with a pass) may do so provided he is willing to pay the penalty (price). On this view, penalties are in effect licensing fees, different from other purchased permits in that the price is often paid afterward rather than in advance. Since a similar interpretation of punishments seems implausible, it might be alleged that this is the basis of the distinction between penalties and punishments. However, even though a great number of penalties can no doubt plausibly be treated as retroactive licensing fees, it is hardly possible to view all of them as such. It is certainly not true, for example, of most demotions, firings, and flunkings that they are "prices" paid for some already consumed benefit; and even parking fines are sanctions for rules "meant to be taken seriously as . . . standard[s] of behavior"[5] and thus are more than mere public parking fees.

Rather than look for a characteristic common and peculiar to the penalties on which to ground the distinction between penalties and punishments, we would be better advised, I think, to turn our attention to the examples of punishments. Both penalties and punishments are authoritative deprivations for failures; but, apart from these common features, penalties have a miscellaneous character, whereas punishments have an important additional characteristic in common. That characteristic, or specific difference, I shall argue, is a certain expressive function: punishment is a conventional device for the expression of attitudes of resentment and indignation, and of judgments of disapproval and reprobation, on the part either of the punishing authority himself or of those "in whose name" the punishment is inflicted. Punishment, in short, has a *symbolic significance* largely missing from other kinds of penalties.

The reprobative symbolism of punishment and its character as "hard treatment," though never separate in reality, must be carefully distinguished for purposes of analysis. Reprobation is itself painful, whether or not it is accompanied by further "hard treatment," and hard treatment, such as fine or imprisonment, because of its conventional symbolism, can itself be reprobatory. Still, we can conceive of ritualistic condemnation unaccompanied by any *further* hard treatment, and of inflictions and deprivations which, because of different symbolic conventions, have no reprobative force. It will be my thesis in this essay that (1) both the "hard treatment" aspect of punishment and its reprobative function must be part of the *definition* of legal punishment, and that (2) each of these aspects raises its own kind of question about the *justification* of legal punishment as a general practice. I shall argue that some of the jobs punishment does, and some of the conceptual problems it raises, cannot be intelligibly described unless (1) is true, and that the incoherence of a familiar form of the retributive theory results from failure to appreciate the force of (2).

I

That the expression of the community's condemnation is an essential ingredient in legal punishment is widely acknowledged by legal writers. Henry M. Hart, for example, gives eloquent emphasis to the point:

> What distinguishes a criminal from a civil sanction and all that distinguishes it, it is ventured, is the judgment of community condemnation which accompanies . . . its imposition. As Professor Gardner wrote not long ago, in a distinct but cognate connection:

> "The essence of punishment for moral delinquency lies in the criminal conviction itself. One may lose more money on the stock market than in a court-room; a prisoner of war camp may well provide a harsher environment than a state prison; death on the field of battle has the same physical characteristics as death by sentence of law. It is the expression of the community's hatred, fear, or contempt for the convict which alone characterizes physical hardship as punishment."

> If this is what a "criminal" penalty is, then we can say readily enough what a "crime" is. . . . It is conduct which, if duly shown to have taken place, will incur a formal and solemn pronouncement of the moral condemnation of the community. . . . Indeed the condemnation plus the added [unpleasant physical] consequences may well be considered, compendiously, as constituting the punishment.[6]

Professor Hart's compendious definition needs qualification in one respect. The moral condemnation and the "unpleasant consequences" that he rightly identifies as essential elements of punishment are not as distinct and separate as he suggests. It does not always happen that the convicted prisoner is first solemnly condemned and then subjected to unpleasant physical treatment. It would be more accurate in many cases to say that the unpleasant treatment itself expresses the condemnation, and that this expressive aspect of his incarceration is precisely the element by reason of which it is properly characterized as punishment and not mere penalty. The administrator who regretfully suspends the license of a conscientious but accident-prone driver can inflict a deprivation without any scolding, express or implied; but the reckless motorist who is sent to prison for six months is thereby inevitably subject to shame and ignominy—the very walls of his cell condemn him, and his record becomes a stigma.

To say that the very physical treatment itself expresses condemnation is to say simply that certain forms of hard treatment have become the conventional symbols' of public reprobation. This is neither more nor less paradoxical than to say that certain words have become conventional vehicles in our language for the expression of certain attitudes, or that champagne is the alcoholic beverage traditionally used in celebration of great events, or that black is the color of mourning. Moreover, particular kinds of punishment are often used to express quite specific attitudes (loosely speaking, this is part of their "meaning"); note the differences, for example, between beheading a nobleman and hanging a yeoman, burning a heretic and hanging a traitor, hanging an enemy soldier and executing him by firing squad.

It is much easier to show that punishment has a symbolic significance than to state exactly what it is that punishment expresses. At its best, in civilized and democratic countries, punishment surely expresses the community's strong *disapproval* of what the criminal did. Indeed, it can be said that punishment expresses the *judgment* (as distinct from any emotion) of the community that what the criminal did was wrong. I think it is fair to say of our community, however, that punishment generally expresses more than judgments of disapproval; it is also a symbolic way of getting back at the criminal, of expressing a kind of vindictive resentment. To any reader who has in fact spent time in a prison, I venture to say, even Professor Gardner's strong terms—"hatred, fear, or contempt for the convict"—will not seem too strong an account of what imprisonment is universally taken to express. Not only does the criminal feel the naked hostility of his guards and the outside world—that would be fierce enough—but that hostility is self-righteous as well. His punishment bears the aspect of legitimized vengefulness. Hence there is much truth in J. F. Stephen's celebrated remark that "The criminal law stands to the passion of revenge in much the same relation as marriage to the sexual appetite."[7]

If we reserve the less dramatic term "resentment" for the various vengeful attitudes and the term "reprobation" for the stern judgment of disapproval, then perhaps we can characterize *condemnation* (or denunciation) as a kind of fusing of resentment and reprobation. That these two elements are generally to be found in legal punishment was well understood by the authors of the *Report of the Royal Commission on Capital Punishment*:

> *Discussion of the principle of retribution is apt to be confused because the word is not always used in the same sense. Sometimes it is intended to mean vengeance, sometimes reprobation. In the first sense the idea is that of satisfaction by the State of a wronged individual's desire to be avenged; in the second it is that of the State's marking its disapproval of the breaking of its laws by a punishment proportionate to the gravity of the offense.*[8]

II

The relation of the expressive function of punishment to its various central purposes is not always easy to trace. Symbolic public condemnation added to deprivation may help or hinder deterrence, reform, and rehabilitation—the evidence is not clear. On the other hand, there are other functions of punishment, often lost sight of in the preoccupation with deterrence and reform, that presuppose the expressive function and would be difficult or impossible without it.

Authoritative disavowal Consider the standard international practice of demanding that a nation whose agent has unlawfully violated the complaining nation's rights should punish the offending agent. For example, suppose that an airplane of nation *A* fires on an airplane of nation *B* while the latter is flying over international waters. Very likely high authorities in nation *B* will send a note of protest to their counterparts in nation *A* demanding, among other things, that the transgressive pilot be punished. Punishing the pilot is an emphatic, dramatic, and well-understood way of *condemning* and thereby *disavowing* his act. It tells the world that the pilot had no right to do what he did, that he was on his own in doing it, that his government does not condone that sort of thing. It testifies thereby to government *A*'s recognition of the violated rights of government *B* in the affected area and, therefore, to the wrongfulness of the pilot's act. Failure to punish the pilot tells the world that government *A* does not consider him to have been personally at fault. That in turn is to claim responsibility for the act, which in effect labels that act as an "instrument of deliberate national policy" and hence an act of war. In that case either formal hostilities or humiliating loss of face by one side or the other almost certainly will follow. None of this scenario makes any sense without the clearly understood reprobative symbolism of punishment. In quite parallel ways punishment enables employers to disavow the acts of their employees (though not civil liability for those acts), and fathers the destructive acts of their sons.

Symbolic nonacquiescence "Speaking in the name of the people"   The symbolic function of punishment also explains why even those sophisticated persons who abjure resentment of criminals and look with small favor generally on the penal law are likely to demand that certain kinds of conduct be punished when or if the law lets them go by. In the state of Texas, so-called paramour killings were regarded by the law as not merely mitigated, but completely justifiable.[9] Many humanitarians, I believe, will feel quite spontaneously that a great injustice is done when such killings are left unpunished. The sense of violated justice, moreover, might be distinct and unaccompanied by any frustrated *Schadenfreude* toward the killer, lust for blood or vengeance, or metaphysical concern lest the universe stay "out of joint." The demand for punishment in cases of this sort may instead represent the feeling that paramour killings deserve to be *condemned*, that the law in condoning, even approving of them, speaks for all citizens in expressing a wholly inappropriate attitude toward them. For in effect the law expresses the judgment of the "people of Texas," in whose name it speaks, that the vindictive satisfaction in the mind of a cuckolded husband is a thing of greater value than the very life of his wife's lover. The demand that paramour killings be punished may simply be the demand that this lopsided value judgment be withdrawn and that the state *go on record* against paramour killings and the law *testify to the recognition* that such killings are wrongful. Punishment no doubt would also help deter killers. This too is a desideratum and a closely related one, but it is not to be identified with reprobation; for deterrence might be achieved by a dozen other techniques, from simple penalties and forfeitures to exhortation and propaganda; but effective public denunciation and, through it, symbolic non-acquiescence in the crime seem virtually to require punishment.

This symbolic function of punishment was given great emphasis by Kant, who, characteristically, proceeded to exaggerate its importance. Even if a desert island community were to disband, Kant argued, its members should first execute the last murderer left in its jails, "for otherwise they might all be regarded as participators in the [unpunished] murder. . . ."[10] This Kantian idea that in failing to punish wicked acts society endorses them and thus becomes *particeps criminis* does seem to reflect, however dimly, something embedded in common sense. A similar notion underlies whatever is intelligible in the widespread notion that all citizens share the responsibility for political atrocities. Insofar as there is a coherent argument behind the extravagant distributions of guilt made by existentialists and other literary figures, it can be reconstructed in some such way as this: to whatever extent a political act is done "in one's name," to that extent one is responsible for it; a citizen can avoid responsibility in advance by explicitly disowning the government as his spokesman, or after the fact through open protest, resistance, and so on; otherwise, by "acquiescing" in what is done in one's name, one incurs the responsibility for it. The root notion here is a kind of "power of attorney" a government has for its citizens.

Vindication of the law   Sometimes the state goes on record through its statutes, in a way that might well please a conscientious citizen in whose name it speaks, but then owing to official evasion and unreliable enforcement gives rise to doubts that the law really means what it says. It is murder in Mississippi, as elsewhere, for a white man intentionally to kill a Negro; but if grand juries refuse to issue indictments or if trial juries refuse to convict, and this fact is clearly recognized by most citizens, then it is in a purely formal and empty sense indeed that killings of Negroes by whites are illegal in Mississippi. Yet the law stays on the books, to give ever less convincing lip service to a noble moral judgment. A statute honored mainly in the breach begins to lose its character as law, unless, as we say, it is *vindicated* (emphatically reaffirmed); and clearly the way to do this (indeed the only way) is to punish those who violate it.

Similarly, *punitive damages,* so called, are sometimes awarded the plaintiff in a civil action, as a supplement to compensation for his injuries. What more dramatic way of vindicating his violated right can be imagined than to have a court thus forcibly condemn its violation through the symbolic machinery of punishment?

Absolution of others   When something scandalous has occurred and it is clear that the wrongdoer must be one of a small number of suspects, then the state, by punishing one of these parties, thereby relieves the others of suspicion and informally absolves them of blame. Moreover, quite often the absolution of an accuser hangs as much in the balance at a criminal trial as the inculpation of the accused. A good example of this point can be found in James Gould Cozzens's novel *By Love Possessed.* A young girl, after an evening of illicit sexual activity with her boy friend, is found out by her bullying mother, who then insists that she clear her name by bringing criminal charges against the boy. He used physical force, the girl charges; she freely consented, he replies. If the jury finds him guilty of rape, it will by the same token absolve her from (moral) guilt; and her reputation as well as his rides on the outcome. Could not the state do this job without punishment? Perhaps, but when it speaks by punishing, its message is loud and sure of getting across.

III

A philosophical theory of punishment that, through inadequate definition, leaves out the condemnatory function not only will disappoint the moralist and the traditional moral philosopher; it will seem offensively irrelevant as well to the constitutional lawyer, whose vital concern with punishment is both conceptual, and therefore genuinely philosophical, as well as practically urgent. The distinction between punishment and mere penalties is a familiar one in the criminal law, where theorists have long engaged in what Jerome Hall calls "dubious dogmatics distinguishing 'civil penalties' from punitive sanctions, and 'public wrongs' from crimes."[11] Our courts now regard it as true (by definition) that all criminal statutes are punitive (merely labeling an act a crime does not make it one unless sanctions are specified); but to the converse question whether all statutes specifying sanctions are *criminal* statutes, the courts are reluctant to give an affirmative reply. There are now a great number of statutes that permit "unpleasant consequences" to be inflicted on persons and yet surely cannot be regarded as criminal statutes—tax bills, for example, are aimed at regulating, not forbidding, certain types of activity. How to classify borderline cases as either "regulative" or "punitive" is not merely an idle conceptual riddle; it very quickly draws the courts into questions of great constitutional import. There are elaborate constitutional safeguards for persons faced with the prospect of punishment; but these do not, or need not, apply when the threatened hard treatment merely "regulates an activity."

The 1960 Supreme Court case of *Flemming* v. *Nestor*[12] is a dramatic (and shocking) example of how a man's fate can depend on whether a government-inflicted deprivation is interpreted as a "regulative" or "punitive" sanction. Nestor had immigrated to the United States from Bulgaria in 1913 and became eligible in 1955 for old-age benefits under the Social Security Act. In 1956, however, he was deported in accordance with the Immigration and Nationality Act for having been a member of the Communist Party from 1933 to 1939. This was a harsh fate for a man who had been in America for forty-three years and who was no longer a Communist; but at least he would have his social security benefits to support him in his exiled old age—or so he thought. Section 202 of the amended Social Security Act, however, "provides for the termination of old-age, survivor, and disability insurance benefits payable to . . . an alien individual who, after September 1, 1954 (the date of enactment of the section) is deported under the Immigration and Nationality Act on any one of certain specified grounds, including past membership in the Communist Party."[13] Accordingly, Nestor was informed that his benefits would cease.

Nestor then brought suit in a district court for a reversal of the administrative decision. The court found in his favor and held Section 202 of the Social Security Act unconstitutional, on the grounds that "termination of [Nestor's] benefits amounts to punishing him without a judicial trial, that [it] constitutes the imposition of punishment by legislative act rendering § 202 a bill of attainder; and that the punishment exacted is imposed for past conduct not unlawful when engaged in, thereby violating the constitutional prohibition on *ex post facto* laws."[14] The Secretary of Health, Education, and Welfare, Mr. Flemming, then appealed this decision to the Supreme Court.

It was essential to the argument of the district court that the termination of old-age benefits under Section 202 was in fact punishment, for if it were properly classified as non-punitive deprivation, then none of the cited constitutional guarantees was relevant. The Constitution, for example, does not forbid all retroactive laws, but only those providing punishment. (Retroactive tax laws may also be harsh and unfair, but they are not unconstitutional.) The question before the Supreme Court, then, was whether the hardship imposed by Section 202 was punishment. Did this not bring the Court face to face with the properly philosophical question "What is punishment?" and is it not clear that, under the usual definition that fails to distinguish punishment from mere penalties, this particular judicial problem could not even arise?

The fate of the appellee Nestor can be recounted briefly. The five-man majority of the Court held that he had not been punished—this despite Mr. Justice Brennan's eloquent characterization of him in a dissenting opinion as "an aging man deprived of the means with which to live after being separated from his family and exiled to live among strangers in a land he quit forty-seven years ago."[15] Mr. Justice Harlan, writing for the majority, argued that the termination of benefits, like the deportation itself, was the exercise of the plenary power of Congress incident to the regulation of an activity.

> Similarly, the setting by a State of qualifications for the practice of medicine, and their modification from time to time, is an incident of the State's power to protect the health and safety of its citizens, and its decision to bar from practice persons who commit or have committed a felony is taken as evidencing an intent to exercise that regulatory power, and not a purpose to add to the punishment of ex-felons.[16]

Mr. Justice Brennan, on the other hand, contended that it is impossible to think of any purpose the provision in question could possibly serve except to "strike" at "aliens deported for conduct displeasing to the lawmakers."[17]

Surely, Justice Brennan seems right in finding in the sanction the expression of Congressional reprobation and, therefore, "punitive intent"; but the sanction itself (in Justice Harlan's words, "the mere denial of a noncontractual governmental benefit"[18]) was not a conventional vehicle for the expression of censure, being wholly outside the apparatus of the criminal law. It therefore lacked the reprobative symbolism essential to punishment generally and was thus, in its hybrid character, able to generate confusion and judicial disagreement. It was as if Congress had "condemned" a certain class of persons privately in stage whispers, rather than by pinning the infamous label of criminal on them and letting that symbol do the condemning in an open and public way. Congress without question "intended" to punish a certain class of aliens and did indeed select sanctions of appropriate severity for that purpose; but the deprivation they chose was not of an appropriate kind to perform the function of public condemnation. A father who "punishes" his son for a displeasing act the father had not thought to forbid in advance, by sneaking up on him from behind and then throwing him bodily across the room against the wall, would be in much the same position as the legislators of the amended Social Security Act, especially if he then denied to the son that his physical assault on him had had any "punitive intent," asserting that it was a mere exercise of his paternal prerogative to rearrange the household furnishings and other objects in his own living room. To act in such a fashion would be to tarnish the paternal authority and infect all later genuine punishments with hollow hypocrisy. The same effect is produced when legislators go outside the criminal law to do the criminal law's job. . . .

IV

The distinction between punishments and mere penalties, and the essentially reprobative function of the former, can also help clarify the controversy among writers on the criminal law about the propriety of so-called strict liability offenses—offenses for the conviction of which there need be no proof of "fault" or "culpability" on the part of the accused. If it can be shown that he committed an act proscribed by statute, then he is guilty irrespective of whether he had any justification or excuse for what he did. Perhaps the most familiar examples come from the traffic laws: leaving a car parked beyond the permitted time in a restricted zone is automatically to violate the law, and penalties will be imposed however good the excuse. Many strict liability statutes do not even require an overt act; these proscribe not certain conduct, but certain *results*. Some make mere unconscious possession of contraband, firearms, or narcotics a crime, others the sale of misbranded articles or impure foods. The liability for so-called public welfare offenses may seem especially severe:

> . . . with rare exceptions, it became definitely established that mens rea *is not essential in the public welfare offenses, indeed that even a very high degree of care is irrelevant. Thus a seller of cattle feed was convicted of violating a statute forbidding misrepresentation of the percentage of oil in the product, despite the fact that he had employed a reputable chemist to make the analysis and had even understated the chemist's findings.*[19]

The rationale of strict liability in public welfare statutes is that violation of the public interest is more likely to be prevented by unconditional liability than by liability that can be defeated by some kind of excuse; that, even though liability without "fault" is severe, it is one of the known risks incurred by businessmen; and that, besides, the sanctions are *only fines*, hence not really "punitive" in character. On the other hand, strict liability to *imprisonment* (or "punishment proper") "has been held by many to be incompatible with the basic requirements of our Anglo-American, and indeed, any civilized jurisprudence."[20] What accounts for this difference in attitude? In both kinds of case, defendants may have sanctions inflicted upon them even though they are acknowledged to be without fault; and the difference cannot be merely that imprisonment is always and necessarily a greater harm than a fine, for this is not always so. Rather, the reason why strict liability to imprisonment (punishment) is so much more repugnant to our sense of justice than is strict liability to fine (penalty) is simply that imprisonment in modern times has taken on the symbolism of public reprobation. In the words of Justice Brandeis, "It is . . . imprisonment in a penitentiary, which now renders a crime infamous."[21] We are familiar with the practice of penalizing persons for "offenses" they could not help. It happens every day in football games, business firms, traffic courts, and the like. But there is something very odd and offensive in *punishing* people for admittedly faultless conduct; for not only is it arbitrary and cruel to *condemn* someone for something he did (admittedly) without fault, it is also self-defeating and irrational.

Although their abundant proliferation[22] is a relatively recent phenomenon, statutory offenses with nonpunitive sanctions have long been familiar to legal commentators, and long a source of uneasiness to them. This discomfort is "indicated by the persistent search for an appropriate label, such as 'public torts,' 'public welfare offenses,' 'prohibitory laws,' 'prohibited acts,' 'regulatory offenses,' 'police regulations,' 'administrative misdemeanors,' 'quasi-crimes,' or 'civil offenses.'"[23] These represent alternatives to the unacceptable categorization of traffic infractions, inadvertent violations of commercial regulations, and the like, as *crimes*, their perpetrators as *criminals*, and their penalties as *punishments*. The drafters of the new Model Penal Code have defined a class of infractions of penal law forming no part of the substantive criminal law. These they call "violations," and their sanctions "civil penalties."

Section 1.04. Classes of Crimes: Violations

(1) An offense defined by this code or by any other statute of this State, for which a sentence of [death or of] imprisonment is authorized, constitutes a crime. Crimes are classified as felonies, misdemeanors, or petty misdemeanors.

[(2), (3), (4) define felonies, misdemeanors, and petty misdemeanors.]

(5) An offense defined by this Code or by any other statute of this State constitutes a violation if it is so designated in this Code or in the law defining the offense or if no other sentence than a fine, or fine and forfeiture or other civil penalty is authorized upon conviction or if it is defined by a statute other than this Code which now provides that the offense shall not constitute a crime. A violation does not constitute a crime and conviction of a violation shall not give rise to any disability or legal disadvantage based on conviction of a criminal offense.[24]

Since violations, unlike crimes, carry no social stigma, it is often argued that there is no serious injustice if, in the interest of quick and effective law enforcement, violators are held unconditionally liable. This line of argument is persuasive when we consider only parking and minor traffic violations, illegal sales of various kinds, and violations of health and safety codes, where the penalties serve as warnings and the fines are light. But the argument loses all cogency when the "civil penalties" are severe—heavy fines, forfeitures of property, removal from office, suspension of a license, withholding of an important "benefit," and the like. The condemnation of the faultless may be the most flagrant injustice, but the good-natured, noncondemnatory infliction of severe hardship on the innocent is little better. It is useful to distinguish violations and civil penalties from crimes and punishments; yet it does not follow that the safeguards of culpability requirements and due process which justice demands for the latter are always irrelevant encumbrances to the former. Two things are morally wrong: (1) to condemn a faultless man while inflicting pain or deprivation on him however slight (unjust punishment); and (2) to inflict unnecessary and severe suffering on a faultless man even in the absence of condemnation (unjust civil penalty). To exact a two-dollar fine from a hapless violator for overtime parking, however, even though he could not possibly have avoided it, is to do neither of these things.

V

Public condemnation, whether avowed through the stigmatizing symbolism of punishment or unavowed but clearly discernible (mere "punitive intent"), can greatly magnify the suffering caused by its attendant mode of hard treatment. Samuel Butler keenly appreciated the difference between reprobative hard treatment (punishment) and the same treatment without reprobation:

> . . . we should hate a single flogging given in the way of mere punishment more than the amputation of a limb, if it were kindly and courteously performed from a wish to help us out of our difficulty, and with the full consciousness on the part of the doctor that it was only by an accident of constitution that he was not in the like plight himself. So the Erewhonians take a flogging once a week, and a diet of bread and water for two or three months together, whenever their straightener recommends it.[25]

Even floggings and imposed fastings do not constitute punishments, then, where social conventions are such that they do not express public censure (what Butler called "scouting"); and as therapeutic treatments simply, rather than punishments, they are easier to take.

Yet floggings and fastings do hurt, and far more than is justified by their Erewhonian (therapeutic) objectives. The same is true of our own state mental hospitals where criminal psychopaths are often sent for "rehabilitation": solitary confinement may not hurt *quite* so much when called "the quiet room," or the forced support of heavy fire extinguishers when called "hydrotherapy";[26] but their infliction on patients can be so cruel (whether or not their quasimedical names mask punitive intent) as to demand justification.

Hard treatment and symbolic condemnation, then, are not only both necessary to an adequate definition of "punishment"; each also poses a special problem for the justification of punishment. The reprobative symbolism of punishment is subject to attack not only as an independent source of suffering but as the vehicle of undeserved responsive attitudes and unfair judgments of blame. One kind of skeptic, granting that penalties are needed if legal rules are to be enforced, and also that society would be impossible without general and predictable obedience to such rules, might nevertheless question the need to add condemnation to the penalizing of violators. Hard treatment of violators, he might grant, is an unhappy necessity, but reprobation of the offender is offensively self-righteous and cruel; adding gratuitous insult to necessary injury can serve no useful purpose. A partial answer to this kind of skeptic has already been given. The condemnatory aspect of punishment does serve a socially useful purpose: it is precisely the element in punishment that makes possible the performance of such symbolic functions as disavowal, nonacquiescence, vindication, and absolution. . . .

NOTES

[1]See esp. the following: A.G.N. Flew, "The Justification of Punishment," *Philosophy*, 29 (1954), 291–307; S. I. Benn, "An Approach to the Problems of Punishment," *Philosophy*, 33 (1958), 325–341; and H.L.A. Hart, "Prolegomenon to the Principles of Punishment," *Proceedings of the Aristotelian Society*, 60 (1959/60), 1–26.

[2]Hart and Benn both borrow Flew's definition. In Hart's paraphrase (*op.cit.*, 4), punishment "(i) . . . must involve pain or other consequences normally considered unpleasant. (ii) It must be for an offense against legal rules. (iii) It must be of an actual or supposed offender for his offense. (iv) It must be intentionally administered by human beings other than the offender. (v) It must be imposed and administered by an authority constituted by a legal system against which the offense is committed."

[3]The distinction between punishments and penalties was first called to my attention by Dr. Anita Fritz of the University of Connecticut. Similar distinctions in different terminologies have been made by many. Sir Frederick Pollock and Frederic Maitland speak of "true afflictive punishments" as opposed to outlawry, private vengeance, fine, and emendation. *The History of English Law Before the Time of Edward I*, and edn. (Cambridge: At the University Press, 1968), 11, 451 ff. The phrase "afflictive punishment" was invented by Bentham: "These [corporal] punishments are almost always attended with a portion of ignominy, and this does not always increase with the organic pain, but principally depends upon the condition [social class] of the offender." *The Rationale of Punishment* (London: Heward, 1830), 83. Sir James Stephen says of legal punishment that it "should always connote . . . moral infamy." *A History of the Criminal Law of England*, 3 vols. (London: Macmillan & Co., 1883), 11, 171. Lasswell and Donnelly distinguish "condemnation sanctions" and "other deprivations." "The Continuing Debate over Responsibility: An Introduction to Isolating the Condemnation

Sanction," *Yale Law Journal*, 68 (1959). The traditional common law distinction is between "infamous" and "non-infamous" crimes and punishments. Conviction of an "infamous crime" rendered a person liable to such postpunitive civil disabilities as incompetence to be a witness.

[4]That even punishments proper are to be interpreted as taxes on certain kinds of conduct is a view often associated with O. W. Holmes, Jr. For an excellent discussion of Holmes's fluctuations of this question, see Mark De Wolfe Howe, *Justice Holmes, The Proving Years* (Cambridge: *Harvard University Press*, 1965), 74–80. See also Lon Fuller, *The Morality of Law* (New Haven: Yale University Press, 1964), Ch. 2, Part 7, and H. L. A. Hart, *The Concept of Law* (Oxford: Clarendon Press, 1961), 39, for illuminating comparisons and contrasts of punishment and taxation.

[5]H. L. A. Hart, *loc. cit.*

[6]Henry M. Hart, "The Aims of the Criminal Law," *Law and Contemporary Problems*, 23 (1958), 11, A, 4.

[7]*General View of the Criminal Law of England* (London: Macmillan & Co., 1863), 99.

[8](London, 1953), 17–18, *My italics.*

[9]The Texas Penal Code (Art. 1220) until recently stated: "Homicide is justifiable when committed by the husband upon one taken in the act of adultery with the wife, provided the killing takes place before the parties to the act have separated. Such circumstances cannot justify a homicide when it appears that there has been on the part of the husband, any connivance in or assent to the adulterous connection." New Mexico and Utah have similar statutes. For some striking descriptions of perfectly legal paramour killings in Texas, see John Bainbridge, *The Super-Americans* (Garden City: Doubleday, 1961), 238ff.

[10]*The Philosophy of Law*, tr. W. Hastie (Edinburgh: T. & T. Clark, 1887), 198.

[11]*General Principles of Criminal Law*, and edn. (Indianapolis: The Bobbs-Merrill Co., 1960), 328.

[12]*Flemming v. Nestor*, 80 S. Ct. 1367 (1960).

[13]*Ibid.*, 1370.

[14]*Ibid.*, 1374 (interspersed citations omitted).

[15]*Ibid.*, 1385.

[16]*Ibid.*, 1375–76.

[17]*Ibid.*, 1387.

[18]*Ibid.*, 1378.

[19]Hall, *op. cit.*, 329.

[20]Richard A. Wasserstrom, "Strict Liability in the Criminal Law," *Stanford Law Review*, 12 (1980), 730.

[21]*United States v. Moreland*, 258 U.S. 433, 447–448 (1922). Quoted in Hall, *op. cit.*, 327.

[22]"A depth study of Wisconsin statutes in 1956 revealed that of 1113 statutes creating criminal offenses [punishable by fine, imprisonment, or both] which were in force in 1953, no less than 660 used language in the definitions of the offenses which omitted all reference to a mental element, and which therefore, under the canons of construction which have come to govern these matters, left it open to the courts to impose strict liability if they saw fit." Colin Howard, "Not Proven," *Adelaide Law Review*, 1 (1962), 274. The study cited is: Remington, Robinson, and Zick, "Liability Without Fault Criminal Statutes." *Wisconsin Law Review* (1956), 625, 636.

[23]Rollin M. Perkins, *Criminal Law* (Brooklyn: The Foundation Press, 1957), 701–702.

[24]American Law Institute, *Model Penal Code, Proposed Official Draft* (Philadelphia, 1962).

[25]*Erewhon*, new and rev. edn. (London: Grant Richards, 1901), Ch. 10.

[26]These two examples are cited by Francis A. Allen in "Criminal Justice, Legal Values and the Rehabilitative Ideal," *Journal of Criminal Law, Criminology and Police Science*, 50 (1959), 229.

INTRODUCTION TO THE PRINCIPLES OF MORALS AND LEGISLATION

—Jeremy Bentham—

CHAPTER XIV OF THE PROPORTION BETWEEN PUNISHMENTS AND OFFENCES

1. We have seen that the general object of all laws is to prevent mischief; that is to say, when it is worth while; but that, where there are no other means of doing this than punishment, there are four cases in which it is not worth while.

2. When it is worth while, there are four subordinate designs or objects, which, in the course of his endeavours to compass, as far as may be, that one general object, a legislator, whose views are governed by the principle of utility, comes naturally to propose to himself.

3. His first, most extensive, and most eligible object, is to prevent, in as far as it is possible, and worth while, all sorts of offences whatsoever: in other words, so to manage, that no offence whatsoever may be committed.

4. But if a man must needs commit an offence of some kind or other, the next object is to induce him to commit an offence less mischievous, rather than one more mischievous: in other words, to choose always the least mischievous, of two offences that will either of them suit his purpose.

5. When a man has resolved upon a particular offence, the next object is to dispose him to do no more mischief than is necessary to his purpose: in other words, to do as little mischief as is consistent with the benefit he has in view.

6. The last object is, whatever the mischief be, which it is proposed to prevent, to prevent it at as cheap a rate as possible.

7. Subservient to these four objects, or purposes, must be the rules or canons by which the proportion of punishments to offences is to be governed.

8. Rule 1. The first object, it has been seen, is to prevent, in as far as it is worth while, all sorts of offences; therefore,

   The value of the punishment must not be less in any case than what is sufficient to outweigh that of the profit of the offence.

If it be, the offence (unless some other considerations, independent of the punishment, should intervene and operate efficaciously in the character of tutelary motives) will be sure to be committed notwithstanding: the whole lot of punishment will be thrown away: it will be altogether inefficacious.

9. The above rule has been often objected to, on account of its seeming harshness: but this can only have happened for want of its being properly understood. The strength of the temptation, caeteris paribus, is as the profit of the offence: the quantum of the punishment must rise with the profit of the offence: caeteris paribus, it must therefore rise with the strength of the temptation. This there is no disputing. True it is, that the stronger the temptation, the less conclusive is the indication which the act of delinquency affords of the depravity of the offender's disposition. So far then as the absence of any aggravation, arising from extraordinary depravity of disposition, may operate, or at the utmost, so far as the presence of a ground of extenuation, resulting from the innocence or beneficence of the offender's disposition, can operate, the strength of the temptation may operate in abatement of the demand for punishment. But it can never operate so far as to indicate the propriety of making the punishment ineffectual, which it is sure to be when brought below the level of the apparent profit of the offence.

The partial benevolence which should prevail for the reduction of it below this level, would counteract as well those purposes which such a motive would actually have in view, as those more extensive purposes which benevolence ought to have in view: it would be cruelty not only to the public, but to the very persons in whose behalf it pleads: in its effects, I mean, however opposite in its intention. Cruelty to the public, that is cruelty to the innocent, by suffering them, for want of an adequate protection, to lie exposed to the mischief of the offence: cruelty even to the offender himself, by punishing him to no purpose, and without the chance of compassing that beneficial end, by which alone the introduction of the evil of punishment is to be justified.

10. Rule 2. But whether a given offence shall be prevented in a given degree by a given quantity of punishment, is never any thing better than a chance; for the purchasing of which, whatever punishment is employed, is so much expended in advance. However, for the sake of giving it the better chance of outweighing the profit of the offence,

The greater the mischief of the offence, the greater is the expense, which it may be worth while to be at, in the way of punishment.

11. Rule 3. The next object is, to induce a man to choose always the least mischievous of two offences; therefore

Where two offences come in competition, the punishment for the greater offence must be sufficient to induce a man to prefer the less.

12. Rule 4. When a man has resolved upon a particular offence, the next object is, to induce him to do no more mischief than what is necessary for his purpose: therefore

The punishment should be adjusted in such manner to each particular offence, that for every part of the mischief there may be a motive to restrain the offender from giving birth to it.

13. Rule 5. The last object is, whatever mischief is guarded against, to guard against it at as cheap a rate as possible: therefore The punishment ought in no case to be more than what is necessary to bring it into conformity with the rules here given.

14. Rule 6. It is further to be observed, that owing to the different manners and degrees in which persons under different circumstances are affected by the same exciting cause, a punishment which is the same in name will not always either really produce, or even so much as appear to others to produce, in two different persons the same degree of pain: therefore,

That the quantity actually inflicted on each individual offender may correspond to the quantity intended for similar offenders in general, the several circumstances influencing sensibility ought always to be taken into account.

15. Of the above rules of proportion, the four first, we may perceive, serve to mark out the limits on the side of diminution; the limits below which a punishment ought not to be diminished: the fifth, the limits on the side of increase; the limits above which it ought not to be increased. The five first are calculated to serve as guides to the legislator: the sixth is calculated, in some measure, indeed, for the same purpose; but principally for guiding the judge in his endeavours to conform, on both sides, to the intentions of the legislator.

16. Let us look back a little. The first rule, in order to render it more conveniently applicable to practice, may need perhaps to be a little more particularly unfolded. It is to be observed, then, that for the sake of accuracy, it was necessary, instead of the word quantity to make use of the less perspicuous term value. For the word quantity will not properly include the circumstances either of certainty or proximity: circumstances which, in estimating the value of a lot of pain or pleasure, must always be taken into the account. Now, on the one hand, a lot of punishment is a lot of pain; on the other hand, the profit of an offence is a lot of pleasure, or what is equivalent to it. But the profit of the offence is commonly more certain than the punishment, or, what comes to the same thing, appears so at least to the offender. It is at any rate commonly more immediate. It follows, therefore, that, in order to maintain its superiority over the profit of the offence, the punishment must have its value made up in some other way, in proportion to that whereby it falls short in the two points of certainty and proximity. Now there is no other way in which it can receive any addition to its value, but by receiving an addition in point of magnitude. Wherever then the value of the punishment falls short, either in point of certainty, or of proximity, of that of the profit of the offence, it must receive a proportionable addition in point of magnitude.

17. Yet farther. To make sure of giving the value of the punishment the superiority over that of the offence, it may be necessary, in some cases, to take into the account the profit not only of the individual offence to which the punishment is to be annexed, but also of such other offences of the same sort as the offender is likely to have already committed without detection. This random mode of calculation, severe as it is, it will be impossible to avoid having recourse to, in certain cases: in such, to wit, in which the profit is pecuniary, the chance of detection very small, and the obnoxious act of such a nature as indicates a habit: for example, in the case of frauds against the coin. If it be not recurred to, the practice of committing the offence will be sure to be, upon the balance of the account, a gainful practice. That being the case, the legislator will be absolutely sure of not being able to suppress it, and the whole punishment that is bestowed upon it will be thrown away. In a word (to keep to the same expressions we set out with) that whole quantity of punishment will be inefficacious.

18. Rule 7. These things being considered, the three following rules may be laid down by way of supplement and explanation to Rule 1.

    To enable the value of the punishment to outweigh that of the profit of the offence, it must be increased, in point of magnitude, in proportion as it falls short in point of certainty.

19. Rule 8. Punishment must be further increased in point of magnitude, in proportion as it falls short in point of proximity.

20. Rule 9. Where the act is conclusively indicative of a habit, such an increase must be given to the punishment as may enable it to outweigh the profit not only of the individual offence, but of such other like offences as are likely to have been committed with impunity by the same offender.

21. There may be a few other circumstances or considerations which may influence, in some small degree, the demand for punishment: but as the propriety of these is either not so demonstrable, or not so constant, or the application of them not so determinate, as that of the foregoing, it may be doubted whether they be worth putting on a level with the others.

22. Rule 10. When a punishment, which in point of quality is particularly well calculated to answer its intention, cannot exist in less than a certain quantity, it may sometimes be of use, for the sake of employing it, to stretch a little beyond that quantity which, on other accounts, would be strictly necessary.

23. Rule 11. In particular, this may sometimes be the case, where the punishment proposed is of such a nature as to be particularly well calculated to answer the purpose of a moral lesson.

24. Rule 12. The tendency of the above considerations is to dictate an augmentation in the punishment: the following rule operates in the way of diminution. There are certain cases (it has been seen) in which, by the influence of accidental circumstances, punishment may be rendered unprofitable in the whole: in the same cases it may chance to be rendered unprofitable as to a part only. Accordingly,

In adjusting the quantum of punishment, the circumstances, by which all punishment may be rendered unprofitable, ought to be attended to.

25. Rule 13. It is to be observed, that the more various and minute any set of provisions are, the greater the chance is that any given article in them will not be borne in mind: without which, no benefit can ensue from it. Distinctions, which are more complex than what the conceptions of those whose conduct it is designed to influence can take in, will even be worse than useless. The whole system will present a confused appearance: and thus the effect, not only of the proportions established by the articles in question, but of whatever is connected with them, will be destroyed. To draw a precise line of direction in such case seems impossible. However, by way of memento, it may be of some use to subjoin the following rule.

Among provisions designed to perfect the proportion between punishments and offences, if any occur, which, by their own particular good effects, would not make up for the harm they would do by adding to the intricacy of the Code, they should be omitted.

26. It may be remembered, that the political sanction, being that to which the sort of punishment belongs, which in this chapter is all along in view, is but one of four sanctions, which may all of them contribute their share towards producing the same effects. It may be expected, therefore, that in adjusting the quantity of political punishment, allowance should be made for the assistance it may meet with from those other controlling powers. True it is, that from each of these several sources a very powerful assistance may sometimes be derived. But the case is, that (setting aside the moral sanction, in the case where the force of it is expressly adopted into and modified by the political) the force of those other powers is never determinate enough to be depended upon. It can never be reduced, like political punishment, into exact lots, nor meted out in number, quantity, and value. The legislator is therefore obliged to provide the full complement of punishment, as if he were sure of not receiving any assistance whatever from any of those quarters. If he does, so much the better: but lest he should not, it is necessary he should, at all events, make that provision which depends upon himself.

27. It may be of use, in this place, to recapitulate the several circumstances, which, in establishing the proportion betwixt punishments and offences, are to be attended to. These seem to be as follows: 1. On the part of the offence: 1. The profit of the offence; 2. The mischief of the offence; 3. The profit and mischief of other greater or lesser offences, of different sorts, which the offender may have to choose out of; 4. The profit and mischief of other offences, of the same sort, which the same offender may probably have been guilty of already. 2. On the part of the punishment: 5. The magnitude of the punishment: composed of its intensity and duration; 6. The deficiency of the punishment in point of certainty; 7. The deficiency of the punishment in point of proximity; 8. The quality of the punishment; 9. The accidental advantage in point of quality of a punishment, not strictly needed in point of quantity; 10. The use of a punishment of a particular quality, in the character of a moral lesson. 3. On the part of the offender: 11. The responsibility of the class of persons in a way to offend; 12. The sensibility of each particular offender; 13. The particular merits or useful qualities of any particular offender, in case of a punishment which might deprive the community of the benefit of them; 14. The multitude of offenders on any particular occasion. 4. On the part of the public, at any particular conjuncture: 15. The inclinations of the people, for or against any quantity or mode of punishment; 16. The inclinations of foreign powers. 5. On the part of the law: that is, of the public for a continuance: 17. The necessity of making small sacrifices, in point of proportionality, for the sake of simplicity.

28. There are some, perhaps, who, at first sight, may look upon the nicety employed in the adjustment of such rules, as so much labour lost: for gross ignorance, they will say, never troubles itself about laws, and passion does not calculate. But the evil of ignorance admits of cure: and as to the proposition that passion does not calculate, this, like most of these very general and oracular propositions, is not true. When matters of such importance as pain and pleasure are at stake, and these in the highest degree (the only matters, in short, that can be of importance) who is there that does not calculate? Men calculate, some with less exactness, indeed, some with more: but all men calculate. I would not say, that even a madman does not calculate. Passion calculates, more or less, in every man: in different men, according to the warmth or coolness of their dispositions: according to the firmness or irritability of their minds: according to the nature of the motives by which they are acted upon. Happily, of all passions, that is the most given to calculation, from the excesses of which, by reason of its strength, constancy, and universality, society has most to apprehend: I mean that which corresponds to the motive of pecuniary interest: so that these niceties, if such they are to be called, have the best chance of being efficacious, where efficacy is of the most importance.

THE MORAL EDUCATION THEORY OF PUNISHMENT

—*Jean Hampton*—

There are few social practices more time-honored or more widely accepted throughout the world than the practice of punishing wrongdoers. Yet if one were to listen to philosophers discussing this practice, one would think punishment impossible to justify and difficult even to understand. However, I do not believe that one should conclude that punishment as a practice is morally unjustifiable or fundamentally irrational. Instead I want to explore the promise of another theory of punishment which incorporates certain elements of the deterrence, retributivist, and rehabilitation views, but whose justification for punishment and whose formula for determining what punishment a wrongdoer deserves are distinctive and importantly different from the reasons and formulas characterizing the traditional theories.

This view, which I call the moral education theory of punishment, is not new. There is good reason to believe Plato and Hegel accepted something like it,[1] and more recently, Herbert Morris and Robert Nozick have maintained that the moral education which punishment effects is at least part of punishment's justification.[2] I want to go farther, however, and suggest that by reflecting on the educative character of punishment we can provide a full and complete justification for it. Hence my discussion of the moral education theory in this paper is meant to develop it as a complete justification of punishment and to distinguish it from its traditional rivals. Most of my discussion will focus on the theory's application to the state's punishment of criminal offenders, but I will also be looking at the theory's implications for punishment within other societal institutions, most notably the family. . . .

THE JUSTIFICATION

Philosophers who write about punishment spend most of their time worrying about whether the state's punishment of criminals is justifiable, so let us begin with that particular issue.

When does punishment by the state take place? The answer to this question seems simple: the state carries out punishment upon a person when he or she has broken a *law*. Yet the fact that the state's punishment always follows the transgression of a law is surely neither coincidental nor irrelevant to the understanding and justification of this practice. What is the nature of law? This is a thorny problem which has vexed philosophers for hundreds of years. For the purposes of this article, however, let us agree with Hart that there are (at least) two kinds of law, those which are power-conferring rules, for example, rules which specify how to make a contract or a will, and those which are "rules of obligation."[3] We are concerned with the latter kind of rule, and philosophers and legal theorists have generally analyzed the structure of this sort of law as "orders backed by threats" made by the state.

What is the subject matter of these orders? I will contend (consistent with a positivist account of law) that the subject matter *ought* to be (although it might not always be) drawn either from ethical imperatives, of the form "don't steal," or "don't murder," or else from imperatives made necessary for moral reasons, for example, "drive on the right"—so that the safety of others on the road is insured, or "advertise your university job in the professional journals"—so that blacks and women will not be denied an opportunity to secure the job.[4] The state makes these two kinds of commands not only to define a minimal set of duties which a human being in that community must follow in his or her dealings with others, but also to designate actions which, when followed by all members of the society, will solve various problems of conflict and coordination.[5]

And the threat? What role does it play? In the end, this is the central question for which we must have an adequate answer if we are to construct a viable theory of punishment.

The threat, which specifies the infliction of pain if the imperative is not obeyed, gives people a nonmoral incentive, that is, the avoidance of pain, to refrain from the prohibited action. The state hopes this incentive will block a person's performance of the immoral action whenever the ethical incentive fails to do so. But insofar as the threat given in the law is designed to play this kind of "deterring" role, carrying out the threat, that is, punishing someone when he or she has broken the law, is, at least in part, a way of "making good" on the threat. The threat will only deter the disobedience of the state's orders if people believe there is a good chance the pain will be inflicted upon them after they commit the crime. But if the state punishes in order to make good on its threats, then the deterrence of future crime cannot be wholly irrelevant to the justification of punishment. And anyone, including Kant, who analyzes laws as orders backed by threats must recognize that fact.[6]

Moreover, I believe we must accept the deterrence theorist's contention that the justification of punishment is connected with the fact that it is a necessary tool for preventing future crime and promoting the public's well-being. Consider standard justifications of the state: philosophers from Plato to Kant to Hart have argued that because a community of people cannot tolerate violent and destructive behavior in its midst, it is justified in establishing a state which will coercively interfere in people's lives for publicly announced and agreed-upon reasons so that an unacceptable level of violence and harm can be prevented. Whereas we normally think the state has to respect its citizens' choices about how to live, certain choices, for example, choices to rape, to murder, or to steal, cannot be respected by a community which is committed to preserving and pursuing the well-being of its members. So when the state annexes punishment to these damaging activities, it says that such activities are not a viable option for anyone in that community.

But to say that the state's punishment is needed to prevent crime is not to commit oneself to the deterrence justification of punishment—it all depends on what one takes prevention to entail. And, as Hegel says, if we aimed to prevent wrongdoing only by deterring its commission, we would be treating human beings in the same way that we treat dogs.[7] Consider the kind of lesson an animal learns when, in an effort to leave a pasture, it runs up against an electrified fence. It experiences pain and is conditioned, after a series of encounters with the fence, to stay away from it and thus remain in the pasture. A human being in the same pasture will get the same message and learn the same lesson—"if you want to avoid pain, don't try to transgress the boundary marked by this fence." But, unlike the animal in the pasture, a human being will also be able to reflect on the reasons for that fence's being there, to theorize about *why* there is this barrier to his freedom.

Punishments are like electrified fences. At the very least they teach a person, via pain, that there is "barrier" to the action she wants to do, and so, at the very least, they aim to deter. But because punishment "fences" are marking *moral* boundaries, the pain which these "fences" administer (or threaten) conveys a larger message to beings who are able to reflect on the reasons for these barriers' existence: they convey that there is a barrier to these actions *because* they are morally wrong. Thus, according to the moral education theory, punishment is not intended as a way of conditioning a human being to do what society wants her to do (in the way that an animal is conditioned by an electrified fence to stay within a pasture); rather, the theory maintains that punishment is intended as a way of teaching the wrongdoer that the action she did (or wants to do) is forbidden because it is morally wrong and should not be done for that reason. The theory also regards that lesson as public, and thus as directed to the rest of society. When the state makes its criminal law and its enforcement practices known, it conveys an educative message not only to the convicted criminal but also to anyone else in the society who might be tempted to do what she did.

Comparing punishments to electrical fences helps to make clear how a certain kind of deterrent message is built into the larger moral point which punishment aims to convey. If one wants someone to understand that an offense is immoral, at the very least, one has to convey to him or her that it is prohibited—that it ought not to occur. Pain is the way to convey that message. The pain says "Don't!" and gives the wrongdoer a reason for not performing the action again; an animal shocked by a fence gets the same kind of message and the same kind of incentive. But the state also wants to use the pain of punishment to get the human wrongdoer to reflect on the moral reasons for that barrier's existence, so that he will make the decision to reject the prohibited action for *moral* reasons, rather than for the self-interested reason of avoiding pain.

If those who are punished (or who watch the punishment take place) reject the moral message implicit in the punishment, at least they will learn from it that there is a barrier to the actions they committed (or are tempted to commit). Insofar as they choose to respond to their punishment (or the punishment of others) merely as a threat, it can keep them within moral boundaries in the same way that fences keep animals in a pasture. This deterrent effect of punishment is certainly welcome by the state whose role is to protect its citizens, and which has erected a "punishment barrier" to certain kinds of actions precisely because those actions will seriously harm its citizens. But on the moral education view, it is incorrect to regard simple deterrence as the aim of punishment; rather, to state it succinctly, the view maintains that punishment is justified as a way to prevent wrongdoing insofar as it can teach both wrongdoers and the public at large the moral reasons for *choosing* not to perform an offense.

I said at the outset that one of the reasons any punishment theory is complicated is that it involves one in taking stands on many difficult ethical and legal issues. And it should be quite clear already that particular positions on the nature of morality and human freedom are presupposed by the moral education view which distinguish the theory from its traditional rivals. Given that the goal of punishment, whether carried out by the state on criminals or by parents on children, is the offender's (as well as other potential offenders') realization of an action's wrongness, the moral education view naturally assumes that there is a fact of the matter about what is right and what is wrong. That is, it naturally rests on ethical objectivism. Perhaps certain sophisticated subjectivists could adapt the theory to accommodate their ontological commitments (punishment, they might say, teaches what society defines as right and wrong). But such an accommodation, in my view, does real damage to the theory, which purports to explain punishment as a way of conveying when an action *is* wrong. Given that the theory holds that punishment is a way of teaching ethical *knowledge*, if there is no such thing, the practice seems highly suspect.

The theory also takes a strong stand on human freedom. It rests on the idea that we can act freely in a way that animals cannot. If we were only like animals, attempts at punishment would affect us in the way that electrical fences affect animals—they would deter us, nothing more. But this theory assumes that we are autonomous, that we can choose and be held accountable for our actions. Thus it holds that punishments must attempt to do more than simply deter us from performing certain offenses; they must also, on this view, attempt to provide us with moral reasons for our *choosing* not to perform these actions. Only creatures who are free to determine their lives according to their moral values can choose not to do an action because it is wrong. Insofar as the moral education view justifies punishment as a way of promoting that moral choice, it assumes that punishment is (and ought only to be) inflicted on beings who are free in this sense.[8] It might be that human beings who have lost their autonomy and who have broken a law can be justifiably treated in a painful way so as to deter them (even as we would deter dangerous animals) from behaving similarly in the future, but this theory would not call such treatment punishment.

Thus one distinction between the moral education view and the deterrence justification of punishment is that on the moral education view, the state is not concerned to use pain coercively so as to progressively eliminate certain types of behavior; rather, it is concerned to educate its citizens morally so that they choose to engage in this behavior. Moreover, there is another important difference between the two views. On the deterrence view, the infliction of pain on certain individuals is justified as a way of promoting a larger social end. But critics of the deterrence view have pointed out that this is just to say that it is all right to *use* certain individuals to achieve a desirable social goal. The moral education theory, however, does not sanction the use of a criminal for social purposes; on the contrary, it attempts to justify punishment as a way to benefit the person who will experience it, a way of helping him to gain moral knowledge if he chooses to listen. Of course other desirable social goals will be achieved through his punishment, goals which include the education of the larger community about the immorality of the offense, but none of these ends is to be achieved at the expense of the criminal. Instead the moral good which punishment attempts to accomplish within the wrongdoer makes it something which is done *for* him, not *to* him.

There are also sharp differences between the moral education view and various rehabilitative theories of criminal "treatment." An advocate of the moral education view does not perceive punishment as a way of treating a "sick" person for a mental disease, but rather as a way of sending a moral message to a person who has acted immorally and who is to be held responsible for her actions.[9] And whereas both theorists are concerned with the good which punishment can do for the wrongdoer, they disagree about what that good is, one defining it as moral growth, the other as the wrongdoer's acceptance of society's mores and her successful operation in the community. In addition, as we shall discuss in Section II, they disagree about what methods to use to achieve these different ends.

Some readers might wonder how close the moral education view is to the old retribution theory. Indeed references in the literature to a view of this type frequently characterize it as a variant of retribution.[10] Nonetheless, there are sharp and important differences between the two views, which we will explore in more detail in Section II. Suffice to say now that whereas retributivism understands punishment as performing the rather metaphysical task of "negating the wrong" and "reasserting the right," the moral education theorist argues that there is a concrete moral goal which punishment should be designed to accomplish, and that goal includes the benefiting of the criminal himself. The state, as it punishes the lawbreaker, is trying to promote his moral personality; it realizes that "(h)is soul is in jeopardy as his victim's is not."[11] Thus, it punishes him as a way of communicating a moral message to him, which he can accept or not, as he chooses.

Certain retributivists have also been very attracted to the idea that punishment is a kind of speech act. For example, Robert Nozick in his book *Philosophical Explanations* has provided a nice nine-point analysis of punishment which presents it as a kind of communication and which fits the account of meaning put forward by H. P. Grice.[12] Yet if punishment is a way of (morally) speaking with a wrongdoer, then why doesn't this show that it is fundamentally justified as a *communication*, in virtue of what it is trying to communicate, rather than, in Nozick's view, as some kind of symbolic "linkage" of the criminal with "correct values"?[13]

Indeed, I would maintain that regarding punishment as a kind of moral communication is intuitively very natural and attractive. Consider, for example, what we say when we punish others: a father who punishes his child explains that he does so in order that the child "learn his lesson"; someone who has been physically harmed by another demands punishment "so that she will understand what she did to me"; a judge recently told a well-known user of cocaine that he was receiving a stiff sentence because his "matter-of-fact dabbling in cocaine . . . tells the whole world it is all right to use it."[14] These kinds of remarks accompanying our punishment efforts suggest that our principal concern as we punish is to get the wrongdoer to stop doing the immoral action by communicating to her that her offense was immoral. And the last remark by the judge to the cocaine user shows that when the state punishes it is important that these communications be public, so that other members of society will hear the same moral message. Even people who seem to be seeking revenge on wrongdoers behave in ways which show that they too want to make a moral point not only to the wrongdoer, but to anyone else who will listen. The hero seeking revenge in a Western movie, for example, never simply shoots the bad guy in the back when he finds him—he always confronts the bad guy first (usually in the presence of other people) and tells him *why* he is about to die. Indeed, the movie would be unsatisfying if he didn't make that communication. And surely, the hero's desire to explain his actions is linked with his desire to convey to the bad guy and to others in society that the bad guy had "done him wrong."[15]

Moreover, if one understands punishment as a moral message aimed at educating both the wrongdoer and the rest of society about the immorality of the offense, one has a powerful explanation (at least as powerful as the one offered by retributivism) of why victims so badly want their assailants punished. If the point of punishment is to convey to the criminal (and others) that the criminal *wronged* the victim, then punishment is implicitly recognizing the victim's plight, and honoring the moral claims of that individual. Punishment affirms as a *fact* that the victim has been wronged, and as a *fact* that he is owed a certain kind of treatment from others. Hence, on this view, it is natural for the victim to demand punishment because it is a way for the community to restore his moral status after it has been damaged by his assailant.

Thus far, I have concentrated on how the state's punishment of criminals can be justified as an attempt at moral education. But I want to contend that punishment efforts by *any* institution or individual should be perceived as efforts at moral education, although the nature and extensiveness of the legitimate educative roles of these institutions and individuals might differ sharply. For example, I believe it is quite clear that parents want to make such a moral communication through their punishments. . . . [16]

However, although both state and parental punishment should, according to this theory, be understood as efforts at moral communication and education, the theory does not regard the two kinds of punishment as exactly the same. While punishment should always be regarded as moral education, the "character" of that education can vary enormously, depending in particular on the nature of the institution or individual charged with inflicting the punishment. For example, a parent who is responsible for the full maturation and moral development of her child is naturally thought to be entitled to punish her children for many more offenses and in very different ways, than the children's schoolteacher, or the neighbor down the street. . . .

None of us, I believe, thinks that the state's role is to teach its citizens the entire contents of morality—a role we might characterize as "moral paternalism." A variety of considerations are important in limiting the mode and extent of the state's punishment.

Nonetheless, some readers still might think the moral education theory implies a paternalistic theory of the state—after all, doesn't it maintain that the state can interfere in people's lives for their own good? But when such philosophers as John Stuart Mill have rejected paternalism, what they have rejected is a certain position on what should be law; specifically, they have rejected the state's passing any law which would restrict what an individual can do to *himself* (as opposed to what he can do to another). They have not objected to the idea that when the state justifiably interferes in someone's life *after* he has broken a law (which prohibited harm to another), it should intend good rather than evil towards the criminal. Now it is possible they might call this theory paternalistic anyway, not because it takes any stand on what should be law, but because it views the state's punishment as interference in his life plans without his consent for his own good. But why should paternalism in this sense be offensive? It would be strange indeed if philosophers insisted that the state should only try to prevent further harm to the community by actively intending to harm, or at least be indifferent to, the people it punishes! . . .

But, critics might insist, isn't this theory arguing that the state should be in the business of deciding and enforcing morality, overriding the autonomous moral decisions of its citizens? Yes, that is exactly the theory's point, the state *is* in that business in a very limited way. Imagine a murderer saying: "You, the state, have no right to tell me that my murder of this man is wrong," or a rapist protesting: "Who is the state to tell me that my rape of this woman is immoral?" These statements sound absurd, because we believe not merely that such actions are wrong, but that they are also heinous and morally appalling. The state is justified in punishing rapists and murderers because their choices about what to do betray a serious inability to make decisions about immoral and moral actions, which has resulted in substantial harm to some members of that community. And while some readers might find it offensive to contemplate the state presuming to morally educate anyone but serious felons, is this not exactly the kind of sentiment behind the libertarians' call for extensive constraints on the state's role and power? . . .

QUESTIONS AND CRITICISMS

Although I will not fully develop and defend the moral education view in this article, I now want to put some flesh on the skeletal presentation of the view just given by considering some questions which spring naturally to mind as one reflects on the theory.

1. *What is this theory's punishment formula?* Punishment formulas always follow directly from punishment justifications. If punishment is justified as a deterrent, then it follows from that justification that particular punishments

should be structured so as to deter. But if punishment is justified as a way of morally educating the wrongdoer and the rest of society about the immorality of the act, then it follows that one should punish in ways that promote this two-part goal. But how do we go about structuring punishments that morally educate? And would this way of determining punishments yield intuitively more just punishments than those yielded by the formulas of the traditional theories?

One reason these formulas of all the traditional theories have been attacked as unjust is that all of them fail to incorporate an acceptable upper bound on what punishments can be legitimately inflicted on an offender. Consider that, once the deterrence theorist has defined his deterrence goal, any punishment that will achieve this goal is justified, including the most brutalizing. Similarly, the retributivist's *lex talionis* punishment formula (dictating that punishments are to be somehow equal to the crime) would seem to recommend, for example, torturing the torturer, murdering *all* murderers, and such recommendations cast serious doubt on the formula's moral adequacy.[17] Even the rehabilitation theory does not place strict limits on the kinds of "treatments" which can legitimately be given to offenders. If the psychiatric "experts" decide that powerful drugs, shock treatments, lobotomies or other similar medical procedures are legitimate and necessary treatments of certain criminals, why shouldn't they be used? The only upper bound on the treatments inherent in this theory derives from the consciences of psychiatrists and the consensus about what constitutes "reasonable" treatment, and many contend that history has shown such an upper bound to be far too high.[18]

The moral education theory, however, does seem to have the resources to generate a reasonable upper limit on how much punishment the state can legitimately administer. Because part of the goal of punishment is to educate the criminal, this theory insists that as he is educated, his autonomy must be respected. The moral education theorist does not want "education" confused with "conditioning." Shock treatments or lobotomies that would damage or destroy the criminal's freedom to choose are not appropriate educative techniques. On this view the goal of punishment is not to destroy the criminal's freedom of choice, but to persuade him to use his freedom in a way consistent with the freedom of others. Thus, any punishment that would damage the autonomy of the criminal is ruled out by this theory.

In addition, it is important to remember that, on this view, punishments should be designed to convey to the criminal and to the rest of society the idea that the criminal's act was wrong. And it seems difficult if not impossible for the state to convey this message if it is carrying out cruel and disfiguring punishments such as torture or maiming. When the state climbs into the moral gutter with the criminal in this way it cannot credibly convey either to the criminal or to the public its moral message that human life must always be respected and preserved, and such actions can even undercut its justification for existing. Note that both of these considerations indicate this theory rules out execution as punishment.[19] (Of course, the moral education theory says nothing about whether the execution of criminals might be justified not as punishment but as a method of "legitimate elimination" of criminals who are judged to have lost all of their essential humanity, making them wild beasts of prey on a community that must, to survive, destroy them. Whether such a justification of criminal execution can be morally tolerable is something I do not want to explore here.)

But, the reader might wonder, how can inflicting *any* pain upon a criminal be morally educational? And why isn't the infliction of mild sorts of pains and deprivations also climbing into the moral gutter with the criminal? The moral education theorist must provide an explanation of why certain sorts of painful experiences (whose infliction on others we would normally condemn) may legitimately be inflicted in order to facilitate moral growth. But is such an explanation possible? And even if it is, would the infliction of pain always be the right way to send a moral message? If a criminal's psychological makeup is such that pain would not reform him, whereas "inflicting" a pleasurable experience would produce this reform, are we therefore justified only in giving him that pleasurable experience? Retributivists like Robert Nozick think the answer to this last question is yes, and thus reject the view as an adequate justification of punishment by itself.[20]

All three of these worries would be allayed if the moral education theorist could show that only the infliction of pain of a certain sort following a wrongdoing is *necessarily* connected with the promotion of the goal of moral education. In order to establish this necessary connection between certain sorts of painful experiences and moral growth, the moral education theorist needs an account of what moral concepts are, and an account of how human beings come to acquire them (that is, what moral education is). I cannot even attempt to propose, much less develop, answers to these central ethical issues here. But I will try to offer reasons for thinking that painful experiences of a particular sort would seem to be necessary for the communication of a certain kind of moral message.

It is useful to start our discussion by getting a good understanding of what actions count as punishment. First, if we see punishment from the offender's standpoint, we appreciate that it involves the loss of her freedom. This is obviously true when one is locked up in a penitentiary, but it is also true when, for example, parents stop their child's allowance (money that has previously been defined as hers is withheld—whether she likes it or not) or when they force her to experience a spanking or a lecture. I would argue that this loss of freedom is why (autonomous) human beings so dislike punishment. Second, whereas it is very natural to characterize punishment as involving pain or other unpleasant consequences, the infliction of what we intuitively want to call punishment might involve the wrongdoer in performing actions which one would not normally describe as painful or unpleasant. For example, a doctor who cheated the Medicare system and is sentenced to compulsory weekend service in a state-supported clinic would not be undergoing what one would normally describe as a painful or unpleasant experience (he isn't being incarcerated, whipped, fined). Nonetheless, insofar as some of his free time is being taken away from him, the state is depriving him of his freedom to carry out his own plans and to pursue the satisfaction of his own interests. In this case, the state is clearly punishing an offender, but it sounds distorted to say that it is inflicting pain on him. Thus we need a phrase to describe punishment which will capture better than "infliction of pain" all of the treatments which we intuitively want to call punishment. For this purpose I propose the phrase "disruption of the freedom to pursue the satisfaction of one's desires," a phrase which is suitably general and which fits a wide variety of experiences that we want to call experiences of *punishment*. (It may well be *too* general, but I do not want to pursue that issue here.)[21]

Thus I understand punishment as an experience which a wrongdoer is forced by an authority to undergo in virtue of the fact that he has transgressed (what ought to be) a morally derived rule laid down by that authority, and which disrupts (in either a major or a minor way) the wrongdoer's freedom to pursue the satisfaction of his desires. Given that punishment is understood in this way, how do coercion and disruption of one's self-interested pursuits convey a *moral* message?

Before answering this question, it is important to make clear that punishment is only *one* method of moral education. Upon reflection, it is clear, I think, that we choose to employ this method only when we're trying to teach someone that an action is *wrong*, rather than when we are trying to teach someone what (imperfect) moral duties he or she ought to recognize. (We punish a child when he kicks his brother: we don't punish him in order to get him to give Dad a present on Father's Day.)

What is one trying to get across when one wants to communicate an action's wrongness? The first thing one wants to convey is that the action is forbidden, prohibited, "fenced off." Consider a mother who sees her child cheating at solitaire. She might say to the child, "You mustn't do that." Or if she saw her child putting his left shoe on his right foot, she would likely say, "No, you mustn't dress that way." In both cases it would be highly inappropriate for her to follow these words with punishment. She is communicating to her child that what he is doing in these circumstances is inadvisable, imprudent, not playing by the rules, but she is not communicating (and not trying to communicate) the idea that such actions violate one's moral duty to others (or, for that matter, one's moral duty to oneself). Now consider this mother seeing her son kick the neighbor's young daughter. Once again she might say, "You mustn't do that," to the child, but the "mustn't" in the mother's words here is unique. It is more than "you shouldn't" or "it isn't advisable" or "it's against the rules of the game." Rather, it attempts to convey the idea that the action is forbidden, prohibited, intolerable.

But merely telling the child that he "mustn't do that" will not effectively convey to the child that there is this profound moral boundary. Without punishment why shouldn't the child regard the "mustn't" in the parent's statement just as he did the "mustn't" in "You mustn't cheat at solitaire"? The mother needs to get across to the child the very special nature of the prohibition against this immoral act. How can she do this? Consider the fact that someone who (for no moral reason) violates a positive duty to others is not acting out of any interest in the other's well-being. A teenager who steals from a passer-by because she needs the money, a man who rapes a woman so that he can experience a sense of power and mastery—such people are performing immoral acts in order to satisfy their own needs and interests, insensitive to the needs and interests of the people they hurt. The way to communicate to such people that there is a barrier of a very special sort against these kinds of actions would seem to be to link performance of the actions with what such people care about most—the pursuit of their own pleasure. Only when disruption of that pursuit takes place will a wrongdoer appreciate the special force of the "mustn't" in the punisher's communication. So the only effective way to "talk to" such people is through the disruption of their own interests, that is, through punishment (which has been defined as just such a disruption.)

What conclusions will a person draw from this disruption of his pleasure? At the very least he will conclude that his society (in the guise of the family, the state, the university, etc.) has erected a barrier to that kind of action, and that if he wants to pursue the satisfaction of his own desires, he won't perform that action again. So at the very least, he will understand his punishment as society's attempt to deter him from committing the action in the future. Such a conclusion does not have moral content. The person views his punishment only as a sign of society's condemnation of the act, not as a sign of the act's *wrongness*. But it is a start, and a *necessary first start*. If a wrongdoer has little or no conception of an action's wrongness, then the first thing one must do is to communicate to him that the action is prohibited. We must put up the electrical fence in an attempt to keep him out of a forbidden realm.

But given that we want the offender to understand the moral reasons for the action's condemnation, how can punishment communicate those reasons? The punisher wants the wrongdoer to move from the first stage of the educative process initiated by punishment—the realization that society prohibits the action—to a second stage, where the moral reasons for the condemnation of the action are understood and accepted. Can punishment, involving the disruption of a person's self-interested pursuits, help an offender to arrive at this final moral conclusion, to understand, in other words, why this fence has been erected?

What is it that one wants the wrongdoer to see? As we noted before, someone who (for no moral reason) violates her (perfect) moral duty to others is not thinking about the others' needs and interests, and most likely has little conception of, or is indifferent to, the pain her actions caused another to suffer. Hence, what the punisher needs to do is to communicate to the wrongdoer *that* her victims suffered and how much they suffered, so that the wrongdoer can appreciate the harmfulness of her action. How does one get this message across to a person insensitive to others? Should not such a person be made to endure an unpleasant experience designed, in some sense, to "represent" the pain suffered by her victim(s)? This is surely the institution behind the *lex talionis* but it best supports the concept of punishment as moral education. As Nozick admits,[22] it is very natural to regard the pain or unpleasantness inflicted by the wrongdoer as the punisher's way of saying: "This is what you did to another. You hate it; so consider how your victim felt." By giving a wrongdoer something like what she gave to others, you are trying to drive home to her just how painful and damaging her action was for her victims, and this experience will, one hopes, help the wrongdoer to understand the immorality of her action.

Of course, the moral education formula does not recommend that punishments be specifically *equal* to the crime—in many instances this doesn't even make sense. But what does the "representation" of the wrongful act involve, if not actual equality? This is a terribly difficult question, and I find I can only offer tentative, hesitant answers. One way the moral education theorist can set punishments for crimes is to think about "fit." Irrespective of how severe a particular crime is, there will sometimes be a punishment that seems naturally suited to it; for example, giving a certain youth charged with burglarizing and stealing money from a neighbor's house the punishment of supervised compulsory service to this neighbor for a period of time, or giving a doctor charged with cheating a government medical insurance program the punishment of compulsory unremunerated service in a state medical institution. And probably such punishments seem to fit these crimes because they force the offender to compensate the victim, and thus help to heal more effectively the "moral wound" which the offense has caused. Another way the moral education theorist can make specific punishment recommendations is to construct an ordinal scale of crimes, going from most offensive to least offensive, and then to link determinate sentences to each crime, respecting this ordinal comparison, and insuring proportionality between crime and punishment. But it is not easy to use either method to fashion a tidy punishment table because it is not easy to determine which painful experiences will be educative but not cruel, both proportional to the offense committed and somehow relevant to that offense. Indeed, our society has been notoriously unsuccessful in coming up with punishments that are in any way morally educative. And I would argue that it speaks in favor of this theory that it rejects many forms of incarceration used today as legitimate punishments, insofar as they tend to make criminals morally worse rather than better.

But even if this theory can tell us how to represent wrongdoing in a punishment, it must still handle other questions which I do not have time to pursue properly in this article. For example, how does that representation help the wrongdoer to understand and *accept* the fact that she did wrong and should do otherwise in the future? And if we want to send the most effective message possible in order to bring about this acceptance, should we try to tailor punishments to the particular psychological and moral deficiencies of the wrongdoer, or must considerations of equal treatment and fairness override this? Finally, does the view justify the state's punishing people who are innocent of any illegal act but who seem to need moral education?

The theory has a very interesting and complicated response to this last question. We have said that punishment is not the appropriate method to teach every sort of moral lesson, but only the lesson that a certain action is wrong. But on whom is the state justified in imposing such a lesson?—clearly, a person who has shown she needs the lesson by committing a wrong which the state had declared illegal, and clearly *not* a person who has shown she already understands this lesson (at least in some sense) by conscientiously obeying that law. We also believe that the state is justified in imposing this lesson on a person who has not broken that law but who has *tried* to do so. She might, for example, be punished for "attempted murder" or "attempted kidnapping." (And do we make the punishments for such attempts at wrongdoing less than for successful wrongdoings because we're not sure the attempts provide conclusive evidence that such people would have carried through?) But what about a person who has not broken a law or even attempted to do so but who has, say, talked about doing so publicly? Is that enough evidence that she needs a moral education? Probably—by *some* person or institution, but not by the state. The point is that we believe the state should refrain from punishing immoral people who have nonetheless committed no illegal act, not because they don't need moral education but because the state is not the appropriate institution to effect that education. Indeed, one of the reasons we insist that the state operate by enacting laws is that doing so defines when it may coercively interfere in the lives of its citizens and when it may not; its legislation, in other words, defines the extent of its educative role (and there might exist constitutional rules guiding this legislation). So if the state were to interfere with its citizens' lives when they had not broken its laws, it would exceed its own legitimate role. In the end, the state may not punish immoral people who are innocent of any crime not because they don't need moral education, but because the state is not justified in giving it to them.

However, there is another question relevant to the issue of punishing the innocent. Given that I have represented the moral education theory as having a two-part goal—the moral education of the criminal and the moral education of the rest of society—it might be that a punishment which would achieve one part of this goal would not be an effective way of realizing the other part. Must we choose between these two objectives, or is it possible to show that they are inextricably linked? And if they are not, could it be that in order to pursue the goal of morally educating *society*, it would be necessary to punish an innocent person? More generally, could it be justifiable on this view to punish a wrongdoer much more (or much less) severely than her offense (if any) would seem to warrant if doing so would further society's moral education? If this were true, the theory would not preserve proportionality between crime and punishments. However, there are reasons for thinking that educating the criminal and educating the community are inextricably linked. For example, if the state aims to convey a moral lesson to the community about how other human beings should be treated, it will completely fail to do so if it inflicts pain on someone innocent of any wrongdoing—indeed, it would send a message exactly contrary to the one it had intended. But even if we suppose, for the sake of argument, that these educational objectives could become disengaged, we can preserve proportionality between a person's crime and her punishment by making the moral education of the criminal lexically prior to the moral education of the community (after all we *know* she needs the lesson, we're less sure about the community.)[23] . . .

2. *Is the moral education of most criminals just a pipe dream?* How can we really expect hard-core criminals convicted of serious offenses to be able to change and morally improve? In answer to this last question, the moral education theorist will admit that the state can predict that many of the criminals it punishes will refuse to accept the moral message it delivers. As I have stressed, the moral education theory rests on the assumption of individual autonomy, and thus an advocate of this theory must not only admit but insist that the choice of whether to

listen to the moral message contained in the punishment belongs to the criminal. Thus it is very unlikely that society will be 100 percent successful in its moral education efforts, no matter how well it uses the theory to structure punishments.

But at least the punishment the state delivers can have a deterrent effect; even if the criminal refuses to understand the state's communication about why there is a barrier to his action, at least he will understand *that* the barrier exists. Hegel once wrote that if a criminal is coerced by a punishment, it is because he *chooses* to be so coerced; such a person rejects the moral message and accepts instead the avoidance of pain as his sole reason for avoiding the action.[24] In the end, punishments might only have deterrent effects because that is all wrongdoers will let them have.

However, neither the state nor anyone else can determine who the "losers" are. None of us can read another's mind, none of us knows the pressures, beliefs, and concerns motivating another's actions and decisions. The state cannot, even with the help of a thousand psychiatrists, *know for sure* who is a hopeless case and who isn't. Nor is this just a simple epistemological problem. Insofar as the state, on this view, should regard each person it punishes as autonomous, it is committed to the view that the choice of whether to reform or not is a free one, and hence one the state cannot hope to predict. Finally, the state's assumption that the people it is entitled to punish are free means it must never regard any one it punishes as hopeless, insofar as it is assuming that each of these persons still has the ability to choose to be moral. Thus, as Hegel puts it,[25] punishment is the criminal's "right" as a free person—to refuse to punish him on the grounds that he has been diagnosed as hopeless is to regard him as something other than a rational human being.

But even if it seems likely that punishing some criminals will not effect their moral growth, and may not even deter them, the moral education of the community about the nature of their crimes can still be promoted by their punishment. Indeed any victim of crime is going to be very sensitive to this fact, insofar as he has been the one against whom the wrong has been committed, and is the one who is most interested in having the community acknowledge that what happened to him *shouldn't* have happened. And as long as the person whom we punish is admitted to be an autonomous human being, we cannot be convicted of using her as we educate the community about the wrongness of her offense, because we are doing something to her which is *for* her, which can achieve a great deal of good for her, if she will but let it.

3. *Shouldn't the moral education theory imply an indeterminate sentencing policy?* Throughout your discussion, rehabilitationists might complain, you have been assuming that punishment by the state should proceed from determinate sentences for specific crimes. But isn't indeterminate sentencing fairer? Why keep a criminal who has learned his moral lesson in jail just because his sentence has not run out, and why release a criminal who is unrepentant and who will probably harm the public again, just because his sentence has run out?

However, the moral education theorist has very good reasons, provided by the foundations of the theory itself, for rejecting the concepts of indeterminate sentences and parole boards. First, this theorist would strongly disagree with the idea that a criminal should continue to receive "treatment" until his reform has been effected. Recall that it is an important tenet of the view that the criminals we punish are free beings, responsible for their actions. And you can't *make* a free human being believe something. In particular, you can't coerce people to be just for justice's sake. Punishment is the state's attempt to teach a moral lesson, but whether or not the criminal will listen and accept it is up to the criminal himself.

The moral education theorist takes this stand not simply because she believes one ought to respect the criminal's autonomy, but also because she believes one has no choice but to respect it. The fact that parole boards in this country have tried to coerce repentance is, from the standpoint of this theorist, a grave and lamentable mistake. (Consider James McConnell's claim, in an article in *Psychology Today*, that "Somehow we've got to *force* people to love one another, to force them to want to behave properly.")[26] Indeed, critics of present parole systems in the United States maintain that these systems only open the way for manipulation.[27] The parole board uses the threat of the refusal of parole to get the kind of behavior it wants from the criminal, and the criminal manipulates back—playing the game, acting reformed, just to get out. In the process, no moral message is conveyed to the criminal, and probably no real reformation takes place. The high recidivism rate in the United States tells the tale of how successful parole boards have been in evaluating the rehabilitation of prisoners.

As one prisoner put it: "If they ask if this yellow wall is blue, I'll say, of course it's blue. I'll say anything they want me to say if they're getting ready to let me go."[28]

The moral education theorist doesn't want the state to play this game. A sentence for a crime is set, and when the criminal breaks a law, the sentence is inflicted on him as a way of teaching him that what he did was wrong. When the sentence is up, the criminal is released. The state hopes its message was effective, but whether it was or not is largely up to the criminal himself.

There is another important reason why the moral education theorist does not want to insist on repentance before release. Even a good state can make mistakes when it enacts law. It is not just possible but probable that the state at one time or another will declare a certain action immoral which some of its citizens will regard as highly moral. These citizens will often decide to disobey this "immoral" law, and while being punished, will steadfastly refuse to repent for an action they believe was right. Martin Luther King, Jr. never repented for breaking various segregation laws in the South while he was in jail; few draft resisters repented for refusing to go to Vietnam when they were in prison. By not insisting on the repentance of its criminals, the state is, once again, respecting the freedom of its citizens—particularly each citizen's freedom of conscience, and their right, as free beings, to disagree with its rulings. Hence, the moral education theorist doesn't want the state to insist on repentance because it doesn't want Solzhenitsyns rotting in jail until they have "reformed."[29]

How can the moral education theorist justify the punishment of a criminal who is already repentant prior to his sentencing, or who repents before his sentence is completely served? The theorist's response to this question is complicated. Because it is difficult to be sure that a seemingly repentant criminal is *truly* repentant, and thus because a policy of suspending or shortening sentences for those who seem repentant to the authorities could easily lead the criminal to fake repentance before a court or a parole board, the moral education theorist would be very reluctant to endorse such a policy.

Moreover, it might well be the case that, prior to or during sentencing, a criminal's experience of repentance is produced in large part by the expectation of receiving the full punishment, so that the state's subsequent failure to inflict it could lead to a weakening of the criminal's renunciation of the action. Like a bad but repentant child who will conclude, if he is not punished by his parents, that his action must not have been so bad, the repentant criminal might well need to experience his complete sentence in order to "learn his lesson" effectively.

Finally, the lesson learning effected by punishment can also involve a purification process for a wrongdoer, a process of healing. As Herbert Morris has written, experiencing the pain of punishment can be a kind of catharsis for the criminal, a way of "burning out" the evil in his soul.[30] Novelists like Dostoyevsky have explored the criminal's need, born of guilt and shame, to experience pain at the hands of the society he has wronged in order to be reconciled with them. Thus the rehabilitationist who would deny the criminal the experience of pain at the hands of the state would deny him what he may want and need to be forgiven—both by society and by himself. And punishment understood as moral education would explain how it could be perceived as a purification process. For how is it that one overcomes shame? Is it not by becoming a person different from the one who did the immoral action? The subsiding of shame in us seems to go along with the idea. "Given who I was, I did the action then, but I'm different now—I'm *better* now—and I wouldn't do the same act again." But how do we become different, how do we change, improve? Insofar as punishment is seen as a way of educating oneself about the offense, undergoing that experience is a way of changing for the better. It might well be the yearning for that change which drives a person like Raskolnikov towards his punishment.

Nonetheless, if there were clear evidence that a criminal was very remorseful for his action and had already experienced great pain because of his crime (had "suffered enough"), this theory would endorse a suspension of his sentence or else a pardon (*not* just a parole). His moral education would have already been accomplished, and the example of his repentance would be lesson enough for the general public. (Indeed, punishment under these circumstances would make the state appear vindictive.) In addition, because the state conceives itself to be punishing a wrong, it is appropriate for it to allow certain sorts of excuses and mitigating circumstances to lessen the penalty normally inflicted for the crime in question.

4. *Does the moral education theory actually presuppose the truth of retribution?* Retributivists have a very interesting criticism of the moral education theory available to them. Granted, they might maintain, that punishment is connected with moral education, still this only provides an additional reason for punishing someone—it does not provide the fundamental justification of punishment. That fundamental justification, they would argue, is retributive: wrongdoers simply deserve to experience pain for the sake of the wrong they have committed. As Kant has argued, however much good one intends one's punishment to effect,

> yet it must first be justified in itself as punishment i.e. as mere harm, so that if it stopped there, and the person punished could get no glimpse of kindness hidden behind this harshness, he must yet admit that justice was done him, and that his reward was perfectly suitable to his conduct.[31]

Moreover, such modern retributivists as Walter Moberly have argued that it is only when the wrongdoer can assent to his punishment as already justified in virtue of his offense that the punishment can do him any good.[32]

In a certain sense, Moberly's point is simply that a criminal will perceive his punishment as vindictive and vengeful unless he understands or accepts the fact that it is justified. But should the justification of punishment be cashed out in terms of the retributive concept of desert, given that it has been difficult for retributivists to say what they mean by the criminal's "deserving" punishment simply in virtue of his offense? Robert Nozick tries to cash out the retributive link between crime and "deserved" punishment by saying that the punishment represents a kind of "linkage" between the criminal and "right values."[33] But why is inflicting pain on someone a way of effecting this linkage? Why isn't the infliction of a pleasurable experience for the sake of the crime just as good a way of linking the wrongdoer with these right values? And if Nozick explains the linkage of pain with crime by saying that the pain is necessary in order to communicate to the criminal that his action was wrong, he has answered the question but lost his retributive theory.

Other philosophers, like Hegel,[34] speak of punishment as a way of "annulling" or "canceling" the crime and hence "deserved" for that reason. But although Hegel's words have a nice metaphorical ring to them, it is hard to see how they can be given a literal force that will explain the retributivist concept of desert. As J. L. Mackie has written, insofar as punishment occurs after the crime, it certainly cannot cancel it—past events are not eliminated by later ones.[35]

It is partly because retributivists have been at a loss to explain the notion of desert implicit in their theory of punishment that I have sought to propose and explore a completely nonretributivist justification of punishment. But my reasons for rejecting retributivism are deeper. The retributive position is that it is somehow morally appropriate to inflict pain for pain, to take an eye for an eye, a tooth for a tooth. But how is it ever morally appropriate to inflict one evil for the sake of another? How is the society that inflicts the second evil any different from the wrongdoer who has inflicted the first? He strikes first, they strike back; why is the second strike acceptable but the first not? Plato, in a passage quoted at the start of this article, insists that both harms are wrong; and Jesus attacks retributivism[36] for similar reasons:

> You have learned that they were told, 'Eye for eye, tooth for tooth'. But what I tell you is this: Do not set yourself against the man who wrongs you. . . . You have heard that they were told 'Love your neighbor, hate your enemy'. But what I tell you is this: Love your enemy and pray for your persecutors; only so can you be children of your heavenly father, who makes the sun rise on good and bad alike, and sends the rain on the honest and dishonest. [Matt. 5:38-9, 43-6]

In other words, both reject retributivism because they insist that the only thing human beings "deserve" in this life is *good*, that no matter what evil a person has committed, no one is justified in doing further evil to her.

But if one accepts the idea that no one can ever deserve ill, can we hope to justify punishment? Yes, if punishment can be shown to be a good for the wrongdoer. The moral education theory makes just such an attempt to explain punishment as a good for those who experience it, as something done *for* them, not to them, something designed to achieve a goal that includes their own moral well-being. This is the justification of punishment the criminal needs to hear so that he can accept it as legitimate rather than dismiss it as vindictive. Therefore, my interest in the moral education theory is connected with my desire to justify punishment *as a good* for those who experience it, and to avoid any theoretical justification of punishment that would regard it as a deserved evil.[37] Reflection on the punishment activities of those who truly love the people they punish, for example, the infliction of pain by a parent on a beloved but naughty child, suggests to me that punishment should not be justified as a deserved evil, but rather as an attempt, by someone who cares, to improve a wayward person.

Still, the moral education theory can incorporate a particular notion of desert which might be attractive to retributivists. Anyone who is punished according to this theory would know that his punishment is "deserved," that is, morally required, insofar as the community cannot morally tolerate the immoral lesson that his act conveys to others (for example, the message that raping a woman is all right if it gives one a feeling of self-mastery) and cannot morally allow that he receive no education about the evil of his act.

So the theory's point is this: Wrong occasions punishment not because pain deserves pain, but because evil deserves correction.

NOTES

[1] See Hegel, *Philosophy of Right*, tran. T. Knox (Oxford: Clarendon Press, 1952), sections 90–104 (pp. 66–74); and see Plato, in particular the dialogues: *The Laws* (bks. 5 and 9), *Gorgias* (esp. pp. 474ff.), *Protagoras* (esp. pp. 323ff.) and Socrates's discussion of his own punishment in the *Apology* and the *Crito*. I am not convinced that this characterization of either Hegel's or Plato's views is correct, but I do not have time to pursue those issues here. J. E. McTaggart has analyzed Hegel's position in a way that suggests it is a moral education view. See his "Hegel's Theory of Punishment," *International Journal of Ethics* 6 (1896), pp. 482–99; portions reprinted in *Philosophical Perspectives On Punishment*, ed. Gertrude Ezorsky (Albany, NY: State University of New York Press, 1972). In her *Plato on Punishment*, M. M. Mackenzie's presentation of Plato's position suggests it is not a strict moral education view.

[2] Recently Morris has been explicitly advocating this view in "A Paternalistic Theory of Punishment," *American Philosophical Quarterly* 18, no. 4 (October 1981), but only as *one aspect* of the justification of punishment. Morris argues that punishment is sufficiently complicated to require a justification incorporating all of the justificatory reasons offered by the traditional theories of punishment as well as by the moral education view. I do not think this sort of patchwork approach to punishment will work and, in this article, I explore the idea that the moral education view can, by itself, give an adequate justification of punishment.

See also Nozick's recent book *Philosophical Explanations* (Cambridge: Harvard University Press, 1981), pp. 363–97.

[3] See Hart, *The Concept of Law* (Oxford: Clarendon Press, 1961), chaps. 5 and 6.

[4] As stated, this is a positivist definition of law. However, with John Chipman Gray I am maintaining that morality, although not the same as law, should be the source of law. (See Gray's *The Nature and Source of Law* [New York: Macmillan, 1921], p. 84.)

[5] See Edna Ullman-Margalit, *The Emergence of Norms* (Oxford: Clarendon Press, 1977) for a discussion of how law can solve coordination and conflict problems.

[6] Although Kant's position on punishment is officially retributive (see his *Metaphysical Elements of Justice*, trans, J. Ladd [Indianapolis: Bobbs-Merrill, 1965], p. 100, Academy edition, p. 331), his definition of law conflicts with his retributivist position. Note, for example, the deterrent flavor of his justification of law:

> if a certain use of freedom is itself a hindrance to freedom according to universal laws (that is, unjust), then the use of coercion to counteract it, inasmuch as it is the prevention of a hindrance to freedom according to universal laws, is consistent with freedom according to universal laws; in other words, this use of coercion is just (p. 36, Academy edition, p. 231; see also *Metaphysical Elements of Justice* pp. 18–19, 33–45; Academy edition, pp. 218–21, 229–39).

[7] Hegel, *Philosophy of Right*, addition to par. 99, p. 246.

[8] Kantians who see a close connection between autonomy and moral knowledge will note that this connection is suggested in these remarks.

[9] Rehabilitationists disagree about exactly what disease criminals suffer from. See for example the various psychiatric diagnoses of Benjamin Karpman in "Criminal Psychodynamics: A Platform," reprinted in *Punishment and Rehabilitation*, ed. J. Murphy (Belmont, CA: Wadsworth, 1973) as opposed to the behaviorist analysis of criminal behavior offered by B. F. Skinner in *Science and Human Behavior* (New York: Macmillan, 1953), pp. 182–93 and 446–49.

[10] See for example Nozick's characterization of the view as "teleological retributivism," pp. 370–74 and Gertrude Ezorsky's use of that term in *Philosophical Perspectives on Punishment*.

[11] Morris, "The Paternalistic Theory of Punishment," p. 268.

[12] Nozick, pp. 369–80.

[13]Ibid, pp. 374ff. The point is that if one is going to accept the idea that punishment is a communication, one is connecting it with human purposive activity, and hence the *purpose* of speaking to the criminal (as well as to the rest of society) becomes central to the justification of the communication itself. To deny this is simply to regard punishment as something fundamentally different from a species of communication (for example, to regard it as some kind of "value-linkage device") which Nozick seems reluctant to do.

[14]*Los Angeles Times*, 30 July 1981, part 4, p. I.

[15]Nozick has also found the "communication" element in comic book stories about revenge; see *Philosophical Explanations*, pp. 368–69.

[16]Parental punishment can take many forms; although spanking and various kinds of corporal punishment are usually what spring to mind when one thinks of parental punishment, many parents punish through the expression of anger or disapproval, which can be interpreted by the child as a withdrawal of love or as the (at least temporary) loss of the parent's friendship. Such deprivations are in many ways far more serious than the momentary experience of bodily pain or the temporary loss of certain privileges, and hence, although they seem to be mild forms of punishment, they can in actuality be very severe. I am indeed indebted to Herbert Morris for suggesting this point.

[17]Some retributivists have tried to argue that the *lex talionis* needn't be regarded as a formula whose upper bound *must* be respected; see, for example, K. C. Armstrong, "The Retributivist Hits Back," *Philosophy of Punishment*, ed. H. B. Acton (London: Macmillan, 1969). However, critics can object that Armstrong's weaker retributivist position still does not *rule out* barbaric punishments (like torture) as permissible, nor does it explain why and when punishments which are less in severity than the criminal act can be legitimately inflicted.

[18]Consider the START program used in a Connecticut prison to "rehabilitate" child molesters: electrodes were connected to the prisoner's skin, and then pictures of naked boys and girls were flashed on a screen while electric shocks were applied. The Federal Bureau of Prisons canceled this program just before they were about to lose a court challenge to the program's constitutionality (see David J. Rothman's discussion of this in "Behavior Modification in Total Institutions," *Hastings Center Report* 5, no. I [1975]: 22]).

[19]Apart from the fact that killing someone is hardly an appropriate technique for educating him, it is likely that this action sends a poor message to the rest of society about the value of human life. Indeed, in one of their national meetings, the Catholic bishops of the United States argued that repeal of capital punishment would send "a message that we can break the cycle of violence, that we need not take life for life, that we can envisage more human and more hopeful and more effective responses to the growth of violent crime." ("Statement on Capital Punishment," *Origins* 10, no. 24 [27 November 1980]: 374.)

[20]Nozick, pp. 373–74.

[21]George Fletcher, in *Rethinking Criminal Law* (Boston: Little, Brown, 1978), p. 410, worries about defining punishment so that it doesn't include too much (for example, it should not include the impeachment of President Nixon, despite the fact that it would be a case of unpleasant consequences inflicted on Nixon by an authority in virtue of a wrongdoing). I do not have time here to consider how to hone my definition such that it will not encompass impeachments, deportation, tort damages, and so forth. Indeed, perhaps the only way one can do this is to bring into the definition of punishment its justification as moral education.

[22]Compare Nozick's discussion of the content of the Gricean message of punishment. pp. 370–74.

[23]I have profited from discussions with Katherine Sharney on this point.

[24]See Hegel, *Philosophy of Right*, sec. 91.

[25]Ibid, sec. 100, p. 70.

[26]From "Criminals Can be Brainwashed—Now," *Psychology Today*, April 1970, p. 14: also quoted in Rick Carlson's *The Dilemma of Corrections* (Lexington, MA: Lexington Books, 1976), p. 35.

[27]See "The Crime of Treatment," American Friends Service Committee from *The Struggle for Justice*, chap. 6 (New York: Hill and Wang, 1971) reprinted in *Punishment: Selected Readings*, eds., Feinberg and Gross.

[28]Quoted by Carlson, p. 161; from David Fogel, *We Are the Living Proof* (Cincinnati: W. H. Anderson, n.d.).

[29]Jeffrie Murphy has argued that instituting a rehabilitationist penal system would deny prisoners many of their present due process rights. See "Criminal Punishment and Psychiatric Fallacies," especially pp. 207–209, in *Punishment and Rehabilitation*, ed. J. Murphy. The American Friends Service Committee has also charged that the California penal system, which was heavily influenced by the rehabilitation theory, has in fact done this. See "The Crime of Treatment," pp. 91–93, in Feinberg et al.

[30]See Morris's discussion of certain wrongdoers' need to experience punishment in "The Paternalistic Theory of Punishment," p. 267.

[31]Kant, *Critique of Practical Reason*, "The Analytic of Pure Practical Reason," Remark II. (Abbott trans, in Kant's *Theory of Ethics* [London: Longman, 1959], p. 127; Academy edition, p. 38.)

[32]Walter Moberly, *The Ethics of Punishment*, (London: Faber & Faber, 1968), p. 141.

[33]Nozick. pp. 374ff.

[34]For example, see Hegel, *The Philosophy of Right*, sec. 101–103.

[35]J. L. Mackie, "Morality and the Retributive Emotions, "in *Criminal Justice Ethics* I, no. I (Winter/Spring 1982): 3–10. In the face of the retributivists' failure to explain why punishment is deserved, Mackie wants to argue that our retributive intuitions spring from fundamental retributive emotions, which are part of a human being's fundamental moral make-up (and he gives a sketch of how our evolution as a species could have generated such emotions). But many retributivists, particularly the Kantian sort, would eschew such an explanation which, in any case, is hardly *justification* of the retributive impulse itself.

[36]Jesus rejected not only "negative retributivism," that is, the idea that we deserve bad for doing bad, but also "positive retributivism," that is, the idea that we deserve good for doing good, but I cannot go into that here.

[37]Indeed, I believe that it is because retribution would justify punishment as a deserved evil that it strikes many as much too close to revenge.

HARSH JUSTICE

CRIMINAL PUNISHMENT AND THE WIDENING DIVIDE BETWEEN AMERICA AND EUROPE

—*James Q. Whitman*—

HARSHNESS IN THE LAW OF PUNISHMENT

The measure of the explosive power of mass politics in America can indeed be taken from the law of punishment, where the push for a tough retributivism has had an extraordinary effect. Numerous statutes have lengthened prison sentences. Most especially, certain morals offenses have been the target of particularly increased—sometimes drastically increased—legislated sentencing. Drug offenses especially fall into this category, for example in the much-debated Rockefeller laws of New York State that date to the mid-1970s, the beginning of our era of crackdown. Federal drug laws, too, requiring sentences of sometimes awesome length, have had a tremendous (though somewhat difficult to analyze) impact on the federal prison population. Indeed, it is a striking fact about the growth of the American prison population—particularly striking by contrast with Europe, as we shall see—that most of that growth has involved the incarceration of *nonviolent* criminals. Historically, violent crime is what has lain at the core of what Western legal cultures regard as "criminal." Yet in the United States, a vast disproportion of the immense growth of the prison population between 1980 and 1992 was for drug offenses, nonviolent property crimes, and (occasionally) minor offenses of kinds that Europeans regard as forms of disorderly conduct. The same tendency can be detected in the intensification of criminal liability for American minors: the growth in classification of juveniles as "adults" since 1992 has apparently involved mostly nonviolent offenses.

Other statutes have also brought dramatically longer terms. There are, first and foremost, "three-strikes-and-you're-out" laws, which require fixed long terms, often life terms, for three-time offenders. Legislation of this type actually has a long history in the United States, running as far back as 1797 in New York; and by the late 1960s, twenty-three states had repeat offender statutes that permitted life imprisonment. The American tradition of this kind of harshness runs deep. Nevertheless, the newest generation of these laws, dating to the mid-1990s, in twenty-four states as well as on the federal level, differs in a telling way: old life-imprisonment statutes were directed only at certain serious crimes. The new "three-strikes-and-you're-out" laws, by contrast, frequently apply even to those who have committed what were once regarded as minor offenses. Most notably, these include drug and nonviolent property offenses. This is particularly true where these laws interact with enhancement statutes, which regrade prior misdemeanors as more serious felonies. (I will return to these enhancement statutes shortly.) The interaction between these two statutory schemes has resulted in some much-reported scandals—one notorious sentence of twenty-five years to life, in particular, imposed in California for the theft of a slice of pizza. That sentence, at least, was revisited. Nevertheless, "three-strikes-and-you're-out" laws are particularly dramatic evidence of a new style of American toughness.

These statutes have had an impact on American law that would be strictly impossible under prevailing doctrine in continental Europe. The European systems all subscribe to some version of the principle of proportionality. This principle holds that sentences, though indeterminate, cannot be disproportionate to the gravity of the offense; the legal profession takes it very seriously; and it means that sentences of American severity are effectively impossible. That principle is, by contrast, generally absent from American sentencing practices, and long has been. Indeed, long before the rise of determinate sentencing, the absence of a proportionality principle produced what seemed to many egregious injustices under older indeterminate sentencing statutes. In the California case of *In re Lynch*, to take a well-known example, the petitioner was a prisoner serving an indeterminate sentence after being caught masturbating in his car in 1967, with a prior conviction for indecent exposure from 1958. A substantial part of this sentence had been served in the tough conditions of the maximum security prison in Folsom, and there was no way of being certain when Lynch would ever be released. The California Supreme Court responded to his situation by creating, in 1972, a constitutionalized proportionality doctrine. This doctrine has not effectively survived in the later jurisprudence of the California court, though; and its absence is palpable in the world of determinate sentencing that has sprung up since 1972. Proportionality suffered, indeed, a grievous blow in the Supreme Court's 1991 decision of *Harmelin v. Michigan*, in which the court saw no unconstitutional disproportion in a life sentence imposed for possession of 672 grams of cocaine.

With proportionality setting no clear limit, the promulgation of the new penal statutes of the last twenty-five years has had, it is generally agreed, a tremendous impact on American incarceration rates. Longer sentences mean larger prison populations; and sentences have been getting steadily longer in America. Indeed, we have now reached the point where American convicts, as we shall see, serve sentences roughly *five to ten times* as long as similarly situated French ones; and almost certainly even longer by comparison with German convicts. The results tell in our prisons and jails. The growth in the American incarcerated population over the last twenty-five years has been extraordinary, roughly tripling from the early 1970s until the mid-1990s, and continuing to grow apace since, reaching 2 million in 2000—up from a (then unprecedented) 1 million in 1990. This has a consequence of immense significance for punishment culture in America: massive overcrowding. On both sides of the Atlantic, prison overcrowding is a problem. But the crowd of American prisoners has come to be vastly larger. Depending on how you reckon it, the American incarceration rate now stands at somewhere between 450 and 700 per 100,000 of the general population—on a rough par with Russia; and in certain parts of the United States, like Louisiana and the District of Columbia, the rate stands as high as 760 or 1,700 per 100,000. The typical European incarceration rate, by contrast, stands somewhere between 65 and 100 per 100,000.

Incarceration is by far the most important part of the story of the changing American law of punishment, but it is not the only part. Indeed, it is not the only place where we see a new willingness to treat offenders with a kind of unbridled lack of respect. There is also what we might call a new inventiveness in punishment. In particular, American criminal justice has seen the revival of two styles of punishment that had almost entirely vanished from the Western world: public shaming and public forced labor of an ostentatiously degrading kind. These are developments that date, like most of what I have discussed, to the late 1970s, when they reappeared on the American scene in a completely unexpected way. Since that time, publicly inflicted shaming in particular has been imposed in a new-old class of penalties, which have been crafted by low-level American judges in all parts of the country. The new shame sanctions, imposed for the most part as probation conditions, are often fashioned in ways that deliberately echo the scarlet letter and pillory of the premodern past. Defendants have thus been obliged to parade themselves wearing signs, shirts, or bumper stickers describing their offenses. Accused offenders have been displayed to the press and the public in humiliating ways. Alongside these punishments come chain gangs, for example, the most striking form of public forced labor. Also worthy of note, though not involving public labor, is the reintroduction of forced labor at the rock pile, reintroduced as part of chain gang practice in Alabama, Arizona, and Florida. This practice too is of course rich in associations with a preliberal past in American punishment.

All of these new/old punishments reflect one revealing. If hard-to-interpret, feature of the new American punishment law: a kind of inventiveness in punishment—and of a species of inventiveness that has not been seen in Europe since the fascist era. For Europeans, the notion that Judges might try to think up new punishments, or even revive forgotten ones, has something offensive and even bizarre about it. Indeed, as long ago as the eighteenth century, continental Europeans were expressing discomfort with the notion of inventive punishing: "It is not permitted," wrote one 1767 authority flatly, "for judges to invent punishments." Punishment, on the continent, is expected to be surrounded with a kind of sad solemnity and a sobriety that exclude judicial and legislative creativity. That attitude of solemnity and sobriety is noticeably less present in the United States than it was thirty years ago. In the common law world too, "invention" of punishments was once considered unacceptable. Indeed, the Supreme Court has observed that the very prohibition on "cruel and unusual" punishment began its life largely as a prohibition on the invention of novel punishments. Yet novelty in punishment has reappeared in America. Let us call this a shift, in America, away from the bureaucratic mentality. Punishment, in Europe, is for weary professionals, who do not imagine that it is their job to devise ingenious new practices. In America we have come, at least at times, to view things differently.

HARSHNESS IN THE APPLICATION OF PUNISHMENT

If the law of punishment in the United States shows a fairly unadulterated picture of growing harshness, the *application* of punishment presents a somewhat more mixed story—though it is still a story of deepening harshness.

Here the most important questions involve prison conditions.

Readers of American novels and viewers of American movies may acquire a thoroughly Dantesque idea of the hellishness of American prisons. Indeed, much of what most strikingly colors current American legal culture is a horror of prisons, and a sense that conditions behind bars are unspeakably barbaric. It is impossible to describe the culture of punishment in America without making some reference to the popular image of prisons. Movies and popular literature convey a fascination with the degradation and violence of prison life; the sense that imprisonment is spectacularly horrific lies near the heart of what makes punishment harsh in the American mind. Here the fear of homosexual rape, which in many societies causes irreversible status degradation, features prominently, and suggestively. In the Roman Empire, according to the books of dream interpretation, people used to have nightmares about being crucified. As classicists observe, this tells us something peculiarly intimate and revealing about how omnipresent harsh punishment was in ancient lives. People in the United States watch movies and read novels about beatings, stabbings, and violent homosexual rape in prison. This also seems to tell us something intimate and revealing about an American culture of harsh punishment.

It is all the more important to observe, then, that conditions in American prisons are a lot better than they used to be, and in some ways even better than conditions in France (though not in Germany). American prisons went through a period of court-ordered reform, some of it massive, that began relatively abruptly in the mid-1960s. During the 1970s, courts actively tested prison practices against a developing Eighth Amendment Jurisprudence, abandoning the traditional harsh view that inmates were simply "slaves of the state." Those reforms—which paralleled contemporary reforms in Europe, as we shall see—eliminated some spectacularly frightening and dangerous conditions, especially in prisons in the American South. The impulse toward reform reached its high-water mark in 1980, when Congress passed the Constitutional Rights of Incarcerated Persons Act. This era of reform undoubtedly achieved much of importance. As summarized by Chief Justice Rehnquist, American prisons today, unlike their predecessors of fifty years ago, must provide a certain minimum: "When the State by the affirmative exercise of its power so restrains an individual's liberty that it renders him unable to care for himself, and at the same time fails to provide for his basic human needs—e.g., food, clothing, shelter, medical care and reasonable safety—it transgresses the substantive limits on state action set by the Eighth Amendment." This, at least according to its letter, is by no means nothing—though as we shall see, its letter provides for significantly less than the letter of European law. . . .

The era of reform proved brief in the United States, and this aspect of American punishment practice too has settled into a mood of harshness typical of the last several decades. By the late 1970s, the flush of prison reform had already begun to recede. To be sure, in 1994, the United States ratified the Convention against Torture and Other Cruel, Inhuman or Degrading Treatments—the document that is a principal font of punishment reform in continental Europe. However, the United States made its ratification subject to the express reservation that the dictates of the convention would be interpreted to conform to the American constitutional limitations found especially in the Eighth Amendment. As it turns out, those limitations have proved to be few. The Supreme Court handed down an especially critical decision in *Wilson v. Seiter*, of 1991, which set a high hurdle for court action in cases of alleged inmate abuse, requiring that inmates demonstrate "deliberate indifference" on the part of prison officials. As the court's jurisprudence stands under *Wilson*, complaining inmates must prove in effect that prison officials had a subjective intent to subject an inmate to the "cruel and unusual" punishment condemned by the Eighth Amendment, no matter how objectively bad their prison conditions may be. This is very tough on prisoners, representing a real bar to litigation over objectively bad prison conditions and putting an almost impossible burden of proof on the complainant. In other respects, too, the court has established a deferential standard, denying federal courts that power to intervene to end any practice for which prison officials can claim a reasonable relationship to the management of their institutions. Inmates do retain some protection against "malicious" excessive force by guards, held by the court to violate "contemporary standards of decency." In this as in other things, American law has a special sensitivity to violence. Inmates have benefited from some other decisions too. In particular, bizarrely, but typically of contemporary American legal culture, the Supreme Court has held that inmates may also have a right to protection against secondhand smoke. On the whole, though, conditions have not improved for prisoners in the 1990s. Congressional legislation of the mid-1990s did away with much of the courts' authority to intervene, and more broadly the period of general growing harshness in American punishment has thus also been one in which judicial prison reform "has suffered a succession of heavy blows from the Supreme Court, the Administration, and Congress."

GRADING, ENFORCEMENT, AND DOCTRINAL FLEXIBILITY

Let me turn now to my three final measures of harshness: harshness in grading and enforcement; and harshness in inflexible doctrines of liability. These present varying pictures of the state of American criminal punishment.

Harshness in Grading and Enforcement

Harshness in grading and harshness in enforcement can profitably be viewed together. While neither measure is entirely easy to assess, both suggest once again the same relatively strong tendency. It is the quasi-Kantian tendency I described above: the tendency to seek out evil wherever it may be found.

American law clearly shows a trend toward harshness in grading, especially by contrast with continental Europe. As I suggested in the last chapter this is a measure that can reveal a great deal about a given punishment culture. When criminal justice systems grade offenses high—as felonies, in common-law terms—it is typically because they regard those offenses as *mala in se*, as evils in themselves. The attitude toward grading in a given system thus has something to do with its attitude toward the problem of evil.

Now, it is hardly the case that American criminal justice displays no wisdom on the topic of grading. On the contrary, the Model Penal Code in particular, promulgated in 1962, is indeed a model effort to use grading wisely, especially in its treatment of "violations," its lowest grade of offense. It is not that American criminal justice does not see the importance of grading; it is rather that American justice has shown, over the last twenty-five years, a tendency to grade offenses comparatively high. This is a tendency that has taken several forms. Some acts have been graded upward. California, for example, in its epochal crackdown, has been classifying more and more offenses as "felonies," with the total at more than five hundred as of 1998. The same strategy has appealed to other Americans as well during the same period: The U.S. Advisory Board on Child Abuse and Neglect has demanded, for example, that states reclassify child abuse misdemeanors as felonies. Here again, we see typically American strategies appearing both on the right and on the left. Most important, so-called "enhancements" show a similar tendency to grade offenses more severely. Under enhancement doctrine, low-grade offenses can be graded up for sentencing purposes if the offender commits a subsequent offense; and subsequent offenses can themselves be graded up if there is a prior history of convictions. Thus it is that in California, as widely reported in Europe, minor prior thefts can lead to longer sentences, and even life sentences. This, if you like, represents right-wing enhancement doctrine. There is also left-wing enhancement doctrine: it is also a variety of enhancement that is used to penalize bias crimes more severely.

American criminal law is thus in a variety of ways engaged in grading offenses up. Something similar is arguably at work in American enforcement. The question of whether American enforcement has grown harsher is too empirically difficult to resolve: an adequate answer would require too much close study of too many prosecutorial and police practices. Nevertheless, there are some examples of intensified enforcement that deserve to be mentioned because they seem so manifestly symptomatic of the broader changes that have come to American law. One example is renewed efforts to crack down on prostitution. We can also see it in many scattered exercises of prosecutorial discretion, such as the recent decision by a Colorado prosecutor to treat a skiing accident as a case of felony reckless manslaughter. The pursuit of drunk driving is also a matter of changing enforcement rather than changing grading: on the books, drunk driving has long been treated as quite grave. But it is since the early seventies, in this as in so many other aspects of American criminal justice, that the systematic prosecution has come. Perhaps most interestingly, we can see intensifying enforcement in the slow growth of concern about date rape. . . .

THE MILDNESS OF RESPECT AND PARDONS

Let me now turn, finally, to the two forms of mildness: the mildness of respectful treatment and the mildness of mercy.

The Mildness of Respectful Treatment

This species of mildness is dramatically absent in American punishment, by contrast with continental European punishment. Prison life and public shaming make the best examples.

American high-security prisons are characterized by a number of practices that have waned or entirely vanished in Europe. Among these are a variety of aspects of prison life that go mostly unquestioned, and even unnoticed, in the United States, but that have been wholly or largely eliminated across the Atlantic. First is the practice of keeping inmates in cells with barred doors and the like through which they are not just *observed* (as they would be through peepholes) but thoroughly *exposed*—inmates having as the Supreme Court has held, "no reasonable expectation of privacy." Second is the common obligation to wear prison uniforms, a practice with especially interesting psychological consequences. Along with uniforms go prison regulations on personal grooming, regulating hair length, facial hair, and the like. Transvestites in particular (unlike their European counterparts) have been denied the right to wear female clothing and cosmetics. These are all measures through which American inmates are essentially denied all control over their "presentation of self," to borrow a famous phrase of Erving Goffman. Also important are a range of restrictions on visitation, including in some cases the practice of separating inmates from their visitors behind a glass partition; and a spirit of regimentation represented notably by the practice of common dining in a common mess hall where prisoners may have no choice of foods and may be hustled out after as short a time as twelve minutes.

All of these are practices that Europeans have, in one measure or another, condemned as incompatible with inmate "dignity." They are all practices that show our lack of concern for respect for persons in the second of the two senses with which I began: they all diminish the respect with which inmates are treated. These are, as it were, the outward dramatizations of the "hatred, fear [and] contempt for the convict" that characterize our attitude toward these offenders. There are others, too. One of the most frequently discussed is the deprivation of the right to vote and like civic rights, still widespread in various forms and having a striking impact on the African-American population. Odd reports of prison life, some of them wholly bizarre, further testify to a new spirit of indignity in the American prisons—such as the organization by guards in one California state prison of "gladiator days," during which fights were arranged between inmate members of rival gangs, complete with audiences—fights that often ended in shootings.

More generally—and of particular importance for the contrast with Europe, as we shall see—the expectation of privacy for American convicts is effectively nil. The Supreme Court has held that "it would be literally impossible to accomplish the prison objectives of preventing the introduction of weapons, drugs, and other contraband into the premises if inmates retained a right of privacy in their cells." As one recent reform-minded author describes the resulting situation in American prisons: "Prison and privacy often appear to be antithetical entities. For non-prisoners, privacy is an umbrella concept, protecting a variety of disparate activities. For prisoners, lack of privacy may seem equally wide-ranging. Surveillance in prison can be unremitting and escape to the privacy of one's cell is often impossible. Cell and strip searches occur with no notice. Visits are monitored and private letters are intercepted and read. Personal possessions are strictly limited." The Fourth Amendment guarantee against searches and seizures, principal font of privacy rights in the United States, is at best problematically applicable to prisoners.

Non-Fourth-Amendment-based privacy rights are essentially denied to them. No warrants are required for cell searches, which may be conducted without notice, or for searches of personal property. Much of Fourth Amendment jurisprudence revolves around the question of whether items are in "plain view"; and as American prisoners are often placed in cells with barred doors, their belongings are of course often in "plain view." But even items not in plain view enjoy no protection. As Gresham Sykes observed thirty years ago, this deprivation of control over basic possessions is difficult to bear: "In modern Western culture, material possessions are so large a part of the individual's conception of himself that to be stripped of them is to be attacked at the deepest layers of personality." Inmates may be obliged to use toilets within the view of guards of the opposite sex. With regard to privacy, overcrowding is of course again a major factor. Overcrowding has led to multiple occupancy of tiny prison cells, which, as one court observed, "rips away the sense of privacy—of dignity which can make bearable many things which could not otherwise be endured."

There is of course more: body cavity searches, for example, and seizure of inmates' property. Taken together, it amounts to a jurisprudence that, as we shall see, is far less sensitive to dignitary issues—one is tempted to say infinitely less sensitive—than the jurisprudence of continental Europe.

The same can be said of public shaming. The new shame sanctions take a variety of forms. In most cases, they are inflicted on persons who have actually been convicted of an offense. In other cases, though, these sanctions have been visited on persons who have been arrested but not yet convicted. Especially important here is the Supreme Court's decision in *Paul v. Davis*, a case decided in 1976, early on in the recent American secular shift toward greater harshness in punishment. *Paul v. Davis* involved a local sheriff who circulated photographs of "known shop-lifters" to be posted at cash registers in Iowa markets. This practice was challenged by one "known shop-lifter" against whom all charges had been dropped, and who understandably wanted to avoid the ugly publicity created by the posting of his photograph. The Supreme Court rejected his claim, strikingly holding that there is no constitutional right to protection of reputation. That decision opened the door to a whole variety of politically popular practices. Most widespread of these, probably, is the practice of televising the names of johns arrested for soliciting prostitutes. One enterprising sheriff broadcasts scenes from his jail 24 hours a day on the Internet.

There are other classes of cases too. One class in particular runs strongly at odds with the policies of rehabilitation and resocialization that were the bread and butter of individualization in an earlier era: public exposure visited on persons who have completed their prison terms. An example of this is the class of so-called "Megan's Laws" involving sex offenders whose names and whereabouts are disclosed to the public after their release. Perhaps more revealing, though, is a different class. States have been moving to change what had been a deeply rooted practice in American justice: the practice of sealing juvenile criminal records, so that persons could leave youthful transgressions behind. Between 1992 and 1995, forty states enacted legislation making juvenile criminal records more easily accessible.

It is important not to exaggerate the role of most of these new sanctions in American criminal justice. Most forms of public shaming probably remain relatively rare. Nevertheless, they are indicative of an attitude that sharply distinguishes Americans from continental Europeans. It is an attitude that reflects, once again, our relative lack of concern for shows of respect. Shameful public exposure is antithetical to the display of respect. Persons who are exposed to the derision of those around them have been deprived a basic measure of self-respect. To be sure, Americans have never been as sensitive to public exposure as continental Europeans are. The contrast is one that we can see most notably in the comparative law of privacy. Continental concepts of the protection of privacy revolve around shielding people from public exposure in ways that are quite alien to the American sensibility. Nevertheless, Americans too have their dread of being publicly shamed; and even in the American context it is fair to describe the return of public shame sanctions as symptomatic of a reduced commitment to respect for criminal offenders. The decline of respect for persons can thus be detected in the rise of shame sanctions, just as it can be detected in the rise of formal equality in American criminal law.

The Mildness of Pardons

The application of the power of pardoning is so relatively rare in the United States that one would hardly mention it at all, if one were not laying the groundwork for a comparison with continental Europe.

All executives—state governors and the president of the United States—possess a pardoning power; and it is certainly in use. But it is used overwhelmingly for one purpose: to remove the civil and political disabilities that generally attach to a felony conviction in the United States. There are occasional cases in which pardons are issued to mitigate the harshness of some of the new sentencing statutes. There are also occasional commutations of the death penalty; and of course, there remains an appeal for mercy as of right for all persons condemned to die. There are some famous cases of political pardons—the pardon of Richard Nixon; and of the Vietnam-era draft dodgers.

For the most part, though, the pardoning power is little in evidence. The most highly publicized use of it in recent years is testimony, in fact, to its relative weakness. The presidential pardoning power is at the heart of the scandal over outgoing President Clinton's pardon of fugitive Marc Rich, along with other favored recipients. These Clinton pardons have stirred strong American suspicions that the pardoning power is used to benefit the rich and well connected. The Clinton pardons thus touched an egalitarian nerve. As we shall see, this was not unprecedented: such scandals over the pardoning power have a long history in the United States.

Harshness in Inflexible Doctrines of Liability

This is an area in which European criminal law has come, at first glance, to look somewhat harsher. Doctrines of extenuating circumstances have been abandoned, in the new French Code, in favor of individualization in punishment. In similar ways, the German Criminal Code aims to guarantee that offenders will not benefit from double-counting, receiving milder treatment both at the sentencing phase and in the course of the individualization of their punishment. These do not reflect any drive toward increased harshness, though. Rather, in both countries, flexibility in doctrines of liability is gradually being replaced by flexibility in the application of punishment.

Harshness in Enforcement

It is too empirically difficult to form any firm sense of how continental law should be measured by this category.

RESPECT AND MERCY

Let me come, finally, to my last two measures of mildness.

The Mildness of Respectful Treatment

We have seen that prison life is probably less violent on the continent than it is in the United States. Focusing exclusively on the question of violence would however be a mistake. For a large part of what most strikingly characterizes the law of European prisons is its concern with something that is almost entirely missing in the law of American ones: a concern with the *dignity* of prisoners. With this indeed we come to the matter of central importance for my argument. Dignitary concerns are pursued in Europe with an intensity unlike anything to be found in the United States, and it is to those concerns I now turn.

The intense interest that surrounds dignitary questions in European prison law can be disconcerting to Americans; reading the European literature is, from time to time, a strange experience. What can Americans think, when they discover that one of the most lively controversies in the German prison law of the late 1990s turned on the question of whether guards should be required to *knock* in all cases before entering prisoners' cells? What can they think when they discover that the very first of complaints about prison conditions raised by Mme. Baste-Morand, a prominent French reformer in 1982, was the absence of—a "right to respect"? "The Right to Respect. Guards are forbidden to address a prisoner as 'Monsieur.' Exactly the opposite should be the rule."

Other reformers have certainly detected worse scandals in French prisons. Nevertheless, the very fact that anyone could give first priority to the proposition that prisoners need to be addressed as "Monsieur" shows that matters are different in France from what they are in the United States—and in a way that we need the resources of a cultural anthropology to explain. Even harsher denunciations of French prisons can fall oddly on American ears. Thus a 1999 exposé in *Le Monde*, during the initial run-up to the current round of prison reform, deplored behavior by guards that included "racist insults, sexual harassment, and regular beatings." How striking that, in a summary that is meant to express outrage, two varieties of disrespectful insult should precede any mention of violence! What denunciatory account of an American high-security facility would ever begin by complaining of insults? Violence is, in fact, only a part of what European reformers care about. As the German debate over knocking, and Mme. Baste-Morand's list of complaints suggest, the right to "respect" and the right to "dignity" also play a large role in the humanitarian law of European prisons—and it is dignity of a deeply different kind from the kind pursued by American reformers.

That "dignity" matters in European prisons is, of course, not news. European thinking has produced a number of much-admired declarations and recommendations on safeguarding "human dignity" in prison conditions. It is easy to cite regulations according to the letter of which, at least, to be a convict in continental Europe is to enjoy safeguards for one's "dignity" that few would claim for American prisoners. But what exactly does this "dignity" consist in? The important answer is that dignity in European imprisonment is much like the "dignity" that prevails in other corners of European legal culture: It is a dignity that blends concepts of entitlement in the modern social state with much older ideas of personal honor. Moreover, it is "dignity" that pursues one extremely revealing goal: it aims to avoid the sort of *status-degradation* that is a prime feature of American criminal justice culture.

Indeed, by contrast with American punishment law, the punishment law of both France and Germany is expressly designed to avoid any sort of punishment practice that would create any sense of status differentiation between prisoners and the general population. On the contrary, practices in both countries are supposed to dramatize the fact that inmates are *just like everybody else*. In part this has involved one reform in the technical legal consequences of conviction: Europeans have fully abolished "civil death," the old erasure of civil personality and political rights that used to be a consequence of many criminal convictions. (Full-scale "civil death" is gone in the United States too; but loss of political rights remains common.) The contrast is striking. Very few European offenders suffer the expulsion from political and public life that can come with a felony conviction and its attendant disabilities in the United States. European judges still deprive some offenders of their civic rights for some period of time. But this is never done automatically, and it is always imposed as a temporary measure. There is none of the American notion that every felon should instantly be classed as something less than a full citizen. (Quite the contrary: in both France and Germany, efforts are made to encourage convicts to exercise political rights as a way of reintegrating them into normal society.) European offenders do not lose membership in the political community.

But it is perhaps even more important that they do not lose membership in what we might call the *social* community. The effort to keep offenders symbolically integrated into society involves what sometimes are some very striking measures. Most notable of all, perhaps, is one measure that has much preoccupied both French and German law, and that shows that there are ideas coursing under the surface of the continental idea of dignity that are alien to any we can find in America. Under modern reforms, the obligation of wearing prison uniforms has been generally eliminated, on the grounds that this practice diminishes the dignity of prisoners. Though practices differ somewhat under the letter of French and German law, and according to the rules in different continental prisons, the general tendency is the same everywhere. Where uniforms are required at all, they are required only in the prison workplace; and where they are required, efforts are made to guarantee that they resemble ordinary clothing in the outside world. This is, from the point of view of cultural anthropology, a revealing reform: changes in dress are a classic means of signaling a change in status.

The question of uniforms has played a particularly prominent role in French reform discussions; there is in fact a kind of horror of uniforms that runs through the French law. Moreover, French punishment professionals also see the same sorts of dignitary issues at play in other questions too—such as whether visitors may be kept behind a glass partition. (In both Germany and France, the use of glass partitions is restricted, and the partitions themselves are frequently low panes of glass that divide an otherwise open table.) This hostility both to the wearing of uniforms and to isolation behind glass partitions are central to the atmosphere of French reforms, and both suggest something important. There is a deep disinclination, in French law, to accept an idea that has a powerful grip on American punishment culture: the idea that conviction works a deprivation of the offender's humanity, as measured by isolation from other human beings and loss of control over the presentation of self. Prison uniforms and isolation in various forms, like routine searches and other lack of privacy protections, are part of what makes American convicts feel that they have been branded as lesser human beings.

Now, it should be emphasized that these ambitions do not make French prisons humane places. Life in French prisons is very rough. Nevertheless, the ambitions certainly make some difference, and they are revealing about the reigning spirit in French criminal justice. French convicts, at least in theory, are indeed not supposed to feel *branded*. On the contrary, it is the drive of French dignitary legislation to insist that convicts are just like everybody else. The same drive is to be found in Germany—strikingly captured, in the German Code of Punishment Practice, by what is called the *Angleichungs-grundsatz*, the principle of approximation, or, as I will call it, the "principle of normalcy." This principle, enshrined in the third paragraph of the Code of Punishment and worked out with typical juristic care by the German legal profession, holds that prison life must resemble as closely as possible life in the outside world. In some respects, the principle of normalcy has left German inmates a shade less well off than French ones, at least in theory. Thus the letter of German regulations says that they, unlike French prisoners, must ordinarily wear prison uniforms. (Prison officials do have discretion to lift this requirement, though, and in the maximum security prison that I visited in Berlin, inmates did not in fact wear uniforms. Only in the investigative custody facility that I visited in Munich were uniforms in use, and there only in the workplace.) The story does not end there, though. Even where they are obliged to wear uniforms, dignitary concerns set German practices apart from American: German uniforms must resemble the clothing worn in the outside world. American-style day-glo uniforms are carefully avoided on dignitary grounds, as are stripes or anything else that might make convicts feel branded. German rules also carefully specify that inmates, at their initial admission, are to be dressed in their uniforms outside the presence of third parties. Explicitly sensitive to the idea that special dress works a status degradation, German reformers have tried to eliminate whatever is most humiliating about uniforms. Many other provisions reflect a far-reaching concern, in German law, that prisoners should not feel that they have been cast out from ordinary society. Any regulation that could be understood as in any way symbolically branding prisoners is out. Such an approach is unimaginable in the world of American jurisprudence—a world in which the Supreme Court takes it for granted that prisoners could not conceivably expect to live in the way persons in the outside world do. The German code does not "mandate comfortable prisons" any more than the United States Constitution does; but it does mandate circumstances that will minimize the degree to which inmates feel themselves assigned to a subclass of human beings, different from those on the outside.

This idea of "normalcy" for convicts, shared by both French and German systems, this ambition to guarantee that inmates will not undergo symbolic status-degradation, may seem a minor thing to my American readers, who will think of problems in prison conditions primarily as problems of *violence*. Who cares, they may ask, if prisoners do or do not wear uniforms? Yet if my American readers find these dignitary issues to be minor matters, that only shows that they are American readers. If American readers find these issues to be minor ones, that fact only effectively poses the question of this book all the more sharply. Why are American perceptions different, and with what consequences?

At any rate, the continental commitment to normalcy, to the proposition that prisoners should be just like everybody else, also expresses itself in some further revealing dignitary measures. Deserving special emphasis are two programmatic efforts in both France and Germany: an effort to guarantee convicts the privileges of the social welfare state; and an effort to guarantee them the privileges of ordinary legal protections for their dignity and honor.

Thus "resocialization," in prisons both French and German, involves, first of all, a complex effort to integrated inmates into the same system of state socialism that everybody else is integrated into. In France the 1981 law that is the main basis of the current regime of prison regulations established a large variety of new rights that were conceived by the government as "social" rights in the fullest sense of the term—including, for example, not only a "right to information" but also a "right to leisure and culture." The avowed ambition behind this grant of rights was to avoid any kind of fundamental status differentiation between "criminals" and "noncriminals"—to guarantee that "the rights that prisoners enjoy by virtue of their status as citizens (right to work, right to culture) are not, in the absence of particular circumstances, suppressed or suspended solely on account of incarceration." As the "right to leisure and culture" in particular was described in 1982:

Our society must furnish the means (both in terms of finances and of time) for the collectivity of individuals to cultivate and amuse themselves. This obligation to society in general cannot exclude the prisons. It is true that, for a long time, many believed that there was an irreducible incompatibility between prison and leisure. Notions of austerity had primacy in policies of incarceration, which made any serious cultural development impossible. . . .

It is in this spirit that we are trying to develop those manual activities that will be maximally accessible to the great number of prisoners. A series of projects is being worked out at this time that aim to allow prisoners in numerous institutions to exercise a meaningful choice between artisanal and artistic activities such that they can explore a mode of expression through basket-weaving, pottery, drawing, painting etc.

It is easy to laugh at this, with its earnest Marxist humanism—this sounds very much like what French politicians today decide as "gauchisme laxiste," "leftism gone soft." Nevertheless, this passage represents something significant about French penal ambitions. When the French socialist government set about to reaffirm the national commitment to a socialized state that would raise the cultural status of all, it did not hesitate to include prison inmates. (It also reflects an important fact about French theories of the personality: their intimate connection with ideals of artistic self-expression.)

In Germany, too, prison reform is thoroughly entangled with the "social state" and its constitutionalized values of human dignity. The statutory requirement of fostering a "socially responsible way of life" for convicts is understood to derive directly from the constitutional sanctifications of human dignity and of the social state principle that protects everybody. Integration of inmates into the German social welfare state has some important corollaries. Notably, when German inmates work—and they are, at least in principle, all entitled (and indeed required) to work—they receive unemployment insurance contributions at the going rate for the outside world. This means that they can expect to draw unemployment benefits on their release. (They receive health coverage too—indeed, one recent newspaper article complained that inmates were better covered than civilians.) Even more strikingly, they are subject to a slightly modified version of ordinary labor law. Among other consequences, this means that, while at work, they are supervised by outside entrepreneurs rather than guards. They receive a version of ordinary protections against discharge. (In conversation with employers at two German prisons, I was told that it can be difficult indeed to fire prisoners.) They even receive paid vacation, just like Germans in the outside world. Until recently this totaled only three weeks—half of the six that are customary for most Germans. But efforts to improve the working conditions of inmates have continued. New legislation raised their wages as of January 1, 2001, and they have also now received six further vacation days, which they may either use as vacation time or bank toward eventual early release.

The normalcy of French and German dignity in the prisons does not end with membership in the social welfare state, moreover. Just as they are supposed to be participants in the social welfare state, convicts are supposed to be participants in the general culture of dignity. In particular, it is repeatedly said that they enjoy the same sorts of "personality" and "privacy" rights that reign in the honor culture of the outside world. As a French passage puts it:

The "freedom of personal choice" characterizes the ensemble of rights that aim to guarantee respect for privacy and intellectual freedom. A number of recent prison reforms can be classified as belonging to this model. The generalization of visiting rooms without glass partitions, the improvement of everyday life in the prisons, the extension of contacts with the outside world, and especially with the family, are all illustrations. There are also measures that belong to the same tendency but that are more symbolic or expressive: notably the end, in 1983, of the obligation to wear a prison uniform, as well as the right to correspond with any person, or, finally, as of the 15th of December 1985, the authorization given to prisoners to have a television in their cell.

In all of this, the problems of dignity within prison are not understood as fundamentally different from those outside. French prison regulations include, for example, provisions on insult. (Here American readers may need some background. Continental European legal systems include a category of law that is essentially absent in America: the law of *insult*. This body of law criminalizes insulting or disrespectful speech.) A version of the law of insult is to be found in the French prisons too. Under regulations promulgated in 1996, inmates may be disciplined not only for insulting prison personnel but also for insulting other inmates.

As for Germany, there, too, and there especially, the value of human dignity has been taken to guarantee inmates the same sorts of dignitary rights that Germans in the outside world enjoy. Thus inmates' right to furnish their cells with their own belongings has been held to be dictated by their right to a "private sphere." (In American prisons, by contrast, to repeat, inmate's possessions may effectively be summarily seized by prison officials.) The same is true of German inmates' right to visits—including regular visits with family that are permitted to unmarried as well as married convicts. (German jurists also view the Basic Law as guaranteeing, not only contact with family members, but also the possibility of striking up new romantic relationships with denizens of the outside world.) This commitment to privacy can have some consequences that are quite remarkable from the American point of view. In the maximum-security prison that I visited in Berlin, for example, inmates—almost all housed one to a cell, despite the current overcrowding crisis—had doors without peepholes, behind which they could enjoy a kind of privacy to which maximum-security American prisoners can hardly think of aspiring. During the day, moreover, their cell doors stood unlocked.

Like American prisons, German ones come in more and less harsh varieties: German law distinguishes between "open" and "closed" facilities, with open facilities something like American halfway houses. The letter of the German statute declares that inmates are presumptively to be housed in "open" facilities, with "closed" punishment the exception. This is a dead letter: in a system in which only very serious offenses result in imprisonment, the notion that offenders should routinely be placed in halfway houses never had any hope of success. Nevertheless, the very aspiration to make halfway houses the norm speaks volumes about the statute's attitude toward prisoners.

Not least, as in France, one sees the penetration of the general culture of interpersonal respect into German prisons. A particularly odd example, from the American point of view, is one with which I began: a German requirement that guards *knock* before entering cells. A standard introductory text explains the thinking behind this rule:

> Before entering a place of confinement, prison personnel are obliged to knock. *This does not present a question of mere politeness. . . . Rather, it is the right of the prisoner to protection and respect for his human dignity (Art. 1 GG) as well as his intimate sphere (Art 2 GG), which, taking into account the principle of normalcy, make it appropriate for the managers of the institution to work to create suitable forms of polite interaction between guards and inmates. . . . For entering a place of confinement without first knocking means imposing limits on prisoners which are not necessary as an indispensable consequence of the deprivation of liberty.*

This rule, which was endorsed by a number of appellate courts, was a bit too much for the Constitutional Court, which held in 1997 that it lay within the discretion of prison personnel whether or not to knock. Nevertheless, here as so often, the very fact that an absolute bar on entering without knocking had a few years of life testifies to the strength of an idea of dignity that rests to a remarkable degree on inherited ideas of politeness. So too does the prominence of matter from the law of insult in the prisons. The regulations require German prison guards, to address prisoners as "Sie," the respectful formal form of address. Germans inmates have not infrequently brought successful actions against guards who addressed them disrespectfully; what could be further from the world of American prisons? The application of the law of insult in German prisons is however a more one-sided matter than the application of rules of insult in French prisons. Where it is clear that French convicts may not insult their guards, the vigorous free-speech jurisprudence of the German Constitutional Court has left German guards less well protected. Convicts have protections for their honor, but also for their freedom of speech—with some comical consequences. In one important case, an inmate who had been handed an unfavorable decision of the Constitutional Court burst out at his guard, "Don't be so snotty [vorlaut], you uppity jerk." Subjected to disciplinary measures for this insult, the inmate carried the case to the Constitutional Court once again, which carefully ruled that, while criminal insults were naturally punishable, prison officials had a special obligation to weigh that interest against the inmate's interest in free expression. Strangely enough, German convicts may thus actually be *more* free to hand out insults than ordinary Germans are. Whatever the oddities of insult jurisprudence, the main point remains that the culture of dignity and respect that prevails generally in German society also sets the terms of discussion for "dignity" in imprisonment.

The greater continental concern with dignity in prison is paralleled by a greater continental dislike of *public exposure.*

Both German and French law display a resistance, if only a limited resistance, to public exposure for offenders—a resistance that sets these systems sharply apart from the American criminal justice. This resistance is something we can see, not only in the absence of shame sanctions in Europe, but also in a horror of barred celled doors that characterizes French and German prisons much more than American ones. It is also something we can see in other aspects of French and German criminal law. French and German jurists continue to think of public exposure as a frightening and barbaric thing.

Of course, there are always limits to the extent to which criminal justice systems can avoid subjecting offenders to public exposure. The identity, and the dangerousness, of some offenders has to be publicized, and no system could completely do without public exposure. Abolishing public shame sanctions is one thing: keeping the public in ignorance of the identity of offenders is something else entirely. Nevertheless, in France, and especially in Germany, the law is much more chary of exposing defendants and convicts to publicity than the American system is. The most striking expression of this chariness was the famous *Lebach* decision of the German Constitutional Court, handed down in 1973—roughly contemporaneously with the United States Supreme Court's decision in *Paul v. Davis. Paul v. Davis,* readers will recall, permitted the circulation of the photo of a "known" shoplifter against whom charges had been dismissed. The *Lebach* decision took a very different attitude. The case concerned a 1960s radical who been convicted of the terrorist murder of soldiers stationed in the town of Lebach. This convict had been involved in a homosexual relationship with one of his accomplices. The story was too good for journalists to keep away from, and German television sought to broadcast a film about him. In the *Lebach* case, the convict objected, successfully, on the grounds that broadcasting his story in such a way would both violate his constitutional right of personality and impede the resocialization that was his entitlement as a German prisoner. German constitutional jurisprudence has since retreated a bit from the specific holding in *Lebach,* but the case is still regarded as the font of both dignitary law in German prisons and of modern German privacy law. It reflects, clearly enough, the fact that Germans feel far greater discomfort with public exposure than Americans do. There are other rules and practices that reflect the same discomfort. A German inmate's privacy is now protected, for example, through a rule permitting him to demand the destruction of the file describing his personal characteristics, fingerprints, and the like, after his release from prison. Perhaps most noticeably, for an American experiencing day-to-day life in Germany, newspapers there still frequently avoid naming defendants.

France has a less developed jurisprudence of this kind, but it still shows a much more lively sensibility with regard to public exposure than America does. Most striking here is the law surrounding the codified right to privacy, added to the Code Civil in 1970—again about the same time as the *Lebach* decision. This right, framed in general terms, embodied aspirations that were perhaps not practically achievable with regard to convicts. Nevertheless, the right to privacy of defendants and convicts became a vibrant issue of discussion, and in 1993 the code was modified expressly to protect defendants against adverse publicity. Article 9-1 of the code declares "every person has a right to respect of the presumption of innocence." This provision allows judges to order the publication of a retraction, without prejudice to any other suit for damages. Under the resulting jurisprudence, still developing, newspapers have been successfully sued for coverage that did not carefully make it clear that accused persons had not been found guilty.

In all of these rules, we see the same deep-seated continental sensibility at work—a sensibility that associates any kind of public exposure with a loss of dignity. We also see, once again, the strength of the drive to generalize ordinary social dignity to criminals. Even criminals, these rules hold in effect, should not be subjected to the intense shame and loss of social standing that public exposure carries with it.

The Mildness of Mercy

Alongside all of these aspects of European punishment practice, finally, it is important to mention one last practice that will seem to Americans exceedingly strange: the granting of amnesties. This is, in fact, one of the most telling and characteristic expressions of the broad European urge toward mildness. General amnesties for convicts serving shorter sentences are a regular business in European justice. Mildness in European law is pursued partly through something almost wholly missing in the United States: systematic mercy.

The practice is most noticeable, and most frequently discussed, in France. There, the granting of amnesties has an old historical pedigree. The royal prerogative of granting large-scale celebratory amnesties extends far back into the ancien régime. It was an important aspect of the sacral practices of the prerevolutionary monarchy to grant amnesties, and kings regularly did so, on such events as their coronations or their birthdays. The granting of amnesties was, indeed, closely associated with the king's claim to hold a sovereign power of grace that stood outside the law, and accordingly many Enlightenment reformers, including Beccaria and Kant, objected to it. Nevertheless, despite some strong objections during the revolution, it never died. Indeed, the practice has played a regular role in France ever since. Frequent amnesties have played an important role in limiting the prison population since the World War II. Notably, these amnesties often celebrate the accession to power of a new government, a French republican tradition that continues a distinctly regal ancien régime tradition. (This has some comical results. In 2001, for example, as French citizens expected the election of a new president in a year's time, one kind of lawlessness increased in anticipation of a general amnesty: illegal parking was rampant.) Convicts are also beneficiaries of this tradition: Bastille-day amnesties result in the annual release of some inmates as well.

In Germany, amnesties have had a more complex history, to which I will return later. To focus for the moment only on their place in current punishment practice, while they are less publicized, amnesties are as regular a practice in Germany as they are in France—though illegal parkers and the like do not benefit in Germany. In particular, every German state grants regular Christmas amnesties, which free all inmates serving short sentences. German lawyers, Indeed, can try to plan around these amnesties, in the effort to guarantee their clients the shortest possible stay in prison. It is known, in the various states, that inmates must serve a certain minimum time—typically a month—before they may benefit from any amnesty. Savvy offenders can try to delay their admission to prison until one month before the effective date of the annual Christmas amnesty, effectively shortening their sentences to one month. The fact that the German justice system tolerates these tactics reflects a systematic toleration for relative mildness.

Amnesties, a general reluctance to incarcerate, a strong commitment to individualization and resocialization, a drive to define offenses as mere "contraventions" or *Ordnungswidrigkeiten*, "dignity" of a variety of types for prisoners, a concerted effort to guarantee that convicts will not be regarded as having a different status from anybody else, a resistance to public exposure: these are all measures of an instinct toward mildness that sets Europe sharply apart from the United States. As the United States has entered its late-twentieth-century ice age of harshness, the climate has become somewhat colder in Europe, too, as we have seen. Nevertheless, there is a warm counter-current in Europe as well, a tendency toward compensating mildness in the criminal justice systems of France and Germany—a tendency that shows especially in French and German commitment to relatively dignified, and relatively easy, sentences of punishment.

WHAT DO ALTERNATIVE SANCTIONS MEAN?

—Dan M. Kahan—

[excerpts, notes omitted]

Imprisonment is the punishment of choice in American jurisdictions. In everyday life, the modes of human suffering are numerous and diverse: when we lose our property, we experience need; when we are denounced by those whose opinions we respect, we feel shame; when our bodies are tormented, we suffer physical pain. But for those who commit serious criminal offenses, the law strongly prefers one form of suffering—the deprivation of liberty—to the near exclusion of all others. Some alternatives to imprisonment, such as corporal punishment, are barely conceivable. Others, including fines and community service, do exist but are used sparingly and with great reluctance. [*592]

The singularity of American criminal punishments has been widely lamented. Imprisonment is harsh and degrading for offenders and extraordinarily expensive for society. Nor is there any evidence that imprisonment is more effective than its rivals in deterring various crimes. For these reasons, theorists of widely divergent orientations—from economics-minded conservatives to reform-minded civil libertarians—are united in their support for alternative sanctions.

The problem is that there is no political constituency for such reform. If anything, the public's commitment to imprisonment has intensified in step with the theorists' disaffection with it. In the last decade, prison sentences have been both dramatically lengthened for many offenses and extended to others that have traditionally been punished only with fines and probation.

What accounts for the resistance to alternative sanctions? . . . .

The political unacceptability of alternative sanctions, I will argue, reflects their inadequacy along the expressive dimension of punishment. The public rejects the alternatives not because they perceive that these punishments won't work or aren't severe enough, but because they fail to express condemnation as dramatically and unequivocally as imprisonment. . . .

[However,] the meaning of alternative sanctions can be reformed. Shaming penalties unambiguously express condemnation and are a feasible alternative to imprisonment for many offenses.

FINES VS. IMPRISONMENT

Fines are the most commonly defended alternative sanction. Proponents make an optimal-deterrence argument: fines are comparably effective to imprisonment, and enrich rather than [*618] impoverish society. Accordingly, society should impose fines rather than imprisonment whenever feasible.

This well rehearsed defense of fines has carried little weight in the political process. Indeed, the law has moved in exactly the opposite direction. Before 1984, white-collar offenders were much more likely to be fined and much less likely to be imprisoned than common offenders. Optimal deterrence theorists applauded this pattern. Far from ratifying it, however, Congress invited the United States Sentencing Commission to consider requiring judges to sentence white-collar offenders to prison terms; the Commission thereafter issued guidelines doing exactly that. Congress also substantially increased the maximum fines for white-collar offenses. But these penalties were authorized as supplements to and not as substitutes for the prison terms required by the Guidelines.

Is there an explanation for American jurisdictions' traditional reluctance to make greater use of fines? . . . .

Fines, I will argue, are politically unacceptable not because the public perceives that they are insufficiently severe, but because it believes that fines are insufficiently expressive of condemnation. . . . . .

[A]fflictions can be equivalent along many dimensions—including pain and deterrent effect—but still differ radically in meaning. Robert Cooter recognizes this when he distinguishes between a "sanction"—which he defines as "a detriment imposed for doing what is forbidden"—and a "price"—which he defines as a detriment that an actor is required to endure "in order to do what is permitted." Prison, on this account, is clearly a sanction; because liberty is so universally and intensely valued, taking it away is our society's most potent symbol of moral condemnation. Fines condemn much more ambivalently. When combined with a term of imprisonment, no one doubts that fines convey moral disapproval. But when fines are used as a substitute for imprisonment, the message is likely to be that the offenders' conduct is being priced rather than sanctioned. And while we might believe that charging a high price for a good makes the purchaser suffer, we do not condemn someone for buying what we are willing to sell.

Cooter examines the respective regulatory properties of sanctions and prices; I want to show how their respective meanings affect their political acceptability. Imprisonment, as a sanction, invariably condemns; fines, when viewed as prices, do not. Accordingly, when it lacks this signification, a fine, no matter how large, won't be viewed as an adequate substitute for an appropriate term of imprisonment. . . .

[T]he expressive inadequacy of fines is directly borne out by opinion surveys. Such studies consistently show that the public and (democratically accountable) decision makers view fines, by themselves, as insufficiently condemnatory for "serious" offenses. As the authors of one such study put it, "many people believe that the idea of an offender paying for his immorality is offensive, and that a fine is 'a pretty timid expression of moral indignation.'" . . .

ENRICHING OUR PUNITIVE VOCABULARY: THE REDISCOVERY OF SHAME

So far I have concentrated on showing how the social meaning of alternative sanctions, in the form in which they are conventionally proposed, makes them politically unacceptable. I will now examine how the expressive dimension of punishment can be used to identify politically acceptable reforms.

The Shaming Alternative

Early Americans turned to imprisonment in large part because they believed that existing criminal penalties had lost the power to shame. It is perfectly fitting, then, that contemporary Americans are rediscovering shaming penalties as they attempt to extricate themselves from their excessive reliance on imprisonment. In this Part, I offer an overview of what those penalties are and why they are more likely to be embraced by the public than conventional alternative sanctions.

What Shaming Penalties Are

The last decade has witnessed the advent of a wide variety of shaming sanctions. Although categorizing them risks understating their diversity and richness, these penalties can be grouped into four classes: stigmatizing publicity, literal stigmatization, self-debasement, and contrition.

Stigmatizing publicity is the most straightforward. Penalties in this class attempt to magnify the humiliation inherent in con- [*632] viction by communicating the offender's status to a wider audience. Some municipalities, for example, publish offenders' names in newspapers or even on billboards, a disposition that is especially common for men convicted of soliciting prostitutes. Other jurisdictions broadcast the names of various types of offenders on community-access television channels.

Literal stigmatization is just that—the stamping of an offender with a mark or symbol that invites ridicule. Some judges order petty thieves to wear t-shirts announcing their crimes. Others achieve the same effect with brightly colored bracelets that read "DUI Convict," "I Write Bad Checks," and the like. One judge ordered a woman to wear a sign declaring "I am a convicted child molester."

Less dramatic but even more common are penalties that attach stigmatizing marks to property. Some jurisdictions now require persons guilty of drunk driving to display special license plates or bumper stickers. Courts have also ordered those [*633] convicted of sexual assaults and other crimes to post signs at their residences warning others to steer clear.

Self-debasement penalties involve ceremonies or rituals that publicly disgrace the offender. In a contemporary version of the stocks, for example, some communities require offenders simply to stand in public spaces, such as the local courthouse, with signs describing their offenses. More imaginative forms of self-debasement attempt to match the penalty to the character of the offense. A judge in Tennessee orders convicted burglars to permit their victims to enter their homes and remove items of their choosing. n166 In New York, a slumlord was sentenced to house arrest in one of his rat-infested tenements (where tenants greeted him with the banner, "Welcome, You Reptile!"). Hoboken, New Jersey, requires Wall Street brokers and others who urinate in public to clean the city's streets. This is only a small sam- [*634] ple; self-debasement sanctions are as diverse and particular as the crimes that they are used to punish.

Contrition penalties come in two forms. The first requires offenders to publicize their own convictions, describing their crimes in first-person terms and apologizing for them. These penalties combine stigmatizing publicity with an element of self-debasement; the sincerity of the offenders' remorse seems largely irrelevant.

Another form of contrition is the apology ritual. In Maryland, for example, juvenile offenders must apologize on their hands and knees and are released from confinement only if they persuade their victims that their remorse is sincere. Other jurisdictions use community-based sanctions that include public apologies and appropriate reparations. Because many of these penalties contemplate genuine rapprochement, apology rituals seem to be used primarily in cases in which the offender is connected to the victim by family or close community ties. [*635]

What Shaming Penalties Mean

The proponents of alternative sanctions shouldn't be entirely surprised by the growing popularity of shaming penalties. Much of their appeal is simply that they are cheaper than imprisonment. Not all offenders who receive shaming penalties would otherwise have been incarcerated, but many of them would have. Courts use shaming penalties to punish a wide array of offenses, including drunk driving, larceny, embezzlement, assault (sexual and nonsexual), burglary, perjury, toxic-waste dumping, and drug distribution. When imposed for crimes such as these, shaming penalties free up imprisonment resources for offenders who more urgently demand incapacitation.

But shaming penalties are also emerging as a serious rival of imprisonment because they do something that conventional alternative sanctions don't do: express appropriate moral condemnation. Such penalties, one court explained, "inflict[] disgrace and contumely in a dramatic and spectacular manner." This dimension of meaning sets shaming penalties apart from fines and community service, which seem unsatisfactory precisely because they condemn the offender's acts only equivocally. [*636]

In fact, the expression of condemnation is at least as central to shaming penalties as the infliction of shame itself. Shame is the emotion that a person experiences when she believes that she has been disgraced in the eyes of persons whom she respects. Most offenders punished by shaming penalties are likely to feel shame. But some probably do not, just as some offenders do not view imprisonment as vitiating the respect of their peers. The public's realization that not all offenders view such punishments as disgraceful, however, does not diminish the resonance of either shaming penalties or imprisonment as symbols of the community's moral disapproval. If anything, the perception that the offender is not shamed by what is commonly understood to be shameful would reinforce onlookers' conclusion that he is depraved and worthy of condemnation.

Shaming penalties might even more accurately be described as degradation penalties. All of them satisfy what Harold Garfinkel identifies as the "conditions of successful status degradation ceremonies": they are imposed by an agent invested with the moral authority of the community; they denounce the wrongdoer and his conduct as contrary to shared moral norms; and they ritualistically separate the wrongdoer from those who subscribe to such norms. It is not a condition of a successful degradation ceremony that it induce any particular belief or emotion on the part of the offender. We might expect the ceremony to cause shame—particularly if the offender identifies with the community that is denouncing him. But to lower the offender's [*637] social status within that community, it is enough that the affliction convey disapproval in terms that its members understand. . . . .

SHAMING ANXIETIES

Showing that shaming penalties are likely to be a politically acceptable alternative to imprisonment does not, in and of itself, show that they are appropriate criminal punishments. Members of the public insist that punishments express appropriate condemnation, but they also expect them to do an adequate job in protecting them from criminality. They also demand (or at least ought to demand) that punishments be consistent with desert, equality, and other values.

I will now address a number of important issues relating to the moral acceptability of shaming penalties. I will argue that the same properties that make shaming penalties express appropriate condemnation are also likely to make them effective and just.

Shame and Deterrence

. . . Does shame deter criminality? The short and simple answer is that we don't know. Shaming penalties have not yet been subject to rigorous empirical evaluation.

The longer and more complicated answer is that shaming penalties should work. There may be little data on the effectiveness of shaming penalties in particular, but the ways in which criminal penalties deter in general have been carefully studied. What we know about deterrence should make us confident that shaming penalties will be reasonably effective by virtue of their character as degradation ceremonies.

Criminal penalties deter, first, by raising the cost of criminal behavior. Potential offenders refrain from committing crimes when the threat of unpleasant consequences offsets the expected gains from breaking the law.

The consequences of shaming penalties are extremely unpleasant. Those who lose the respect of their peers often suffer a crippling diminishment of self-esteem. Moreover, criminal offenders are as likely to be shunned in the marketplace as they are in the public square, leading to serious financial hardship. Indeed, some studies suggest that the prospect of public disgrace exerts greater pressure to comply with the law than does the threat of imprisonment and other formal sanctions. It stands to reason, then, that shaming penalties, which abstract disgrace from the afflictive dimension of formal sanctions, should compare favorably with imprisonment as a deterrent. . . .

Shame and Stigma

Critics argue (somewhat inconsistently) that shaming penalties are likely to be ineffective deterrents not only because they hurt offenders too little but also because they hurt them too much. Such penalties aim to disgrace the offender. Once a person has been so stigmatized, his propensity to commit offenses (it is claimed) is no longer held in check by the prospect that he will lose social status. In fact, at that point, the shamed individual can maintain self-respect only by turning to deviant subcommunities that value and thereby reinforce the very traits for which he has been condemned by society at large. Shame, [*645] the critics maintain, is therefore a self-defeating strategy for preventing criminal behavior.

This claim, however, faces a massive baseline problem. The alternative to shaming penalties, at least for serious offenses, is imprisonment. Imprisonment likewise satisfies the conditions of successful degradation ceremonies precisely because liberty deprivation is such a potent symbol of moral condemnation in American society. Indeed, casual observation and common sense suggest that persons who are imprisoned are more likely to be shunned and driven into criminal subcultures than those who are subjected to shaming penalties. Unless they are prepared to reject the use of imprisonment on the same ground, the critics cannot persuasively challenge shaming penalties based on their stigmatizing effect. . . . .

Shame and Cruelty

Is shaming cruel? Shame works, if it does, because the respect of one's peers is essential to a person's well-being. Can it be just to take this good away from someone? For some critics, the answer is no.

But again, identifying the proper baseline disposes of the objection. However cruel shaming is, imprisonment is much worse. It expresses at least as much condemnation, and it adds a grotesque variety of indignities that shaming cannot hope to rival. . . . .

CONCLUSION

The dominant position of imprisonment is usually attributed either to the public's ignorance or to its appetite for human suffering. My analysis suggests a more complicated and less disturbing explanation: imprisonment is expressively superior to its conventional rivals. The public expects punishment not only to deter crime but to express appropriate moral condemnation. Because of the value of liberty in our culture, imprisonment unequivocally conveys society's denunciation of wrongdoers. The conventional alternatives, however, express condemnation much more ambivalently. Fines, when used in lieu of imprisonment, often imply that society is merely pricing, not sanctioning, offenders' behavior. Community service seems to suggest that society doesn't sincerely believe the offender to be vicious, or, even worse, that it doesn't genuinely respect the virtue of those who voluntarily serve the public. Whatever equivalence there [*653] might be between these sanctions and imprisonment along the dimensions of regulatory effect and pain, they will frequently remain incommensurable with imprisonment along the dimension of meaning. When this is so, they will be inadequate substitutes for imprisonment in whatever amount they are imposed. . . .

American jurisdictions can liberate themselves from their excessive reliance on imprisonment if they can identify alternative sanctions that do express appropriate condemnation. I identified shaming penalties as one possibility. These sanctions, used alone, are already proving to be a politically acceptable alternative to imprisonment for many offenses. If combined with fines and community service, moreover, these sanctions would likely dispel the expressive ambiguity that makes these sanctions politically unacceptable substitutes for imprisonment.

WHAT IS WRONG WITH SHAME SANCTIONS?

—James Q. Whitman—

[excerpts; notes omitted]

We are all aware that there was a time in the western world when punishment frequently revolved around the public humiliation of the offender. Everyone likes to read about the picturesque barbarism of the old punishments: the pillory, the stocks, the ducking stool, branding, and so on. Many of us are also dimly aware that such shame sanctions continue to be used in much of the nonwestern world. . . . Most recently, the media have focused on the humiliation rituals of the Islamic legal revival broadly, and of the Afghan Taliban, in particular.

The scattered reappearance of shame sanctions in the United States is a surprise, however. Most of us, at least as of 1975 or so, would probably have said that sanctions of the premodern type—sanctions whose main purpose is the ritualized humiliation of the offender-had permanently vanished from our legal landscape. Yet, as news magazines and newspapers have eagerly been reporting, just such sanctions have begun to reappear. It is true that these practices do not often assume the lurid shapes they took in the early-modern or Maoist worlds. In particular, modern American shame sanctions lack the air of physical violence that has commonly hung about the shame sanctions of other times and places; American courts do not order offenders flogged, dunked, or branded. The current American practice takes milder forms, such as requiring offenders to wear shirts describing their crimes, publishing the names of prostitutes' johns,' or (in a ritual not that far removed from the Chinese one) making offenders sit outside public courthouses wearing placards. Unlike the premodern punishments, none of these is inflicted in the expectation that offenders will be physically assaulted. Perhaps the new shame sanctions seem more acceptable for that reason. Nevertheless, they do not seem very acceptable. But why not?. . . .

In point of fact, I contend, the most compelling arguments against pure humiliation sanctions—sanctions that involve only public exposure and not corporal violence—do not have to do either with their ineffectuality or with their cruelty. The most compelling arguments against such humiliation sanctions do not, in fact, involve the way they deal with the offender at all. As I try to show, the most compelling arguments against shame sanctions involve the way they deal with the public, with society at large, with the crowd. In the last analysis, we should think of shame sanctions as wrong because they involve a species of lynch justice, and a peculiarly disturbing species of lynch justice at that—a species of official lynch justice. The chief evil in public humiliation sanctions is that they involve an ugly, and politically dangerous, complicity between the state and the crowd. Shame sanctions are wrong in our society for the same reason that we feel they are wrong in China, or in the Afghanistan of the Taliban: They represent an unacceptable style of governance through their play on public psychology. This evil is one that we will never fully appreciate so long as we continue to focus exclusively on the effects of shame sanctions on the offender. In fact, it is of no ultimate importance whether shame sanctions are cruel or not. Shame sanctions would be wrong even if they

Reprinted by permission of The Yale Law Journal Company, Inc., from *The Yale Law Journal*, Vol. 107, pp. 1055.

had no impact on the offender at all; for, no matter what, they would represent an improper partnership between the state and the crowd. Even if shame sanctions were wholly unobjectionable from the point of view of punishment theory, they would still fail the test of a sane political theory. . . . .

So what is the argument against shame sanctions?

[T]here are two aspects to what is troubling about shame sanctions: their effect on the offender and their effect on the crowd. We tend, in our rights-oriented society, to begin by reasoning from the first. But let us try to begin our reasoning from the second.

The classic political objections . . . agree on one proposition: The government cannot control fully the actions and the affect of the crowd as it wishes. . . .

Once the state stirs up public opprobrium against an offender, it cannot really control the way the public treats that offender. Indeed, in the most controversial area of current American practices, the sexual predator notification statutes of the Megan's Law type, debate has come forcefully, and I think rightly, to revolve around the risk of lynching in various forms. The government, in this context, may indeed create something akin to riots, as in the painful case in which an innocent man was assaulted by attackers who wrongly supposed him to be a released child molester. But I do not wish to rest my argument on the danger of literal riots, for it is essential that we grasp what is wrong even with far less dramatic cases than the sorts of child molestation that are the usual stuff of laws like Megan's Law. Even where there is no threat of rioting, the state has no control over the sort of abuse the public will deal out to a shamed offender. When our government dangles a sex offender or a drunk driver before the public, it has vanishingly little control over how the public treats the person. Riots are by no means the only danger. Other things happen too—things that are more difficult to detect and therefore more disturbing. Who knows how private persons will treat the shamed john, the shamed merchant, the shamed shoplifter, the shamed drunk driver? Who knows how private persons, given the right to play policemen, will behave?

It is here, I think, that we begin to approach the heart of what is troubling about shame sanctions: They involve a dangerous willingness, on the part of the government, to delegate part of its enforcement power to a fickle and uncontrolled general populace. Even in their mildest American form, shame sanctions amount to a kind of posse—raising legal politics, with all of the risks that implies. They are, at base, a form of officially sponsored lynch justice, meted out by courts that have given up on the obligation of the state both to define what is criminal and to administer criminal sanctions itself.

Of course, it is easy to understand how courts have come to this point. We all believe the state is doing a bad job of administering criminal sanctions and that our prisons, in particular, are lousy institutions. Why not turn certain limited classes of offenders over to the public? Why not discipline sexual misbehavior, commercial misbehavior, and the like, through techniques of humiliation that are often likely to be effective and to bring many offenders into line with what we think are norms of public comportment? Why not turn such offenders over to be judged by the established norms of public opinion?

The right answer, I think, recognizes shaming as a form of lynch justice and acknowledges both the personal and the political dangers that state encouraged lynch justice raises. The right answer acknowledges three things: first, that it is a mistake to imagine that there are established norms of public opinion that go unaffected by state shaming; second, that we have far too little control over the way the public exercises its enforcement power— far too little control over the tendency of the public to become either a mob or a collection of petty private prison guards; and third, that allowing state—encouraged lynching involves a troubling tolerance for ochlocracy, for a democratic government too susceptible to the pitch and yaw of mob psychology. Particularly where shame sanctions are applied in the realms of sex and commerce, they represent a misguided willingness to let the business of government devolve to an over-volatile public—to make, in the words of a nineteenth-century reformer, their victim a "plaything of the populace."'

With respect to the first point, it is simply wrong to suppose that the shaming state is not a maker of public norms. This is not because the American government engages in propaganda of the Nazi or Maoist kind when it inflicts shame sanctions. The process is subtler than any kind of calculated propagandizing, but it is a powerful process nevertheless. Government actions like shame sanctions change public norms; and, let us not fail to note, public officials often seek to employ shame sanctions in order to change public norms. Is the only effect of publishing the names of prostitutes' johns to expose them to an existing atmosphere of condemnation? Or is the effect to nudge prevailing views in a new, more moralistic, direction—or even simply to consolidate what had hitherto been a more vague and less effective consenus? Are officials who advocate publishing the names of johns simply seeking more effective enforcement measures? Or are they promoting greater political legitimacy for themselves by stirring up some mix of public indignation and public merriment? Is the only effect of publicly shaming Wall Street traders to draw on an existing body of righteous public indignation? Or is it to create, or enhance, a public sense that something sinister is afoot in the financial world and so to stir up the sort of politically powerful anti-banker sentiment that has characterized so much of modern politics (especially in its anti-Semitic incarnations)? These are unavoidable issues in any scheme that involves the dangling of sexual, commercial, and first or minor offenders before the public. Playing with public opinion on dark and volatile psychologies like the psychologies of sex and commerce makes for a distressingly creative politics, a politics of the dark and the volatile. It is a form of legislating and politicking in the realm of morality that goes unchecked by any of our standard ideas about the propriety of legislating or moralizing. It is a stirring up of the public—who knows whither?

It is also a stirring up of the public in who knows what way. The numberless private policemen who enforce shame sanctions play by their own rules or by none. This is a pressing problem and a problem best understood by coming at last to the question of how shame sanctions violate the dignity of the offender. For the dignitary claim I would like to defend is this: Subjecting offenders to the public's unpredictable response to shame sanctions is a violation of our modern sense of what we might call transactional dignity. It is a deeply rooted norm of our society that persons should never be forced to deal with wild or unpredictable partners. We have a sense that no one should be compelled to dance with a madman, that no one should be compelled to trade except under well-understood rules of trading. This is something very different from bodily dignity, something different from status dignity. It is, as it were, marketplace dignity. It is the dignity involved in having the right to know what kind of a deal one has struck, and on what terms. It is the dignity of the one-shot transaction— the dignity that arises from our marketplace right to complete one deal and move on to the next one, the dignity that comes from our right to pay off a debt once and for all and be done with our creditor.

When the state turns an offender over to the public, it robs him of that transactional dignity. There is no way to predict or control the way in which the public will deal with him, no rhyme or limit to the terms the public may impose. Shame sanctions, in this regard, are very different from prisons or fines. However much prisons may have declined into chaos, they are in principle controllable. However monstrous they may have become, we all agree that the state has the duty to manage them: to establish rules, to call review boards, to answer complaints in court. None of that apparatus exists to control the enforcement of shame. This means that, though courts may wish to abandon the prison system and switch to a system of shaming, they must not be permitted to do so. Doing so means abandoning their obligation to maintain a monopoly of the means of power—it means abandoning their duty to be the imposers of measured punishment.

Shame sanctions thus do represent a deprivation of dignity in a sense that is meaningful for our society, and perhaps that is enough to resolve the question. But there is more to the matter than that, and I would not like to end by speaking of the offender's dignity. It is important, even at the risk of sounding what may seem a wild alarm, to recognize that public humiliation of offenders is a politically questionable practice. If we focus only on the offender's dignity, we will never be able to answer the question that should trouble us most: What is it about shame sanctions that made them appealing to Maoists, to the Taliban, to the Nazi SA? What is it that made them appealing to the very movements that define political illiberalism for us?

The answer has to be that shame sanctions lend themselves to a politics of stirring up demons—as the SA tried to stir up demons and as Mao tried to stir up demons. Shame sanctions belong to a style of twentieth-century mass politics that draws its power not from a sober public, but from a fired-up crowd. Innocent though shame sanctions may often seem in our own country, they carry all the dangers of a demagogic democratic politics. Of course, we are not likely to have fascism or Maoism here. Nevertheless, it remains a condition of democratic rule of law, and of the right of a democratic society to punish, that we shy away from mob politics. In defining ourselves as a liberal society, as a society different from Maoist or Nazi society, we must accordingly remain conscious of the dangers of demagogic politics—conscious of the impropriety of any kind of official action that plays on the irrational urges of the public. We must remember something that was apparent to all in the nineteenth century: Democracy is never a proper form of government unless it can count on a sober and disciplined populace. Displaying morals offenders, commercial offenders, or first and minor offenders invites the public to rummage in some of the ugliest corners of the human heart. That cannot be good for healthy politics.

All of this provides a metric for judging shame sanctions as they appear in our country. To the extent such sanctions proclaim the message that the public is to serve as the agent of punishment, they will always run counter to the norms of democratic rule of law. By this metric, we can determine which shame sanctions are troubling, and how troubling they are. The most disturbing shame sanctions are those that convey the message that government has abandoned its monopoly of the power to punish crime, allowing the public to do with the offender as it sees fit. The shame attached to a prison sentence is, by this measure, comparatively untroubling; for a prison sentence, by its nature, announces the government's ultimate refusal to abandon the power to punish. Shame sanctions are most objectionable, however, where they most encourage the public to punish in an undisciplined and unthinking way. This means that they are especially objectionable when they are inflicted in the sensational and politically charged realms of sex and commerce, realms in which the public in mass democracies can lose its bearings, just as village societies did in the premodern world.

It is essential that we carve out a realm of the political that is not about dark psychologies of sex, not about dark suspicions directed against commerce and money. It is essential that we carefully limit the powers we confer upon the public to questions upon which the public can pass in a spirit of sanity and good sense. That is why we limit the business of inflicting criminal sanctions to criminal justice professionals. We have worked, over two liberal centuries, to build an ethic of businesslike politics that denies our officials the authority to pluck on the bass strings of public psychology and that makes criminal law the province of trained and disciplined officers. Over many generations of ugly experience, we have worked to build a democratic government that acknowledges the importance of an ethic of restraint and sobriety. The new shame sanctions tend to undermine that ethic, and that is a disturbing thing.

SPEECH GIVEN BEFORE HOUSE OF COMMONS

21 APRIL, 1868

—John Stuart Mill—

It would be a great satisfaction to me if I were able to support this Motion. It is always a matter of regret to me to find myself, on a public question, opposed to those who are called—sometimes in the way of honour, and sometimes in what is intended for ridicule—the philanthropists. Of all persons who take part in public affairs, they are those for whom, on the whole, I feel the greatest amount of respect; for their characteristic is, that they devote their time, their labour, and much of their money to objects purely public, with a less admixture of either personal or class selfishness, than any other class of politicians whatever. On almost all the great questions, scarcely any politicians are so steadily and almost uniformly to be found on the side of right; and they seldom err, but by an exaggerated application of some just and highly important principle. On the very subject that is now occupying us we all know what signal service they have rendered. It is through their efforts that our criminal laws—which within my memory hanged people for stealing in a dwelling house to the value of 40s.—laws by virtue of which rows of human beings might be seen suspended in front of Newgate by those who ascended or descended Ludgate Hill—have so greatly relaxed their most revolting and most impolitic ferocity, that aggravated murder is now practically the only crime which is punished with death by any of our lawful tribunals; and we are even now deliberating whether the extreme penalty should be retained in that solitary case. This vast gain, not only to humanity, but to the ends of penal justice, we owe to the philanthropists; and if they are mistaken, as I cannot but think they are, in the present instance, it is only in not perceiving the right time and place for stopping in a career hitherto so eminently beneficial. Sir, there is a point at which, I conceive, that career ought to stop. When there has been brought home to any one, by conclusive evidence, the greatest crime known to the law; and when the attendant circumstances suggest no palliation of the guilt, no hope that the culprit may even yet not be unworthy to live among mankind, nothing to make it probable that the crime was an exception to his general character rather than a consequence of it, then I confess it appears to me that to deprive the criminal of the life of which he has proved himself to be unworthy—solemnly to blot him out from the fellowship of mankind and from the catalogue of the living—is the most appropriate, as it is certainly the most impressive, mode in which society can attach to so great a crime the penal consequences which for the security of life it is indispensable to annex to it. I defend this penalty, when confined to atrocious cases, on the very ground on which it is commonly attacked—on that of humanity to the criminal; as beyond comparison the least cruel mode in which it is possible adequately to deter from the crime. If, in our horror of inflicting death, we endeavour to devise some punishment for the living criminal which shall act on the human mind with a deterrent force at all comparable to that of death, we are driven to inflictions less severe indeed in appearance, and therefore less efficacious, but far more cruel in reality. Few, I think, would venture to propose, as a punishment for aggravated murder, less than imprisonment with hard labour for life; that is the fate to which a murderer would be consigned by the mercy which shrinks from putting him to death.

But has it been sufficiently considered what sort of a mercy this is, and what kind of life it leaves to him? If, indeed, the punishment is not really inflicted—if it becomes the sham which a few years ago such punishments were rapidly becoming—then, indeed, its adoption would be almost tantamount to giving up the attempt to repress murder altogether. But if it really is what it professes to be, and if it is realized in all its rigour by the popular imagination, as it very probably would not be, but as it must be if it is to be efficacious, it will be so shocking that when the memory of the crime is no longer fresh, there will be almost insuperable difficulty in executing it. What comparison can there really be, in point of severity, between consigning a man to the short pang of a rapid death, and immuring him in a living tomb, there to linger out what may be a long life in the hardest and most monotonous toil, without any of its alleviations or rewards—debarred from all pleasant sights and sounds, and cut off from all earthly hope, except a slight mitigation of bodily restraint, or a small improvement of diet? Yet even such a lot as this, because there is no one moment at which the suffering is of terrifying intensity, and, above all, because it does not contain the element, so imposing to the imagination, of the unknown, is universally reputed a milder punishment than death—stands in all codes as a mitigation of the capital penalty, and is thankfully accepted as such. For it is characteristic of all punishments which depend on duration for their efficacy—all, therefore, which are not corporal or pecuniary—that they are more rigorous than they seem; while it is, on the contrary, one of the strongest recommendations a punishment can have, that it should seem more rigorous than it is; for its practical power depends far less on what it is than on what it seems. There is not, I should think, any human infliction which makes an impression on the imagination so entirely out of proportion to its real severity as the punishment of death. The punishment must be mild indeed which does not add more to the sum of human misery than is necessarily or directly added by the execution of a criminal. As my honourable Friend the Member for Northampton (Mr. Gilpin) has himself remarked, the most that human laws can do to anyone in the matter of death is to hasten it; the man would have died at any rate; not so very much later, and on the average, I fear, with a considerably greater amount of bodily suffering. Society is asked, then, to denude itself of an instrument of punishment which, in the grave cases to which alone it is suitable, effects its purpose at a less cost of human suffering than any other; which, while it inspires more terror, is less cruel in actual fact than any punishment that we should think of substituting for it. My honourable Friend says that it does not inspire terror, and that experience proves it to be a failure. But the influence of a punishment is not to be estimated by its effect on hardened criminals. Those whose habitual way of life keeps them, so to speak, at all times within sight of the gallows, do grow to care less about it; as, to compare good things with bad, an old soldier is not much affected by the chance of dying in battle. I can afford to admit all that is often said about the indifference of professional criminals to the gallows. Though of that indifference one-third is probably bravado and another third confidence that they shall have the luck to escape, it is quite probable that the remaining third is real. But the efficacy of a punishment which acts principally through the imagination, is chiefly to be measured by the impression it makes on those who are still innocent: by the horror with which it surrounds the first promptings of guilt; the restraining influence it exercises over the beginning of the thought which, if indulged, would become a temptation; the check which it exerts over the gradual declension towards the state—never suddenly attained—in which crime no longer revolts, and punishment no longer terrifies. As for what is called the failure of death punishment, who is able to judge of that? We partly know who those are whom it has not deterred; but who is there who knows whom it has deterred, or how many human beings it has saved who would have lived to be murderers if that awful association had not been thrown round the idea of murder from their earliest infancy? Let us not forget that the most imposing fact loses its power over the imagination if it is made too cheap. When a punishment fit only for the most atrocious crimes is lavished on small offences until human feeling recoils from it, then, indeed, it ceases to intimidate, because it ceases to be believed in. The failure of capital punishment in cases of theft is easily accounted for: the thief did not believe that it would be inflicted. He had learnt by experience that jurors would perjure themselves rather than find him guilty; that Judges would seize any excuse for not sentencing him to death, or for recommending him to mercy; and that if neither jurors nor Judges were merciful, there were still hopes from an authority above both. When things had come to this pass it was high time to give up the vain attempt. When it is impossible to inflict a punishment, or when its infliction becomes a public scandal, the idle threat cannot too soon disappear from the statute book. And in the case of the host of offences which were formerly capital, I heartily rejoice that it did become impracticable to execute the law. If the same state of public feeling comes to exist in the case of murder; if the time comes when jurors refuse to find a murderer guilty; when Judges will not sentence him to death, or will recommend him to mercy; or when, if juries and Judges do not flinch from their duty, Home Secretaries, under pressure of deputations and memorials, shrink from theirs, and the threat becomes, as it became in the other cases, a mere brutum fulmen; then, indeed, it may become necessary to do in this case what has been done in those—to abrogate the penalty. That time may come—my honourable Friend thinks that it has nearly come. I hardly know whether he lamented it or boasted of it; but he and his Friends are entitled to the boast: for if it comes it will be their doing, and they will have gained what I cannot but call a fatal victory, for they will have achieved it by bringing about, if they will forgive me for saying so, an enervation, an effeminacy, in the general mind of the country. For what else than effeminacy is it to be so much more shocked by taking a man's life than by depriving him of all that makes life desirable or valuable? Is death, then, the greatest of all earthly ills? Usque adeone mori miserum est? Is it, indeed, so dreadful a thing to die? Has it not been from of old one chief part of a manly education to make us despise death—teaching us to account it, if an evil at all, by no means high in the list of evils; at all events, as an inevitable one, and to hold, as it were, our lives in our hands, ready to be given or risked at any moment, for a sufficiently worthy object? I am sure that my honourable Friends know all this as well, and have as much of all these feelings as any of the rest of us; possibly more. But I cannot think that this is likely to be the effect of their teaching on the general mind. I cannot think that the cultivating of a peculiar sensitiveness of conscience on this one point, over and above what results from the general cultivation of the moral sentiments, is permanently consistent with assigning in our own minds to the fact of death no more than the degree of relative importance which belongs to it among the other incidents of our humanity. The men of old cared too little about death, and gave their own lives or took those of others with equal recklessness. Our danger is of the opposite kind, lest we should be so much shocked by death, in general and in the abstract, as to care too much about it in individual cases, both those of other people and our own, which call for its being risked. And I am not putting things at the worst, for it is proved by the experience of other countries that horror of the executioner by no means necessarily implies horror of the assassin. The stronghold, as we all know, of hired assassination in the eighteenth century was Italy; yet it is said that in some of the Italian populations the infliction of death by sentence of law was in the highest degree offensive and revolting to popular feeling. Much has been said of the sanctity of human life, and the absurdity of supposing that we can teach respect for life by ourselves destroying it. But I am surprised at the employment of this argument, for it is one which might be brought against any punishment whatever. It is not human life only, not human life as such, that ought to be sacred to us, but human feelings. The human capacity of suffering is what we should cause to be respected, not the mere capacity of existing. And we may imagine somebody asking how we can teach people not to inflict suffering by ourselves inflicting it? But to this I should answer—all of us would answer—that to deter by suffering from inflicting suffering is not only possible, but the very purpose of penal justice. Does fining a criminal show want of respect for property, or imprisoning him, for personal freedom? Just as unreasonable is it to think that to take the life of a man who has taken that of another is to show want of regard for human life. We show, on the contrary, most emphatically our regard for it, by the adoption of a rule that he who violates that right in another forfeits it for himself, and that while no other crime that he can commit deprives him of his right to live, this shall. There is one argument against capital punishment, even in extreme cases, which I cannot deny to have weight—on which my honourable Friend justly laid great stress, and which never can be entirely got rid of. It is this—that if by an error of justice an innocent person is put to death, the mistake can never be corrected; all compensation, all reparation for the wrong is impossible. This would be indeed a serious objection if these miserable mistakes—among the most tragical occurrences in the whole round of human affairs—could not be made extremely rare. The argument is invincible where the mode of criminal procedure is dangerous to the innocent, or where the Courts of Justice are not trusted. And this probably is the reason why the objection to an irreparable punishment began (as I believe it did) earlier, and is more intense and more widely diffused, in some parts of the Continent of Europe than it is here. There are on the Continent great and enlightened countries, in which the criminal procedure is not so favourable to innocence, does not afford the same security against erroneous conviction, as it does among us; countries where the Courts of Justice seem to think they fail in their duty unless they find somebody guilty; and in their really laudable desire to hunt guilt from its hiding-places, expose themselves to a serious danger of condemning the innocent. If our own procedure and Courts of Justice afforded ground for similar apprehension, I should be the first to join in withdrawing the power of inflicting irreparable punishment from such tribunals. But we all know that the defects of our procedure are the very opposite. Our rules of evidence are even too favourable to the prisoner: and juries and Judges carry out the maxim. "It is better that ten guilty should escape than that one innocent person should suffer," not only to the letter, but beyond the letter. Judges are most anxious to point out, and juries to allow for, the barest possibility of the prisoner's innocence. No human judgment is infallible: such sad cases as my honourable Friend cited will sometimes occur; but in so grave a case as that of murder, the accused, in our system, has always the benefit of the merest shadow of a doubt. And this suggests another consideration very germane to the question. The very fact that death punishment is more shocking than any other to the imagination, necessarily renders the Courts of Justice more scrupulous in requiring the fullest evidence of guilt. Even that which is the greatest objection to capital punishment, the impossibility of correcting an error once committed, must make, and does make, juries and Judges more careful in forming their opinion, and more jealous in their scrutiny of the evidence. If the substitution or penal servitude for death in cases of murder should cause any relaxation in this conscientious scrupulosity, there would be a great evil to set against the real, but I hope rare, advantage of being able to make reparation to a condemned person who was afterwards discovered to be innocent. In order that the possibility of correction may be kept open wherever the chance of this sad contingency is more than infinitesimal, it is quite right that the Judge should recommend to the Crown a commutation of the sentence, not solely when the proof of guilt is open to the smallest suspicion, but whenever there remains anything unexplained and mysterious in the case, raising a desire for more light, or making it likely that further information may at some future time be obtained. I would also suggest that whenever the sentence is commuted the grounds of the commutation should, in some authentic form, be made known to the public. Thus much I willingly concede to my honourable Friend; but on the question of total abolition I am inclined to hope that the feeling of the country is not with him, and that the limitation of death punishment to the cases referred to in the Bill of last year will be generally considered sufficient. The mania which existed a short time ago for paring down all our punishments seems to have reached its limits, and not before it was time. We were in danger of being left without any effectual punishment, except for small offences. What was formerly our chief secondary punishment—transportation—before it was abolished, had become almost a reward. Penal servitude, the substitute for it, was becoming, to the classes who were principally subject to it, almost nominal, so comfortable did we make our prisons, and so easy had it become to get quickly out of them. Flogging—a most objectionable punishment in ordinary cases, but a particularly appropriate one for crimes of brutality, especially crimes against women—we would not hear of, except, to be sure, in the case of garotters, for whose peculiar benefit we re-established it in a hurry, immediately after a Member of Parliament had been garotted. With this exception, offences, even of an atrocious kind, against the person, as my honourable and learned Friend the Member for Oxford (Mr. Neate) well remarked, not only were, but still are, visited with penalties so ludicrously inadequate, as to be almost an encouragement to the crime. I think, Sir, that in the case of most offences, except those against property, there is more need of strengthening our punishments than of weakening them: and that severer sentences, with an apportionment of them to the different kinds of offences which shall approve itself better than at present to the moral sentiments of the community, are the kind of reform of which our penal system now stands in need. I shall therefore vote against the Amendment.

ON DETERRENCE AND THE DEATH PENALTY

—Ernest van den Haag—

I

If rehabilitation and the protection of society from unrehabilitated offenders were the only purposes of legal punishment the death penalty could be abolished: it cannot attain the first end, and is not needed for the second. No case for the death penalty can be made unless "doing justice," or "deterring others," are among our penal aims. Each of these purposes can justify capital punishment by itself; opponents, therefore, must show that neither actually does, while proponents can rest their case on either.

Although the argument from justice is intellectually more interesting, and, in my view, decisive enough, utilitarian arguments have more appeal: the claim that capital punishment is useless because it does not deter others, is most persuasive. I shall, therefore, focus on this claim. Lest the argument be thought to be unduly narrow, I shall show, nonetheless, that some claims of injustice rest on premises which the claimants reject when arguments for capital punishment are derived therefrom; while other claims of injustice have no independent standing: their weight depends on the weight given to deterrence.

II

Capital punishment is regarded as unjust because it may lead to the execution of innocents, or because the guilty poor (or disadvantaged) are more likely to be executed than the guilty rich.

Regardless of merit, these claims are relevant only if "doing justice" is one purpose of punishment. Unless one regards it as good, or, at least, better, that the guilty be punished rather than the innocent, and that the equally guilty be punished equally unless, that is, one wants penalties to be just, one cannot object to them because they are not. However, if one does include justice among the purposes of punishment, it becomes possible to justify any one punishment—even death—on grounds of justice. Yet, those who object to the death penalty because of its alleged injustice, usually deny not only the merits, or the sufficiency, of specific arguments based on justice, but the propriety of justice as an argument: they exclude "doing justice" as a purpose of legal punishment. If justice is not a purpose of penalties, injustice cannot be an objection to the death penalty, or to any other; if it is, justice cannot be ruled out as an argument for any penalty.

Consider the claim of injustice on its merits now. A convicted man may be found to have been innocent; if he was executed, the penalty cannot be reversed. Except for fines, penalties never can be reversed. Time spent in prison cannot be returned. However a prison sentence may be remitted once the prisoner serving it is found innocent; and he can be compensated for the time served (although compensation ordinarily cannot repair the harm). Thus, though (nearly) all penalties are irreversible, the death penalty, unlike others, is irrevocable as well.

Despite all precautions, errors will occur in judicial proceedings: the innocent may be found guilty; or the guilty rich may more easily escape conviction, or receive lesser penalties than the guilty poor. However, these injustices do not reside in the penalties inflicted but in their maldistribution. It is not the penalty—whether death or prison—which is unjust when inflicted on the innocent, but its imposition on the innocent. Inequity between poor and rich also involves distribution, not the penalty distributed. Thus injustice is not an objection to the death penalty but to the distributive process—the trial. Trials are more likely to be fair when life is at stake—the death penalty is probably less often unjustly inflicted than others. It requires special consideration not because it is more, or more often, unjust than other penalties, but because it is always irrevocable.

Can any amount of deterrence justify the possibility of irrevocable injustice? Surely injustice is unjustifiable in each actual individual case; it must be objected to whenever it occurs. But we are concerned here with the process that may produce injustice, and with the penalty that would make it irrevocable—not with the actual individual cases produced, but with the general rules which may produce them. To consider objections to a general rule (the provision of any penalties by law) we must compare the likely net result of alternative rules and select the rule (or penalty) likely to produce the least injustice. For however one defines justice, to support it cannot mean less than to favor the least injustice. If the death of innocents because of judicial error is unjust, so is the death of innocents by murder. If some murders could be avoided by a penalty conceivably more deterrent than others—such as the death penalty—then the question becomes: which penalty will minimize the number of innocents killed (by crime and by punishment)? It follows that the irrevocable injustice, sometimes inflicted by the death penalty would not significantly militate against it, if capital punishment deters enough murders to reduce the total number of innocents killed so that fewer are lost than would be lost without it.

In general, the possibility of injustice argues against penalization of any kind only if the expected usefulness of penalization is less important than the probable harm (particularly to innocents) and the probable inequities. The possibility of injustice argues against the death penalty only inasmuch as the added usefulness (deterrence) expected from irrevocability is thought less important than the added harm. (Were my argument specifically concerned with justice, I could compare the injustice inflicted by the courts with the injustice—outside the courts—avoided by the judicial process. *I.e.*, "important" here may be used to include everything to which importance is attached.)

We must briefly examine now the general use and effectiveness of deterrence to decide whether the death penalty could add enough deterrence to be warranted.

III

Does any punishment "deter others" at all? Doubts have been thrown on this effect because it is thought to depend on the incorrect rationalistic psychology of some of its 18th and 19th century proponents. Actually deterrence does not depend on rational calculation, on rationality or even on capacity for it; nor do arguments for it depend on rationalistic psychology. Deterrence depends on the likelihood and on the regularity—not on the rationality—of human responses to danger; and further on the possibility of reinforcing internal controls by vicarious external experiences.

Responsiveness to danger is generally found in human behavior; the danger can, but need not, come from the law or from society; nor need it be explicitly verbalized. Unless intent on suicide, people do not jump from high mountain cliffs, however tempted to fly through the air; and they take precautions against falling. The mere risk of injury often restrains us from doing what is otherwise attractive; we refrain even when we have no direct experience, and usually without explicit computation of probabilities, let alone conscious weighing of expected pleasure against possible pain. One abstains from dangerous acts because of vague, inchoate, habitual and, above all, preconscious fears. Risks and rewards are more often felt than calculated; one abstains without accounting to oneself, because "it isn't done," or because one literally does not conceive of the action one refrains from. Animals as well refrain from painful or injurious experiences presumably without calculation; and the threat of punishment can be used to regulate their conduct.

Unlike natural dangers, legal threats are constructed deliberately by legislators to restrain actions which may impair the social order. Thus legislation transforms social into individual dangers. Most people further transform external into internal danger: they acquire a sense of moral obligation, a conscience, which threatens them, should they do what is wrong. Arising originally from the external authority of rulers and rules, conscience is internalized and becomes independent of external forces. However, conscience is constantly reinforced in those whom it controls by the coercive imposition of external authority on recalcitrants and on those who have not acquired it. Most people refrain from offenses because they feel an obligation to behave lawfully. But this obligation would scarcely be felt if those who do not feel or follow it were not to suffer punishment.

Although the legislators may calculate their threats and the responses to be produced, the effectiveness of the threats neither requires nor depends on calculations by those responding. The predictor (or producer) of effects must calculate; those whose responses are predicted (or produced) need not. Hence, although legislation (and legislators) should be rational, subjects, to be deterred as intended, need not be: they need only be responsive.

Punishments deter those who have not violated the law for the same reasons—and in the same degrees (apart from internalization: moral obligation) as do natural dangers. Often natural dangers—all dangers not deliberately created by legislation (*e.g.*, injury of the criminal inflicted by the crime victim) are insufficient. Thus, the fear of injury (natural danger) does not suffice to control city traffic; it must be reinforced by the legal punishment meted out to those who violate the rules. These punishments keep most people observing the regulations. However, where (in the absence of natural danger) the threatened punishment is so light that the advantage of violating rules tends to exceed the disadvantage of being punished (divided by the risk), the rule is violated (*i.e.*, parking fines are too light). In this case the feeling of obligation tends to vanish as well. Elsewhere punishment deters.

To be sure, not everybody responds to threatened punishment. Non-responsive persons may be a) self-destructive or b) incapable of responding to threats, or even of grasping them. Increases in the size, or certainty, of penalties would not affect these two groups. A third group c) might respond to more certain or more severe penalties. If the punishment threatened for burglary, robbery, or rape were a $5 fine in North Carolina, and 5 years in prison in South Carolina, I have no doubt that the North Carolina treasury would become quite opulent until vigilante justice would provide the deterrence not provided by law. Whether to increase penalties (or improve enforcement), depends on the importance of the rule to society, the size and likely reaction of the group that did not respond before, and the acceptance of the added punishment and enforcement required to deter it. Observation would have to locate the points—likely to differ in different times and places—at which diminishing, zero, and negative returns set in. There is no reason to believe that all present and future offenders belong to the *a priori* non-responsive groups, or that all penalties have reached the point of diminishing, let alone zero returns.

IV

Even though its effectiveness seems obvious, punishment as a deterrent has fallen into disrepute. Some ideas which help explain this progressive heedlessness were uttered by Lester Pearson, then Prime Minister of Canada, when, in opposing the death penalty, he proposed that instead "the state seek to eradicate the causes of crime—slums, ghettos and personality disorders."

"Slums, ghettos and personality disorders" have not been shown, singly or collectively, to be "the causes" of crime.

(1) The crime rate in the slums is indeed higher than elsewhere; but so is the death rate in hospitals. Slums are no more "causes" of crime, than hospitals are of death; they are locations of crime, as hospitals are of death. Slums and hospitals attract people selectively; neither is the "cause" of the condition (disease in hospitals, poverty in slums) that leads to the selective attraction.

As for poverty which draws people into slums, and, sometimes, into crime, any relative disadvantage may lead to ambition, frustration, resentment and, if insufficiently restrained, to crime. Not all relative disadvantages can be eliminated; indeed very few can be, and their elimination increases the resentment generated by the remaining ones; not even relative poverty can be removed altogether. (Absolute poverty—whatever that may be—hardly affects crime.) However, though contributory, relative disadvantages are not a necessary or sufficient cause of crime: most poor people do not commit crimes, and some rich people do. Hence, "eradication of poverty" would, at most, remove one (doubtful) cause of crime....

Whether any activity—be it lawful or unlawful—takes place depends on whether the desire for it, or for whatever is to be secured by it, is stronger than the desire to avoid the costs involved. Accordingly people work, attend college, commit crimes, go to the movies—or refrain from any of these activities. Attendance at a theatre may be high because the show is entertaining and because the price of admission is low. Obviously the attendance depends on both—on the combination of expected gratification and cost. The wish, motive or impulse for doing anything— the experienced, or expected, gratification—is the cause of doing it; the wish to avoid the cost is the cause of not doing it. One is no more and no less "cause" than the other. (Common speech supports this use of "cause" no less than logic: "Why did you go to Jamaica?" "*Because* it is such a beautiful place." "Why didn't you go to Jamaica?" "*Because* it is too expensive."—"Why do you buy this?" "*Because* it is so cheap." "Why don't you buy that?" "*Because* it is too expensive.") Penalties (costs) are causes of lawfulness, or (if too low or uncertain) of unlawfulness, of crime. People do commit crimes because, given their conditions, the desire for the satisfaction sought prevails. They refrain if the desire to avoid the cost prevails. Given the desire, low cost (penalty) causes the action, and high cost restraint. Given the cost, desire becomes the causal variable. Neither is intrinsically more causal than the other. The crime rate increases if the cost is reduced or the desire raised. It can be decreased by raising the cost or by reducing the desire.

The cost of crime is more easily and swiftly changed than the conditions producing the inclination to it. Further, the costs are very largely within the power of the government to change, whereas the conditions producing propensity to crime are often only indirectly affected by government action, and some are altogether beyond the control of the government. Our unilateral emphasis on these conditions and our undue neglect of costs may contribute to an unnecessarily high crime rate.

V

The foregoing suggests the question posed by the death penalty: is the deterrence added (return) sufficiently above zero to warrant irrevocability (or other, less clear, disadvantages)? The question is not only whether the penalty deters, but whether it deters more than alternatives and whether the difference exceeds the cost of irrevocability. (I shall assume that the alternative is actual life imprisonment so as to exclude the complication produced by the release of the unrehabilitated.)

In some fairly infrequent but important circumstances the death penalty is the only possible deterrent. Thus, in case of acute *coups d'état*, or of acute substantial attempts to overthrow the government, prospective rebels would altogether discount the threat of any prison sentence. They would not be deterred because they believe the swift victory of the revolution will invalidate a prison sentence and turn it into an advantage. Execution would be the only deterrent because, unlike prison sentences, it cannot be revoked by victorious rebels. The same reasoning applies to deterring spies or traitors in wartime. Finally, men who, by virtue of past acts, are already serving, or are threatened, by a life sentence, could be deterred from further offenses only by the threat of the death penalty.

What about criminals who do not fall into any of these (often ignored) classes? Prof. Thorsten Sellin has made a careful study of the available statistics: he concluded that they do not yield evidence for the deterring effect of the death penalty. Somewhat surprisingly, Prof. Sellin seems to think that this lack of evidence for deterrence is evidence for the lack of deterrence. It is not. It means that deterrence has not been demonstrated statistically—not that non-deterrence has been.

It is entirely possible, indeed likely (as Prof. Sellin appears willing to concede), that the statistics used, though the best available, are nonetheless too slender a reed to rest conclusions on. They indicate that the homicide rate does not vary greatly between similar areas with or without the death penalty, and in the same area before and after abolition. However, the similar areas are not similar enough; the periods are not long enough; many social differences and changes, other than the abolition of the death penalty, may account for the variation (or lack of) in homicide rates with and without, before and after abolition; some of these social differences and changes are likely to have affected homicide rates. I am unaware of any statistical analysis which adjusts for such changes and differences. And logically, it is quite consistent with the postulated deterrent effect of capital punishment that there be less homicide after abolition: with retention there might have been still less.

Homicide rates do not depend exclusively on penalties any more than do other crime rates. A number of conditions which influence the propensity to crime, demographic, economic or generally social, changes or differences—even such matters as changes of the divorce laws or of the cotton price—may influence the homicide rate. Therefore variation or constancy cannot be attributed to variations or constancy of the penalties, unless we know that no other factor influencing the homicide rate has changed. Usually we don't. To believe the death penalty deterrent does not require one to believe that the death penalty, or any other, is the only, or the decisive causal variable; this would be as absurd as the converse mistake that "social causes" are the only, or always the decisive factor. To favor capital punishment, the efficacy of neither variable need be denied. It is enough to affirm that the severity of the penalty may influence some potential criminals, and that the added severity of the death penalty adds to deterrence, or may do so. It is quite possible that such a deterrent effect may be offset (or intensified) by non-penal factors which affect propensity; its presence of absence therefore may be hard, and perhaps impossible to demonstrate.

Contrary to what Prof. Sellin *et al.* seem to presume, I doubt that offenders are aware of the absence of presence of the death penalty state by state or period by period. Such unawareness argues against the assumption of a calculating murderer. However, unawareness does not argue against the death penalty if by deterrence we mean a preconscious, general response to a severe, but not necessarily specifically and explicitly apprehended, or calculated threat. A constant homicide rate, despite abolition, may occur because of unawareness and not because of lack of deterrence: people remain deterred for a lengthy interval by the severity of the penalty in the past, or by the severity of penalties used in similar circumstances nearby.

I do not argue for a version of deterrence which would require me to believe that an individual shuns murder while in North Dakota, because of the death penalty, and merrily goes to it in South Dakota since it has been abolished there; or that he will start the murderous career from which he had hitherto refrained, after abolition. I hold that the generalized threat of the death penalty may be a deterrent, and the more so, the more generally applied. Deterrence will not cease in the particular areas of abolition or at the particular times of abolition. Rather, general deterrence will be somewhat weakened, through local (partial) abolition. Even such weakening will be hard to detect owing to changes in many offsetting, or reinforcing, factors.

For all of these reasons, I doubt that the presence or absence of a deterrent effect of the death penalty is likely to be demonstrable by statistical means. The statistics presented by Prof. Sellin *et al.* show only that there is no statistical proof for the deterrent effect of the death penalty. But they do not show that there is no deterrent effect. Not to demonstrate presence of the effect is not the same as to demonstrate its absence; certainly not when there are plausible explanations for the non-demonstrability of the effect.

It is on our uncertainty that the case for deterrence must rest.

VI

If we do not know whether the death penalty will deter others, we are confronted with two uncertainties. If we impose the death penalty, and achieve no deterrent effect thereby, the life of a convicted murderer has been expended in vain (from a deterrent viewpoint). There is a net loss. If we impose the death sentence and thereby deter some future murderers, we spared the lives of some future victims (the prospective murderers gain too; they are spared punishment because they were deterred). In this case, the death penalty has led to a net gain, unless the life of a convicted murderer is valued more highly than that of the unknown victim, or victims (and the non-imprisonment of the deterred non-murderer).

The calculation can be turned around, of course. The absence of the death penalty may harm no one and therefore produce a gain—the life of the convicted murderer. Or it may kill future victims of murderers who could have been deterred, and thus produce a loss—their life.

To be sure, we must risk something certain—the death (or life) of the convicted man, for something uncertain—the death (or life) of the victims of murderers who may be deterred. This is in the nature of uncertainty—when we invest, or gamble, we risk the money we have for an uncertain gain. Many human actions, most commitments—including marriage and crime—share this characteristic with the deterrent purpose of any penalization, and with its rehabilitative purpose (and even with the protective).

More proof is demanded for the deterrent effect of the death penalty than is demanded for the deterrent effect of other penalties. This is not justified by the absence of other utilitarian purposes such as protection and rehabilitation; they involve no less uncertainty than deterrence.

Irrevocability may support a demand for some reason to expect more deterrence than revocable penalties might produce, but not a demand for more proof of deterrence, as has been pointed out above. The reason for expecting more deterrence lies in the greater severity, the terrifying effect inherent in finality. Since it seems more important to spare victims than to spare murderers, the burden of proving that the greater severity inherent in irrevocability adds nothing to deterrence lies on those who oppose capital punishment. Proponents of the death penalty need show only that there is no more uncertainty about it than about greater severity in general.

The demand that the death penalty be proved more deterrent than alternatives can not be satisfied any more than the demand that six years in prison be proved to be more deterrent than three. But the uncertainty which confronts us favors the death penalty as long as by imposing it we might save future victims of murder. This effect is as plausible as the general idea that penalties have deterrent effects which increase with their severity. Though we have no proof of the positive deterrence of the penalty, we also have no proof of zero, or negative effectiveness. I believe we have no right to risk additional future victims of murder for the sake of sparing convicted murderers; on the contrary, our moral obligation is to risk the possible ineffectiveness of executions. However rationalized, the opposite view appears to be motivated by the simple fact that executions are more subjected to social control than murder. However, this applies to all penalties and does not argue for the abolition of any.

INDEX

R

S

T

U